The Life of the Mind

Selected Papers

Jason W. Brown, M. D.

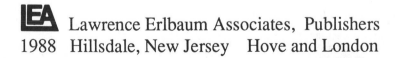 Lawrence Erlbaum Associates, Publishers
1988   Hillsdale, New Jersey   Hove and London

Lawrence Erlbaum Associates, Inc., Publishers
365 Broadway
Hillsdale, New Jersey 07642

Library of Congress Cataloging in Publication Data

Brown, Jason W.
    The life of the mind : selected papers / Jason W. Brown.
        p.   cm.
    Bibliography: p.
    Includes index.
    ISBN 0-8058-0236-3 :
    1. Neuropsychiatry.   2. Neuropsychology.   3. Aphasia.   4. Higher
nervous activity.   I. Title.
    RC343.B74 1988
    152--dc19   66262   88-12111
                                                                  CIP
Printed in the United States of America
10 9 8 7 6 5 4 3 2 1

Contents

Preface

With a few exceptions, the history of neuropsychology is the story of psychological theory translated into practical neurology. It is probably not an exaggeration to say that brain pathology has been of concern to psychology mainly to the extent that philosophy of mind, introspection, and inferences from experiments on normal subjects could be supported or disconfirmed by patterns of function breakdown. On the other hand, neurologists interested in more than case reports and anatomical localization have looked to psychological theory—behavioral, gestalt, cognitive—for explanations of clinical findings. Yet, for a long time I have thought this not to be the proper approach to the pathological material. It seemed that a psychology was lurking in the neurological clinic, one waiting to be built up directly on the study of pathological symptoms.

For me, as for others (notably Freud), the problem of aphasia pointed the way to psychological theory. The aphasias are a window into cognitive structure, and the search for a theory that explains the diversity of aphasic disorders leads to a theory that accounts, more generally, for disorders of action and perception. In other words, the aphasias provide the insight that principles underlying language and its disorders are fundamentally the same as those of other cognitive domains. This book is the record of a search for such a theory. In part, it grew out of questions that were raised by Karl Pribram in a gracious review of my book *Mind, Brain and Consciousness* and the obvious need that he exposed for me to delve more deeply into disorders of action and perception. In many ways, this collection is a response to that review, an effort to document and to extend the theory outlined in that monograph.

The opportunity to begin the documentation was provided by an NIH research grant —not of course for the study that was funded, but for the free time to do other things—and the hospitality of George Miller during a year at Rockefeller. It was during this year that I realized that cognitive science, for all the euphoria, has little to offer to clinical study, although it does provide a good illustration of my opening contention.

It is a prosaic fact that much of my writing has been done away from home in circumstances less pedestrian than grazing through the stacks or slouching over a word processor. In bits and pieces, and in an assortment of places, this book has assembled itself. Perhaps anticipating liquidation, the Foundation's Fund for Research in Psychiatry supported a year with Henry Hécaen in Paris. The Fogarty Center sent me to Bucharest with Alexandru Fradis, and to Moscow, where I passed some weeks on the beautiful birch-covered grounds of the Troubetsky estate, now converted into a convalescent hospital, walking with Luria and discussing a whole range of neuropsychological issues. There were periods over the years with Anton Leischner in Bonn, through the continuing generosity of the Alexander von Humboldt Foundation, and summer vacations in locales as diverse as the Thames valley, the crowded beaches of Antibes and Lerici, a spectacular terrace in Positano, and a very special river-side park on Sutton Place in New York.

After the pain of writing, comes the agony of revision. For me, a deletion is a kind of wound—and one needs the tact and good sense of friends to survive the errors, the cherished ambiguities, and non sequiturs that would vitiate whatever of value remains. Mostly, I owe a debt to the friendly spirits of Paul Schilder, Arnold Pick, William James, Paul Yakovlev, and Henri Bergson who set me on this path. I hope this work pleases them. Among the living, Ellen Perecman and Avram Schweiger kept me on the track and even deepened my understanding of my own writing. Steve Levick, Eran Zaidel, Dee Pandya, and Hugh Buckingham helped me to see the trees as well as the forest. Joe Jaffe, the late Silvano Arieti, Diana van Lancker, Paul MacLean, Terry Deacon, Gary Goldberg, and Ralph Hoffman: all comrades in the trenches. Karen Chobor and Adam Wechsler reminded me that the truth of a theory, like the test of a friendship, is in the harmony of its elements. If, as Emily Dickinson wrote, "The brain is just the weight of God," then harmony is His language, though in a land of pagans it helps to have some data.

In compiling this book, I have deleted many of the figures, especially CT scans and case reports, which do not add materially to the presentation, along with some of the text that may have been duplicated in other sections. In instances where that material is sought, the reader is advised to refer to the original papers. I have attempted to collect mainly those papers that best illustrate the theoretical framework, that of microgenesis, about which the clinical material is organized. It is my hope that this volume will serve as a reference for those interested in microgenetic theory, whereas for me, personally, it is an opportunity to set out in some detail the clinical record that supports and documents the theory, so as to provide a basis for future work on a theory of mind that is firmly based in brain study.

I wish to express my gratitude to the following individuals, journals, and publishers for permission to reproduce material from prior publications: *Contemporary Psychology*; Charles C. Thomas, Publisher; the World Rehabilitation Fund; the Department of Health, Education and Welfare, Washington, DC; Plenum Press; Grune & Stratton; *Journal of Mental*

Imagery, Neurology, Dick van Frank for *Brain and Language* and Academic Press; Fred C C. Peng for the *Journal of Neurolinguistics*; Elsevier and the *Handbook of Clinical Neurology*; Michael Arbib and *Cognition and Brain Theory*; *Journal of the American Academy of Psychoanalysis*; Gene Brody and the *Journal of Nervous and Mental Disease*; Pergamon Press and *Neuropsychologia*; and MIT Press.

Finally, there is a debt I can never repay, to my wife, my friend, and my loving partner, of whom Dante wrote: "If all of her that heretofore is said/Could in a single perfect praise be quit/'Twere still too narrow to suffice my need."

Jason W. Brown

Introduction: Microgenetic Theory

The papers represented in this collection are the outcome of a program of clinical research initiated about 10 years ago with the publication of my book *Mind, Brain and Consciousness* (Brown, 1977). This monograph—little more than an outline of a theory at the time—sought to develop a new approach to the interpretation of symptoms of brain injury, one based on the concept of microgenesis. A central feature of this approach is the assumption that the symptoms of brain damage represent *normal* stages in the microtemporal processing of cognitions and behaviors. Symptoms are not aberrations that point to defective mechanisms, but have a deeper meaning. The abnormal behavior that constitutes the symptom is, in reality, a normal processing stage beneath the surface representation. The significance of this interpretation is that the various types of symptoms associated with brain damage—since they represent stages in normal function—can be aligned in a series that captures the formative direction of normal processing. Symptoms are data points in clinical investigation, experiments in nature that help us to see—as research studies often do not—the processes that occur *within* cognitive structure.

Working with symptoms in this way, it was possible in broad strokes to reconstruct the stages—or a theory of the stages—involved in the production and perception of language. The theory is based on processing rather than on content; that is, on the process through which representations are generated, as opposed to the content of a particular representation—and it is an approach that is clearly incompatible with existing anatomical models. For one thing, the concept of a flow from one state to the next cannot easily be related to the prevalent notion of centers and connecting pathways. Such concepts are too static to capture the moment-to-moment change inherent in a processing account. The idea that a mechanism or output device located in a special piece of brain tissue is prewired for a given cognitive operation cannot be resolved with changing lesion effects over time—in recovery or deterioration, as well as over the life span—nor for that matter with changes in symptom pattern in the course of a single examination.

Another problem with the traditional interpretation of brain/behavior relations has to do with the evolutionary perspective upon which microgenesis is

1

based. There is a need for a more fluid account of both lesion effects and the anatomical substructure of language (or other cognitive functions) from which pathological effects obtain. Anatomy is not a rigid skeleton on which function is superimposed but is a living system in constant flux. One can say the anatomy has to be just as alive as the cognitive processing to which it is mapped. Even more than the psychology, the anatomy poses a special problem. No wonder that prior to microgenetic theory, in spite of many psychological accounts of aphasia, only one anatomical model, that of Wernicke, had ever been proposed!

The shift in anatomical thinking came about with a recognition of an ontogenetic dimension in lesion effects. Through a series of inferences from aphasia in children and adults with atypical dominance, it was possible to rethink anatomy in relation to phyletic and maturational growth trends. Continuing specification of the brain—especially of the language areas—was inferred to occur over the life span. While there is still insufficient data to draw a firm conclusion, it is worth noting that the controversy between prewiring and continuing specification in neurological development is similar to the debate between preformation and epigenesis in evolutionary theory.

Another idea arising in relation to observation of children is that areas of the brain linked to language disorders can be conceived as levels in a "vertical" structure, not as centers in a two-dimensional network. These levels constitute a stratified system of phyletic growth planes. Language maps onto this structure. Language is not the result of operations mediated by discrete neocortical centers, but the outcome of a multitiered system distributed over levels in the evolution of brain and behavior. Thus, from the beginning, the developing psychological theory led to fresh anatomical insights; and as one line of study progressed, it enriched the other.

In early papers, microgenetic theory was explored mainly in the field of language pathology. However, it later became clear that the microgenetic concept provided a unitary framework for the understanding not only of language disorders but of a diversity of other clinical problems. This, in fact, is one of the more compelling arguments in its favor, that the microgenetic concept applies "across the board" to all cognitive domains. Within the complexity of the anatomy and the richness of the clinic, there is an esthetic in a theory that is uniform across various components and even, as discussed below, across the process of cognition and the pattern of physiological growth. This collection of papers, therefore, though it begins with and is indebted to studies of cerebral dominance and language pathology, is the record of a search for a general theory of behavior. More than this, however, the papers point to a body of data that can no longer be ignored by those working in behavioral neurology—from whatever theoretical perspective—nor for that matter by allied fields of philosophy and experimental cognition.

I

What Is Microgenesis?

The idea of microgenesis developed in the Würzburg school of psychology (Humphrey, 1963) but the term was coined from the German *Aktualgenese* by Heinz Werner for the microtemporal unfolding of object representations, conceived as a more or less instantaneous recapitulation in cognition of patterns laid down in phylo-ontogeny. The approach was explored in aphasia studies by Arnold Pick (1913) and, though not well appreciated, in apraxia theory by Liepmann (1920), who held that the different types of apraxia (ideational, ideomotor) were moments in the action development. Yakovlev (1948) contributed a seminal paper on the microgeny of action systems.

The basic assumption of microgenesis is that mental representations (perceptions, ideas), as well as actions and affects, have a prehistory that forms the major part of their structure. There is an unfolding in microtime—in seconds or in a fraction of a second—leading to an action or an idea. This unfolding process is concealed from the individual, who is only aware of events in consciousness. The surface events that articulate consciousness—limb movements, utterances, objects and mental images—are like the tip of an iceberg in cognitive structure. They are the outcome of a more or less instantaneous development, a process that is reiterated in the occurrence of every representation.

The implication for a theory of mind is that mental states, as well as consciousness—including the self-concept—are elaborated over a series of vertical modules that develop "bottom-up" over evolutionary structure. These modules have brief durations and may overlap. This entails that the active or causal agent in cognition is the process leading to the representation, not the representation itself. That is, mind unfolds from depth to surface, not from one representation to another. The activation leading to the content in a conscious representation owes to subsurface mentation, not to the preceding conscious content. This is why, if mind is taken to consist in the objects, acts and inner states that fill our conscious awareness (or conversely, if attention is on the content of representations rather than on the process through which the content develops), mind will be missed entirely. Instead, we must go to the antecedents of representations, to their microgenesis.

There is an important difference in focus between microgenetic theory and experimental cognition. This concerns the distinction between the final (conscious) content of a mental representation—which is of concern to cognitive psychology—and the stages through which that representation unfolds, which is the core of microgenetic theory. Microgenesis looks at processing stages underlying representations, a representation being a slice through a processing continuum. The final content of a processing sequence is prefigured by stages that are very different from that of the final representation; and all of the stages given up in the derivation of the final stage are conceived as persisting, abstractly, in the final performance. Microgenetic theory holds that the content of an idea is detritus at the surface of a dying representation as it gives way to new forms rising from deeper strata. On the other hand, this evanescent content is the substance of cognitive psychology, where it has an active—indeed, a central—role in shaping new representations.

The microgenetic process is hierarchical; later levels differentiate out of earlier ones. The series of levels leading from the inception of a mental state to the final representation forms a complex structure. Mind does not appear at the surface of this structure but obtains at each in a series of emergent states. The complete structure—the series of unfolding stages, not their outcome, the representation—is the neuropsychological correlate of a cognitive state. The representation incorporates into its structure, and is part of, the whole hierarchic series which precedes it. In other words, processing stages that underlie or are submerged within a performance constitute part of the structure of that performance, just as stages of development in childhood persist as the "subconscious" motives or the experiential context guiding the cognition of the adult.

Microgenesis and Evolution

The idea that phyletic and ontogenetic growth patterns are retraced in microgeny implies that microgenesis may be an expression of a single process extending over different time frames. When the time frame is millions of years, the process is referred to as phylogenesis. When the period is measured in decades, ontogenesis, and when these processes are collapsed over a second or so, microgenesis. In fact, the idea that the phyletic sequence is condensed in microgeny is similar to the idea of a condensation of phyletic forms in ontogeny, though the microgenetic progression is more closely linked to phyletic than ontogenetic growth planes. Specifically, growth processes in phylo-ontogeny correspond with the sequence of stages in cognitive processing. Morphological growth over long time periods and ongoing physiological change are manifestations of the same process.

The similarities between growth and cognitive processing can be seen in several areas. In the process through which the coupled growth of brain and behavior builds up phyletic structure, the transition to new anatomical levels is characterized by the appearance of growth planes. These planes develop as regions of "bud formation" or "core differentiation" within more generalized background fields (Sanides, 1970; Braak, 1980). The description of this pattern of growth provides a thematic link between phyletic and microgenetic theory. For example, object formation or lexical selection both involve a kind of "functional" core differentiation, a zeroing in on target representations. Mental contents individuate through a type of center:surround or figure:ground transformation that is reiterated at successive points and this process is similar to that in evolutionary brain growth.

Phylogenetic trends continue into the maturational period. The time frame now is not millions of years but the life span of an organism. Here we find parallels between the theory of core differentiation in evolution and the concept of progressive regional specification of the dominant hemisphere in the course of maturation. There is evidence for a type of diffuse to focal change in brain organization over the developmental period. Functional representation may be more generalized in the right hemisphere than in the left hemisphere. Lateral asymmetry and intrahemispheric specificity appear to be tightly correlated. These changes may be due to a type of selective inhibition rather than to preferential growth. The specification or parcelation of the left hemisphere may reflect the survival of some cell populations over others. In fetal development, growth is exuberant and specificity may be accomplished through a dropping out of superfluous connections. Thus, in both fetal and postnatal development, the shift to a more discrete representation may reflect the loss of cellular elements. In this there is an important parallel to patterns of cognitive processing, since the emergence of representations through inhibition of competing alternatives is central to the microgenetic theory of perception. In fact, the process of percept formation can be viewed, not as a constructive series but as the derivation of objects through successive levels of sensory constraint.

Phyletic and ontogenetic processes converge in the idea of microgenesis. The time frame is now in milliseconds. Microgenesis is a type of instantaneous evolution. Like evolution and maturation, it is assumed to proceed in a forward direction. Systems are entrained in cognitive activity in a sequence that mirrors their appearance in evolution. The idea of a unidirectional flow from archaic structures to those of evolutionary recency is a key element in microgenetic theory. Every percept and response of the organism reiterate phyletic structure. Core differentiation in phylogeny, regional specification and neural selectivity in ontogeny, and the specification of target representations in microgeny, reflect a *single process affecting structural and functional growth over different time periods*.

Another basic element in microgenetic theory is the idea that subsurface events that immediately precede surface representations are part of the structure of the representation and not purely anticipatory or preparatory stages, a concept identical to that in evolutionary theory. An individual is the product of his past, structurally, culturally and, one can say, cognitively as well. The past is continuously active as the present is elaborated. This is not a simple concept to grasp. In the evolution of a physical structure, a lamination is deposited as a visible trace of what has gone before. The contour of a hill is not what we call the hill: The hill is the subterranean mass within that contour; the contour is only its surface appearance. Similarly, evolution has its markers in the development of an organism; there is a stratification in the brain that points to this process. This is not a series of phyletic encrustations, but a dynamic system continually pouring out new form. Evolution is more than an account of past happenings, and evolutionary structure in the brain is more than a relic of ancestral behavior. The evolutionary history of an organism constitutes a kind of *abstract* structure through which behavior unfolds.

An organism is active in the present. The ontogenesis of the organism is a record in the experience of living things; its phylogenesis, a theory about a period before the living record. We accept that maturation goes into the shaping of a particular stage in behavior, and that ontogenetic form has an evolutionary background. But to comprehend the structural role of phyletic and maturational antecedents is still less difficult to understand than the comparable role of these antecedents in the microgenesis of a mental representation. We infer the derivation of the organism through an ontogenetic process, but we have to understand abstractly the continuing activity of evolutionary form.

Relation to Ontogeny

Implicit in the microgenetic idea is the concept of a recapitulation of evolutionary and, to a lesser extent, ontogenetic development. In early formulations such as that of Werner, phylo-ontogeny was thought to leave a track that was retraced each moment in the process of object formation. The implication is that pathological destructuration unravels cognition in the reverse of the sequence of evolutionary and maturational development. This is sometimes referred to as the regression hypothesis.

With regard to ontogeny, there are some points of contact between patterns of symptom formation in pathological cases and patterns of development in, say, Piagetian theory, and some developmental milestones can be identified in the course of pathological decay; but more often than not the correlations are weak. Indeed, there is considerable evidence against the idea, in its simple form, that pathology unravels the maturational sequence. However, the relation of microgenesis to ontogeny is more subtle than refutations of the regression hypothesis suppose. There is an important insight in the idea of regression that can be missed if we throw out the ontogenetic perspective. The problem is that neither a deficit at a given maturational stage nor the pattern of pathological breakdown at any age clearly reflect the order in which capacities are acquired.

This is because the regression that occurs in pathology is *micro*structural, not ontogenetic. Pathological symptoms are levels in cognition, not stages in cognitive development. The cognition of a child unfolds over all levels in microgenesis, the structure maturing as a whole so that acquisitional stage refers to the system generally and not its level-specific components. In other words, developmental psychology looks at growth of cognition, while neuropsychology looks at levels in cognitive structure.

For this reason one would expect only the most general correspondence between the two fields of study. An example might be the traversal early on in the course of object formation of preprocessing stages bound up with a phase of experiential relations, or the emergence of object representations out of long-term memory into short-term memory and perception, or the form-building role in early perception of "buried" contents from the first several years of life, that period of development for which there is a childhood amnesia. In other words, certain categories of early experience form the foundation out of which object representations develop. Put differently, the microgeny of objects—indeed, the structure of an object representation—leads from archaic percepts to current ones.

Another example might be the growth of sucking behavior in the infant, where a rhythmic axial movement organized about the body space at a drive level in cognition, associated with appetitive and hypnic states, proceeds outward to limb movements and increasingly more differentiated asymmetric and affect-free digital movements in extrapersonal space. Motility in the adult recapitulates this progression each moment. One can say that this recapitulation forms the structure of an action. But clearly in development this "structure" is undergoing growth as a whole. Each new performance is not grafted to the preceding stage but issues from the depths of the structure. Pathology in the adult exposes different moments or structural levels in the unfolding of the action, while developmental stage is related to the maturation of the entire action structure.

Microgenesis and Jacksonian Theory

The concept of regression in neuropsychology owes much to Hughlings Jackson, as well as to Freud who elaborated on many of Jackson's ideas. It is well, however, to point out some of the differences between microgenetic theory and Jacksonian concepts. For Jackson, cognition was layered (re-represented) over successively "higher" stages in development. A given function mediated, say, by brainstem mechanisms was (re)represented at neocortical levels in a progressively more individuated state. Thus, deep or developmentally early levels elaborate automatic functions, whereas "higher" levels elaborate volitional performances. This concept differs from that of encephalization, which postulates a transfer of function to stages of greater evolutionary recency. For Jackson, function was not transferred but represented again in a different form. According to Jackson, damage to superficial levels in the hierachy of representational stages released or disinhibited archaic systems normally held in check. A persistent release of a lower level would be construed as a regression to a more primitive mode of behavior. This concept of a stratified cognition with descending inhibitory effects—with suppression of deep or early layers by more superficial ones—is the origin of Freud's topographic model.

In contrast, the microgenetic idea is that preliminary stages are not released or disinhibited from above, but exhibit a form of cognition consistent with a certain level of derivation. The structure of cognition is not that of "higher," more volitional stages controlling lower automatic ones. Early processing stages are transformed to later ones, but the early stages also persist, in some sense, in the structure of the ones that follow. The direction of processing is not one of control by higher centers over lower output levels but an emergent process from depth to surface. In this account, the more labile, precipitous and global nature of archaic reactions is not a released automatism but a characteristic of early cognition that is normally derived to a more differentiated manifestation.

For example, a Jacksonian interpretation of "sham" display—rage, laughing, crying—in cases of brain damage entails an interruption of descending fiber pathways that inhibit mechanisms subserving the display. These pathways serve to inhibit reactions organized at archaic levels. When they are interrupted the reactions are disinhibited, or released, and there is an automatic display. The absence of an appropriate inner affect accompanying the display confirms that archaic automatisms are involved. Conversely, the microgenetic hypothesis is that early stages in affect development appear as symptoms when regions mediating those stages are disrupted or, with extensive pathology, there is an attenuated "ceiling" on cognitive unfolding. In this view, the inability to verbalize internal affect consistent with the display results from impaired access to subsurface mentation, while the display itself is not a mechanism but a phase in the development of emotional expression. In other words, the sham display is the preliminary core of what later individuates to more subtle expressions of emotion and finely tuned affective states.

Mind and Evolution

We see the process of evolution reasserted each moment in the mental life of the organism. Evolution is an account of the history of mind and its interaction with the external world. Microgenesis is an account of the evolution of acts and objects in the resurgence and flow of cognition. The process of evolution leads to the formation of the organic world. The process of microgenesis leads to the world of cognition. The products of microgenetic activity appear as contents exteriorizing into the world that evolution has given us.

Put differently, evolutionary theory gives us an account of how living objects were formed; it is an explanation of diversity. In perception, we are also confronted with diversity. The objects which evolution had deposited along the way are like representations in the mind of a perceiver. Evolution is a theory positioned in a world of adaptation and survival. This evolutionary process is played out again in the microgenesis of the world of cognition. Mental representations appear and disappear—as do organisms—yet we are unaware of the struggle through which these representations develop. In a very real sense, the differentiation of a species in evolution is like the selection of an object in perception. Once we have a representation, an act or an utterance, it is no more a part of the cognitive process. The real work of cognition is over.

This is because microgeny, like the evolutionary process, is propelled by organic forms that do not materialize. Speciation in evolution takes its origin at primitive or rudimentary stages, not at fully developed points, as a tree branches from its basal structure. Evolutionary progression is a continuity across embryonic forms, not the adult expressions of those forms. The phenotype of an organism is a dead end in the evolutionary process. In modern concepts of the evolution of the brain, new regions develop out of more generalized older zones, not the immediately preceding stage. Neither in the evolution of an organism nor in the evolution of the brain is growth a result of terminal addition. This is also the case in microgenesis. New objects emerge from deeper layers through a process of selection. Creative thinking is like a divergence in phyletic development; it involves a type of subsurface branching. The object of a perception, like an organism in the world, is what survives of a developmental series. The variety of objects in the mind's representation of space are the distal segments or twigs in a microgenetic tree. In both evolution and microgeny, the formative or developmental stages are obscured, while the final stages—object representations or living organisms—are no longer active in the formative process. One can say that an object in perception is like an extinct organism in evolution.

This evolutionary approach shifts our attention away from the final contents of mind to the process though which these contents are generated. We are also directed away from the static architecture of the brain to the dynamic activity underlying its structure. The dimensions of, say, the language areas and their interconnections have as little to do with the process of language production as the size, shape and relations between objects in perception have to do with the process of percept formation. There are any number of ways to describe a table or a brain. These descriptions constrain a theory of object formation but are not themselves components of the formative process. The brain is not just an object in perception, it is a microgenetic process through which representations unfold. If we look into the problem deeply enough we come at last to see that evolution and mind are terms for a common process. At the very heart of the matter there is in living systems only one law, an evolutionary law, which is everywhere the same but in a different mode of concealment.

II

Symptoms and Deficits

One of the more intractable problems of behavioral neurology concerns the nature of the lesion effect on linguistic or cognitive function. What does a lesion do? Does it destroy a process or an operation? Does it knock out a strategy or a representation located in the damaged area? Does it interrupt flow or disconnect two or more regions, produce a local or distant inhibition, a disinhibition? These are the usual ways of thinking about lesion effects. Of course, this interpretation works best for deficits. The preoccupation with deficits—with what the patient can't do, rather than with the errors he makes—leads to this view and reinforces it.

In clinical case study the deficit method has usually been framed in terms of syndrome description. What this really involves is a lateral expansion from a target symptom to associated disturbances, to bundles of deficits that may or may not be inwardly related. A focus on deficits is also inherent in assessment-based approaches where impaired performances are viewed as insufficiencies relative to norms. Such approaches provide little more than *ad hoc* conclusions about the normal state or the nature of the deficit. It is not possible to penetrate into the actual processing. More recently, so-called theory-driven methods have emphasized the need for a kind of cross-sectional expansion within the deficient performance. This method seeks to define processing defects through single-case analysis. Thus far, the results have not been encouraging, tending largely to confirm clinical observation as to individual variability. Moreover, predictions as to site of deficit derived from flow models in other fields of research have not found much support.

While from the standpoint of the examiner the deficit is a deviance or discrepancy from the normal, the error is an achievement of the cognition of the patient. The analysis of deficiency states differs from error-based approaches in that, in the latter, a defective stage is assumed to actualize directly in aberrant behavior. At least, this is my own view of the meaning of errors. Specifically, an error or positive symptom is a moment in flow prematurely displayed. Both organic and psychopathologic disorders result in the surfacing of behaviors that are abnormal only by virtue of their unexpected appearance. Errors are sub-surface phases in the infrastructure of cognition, manifestations of normally "buried" or submerged processing stages. They differ from deficits in that an error is a slice through a processing series that is momentarily attenuated, while a deficit entails a comparison with the unrealized endpoint. The concept that lesions reveal processing by displaying normal events that are otherwise transparent attempts to forge a series of links between a process, damage to the process, and the resultant symptom.

The Meaning of the Symptom

On the microgenetic approach, symptoms reflect normal subsurface processing mediated by the damaged region. An important point is that symptoms are not attenuations but submerged levels *processed normally* distal to the point of damage. Pathology disrupts the subsurface stage and exposes the normal processing at the disrupted segment. This is why patients with phonemic or lexical-semantic errors have an essentially normal phonological or lexical-semantic system. Cognition is not unpeeled like an onion. Lesions induce a microdissection of cognitive structure with the exposed point carried through successive stages in a normal manner. Symptoms reflect a particular moment in microgeny determined by the degree to which the process unfolds. This account is similar to the idea of the symptom in psychoanalytic theory. Recall that Freud argued that symptoms were not aberrations or states of possession but revelations of normal structure.

It is not difficult to imagine the symptom as a kind of regression effect in functional states, but it requires an imaginative step to accept this idea for organic disorders. Yet, there is some evidence that this is the case. The full range of aphasic errors occurs in normal sleep-talking. Errors typical of aphasics occur in normal speakers, particularly in learning a second language. Studies of phonemic jargon indicate that phoneme frequencies do not differ markedly from the normal. Similar findings have been reported in other types of aphasia.

How Does the Lesion Display Processing?

The precise nature of the lesion effect is not clear. However, the concept of the symptom as a normal but earlier stage in the microgenetic sequence suggests a comparison with developmental "lesions" in which a deviant adult form results from an arrest of embryogenesis. There are parallels between the microgenetic concept of errors (symptoms) and the hypothesis that errors in development are instances of a "prolonged embryology," a local arrest or retardation (or acceleration?). The theory of developmental arrests has been discussed at length by Gould (1977) who writes, "If different parts of the fetus can develop at different rates, then 'monstrosities' will arise when certain parts lag behind and retain, at birth, the character of some lower animal" (p. 49). Of interest is the description by Serres (1860) of two sorts of malformations, the *monstres par défaut* and the *monstres par excès,* recalling the distinction of deficiency states or omissions on the one hand, and errors on the other, or the difference between negative and positive symptoms.

One such mechanism might be that of heterochrony, a change in the onset or timing of a particular stage in development or in the rate of that stage in relation to other systems undergoing simultaneous development. As Gould notes, the effect of heterochrony will depend in part on whether there is a change in the length of ontogeny. If a stage in microgeny is retarded or accelerated in relation to other components, and if the length of the microgenetic sequence is constant, the final product (utterance, action, percept) will reflect the change in the rate of development of the disrupted segment.

For example, if a lesion gives a retardation at a point in lexical selection just prior to the specification of the target item, a semantic paraphasia (e.g., *chair* for table) would represent that moment in the background field or category where there is a kind of equivalence between the two instances (chair, table). The retardation leads to a momentary arrest of the process at a prephonological stage of semantic covalence. The deviant item appears through an incomplete, sluggish(?) traversal of this stage; i.e., a retardation of the stage in comparison with other simultaneously unfolding contents. Of interest is that on this account a representation may be premature semantically even if correct (i.e., *table* for table may be deviant). In any event, subsequent phonological encoding is intact. This is similar to the situation in ontogeny when a body part is deformed (for example, as in fused or webbed fingers), but the deformed part undergoes further development through intact later stages.

In the development of an organism a birth defect can be widespread or specific to a given domain of function. The form of the defect will reflect the focus and severity of the pathology, and the ontogenetic stage at which it occurs. Analogous defects occur in the brain damaged. A microgeny can be truncated and the distal segment incomplete, or a pathological level can be embedded in a microgeny completed through other systems. For example, a lesion involving object representation without affecting other components might lead to hallucination, while a more global expression of the same level occurs normally in dream. The stage affected—the depth of the retardation—also accounts for the generality or focality of the defect. For example, akinetic mutism involves the entire action system at its base and spills into other cognitive domains, while selective impairments of limb initiation occur with damage to later processing stages.

Heterochrony and Symptom Formation

Focal lesions induce a local retardation but the processing mediated by the damaged area still takes place. How can we understand this effect? One possibility is that the lesion acts like an obstruction or partial blockage in a river producing an eddy about the interrupted point (Figure I-1). The flow diverges around the obstruction and regroups when the obstruction is passed. Flow continues in neighboring regions with minimal if any change.

Something of this sort in brain-injured patients would explain why processing is continuous but delayed. Flow is retarded but not blocked; the segment of the stream that is derailed arrives beyond the point of the derailment after a slight delay. The delay is important because it leads to a retardation of that segment relative to other regions. The argument is that in brain pathology the symptom reflects the point in the stream where the delay occurs. Through this interpretation, the neural correlates of mental contents have configurational properties. The configuration envelops the lesion and is preserved even as the process flows around the obstruction. The critical factor is the delay in transmission, not the distortion of the configuration or a loss of elements.

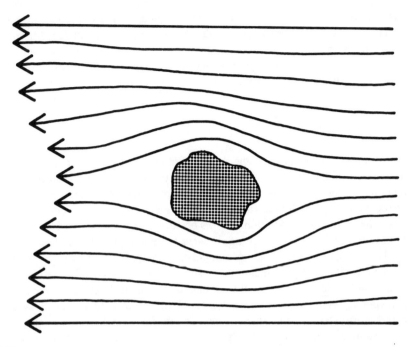

FIGURE I-1. The lesion retards but does not interrupt cognitive flow. See text.

There are several implications of this idea for brain study. First, it entails an account of neural states underlying cognitive functions in terms of wave fronts or fields rather than centers or modules and connections. The mental content is not transmitted from one site to another through a system of wires that can be interrupted, but is conveyed through a network dynamic that "wraps around" a lesion in its course. Eccles has speculated that cognitive functions are mediated by fieldlike effects, and of course this was the contribution of the Gestalt school. Field theory entails that the neural functions and processes that mediate perceptual events are located in a continuous medium. Attempts to test Kohler's concept of direct current fields by Lashley, Sperry and others (Pribram, 1982) by placing gold foil on the cortex, mica insulation, and aluminum hydroxide cream injections, failed to show a change in performance. Whether holographic theory and/or waveform mathematics can capture the described fieldlike effects remains to be seen.

Second, the concept of pathology as a delay rather than an interruption or loss implies that, barring very extensive lesions, functions are not destroyed or eliminated from the repertoire of behavior, but persist and play a role and have the potential to be retrieved. This means that recovery is at least a theoretical possibility.

Another implication, it would seem, is that microgeny has a fixed duration. Systems in parallel to the damaged system complete their development slightly in advance of the latter, which appears defective because it is delayed. Microgeny is not open-ended; rather, it is a sequence—in my view, an obligatory sequence—that is reiterated each moment. This means that the obstruction is not bypassed as in the flow of a river but is encountered anew for every iteration.

III

With this introduction to the theory of microgenesis, we can turn to a brief description of the model and its application to different types of behavior. As mentioned, the microgenetic theory developed out of research on language disorders, but gradually insights from aphasia study came to be seen as relevant to a general theory of cognition. As this occurred, the aphasias—and by implication, normal language organization—came to be interpreted as a subdivision or offshoot of perceptual and action components. Action and perception, however, were viewed as complex hierarchic systems, not as peripheral input: output or sensorimotor devices. The point is that cognition is built up on action and perception, with language a derivation of these more fundamental systems. Neural correlates in the production and comprehension of language evolve out of systems mediating action and perception, as these systems undergo a fractionation within a unified stem or core. Other cognitive functions—thought, affect, and memory—are interpretable in relation to these fundamental components.

On the basis of this theory, language is not mediated by a system appearing *de novo*—a dedicated module in the brain—but is a result of the confluence of systems elaborating action and perception that have undergone an evolutionary advance. This advance is characterized *inter alia* by an increased capacity for cognitive analysis, that is, by the ability to segment or specify the constituent items within a more global or holistic content. The appearance of language is closely associated with this capacity, and is expressed in the ability to achieve a phonemic representation out of an abstract lexical or conceptual frame, as well as the corresponding phonetic realization of an emerging vocal act. With the acquisition of phonology, other aspects of cognition achieve greater specification.

Given the primary components of action, perception, and language, other domains of cognition, such as memory and thinking, can be understood as phenomena linked to moments in the flow of the microgenetic process when a particular configuration emerges. The different types of memory can be viewed as performances at successive moments in perceptual, motor or language microgeny. Similarly, thinking can be approached as a type of productive memory and, like memory, thinking captures moments in the unfolding of linguistic or perceptual representations. Unlike memory, however, we do not yet have a neurology of thinking. The poverty of lesion data, or for that matter clinical studies, on this topic is such as to discourage any attempt at a neural structure of thought to correspond with that of the other components. Some tentative efforts in this direction, however, were described in the aforementioned monograph.

We begin with some speculations on a neural system that might be involved in "primitive cognition," the first appearance of a cognitive representation. This system configures ensuing stages in action and perception, and from these language processes appear. Affect develops in concert with these components. Each of these topics is briefly discussed, to provide a guide for the clinical material to follow.

Speculation on the Neural Origin of Mind

Cognition, or mind, first appears in the stem or core system, out of which acts and objects develop. This archaic system is built up on perceptuomotor function in a primitive or preliminary representation of space. The stem system is assumed to constitute a rudimentary mind that emerges within reflex systems. In lower organisms behavior seems determined by reflex operations and it has been natural to assume that the human mind/brain would be organized on the same basis, namely a complex bundle of reflex mechanisms. The idea that the mind/brain is a compilation of reflexes, which in turn are derived from tropisms, forms the basis of much speculation in neurology, not to mention entire systems of anatomical and psychological thought. However, mind or cognition entails a representation, and in this respect differs fundamentally from reflex.

In reflex, a stimulus is followed by a response that involves a movement or a displacement, and this displacement provides the basis for another stimulus. The *sensory* event is that stimulus which elicits a movement, but a *movement* is also a stimulus. In reflex there is a superficial distinction between sensation and movement—even less between stimulus and response. The events are circular, as in the *Gestaltkreis* of von Weizsaecker (1958). The sequence is determined by the point in the circle where one happens to intervene. A reflex does not require a brain and is extrinsic to cognition. The outcome of a reflex—say, a knee jerk—is perceived as an object; it is not elaborated inwardly.

From the microgenetic view, however, sensations do not provide the "raw material" of percepts or cognitions, but constrain or "sculpt" mind to represent sensory events. In the same way, movement is the physical realization of an action representation and discharges in a space extrinsic to cognition. Since we know only our mental representations, the existence of sensation and movement requires an act of faith in a physical world beyond cognition. One could say that sensation and movement are a type of evolutionary myth about the microgenetic origins of consciousness.

In reflex, sensory and motor phases follow one another. Even in consciousness we infer priority to perception. We see an object and act upon it. But at what point does an event become a perception? Not when a stimulus occurs at the receptors. This is still an external or peripheral phase. The perception appears when a neural configuration first represents a preliminary object. When does action enter? Not when there is muscular contraction. The action appears when a neural configuration represents the nucleus or plan of the act to be performed. In contrast to the circularity of reflex, the neural configuration that represents the preliminary object is part of the same configuration that represents the preliminary action. The departure from reflex occurs when the earliest phase of object representation is the preliminary phase of an action. In other words, unlike reflex, *action and perception develop simultaneously out of the same deep organization.*

A candidate substrate for the inception of a cognitive as opposed to a purely reflex operation might be a population of neurons with short intrinsic connections arising in proximity to sensory and motor pathways. The configuration derived from this neuronal pool would constitute an embryonic act:object. The configuration would develop within a sensorimotor surround distinct from and extrinsic to the cognitive representation emerging at its juncture. The core is modulated by sensation and read off into movement, but these are physical events not experienced in mind/brain. The world of cognition is a unified act:object. This pattern of an emergent representation accompanied at each of a series of levels by a stratified sensory and motor organization becomes the model for all subsequent cognitive layering. The core of this system is probably located in upper brainstem.

Perception: Summary of the Model

The microgenetic account of perception has been framed largely in relation to visual perception, though the interpretation is similar for the auditory and somaesthetic systems. In the case of vision, the perception is thought to arise as a two-dimensional map elaborated through upper brainstem and tectal mechanisms representing the space of the body and body surround. Space consists of a schema for actions on proximate targets. Objects as such have not yet appeared. The space of the target is confluent with the space of the body. Act and percept are tightly bound together, giving almost the appearance of a sensorimotor reflex. Movements involve the proximal or axial musculature, or saccadic eye movements, often in the form of an orientation or rapid ballistic grasp. An example of this stage as a final level in percept formation would be the sudden thrust of the frog's tongue to capture an insect, where the stimulus and the resulting action are locked as a single unit. In human perception, this stage underlies all successive levels of sensory modeling (Figure I-2).

Sensory input to this purely intrinsic system constrains the spatial map to model or represent aspects of the external object. Partial damage to this system leads to impairments in personal space, defective ballistic movements and

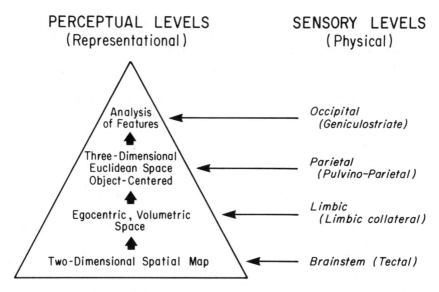

PERCEPTUAL LEVELS
(Representational)

SENSORY LEVELS
(Physical)

Analysis
of Features

Three-Dimensional
Euclidean Space
Object-Centered

Egocentric, Volumetric
Space

Two-Dimensional Spatial Map

Occipital
(Geniculostriate)

Parietal
(Pulvino-Parietal)

Limbic
(Limbic collateral)

Brainstem (Tectal)

FIGURE I-2. Levels of object and space representations with corresponding stages of sensory constraint.

disorders of orientation. Severe damage leads to coma. With a suspension of sensory input, the system operates autonomously and leads to a state of dreamless sleep.

The construct resulting from sensory modulation of brainstem and tectal systems develops to a viewer-centered, volumetric space through mechanisms in limbic and temporal lobe. At this stage the primitive schema is transformed—or the object is selected—through a network of symbolic and experiential relations. There is direct sensory input to limbic-temporal lobe, but the poverty of constraints on the developing representation at this level enables it to undergo selection through a system of personal memory. Image phenomena occur in the absence of sensation at more distal microgenetic stages. Such phenomena have an hallucinatory quality. There are features of dreamwork mentation, and the object is bound up with instinctual drive and a strong affective tonality. This level in the object representation appears normally in dream hallucination. The shift between dream and dreamless sleep reflects the momentary dominance in the perception of limbic-temporal or upper brainstem mechanisms.

The limbic image and its egocentric space are then transformed (selected) through fields of conceptual relationships to a three-dimensional Euclidean or object-centered space. This occurs by way of mechanisms in the parietal lobe. The representation achieves a referential adequacy. There is an object in an external space, but object and space are not fully independent of the viewer. This is a space of the arm's reach, a space bounded by the perimeter of limb action. Damage to parietal lobe mechanisms leads to disorders of spatial perception, impaired size, distance and simultaneity judgments and misreaching—in other words, deficits in the perception of object relations, particularly when object manipulation is involved. Illusions may also occur, and these—the so-called metamorphopsias—reflect distortions of objects or altered spatial relationships. With reduced sensory input, mental imagery rather than object perception may occur. The hallucinatory stage of the preceding level is then transformed to a memory image. The memory image is at the threshold of awareness. The link between hallucination and memory imagery is experienced normally when a memory image survives a dream that is fading as one is awakened.

The object representation that is derived through parietal lobe mechanisms is then submitted for featural modeling and complete exteriorization through mechanisms in striate and circumstriate cortex. Sensory input at this stage constrains an object gestalt to the fine analysis of object form. At the same time, the emerging mental representation of the object is established as an independent thing in the world. This is the surface of our everyday perceptions. On those occasions when the level discharges spontaneously or is deprived of sensory input, there are various forms of imagery, such as elementary hallucinations in migraine, and afterimagery. Damage to this stage leads to deficits in the identification of object features—impaired reading, recognition of form and color—or to "loss of vision" in a field. In the latter case, even with cortical blindness, residual vision points to levels in the object that are completed prior to the surface disruption.

Central to this account is the hypothesis that sensation, a physical effect outside of cognition, enters hierarchically at successive stages and acts to constrain the derivation or selection of the representation—a purely cognitive or mental phenomenon—so as to model an external object. Sensations do not enter directly into the object construction. The different forms of normal and pathological imagery—hallucination and illusion, memory, eidetic and imagination images—and the different types of impairments that occur in space and object perception—the agnosias—are disruptions at specific levels in this unfolding sequence.

Action: Summary of the Model

As in perception, phylogenetically older systems in motor organization mediate early stages in the unfolding of an action. Unlike movement, which by analogy to sensation is activity in physical space, an action is a construct in cognition. An action is not a set of concatenated movements but an hierarchic series of rhythmic levels (Figure I-3) that are entrained sequentially, laying down a dynamic system of oscillators distributed over stages in evolutionary growth.

The action proceeds bottom up from a core in upper brainstem and basal ganglia. This "envelope" of the action linked to tectal-midbrain systems in perception elaborates postural and locomotor activities in relation to other rhythmic functions, such as respiration. In lower forms where rhythmic axial

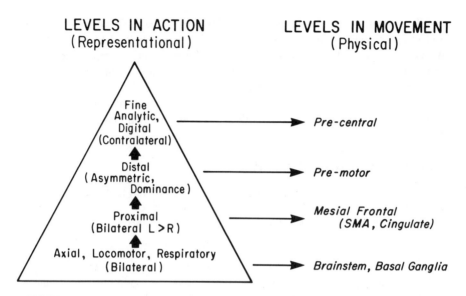

FIGURE I-3. Levels in the structure of an action with discharge into motor keyboards.

motility is the sole or chief manifestation of the action, such as fish or reptiles, it constitutes an end stage in the action development.

This archaic level is derived through mesial paralimbic (anterior cingulate gyrus, supplementary motor area) regions to a stage mediating the proximal limb musculature. As with the correlated level in object formation, the developing action has a strong affective tonality. Instinctual activities (flight and fight responses, drivelike behavior) are related to this phase.

The subsequent differentation of the emerging act leads to premotor cortex on the convexity of the hemisphere and, finally, the act is derived to precentral or motor cortex. In the course of this unfolding, the action undergoes progressive specification, from postural and axial systems to the distal limb and vocal musculature. Finally, the act is transformed through mechanisms in motor cortex to highly individuated actions realized through the articulatory and asymmetric limb and digital musculature.

The direction of processing corresponds with that of evolutionary growth, proceeding from a unitary core to a bilateral representation, passing through an intervening stage of asymmetric representation in which one (usually the left) hemisphere controls actions with either limb, to the motor cortex of the hemisphere opposite the limb. The progression from an inception in archaic structures organized about the midline in a primitive, unextended body-centered space (actions dependent on "internal context") toward discrete asymmetric movements with the distal musculature on ostensibly real objects in the external world ("goal oriented" actions) corresponds with levels in affect, language, and object and space representation.

The action microgeny is exactly parallel to the object microgeny. Both act and object begin "within the body" and differentiate outward to the external world. The space of successive levels in the forming action corresponds with levels in the forming object. The zeroing-in on target movements in the action specification has its perceptual correlate in the featural analysis of object form. The primary motor cortex mediates the endpoint of the action development just as the primary visual cortex is hypothesized to mediate an endpoint in object representation.

Language: Summary of the Model

According to the model, language develops in relation to anterior (action) and posterior (perception) structures. There are a series of levels of perceptual representation that emerge together with levels in articulatory realization (Figure I-4).

The Anterior Component The motor component of the utterance develops from depth to surface over stages in the evolution of the forebrain. Initial stages bound up with respiratory timing—breath groups—and locomotor and postural rhythms are linked to axial motor systems and archaic strata in perceptual space. Upper brainstem and basal ganglia mediate an early stage of motor planning in

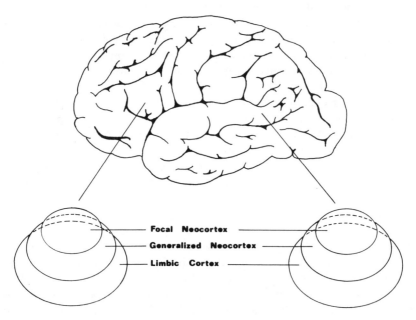

FIGURE I-4. Hierarchic systems mediating anterior and posterior sectors of language processing. See text.

which vocal, limb and body actions appear *in statu nascendi,* part of a "motor envelope" that fractionates to part-acts at subsequent stages. Oscillatory or kinetic rhythms in the motor envelope anticipate the appearance of discrete vocal, limb and axial motility.

The action develops through mesial limbic cortex with progressive individuation of vocal, limb and body gestures. Damage at this point gives disorders of vocal and limb initiation, transcortical motor aphasia and the alien hand syndrome. Vocal and somatic automatisms may also occur. Conceivably, an oscillator mediating the preliminary tonal or breath group of the utterance is derived to one that elaborates the speech melody, a cognitive rhythm laying down the prosodic contour or rhythmic structure of the phrase. Damage at this point gives the impression of a loss of grammatical knowledge, though the condition can be explained through variables of motor timing, parsing, prosody and stress rather than damage to a module for the rules of grammar.

The continued microgenesis of the vocal act leads through dominant premotor (Broca) and precentral cortices, which elaborate the fine temporal programmation of sound sequences and, finally, to the motor implementation of the utterance through the articulatory musculature. Damage at this point in the sequence gives rise to phonetic/articulatory defects.

From the pathological case material one can infer the motor structure of an utterance to consist of an hierarchic series of rhythmic levels or oscillators. This series, which may arise out of periodic or circadian rhythms elaborated through hypothalamic mechanisms, begins with a ?fundamental frequency bound up with low-level automatisms, respiration and axial motility, and is hypothesized to derive to a ?harmonic of this rhythm at successive levels, laying down sequentially the speech melody or prosodic contour of the utterance and a phonetic program leading to a motor keyboard for the articulators. The utterance unfolds over layers of progressive specification, comparable to levels of selection or analysis in percept formation.

The Posterior Component In parallel with the motor series, a posterior hierarchic system lays down levels in lexical representation. The perceptual component of the utterance evolves from a spatial construct arising most likely through upper brainstem mechanisms, with initial stages in language representation bound up with early levels in object development. From this stage there arises through limbic-derived neocortex a conceptual (symbolic, experiential) and affective layer out of which the forming lexical item is selected. The lexical item begins with a traversal of this stage regardless of whether the process leads to speech or speech perception. Damage at this point gives rise to unusual (at times even schizophreniclike) word substitution and confabulatory responses.

The subsequent microgenesis of the emerging representation involves the specification of the lexical item through layered semantic fields, with a gradual honing in on the lexical target. The word is not retrieved but realized or derived and all of the stages in this derivational process (experiential, affective, semantic category) persist as a background of personal and lexical meaning. Lexical representation occurs by way of auditory belt or posterior integration cortex of dominant hemisphere. Damage to this area gives rise to word-finding difficulty or word substitutions where category relations are prominent.

From this stage the perceptual (lexical) representation is derived through mechanisms in para-auditory cortex (supramarginal gyrus, posterior T1) to a phonemic representation of the selected item. This involves the analysis or segmentation of abstract lexical frames analagous to the realization of articulatory or fine digital movements in the motor hierarchy. Damage at this point gives rise to phonemic errors in otherwise correctly selected lexical targets.

In speech *production* there is a simultaneous unfolding over anterior and posterior microgenetic trees. In both anterior and posterior components this leads from bilaterally organized (mesial or lateral) limbic-derived cortex, through asymmetric "integration" (frontal or temporoparietal) neocortex to focal left frontal (Broca) and temporal (Wernicke) regions. The various aphasic syndromes represent moments in this unfolding process, with brain damage viewed as disrupting levels in a continuum rather than centers in an interactive or functional system.

In speech *perception* the described series of posterior levels is constrained at successive levels by auditory sensation to model the physical stimulus. The autonomous system of cognitive representation active in speech production is given over to speech perception. The anterior (action) component is attenuated so that the phonemic representation derived through this system is apprehended as external or perceptual in origin. In other words, the same series of posterior hierarchic levels elaborates language production and perception, but it is the relative activity of the anterior system that determines whether the subject apprehends the achieved lexical representation as self-generated or perceived. Intermediate stages in this process are bound up with imagery and elaborate inner speech or auditory hallucination, again depending on the degree of completion of the action microgeny (Figure I-5). In either case, whether the process leads to speech or to perception, the progression is from internal representation to an exteriorized and ostensibly independent source, or object.

Put differently, it is the unfolding of the motor component that provides the feeling of intention or agency that enables the subject to distinguish an active, self-initiated representation from one that is "passive" or perceptual. In speech production, a phonemic representation is realized together with a phonetic program, and the latter carries the representation outward from speaker to external world. In perception, the action development is attenuated and the perceptual series is carried outward. Inner speech and auditory verbal hallucination—intertwined in pathology, normal in the hypnagogic state—are linked to the relative degree of act and percept development over these systems. These relationships are diagrammed in Figure I-5.

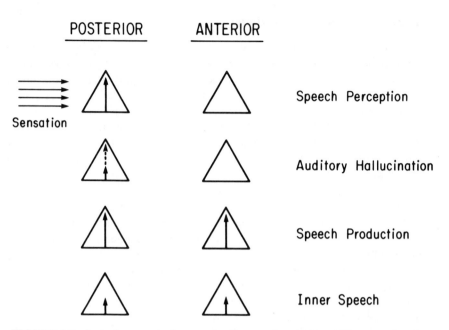

FIGURE I-5. A single perceptual system mediates various aspects of language function depending on its degree of autonomy, and linkage with the anterior (action) component. See text.

Naturally, this model is but an outline for a theory of language organization in the brain. The pathological material is unclear as to the structures involved in syntax; and other complex aspects of language—inference, language at the sentence or intersentential level, etc.—cannot yet be approached from the neurological standpoint. What the theory can do is map some elements of language to brain structure and establish links between language processing and more fundamental components of cognition; it can account for a range of associated phenomena (e.g., problems of affect, imagery, and awareness) not dealt with in linguistic models, and it can motivate studies of the transition from lower organisms.

For example, the concept that lexical items are not looked up or retrieved from a store but are selected through a layered net of word-meaning relationships—(a process that involves a kind of zeroing in on target items, one that is disrupted by lesions of temporal lobe—has points of contact with observations in monkey that temporal lobe lesions impair the selection of object targets in an array of objects. In the microgenetic account, object naming is not mere labeling or association. Lexical items, like objects, are selected as central elements in language representation, developing from preliminary levels in object and space perception.

Affect: Summary of the Model

Affect is intrinsic to the microgeny of acts and objects. Deep levels elaborate states of instinctual drive, which fractionate to flight, fight, and sexual drive through limbic mechanisms. At this stage the developing affect is bilaterally organized. From this point the affect microgeny is transformed to polar affects or moods at a neocortical stage such as euphoria or depression. The probable right hemisphere bias at this stage reflects the advantage of that hemisphere for (or rather, the left hemisphere disadvantage in access to) preliminary processing. Subsequently, the affect undergoes further specification, presumably through left hemisphere mechanisms, to the more highly derived partial affects or affect-ideas.

The sequence of processing in the microgeny of affect maps to the sequence of stages in forebrain evolution. The different forms of emotion (drive, feeling, and affect-ideas) represent points in a processing continuum that leads with diminishing intensity from internal affective states—where the affect is in the observor—toward a "location" in an extrapersonal object. The diminishing intensity of affect over the microgenetic series suggests an answer to the question of what an affect is. Its intensity must in some way reflect the unrealized content of a cognitive representation. In other words, the more completely developed or unfolded the representation, or the more explicit its perceptual or propositional content, the less intense the affect. Conversely, the more intense or emphatic emotions point to representations at early and relatively unanalyzed stages of processing.

At these early stages the range of emotions is limited, whereas at subsequent stages a large number of feelings can be experienced. As affect develops it fractionates to partial expressions, which retain fragments of the more global and archaic representations within which they develop. Thus, drivelike states such as fear contain in some sense the nucleus of what, at subsequent processing stages, becomes affectlike states or feelings such as timidity, shame or humiliation. It should be emphasized that, in this account, affect is not cathected or attached in some way to developing representations but is "articulated" from within into the endpoints of linguistic and perceptual representations, drawn out from the viewer into his own exteriorized objects.

Finally, the transformation of a restricted set of intense emotions (drives, instincts) to a wider set of less intense but qualitatively richer and more distinct moods and feelings occurs parallel with the specification of representations in language and perception. This shows that the affect is not simply the undischarged portion of the representation but is bound up with the representation itself. Affect is generated by the representation through which it takes on its qualitative features. The affect derives its specificity or uniqueness from the way a particular cognitive representation is configured, and its intensity from the degree to which the representation is processed. One implication of this idea is that the deepest or most archaic affects (drives) correspond with a set of cognitive primitives or archaic concepts. If one holds that there is a small, finite set of drives that are distinct from the beginning, this would also hold for our notion of primitive concepts.

IV

This general introduction to the theory of microgenesis should serve to guide the reader through the chapters that follow. In these chapters, details of the application of the theory to each component of cognition are addressed, while some of the final papers, those on action and perception and the experience of memory and time, explore some of its philosophical implications. These articles constitute a theory of mind, or at least the groundwork for a theory, that is based on patterns of functional dissolution.

The history of neuropsychological study has been characterized by a long controversy between unitary (or holistic) and association (or localization) models of aphasia and, by implication, other cognitive functions, a controversy that has usually taken the form of a choice between focal and diffuse representation of function. Over the past 20 years, however, the influence of work in behavioral neurophysiology, the appearance of modularity theory, and the presumed heuristic value of componential accounts have brought about a gradual shift in neuropsychology to localization models. But the other side of this is the failure of holistic or regression models to incorporate advances in neuropsychological study and thus provide a satisfactory framework for contemporary behavioral research. Such theories as Karl Lashley's mass action and equipotentiality, the Jacksonian concept of re-representational levels, Roman Jakobson's idea of linguistic regression, Kurt Goldstein's "abstract attitude" or a process of gestalt formation have at best limited applications, for they address neither the facts of brain specialization nor the problem of the diversity of behavior and pathological change. Here, componential theories have an advantage, for it is easier to add an extra arrow and box to a process diagram than to integrate new phenomena to a unitary concept. Unitary models have to deal with both the unity and the diversity of mental life, local models only with diversity.

In contrast, the microgenetic account is a unitary model that is sensitive to neurological and behavioral complexity. The model is coherent across different cognitive domains—that is, language, perception, action and other functions are interpretable in fundamentally the same way. Whereas AI or componential models tend to disclaim the value of anatomical documentation, and localization models freeze functions in static brain areas, there is a deep inner relationship between the process of microgeny and the building up of anatomical structure. Brain and cognition are interpreted from an equally dynamic standpoint.

Toward a New Holism

Many scientists would agree that the choice of a theory is best determined by the facts it seeks to explain, and that the interpretation of a behavior is independent of its description. But it is well to recognize that scientific enterprises are centered in a certain domain of thought. Einstein said, "It is the theory which decides what we can observe." A point of view is implicit in every scientific demonstration. In a very real sense, a theory has to be accepted, has to fully infiltrate our thinking and influence our view of the world before it can be tested experimentally. This is especially true for psychological investigation. Componential approaches and associationism obligate general theories that are compilations of local models, motivating chiefly those observations by which they can be confirmed. A behavior is fractionated into components that are independently studied and eventually articulated into explanatory models. Indeed, the autonomy of the component is implicit in the derivation of the model.

Microgenetic theory takes a different stand on this question. The richness of the world is not brought together in the mind, an object is not constructed out of sensory elements, a mental state is not the sum of its component parts. The structure of mind is largely inaccessible beneath the representations of waking awareness. We have intuitions about the nature of subconscious processing and we infer its organization from psychological experimentation and daily life events, but these are indirect routes. The symptoms of brain pathology are a *direct* path to mental structure. They reveal a series of microtemporal planes in the unfolding of mental representations and, parenthetically, suggest the existence of a corresponding set of physical levels constraining the unfolding sequence. According to microgenetic theory, an explanation for the flow of events in the world begins and ends in mind. The theory explains how the deception of a real physical world and the exteriorization of action and perception come about. There is a continuum from inner states to "external" phenomena. The theory accounts for the fact that minds develop and degrade; that is, that mind in its instability has an objectlike character. The acts and objects by which we think to interact with this world are not in the world where they appear but in the mind where they originate, the investitures of mind as it distributes itself into a world of its creation. The unity of the mind is not something to be achieved, to be built up from outside. It does not come from the world but is there at the very beginning. The growth of mind over levels leads from unity and centrality toward diversity and elaboration.

I
LANGUAGE

1
Language Representation in the Brain*

A Brain Model of Language

Though there have been various psychological accounts of aphasia over the years, only one—Wernicke's—anatomical theory has ever been proposed. According to this theory, speech perception occurs over a series of stages in the posterior-superior temporal region (Wernicke's area), which both transmits to (for repetition) and modulates Broca's area. Language produced in the posterior brain is conveyed by an uncertain path to Broca's area for articulation. In more modern accounts, mechanisms are assumed to be located within the anterior and posterior regions, which can account for the diversity of clinical symptomatology: for example, mechanisms for sound, word, and meaning perception; for discrimination and sequencing; for various short-term memory and long-term memory processes; a parietal dictionary attached to Wernicke's area accounting for anomia; impaired verbal or auditory feedback. Luria's classification is derived from Wernicke's approach, since similar mechanisms are inferred ad hoc from the clinical picture. In such theories, every new observation implies a new mechanism and results in a chaotic patchwork of areas, mechanisms, and interconnecting paths.

The anatomical model of aphasia presented in this chapter differs fundamentally from this classical account. Limbic and neocortical zones identified with aphasic disturbances are viewed as strata or levels in the evolutionary and maturational structure of the brain. In this model, there is no rostral conveyance of language content, but rather a simultaneous realization of the entire hierarchical system within its anterior and posterior sectors. Nor are there separate processes or strategies operating on language content; instead, there is a resubmission of emerging abstract content at each hierarchical level to the same reiterated process—in other words, one process at multiple levels, rather than multiple processes at the same level. These differences from the traditional approach will become more apparent as we proceed into the actual model.

*Reprinted from "Language Representation in the Brain" by J. W. Brown, 1979. In H. Steklis and M. Raleigh (Eds.), *Neurobiology of Social Communication in Primates*. New York: Academic Press. Copyright 1979 by Academic Press. Adapted by permission.

Evolution of the Language Area

The neural substrate of language consists of a complex hierarchical system of levels corresponding to stages in neocortical evolution. The system has an anterior (frontal) and posterior (temporo-parieto-occipital) component. The two main classes of aphasia, the nonfluent and the fluent aphasias, refer to these components, while the various aphasic syndromes within each class point to different levels within the anterior or posterior sector. The structure as a whole develops out of medial and paraventricular formations through several growth planes of limbic and paralimbic (transitional) cortex to a stage of generalized ("association," "integration") cortex. Within the latter, developing through a process of core differentiation, the primary motor (gigantopyramidalis) and sensory (koniocortical) zones appear. For example, with respect to motor cortex, the evolutionary wave that had been assumed to lead from precentral to premotor area (Campbell, 1905; Bailey & Bonin, 1951) may actually be the reverse of the true direction of neocortical growth. The premotor area may in fact be the older of the two areas.

Evidence for this reinterpretation of neocortical morphology has been steadily accumulating in recent years. An important element of this new approach is the view that fiber size is related to evolutionary stage. This notion derives largely from the work of Bishop (1959), who noted a tendency for small fibers to project to phylogenetically older sites in brainstem, and larger fibers to project directly to newer targets in the dorsal thalamus, suggesting an evolutionary trend toward increasing fiber diameter. Diamond and Hall (1969) reported studies of the optic system which were in support of this idea. Drawing on work in comparative anatomy and perceptual physiology, they proposed that the geniculo-striate system develops in evolution subsequent to a system relating tectum and pulvinar to the association cortex; that is, the primary visual area is the more recent zone in neocortical phylogenesis. They noted that the cytoarchitecture of the secondary visual area is more primitive than the primary visual area, and its neurons have larger (more primitive) receptive fields.

A similar view has been expressed by Sanides (1975): "What has been recognized as a main feature of neocortex evolution in primates, namely the enormous development of the supposedly secondary integration cortices was actually not understood . . . the most *generalized* neocortical structure is bound to become the most predominant one with the widest scope for further differentiation." The myelinogenetic studies of Flechsig (1920), which showed that the classical motor and sensory areas were among the first to begin myelination in the perinatal period, while the secondary or "association" areas showed a more drawnout pattern of myelination, were misinterpreted to indicate the evolutionary priority of the primary sensorimotor areas. In fact, these areas have the *heaviest* definitive myelin content (Vogt & Vogt, 1919) and for this reason show early myelination. The more heavily myelinated systems are more recent in phylogenesis. Thus, the area gigantopyramidalis, which forms the heaviest myelinated core of the motor region, represents the most recent stage in motor cortex evolution, while the hypergranular koniocortex, forming the heaviest myelinated core of the sensory region, represents the most recent stage in sensory cortex evolution. According to Pandya and Sanides (1973), the "development of koniocortex cores as the last wave of sensory neocortex differentiation occurred during evolution only in the *visual, auditory* and *somatic* sensory systems mediating the sharpest objectifying and localizing representations of the periphery."

This is consistent with observations in cat of a two-stage development of visual cortex, an early primitive stage characterized by the activity of a system of fine fibers projecting to a wider extent of cortex, and a later more differentiated stage of large fibers projecting to the primary visual cortex only (Marty, 1962). In the cat there is evidence for a more diffuse geniculocortical projection on both anatomical (Niimi & Sprague, 1970) and electrophysiological (Bignall, Imbert, & Buser, 1966) grounds. In contrast, in monkey the geniculate projection is exclusively to the striate cortex. These findings are in agreement with the concept of an evolutionary and maturational progression from a diffuse to a focal organization, and with the evolutionary concept that in neocortical phylogenesis the primary "sensory" cortex differentiates *out* of the generalized "association" cortex, as at the thalamic level the geniculate bodies develop out of the lateral-posterior: pulvinar complex. Thus, we might consider the frontal sector to be organized into several evolutionary tiers or planes, leading from limbic to paralimbic (e.g., parts of cingulate gyrus) cortex, to generalized ("association") neocortex, and finally to the primary precentral motor area (gigantopyramidalis) (Figure 1-1). Moreover, levels in brain structure correspond to levels in behavior. The paralimbic region supports a preliminary stage in the development of the motor act. Here the motor pattern is global and organized about the axial and proximal musculature in relation to drive or motivational systems. This stage is more bilaterally organized. At the subsequent level of generalized neocortex, the act develops outward toward the distal muscles. Finally, in primary motor cortex, the most highly differentiated phase (the fine paw or digital movements of the contralateral limb) is achieved.

Accordingly, studies of motor cortex demonstrating a rostrocaudad topography (Woolsey et al. 1952) may indicate that the proximal movements associated with more rostral stimulation represent phylogenetically and ontogenetically older (i.e., earlier) phases in the elaboration of the act than the fine distal movements elicited on precentral stimulation. In general, it appears that, as one goes from limbic cortex to premotor to precentral area, stimulation tends to elicit a progressively more distal and more contralateral response. These findings are consistent with the idea of a microgenetic (moment-to-moment) elaboration of the motor act up through this sequence of evolutionary levels.

The temporo-parieto-occipital sector is organized in a manner parallel to that of the frontal zone (Figure 1-1). With regard to language, limbic-derived insular and medial temporal cortex form a preliminary stage leading to generalized

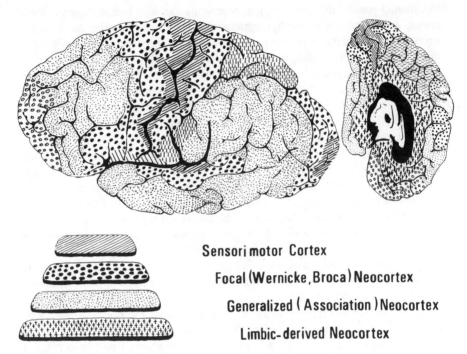

Sensori motor Cortex

Focal (Wernicke, Broca) Neocortex

Generalized (Association) Neocortex

Limbic- derived Neocortex

FIGURE 1-1. Levels in brain evolution and cognitive microgenesis and corresponding regions on an early cytoarchitectural map. The map is quite general and serves to illustrate a conceptual organization. (Modified after Campbell, 1905.)

posterior "association" cortex. The primary sensory (e.g., auditory) cortex differentiates—together with its thalamic (medial geniculate body) nucleus—out of this posterior isocortical field. The organization of perceptual systems is identical to that of motility. Perception does not occur through a constructive phase of in-processing that begins in koniocortex. Rather, *it develops in the reverse direction over a series of levels to a koniocortical end phase.* In other words, the process of object formation unfolds in a cognitive sequence leading from a brainstem preobject through a limbic and generalized neocortical phase, to a final modeling achieved through "primary" visual cortex (Brown, 1977). In a fashion similar to that of the frontal sector, the perception leads from a global pre-object in a unitary field at a preliminary level to the final more or less contralateral hemifield representation at a koniocortical end stage.

A series of recent studies (Jacobsen & Trojanowski, 1977; Jones & Powell, 1970; Pandya & Sanides, 1973; Petras, 1971) has helped to clarify the relationship between various levels in the described infrastructure. Connections, direct and reciprocal, have been shown to exist in a "vertical" direction from one level to the next and across levels; in a "horizontal" direction, excepting sensorimotor cortex, there are connections between homologous levels in the anterior and posterior systems of the same hemisphere, as well as commissural connections to the corresponding anterior or posterior level of the opposite hemisphere. In other words, long intrahemispheric fibers run between the anterior and posterior sectors joining the first three levels in each system. Commissural fibers connect each of these levels, excepting sensorimotor cortices, to the same level in the other hemisphere, and within each of the four sectors (right/left, anterior/posterior), there are reciprocal connections between each level. It is maintained that these various intra- and interhemispheric connections do not serve to transfer contents, percepts or verbal commands, from one point on the surface to another. Rather, it is proposed that they link up temporally, that is, maintain *in-phase,* homologous levels of different brain regions (Figure 1-2).

Maturation and Theory of Lateralization

The nature of cerebral dominance is the central problem for an anatomical theory of language organization. Studies that demonstrate a fixed or native hemispheric asymmetry, whether structural (Teszner, Tzavaras, Gruher, & Hécaen, 1972) or functional (Molfese, Freeman, & Palermo, 1975; Kinsbourne & Hiscock, 1977), lend support to a "prewiring" concept of language mechanisms.

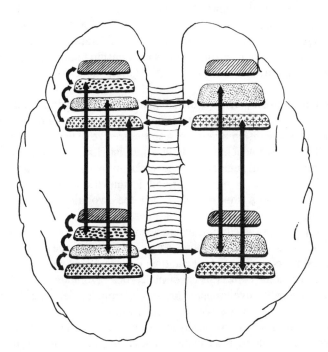

FIGURE 1-2. Cortico-cortical fibers connect homologous levels within and between the hemispheres. The areas are defined on Figure 1-1.

On the other hand, there is considerable evidence (Brown & Jaffe, 1975) that language is gradually biased to one (the left) hemisphere. This argues for a more dynamic model of dominance establishment. However, a theory of continuing lateralization is not necessarily inconsistent with a theory of early structural or functional specialization. Indeed, some combination of the two seems to be required. According to the "prewiring" model, it is difficult to explain findings of considerable right-hemispheric language capacity in commissurotomized adults (Zaidel, 1976), not to mention the longstanding problem of right-hemispheric compensation following aphasia and/or left hemispherectomy. Similarly, the genetic model depends to some extent on the nativist theory to account for the consistent left-side tendency.

In previous articles, an ontogenetic model of the differentiation of the language area has been proposed based on studies of age specificity in aphasia (Brown, 1975). In brief, the model sought to account for age-dependent qualitative differences in aphasia type on the basis of degree of dominance establishment. Confirmation of the model was obtained through a study of aphasia in states of atypical dominance, that is, crossed aphasic dextrals and aphasic left-handers (Brown & Hécaen, 1976).

The evidence was consistent with the following hypothesis: that the degree of dominance reflects the degree of completion of a process of "core differentiation" of focal zones within generalized neocortex of the left hemisphere. These focal zones are conceived as levels that, in the course of development, build up both language and neural structure. Further consideration of this ontogenetic "building up" of the language zone, and its relationship to the described stages in neocortical evolution, has led to a more explicit model of the lateralization process.

According to this model, the differentiation of asymmetric focal neocortex repeats in ontogenesis the pattern established in the evolution of the sensorimotor areas, namely, a core differentiation of a specialized zone within a more generalized field. This phase, which may continue into late life, is characterized by the gradual appearance, in generalized neocortex of both anterior and posterior sectors, of an increasingly more focal and asymmetric (left-lateralized) zone.

One implication of this model is that the evolutionary sequence from transitional to generalized to sensorimotor cortex, which is characteristic of the development of the primate brain, would become, in man, one from transitional to generalized *to focal* to sensorimotor cortex. The emergence of this interposed level (of focal neocortex) out of a penultimate (generalized neocortex) and not a terminal (sensorimotor cortex) phase of neocortical evolution is consistent with the general pattern of evolutionary branching from earlier, less individuated forms rather than from end stages of specialization.

The progression of encephalized neocortex from a bilateral to a unilateral (contralateral) hemispheric organization is described in chapter 7. The essential feature of this model is that cerebral dominance does not come about as a (higher) stage beyond that of the contralateral representation of sensorimotor cortex. Rather, cerebral dominance—or lateral representation—occurs as an intermediate step between bilateral and contralateral representation. The bilateral organization that is characteristic of limbic and transitional cortex develops, in man, through a stage of (left) lateral representation to one of contralateral or crossed representation. Thus, while cerebral dominance constitutes a final phase in neocortical evolution, it is the stage of crossed representation and not that of cerebral dominance that is the end point of motor and perceptual realization (microgenesis).

The Fate of the Right Hemisphere

What is the nature of right-hemispheric organization in the face of continued specification of the left-hemispheric language zone? According to the proposed model, the differentiation of asymmetric or focal neocortex out of generalized neocortex would occur primarily in the left hemisphere, at least in the average right-hander. In dextrals, this implies that in the right hemisphere a direct path exists from generalized to sensorimotor cortex without, or with minimal development of, the intervening stage of focal neocortex (see Figure 1-2.). The evolutionary level of generalized neocortex would then typify the organization of the right hemisphere. This is consistent with evidence concerning the possibility of a more diffuse organization in the right hemisphere (Hécaen, Penfield, & Bertrand, 1956; Semmes, 1968), with a demonstration of a semantic but not phonological processing in the "isolated" right hemisphere (Zaidel, 1976), and with the demonstration of "right-hemispheric language" in a language-deprived adolescent with presumed "disuse" of the focally differentiating left-hemispheric language zone (Curtiss, 1977). Moreover, the nature of "right-hemispheric language" demonstrated in the above studies corresponds in certain respects with that mediated by generalized neocortex in the left hemisphere as inferred from the aphasia material (see below).

It is probable that the degree of focal differentiation within generalized neocortex of the right hemisphere is variable from one individual to another with some relation to handedness. It seems likely that the degree of focal differentiation in the right hemisphere is linked to that in the left hemisphere, such that some "balance" between the hemispheres is achieved. The nature of this balance would determine right- (and consequently left-) hemispheric language capacity, as well as the potential for recovery in aphasia.

The Neural Structure of Language

Through the described process of neocortical phylogenesis, and its ontogenetic continuation in the formation of focal asymmetric neocortex (lateralization), a dynamic system is constructed that mediates the process—the microgenesis—of language production. The anterior and posterior components of this system develop in parallel, symmetrically, supporting complementary constituents of the unfolding *language act.*

Each level in the anterior component is in relation to the corresponding level in the posterior system, as well as to the homologous anterior or posterior level of the opposite hemisphere, through long intra- and interhemispheric fibers. These connections maintain a simultaneity across levels as the content unfolds, in both the anterior and the posterior sector, and between the hemispheres. Both the anterior and posterior components of this system show a progression from bilateral through lateral to contralateral organization. This is inferred from the effects of pathology. In general, symptoms referable to an early (e.g., limbic) level require bilateral lesions; symptoms referable to an intermediate level (e.g., generalized neocortex) result from lesions that are relatively left-lateralized but not strongly focal. This proceeds to an association with focal left-sided lesions at the level of asymmetric neocortex and finally to focal lesions of sensorimotor cortex with a still more restricted predominantly contralateral expression.[1]

Language is elaborated through a process of development over this sequence of anatomical levels. This process can be dissected through a close study of pathological cases. These reveal the infrastructure of normal language, its preliminary levels, and the transitions between them. The aphasias reflect a destructuration within the anterior or posterior component, or sometimes within both. Or there is disruption at a specific level within one component. There is a constant relationship between symptom and level of pathological involvement. The symptom points to the level; the level mediates the language content to which the symptom refers. Thus, we can say that the described sequence of anatomical levels corresponds—in pathology—to a transitional series of symptoms, and these in turn reflect stages in the production of normal language.

Clinical Pathology of Language

Language is not composed of elements, but unfolds in a direction toward those elements. This process of unfolding transforms abstract content to a new state at each successive level. These levels also correspond to stages in the phyletic history of the brain. At each stage, abstract content presents itself in a cognitive mode expressive of that evolutionary level. To the extent that language represents that cognitive mode, it can be said, according to its level, to have a different existence in the world.

This microgenetic sequence leads from a semantic to a phonological level.

---

[1]The lesser degree of contralateral representation in auditory cortex, in comparison with somaesthetic, visual, and motor cortices, raises the possibility of selective pressures acting on the evolution of this region. The contralateral advantage, however, points in the direction of the major trend in sensorimotor cortex evolution, namely, toward contralateral representation.

These levels are really states of the emerging abstract form. In pathology, they are the expressions of this form as a continuous process is "sliced" at successive moments. The dynamic nature of this process will become clearer when we focus on its infratemporal or transitional characteristics.

A description of syndromes of the posterior component follows. First to be considered is the possibility of a limbic disorder of language. *Confabulation* is taken to represent the most prominent *posterior limbic* symptom of language change. There is a transition from confabulation to semantic jargon. This transition is illustrated through a consideration of the expositional (conversational, contextual) speech of patients.

Subsequently, the focus shifts to referential (naming) defects. The sequence of language disorders, in relation to structural brain levels, is then displayed through the varieties of naming errors. A central point is that the language form, the utterance, or the naming error always refers to a level in the described structure. At early levels, bilateral lesions are essential for symptom formation. At later levels, symptoms occur with an increasingly more unilateral (and focal) lesion.

Language Disorders of the Posterior Sector

Limbic-Level Disorders

A limbic core underlies and provides a foundation for the anterior and posterior systems. It serves as a common base out of which these components will arise. Structures of the limbic core support an early, perhaps initial, stage in language production. This limbic role in language, though suggested by stimulation studies in subhuman primates (Myers, 1976), has not been adequately demonstrated in man. It is known that bilateral lesions of the human limbic system produce a severe amnesic syndrome (Scoville & Milner, 1957), but there are also important effects on speech and language. In the posterior system, bilateral lesions of inferomedial and lateral temporal cortex lead to confabulatory states and/or semantic jargon. The failure to find such changes in the "surgical" amnesic probably reflects the anterior location and more limited extent of the lesion. The effect of lesions of medial transitional cortex (e.g., insular cortex) is not fully established (see below).

One of the most striking clinical symptoms of bilateral lesion of posterior limbic-derived cortex is *confabulation*. The confabulation that accompanies an amnesic (Korsakoff) state is not something "added on" to the memory deficit. Rather, it represents a disruption at a stage in cognition where the intimate relationship between the linguistic and mnemic aspects of the deficit is most apparent. Confabulation may be thought of as a "deep-level" aphasia.

Amnesia and Confabulation Confabulation, or false recollection, is characteristic of the amnesic (Korsakoff) syndrome, but occurs in other pathological states as well. Confabulation is usually explained as an attempt by the patient to compensate for or "fill in" an unrecollected gap in memory. It is true that confabulation may signal the restitution of an amnesic syndrome. However, the occurrence of spontaneous confabulation, confabulation for *future* as well as past events, and the dynamic features of the confabulatory content all argue against a compensatory mechanism. In the course of recovery, a patient may progress from an encapsulated amnesia through a confabulatory stage to partial and then more or less complete recall. In such cases, the confabulation points to a stage in the retrieval of a content. The following case is instructive in this regard.

> *Case 1:* An 80-year-old woman had sudden dizziness and collapse, with a brief period of unconsciousness. Neurological examination was negative except for amnesia surrounding the spell; otherwise behavior and language were normal. The following day, marked confusion and confabulation were noted. She described an attack at home by a band of robbers and said her home had been vandalized and that she had been hit over the head and beaten. She suspected the nurses to be in collusion with her assailants, and felt they were trying to kill her. The following day, this picture completely disappeared. She was able to correctly recall events just up to, and immediately following, the period of unconsciousness.

In this patient, a short period of retrograde amnesia led to a state of agitated confusion and confabulation in the course of recovery. This was interpreted by some physicians as a sign of deterioration, when in fact it represented a phase in the resolution of the amnesic segment. Cases of this type indicate that confabulation refers to a level between complete irreminiscence and full recall.

Banal Confabulation Confabulation is something that happens to a content in the course of its retrieval. In the amnesic without confabulation, the content simply is not evoked. The patient may state that he cannot remember the test material. However, some confabulation can almost always be induced by a strong insistence on full recall during the "decay" period. This is briefly illustrated in Case 2.

> *Case 2:* This 53-year-old man had the subacute onset of a profound amnesic syndrome and spinal fluid findings suggestive of herpetic encephalitis. Past memory, digit span, and intelligence were preserved in the presence of severe anterograde (learning) deficit. Except for two or three events there was no recollection for any experiences subsequent to the onset of the amnesia.

The patient was given the following story to read and immediately after relate it back to the examiner:

> *The Hen and the Golden Eggs:* A man had a hen that laid golden eggs, Wishing to obtain more gold without having to wait for it he killed the hen but he found nothing inside of it for it was just like any other hen.

P: It's about a golden hen. . . . The owner of the hen wanted the hen to lay a golden egg . . . so that he could get prosperous I guess. . . . Somehow the hen refused to lay the egg.

This story was repeatedly read to and by the patient, and initially there was no ostensible improvement in immediate recall, though there was a diminution in the (weak) confabulatory response. When the story was shown to him again after several minutes of distraction, there was evidently a type of déjà vu feeling for the story, though he could not say definitely whether he had seen or heard it before. Over a longer time this receded into a complete amnesia.

Semantic Errors in Confabulation The link from a banal confabulatory amnesia to semantic jargon occurs through a semantic elaboration of the confabulatory content. The content of the confabulation in the spontaneous speech of Korsakoff patients does not always show the disarray that characterizes jargon.[2] However, this can often be brought out by tests of story recall. Such tests provide a standard against which the recollection (spontaneous speech) can be judged.

The following patient had relatively normal conversational speech and an obvious amnesic syndrome with banal confabulation. On story recall, there was a marked deterioration approaching a jargon pattern.

P: [Reads story of *Hen and Golden Eggs* corectly.]
E: Can you tell me that story?
P: It's an old hunk of mythology. You have four or five of the same thing don't you. . . . It was about a horse that bred one year or something like that but then didn't breed anything because there was no contact . . . ya, it comes from a thing out of modern politics too. . . . It's sort of an esophagus deal they're trying to sell today. [E: What's an esophagus deal?]. . . . Do you remember the old esophagus [Aesop?] stories? If you've read some, they're very much like that.

Later that day, the patient was again tested with the same story. As before, he read it aloud correctly.

P: It might be, it sounds like . . . I don't know. . . . Well, the old missions about all sorts of things . . . about the old hen, what do you mean, about Colorado, the hen out there, what was the name of that hen? [E: The one with the golden eggs?] No, it wasn't and the thing was written by Charles Dickens, but he didn't write full verse and all that. It wasn't accepted as a literary piece.

In this sample, there is relative preservation at the sentence level, but the lack of intersentential relatedness and the propagatory nature of the confabulation lead to rather striking productions that, from the point of view of the material to be recalled, would have to be judged as semantic jargon. There are also occa-

---

[2]Schizophrenic paramnesia also appears to be linked to semantic errors in retrieval, differing from confabulation, at least in part, by its more subjective (i.e., less manipulable) character (Brown, 1977).

sional word substitutions, for example, "esophagus deal," which foreshadow the lexical errors characteristic of aphasic jargon.

Semantic Jargon

The patient with semantic jargon produces utterances with fairly good or correct syntax but aberrant meaning. There are three major error types: noun substitution, derailments in the speech flow, and circumlocution. The disorder is present in referential speech (naming) and in conversation. As with all of the jargonaphasias, the condition is rare in young patients and when it does occur is generally associated with bilateral lesions of the temporal lobe, possibly involving underlying limbic structures (Weinstein, Lyerly, Cole, & Ozer, 1966). In older aphasics, as in the present case, the disorder can result from a lesion about Wernicke's area or (deep?) lesion of posterior T2, though precise anatomical studies are lacking. Semantic jargon also occurs in acute confusional states and resembles the word-salad of schizophrenia.

> *Case 3:* This 72-year-old man had a left temporoparietal infarction. Although neurological examination was normal, except for the aphasia, there was evidence for bilateral involvement. An electroencephalogram demonstrated some degree of right posterior slowing, and a history was obtained of several left-sided seizures postonset. Initially there was severe semantic jargon with occasional neologism. The following is an example of the conversational speech of this patient.

> And I say, this is wrong. I'm going out and doing things and getting ukeleles taken every time and I think I'm doing wrong because I'm supposed to take everything from the top so that we do four flashes of four volumes before we get down low. . . . Face of everything. This guy has got to this thing—this thing made out in order to slash immediately to all of the windpails . . . This is going right over me from there—That's up to is 5 station stuff from manatime—and with that put it all in and build it all up so it will all be spent with him conversing his condessing [condessing?]. Condessing his treatment of this for he has got to spend this thing. [E holds up handkerchief: What is that?] Well—this is a lady's line—and this is no longer what he wants. He is now leaving their mellonpush ["mellonpush"?]. Which is spelled "U" something or other which also commence the fact that they're gonna finish the end of that letter which is spelled in their stalegame and opens up here and runs across what "M"—it wasn't "M" it's "A" and "M" is the interval title and it is spelled out with all of this.

On tests of naming, the patient named some objects correctly, but many objects were misnamed. These misnamings, or paraphasias, often showed a semantic link to the target object:

earring	"haircone"
pipe	"smokin mob"

At other times no clear relationship to the target object could be ascertained:

ashtray	"mouse looker-atter"
wallet	"lover lob"

In cases such as this, there is generally little or no recognition by the patient of the erroneous nature of the verbal substitution. One has the impression that the closer to target the substitution, the greater the awareness of the error, and the greater the tendency toward self-correction. Immediately following a misnaming, presenting the erroneous name to the patient, for example, asking the patient if the object is a "haircone," will usually elicit a positive response. If the examiner invents a word or a compound such as the above, it is more likely to be rejected by the patient than his own substitution. The ability of patients to reject the examiner's substitution may also increase as the substitution approaches in meaning the target item. Patients also seem better able to reject "words" that do not closely approximate those in their own language than words that are, or could reasonably be expected to be, items or possible items in their own lexicon. Patients are generally able to reject "jabberwocky," as well as sound errors in otherwise correct words. If one speaks in semantic jargon to such a patient there is no clear indication that the jargon is perceived as such by the patient. The patient may recognize when he is addressed in a foreign language but may respond as if he has just heard a meaningful utterance. Bilingual patients, both semantic and neologistic jargonaphasics, may switch their jargon to the language in which they are addressed. From such observations, one forms the impression that patients more readily reject phonological than semantic errors and, within the latter, better reject those closest in meaning to the target item, and that this is true for both speech production and the perceived speech of others.

In addition, patients with semantic jargon are usually euphoric, or at least have a heightened mood without frustration over a poor performance. It seems that the affective tonality is specific to the utterance, as is the awareness experience, so that one sees a change in these parameters moment to moment depending on the predominating error type.

With regard to comprehension, this is usually only moderately impaired, or at least not so severely involved as in neologistic cases, and repetition may be fairly good at times. There also appears to be a Korsakoff-like state with defective verbal (and visual) memory. Cases of this type have been described by Clarke, Wyke, and Zangwill (1958) and Kinsbourne and Warrington (1963a). The present case was also an example of this and in the course of recovery evolved into a fairly characteristic Korsakoff state. During the initial stage, reading showed semantic jargon as severe as in expositional speech, but gradually reading improved to the point where it was relatively intact, and speech became more intelligible with some word-finding difficulty and semantic paraphasias. At this time, the patient was given the story *The Hen and the Golden*

Eggs to read, which he did so correctly and was then asked immediately to recall the story. His performance was as follows.

> *Story:* A man had a hen that laid golden eggs. Wishing to obtain more gold without having to wait for it he killed the hen but he found nothing inside of it for it was just like any other hen.

> P: It seems to be a lot about something . . . it was a command on the hen and he told her to do certain things and she didn't do anything . . . and he tried to get everybody to do things and nobody did. He turned everything over to the marine base. He couldn't see out of this eye [patient had been discussing his visual problem before] doesn't see anything the way it should [E: What about that story?] That's what I'm trying to come back to. He gave it to other people and something took charge and he liked the pieces. He had to put this thing like this because he had to keep this not looked at . . . and then he began to hear things from the outside, which he liked very much, and he let the thing go through because horn [?] this horse he was able to tell exactly who did what with her and who did the wrong with her. [Reads story again, correctly.]

> E: Can you tell the story now?

> P: I'll try to though I have to keep things . . . centered. There was a man who had a hen, and she gave golden eggs and they collected the water and sent it into the water and brought it out, and he had to keep it this way or he couldn't see it and when he sent her into the water other things took charge and he had to hide this from them all the time.

> E: Do you think he did the right thing in killing the hen?

> P: No, I do not. . . . Well, because it distributed itself and brought up everything out of there, not only brought every other hen but it brought any other thing that might be invested by it, and he did that despite my keeping this thing normal. I don't know whether I'm saying it to you or not.

This type of language is similar to the confabulation of Korsakoff patients, especially that seen during the acute confusonal prelude to the disorder. It is probable that there is a close link between semantic jargon and confabulation. In the latter, the memory defect is in the foreground of the clinical picture, and confabulation might be considered a mild or attenuated form of semantic jargon. Semantic jargonaphasia, on the other hand, may be thought of as a deteriorated confabulation where the language defect becomes more prominent. One can say that in semantic jargon there is an amnestic syndrome embedded in the language disorder, whereas in the amnestic syndrome there is an aphasia embedded in the confabulation. Put another way, in banal confabulation the intrasentential organization is relatively intact. The defect is at the intersentential level. This gives the impression of a cognitive or memory defect. The flow of discourse is more comprehensible; the derailment is ideational, not linguistic. However, as the disturbance approaches in the direction of word selection, substitution *within* the sentence becomes more pronounced and the goal of the utterance becomes uncertain to the listener. Now the defect is intrasentential and seems to be linguistic rather than conceptual. However, these disorders lie along a continuum. The Korsakoff patient in the acute stage may have typical semantic jargon, which may be indistinguishable from the semantic jargonaphasic. Ordinary amnesics commonly show aphasic misnaming during this stage (Victor, 1974), and errors tend to be of the semantic type, that is, verbal paraphasias. Such patients have been shown to have a deficit in semantic encoding (Cermak & Butters, 1973). On the other hand, semantic jargonaphasics have an amnesic disturbance. This is apparent on clinical study of such patients but has not yet been the subject of careful investigation. It is of interest, however, that patients generally do not recall the period of their aphasia after recovery.

Levels of Semantic Realization

The transition from confabulation to semantic jargon takes us into aphasia proper. In order to simplify the account of transitions from one aphasic pattern to another, we will set aside our descriptions of conversational speech and turn to an examination of naming.

The errors that patients make on naming tests reflect very closely the nature of their aphasic disorder. When asked to name an object, an aphasic may make one of several types of paraphasic (substitutive) errors. His response may vary greatly from moment to moment. At one time the patient will produce a semantic or verbal (word) substitution, at another a phonological error. However, the response pattern tends to be clustered around predominantly one type of error, and the nature of this error determines what "syndrome" the patient is said to "fit." Syndromes, therefore, are not stable entities but rather refer to the qualitative mean of performance.

To my mind it is preferable to consider separately each utterance or performance of an aphasic patient. These represent a kind of momentary slice through the infrastructure of the patient's cognition. In other words, a paraphasia reveals the level at which—for the instant of that paraphasia—the cognitive structure has actualized. In a sense, therefore, the utterance—the paraphasia—is only the focal point in a cross section of cognition. The paraphasia is seen in relation to other aspects of cognition that, though more subtle in their presentation, accompany and are simultaneous with the paraphasia at the same cognitive level.

The repertoire of paraphasic errors can be viewed along a continuum that leads from an asemantic (or nonmeaningful) substitution, through a substitution in which there are unusual "associative" bonds to the correct item, to categorical or "in-class" errors, and finally to correct selection of the word but failure in its evocation (Figures 1-3 and 1-4). This progression can be conceived as an emergence of an abstract representation of the utterance-to-be up through a series of semantic fields, from those of wide "psychological distance" (asemantic)

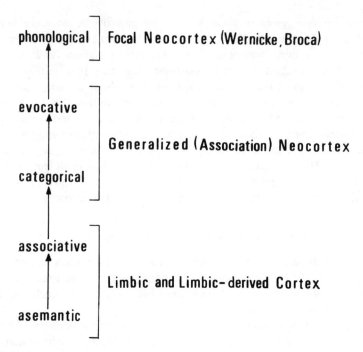

FIGURE 1-3. Levels in language production in the posterior sector correspond to phylogenetic and maturational levels in brain structure.

through a level of (?) experiential and/or affective bonding ("associative") to a categorical selection and finally correct word choice. At this final stage, the lexical item, the word, or an abstract representation of that word has been correctly selected but cannot be evoked. At the next level, the stage of evocation has been adequately traversed but the phase of phonemic encoding, the realization of that word in phonological form, is deficient. This results in phonemic errors in otherwise correctly selected words.

Asemantic In semantic jargon, paraphasic errors are characteristically *asemantic*. This means that the link between the substitution and the object to be named is obscure. Sometimes there are shared elements or attributes ("smokin mob" for pipe), while at other times there is no clear relationship to the required object name (e.g., "wheelbase" for chair). The morphological features of the object do not appear to play a prominent role in determining the paraphasic response. Asemantic errors may occur as "clang" or rhyming responses (e.g., "hair" for chair), but this usually occurs in the context of phonological rather than verbal substitution.

In younger patients, semantic jargon (asemantic paraphasia) may be due to a *bilateral* lesion of limbic transitional cortex. The condition may also occur with a left temporal lesion in the presence of a "physiological" depression of the

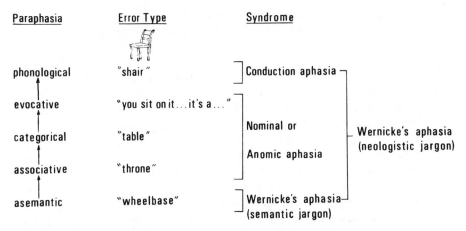

FIGURE 1-4. Aphasic syndromes correspond to levels in semantic or phonological realization.

opposite hemisphere. In older aphasics the disorder may result from a unilateral left temporal lesion, though anatomical studies of such cases are lacking. The disorder also occurs in acute confusional states. There is some resemblance to the word-salad of schizophrenia, where limbic system dysfunction seems likely (Torrey & Peterson, 1974).[3]

Paraphasia in which there is a special type of "associative" relationship to the target item occurs in semantic jargon and in confusional states. The misnaming may reflect situational, experiential, and affective factors. The substitution shares an attribute with the correct object name and commonly has a pedantic or facetious quality, as in the following examples:

bedpan   "piano stool"
doctor   "butcher"

At times the misnaming is correct or vaguely acceptable but of an unexpected nature. In such instances, the paraphasia may be of a considerably lower word frequency than the required name, as in:

---

[3]Recent papers that sharply distinguish schizophasic language from aphasia make the error, in my judgment, of considering only relatively mild schizophrenics, and not the more deeply regressed (and nowadays rare) cases in which word-salad occurs. Schizophasia is not be be compared to aphasia in general, but only to semantic jargon and "associative" paraphasias. Goldstein (1943) has described patients of this type. Whatever differences exist between such forms of schizophrenic and aphasic language can be attributed to the chronicity of the former, the co-occurrence of delusional and/or paranoid trends in schizophrenia, and its fluctuation over time. In addition, in contrast to the schizophrenic, the aphasic brings a normal personality to the (abrupt) pathological change.

glasses	"spectacles"
matches	"ignition system"
red	"fuchsia"

In spite of the low frequency response, the errors may tend to involve lower frequency object names (Rochford, 1974). Accompanying such errors is usually a euphoric mood with little or no insight into the aberrant or tangential nature of the misnaming. Having (mis)named an object, the patient rarely accepts the correct name from the examiner and steadfastly refuses to alter his performance. However, it does seem that such patients are less willing than those of the previous group to accept the asemantic productions of the examiner.

As is the case in semantic jargon, there is generally a bilateral lesion, probably involving medial or inferolateral temporal or limbic structures. The disorder frequently occurs in the acute stage of the Korsakoff syndrome and is common in postconcussive or postanesthetic states.

Categorical The progression from asemantic substitutions to those with an experiential and/or "associative" relationship to the intended or demanded object name leads to substitutions within the object class or category.[4] At this stage the utterance has achieved (or been selected to) the category of the object name, as in:

comb	"brush"
table	"chair"
red	"green"

Categorical substitutions do not show the ease and lability of asemantic and associative paraphasias. There is an impression of word search and, at times, a hesitancy or a tentative quality in the naming response that, though not approaching the next stage, that of evocative difficulty, does signal a change from the more fluent and effortless paraphasias of the preceding level. With utterances of this type, there is also a mitigation of the euphoric mood in the direction of a more appropriate affective stage. There is also increased awareness of error. The patient tends to be dissatisfied with his performance and makes attempts at self-correction.

The pathological correlation is with a lesion of left generalized neocortex, especially middle temporal gyrus (T2) and its (usual) posterior continuation into angular gyrus. The fact that a naming disturbance of this type is also seen in

---

[4]Paraphasias of this type represent the most common responses on word association tests in normal subjects. One can say that the word association technique usually penetrates only to a limited depth in the described system, while aphasic responses (e.g., "associative," asemantic) reflect lexical organization at deeper strata.

diffuse pathological states and with lesions throughout and beyond the classical language zone is consistent with an association with the more widely distributed level of generalized neocortex.

Evocative This refers to the anomic who can "block" a paraphasia and gives descriptive or tip-of-the-tongue responses, but is unable to produce the correct object name. This is not a result of the capacity to suppress a potentially erroneous response. Rather, the abstract representation of the word has achieved its correct lexical form; that is, it has been selected beyond the point of a category error, but the item, the word, cannot be evoked. One can say that such patients have intact word meaning in the presence of word-finding difficulty, whereas those patients at a more preliminary level (asemantic, associative) have facile word production with impairment of word meaning.

The affective state accompanying this disturbance is one of frustration, with relief on success and at times catastrophic reaction on failure. Awareness of the difficulty is more acute and self-critical, with corrections and efforts to achieve an adequate response. The anatomical correlation is, as in the preceding form, a lesion of generalized neocortex somewhat peripheral to, or less severely involving, the central language zone. This form of anomia is also the initial aphasic pattern in the atrophic (and other) dementias, where the degeneration preferentially affects "association" (generalized) neocortex.

Phonological Realization

Phonemic (Conduction) Aphasia The final stage in the semantic series corresponds to the realization of an abstract representation of the correct lexical item. At this point, prior to the process of phonemic selection, the word exists incipiently, its evocation into consciousness taking place as it is realized phonologically. This process leads through a phonological selectional operation analogous to that in the semantic component. Disorders at this level are characterized by a disturbance in the phonological realization of otherwise appropriate target items. Among the many errors that may occur are those of substitution, deletion, and transposition (metathesis):

president	"predisent"
kite	"dite"
green	"reen"

The disturbance is typically present in conversational speech as well as in naming and repetition and is often referred to as conduction (phonemic) aphasia. This designation emphasizes the repetition defect as the primary impairment, though in fact the disorder of repetition is only one instance of the central defect in phonemic encoding (Brown, 1975). There is evidence that in such cases substitution errors respect distinctive feature distance (Blumstein, 1970). Clinically, this does seem to be true for the mild case with a restricted phonological disorder. However, it may not be true of the phonological errors in neologistic jargon, where phoneme substitutions often violate the expectations of distinctive feature theory. Such cases suggest that there may be a narrowing or targeting down in the phonological sphere, from distant to close phonemic paraphasias, comparable to that occurring in the process of lexical selection.

The anatomical correlation of phonemic aphasia is a lesion of the posterior superior temporal gyrus (posterior T1) and especially its continuation into supramarginal gyrus (Ajuriaguerra & Hécaen, 1956). There is no evidence for involvement of underlying white matter in this disorder. Occasionally, phonemic aphasia occurs with lesion of the angular gyrus (Brown, 1972; Green & Howes, 1977).

With regard to neologism, this may represent either a deteriorated (i.e., unintelligible) phonemic paraphasia or a phonemic paraphasia in combination with semantic paraphasia. The former is a type of phonemic or undifferentiated jargon (see below); the latter is neologistic jargon.

Neologism and Neologistic Jargon   Isolated neologisms are not uncommon in a variety of aphasic forms. Lecours and Rouillon (1976) have argued that the occasional neologism observed in the Broca aphasic is structurally identical to that of jargonaphasia. This is open to question. Perhaps it may be the case in resolving global aphasics, but it is unlikely that this is so in documented anterior aphasics. In such patients, neologism is more likely determined by distortion or misarticulation. Phonological errors in the presence of dysarthria may result in words judged to be unintelligible.

The isolated neologism preferentially attacks the content word, often with preservation of syntactic agreement over a range of neologistic forms. Thus, a patient of Caplan, Keller, and Locke (1972) said: "They will have to *presite* me . . . [and] yes, because I'm just *persessing* to one." A personal case remarked: "It was my job as a *convince,* a *confoser* not *confoler* but almost the same as the man who was *commerced.*" Another said, "Your *patebelin* like the mother . . . and his mothers got to go in his *stanchen.*" Another patient, asked to name eyeglasses, said, "Those are *waggots,* they have to be *fribbed* in."

Buckingham and Kertesz (1976) give a number of such examples. As can be seen even in these brief excerpts, the preferential attack on the content word often leaves the initial part of the utterance unaffected.

As the incidence of the neologism increases, there is a corresponding decline in the intelligibility of the utterance. At some uncertain point, say, when neologisms constitute 20%–30% of the words in an utterance, the patient is said to have neologistic jargon. It is rare that this incidence goes beyond about 80%. Cases where speech is virtually 100% neologistic should then appear as "undifferentiated" jargonaphasics. In such cases, either the patient is no longer producing wordlike segments or the listener can no longer segment the utterance into wordlike sequences. In fact, undifferentiated jargon is probably *not* a deteriorated neologistic jargon. In addition, we should keep in mind that, as the incidence of neologism increases, the utterance is not simply being filled with more and more nonsense words. The entire fabric of the aphasia is changing, as well as the patient's affective and cognitive state.

In typical cases of neologistic jargon, the jargon invades all language performances more or less equally. Lhermitte and Derousné (1974) have described a case with good writing, but this appears quite exceptional. There is no selective sparing of sung or automatic speech as in the Broca aphasic; that is, lyrics are jargonized even though the melody may be preserved. Comprehension is (invariably?) severely impaired, and the patient may almost seem deaf, though this can usually be ruled out on careful testing. Generally, even in such cases a response of bewilderment occurs when the patient is addressed in jargon. In a number of personal cases this has been the only language-related response that could be obtained. In one patient even a galvanic skin-reflex could not be elicited to abusive comments, though surprise was registered to the examiner's jargon. In spite of the severe disorganization of language, some patients can function fairly well in the world. Performances on tests such as Ravens Matrices may be quite good. A personal case was able to continue playing chess, albeit at a rather unsophisticated level. Affect is generally heightened; the patient may be euphoric, even manic. This may change with the utterance. A patient may be euphoric during jargon and depressed when speaking *correctly* about his illness or family.

Frequently during the acute stage patients produce sequences of numbers instead of words. In time, this will develop into a more typical jargon pattern. At this point there is often a relative preservation of some thematic material. For example, a patient with completely unintelligible jargon might produce a (usually short) series of correct though often stereotyped utterances about his illness or his work. A personal case spoke incessant jargon except when describing the accident that brought about his condition. He was run over by a car driven by his (jilted) girlfriend and was ordinarily quite lucid in his repetitive accounts of this incident. Commonly, patients lapse into these islands of speech preservation when asked to produce utterances that would otherwise result in jargon. The affective element in such phenomena should not be overlooked.

Lecours and Rouillon (1976) have described predilection units and predilection themes in jargon patients. This means frequently recurring neologistic segments and topics and is confirmed by my own experience. Conceivably there is a relationship between the islands of preserved speech and those of preferential impairment. One may inhibit the other since each seems to occur at widely separated linguistic moments or at different stages in resolution. In spite of the occurrence of predilection units, there is little or no consistency in the jargon on a word-by-word basis. There is no evidence that jargon constitutes a private language. However, it is of interest that neologistic jargonaphasics may engage each other in "conversation" though rejecting a jargon produced by the examiner.

Cases have been cited where the jargonaphasic has seemed to accept his own recorded jargon, but not the same jargon after is has been transcribed and rerecorded by another person. Other well-known features of this type of jargon include the relative preservation of intonation and probably word stress even when it falls on a neologism. Augmentation is common in such patients; that is, they produce more syllables than in the target words. This may also affect intact as well as jargonized utterances, though possibly not to the same degree, and may account in part for the logorrhea.

Within the group of neologistic jargonaphasics several subtypes can be distinguished. There are fluent productive forms with only a slight tendency for alliteration or sound association, while in other patients, or in the same patients at other moments, reiteration on the basis of sound similarity can become quite prominent (e.g., "much tereen, will I could talk, sorlip, gorrip, grip, grip, stick, eye, grin, grim, greeda"). This has been discussed by Kreindler, Calavrezo, and Mihailescu (1971) and Lecours and Rouillon (1976). In cases of this type, fluency is impeded and this limits the jargon to a restricted repertoire of sounds. These patients will approximate the jargon stereotypy of the global or motor aphasic. In such patients Lecours and Rouillon (1976) have argued, correctly I believe, that this error points to a phonological element. In the neologistic jargon case it also reflects the involvement of the phonological system.

The anatomical lesion of jargonaphasia was discussed by Henschen (1922). It was found that a *focal* lesion of the left superior temporal gyrus (T1), regardless of whether it involved a more anterior or posterior section, might cause word deafness in the presence of normal speech. This was also true for combined lesions of T1 and T2, even if subcortex was involved. However, diffuse softening of left T1 and T2 was invariably accompanied by jargonaphasia. More recently, the problem was studied by Kertesz and Benson (1970) in light of several anatomical cases. These authors found involvement of the classical Wernicke zone. In view of the fact that jargon is associated with the late-life aphasic, it is conceivable that in younger patients the disorder may require bilateral pathology. This anatomical correlation can be understood if we interpret neologistic jargon as a combined phonological and semantic defect. For the reason of this constituent phonological disorder, the lesion correlation of neologistic jargon is similar to that of the more restricted phonological disturbance in phonemic aphasia. This corresponds to the level of focal asymmetric neocortex.

Some Problems Concerning the Posterior Aphasias

Classification There are various classifications of the posterior aphasias (Leischner & Peuser, 1975). In some laboratories, there is a subdivision into several independent types (e.g., anomia, conduction aphasia, Wernicke's aphasia), whereas in other laboratories these forms are treated as varieties of a single

Wernicke aphasia, differing along a gradient of severity. However, there is no agreement as to what constitutes Wernicke's aphasia. For some, this refers only to the comprehension impairment, which may or may not be associated with an expressive deficit. According to this view, word deafness would represent the "pure" form of Wernicke's aphasia and the nucleus of the comprehension impairment in the posterior aphasias; that is, there would be either a severe or a mitigated word deafness in association with one or more other component disturbances. For others, however, Wernicke's aphasia is as much characterized by the pattern of expressive speech as by the comprehension deficit. In some classifications jargonaphasia is considered to be the chief expression of Wernicke's aphasia or at least a severe form of Wernicke's aphasia, with conduction aphasia and anomia representing milder or recovering forms. It is recognized that there are several different types of jargon—semantic, neologistic, and un-differentiated—though it is unclear whether all of these belong to the group of Wernicke's aphasias.

The difficulty in the classification of individual cases and the complexity of the literature on the subject have led some workers to revive the simpler distinction of fluent (posterior) and nonfluent (anterior) forms. This is an expeditious way of segregating experimental populations, but it has the effect of lumping together quite different clinical syndromes under a generic label of little or no theoretical value. To say that a patient is fluent is to say that with respect to fluency he is normal, fluency being the normal state and the goal of recovery. Patients evolve toward fluency in recovery and only exceptionally in the reverse direction. Moreover, we occasionally see fluent anteriors and nonfluent posteriors, the latter especially during the acute stage (Karis & Horenstein, 1976); patients may be fluent for some performances and nonfluent for others, while in many patients fluency is not clearly determinable and may fluctuate greatly. Certain cases classified as fluent (e.g., conduction aphasics with phonological errors) may resemble more closely—both clinically and on experimental testing—the behavior of cases classified as nonfluent (e.g., the Broca aphasic with articulation errors) than either resembles other aphasic types within the same category. Fluency is always performance specific and is always a question of degree. For these various reasons, it seems preferable to develop a classification based on predominant error type, for example, semantic, phonological, whether expressed in expositional or referential speech or both, and so on, rather than on the traditional basis of syndromes or on a meaningless fluent-nonfluent dichotomy. Were agreement to be reached on such a classification, patients could then be grouped in such a way as to satisfy both the clinical valuation of individual differences and single case study and the experimental demand for analysis by groups.

The Role of the Insula An important but still unsettled question in aphasia study is that of the relationship of insula to language pathology. Wernicke postulated on a theoretical basis only that a lesion of insula would produce an aphasia. Dejerine (1885) argued that an aphasia secondary to insula lesion would result not from damage to insula cortex but from the interruption of subcortical association fibers traversing this region. Among the early case reports, a widely quoted case was that of a left-handed boy with a type of pure motor aphasia and destruction of righ insula, described by Wadham (1869). Saundby (1911) described a questionable case with a similar aphasia and softening of the left insula. Additional cases were reviewed by Dufour (1881) and then by Monakow (1905, 1914), who could not come to a definite conclusion. The problem was not greatly clarified by Henschen (1922), and there have been few if any cases reported since his comprehensive review.

The frequent involvement of insula in cases of aphasia and the continuity of this area with the cortical language zones led some workers to include it as part of these latter regions. Thus, Niessl von Mayendorff (1911) considered the anterior insula to be part of Broca's area, and Pick (1973) included the posterior insula with Wernicke's area. In more recent times the strongest advocate of a role for the insula in language has been Goldstein (1948), who claimed that it represented a central zone in the anatomical organization of language and that lesions of insula interrupted the language process at a (central) stage in the "thought-speech transition." He even reported (Riese & Goldstein, 1950) a case of a skilled orator with asymmetric enlargement of the insula.

Subsequent work, however, has not confirmed Goldstein's thesis. Penfield and Faulk (1955) did not obtain speech arrest on stimulation in insula, nor did they find aphasia after unilateral—chiefly right-sided—excision in a few cases. Evidently, there are no cases of bilateral surgical lesion of insula on record. Rasmussen (1978) notes that transient aphasia may follow surgical ablation of the left insula. This is similar to that after anterior lobectomy and is attributed to postoperative edema. However, these observations may have to be reconsidered in view of a recent report of dysphasia in a patient during stimulation in the anterior left insula (Ojemann & Whitaker, 1977).

The following case is of interest for several reasons, in addition to the presence of a lesion in the left insula. It is presented in the hope of renewing a dialogue on this basic, and in recent years neglected, problem in the pathological anatomy of aphasia.

Case: A 21-year-old right-handed man, deaf since age 8 following a high fever, developed sudden right-side paralysis. Previously, he used sign language with some speech accompaniment. According to hospital notes, and friends who visited him daily during his hospitalization, he was unable to express himself vocally or in sign with the left hand for the first few days. He was unable to form words with his mouth. He was unable to spell with the left hand. This lasted for about 10 days, at which time he was said to have shown some recovery in signing with the left hand. At 2 weeks post-onset, spelling and signing with the left hand were said to be normal. The right arm and leg showed gradual improvement in strength over 4–6 weeks. Evidently, there was a point where strength had returned but signing was poor with that hand. By 6 weeks post-onset, he was normal, with respect to both signing and vocalization and the neurological examination. The patient was strongly right-handed with no family history of left-handedness. The CT scan showed a lesion in the left insula. Subsequent angiography was normal.

This case indicates that a lesion of the left insula can produce at least a transient aphasia. It also demonstrates that, in deafness acquired at least as early as age 8, the temporal region may persist as a language zone.

Some studies of forebrain development (e.g., Yakovlev, 1972) have shown that the insula is a preliminary stage toward (i.e., in evolutionary continuity with) the generalized neocortex of the posterior hemisphere. In view of this, it would be surprising if the insula were completely unassociated with language or cognitive function. Part of the insula is transitional or *meso*cortex and corresponds to cingulate gyrus on the medial surface of the hemisphere. Unilateral lesion of anterior cingulate gyrus is not, so far as I know, firmly identified with any clinical symptomatology, whereas a bilateral lesion leads to profound mutism and akinesia. Since bilateral lesions are required for symptom formation in anterior mesocortex (cingulate gyrus), it is likely that a similar requirement obtains for posterior mesocortex (insula). If so, this would explain the mild or transient nature or even the lack of symptoms with left insula lesion and emphasizes the need for well-studied bilateral cases.

Language Perception and Production: A Comment and a Speculation
Clinical study suggests that in the posterior aphasias there is an inner bond between the production error and the disturbance in comprehension. One has the impression that a change in one determines a change in the other. If this is so, then we can say that, even when we look at production only, we are indirectly assaying the status of comprehension. This observation raises the first and perhaps most central problem regarding these disorders, namely, the relationship between language comprehension and the language *corpus* that is so prominently affected in posterior aphasia.

Language is organized in the brain largely within a perceptual field. Wernicke's area and its wider extent develop in relation to perceptual areas. The anterior (Broca) zone is in relation to motor systems. Speech errors resulting from pathology in this region are generally those of misarticulation or omission. One has always the question of a (probably systematic) dissolution or impoverishment of motor structure rather than a specific disruption of language. Certainly, experimental studies of syntax in the anterior aphasic have been inconclusive with regard to the specificity of syntactic deficits in these patients (e.g., Kellar, 1978). This is not the case with involvement of the posterior sector. Here the rich inventory of error types points to a selective language disorder. It is of interest, therefore, that morphological studies of the hemispheres have demonstrated asymmetry primarily in the posterior zone (see Rubens, 1977, for a review). This is the main *language* area.

What is the nature of the relationship between perception and production? Clearly the perception of language involves more than listening to the speech of others. The speaker can only have knowledge of his own utterance through his perception of that utterance. For the speaker, the mental representation of the utterance is largely if not completely perceptual. There is little or no motor experience. More than this, the utterance itself appears to be generated or realized through perception. The motor region seems to contribute the initial kinetic and its derived intonational pattern, the final programming of sound sequences, and perhaps also the feeling of intentionality that (except in some pathological cases) accompanies the utterance, but this motor aspect unfolds too rapidly to persist in awareness as a stable content. The problem here is the same as that posed in relation to the perception of limb or eye movements and in past discussions of feelings of effort (Innervationsgefühle). In more recent times this has been treated as a feedback or corollary discharge phenomenon (see Roland, 1978, and discussion). However, at least in the case of language and insofar as we can infer from the aphasia material, the perception of an utterance is not a secondary or following effect of the motor discharge; it is, for the speaker, the primary event. Thus, it would seem that every language act involves a simultaneous discharge over levels in both perception and motility. I believe that the content of an utterance is represented as an end stage in a perceptual development, its articulation being a manifestation of the transition leading to this end stage. In other words, in perception there is an awareness of content without an awareness of the development leading to that content; in action, there is a development—the act itself—without a content. These represent two phases of a common process.

We may recall Bastian's (1898) idea that the motor speech center is really a kinaesthetic area, and that motor aphasia is really a kind of sensory disorder. This is related to Luria's (1966) syndrome of kinaesthetic aphasia. The present argument is in some ways the reverse, that the sensory language area is concerned with language production, and that the comprehension disturbance in the sensory aphasias presents itself in the form of a production deficit. This is offered only as a speculation for the reader without a fuller discussion, as this would take us far from the objective of this chapter. The nature of acts and objects (perceptions) and their derivations in language will be the subject of a monograph that is currently in preparation.

Language Disorders of the Anterior Sector

Limbic-Level Disorders

As in the posterior system, the anterior sector also develops out of a common limbic core. The anterior division of this core mediates the initial stage in motor speech differentiation and so underlies the anterior aphasias, just as limbic amnesia and confabulation were shown to be transitional to the posterior aphasias. Moreover, as with the posterior limbic disorders, the anterior limbic structures require bilateral lesions for symptom expression, which accounts for the relative scarcity of cases of anterior limbic pathology. The most typical example of an anterior limbic syndrome is the condition of anterior cingulate gyrus mutism.

The most characteristic effect of *stimulation* in anterior cingulate gyrus in man is a state of arousal or vigilance not directed to the external world. Motor responses of the limbs tend to be oriented toward the body, and there are changes in mood—fear, anxiety, or sadness—which are usually not verbalized. The impression is of an affective and instinctual state organized about an archaic level in behavior (Bancaud et al., 1976). These effects of stimulation are consistent with the clinical description of bilateral pathological lesions of the anterior cingulate gyrus. In such cases there is a state of mutism, motor akinesis, apathy, and lack of affective responses. In the first case report of this type (Nielson & Jacobs, 1951), there was no spontaneous speech or movement, but the patient could be aroused for brief periods of time, during which she was said not to be aphasic. Subsequent reports have confirmed this picture, though a case has been described in which the mutism was broken by excited outbursts (Farris, 1969). This problem was reviewed by Buge, Escourelle, Rancurel, and Poisson (1975) in light of three further case reports, and the complete absence of spontaneous speech was emphasized, as well as the rarity with which communication could be established. With strong arousal, an occasional, often fortuitous, command could be elicited. In contrast to these profound effects, bilateral stereotactic lesions of human anterior cingulate gyrus lead mainly to a state of placidity. This is probably a partial expression of the more severe condition seen with anterior cingulate destruction.

These findings are consistent with the view that anterior medial limbic cortex mediates an early or "deep" stage in the anterior component of the cognitive process. This stage is characterized by a consciousness level of arousal or vigilance, while behavior is organized about the proximal and/or axial musculature and is not directed to extrapersonal space. The emotional pattern also suggests a "deep" (drive) level in affect differentiation. This stage is referred to as that of the "motor envelope" in which the various preparatory elements of the final utterance—the utterance itself, its accompanying gestures, the postural tonus within which it emerges—are all present together, incipiently, along with an affective component pointing to a drive level in affect derivation. This (pathological) level prefigures and gives rise to a subsequent cognitive stage that is mediated by (left) generalized frontal neocortex. The most striking defect in the syndrome of the anterior cingulate gyrus, loss of spontaneous vocalization with occasional brief emotional utterances and short repetitions, forms the nucleus of the next syndrome (level) to be discussed, transcortical motor aphasia.

Levels in the Realization of the Motor Component

The developing utterance issues out of a preliminary (limbic) cognition. Simultaneously, the action of the limbs proceeds outward toward objects in extrapersonal space. The diffuse, labile affect of the limbic level is derived into more differentiated partial expressions, while consciousness of speech and action becomes increasingly more critical and acute. The anterior aphasias can be thought of as moments or segments of this process at sequential stages in its emergence.

From the point of view of the speech act,[5] there is a progression from akinetic mutism, an inability to evoke or further realize the motor envelope of the speech act, through an attenuated form in transcortical motor aphasia, to agrammatism and finally Broca's aphasia proper. In this progression, the cognitive stage, as it is revealed in pathology, becomes increasingly more focused as it develops toward the final articulatory units (Figure 1-5).

Differentiation of the Motor Envelope The motor envelope contains the embryonic speech act together with its accompanying gestural and somatic motor

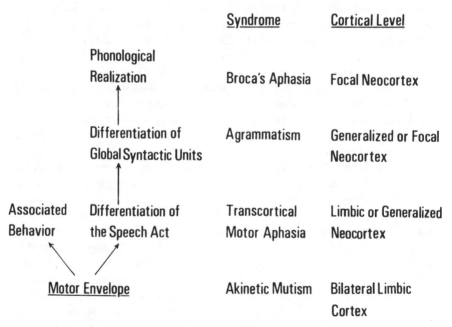

FIGURE 1-5. Syndromes of the anterior sector, with corresponding brain structural level, and level of speech act differentiation.

---

[5]This refers to the utterance as an action that unfolds, emphasizing the fact that the anterior component of language is bound up with motility as a type of specialized motor performance.

elements. At this stage, the elements are only prefigurative, bearing little resemblance to the performances (speech, gesture) to which they give rise. In the microgenesis of this motor configuration, certain elements precipitate out early, for example, postural elements, while others undergo a separate microgenetic fate.

At the point where the speech act differentiates out of this background organization, pathological disruption is characterized by a lack of spontaneous or conversational speech with good repetition. At times, naming and reading aloud are also spared. This constellation of findings has been termed *transcortical motor aphasia;* it is similar to the dynamic aphasia of Luria. In this syndrome there is more than just a lack of spontaneous speech; nonspeech vocalizations and gestures are also reduced and there is often an inertia of behavior generally, which may suggest Parkinsonism. These "associated" symptoms all point to a common level or origin in the unfolding motor act; they are also a sign of its proximity to akinetic mutism.

This disorder reflects an involvement at the level of generation of an utterance, a speech act, without a disruption of the (potential) constituents of that act. This may concern the initiation of the utterance, its organization, and/or its differentiation from other motor elements at that level. Repetition aids in achieving this differentiation and in providing a configuration through which syntactic differentiation can occur. Naming is frequently preserved. The presence of an object may help to provide a structure through which this differentiation may occur. The presence of good naming in this disorder marks a transition to the next level, that of agrammatism, where there is also superior noun production.

The affective state of such patients is usually one of apathy or indifference. The apparent lack of emotional responsiveness is another feature indicating a link with cingulate gyrus disorders. However, the pathological anatomy is uncertain. At least it can be said that the preservation of repetition is not to be understood by the sparing of a repetition pathway; that is, it is not a transcortical defect (Brown, 1975). In many cases there is partial involvement of the left Broca area (Goldstein, 1948). I have described a case with subtotal destruction of Broca's area (Brown, 1975). On the other hand, the most frequent cause is probably occlusion of the anterior cerebral artery, which entails damage to the anterior cingulate gyrus, supplementary motor area and contiguous structures on the medial surface of the frontal lobe. Conceivably, the disorder may follow a left cingulate lesion as a partial form of the severe mutism with bilateral cingulate destruction. The association with supplementary motor area is now well-established. These contain limbic-derived neocortical zones. In any event, the correlation is either with limbic-transitional or *meso*cortex or with the next level in neocortical phylogenesis, generalized neocortex of the left frontal region.

Syntactic Realization As the speech act differentiates, the simpler and more global units of the utterance-to-be are the first to emerge. Along with the appearance of nouns and uninflected verbs, there is an unfolding into the forming utterance of the small grammatical or function words. The appearance of the functors is thus delayed to a level of individuation subsequent to that of holophrastic noun and verb production. Disorders at this stage are characterized by incomplete differentiation of emerging syntactic units (agrammatism).

Conceivably, this disturbance can be conceptualized as an incomplete elaboration of a phrase structure tree, with a premature appearance of representations at the noun and verb phrase level. If so, the nouns and verbs of agrammatic patients should not have precisely the same value as those same lexical units in normal speech. Certainly, agrammatics use nouns in a more diffuse, more propositional (holophrastic) way. Their difficulty in classifying nouns (Lhermitte et al., 1971) may reflect an attenuation of noun-phrase differentiation. However, this is only a way of characterizing agrammatic language and may not reflect real psychological events. The preferential sparing of nouns and simple verbs in agrammatism may well have more to do with the initial use of these items as activity concepts, in relation to the cognitive mode of their acquisition. This is not to suggest that the agrammatic has a child's grammar; there is considerable evidence against this point of view. The evidence suggests, rather, that the young child's use of language in relation to activity may play a determining role in the psychological representation of these lexical items.

There is yet another way of looking at agrammatism. In this disorder there is a disruption at an intermediate stage in the unfolding of the kinetic melody of the utterance. We may consider this "melody," at the level of the motor envelope, as a prefigurative rhythmic organization that is derived, at the level of agrammatism, into the intonational pattern, and then into the temporal programmation of sound sequences. Involvement at an intermediate stage in this series might produce a flattened intonational contour, inability to inflect (tones as well as words), and loss of prosodic values. This might be accompanied by an increased salience for stressed content words, reflecting the posterior development of the content words and the lexical basis of word stress. This would give the appearance of an attenuated syntactic differentiation. This might explain the infrequency of agrammatism in French aphasics. In French, the stress pattern is more evenly distributed over the sentence, allowing the production of functors to survive disruption of the intonational pattern. I believe that the correct interpretation of this disorder, as well as the other "motor" aphasias, is to be found in the concept of successive levels in the derivation of a rhythmic series, though this does not necessarily exclude an account on the basis of a syntactic impairment.

The link between the level of agrammatism and the preceding level can be seen from individual case studies. Patients with transcortical motor aphasia may have agrammatic repetitions. As spontaneous speech returns, it often goes through an agrammatic phase, or there may be agrammatism in writing. Similarly, the improved performance on repetition in this disorder carries over into agrammatism proper where performance is generally better on repetition. In fact, cases of agrammatism in conversational speech with normal repetition have led to the view that agrammatism is a type of economical speech. While there does not seem to be any basis for this belief, the frequent dissociation between good repetition and conversational agrammatism establishes a link with the more preliminary disorder.

The anatomical correlation of agrammatism is typically with generalized neocortex of the dominant frontal lobe, that is, a partial or peripheral lesion of Broca's area. It corresponds, therefore, with anomia (evocational stage) in the posterior series, which is also linked to generalized neocortex. Like anomia, agrammatism is imprecisely localized; the possibility of a frontal anomia is as open as the possibility of a posterior agrammatism. Another similarity is that, in anomia, the abstract representation of the lexical item also fails to achieve phonological realization. In anomia this is more pronounced for nouns than functors, whereas in agrammatism it is the reverse. Both levels converge toward a final stage of phonemic encoding.

An intriguing aspect of agrammatism is that it is the chief manifestation of aphasia in young children, and in dextrals with right-hemisphere lesions (crossed aphasics). In such patients, agrammatism occurs with posterior as well as anterior lesions, presumably because their incomplete lateralization goes along with more diffuse intrahemispheric language organization; in other words, there is less focal differentiation (of a "Broca" area) within generalized neocortex of either hemisphere. The relation of agrammatism to generalized neocortex accounts for its occurrence in cases of "right hemispheric speech; for example, in cases of left hemispherectomy in adults, and in the case of a feral child where left-hemispheric regional specification apparently did not develop (see Curtiss, 1977).

Phonological Realization The anterior development terminates as the emerging lexical frames actualize into phonological sequence. This transition corresponds to that of the posterior component, as both systems converge toward a final phonological stage. Disruption at this level gives rise to phonemic-articulatory disturbances in otherwise well-formed utterances. The disorder is taken to represent Broca's aphasia proper[6] and is distinct, though transitional, from agrammatism. Within this final segment, several sublevels have been described (Lecours & Rouillon, 1976; Alajouanine et al., 1939).

The transitional nature of the phonological level out of the agrammatic complex is evident in the overlap between the two disorders. Agrammatics commonly show some phonemic-articulatory deficits, while the latter group commonly have some agrammatic features. Patients with articulation errors in speech may show agrammatism in writing. In both groups, performance is

---

[6]Probably the same as "verbal apraxia," a term that emphasizes the basis in motility but does not otherwise have any explanatory value.

generally improved for repetition. Moreover, in cases where the impairment is mainly phonological, the deficit is more prominent for functors than for content words.

As the utterance achieves a stage of phonemic encoding, there is an improved affective state; mood and awareness of disability are comparable to that in the posterior phonological disorder (phonemic aphasia). One can say that the affective tone has proceeded to the same derivation as the utterance that accompanies it. Patients also show active, at times labile, gesture, though there is little capacity for sign language or pantomine. The prominent gestural activity may be understood by a microgenetic completion which differentiates from the final speech act development.

The anatomical correlation is with Broca's area (mainly postero-inferior F3; see below) of the dominant hemisphere, in other words, with focal asymmetric neocortex. From this point, the further elaboration of the utterance occurs through inferior precentral (motor) cortex, which mediates the terminal (phonetic) phase of the anterior microgenetic sequence. Disruption of this segment gives rise to the "syndrome of phonetic disintegration" (Alajouanine et al., 1939).

Some Problems Concerning the Anterior Aphasias

Comprehension in Anterior Aphasia The inner bond between comprehension and expression, which seems to exist in the posterior aphasias, is not so readily apparent in the anterior disorders. One has the impression that patients with very similar production deficits vary greatly in the severity of oral comprehension. There is also some evidence (Hécaen & Consoli, 1973) that the severity of the comprehension deficit is related to the depth of the pre-Rolandic lesion. However, in the more restricted cases there is a suggestion of a relationship between the comprehension deficit and the *pattern* of expressive speech. Patients with mutism generally do not show comprehension ability, or at least it is difficult to demonstrate. Patients with intermediate-level disorders, such as "transcortical motor aphasia," have a moderate comprehension impairment, especially when this is in association with echolalic repetition. In agrammatism there is evidence that the mild comprehension disorder is specific to the production pattern (Zurif & Caramazza, 1976), whereas Broca aphasics with primarily phonemic-articulatory errors show relatively good comprehension ability. Clearly, further work is needed in this area; yet there is the suggestion that the disruption in aphasia affects a common level in a system elaborating both language production and perception.

Broca's Area: A Brief Review and Conclusions Historically, Broca (1863) maintained that the frontal speech zone included the posterior portion of the inferior or third frontal convolution (F3), that is, the pars opercularis and possibly the pars triangularis, and perhaps also part of the middle frontal gyrus (F2). Various authors have included the inferior precentral convolution (i.e., the "face area"), although this zone is generally distinguished from Broca's area proper. Some writers (e.g., Goldstein, 1948; Mills & Spiller, 1907) included the anterior insula in an extended frontal speech zone. Niessl von Mayendorff (1911) maintained that the frontal operculum was the motor speech center.

For Monakow (1914), Broca's area included F3, anterior insula, the connecting gyrus between F3 and the precentral convolution, and the Rolandic operculum. This is similar to the description given by Dejerine (1914): the posterior part of left F3, frontal operculum, and neighboring cortex ("cap" of F3 and "foot" of F2), extending to the anterior insula but excluding Rolandic operculum. Henschen (1922) argued that the cap of F3 (pars triangularis) was not a part of the motor speech zone on the basis of a negative case with bilateral lesion reported by Bonvicini (1926).

In sum, there has traditionally been general agreement on the importance of the posterior part of F3 (pars opercularis) and neighboring frontal operculum and uncertainty as to pars triangularis, posterior F2, and anterior insula.

However, shortly after the observation by Broca that a lesion of left posterior F2 produced motor aphasia, exceptional cases were described. In fact, Broca (1865) took up this problem himself in relation to a case of Moreau (1864), a 74-year-old nonaphasic epileptic woman found to have congenital atrophy of the left Sylvian area, particularly involving the posterior inferior frontal region.[7] Recently there has been renewed interest in this problem, in light of cases of destruction or removal of Broca's area without or with only transient aphasia.

Cases of destruction of the left Broca area without persistent aphasia are well known from the early literature (Moutier, 1908; Monakow, 1914; Nielsen, 1946), though in the majority handedness was not specified. Such patients tended to be younger, though several cases were recorded with recovery at an advanced age (e.g., a 70-year-old patient of Bramwell, 1898). Moreover, there was no simple relationship between duration of aphasia and lesion size. Persistent aphasia occurred in several patients with small lesions restricted to the foot of F3, while recovery occurred in some patients with extensive destructions. Involvement of the anterior insula in addition to pars opercularis appeared to be a

---

[7]The absence of aphasia in this case with extensive lesion of the motor speech area led Broca to remark that many times before, in studying the brains of aphemics, "a lesion of the left third frontal convolution was not always directly related in intensity with the alteration of language; . . . (having) seen speech completely abolished by a lesion from 8–10 mm in extent, while in other cases lesions ten times larger altered only partly the faculty of articulate language." Broca commented that "in all probability, the two hemispheres contribute to language . . . [and that in this case] it was perfectly evident that the right third convolution had substituted for the absence of the left." He went on to say that he "wondered why this was not the case in all aphasic patients."

factor in many cases. Other cases are described in Mohr (1973) and Hécaen and Consoli (1973).

Of greater interest are patients with bilateral lesions of Broca's area with and without aphasia. Negative cases were described by Moutier (1908). Cases of bifrontal lesion with aphasia are not comparable in that an initial left-side lesion would tend to produce a persistent aphasia so the effect of a second right-side lesion cannot be clearly determined. Thus, only the patient with an initial left-side lesion without aphasia tends to be reported. Such a case was described by Barlow (1877), a 10-year-old boy with speech loss and right hemiparesis following a fall. After 10 days, speech returned except for some paraphasia. Subsequently, he developed a left hemiplegia and permanent motor aphasia. Postmortem examination showed symmetrical lesions in F2 and F3.

Another case was reported by Charcot and Dutil (in Monakow, 1914). This patient developed, at age 44, a right hemiparesis and Broca's aphasia, which resolved to a partial agraphia. Eleven years later he had another attack with right hemiparesis and complete motor aphasia. After 2 years speech returned; then 5 years later there was a third attack with mild articulation difficulty. Shortly after this, he developed a motor aphasia that persisted to death. At postmortem examination, a small focus of softening was found in the left Broca's area and, on the right side, softening of the Rolandic operculum and pars opercularis. In this case, the terminal aphasia was related to the more recent right-side focus.

Tonkonogy (1968) described a 58-year-old woman who developed weakness of the right side and mild motor aphasia. Speech was described as slow with reduction of words. There was complete recovery in 1 month. One year later, she developed a mild left hemiplegia and dysarthria. Speech was unclear but nonaphasic. Autopsy revealed, in the left hemisphere, softening in the triangular and opercular portions of F3 and a 2.5 × 1.5 cm cyst in the underlying white matter involving insula. In the right hemisphere, the lesion involved internal capsule, insula, the inferior portion of the frontal lobe, and the upper temporal lobe.

There are obvious problems in the interpretation of the clinical material, and for this reason cases of surgical excision of Broca's area are of special import. In 1891, Burckhardt reported a series of patients with psychiatric disorders undergoing cortical topectomy. In two of these cases, there was a unilateral surgical excision of Broca's area.

> The patient was a 26-year-old right-handed male psychotic. Prior to surgery, speech fluctuated between logorrhea and mutism, with frequent neologism. Initially, left posterior T1 and T2 were removed, following which the patient spoke little and mumbled, but utterances were well articulated. Auditory comprehension was said to be intact; auditory hallucinations persisted but were diminished in intensity. Six days after surgery, a transient aphasia was noted. Two years later, because of the return of verbigeration, Burckhardt resected the pars triangularis and foot of the left F3.

Following this second operation, the patient spoke with less fluency, with a reduction of words.

This case was a 51-year-old right-handed woman with long-standing maniacal agitation. In the first operation, part of the left superior parietal and supramarginal gyri was resected. Three months later part of the left T1 was removed, and 2 months after this a third operation was done with excision of posterior-superior temporal cortex and angular gyrus on the left side. While no change was noted in speech, auditory hallucinations were diminished. The final operation was a resection of left pars triangularis, with no postoperative aphasia.

With regard to these cases, the first patient, who was relatively young, had a more extensive excision of Broca's area, with a change in fluency and some vocabulary loss. In the second case, only pars triangularis was resected as the fourth in a series of operations. These factors might account for the lack of language change following surgery. It is of interest that Burckhardt decided to carry out only a partial removal in the second patient because of the patient's age, noting that compensation after complete removal might be less pronounced than in a younger patient.

Subsequently, two patients were described with *bilateral* topectomy of Broca's area (Mettler, 1949):

The patient was a 27-year-old woman with regressed catatonic schizophrenia, described as seclusive and nearly mute. At operation, the inferior frontal gyri (Area 45 and parts of Areas 10, 44, and 46) were ablated bilaterally. Following operation the patient was unresponsive for at least 6 days. By the 12th day, she still did not speak spontaneously and a motor aphasia was suspected. Though on psychological examination it was recorded that 1 month following surgery the patient "spoke clearly and distinctly," even on preoperative neurological testing the patient was said to have spoken in monosyllables. At 4 weeks postsurgery, the neurologist noted that she spoke in thick monosyllables with prominent dysarthria and bilateral facial weakness as well as weakness of tongue movements and dysphagia. There was no evidence of aphasia but rather a "severe degree of dysarthria." Reading and writing were intact within educational limits; naming was also preserved.

The patient was a 31-year-old female with hebephrenic schizophrenia. Prior to surgery speech was confused with "word-salad." At operation, Area 44 (pars opercularis) was removed bilaterally. After operation, speech was said to be "greatly improved with little or no babbling." Questions were answered directly and accurately. This improvement lasted only a short time and within 3 months the patient was speaking as before, that is, word-salad. There was no dysarthria or dysphagia.

In the first case, with a somewhat larger topectomy, some degree of postoperative articulation difficulty appears to have been present, though the recorded notes do show discrepancies as to the extent and duration of this difficulty. In the second case, the cortical removal was more restricted, which may account for the lack of postoperative aphasia. Another and somewhat speculative possibility that has not been considered, which could explain the Burckhardt and Mettler cases, concerns the fact that these were all severely regressed schizophrenics. If the cognitive level or state is important in determining symptomatology—and if Broca's area mediates a cognitive as well as language level—then the more preliminary cognition of the psychotic may permit a relative escape following Broca's area lesion.

These are the most dramatic reports; however, other surgical patients have been described by Chavany and Rougerie (1978), Robb (1948), and Zangwill (1975). In addition, Jefferson (1949) observed that excision of Broca's area, avoiding deep undercuts in the white matter, produced no more than a transient speech disorder. Burckland (personal communication, 1975) has stated that "bilateral removal of the frontal lobes, including the frontal opercular cortex, results in temporary mutism which persists for only a few days" and that "unilateral excision of the 'dominant' frontal opercular area produces mutism, lasting from several days to one month, following which a slight dysarthria can be detected in most cases." According to Burckland, dysarthria does *not* occur after bilateral frontal opercular excisions. Finally, Mettler (1972) has emphasized that motor aphasia has not been described following frontal lobotomy in spite of the insertion of the leucotome in many cases through pars opercularis.

From this review we may at least conclude that there are sufficient cases on record to allow us to distinguish a central zone in the posterior frontal operculum, lesions of which cause some motor speech impairment. The question that we are left with, however, and one that we have attempted to deal with in the preceding sections, is how we are to interpret the functional organization of this anterior zone in relation to both aphasic symptoms and normal speech. Certainly, the evidence cited is consistent with the claim that size of lesion and age at time of pathology are of crucial importance. The surgical topectomies producing minimal or no aphasia were limited cortical resections and were carried out in relatively young individuals. There is improved recovery in younger subjects, as well as in left-handers regardless of side of lesion. We have argued that this can be explained by the more diffuse organization of language in younger subjects and in non-right-handers. But what is meant by "more diffuse"? Diffuseness of representation implies an incomplete differentiation of focal neocortex out of background *generalized neocortex.*

Recent studies in pigment architectonics indicate that the Broca area has relatively fixed boundaries in the operculum. This is in contrast with the Wernicke area, which, in agreement with the thesis of this chapter, shows a greater individual and interhemispheric variability (H. V. Braak, personal communication, 1979). However, the differentiation to which we refer is *functional*. It is a conclusion from the lesion data and not purely morphologicial. Moreover, the postulation of a progression from generalized neocortical to focal neocortical representation applies not only to language but probably to other perceptual and motor systems. Studies of evoked potentials might be expected to show a gradual narrowing down of the zone from which such phenomena are elicited in the course of ontogenetic development.

Rather than a circumscribed zone in a geographic map of the hemispheres, Broca's area undergoes a *development* out of homotypical (generalized) isocortex. This development occurs to a variable extent and determines the degree of lateralization in a given individual. This maturational transition is similar to that which occurs in evolution as homotypical isocortex develops out of mesocortical limbic structures. These structures appear to be represented in the anterior forebrain by portions of supplementary motor area and cingulate gyrus. Evidence that these latter zones participate in language production has been discussed above. There is also the recent demonstration of increased cerebral blood flow to supplementary motor area during vocalization (Lassen, Larsen, & Orgogozo, 1978). The result of these lines of evolutionary and maturational development is that a hierarchical structure is built up in the anterior and posterior brain that mediates or supports the process of language formulation. Broca's area does not represent a language center but rather a *phase* in this dynamic stratification.

"Thalamic" Aphasia There is some evidence that lesions of the (left) thalamus can produce an aphasia. Historically, thalamic lesions have been associated with a nonfluent aphasia, actually a type of mutism, but recently a fluent jargon has been described. Both occur with acute left thalamic lesion, but only mutism has been described in progressive bilateral cases. It is unclear whether these disorders reflect the disruption of intrathalamic mechanisms or are referred effects on overlying cortex; we also do not know what mechanisms (nuclei) are involved.

Thalamic differentiation appears to follow an evolutionary course parallel to that of neocortex. For this reason the symptomatology of thalamic lesions should occur as a destructuring of this phyletic organization; that is, thalamic symptoms should show a level-by-level correspondence with those of cortical lesions. Thus, the picture of a lesion of the pulvinar should be of the same general type as that of a temporoparietal lesion, the picture of a lesion of limbic thalamus should resemble that of limbic cortex, and so on.

Studies in primate have demonstrated prominent connections between the inferior parietal lobule and the pulvinar (Walker, 1938). Using the horseradish peroxidase technique, Kasdon and Jacobson (1978) have shown a more heterogeneous input to this area in monkey but have confirmed the presence of major projections to the inferior parietal lobule from the pulvinar. This arrangement is similar to that in man, where strong connections have been shown to exist between the pulvinar and the inferior parietal and posterior temporal region (Van Buren & Borke, 1969). In contrast, the anterior speech area receives the major projection from the dorsomedial nucleus. This has been demonstrated in monkey by Tobias (1975) and appears also to be the case in man. In sum, the pulvinar is in relation to the generalized neocortex of the posterior sector, and the dorsomedial nucleus is in relation to the neocortex of the anterior sector.

Accordingly, we might suppose aphasic jargon to be associated with a pulvinar lesion and the dysnomia that occurs on pulvinar stimulation to correspond to the semantic disorders that occur with lesions of posterior (transitional and generalized) neocortex. Similarly, mutism may be associated with a lesion of the dorsormedial nucleus. This would correspond to the mutism that occurs as a symptom of anterior (transitional and generalized) neocortical lesion. The lack of phonological or articulatory deficit in the thalamic syndromes would indicate that these nuclei are in functional relationship to the generalized neocortex surrounding the Broca and Wernicke areas, *sensu stricto,* since lesions of these latter zones give rise to deficits at the phonological stages in language processing.

General Conclusions

The structure of the anterior and posterior sectors can be inferred from the pathological material. In the *anterior* system the progression is over a series of levels from:

1. A deep bilaterally represented limbic state incorporating the as-yet-undifferentiated speech act in a matrix of instinctuo-motor activity in relation to a rhythmic kinetic pattern about the body midline (akinetic mutism)
2. Separation of the incipient vocal configuration from its simultaneously emerging nonvocal motor and affective accompaniments, represented in transitional and/or dominant generalized neocortex (transcortical motor aphasia)
3. The possible appearance within this configuration of the early-differentiating global (i.e., holophrastic) syntactic units through dominant, that is, *laterally represented,* generalized neocortex; alternatively, the derivation out of the kinetic melody of an intonational pattern, disruption of which leads to a prominence of content words and the (lexically based) stress pattern (agrammatism)
4. Phonological encoding of the terminal units through the further derivation of the intonational pattern into the temporal programmation of sound sequences, represented in dominant *focal neocortex* (Broca's aphasia)
5. The final phonetic realization achieved through *contralaterally represented* motor cortex (phonetic disintegration)

Simultaneous with this progression, there is an unfolding in the posterior system from:

1. A *bilaterally represented* limbic stage at which the utterance is aroused in memory *in statu nascendi* (amnestic syndrome) leading to the separation and entry into a semantic operation of a verbal component (confabulation)
2. The selection of the verbal component through a series of progressively narrowing semantic fields, by way of limbic transitional and dominant, that is, *laterally represented,* generalized neocortex (semantic aphasic disorders)
3. Adequate selection of an abstract representation of the constituent lexical items, possibly with more facile emergence through the semantic layer of the less meaning-laden functors through dominant, that is, *laterally represented,* generalized neocortex; abstract items emerge in anticipation of a stage of phonemic encoding (anomic aphasia)
4. Phonological encoding of the more or less fully realized utterance through dominant *focal neocortex* (phonemic or conduction aphasia)
5. The final perceptual (and expressive?) exteriorization of the "physicalized" percept through (more or less) *contralaterally represented* sensory (konio)cortex ("word-deafness" and related disorders)

Inspection of the complementary sequences of levels in the anterior and posterior sectors strongly suggests a correspondence between homologous levels in each system. This correspondence is presumably maintained by level-specific inter- and intrahemispheric fibers (Figure 1-2). Interruption of these fibers has not been shown to produce aphasia, though there are some speculations to the contrary. The proposed model, though in disagreement with the concept that language or perceptual information is conveyed over these pathways, does predict some effect of pathway interruption, for example, anterior-posterior asynchrony or elevation of discharge thresholds in the interconnected areas. The central point is that the cortico-cortical fibers relate to timing or to phase relationships in separate, conically organized systems, rather than serving as conduits for the transfer of cognitive packets.

According to this theory, aphasia is the result of disruption at some level in either of two distinct systems. The disruption displays that level and does not destroy a specific language mechanism situated in the damaged site. An aphasic symptom is a fragment of a disturbed level that survives into the end stage, or the development of the level is attenuated. This "regression" effect explains why similar aphasic symptoms occur in patients with small or large lesions, since the extent and nature of the regression are determined by individual differences in the degree of regional hemispheric specialization, that is, the degree of the asymmetry of focal neocortex. This is also related to potential right-hemispheric language processing, in other words, to the development of focal neocortex in right-hemispheric generalized neocortex as well.

Thus, according to the described model, the gradual differentiation that takes place in the generalized neocortex of both anterior and posterior sectors biases the bilaterally emerging utterance toward a phonological realization mediated by these newly differentiating zones. As this process continues, it tends to "asymmetrize" earlier levels, for example, generalized neocortex, which are not ordinarily asymmetric. It is in this way that language becomes lateralized, through the emergence of left focal neocortex, and not through a transfer or migration of function to the left hemisphere.

2
Varieties of Aphasic Jargon*

with Ellen Perecman

In 1833, the *Dublin Journal of Medical and Chemical Science* published a case report on a patient demonstrating a language disturbance characterized by strings of meaningless sounds. In that report, Dr. Jonathan Osborne described a 26-year-old university scholar, once proficient in French, Italian, and German, who had apparently suffered a stroke which left him with language that "caused him to be treated as a foreigner." When asked to read the sentence,

> It shall be in the power of the college to examine or not examine any licentiate, previously to his admission to a fellowship, as they shall think fit.

the patient read:

> An the be what in the temother of the trothltodoo to majorum or that emidrate ein einkrastrai mestreit to ketra totombreidei to ra fromtreido asthat kekritest.

Several days later, he read the same passage as,

> Be mather be in the kondreit of the compestret to samtreis amtreit emtreido am temptrest.

At six months following the onset of the disturbance, the patient read the original test sentence as follows:

> It may be in the power of the college to evhavine or not, ariatin any licentiate seviously to his admission to a spolowship, as they shall think fit.

Finally, after one year, Osborne reports the patient to have improved almost totally.

Browne (cited in Bateman 1890) described a patient who incessantly produced uninterpretable sound sequences, an example of which he transcribed as follows: *kalluios, tallulios, kaskos, tellulios, karoka, keke.* In contrast to Osborne's patient

---

*Reprinted from "Ukeleles, Condessors, and Fosetch" by E. Perecman and J. W. Brown, 1985. *Language Sciences*, 7, 177–214. Copyright 1985 by *Language Sciences*. Adapted by permission.

who appeared to be aware of his impairment, displaying normal affect, Browne's patient was evidently surprised that she could not be understood.

Such language, characterized by strings of meaningless sounds, came to be referred to in the medical literature as aphasic *jargon* (Bastian 1869; Kussmaul 1877; Miraillie 1896; Niessl von Mayendorff 1911) and the disorder, as **jargonaphasia.**

Jargonaphasia has typically been associated with poor comprehension, copious, fluent speech which is largely or entirely unintelligible but in which prosody, articulation and (where the determination can be made) syntax are preserved, and anosognosia. The unintelligibility of the jargon depends upon the extent of semantic and/or phonemic paraphasia, and is usually more pronounced in naming than in spontaneous speech. In most cases, the jargon is interspersed with normal, intelligible language.

Eventually, it became apparent that there are at least three conceptually distinct forms of aphasic jargon and that jargonaphasia in fact designates a superordinate category referring to these heterogeneous disturbances. In 1952, Alajouanine, Sabouraud and De Ribaucourt introduced a distinction between jargon consisting of neologistic sequences and jargon consisting of inappropriate word substitutions. Alajouanine (1956) then specified the qualitative differences among types of jargon even further, describing three forms of jargonaphasia differing in degree of meaningfulness or linguistic organization. In what Alajouanine called **paraphasic jargon**, recognizable words were simply used inappropriately; **asemantic jargon** consisted of neologisms in the context of recognizable words and preserved syntax; in **undifferentiated jargon**, stereotyped sequences were totally meaningless and not clearly not segmentable into word-like groupings. As an example of undifferentiated jargon, Alajouanine gave the following brief excerpt: *sanenequedaucquitescapi.* Subsequently, Alajouanine and Lhermitte (1964) emphasized other clinical aspects of this type of jargon, including the tendency to stereotypy and perseveration, oral apraxia and the involvement of repetition and reading aloud. Oral and written comprehension were said to be preserved.

It would appear that Alajouanine's undifferentiated jargon refers to the same entity that Cenac (1925) called **glossolalia.**[1] Glossolalia is described as consisting of long stretches of neologism which include only phonemes of the standard language and in which phonotactic constraints are preserved. Cenac discusses the structural similarities these neologistic units bear to one another, and to other of the patient's utterances, and indicates that his patient showed a predilection for certain segments or sequences.

---

[1]More recently, the term glossolalia has been revived by Lecours and colleagues to refer to forms of phonemically deviant language, including aphasic jargon, schizophrenic speech and tongues spoken by persons said to be in charismatic states. The use of a single term to refer to phenomena of such diverse origins is presumably intended to capture a structural similarity among them.

The classification of jargons provided by Alajouanine and his colleagues constituted an important contribution to the medical literature on jargonaphasia in that subsequently it would be insufficient to speak of jargonaphasia as if it were a unitary deficit. The recognition of several different types of jargon invalidated much of the older literature in which the form of jargon was left unspecified. With the identification of at least three forms of jargon, a heavy burden was placed on correlative anatomical studies to explain the qualitative differences among them. Moreover, theories of jargon were now obligated to account for the heterogeneity of the clinical picture, as well as the links between jargon and other fluent aphasic disorders.

Brown (1972) proposed a classification of aphasic jargons in terms of the level of linguistic description at which the predominant type of deviance occurs in the jargon. Thus, Alajouanine's **paraphasic jargon**, which is characterized by semantic deviance is referred to as **semantic jargon**. When jargon includes neologisms, defined as word-like forms not included in the lexicon of any language and assumed to be a product of combined semantic and phonemic paraphasia, it is referred to as **neologistic jargon**. Finally, **phonemic jargon**[2] refers to semantically uninterpretable phonemic strings originating at the phonological level.

The types of aphasic jargon most commonly described in the literature are semantic and neologistic jargon. Reports of jargon fitting the description of phonemic jargon have for the most part been restricted to an occasional anecdotal reference (Lecours and Rouillon 1976; Wepman and Jones 1964). Extensive descriptions of such jargon are found in Perecman and Brown (1981) and Peuser and Temp (1981).

Clinically, the difference between one form of jargon and another is not very straightforward. As in most cases of aphasia, theoretically pure forms are rarely observed in practice. Phonemic paraphasias commonly occur in the context of semantic paraphasia and it is often difficult to be sure that a verbal paraphasia, e.g., *window* → *door*, is not, in fact, a homophonous neologism, e.g., *window* → [dɔr]. In addition, the greater the degree of phonemic deviance in neologistic jargon, the more opaque the semantic context and the more difficult it is to distinguish a phonemic deficit from a combined phonemic and semantic one.

SEMANTIC JARGON

Semantic paraphasia is typically associated with Wernicke's aphasia, although there are recent studies which argue that semantic paraphasia is related to overall severity and not to aphasic type (Butterworth, Howard, and McLaughlin 1984). Semantic jargon is semantically aberrant language consisting of excessive semantic paraphasia but

---

[2]Certain French authors refer to the phonemic paraphasias of conduction aphasics as phonemic jargon.

no more than occasional phonemic paraphasias or neologisms. This form of jargon is characterized by noun or verb substitution, derailments in the flow of discourse, and circumlocution. When lexical substitution affects syntactically relevant morphemes, e.g., auxilliary verbs, tense markets, articles, and pronouns, there is the appearance of a syntactic deficit. Comprehension is less impaired than in neologistic jargon, and repetition may be fairly good.

Semantic substitutions are typically distant in meaning from their presumed targets, and differ in this way from the circumlocutory errors of the anomic, where the semantic category of the target is often transparent, e.g., *chair→you sit on it*. According to Alajouanine *et al.* (1952), the verbal paraphasias or circumlocutions in semantic jargon are linked to target words through subtle conceptual bonds. Alajouanine *et al.* offer, as an example, a patient who, when asked to define the word *FORK* said, "Ah, fork, that's the need for a schedule." Paraphasias in which compound words are formed (e.g., *featherhair*) recall descriptions of schizophrenic language (Lecours and Vanier-Clement 1976) and sleep speech (Arkin and Brown 1971). Verbal errors in which there is a sound relation to the target (e.g., *pear* for *hair*) are uncommon.

In naming, patients seem to be more aware of a phonological error than a semantic one and, among semantic errors, they are more aware of an erroneous substitution that has a strong semantic relation to the target word; this graded awareness is evident in the incidence of self-correction. These patients are also likely to reject a substitution invented by the examiner when the meaning of the substitution approaches the meaning of the target, when there is a phonemic error in an otherwise correct word, or when the substitution constitutes "jabberwocky." Thus, clinical observations indicate that patients are more aware of phonological errors than semantic errors and that, among semantic errors, those closest in meaning to the target are more reliably rejected. This appears to be the case both in speech perception and production.

As with all of the jargonaphasias, semantic jargon is uncommon in young patients. When it does occur, it is generally associated with bilateral lesions of the temporal lobe, possibly involving underlying limbic structures (Weinstein, Lyerly, Cole and Ozer 1966). In older aphasics, the disorder can result from a lesion about Wernicke's area or posterior T2, though precise anatomical studies are lacking. Semantic jargon also occurs in acute confusional states and in Alzheimer's disease.

Patients with semantic jargon are usually euphoric, or demonstrate a heightened mood, showing no frustration at poor performance. It seems that the affective quality is specific to the utterance (as is awareness of error, described above) such that one sees a change in affect moment-to-moment depending on the predominating error type. Amnestic symptoms, i.e., Korsakoff-like states, have been described by Clarke, Wyke, and Zangwill (1958), and Kinsbourne and Warrington (1963a).

One suspects that there is a close link between semantic jargon and confabulation (see Case 1). In the latter, the memory deficit is in the foreground of the clinical picture; confabulation might be considered a mild or attenuated form of semantic jargon. Semantic jargon, on the other hand, may be thought of as a deteriorated confabulation where the language defect becomes more prominent. One might say that in semantic jargon there is an amnestic syndrome embedded in the language disorder, whereas in confabulation there is an aphasia embedded in the amnestic syndrome. Put another way, in confabulation, **intra**sentential organization is relatively intact; there is no semantic anomaly at the level of the sentence. Rather, the defect is at the **inter**sentential level and any derailment occurs at the discourse level.

In semantic jargon, where the disturbance involves word substitution, intrasentential relations are affected and the meaningfulness of the utterance is called into question. Here, the disorder is properly linguistic in nature, rather than conceptual (see Freedman-Stern, Ulatowska, and Baker 1984, for an example of such a dissociation in the writing of a Wernicke aphasic). Note, however, that the Korsakoff patient in the acute stage may have typical semantic jargon, which is indistinguishable from that of the semantic jargonaphasic. Moreover, ordinary amnesics commonly show aphasic misnamings during this stage (Victor, personal communication) and errors tend to be of the semantic type, that is verbal paraphasias. Such patients have been shown to have a deficit in semantic encoding (Cermak and Butters 1973). On the other hand, clinical observation has shown semantic jargonaphasics to have an amnesic disturbance, although this has not yet been the subject of careful investigation. Note, furthermore, that patients do not recall the period of their aphasia after recovery. What all of these observations suggest is that there is a continuum from linguistic disorders, on the one hand, to conceptual disorders, on the other, and that the midpoint of this continuum is characterized by an overlap between the two, e.g., as seen in the semantic jargon of an acute Korsakoff patient.

Case 1. This 72 year old man had a right temporoparietal infarction. Although neurological examination was normal, except for the aphasia, there was evidence of bilateral involvement. Electroencephalography (EEG) demonstrated some degree of bilateral posterior slowing, and a history indicated several left-sided seizures post-onset. Initially, there was severe semantic jargon with occasional neologism. The following is an example of the conversational speech of this patient (neologisms are in italics):

(1) **P**: And I say, this is wrong. I'm going out and doing things and getting *ukeleles* taken every time and I think I'm doing wrong because I'm supposed to take everything from the top so that we do four flashes of four volumes before we get down low . . . Face of everything. This guy has got to this thing — this

thing made out in order to slash immediately to put all of the *wind-pails*...This is going right over me from there — that's up to is five station stuff from *manatime* — and with that put it all in the build it all up so it will all be spent with him conversing his *condessing.*

E: Condessing?

P: Condessing his treatment of this for he has got to spend this thing.

E: (Holds up handkerchief) What is this?

P: Well, this is a lady's line — and this is no longer what he wants. He is now leaving their *mellonpush.*

E: Mellonpush?

P: What is spelled "U" something or other which also commence the fact that they're gonna finish the end of that letter which is spelled in their *stale-game* and opens up here and runs across what "M" or wasn't "M" it's "A" and "M" is the interval title and it is spelled out of all of this.

Performance on naming tasks was unreliable. Among his misnamings, or verbal paraphasias, some showed semantic link to the target object: "haircone" for earring, "smokin mob" for pipe; others showed no clear relation to the target object: "mouse looker atter" for ashtray, "lover lob" for wallet. There was generally little or no recognition by the patient of the erroneous nature of the verbal substitution.

In the course of recovery, the patient evolved into a fairly characteristic Korsakoff state. During the initial stage, the semantic jargon produced in reading was as severe as that in expositional speech. Gradually, reading improved to the point where it was relatively intact and speech became more intelligible, though some word-finding difficulty and semantic paraphasia remained. At this time, the patient was asked to read and immediately recall the story of *The Hen and the Golden Eggs.* The story is about a man who had a hen that laid golden eggs. Wishing to obtain more gold without having to wait for the hen to lay more eggs, the man killed the hen. Upon opening it, however, he found nothing inside, for it was just like any other hen.

The patient read the story correctly, although his immediate recall was quite poor. This can be seen in the following transcription of his performance:

(2) P: It seems to be a lot about something . . . it was a command on the hen and he told her to do certain things and she didn't do anything . . . and he tried to get everybody to do things and nobody did. He turned everything over to the marine base. He couldn't see out of this eye (patient had been discussing his visual problem before), doesn't see anything the way it should.

E: What about that story?

P: That's what I'm trying to come back to. He gave it to other people and something took charge and he liked the pieces. He had to put this thing like this because he had to keep this not looked at . . . and he began to hear things from the outside, which he liked very much, and he let the things go through because *horm*(?) this horse, he was able to tell exactly who did what with her and who did wrong with her. (Reads story again, correctly.)

E: Can you tell the story now?

P: I'll try to, though I have to keep things . . . centered. There was a man who had a hen, and she gave golden eggs and they collected the water and sent it into the water and brought it out, and he had to keep it this way or he couldn't see it and, when he sent her into the water, other things took charge and he had to hide this from them all the time.

E: Do you think he did the right thing in killing her?

P: No, I do not . . . Well, because it distributed itself and brought up everything out of there, not only brought every other hen, but it brought any other thing that might be invested by it, and he did that despite my keeping this thing normal. I don't know whether I'm saying it or not.

This language is similar to that of confabulating Korsakoff patients, especially those experiencing acute confusion at the onset of the disorder.

Case 1 illustrates the properties of semantic jargon described earlier: semantic anomaly attributable to the inappropriate use of nouns and verbs, derailments in the flow of discourse, perhaps related to the tendency toward confabulation, and an empty circumlocutory quality which contributes to the general incoherence of the discourse. Note that inappropriate utterances fall into three categories: (1) contextually inappropriate use of an otherwise 'legal' word, e.g., *commence the fact*; (2) illegal compounding of real words, e.g., *stale-game*; (3) neologism combined with a bound morpheme, e.g. *condessing*, and (4) word fragment combined with a free morpheme (word), e.g., *mana-time*.

NEOLOGISM AND NEOLOGISTIC JARGON

Isolated neologisms are not uncommon in a variety of aphasia subtypes (Butterworth *et al.* 1984). Lecours and Rouillon (1976) have argued that the occasional neologism observed in the Broca's aphasic is identical to that found in jargon-aphasia. This is open to question. Perhaps, it is the case in resolving global aphasics, but it is unlikely in documented anterior aphasics. In such patients, the apparent neologism is more likely a product of dysarthric distortion or phonetic misarticulation, and is not attributable to a disturbance in phoneme selection, as is presumably the case in jargonaphasia.

The isolated neologism usually replaces content words, i.e., nouns, verbs, adjectives, adverbs, and leaves intact the remaining part of the utterance, including affixes and function words, i.e., prepositions, articles, conjunctions, etc. Thus, a patient of Caplan, Kellar, and Locke (1972) was quoted as saying: "They will have to *presite* me . . ." and "Yes, because I'm just *persessing* to one." In a case seen by one of us, the patient remarked: "It was my job as a *convince*, a *confoser* not *comfoler* but almost the same as the man who was *commerced*." Another said, "Your *patebelin* like the mother . . . and his mothers of to go in his *stanchen*." Another patient, asked to name eyeglasses, said, "Those are *waggots*, they have to be *fribbed* in." [See Buckingham (1981) for additional examples.]

As the incidence of neologism increases, there is a corresponding decline in the intelligibility of the utterance. At some certain point, say, when neologisms constitute 20-30% of the words in an utterance, the patient is said to have neologistic jargon. It is rare that this incidence goes beyond about 80%.

In typical cases of neologistic jargon, the jargon invades all linguistic perform-ances more or less equally. Lhermitte and Derousne (1974) have described a case with good writing, but this is exceptional. There is no selective sparing of sung speech as in the Broca's aphasic; that is, lyrics are jargonized even though the melody may be preserved. During the acute stage, patients frequently produce sequences of numbers instead of words. Comprehension is usually so severely impaired as to suggest deafness. Yet, even in such cases, a response of bewilderment generally occurs when the patient is addressed in jargon (Boller and Green 1972). In a number of cases seen in our lab, this has been the only language-related response that could be obtained. In one patient, even abusive and obscene comments failed to elicit a galvanic skin reflex, though surprise was registered in response to the examiner's jargon.

There is little or no systematicity to jargon, i.e., no consistency of reference from one instance to the next and, thus, no evidence that jargon constitutes a private language. However, it is of interest that neologistic jargonaphasics may engage one another in "conversation" while rejecting jargon produced by the examiner. Lord Brain cited a case report of a jargonaphasic who seemed to accept his own tape-recorded jargon, but did not accept the same jargon after it had been transcribed and rerecorded by another person. Other well-known features of this type of jargon include the relative preservation of intonation contours, and the appropriate stress assignment in neologisms. Such patients are also known to augment, that is, to produce a greater number of syllables than are present in target words or greater number of words than are necessary in a target utterance. Such augmentation may affect neologisms as well as real words and may account, in part, for the logorrhea.

Within neologistic jargonaphasia, one can observe a fluent form, in which there is only a slight tendency toward rhyming or alliterative relations among words produced, and a less fluent, repetitive form in which the phonetic relations among words become quite prominent, e.g., "much tereen, will I could talk, sorlip, gorrip, grip, stick, eye, grin, grim, greeda." Such "rhyming jargon" also occurs in patients with left thalamic lesions.

These different forms may be observed in different patients or within the same patient at different moments (see Kreindler, Calavrezo, and Mihailescu 1971, and Lecours and Rouillon 1976). In cases of the latter type, fluency is impeded and jargon consists of a restricted repertoire of sounds, approximating the jargon stereotypy of the global or motor aphasic. Lecours and Rouillon (1976) have argued that in the global or motor aphasic such stereotypy points to a phonological disturbance. Presumably, in the neologistic jargon case, it also reflects the involvement of the phonological system.

In spite of severe disorganization of language, some patients can function fairly well in the world, demonstrating preserved analogical reasoning, and even continuing to play chess, though perhaps not at a very sophisticated level. Affect is generally heightened during jargon episodes and appears to be associated with the content of speech. Thus, while the patient may be euphoric, even manic when speaking in jargon, he may appear to be depressed when speaking correctly about his illness or family. Commonly, patients lapse into islands of preserved speech when asked to produce utterances that would otherwise result in jargon. The affective element in such phenomena should not be overlooked. In one of our cases the patient spoke incessant jargon, except when describing the accident that brought about his condition. He was run over by a car driven by his former girlfriend and was ordinarily quite lucid in his repetitive accounts of this incident.

Frequently there is a relative preservation of some thematic material even during the acute stage. For example, a patient with completely unintelligible jargon might produce a (usually short) series of correct, though often stereotyped, utterances about his illness or work. Lecours and Rouillon (1976) describe predilection units and predilection themes in jargon patients, where segments of words or whole words recur frequently, or where a specific topic dominates conversation.

Case 2. The patient was a 62-year-old, right-handed male with an intracerebral hematoma surrounded by edema in the temporoparietal region of the left hemisphere. Neurological examination showed no impairment other than the aphasia. Rate, intonation, and articulation of speech were normal. It should be noted that the patient acquired German as a second language when he was in his 20's. Expressive symptoms of the aphasia included fluent speech characterized by logorrhea, a stereotypic quality due to the recurrence of several predilection words and the production of neologisms. Alliteration and assonance were common, more so in reading than in spontaneous speech.

The neologistic content of this patient's speech is exemplified by the following:

(1) **P:**   What is it, uh, what [kɛču] are you talking about?

(2) **P:**   Do you know where my [gaʊ ʟɪ] is?

    E: Your what?

    P: No. Where *my* [kaʊaʊə]. You got something and I'll write it for you.

In fact, his spontaneous writing was almost entirely neologistic jargon. His copying showed evidence of transliteration and augmentation.

In the following utterances, the neologisms seem to be replacing the verb (3), or adjective (4-5):

(3) **P:**   I'm trying to [mətrairim] and you do that.

(4) **P:**   There was no girls [strɛpredɪd] or nothin'.

(5) **P:**   I was small but it was just [mɪziz] here.

    E: It missed you?

    P: It was [mɪsənin] yeah.

An apparent predilection for the words GIRL, MONEY, GOD, and GUESS was observed. The preoccupation with the theme of MONEY is seen in the examples below:

(6) **E:**   How old were you?

    P: For the moneys? Oh, that was 6 [mæʊəliəks] . . . No [dilz] nothing. Every night was something. There was nothing free. Money, money, money, money, money, [mʌnəmi wən wən wʌnʌ] by the American people.

    E: Uh, huh.

    P: You know, from, uh, that's much money here.

(7) **E:**   Where were you in Germany?

    P: 6 [mil]

    E: Uh, huh.

    P: 6 uh. She had. When I [gɛltɪd] her. In [vir] it was 6 [piəlu]. 1 [mil] 1 [mil] 1 [mil] 1 [mil] 1 [mil].

The word [gɛltɪd] in Example 7 is possibly derived from the German word for MONEY, that is *GELT*. In the following examples, the patient demonstrates the use of verbs inappropriately associated with the theme of MONEY.

(8) Well, I [ɔwɪz] to *pay* you at your right side that you're a beautiful girl.

(9) Did she want 'em in [bə] *pay* something for you.

(10) It's hard for [mɛmədi]. Remember these [gadz]. But I'm not *spend* everything right. So I'm just [gɛstɪŋ] right.

(11) And I don't [dil] you know. I'm bought so much *money*.

At one month post-onset of aphasia he was able to copy abstract drawings fairly well, but failed to copy drawings of real objects, such as a house and a chair.

In reading, 50% of words were produced as neologisms, with grammatical function words being preserved. His predilection theme of money was quite prominent in reading. In fact, the word [gɛlt], the German translation of his predilection word MONEY, appears in the reading. What follows is a transcription of the patient's reading of the story *The Hare and the Tortoise*. Below each line of the transcription is given the line of the story which the investigator was pointing to as the patient read. [Single and double bars represent short and long pauses, respectively.]

[dʌfa dəv faðə ǀ æ dərə mudyəfɪld] and a [iyə] fifty by of a ‖
[ɪfi] are a [iyti dæz ǀ bardi tɪd ‖ fərɪg ɪd voev so vɛdz ər ‖
The Hare and the Tortoise: A hare made fun of a tortoise because it was so slow.

[dəer kɪrfuzs seisi] to the [fɪɹɐ fɪn] ɪ will [foɐ fɪtʃ] pay to ǀ
a child that is here these [bʌčəguʃ] there [mʌs swez] to pay a [sɪz oez sə] in [sɛmf] so
Then, the tortoise said to the hare: "I will challenge you to a race." The hare thought this was a silly idea but agreed

to the [bɛdoef] ‖ they [haɹ u? diə di dɹɹɐ
to the competition. They started off but the hare

[fɪ so dɐɹɐ dɪ? ‖ wʌts bəfi bvɛrʏ ‖ fee fuər fɛz ‖]ᵇ
there is no is [su] ‖
ran so quickly that soon he was far ahead. Then, he thought:

[ɛl wɛl] to [oefɛfs fɛllf] on [dee dælɪd ‖ fɔlɐɪt ‖' fʌɹɹən fʌəd fɯ]
"I'll take a nap until that stupid tortoise catches up

---

[3]Note metathesis of final /s/ from *nothing is* (= nothing's) to *happening*.

[4]The majority of speech errors in normals occur on nouns (Browman, 1978).

wɪll all [vɪd dʌ | fɔrɪd | feɹɪd | faɹlʔ | far | ʌʔ ayt hayz ‖
ya]

with me." The tortoise crawled along very, very, slowly,

[faɹɹɪd | dlə vwahea] we wɪll wɪll [purɪd] ‖ and own [pærɪn brlɪ] ‖

passed the hare who was fast asleep and had nearly reached

[də kɪlənfš] ‖ the [fɪlɪv] ten [weɹɪn] where the no [div də |
bɪtɪ3 ‖ də ðlztʌr] so

the finishing line when the hare woke up. The hare

[bɪæd æd gerɪ3] and uh [beɹyut | bəhæt] they'll always [dərɪʔ věn
ɔlɛnt] to spend the hen a [æʔ əʔ gɛlt]

ran as fast as he could but didn't manage to get there first.

də gɛlt] the penny [gɛlt] and [owi dɛn sǒnsusəsi]
The tortoise had won the race.

It was difficult to test comprehension in this case, since the patient's responses
were usually irrelevant. Nevertheless, over the period of observation (2-1/2 months),
improvement in the domain of language as well as affective behavior was noted.

The patient commonly expressed frustration with statements such as: "I'm
not speaking right" and "I don't know what the hell's the matter with me." The
following excerpts from conversations illustrate the patient's awareness of the
language difficulties he was experiencing:

(12) **E:** Can you talk a little louder?
       P: I can't.
(13) **P:** (Mumbling) . . . This wat is [dilz] is better.
       E: Why is it better?
       P: If I try to (opens his mouth), it doesn't work.
(14) **E:** Can you say it? Say Ellen.
       P: No. I can't.
       E: Say Ellen. Say Ellen.
       P: See. Isn't that a funny thing you know. When I want to tell you
things. I'm trying to tell you and nothing happenings.[3] You know.
(15) **E:** What's the matter?
       P: I cannot [dil] with me. I (stuttering) don't know what's the
matter with me these days.

The neologisms in **Case 2** are typical in that they do not violate phonotactic constraints of the speaker's language, i.e., patients rarely produce consonant clusters not found in their native language, or clusters in initial position that are restricted to final position in the native language. Note that neologisms often incorporate standard morphemes of the language, such as plural markers for nouns, e.g., [mæɹəliəks] and tense markers for verbs, i.e., it was [mɪsənin]. The preservation of these affixes, together with the preservation of function words, makes it possible to establish that in most cases neologisms take the place of nouns[4] and to a lesser extent, verbs.

PHONEMIC JARGON

Cases in which speech is virtually 100% neologistic fall into the category of phonemic jargonaphasia. This is not to suggest, however, that phonemic jargon is a deteriorated neologistic jargon. On the contrary, it is important to keep in mind that as the incidence of neologisms increases, the utterance is not simply being filled with more and more nonsense words. Rather, the entire fabric of the aphasia is changing, including the patient's affective and cognitive state.

In phonemic jargonaphasia, as represented in **Case 3**, the meaning-bearing function of speech sounds is entirely absent, and there are few, if any, recognizable words or word-fragments. Fluent, voluble jargon produced with good articulation is characterized by a diversity of meaningless phoneme strings of variable length. Whether or not there are meaningful intentions underlying the jargon is open to question.

Elsewhere (Perecman and Brown 1981), we have described in detail the frequency distribution of phonemes in phonemic jargon, and the preference for labial consonants and the phonemes /r/ and /s/. It is noteworthy that the labial class of sounds provides a foundation for phonological development in the child and for phonological systems in the languages of the world. It is also a category of sounds for which the articulators happen to be most visible and manipulable. Phonemic jargon may, thus, reflect the salience of labials in perception and production. On the other hand, the high frequency of /r/ and /s/ in the jargon, phonemes of relatively high functional load in normal English, may indicate that frequent exposure to sounds in the environment also influences the content of the jargon.

A preference for /r/ and /s/ is not unusual among jargonaphasics. Green (1969) described a stereotypic sequence recurring in the speech of his patient HP, which always included the consonant /r/. Lecours and Lhermitte (1972) divided their patient's neologisms into three classes, each of which was characterized by a stereotypic sequence of phonemes. In all three classes, /r,s,b/ and /m/ always occurred in one position or another. Finally, the phoneme frequency distribution of a corpus of neologisms from Buckingham and Kertesz (1976) also shows a preference for /r/ and /s/.

Case 3. KS, a German-English bilingual male, suffered a CVA resulting in aphasia at the age of 74. At the time of his stroke, KS showed mild, left-sided weakness and EEG slowing over the left temporal lobe. Two months post-stroke, he was found to be neurologically normal except for the aphasia. A CT scan obtained at six months post-onset demonstrated two discrete lesions. One lesion involves the left temporoparietal region; the other involves the temporoparietal region of the right hemisphere. Mild ventricular dilation was noted. After reviewing the CT scan findings it was considered unlikely that both lesions occurred simultaneously. However, this was the patient's first known hospitalization.

KS appears to be right-handed as judged from the preferential use of that hand and dexterity in writing. On examination, he was alert and very cooperative. Indeed, he was eager to participate in testing. He obeyed normal speaker-listener conventions, responding when addressed, and remaining quiet and attentive when others were speaking.

Speech production was, on the whole, clearly articulated consisting of fluent, voluble jargon produced with an apparent logorrhea. KS produced virtually all of the sounds of normal English and German. Although the overall frequency distribution of sounds in his jargon is significantly correlated with the distribution found in normal speakers, the two distributions differ in terms of individual phonemes, largely because KS produces a greater than expected proportion of labials.

The following are examples of KS's spontaneous jargon. The first sample is from an extended monologue.

```
[u ɛt vʊni æ pɪuvwˀɪvwɛnhɪ ɛspɪdə ɛtsəbafɔʁɕɔʁ ɔʁlik bɔts
bimɛnziɔvəmitsʊhaɹa ‖ aɹu aino ʌˀʌɹimɪpaɹ ɱits fɛʁɛɕ i-
səmʊɱ i ɹɛdəmɔfɪɱɪtsi avwɔmamibeɹ fatbamasbiɕɔspailə
etəmezpɔmvɹemhia ‖ bʌ aimʊdɛvəbiastuduautəgaɹn aksɪdeɹvi-
dautʃɛʁ ‖ anɛpɛpɛpeɹasɪpi adoŋɛnimimiɛotbɪlʊz fɔɱ ima
mibi ʊ amasfə əmafɪbianəlidasbeɹɛtsbiu ‖ vwʊibin ɛn ðeðeðeba-
pfaʁbafəbiɛ demeəfəbasfəbɪspaɹetaɹɔfbəbla fɔmababɪspɹ ɪn ‖
map maɹafəɱanaɹ i mʊabiɬoɛɛsənədə ɛbimiviniviaɹ spɪnifumiəobv-
imai ɛbidzɔmiɹʊsfɔmivwɔ bamɪɹ ɪbjɛspimes fɔaməɕ ɛniɕ ambos
fənandi ‖ mɪɹ as pəlemvasibenʊ maɔsbaɹɛniasinimjɛnzəs baɹui
fotəeɹɔfibi ameɹ i veɹstiobaabmotəob]
```

In the second sample, KS is engaged in conversation with the investigator about a passage from Chomsky which he has just read aloud.

E: Good. What was this about?

P: [kɔt ɔt vɔt mɔz mɪmɛzivi] (pointing to neck)

E: Tell me what this was about. What was this about?

P: [ɹɛ no bat avat]

E: What did he write about?

P: [ai ino bɛs ɛsɛ] (begins to read text again)

E: Tell me just tell me in your own words. Tell me. What is this about?

P: [ʌm no no no nɔt həbɪlɐɛs pad bɪs (points to his temple or eye) obɯabɛsɛ bɹɛɓɯofɛɹmaws eis ɔn bot bɪstan estə bɐɐiə]

The jargon is characterized by a stereotypic, repetitious quality attributable to the consistent preference for /r/ and /s/ among consonants and /a/ among vowels. Units of production tend to be initiated and terminated by central consonants. In vowel clusters, there is a transition from low-back to high-front. For consonant clusters, the sequence is typically a centrally articulated stop followed by a centrally articulated fricative. Manner tends to change across a consonant cluster while voicing remains the same. The most common consonant cluster is a voiceless stop followed by a voiceless fricative. In CV clusters, central consonants are followed by back vowels; in VC clusters, back vowels are followed by central consonants.

On reading tasks, KS used his finger to guide himself across a word or sentence indicating that he was indeed going through the motions of reading. The jargon elicited on reading tasks essentially conforms to the pattern found in spontaneously produced jargon, indicating a simple stereotyped mode of production.

Examples of his reading at the simple word level are given below. Note that there is no relationship to the target.

TARGETS		RESPONSE
arm	→	[o ɹaigiɐts]
farm	→	[obɯainstɛspainiɐsdzɛsiɐsovbɯ audzaɪnzdziɹɛstsvosasdɪnsdasdɛɐs]
serve	→	[fo veɐzi]
observe	→	[topvɔdɛnɔnlɐs sofbanefbanlɐs]
back	→	[obaɪnɘsɵɪɐs ogɐanesdiɐs]
bag	→	[vɔʔfɪns vɔd zijes]
rag	→	[aɹaidiɐts seganɔs sambanəliɐsezəm]

Asked to read the story *The Hare and the Tortoise*, he read as follows:

[deʁ heɹa ũnt deʁ haɹɪteɹstʊʤaitsɪsʊs ‖]
The Hare and the Tortoise.

[awɔits vwaits deʁs of a dɛnsdeʁaɹɪ steʁzəs piʁasɔlʁɪvɪyɪnais
ɔɹvaiɹt]
A hare made fun of a tortoise because it was so slow.

[dɪʁdiʁuf deʁʔbainɬiɛsʊsəs oededeɹaibɪɯəfɹɛ ‖   abaɪf
vɹɪdɪmiɹspɯɪs tu dɪʁs]
Then the tortoise said to the hare: "I will challange you to

avwasɛvɛ ‖ ðɛʁ amɛ batplʁi stɛdvaisɛʁvwaisfyzən apeʁvyvɪtɛs
a race." The hare thought this was a silly idea but agreed

əətgamibiɬis ðl eʁs obadambeʁdɪstkʌmeʁɪs mans ɛntɛnəveʁsofɛ-
ʁaɹɪsɪʁs
to the competition. They started off but the hare

[feʁain bɛveʁs pfɛʁɪsɪpʊs dʒɛʁ aivaivwɔsdes emɔsbɛzə ‖ dzɔmdz-
ɛʁɪnɪdzani]
ran so quickly that soon he was far ahead. Then he thought:

[of adθeʁɹɪsovwaɪts ɔmɪmifɔʁ odhaɪmɪtzɔnɪmɛnɪtzeʁtzatzamabiv]
"I'll take a nap until that stupid tortoise catches up

[nuʁbaisbobʁiz ‖ ðɛʁ gamnesɛʁsf fɔmais fɹɔmasfɔɹɪbɔɹavipandɹi-
məmzɪʁs]
with me." The tortoise crawled along very, very, slowly,

[baɹofdɛʁvainɪʁsvɛi iʁso asbeʁɹi ũnz ɛs svandafabʁɛɪndzəm]
passed the hare who was fast asleep and had nearly reached

[ðɛʁ vʊʁsɔənsteʁmɔʁespɩsasfeʁai viəmeʁtzɪpif] ‖
the finishing line when the hare woke up. The hare

[ə aibɛsɛsdeʁ kamɛʁm aʁfdeʁ fɔfts ʁəmemi beʁəʁə indeʁ
menɹə ‖ fiʁt]
ran as fast as he could but didn't manage to get there first.

ðɛɹ kamdɛɹtsInɛɹɪts tsInɛɹɪts faInɛdI vaItsdɛɹ ɹubɛɹ
kɐmIsbos ‖]
The tortoise had won the race.

He did not appear to be aware that his utterances were jargon, but from time to time evidenced frustration, suggesting that he was aware of a failure to communicate. Active gesture was observed both as an accompaniment to speech and as a substitution for speech. Prosody and intonation were quite normal.

Comprehension was severely impaired, initially suggesting cortical deafness. It was difficult to distract him with loud noise, or by calling his name from out of sight. Occasionally, he followed simple whole-body commands, such as "stand up," even when the command was whispered from behind him. There was no response to other body, limb, or facial commands, though the examiner noted a difference in KS's response depending upon whether he was addressed in the form of a statement, a command, or a question. Jargon spoken by the examiner was rejected. At times, KS's jargon would incorporate segments from words spoken by the examiner. He was unable to point to objects named, either when the object was placed before him or when it was somewhere in the room. However, if the object was given a functional context, by means of a pantomimed demonstration of its use, he was sometimes able to point to the target object correctly.

Over the months, comprehension improved to the point where he was able to indicate many single objects named aloud, and even to answer "yes" and "no" to very simple questions. It was apparent that KS's performance on a task was more likely to be successful once a behavioral set for that particular task had been established.

Audiometric testing indicated a mild hearing loss with normal pure tone thresholds.

KS demonstrated no repetition upon request, although, as mentioned above, words or portions of words produced by the examiner were occasionally detected in his jargon output.

Naming was jargonized, and only rarely could the target word be discerned in his utterance. There was considerable augmentation, with the response including many more syllables than the target in fact included. Perseveration was noted.

Reading comprehension was possible to a limited extent. Though unable to follow simple written commands, he was able to match many written words with correct objects or line drawings of those objects. Performance on this task was better in English than in German. When the written words ENGLISH, GERMAN, FRENCH were displayed before him, and he was asked to match a written or spoken word to the word indicating the language in which the item was presented, he was unable to do so. Over a period of several weeks, he was able to complete simple written phrases with a word selected from a choice card, where the choice included nouns, verbs, and functors. Semantic category information appeared to be intact. When shown the word "tool," he pointed to a picture of a hammer, pliers, etc.; in response to the word "fruit," he pointed to an apple, banana, etc.

Writing was poor and jargonized for spontaneous productions, but copying was excellent. He showed an ability to transliterate, correctly matching words written in block letters with the same words written in script. In addition, he could write numbers from one to ten. In contrast to the apparent lack of awareness for the content of his speech, he was often frustrated by the difficulty in written expression.

Limb praxis was difficult to evaluate. Some actions were carried out to imitation, such as eye closure, lifting the hand and standing up. He was able to match body parts from the examiner to himself, but finger identification on a matching test was poor.

Drawing ability was fairly good. Little perseveration was observed in action and drawing, with such behavior more apparent in writing. There was no evidence of neglect. Line bisection was normal.

At present, Case 3 is one of the only cases of phonemic jargonaphasia to have been extensively documented. One must, therefore, proceed with caution in drawing generalizations about the properties of this form of jargonaphasia. Nevertheless, this case material does allow us to formulate hypotheses to be tested by future cases of this type.

RELATIONSHIPS AMONG PHONEMIC JARGON, JARGON STEREOTYPY, AND NEOLOGISTIC JARGON

The phonemic diversity of phonemic jargon stands in contrast to the restricted inventory of sounds found in the jargon stereotypies that form the residual utterances of motor and global aphasics. In the latter patients, whose aphasias are associated with large peri-Sylvian lesions, the jargon usually consists in the repetition of a single CV syllable such as *titi*, but may include a limited extent of phonemic variation with repetition of several CV sequences. These cases may be transitional to others which include a still richer flow of CV strings consisting of all of the phonemes of the speaker's language (Peuser and Temp 1981). Such cases may be similar to the description of jargon with apraxia of Alajouanine and Lhermitte (1964), where comprehension was said to be relatively well preserved and there was severe oral apraxia. However, it is questionable whether a relation exists between the simple reiterated jargon stereotypies of motor and global aphasics and the rich and complex phonemic jargon in KS. The more likely possibility is that there is a relation between phonemic jargon and other fluent jargons.

Consider for a moment the possibility that phonemic jargon is a type of deteriorated neologistic jargon. Certain structural similarities between phonemic jargon and neologistic jargon are indeed apparent: (1) both forms of jargon respect the phonotactic constraints of the standard language; (2) both may be marked by alliteration and assonance[5]; (3) in both, phoneme frequency distributions deviate from the norm (Wepman and Jones 1964: Butterworth 1979; Lecours and Lhermitte, 1972).

It is of note that those studies which purport to show a preservation of distributional properties in aphasic speech, generally either (a) do not include neologisms in the analysis (Blumstein 1973), or (b) determine distributional properties over a heterogeneous group of aphasia patients (Mihailescu, Voinescu, and Fradis 1967), in which case, any differences among aphasia types will have been obscured.

The most obvious difference between neologistic jargon and phonemic jargon is that in neologistic jargon there is a preferential disturbance of nouns and verbs, whereas in phonemic jargon all word classes are equally affected. Note, however, that it is in fact difficult to establish whether or not grammatical morphemes are preserved in phonemic jargon given the virtual absence of any intelligible sequences. Indeed, it is this qualitative difference between the two jargons which has been taken to suggest that phonemic jargon is simply a more severe form of neologistic jargon. Yet, this preferential disturbance of nouns and verbs in neologistic jargon might also suggest a crucial distinction in underlying mechanism between the two jargons. The fact that the parts of the utterance most likely to be affected in neologistic jargon are those with the greatest semantic content, i.e., nouns and verbs, suggests that neologistic jargon entails an underlying semantic disturbance. The phonological deviance is only secondary. In phonemic jargon, on the other hand, deviant phonological processing alone accounts for the jargon. This hypothesis would explain why phonemic jargon affects all word classes regardless of semantic content. According to this view, it is some parameter of semantic content, e.g., imageability, concreteness, that determines which parts of the utterance are affected by neologistic jargon, and not the morpho-syntactic distinction between word classes, i.e., prepositions vs. nouns.

JARGONAPHASIA IN THE POLYGLOT

While jargonaphasia is one of the rarer forms of aphasia, it is quite common to find that patients with jargonaphasia are multilingual. Indeed, there are cases

---

[5]It is of interest that semantic jargon as well is characterized by rhyming and other phonological relationships among verbal paraphasis. Kreindler, Calavrezo, and Mihailescu (1971) describe a semantic jargonaphasic in whom "the criterion for selection of [verbal paraphasias and neologisms] was not the semantic one but exclusively the criterion of auditory similarity determined by the rhyme (1971:221)."

in which polyglot aphasics "mix" their languages, producing utterances which consist of words from different languages. While language mixing is not necessarily a pathological behavior (consider the intrusion of English words in the Spanish spoken by Hispanic Americans and the mixing of English and Yiddish words among the Yiddish-speaking community of American Jews) aphasic language mixing can produce quite abberant linguistic forms.

The mixing of languages subsequent to an aphasia has been observed in spoken as well as written language and at all levels of linguistic description. Patients combine words from several languages in the same word, e.g., 'gelting' from German 'Gelt' and English suffix '-ing' (Perecman 1980); or they simply produce a blend of semantically comparable words from different languages, e.g., 'zwetto' from German 'zwei' and Hungarian 'ketto' (see Paradis 1977). Patients have also been reported to use the syntax of one language with the vocabulary of another or the vocabulary and syntax of one with the intonation pattern of another.

While the mixing itself does not necessarily yield incoherent language (see Case 4 and Perecman (1984) for fuller discussion of this case) it does indeed give rise to a bizarre linguistic product. In the case below, language mixing occurs in the context of semantic jargon, and manifests itself predominantly in a tendency to shift randomly from one language to another and to spontaneously translate portions of utterances into another language.

Case 4. HB, an 80 year old male, was born in Cameroon, West Africa of German parents. He learned German as a native language, French as a second language, and then learned English when he settled in the United States at the age of 18. From that time onward, he spoke primarily English. At the age of 75, HB suffered a bilateral subdural hematoma resulting from a car accident. The patient did not undergo surgery. Several weeks following the accident, his brain scan was normal, his EEG showed abnormal bifrontal diffuse waves, and there was slight spasticity.

The most striking properties of HB's language disturbance were spontaneous translation and failure to maintain a language set, i.e., shifting from one language to another, sometimes within the same utterance. The unsolicited spontaneous translation is of particular interest in view of the fact that HB could not translate upon request (e.g., *the wall* "la [val] est langue francaise;" *seife* "Französiche Auskunft'"). Examples of spontaneous translation and language shifts are given below.

Spontaneous Translation

(1) **P:** verstehen Sie Deutsch‖ do you know German | verstehen do you understand German | verstehen Sie Deutsch | aber nur ein bischen | but only a little

(2) **P:** was sagten Sie sonst | what else did would you say otherwise

(3) **P:** was wollen Sie haben | I would say what do you wish to have | was wollen Sie haben || Ich mochte ein Buch haben || I want to have a book || uh || aber sonst nichts || but otherwise nothing

Language Shifts

(4) **E:** well what happened to the hen?

    P: die [hɛndə] die Henne ist verschwunden

(5) **E:** wie steht es jetzt | ist es . . .

    P: à la | à la | à la | I say

(6) **E:** haben Sie auf Deutsch die Bücher gelesen?

    P: yes I read I read some German books

The language shifts illustrated above appear to indicate interference among the languages in HB's repertoire, where German interferes with English much more than does French. In fact, it was quite difficult for HB to switch to French from another language and he did not maintain it for very long before switching back to one of the other languages. Interference among these languages was particularly pronounced when the examiner shifted from one language to another within the same session, or when HB switched to the French mode.

Interference occurred at the phonological and morphological levels as well as at the semantic level. When asked to translate the French expression LA VIE EST DURE into English, HB responded "[dɔr]" *door*, demonstrating phonological level interference. Another example of interference at this level is the patient's translation of the word GROOM as *der* [bʉum]. When asked to translate the English word BUTTERFLY into French, he produced *la votre fly*, which also demonstrates phonological level interference. At the morphological level, this interference is demonstrated in the production of [gəʃvɛrdəs] *Haus* in response to a request to interpret the phrase SWELLED HEAD. (See Paradis [1977] for examples of similar phenomena.)

Failure to maintain a language set was also evident in reading, where the patient was observed to interject German into English sentences and also to read English sentences entirely in German. Both syntactic and phonological level interference was observed. The phonological level interference took the form of phonological adaptation of one language to another. For example, HB read the word HEARD as *der Hund*, producing instead of the English word, as a phonetic approximation in German. This phenomenon was also observed in solicited translation (i.e., asked to translate the word WALL into German, he produced *la [val] est langue Francaise*) and in repetition (i.e., asked to repeat the Spanish COMO SE LLAMA USTED, he said *kommen sie immer hier*). In each of these cases, HB appears to be perceiving one language in terms of the phonetics of another.

Syntactic level (and arguably semantic level) adaptation is illustrated by the

reading of the sentence I GOT HOME FROM WORK as *I* [*vɪl*] *home* [*kʌmɪn*].
Here the patient has translated the English syntax of the target sentence into German
syntax, placing the main verb in clause-final position and affixing a German
infinitival inflection '-en' on the English verb COME. As another example of
syntactic adaptation or interference, note the reading of the year '1936' in the
context of an English sentence as '1963'. The reversal of the three and the six
suggests interference from German syntax, where thirty-six is literally translated
as six and thirty.

The patient seemed to be preoccupied with languages and the differences among
them. This preoccupation manifested itself in the patient's tendency to comment
on the fact that he was using one language or another. Often, he would identify
the language being addressed to him but would not be able to respond appropriately
to the question being asked in that language. For example, when asked, in German,
to subtract four from twelve, he responded *zwolf weniger weniger weniger vier . . .
ist Deutsch*. Instead of performing the requested calculation, he simply identified
the language of the question. He also appeared to be commenting on the involuntary
quality of the shifts from one language to another when he said:

> P: repeat this | at at [ato anto pri] prevu | un un retrait || I'm speaking
> it more and more in the the French into [eylɛ] into French | ein Deutsches
> Franzosich

Although this patient continued to deny his language impairment, this utterance
suggests that, in fact, he was at some level aware of his language difficulty.

Among the cases cited in the literature, only three have demonstrated spontaneous translation as seen in **Case 4** above. Veyrac (1931) described an echolalic patient
who, on two occasions automatically translated short sentences, with an obvious
lack of understanding for what she had said. Jakobson (1964) reports that after
a car accident, he was aphasic for a few hours and found himself translating each of
his utterances into four languages. Paradis, Goldblum, and Abidi (1982) describe
the recovery pattern of an aphasic whose language competence alternated from day
to day, i.e., she could speak English better on one day, French better the next.
On a day when French was her stronger language, she was asked in French to point
to objects in the room. She responded by spontaneously translating the names of
the objects into English, her weaker language on that day, although she was unable
to point to those objects.

The second striking property of the language disturbance in **Case 4**, inappropriate switching from one language to another, accompanied by an inability to
translate upon request, was also described by Goldstein (1948). The question at
issue with regard to both of these symptoms is how they might relate to the semantic
paraphasias, neologisms, and other symptoms of jargonaphasia in monolinguals.

In our view, language is a psychological event which originates in the nonlinguistic conceptual domain, the realm of ideas, and terminates with phonological encoding at the linguistic level. We would maintain that language mixing symptoms differ from symptoms of jargonaphasia in that the substitution of one language for another refers to the conceptual level, while the substitution of one linguistic unit for another from the same language is referable to the linguistic level. The implications of this interpretation are that cross-linguistic symptoms, such as spontaneous translation and random switching, point to a conceptual disorder, while language specific symptoms indicate a properly linguistic deficit (see Perecman 1984).

APHASIC MUMBLING

Mumbling occurs in aphasia, as well as in severe dementia, Parkinsonism, and other neurological disorders. But while isolated mumbled words are common in aphasia, it is quite unusual to find patients with focal brain damage producing untranscribable mumbling with infrequent, if any, audible words or discrete speech sounds. Although such a disorder is not considered rare among aphasiologists, to our knowledge, the only case report in the literature is that of Kahler and Pick (1879) describing a 42-year-old woman who mumbled constantly. The only utterances articulated sufficiently clearly to be identified were "tschen" and "tscho." There was no evidence of comprehension and no paralysis. The autopsy showed bilateral superior temporal lobe softening.

Lecours (1978) indicates that, though distinct, mumbling is often grouped with the glossolalias. In view of the scarcity of case material, one can only speculate on the pathology. In **Case 5** presented below, a left temporal lesion was demonstrated. However, the severity of the comprehension impairment suggests the possibility of a right temporal lesion as well. We have also seen another case in which a bitemporal lesion was suspected. However, the disorder can probably result from a large left central or posterior lesion in which the mumbling is a kind of vestige of fluency in the context of a global aphasia. It may be that in younger patients (e.g., the case of Kahler and Pick 1879) bilateral temporal lesions are necessary, whereas in older patients (e.g., the present case) a large unilateral (temporal?) lesion will suffice. The following case is an example of this disorder.

Case 5. A 69-year-old French-English bilingual man had right-sided weakness and aphasia for five months following a stroke. Thereafter, spontaneous speech consisted of a continuous stream of quite unintelligible mumbling, with no evidence of neologisms or paraphasias. The patient was right-handed with no family history of left-handedness. During the first six years of his life, he spoke only French. At the time of the stroke, he was said to be equally proficient in French and English.

An EEG revealed left posterior temporal slowing, and a brain scan showed a large area of uptake in the left temporoparietal region. There was gradual recovery of function on his right side but speech remained unchanged over a year of observation. There was no motor or sensory deficit and the patient did not demonstrate dysarthria.

Streams of mumbling were introduced by a consonant, occasionally the first syllable of a word spoken to him, and were characterized by prolonged vowel sounds. There was little or no variation in intonation. However, the amplitude of the mumbling would decrease and trail off, creating a decrescendo pattern, at which time a new burst of mumbling would initiate another decrescendo. A marked speech pressure made it difficult to interrupt the patient's speech flow and the patient did not appear to be aware that his speech was incoherent. Reading aloud was identical to spontaneous speech. Motor series were impossible. When the patient attempted to sing with assistance, the melody was vaguely approximated, but the lyrics were produced no better than in spontaneous speech. On repetition and naming, the first sound of the target word was occasionally produced as the initial sound of the response. Otherwise, there were no correct repetitions or namings.

Comprehension was markedly impaired. However, during moments of spontaneous silence one could occasionally elicit a correct pointing response to a single object. The patient was able to carry out commands such as "lift your arm" and "point to the table," given in French or English, during moments of spontaneous – but not forced – silence. When addressed in French, a definite French accent and an occasional French word were noted. For example, when he was told, *Fermez les yeux*, the word *yeux* was distinctly heard in the mumbled response. There was no echolalia. The patient could not follow simple written commands.

Initially, he was said to be able to write only the letters AUDD and he could not copy these or other letters or shapes. Subsequently, there was some ability to copy and transliterate simple words. Writing to dictation was impossible, but, when given a sentence in French or English, he did attempt to write in the appropriate language. The patient could copy a simple square but had difficulty with three-dimensional figures. Simple calculations were usually impossible; he once summed 12 and 29 correctly, but usually could not add single digits. Praxis could not be evaluated.

There are several aspects of this case that deserve emphasis. The patient was found to assimilate into the mumbling, speech sounds from words which were addressed to him, as well as suprasegmental properties of speech addressed to him. On naming tests, the initial syllable of target nouns was discernible. This behavior was also noted on occasion in the case of phonemic jargon. In our experience, this also occurs in neologistic jargon. The pressured, logorrheic quality of the mumbling as well as the progressive amplitude reduction within an utterance was also observed in the case of phonemic jargon (**Case 3**). The loss of speaker-listener constraints resembles more closely the situation in neologistic jargon. While aphasic mumbling appears to be related to a form of posterior aphasia, the precise nature of the disorder remains to be defined.

ANATOMICAL CORRELATES OF JARGON

The classical anatomical correlation of Wernicke's aphasia is with the posterior superior temporal gyrus (T1) of the dominant hemisphere. Although cases of jargon were documented before Wernicke first described sensory aphasia, the early literature does not isolate jargonaphasia as a phenomenon distinct from sensory aphasia. Starr (1889) reviewed 50 cases of sensory aphasia with and without paraphasic phenomena and found no constant anatomical differences between these clinical forms.

The anatomical lesion of jargonaphasia was discussed by Henschen (1922). He found that a focal lesion of left T1, regardless of whether it involved a more anterior or posterior section, might cause word deafness in the presence of normal speech. This was also true for combined lesions of T1 and T2, even if subcortex was involved. However, diffuse softening of left T1 and T2 was invariably associated with jargonaphasia.

Head (1926) attributed a case with jargon to the posterior region of the Sylvian fissure. Cohn and Neumann (1958) reported bilateral damage in a case in which speech is described as consisting of "little proper syllable or word formation," alternating with correct and appropriate expression. Lesions were found in the posterior superior temporal lobe, supramarginal gyrus and underlying subcortical white matter including the arcuate fasciculus. In addition, there was less extensive subcortical damage in the right posterior frontal region.

Neologistic jargon was specified in two cases reported by Kleist (1962) and attributed to lesions affecting Heschl's gyrus and the neighboring cortex of T1. Kertesz and Benson (1970) reported 10 cases with neologistic jargon and concluded that neologistic jargon appears with lesions of both posterior T1 and arcuate fasciculus. Buckingham and Kertesz (1976) described a case of neologistic jargon associated with an infarction of the left posterior Sylvian region and involvement of T1, supramarginal gyrus and the left parietal lobule. Based on localizations in 10 cases of neologistic jargon, Kertesz (1981) concluded that the most consistently affected regions are the left posterior superior temporoparietal area, the supramarginal gyrus, the posterior parietal operculum, the inferior parietal lobule, the posterior portion of the first temporal gyrus, the posterior temporal operculum and the angular gyrus. Kertesz considered the more peripheral regions of the occipital, temporal and parietal lobes to be optional. Moreover, he regarded the severity of the jargon to be a function of the size and extent of lesion (see Naesser and Hayward 1978).

Whereas there is good evidence that neologistic jargon involves posterior T1 and T2, the anatomical correlation of semantic jargon is less certain. Weinstein, Lyerly, Cole, and Ozer (1966) described 18 cases of jargonaphasia, primarily semantic in quality, with relatively good comprehension. All cases involved bilateral damage. Brown (1972) reported a case with bilateral temporal subdurals and argued that bilateral damage was common in cases of semantic jargon. Mild forms of semantic jargon occur with unilateral lesions, but bilateral lesions are present in younger patients and in those with marked semantic anomaly in speech. The occurrence of an additional right-sided lesion has not been given sufficient attention. For example, one of the best anatomical cases of semantic jargon, that of Kleist (1962), was attributed to left temporal damage even though right temporal lesions were also present. The case of semantic jargon described in this paper also had bilateral temporal lesions.

With regard to phonemic jargon, the bilateral temporoparietal lesions observed in our case (KS), and the large central lesion in Peuser and Temp's (1981) case, constitute the only evidence to date on lesion location in this form of jargonaphasia. Whether or not bilateral damage is necessary to produce the complex jargon found in KS will depend upon anatomical evidence from further case studies.

Kertesz (1981) points out that the lesion associated with neologistic jargon is also associated with conduction aphasia, a disorder characterized by phonemic errors which may, at times, resemble neologistic jargon. Indeed, neologistic jargon may recover to conduction aphasia. The lesions in conduction aphasia are usually smaller and more anteriorly placed. Kertesz suggests a continuum between Wernicke's aphasia with neologistic jargon and conduction aphasia with severe phonemic paraphasia. The good comprehension and less jargon is a result of greater involvement of the inferior-parietal region and supramarginal gyrus and less involvement of the temporal lobe.

Elsewhere (Brown 1979a; Brown and Perecman 1985) we have proposed an anatomical model of the posterior aphasias, including jargon. According to the model, semantic processing is bilaterally mediated through inferolateral temporal neocortex, especially T2 and its usual parietal continuation into angular gyrus, in association with limbic structures. The continuum between confabulation in Korsakoff cases and semantic jargon, and their anatomical correlations, support this localization. In addition, evidence for reasonably good lexical-semantic processing in right hemisphere, together with semantic deficits in many right-damaged patients, suggests that an additional right hemisphere lesion is often necessary for semantically deviant jargon. In contrast, phonological processing is more left lateralized and more focally represented in the Broca (phonetic) and

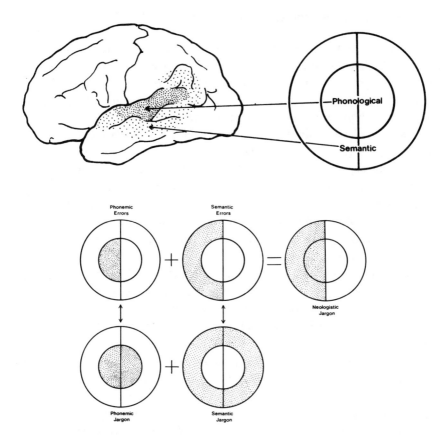

FIGURE 2-1. Schema of the probable lesion site in unilateral and bilateral phonemic and semantic disorders.

Wernicke (phonemic) zones. Lesions of the right hemisphere do not ordinarily produce phonological deficits, though there may be limited phonological processing in the isolated right hemisphere of split-brain cases (see Perecman 1983).

Accordingly, bilateral lesions of temporal lobe (posterior T2, T3) give rise to semantic jargon, though in late life and in mild cases a unilateral left-sided lesion is sufficient (see Figure 2-1). A lesion of left T1 results in fluent phonological errors ("conduction" aphasia), while a lesion of left T1 and T2 results in phonological plus semantic errors (neologistic jargon). Bilateral T1 lesions may be required for a dense 'conduction' aphasia, i.e., the marked phonological errors of phonemic jargon, as in KS, **Case 3**.

LEVELS OF PHONOLOGICAL PROCESSING

The anatomical relation between phonemic (conduction) aphasia and phonemic jargon is also linguistically motivated. Recall that phonemic jargon has no identifiable lexical content. Let us consider this a failure of semantic content to achieve its terminal phonological realization in a sequence of appropriate segments, and assume that phonological processing in phonemic jargon is confined to an early stage, where isolated phonemic segments do not exist and language is encoded in terms of supra-segmental **phonological gestalts**. Semantic information is not encoded into a segmental phonological structure because, given that **both** hemispheres contribute to semantic processing, the bilateral lesion prevents the requisite semantic specification (see Brown and Perecman 1985 for elaboration of the notion of semantic specification) for the emergence (encoding) of segmental structure.

In phonemic (conduction) aphasia associated with unilateral lesions, on the other hand, semantic content is sufficiently specified to facilitate the emergence of a segmental representation and these segmental representations are more likely to be roughly appropriate. Phonemic paraphasias, however, will occur because the left T1 lesion affects the efficiency of the segmental encoding itself. The difference between unilateral and bilateral disruption at the phonological level is a difference between problems in phonological processing of highly specified lexical representations and problems in the phonological processing of poorly specified lexical representations. This hypothesis predicts recovery of phonemic jargon to phonemic (conduction) aphasia.

It is necessary to assume the existence of two distinct stages of phonological processing i.e., level of phonological gestalts, and level of segmental structure, in order to account for why content words and function words are affected differently in neologistic jargon versus phonemic jargon. On the assumption that a neologism results at least in part from incorrect phoneme selection at the segmental level of processing, it is argued that since items subject to neology, namely, content words, are also disrupted in phonemic jargon, they must presumably be processed both at the stage of phonological gestalts *and* at the stage of segmental structuring. Function words, in contrast, which are not neologized but *are* affected by phonemic jargon, are processed only as phonological gestalts.

THE MECHANISM OF JARGON PRODUCTION

Wernicke (1874) offered the first theory of jargon production when he argued that a left temporal lesion could de-afferent Broca's area, thereby allowing it to "run on" uninhibitedly. This view of jargon as the result of an interruption of the feedback control system which normally modulates Broca's area is found also in the works of Alajouanine *et al.* (1964). These authors take the classical position that auditory images are necessary to the normal production of language, and argue that jargonaphasia results from the disturbance of two elementary and distinct mechanisms corresponding to levels in the elaboration of an utterance.

According to Alajouanine *et al.*, jargonaphasia manifests a disruption of the auditory images since speech production depends on the perception of sounds produced. Phonemic paraphasias represent a disinhibition of verbal expression which is normally constrained by these auditory images. Semantic paraphasias represent a disturbance of the process that unites thought and language.

Buckingham and Kertesz (1976) suggest that instances of phonemic jargon in which a target cannot be identified are attributable to (1) failure of lexical selection and consequent disinhibition of a phoneme transformation component; (2) a phonological transformation of an incorrectly selected lexical item (see Brown 1972); or (3) perseveration or postactivation of earlier produced items which "fill in the temporal gaps where actual words are missing" (Buckingham and Kertez 1976, p. 55).

Lecours and Lhermitte (1972) propose that these errors are determined by the phonological context in which they appear, on the basis of an argument that these errors are related to the target either paradigmatically or syntagmatically. But this account explains neither phonologically unrelated errors nor utterances in which a target cannot be identified. Similarly, Buckingham and Kertesz (1976) account for structural relationships between items in the utterance in terms of perseveration but do not attempt to explain why the failure of the phoneme transformation component yields the particular sequence it does.

Others have suggested alternative explanations. Kussmaul (1877) attributed jargon to diminished attention while Pick (1931) believed it resulted from a redistribution of attention over the levels of linguistic representation. Niessl von Mayendorff (1911) proposed that paraphasia and jargon reflected the inferior language ability of the right hemisphere after lesion of the left temporal lobe, a view that predicted an abolition of pre-existing paraphasia by a second lesion in the right Wernicke area. Henschen (1920) gave a critical discussion of this theory. He reported a case with bilateral lesion of T1 but no paraphasia and suggested that, if the right hemisphere did have a role in the residual jargon and paraphasic speech of an aphasic, this was not necessarily through the mediation of the right temporal lobe. Brain (1961) considered jargon the product of a thought disorder and Goldstein (1948) wrote that paraphasia was due to impaired inner speech. Weinstein, Lyerly, Cole, and Ozer (1966) and Kinsbourne and Warrington (1963a) take a psychoanalytic approach, conceiving of jargon as an attempt to mask an uncertainty in the use of language.

In contrast to these explanations of jargon as manifestation of a reorganization of the language processing system is the view expounded here that aphasic jargon (and indeed all aphasic symptoms) reflect the organization of language processing in the normal speaker. Butterworth (1984) argues in favor of such an approach to jargon and paraphasia. He entertains the position taken by Freud (1891) that jargon may reflect "a transient regulatory malfunction" in an intact linguistic system, and interprets aphasic jargon as a blend of alternative well-formed structures generated either simultaneously or in succession by the intact system. For example, he proposes that the paraphasic error in

its *spent* me a year

reflects a blend of two alternative utterance choices

(1) it's taken me a year, and
(2) I spent a year.

Luria (1966) offered a related hypothesis to the effect that paraphasia is caused by an "equalization of associative strengths" among phonemic and semantic alternatives.

FINAL REMARKS

The varieties of jargon discussed above are symptoms of a language disturbance characterized by a breakdown in the emergent process of language. In jargonaphasia, meaning is obscured both in expression and in comprehension, because concepts are no longer represented by sequences of sounds normally used to express their meanings. Thus, a patient may refer to a "thumb" as an "envelope," where the target is replaced by another actual word but where that word has no relation to the target in either sound or meaning. In the case of a patient who refers to a "thumb" as a "[froziz]," not only is there no phonetic relation between the target and the erroneously produced word, but there can be no relation in meaning because the sound sequence uttered has no meaning.

Symptoms of jargonaphasia may provide insight into the relations among levels of representation of linguistic knowledge and particularly into the nature of the emergence, in perception and production, of semantic and phonemic representations. Each of the forms of jargonaphasia is distinct with regard to the locus of the disruption in the system through which those sound and meaning representations develop. In other words, each form of jargonaphasia identifies a level of linguistic representation, and the stage to which it corresponds in the psychological unfolding of a linguistic act.

In semantic jargon, cognitive differentiation of the semantic level of language is disturbed such that the incorrect meaning representation becomes converted into sound. In neologistic jargon, cognitive differentiation at both the semantic and phonemic levels is disturbed. The result is that incorrect meaning representations are converted into incorrect representations of segmental sound structure. In phonemic jargon, where none of the sound sequences transmit linguistic meaning, the cognitive differentiation of a representation of meaning is incomplete and as a result, this representation cannot be translated into an appropriate sound representation.

This model of jargon provides the theoretical framework for a program of research whose goal is three-fold:

(1) to identify the fundamental properties of semantic and phonological processes, as well as their relation to syntactic processes, by reconstructing the normal course of a language act from jargon symptomology; and

(2) to carefully define, both neuropsychologically and linguistically, patterns of recovery or improvement from jargonaphasia, in order to

(3) design a program of language facilitation which is motivated by, and takes full advantage of, the potential offered by those natural lines of recovery.

The achievement of these goals promises an exciting challenge.

NOTES

1. More recently, the term glossolalia has been revived by Lecours and colleagues to refer to forms of phonemically deviant language, including aphasic jargon, schizophrenic speech and tongues spoken by persons said to be in charismatic states. The use of a single term to refer to phenomena of such diverse origins is presumbly intended to capture a structural similarity among them.

2. Certain French authors refer to the phonemic paraphasias of conduction aphasics as phonemic jargon.

3. Note metathesis of final /s/ from *nothing is* (= nothing's) to *happening*.

4. The majority of speech errors in normals occur on nouns (Browman 1978).

5. It is of interest that semantic jargon as well is characterized by rhyming and other phonological relationships among verbal paraphasis. Kreindler, Calavrezo, and Mihailescu (1971) describe a semantic jargonaphasic in whom "the criterion for selection of [verbal paraphasias and neologisms] was not the semantic one but exclusively the criterion of auditory similarity determined by the rhyme (1971: 221)."

3
Thalamic Mechanisms in Language*

Introduction

Although there are reports in the early literature of lesions of the thalamus in association with disorders of perception, for example, Morsier's (1938) case of pulvinar lesion with "peduncular hallucinosis," as well as with disorders of cognition, such as Grunthal's (1942) case of "thalamic dementia," it was not until the monograph by Penfield and Roberts (1959) that attention was focused on the thalamus in relation to language organization. In this monograph, it was proposed that the thalamus, specifically the nucleus pulvinaris, was a way station in language processing between the anterior and posterior speech zones. While no persuasive evidence was presented in support of this hypothesis, it was at least consistent with the enormous expansion of pulvinar over the mammalian series leading to man, as well as with the presence of major fiber pathways between pulvinar and the posterior temporoparietal cortex.

Subsequently, the development of stereotactic surgery for the treatment of movement disorders, particularly for Parkinson's disease and dystonia, led to the investigation of psychological function following surgical lesion in various thalamic sites. In spite of the obvious importance of and interest in this region, it is striking how little we still know of the behavioral consequences of thalamic lesions in man. Unlike other areas, the thalamus is not often preferentially involved in neurological disease, nor is it commonly the site of localized vascular lesion. Surgical ablation has been carried out only in a few nuclear groups and only in subjects with preexisting neurological disorders, so that even there we see the effects on an ongoing pathological state rather than in a normal brain.

Nonetheless, over the last 20 years renewed interest in the role of the thalamus in language and cognition has given rise to new observations and experimental studies. It is the purpose of this chapter to review some of this material in relation to present concepts of language-brain relationships.

---

*From "Thalamic Mechanisms in Language" by J. W. Brown, 1979. In M. Gazzaniga (Ed.), *Handbook of Neuropsychology*. New York: Plenum Press. Adapted by permission.

In man, the pertinent observations can be grouped into the following categories: lesions which result from (1) degenerative, (2) vascular, or (3) neoplastic involvement of the thalamus, or (4) surgical thalamotomy.

Degenerative Lesions

Several patients have been described with progressive symmetrical bilateral degeneration of the thalamus. The first case was reported by Stern (1939) in a 41-year-old man with a dementia progressing rapidly over a 1-year period. The principal features were severe impairment of memory, orientation, and attention, with perseveration, confabulation, drowsiness, inertia, and lack of initiative; peculiar mannerisms, sucking of the lips, and extreme restlessness were also described. The patient was uncommunicative and showed little attention to questions or commands, but did not use wrong words. There was no difficulty in expression; the patient simply spoke less and less. Understanding became impaired and he was eventually unable to read or write. There was also a tendency to repeat actions and words (echopraxia, echolalia), and "the whole mental atmosphere was weird, uncanny and crafty." Aphasia, apraxia, and agnosia were said to be absent. Neurological findings were limited to mild left lower facial weakness, loss of the pupillary and convergence reflex, and bilateral grasping and sucking reflexes. The autopsy revealed no evidence of gross cortical atrophy, but on microscopic examination there was severe bilateral symmetrical degeneration of the thalamus, primarily involving the anterior, medial, and lateral nuclei and centromedian. Posterior ventral, reticular, and midline nuclei and geniculate bodies were spared. The cerebral cortex showed some lipoid neuronal atrophy and recent gliosis, with dense subcortical gliosis considered to be senile changes. There was some bilateral atrophy of the medial sector of dorsal and ventral inferior olivary laminae and gliosis of the superior colliculi. Stern (1939) commented that this was a system degeneration in the thalamus, sparing the phylogenetically older nuclear groups (e.g., midline nuclei, ventral nucleus, and geniculate bodies), possibly an atypical form of Creutzfeldt-Jakob disease.

A few years later, Grunthal (1942) reported another case, unsatisfactory for the reason of mental deficiency prior to the development of dementia and a course of 26 years. Grunthal considered a vascular pathology in the thalamus, but subsequent authors have argued that atrophic dementia was present. These cases are both discussed in a paper by Schulman (1957) in which a further case is described, a 50-year-old man with a rapidly progressive dementia leading to death in 7 months. The picture was characterized by recent memory impairment, reduced digit span, difficulty with simple arithmetic, and hesitancy or blocking in speech, although neither dysarthria nor aphasia was present. The patient showed no concern about his illness, and was facetious, with frequent smiling and laughing. Moderate ataxia was present in all limbs, with choreoathetosis and increased deep reflexes on the right side. The patient's behavior gradually became more bizzare, with episodes fluctuating between quiet stupor and sudden crying, shouting, and violent laughter. Speech was ultimately reduced to a state of virtual muteness. On postmortem study, serial sections of the thalamus demonstrated severe degeneration in n. dorsomedialis, n. ventralis, posterolateralis, dorsolateralis, reticularis, and anterior pulvinar. Moderate degeneration was found in n. anterodorsalis and ventralis anterior, and mild changes were found in the centromedian. No changes were noted in intralaminar and midline nuclei, geniculate bodies, or posterior pulvinar, and the remainder of the brain was essentially normal except for mild gliosis in the rostrodorsal periphery of the red nucleus and in the bilateral rubrothalamic radiations. Following Stern, Schulman noted the preferential involvement of the neothalamus, but he also mentioned certain inconsistencies such as the severe involvement of the reticular nucleus and the sparing of the posterior pulvinar. He did not emphasize a relation to Creutzfeldt-Jakob disease, although, according to Garcin, Brion, and Khochneviss (1963), when this case was presented to the American Association of Neuropathology in December 1955, this possibility was specifically mentioned by Adams in the ensuing discussion.

Garcin et al. (1963) subsequently reported a further case and concluded that the disorder was a localized form of Creutzfeldt-Jakob disease. Their patient, a 56-year-old man, developed apathy, memory difficulty, dysarthria, and choreoathetosis leading to coma and death in 9 months. Pathological findings were mainly in the thalamus, with bilateral symmetrical neuronal loss and gliosis especially affecting n. dorsomedialis, ventralis lateralis, and pulvinar. Minor lesions in F_3, insula, and inferior olives were present. The striatum was normal, with no senile or inflammatory changes.

Subsequent papers dealing with this subject include those of Nayrac, Arnott, and Warot (1965), Castaigne et al. (1966), and Martin (1966). A report by Daniels (1969) described a 55-year-old man with personality change, irritability, and impairment of recent memory which rapidly progressed to confusion, global dementia, and death over a 5-month period. This patient also had a syndrome of inappropriate antidiuretic hormone secretion in association with bronchogenic carcinoma. Pathological examination disclosed symmetrical bilateral degeneration of the thalamus, with neuronal loss and gliosis most severely affecting n. dorsomedialis. Moderate involvement of the anterior group, centromedian, n. ventralis lateralis, posteromedialis, and pulvinar was present. The disorder was considered a remote effect of the carcinoma.

Reyes, Chokroverty, and Masdeu (1976) reported a 38-year-old woman with Hodgkin's disease who developed an impairment in recent and remote memory and diminished attention span. The patient showed "withdrawn behavior," continued to deteriorate, and died several weeks later. Postmortem examination disclosed a neuroaxonal dystrophy involving primarily the thalamus symmetrically, and presumed to be a secondary effect of the Hodgkin's disease.

In sum, although there are few reported instances of degenerative change limited to the thalamus, it is nevertheless possible to delineate some general features of the resultant dementia. The onset is characterized by apathy and indifference, with gradual uninterest and slowing of activity. Speech also becomes slowed, although dysarthria is not apparently a prominent feature. There is loss of recent memory, and the patient does not have full insight into the nature of his condition. Although the mental state is characterized by a progressive retardation of all functions, restlessness, bizarre behavior, inappropriate laughing, and echo reactions may also occur. It is evident that while the tendency toward a catatonic state may be punctuated by psychotic episodes the overall course is rapid and generally leads to coma and death within a year. Pathological changes tend to be limited to the thalamus, with symmetrical bilateral degeneration affecting principally, although not exclusively, the neothalamic groups, n. dorsomedialis, anterior nucleus, centromedian, and pulvinar. A relation to Creutzfeldt-Jakob disease has been stressed in a few reports, and in two cases the syndrome has been considered a remote effect of cancer. It appears likely that the principal nuclei involved in the dementia of thalamic degeneration are n. dorsomedialis, pulvinar, and/or anterior nucleus. The recent correlation by Victor, Adams, and Collins (1971) of Korsakoff amnesia with lesions in n. dorsomedialis and perhaps pulvinar is consistent with this conclusion. There are also important negative cases, such as the patient of Adams and Malamud (1971) with bilateral symmetrical degeneration of centrum medianum without language disorder or dementia.

Vascular Lesions

Another line of evidence pointing to the possible role of the thalamus in cognition and language function concerns those patients with documented unilateral and/or bilateral thalamic vascular lesions. This material can be discussed under two major categories, patients with bilateral thalamic encephalomalacia and patients with unilateral hemorrhagic or ischemic damage to the thalamus.

Unilateral Cases It is generally considered that thalamic infarction may be accompanied by some language disturbance, although few pertinent cases are available. Most of the early work developed out of the description by Dejerine and Roussy (1906) of a thalamic syndrome, and the occurrence in some cases of defects in speech. Perhaps the first case to be studied from this point of view was the report by Walther (1945) of a 54-year-old right-handed man with two apoplectic attacks leading ultimately to a syndrome characterized by dullness, apathy, confusion, and difficulty in formulating thought and finding words.

Certainly, the most publicized case of unilateral thalamic lesion is that of Penfield and Roberts (1959). Their patient, said to be aphasic, was diagnosed as having a small hemorrhage in the pulvinar on the basis of clinical studies.

However, the brevity of the clinical description and the lack of postmortem verification leave both the diagnosis and localization in some doubt. About the same time, Fisher (1959) noted the occurrence of dysphasia as a cardinal feature of thalamic hemorrhage.

Two cases of unilateral thalamic lesion were described by Sager, Mares, and Nestianu (1965, in Botez & Barbeau, 1971). Both patients were said to show "receptive dysphasia" following cerebrovascular accidents of 7 and 14 days' duration. Postmortem examination disclosed hemorrhagic softening in the left posterior thalamus without cortical involvement.

Subsequently, Ciemins (1970) described two patients with aphasia and left thalamic hemorrhage. The first case was of a 53-year-old man with incomplete and fragmentary sentences. There was little spontaneous speech and the patient responded only to questions. Repetition was normal, simple objects could be named, and simple commands could be carried out. A large hemorrhagic lesion was found in the left thalamus. In this case, the description suggests as much an aspontaneity of speech as a true aphasia. Moreover, the course was rapid, only 22 days, and the patient was somnolent, with bilateral Babinski responses suggesting bilateral involvement. The second case was of a 61-year-old woman with some speech disturbance, e.g., speech was "feeble" for several years prior to death; a thalamic infarct was found at necropsy.

Mohr, Watters, and Duncan (1975) reported two cases of hemorrhage involving, but not confined to, the left thalamus (localization by CT scan). Both patients showed paraphasic speech and good (echolalic) repetition, but in the context of obvious somnolence or disorientation. While the authors make a claim for a specific language disorder associated with a left thalamic lesion, it is not unlikely that the language disorder was part of a general confusional state related to the acute mass lesion rather than to a lesion specifically in the thalamus. Certainly, the intermittent nature of the language disorder seems to argue against an effect of a fixed lesion.

Luria (1977) has observed two cases in which a left thalamic lesion was inferred from the clinical picture, with paraphasic impairments in speech and repetition. These "quasiaphasic" symptoms are presumed secondary to a defect in stimulus filtration rather than to a primary disruption of language.

Recently, Rubens and Johnson (1976) have described another case, with CT scan demonstration of a left thalamic hemorrhage. This patient had "bursts of almost entirely unintelligible logorrheic speech with frequent phonemic paraphasia often resulting in neologisms." In contrast to Luria's case, but similar to those of Mohr, repetition was correct but echolalic. Also, as with Mohr's cases, the intermittent nature of the symptoms could reflect pressure or other effects from an acute mass lesion, i.e., acute confusion, rather than an aphasia of thalamic origin. This is further suggested by the fact that the patient improved into a more typical confusional state.

It would appear that at least two different "syndromes" can occur with an acute left vascular lesion of the thalamus, either a state of mutism, which may or may not be aphasic in nature, or a picture of intermittent logorrheic jargon with or without echolalia, which may or may not be a confusional state. The following personal cases are examples of each of these types.

CASE REPORT. A 68-year-old hypertensive right-handed woman had a sudden collapse in December 1970, with flaccid right hemiparesis, right visual field defect, and diminished sensation on the right side. Initially, she was mute and unable to follow commands. Repeated lumbar punctures revealed elevated opening pressure and bloody fluid; EEG showed left hemispheric slowing. Over the subsequent weeks, there was no change in her status. On repeat examination 8 weeks later, she was alert but inattentive to the right side. There was still a flaccid right hemiplegia, absent response to pain on the right side, and loss of response to visual threat in the right visual field. Deep reflexes were brisk on the right, with bilateral Babinski responses.

The patient was aphonic, with no attempt at vocalization. There was no response to repetition, naming, or verbal or written commands. She was unable to write or draw, and made no response to whole-body commands or tests utilizing imitation. The family was questioned and confirmed the total lack of speech and speech comprehension. There was no change in her condition until death 2 months after admission.

Pathological examination revealed a brain weight of 1300 g; macroscopic sections showed possible slight thinning of the cortical mantle. There was a hemorrhagic lesion restricted largely to the region of the left thalamus. The lesion extended posteriorly to a thin ribbon involving the tapetum and optic radiations, and anteriorly up to, although sparing, the anterior nucleus of the thalamus. Major thalamic groups involved were pulvinar, ventralis posterior, and lateralis, and the posterolateral portion of n. dorsalis medialis and centrum medianum. The posterior limb of the internal capsule and part of the putamen and left hippocampal commissure were involved. A small area (4 mm) of cystic encephalomalacia was present in the right internal capsule. The midbrain, pons, and medulla were normal except for a slight decrease in size of the left corticospinal tract. The cerebellum was normal. Microscopic examination of the left temporoparietal cortex was negative. Basal ganglia and the thalamus showed accumulation of gitter cells, with fragmentation of myelin and areas of necrosis. There were large amounts of hemosiderin deposit present at the periphery of the infarct and left lateral ventricle. Some vacuolation and decrease of myelin were noted in the left corticospinal tract.

CASE REPORT. A 76-year-old man developed an acute intracerebral hemorrhage, with mild right hemiparesis, no sensory impairment, and difficulty with speech. The patient was not personally examined, but was described as "speaking in an unknown language or in gibberish." It was said that he "made no sense in

English." Some observers thought he may have been trying to speak in German, but there is no indication of prior facility with this language. Repetition was not described, but he was reported to have followed verbal commands well. A CT scan showed a left thalamic hemorrhage. Over the next few days, the aphasia resolved to a state of confusion and disorientation. Six days later, he developed a recurrent left thalamic hemorrhage, again confirmed by CT scan. At this time, he was said to have an "expressive aphasia." One day later, he was noted to be dysarthric and "not clear mentally." Another observer stated that he was able to speak and complained of weakness in his limbs. The following day he was "talking more clearly," and the next was "conversing in English," although it would seem that complete recovery from the aphasia had not yet occurred. Shortly after, the patient went into coma and expired.

On postmortem examination (Dr. G. Budzilovich), the brain weight was 1300 g, and the external appearance was unremarkable. Coronal sections confirmed the presence of a hemorrhage in the left thalamus extending into the left lateral ventricle. Moderate generalized ventricular dilatation was noted. The overlying cortex was grossly normal, although full histological study was not carried out.

DISCUSSION. Of these two cases, the first is more characteristic of unilateral thalamic vascular lesion, with a picture of mutism and failure to respond to comprehension testing. In this respect, such cases are comparable to those of thalamic degeneration or tumor (see below), where apathy, disorientation and confusion, word-finding difficulty, and aspontaneity of speech lead to an end state of (akinetic) mutism. The picture may be difficult, if not impossible, to distinguish from a global aphasia, especially in view of the apparent relationship to left-sided vascular lesions. It would be important to study recovery in patients of this type, to determine if the evolution is through an aphasic stage. If it should prove that such patients are truly mute rather than aphasic, the predilection for left thalamic lesions could be explained through the tendency for acute involvements of the dominant hemisphere to produce bilateral manifestations, while the effects of acute right hemispheric pathology tend to be limited to that hemisphere.

In the second case, the description of "gibberish" speech suggests a possible correspondence to cases with logorrheic jargon. In this case, as in the others described, the thalamic lesion has generally been hemorrhagic in nature. In such cases, symptoms fluctuate due to pressure shifts. Logorrheic jargon is well known in patients with marked confusion; neologisms and paraphasias may also occur. In the second patient, the aphasia resolved into a confusional state after several days, suggesting that the initial language disorder was a manifestation of the more profound degree of confusion.

Bilateral Cases Bilateral cases are among the earliest reports of vascular involvement of the thalamus giving rise to language disorder and are generally included as instances of the so-called arteriopathic thalamic dementia, with descriptions of thalamic degeneration. Even the original case of Grunthal (1942) has been classified with both the vascular and the atrophic dementias. The initial description was Schuster's (1936, 1937) case (No. 11) of a 49-year-old woman with a sudden onset of coma resolving into a state of aspontaneity, apathy, indifference, and memory disorder. There was no evidence of aphasia, but speech was described as atonal, poorly articulated, and similar to parkinsonian speech. The author suggested a comparison with akinetic mutism. Postmortem findings were of bilateral necrosis involving the paraventricular region, the internal nuclei, the medial portion of the lateral nucleus, and the centrum medianum.

According to Botez and Barbeau (1971), the only two cases on record of bilateral thalamic softening with impaired speech fluency are those of Marinesco, Nicolesco, and Nicolesco (1935) and Kreindler, Neriantiu, and Botez (1962). The patients in these studies were not thought to represent instances of pure aphasia but rather of speech aspontaneity and/or mutism.

In an excellent review, Castaigne et al. (1966) described two patients, the first a 76-year-old woman with left hemiparesis, inattention, and a dementia characterized by aspontaneity of movement and speech with severe memory disturbance. Speech consisted of incessant mumbling, which was stereotyped in a weak voice without intonation. Repetition of words and short phrases was possible, naming was good for objects, and there was no disturbance of comprehension at a simple level, both for written and for spoken language. It was specifically mentioned that aphasic disturbances were absent. Postmortem findings were of bilateral thalamic softening restricted to the retromammillary peduncle and intralaminar formation, affecting the left ventralis anterior and part of the dorsolateral and paracentral nuclei. Their second case was of a 67-year-old woman with the sudden onset of a vascular accident and coma which evolved into dementia persisting over 3 years until death. There was marked disturbance of attention and memory; WAIS IQ was 70; there was no evidence of aphasia. Postmortem examination showed bilateral softening in the thalamus involving on the left especially the paracentral group and the inferior part of n. dorsomedialis and ventralis anterior, and on the right n. parafascicularis and dorsomedialis.

Recently, Delay and Brion (1962) described a case of true aphasia with thalamic lesion. This 48-year-old woman had a rapid onset of delirium and depression leading to dementia with paranoia, auditory hallucinations, intellectual reduction, and impaired memory. Paramnesia was present, and there was only partial awareness of the disorder. There were no neurological signs. The authors noted that a Wernicke's aphasia was present, although details were not given. The patient showed progressive deterioration, and terminated in a state of epileptic seizures with a right hemiparesis. Postmortem findings were of diffuse arteriosclerosis, but the cortex was intact. There were a small area of old encephalomalacia in the white matter of T_4 on the left, vascular lesions in the left amygdaloid region, and lacunae in the putamen and cerebellum. The major lesions involved the thalamus in a bilateral and symmetrical fashion, with old areas of softening in the left and right n. dorsomedialis and right pulvinar and an organized thrombus in the right lateral nuclear group. In view of the finding of Wernicke's aphasia, it is regretable that the pathological picture was so diffuse.

Apart from these cases, there are only anecdotal references to thalamic dementia on an arteriopathic basis. Nielson (1946) commented on the occurrence of defects in attention with bilateral thalamic degeneration, and there are scattered cases of stupor, apathy, and/or indifference with similar pathology. In a related study, Segarra (1970) discussed akinetic mutism as a manifestation of small lesions in the midbrain and the thalamus. Particularly important are the midline nuclei, both of his cases having lesions of n. dorsomedialis and centrum medianum. This is further evidence for the essential similarity of thalamic apathy and the akinetic mute state.

Neoplastic Lesions

There are numerous cases in the literature of unilateral and bilateral thalamic neoplasms in which dementia was a prominent symptom. Smyth and Stern (1938) reported two cases of small intrinsic thalamic tumor without somnolence in which dementia was the presenting complaint. The dementia was characterized by inattention, forgetfulness, and disorientation, and the pathology concerned the medial portion of the thalamus, possibly n. dorsomedialis. Cheek and Taveras (1966) agreed with this conclusion and insisted that dementia could occur with thalamic tumor without hydrocephalus or massive white matter involvement. Delay and Brion (1962) concluded that bithalamic tumor can present with early dementia as a specific sign prior to increased intracranial pressure. Other references are Cremieux, Alliez, Toga, and Bruno (1959), Nayrac et al. (1965), and McEntee, Biber, Perl, and Benson (1976).

The picture that emerges is of a generally bilateral but occasionally unilateral thalamic glioma, usually in the region of the third ventricle, presenting with early mental change. The dementia is characterized by slowness of activity and ideation, apathy, aspontaneity, and moderate to marked impairment of memory. Catatonic or delirious episodes or even frank psychosis may occur. Attention is certainly reduced, and in many cases it is unclear whether a confusional state or a true dementia is present. In cases where the tumor originates extrinsic to the thalamus, there is gradual encroachment on the lateral nuclei. Here, dementia is apparently a part of late confusion, somnolence, or obtundation. However, with intrinsic tumor, especially if the tumor originates medially, the dementia may be the earliest sign and will be apparent well before there is demonstrable ventricular enlargement or elevated intracranial pressure.

In sum, there is little to distinguish the dementia of thalamic glioma from the vascular or degenerative states which have been discussed. Diagnosis depends on the history and on the ancillary findings of hydrocephalus and elevated intracranial pressure.

Surgical Lesions

Various thalamic nuclei have been explored surgically for the treatment of psychiatric disease, pain states, seizures, and movement disorders. Regarding lesions of n. ventralis lateralis, a large literature has accumulated (e.g., Bell, 1968; Riklan & Levita, 1969) and will not be discussed at length in this chapter. Most authors have demonstrated mild general decrement on intellectual testing following bilateral lesions, with some evidence (Ojemann & Ward, 1971; Riklan & Levita, 1969) that lesions in the speech-dominant hemisphere entail further deficit in verbal memory and in verbal IQ. In various series (e.g., Allen, Turner & Gadea-Ciria, 1966; Hermann, Turner, Gillingham, & Gaze, 1966; Waltz, Riklan, Stellar, & Cooper, 1966) aphasia has been reported as a sequel in anywhere from 2% to 10% of cases, and relates especially to procedures in the dominant hemisphere. However, careful studies of post-thalamotomy "dysphasia" have not been carried out, and it is not clear whether they simply represent speech reduction and/or dysarthria. When present, aphasia usually lasts only a week or two following surgery, rarely persisting beyond the third or fourth week. Since testing has usually been carried out several days after surgery without immediate postoperative observation, it has not been possible to eliminate general factors such as edema, subsequent hemorrhage into a lesion, and general effects of ventriculography. Moreover, most reports concern parkinsonian patients, many no doubt with preexisting mild dementia in association with diffuse brain pathology, and comparisons are lacking with thalamotomy effects in subjects without such preexisting problems.

In other studies, Spiegel, Wycis, Orchinik, and Freed (1955) have reported a variety of changes following bilateral surgical lesions of n. dorsomedialis. Disturbances of memory and orientation have been described, as well as a disorder in the "time sense," chronotaraxis. Mark, Ervin, and Yakovlev (1963) have described relief of pain without apparent change in mentation following surgical lesions in the parafascicular and intralaminar nuclei; lesions in the anterior nucleus produced euphoria with some change in affect and pain relief. Alterations in mentation were not described. Sugishita, Ishijima, Hori, Fukushima, and Iwata (1973) described a 62-year-old man who developed a "pure agraphia" which persisted for 6 weeks following left CM-thalamotomy for intractable facial pain. Mild constructional disability was present, but no disorder of language was observed. In contrast, Jurko and Andy (1973) noted few cognitive changes following surgical lesion of the centrum medianum. These authors did note varying degrees of impairment on cognitive tests with lesions in other thalamic sites. Of interest was their finding of greater impairment on the Bender-Gestalt Test after right thalamic lesion.

Pulvinectomy Surgical interest in the pulvinar developed largely out of the theory of Penfield and Roberts (1959) that the speech functions of the various cortical language areas are coordinated by way of reciprocal projections to the pulvinar. This hypothesis led to studies by Ojemann, Fedio, and Van Buren (1968), who described "dysnomia" on stimulation in three subcortical sites in right-handed (mainly parkinsonian) subjects, the left pulvinar and deep parietal white matter of both hemispheres. However, stimulation in parietal white matter produced a more densely anomic state (omissions) than stimulation in pulvinar (misnaming), and white matter stimulation also had the more severe effect on verbal memory, findings which might have suggested the dysnomia to be a cortical rather than subcortical effect. The recent demonstration by Ojemann (personal communication, 1976a) of similar effects on direct cortical stimulation is consistent with this interpretation.

There is also evidence (Ojemann, 1976b) that stimulation in the dominant thalamus enhances later retrieval of material presented during the stimulation period, an effect which has apparently not been duplicated by neocortical stimulation. Whether this also represents a distant effect—in this case on limbic structures—or is attributable to thalamic mechanisms concerned directly with memory or with attentional processes has not yet been determined.

In a more recent paper, Van Buren and Borke (1969) studied serial sections of thalamus in several patients with cerebral lesions and aphasia. Marked degeneration of the pulvinar was found in a case of global aphasia and moderate degeneration in another case. On the basis of these findings, the authors argued that the anterior superior pulvinar was important in language function. Subsequently, Ojemann and Ward (1971) concluded from stimulation studies that the anatomical substrate for speech includes the pulvinar and *en passage* fibers related to the centrum medianum and n. dorsomedialis (for comment on these studies, see Brown, 1973).

We have had the opportunity to study over 30 patients with cryogenic surgical lesion in the pulvinar (Brown, 1972, 1973). This procedure was initially carried out in the hope of benefit for severe permanent aphasia, but was extended to incapacitated dystonic patients when some favorable effect on motor tone was observed.

UNILATERAL. Most of the 30 patients in the unilateral group were right-handed. There were also several instances of structural brain damage (vascular, traumatic) and cerebral palsy. It was found that subjects with normal preoperative language and cognitive function, and without structural brain damage, showed no evidence of aphasia or dementia following cyropulvinectomy in the presumed speech-dominant hemisphere. Moreover, there was no evidence of spatioconstructional disturbance in patients undergoing surgery in the presumed nondominant hemisphere. Some patients showed immediate postoperative decrement in verbal learning on supraspan word recall and paired associates, but there was no indication that verbal material learned prior to surgery was affected by the operation. This alteration was not absolutely related to dominant-side surgery, although statistical analysis of side preference was not carried out. Mild reduction in digit span was also noted. In a few patients with preexisting structural lesion and with borderline language or cognitive function, cryopulvinectomy in the dominant hemisphere did induce further deterioration. In one such patient with head trauma and bilateral brain damage, right hemiparesis, mild dementia, and some word-finding difficulty, a marked dysonomic state at times approximating semantic jargon followed left cryopulvinectomy. There was gradual improvement over a 4- to 6-week period to the preoperative level. A second patient with long-standing hemispheric atrophy and right hemiparesis but without preoperative language defect developed dysnomia following pulvinectomy in the atrophic hemisphere. This patient also showed resolution over a period of a few weeks. A third patient with a cerebrovascular accident, right hemiparesis, and resolved anterior aphasia had transient postoperative hesitation on naming and mild vocabulary impairment, particularly noticeable on tests utilizing low-frequency words. However, in the more optimal surgical group, the dystonics, the majority of whom had normal or above-average IQ and intact preoperative language function, no deterioration in language was observed. Some degree of aspontaneity and mild inconstant mood changes were also noted.

BILATERAL. In three cases studies with extensive pre- and postoperative language testing, there was no evidence of an aphasic impairment following bilateral cryopulvinectomy. In two patients, the presence of severe limb dystonia prevented thorough evaluation of writing and spatioconstructional ability, although no postoperative change was judged to be present. This was corroborated in a third case where more extensive evaluation was possible. Moreover, there was no right-left disorientation, misidentification of fingers, alexia, or dyscalculia; visual imagery was unchanged, and there was no hallucinatory or psychotic behavior. In two patients, IQ testing showed a slight decrement. In a third case, marked decrement occurred in the period following left pulvinectomy and prior to right pulvinectomy, a time during which no surgery occurred. Subsequent repeat testing demonstrated moderate return. The principal findings, as in the unilateral cases, were of some impairment on tests of verbal learning, e.g., supraspan word recall and paired associates, and reduced digit span (see Brown, 1974).

The study of these cases has demonstrated relatively minor changes in language function following unilateral or bilateral pulvinectomy. This finding has been confirmed in a recent paper by Vilkki and Laitinen (1976). The principal postoperative changes were restricted to a slight reduction in digit span, mild aspontaneity, and some impairment on tests of verbal learning. Some patients gave the impression of mild dullness, expressed in slowness of response, hesitation, or in the general appearance and manner of the patient, but this could not be specified on psychological testing. A comparison of the subtest scores for pulvinectomy and routine thalamotomy (Riklan & Cooper, 1975) did not show an appreciable difference in the pattern of impairment. Spatioconstructional ability, imagery, praxis, and calculations were judged to be essentially unchanged. In one patient, macrographic drawing was noted after right cryopulvinectomy, and, in another patient, micrography was found following the second side of a bilateral procedure. These alterations are discussed by Mendilaharsu et al. (1968) in relation to parietal lobe involvement. Some tendency toward simplification of drawing was occasionally found in the absence of other signs of constructional disability.

Apart from the above, postoperative changes in affect were not observed. However, the procedure was carried out in only a few subjects with preexisting emotional disorder. In two patients with a left hemispheric lesion, pulvinectomy in the damaged hemisphere accentuated preexisting aggressive behavior. In two other patients with pathological lability, there was mitigation of the emotionality following right pulvinectomy. These patients all had preexisting structural brain damage.

In general, the findings in these cases, impairment of verbal memory and a suggestion of mental dulling and aspontaneity, correspond quite well with the symptoms of nonsurgical lesion in other neothalamic groups, Review of our pathological material indicates that ordinarily only about 20% of the pulvinar was involved by the cryogenic lesion. This might account for the relative lack of major deficit following surgery.

The possible importance of lesion size is illustrated by the following unique case in which pulvinectomy was done together with ablation in other thalamic sites.

Case Report

PREOPERATIVE EVALUATION (JULY 20, 1971). The patient was a 45-year-old man with longstanding dystonia; he had an eighth-grade education, could read and write, and was strongly right-handed with no family history of left-handedness. Conversational speech and comprehension were relatively normal, although the patient appeared somewhat dull. Proverbs were done concretely, there was difficulty with dates, and he could not remember the names of many previous presidents. Given three words and tested 5 min later for recall, he produced all three correctly. On a test of supraspan recall with ten items, scores were 4, 5, 6, 7, and 8 over five trials. The impression was of some memory impairment with either mental retardation or mild dementia.

OPERATION (JULY 21, 1971). The patient underwent stereotaxic surgery with the placement of extensive cryogenic lesions in the ventralis lateralis, ventralis posterolateralis, centrum medianum, and pulvinar on the left side.

POSTOPERATIVE EVALUATION (JULY 28, 1971). At this time, speech appeared greatly reduced in quantity and articulation was slightly more impaired than prior to surgery but dysarthria was not clearly present. Utterances consisted for the most part of one- or two-word phrases, generally monotonous, grammatically correct, and with perseveration. Asked how he was feeling, he replied, "Okay" or "Better"; when asked about his work, he said, "My work has got better." Asked to describe the job of a policeman, he said, "A policeman has got a better job than the average guy." Many questions were not answered at all, and all responses showed an extremely long latency. Motor series were done slowly but correctly. He followed a conversation but failed on many tests of speech comprehension. For example, asked to point to the door, he sat blankly without a response. Asked to point to each of three objects on command, he correctly pointed to only two, and could not point to objects on a functional description.

Repetition was excellent. He named about 80% of objects and showed excellent phonemic cueing to objects not named spontaneously. Occasionally, there was complete blocking without response. There did not appear to be a difference in performance on visual or tactile naming. However, there was some difficulty in object identification beyond a naming disorder. For example, he was able to correctly identify a spoon, a lock, a football, a comb, and a battery, respectively, but when shown a toothbrush he stated that he did not know what it was, could not describe it or demonstrate its use, was unable to select the correct name from a group of names offered, and, when finally given the correct name, rejected it. When he was then asked to demonstrate how a toothbrush should be used, he did so correctly, and finally agreed that the object might be a toothbrush. No paraphasias were heard, either the object being named correctly or the patient saying, "I don't know."

On tests of color naming, substitution of color names was noted. The patient could not point correctly to colors on command. Naming of body parts was similarly impaired. He was able to read simple words but could not indicate objects whose names he had just read. When shown an object and given a choice of four written names, he was unable to select the correct name. Constructional ability was extremely poor. He was unable to write his first name with his left hand (severe dystonia on the right side). Simple commands were done well, such as making a fist or saluting, but inappropriate movements were noted. Facial praxis could not be evaluated because of dystonic grimacing.

Visual fields appeared intact, but there was difficulty with voluntary gaze to the right. The patient did not attend well to objects on the right side. There was a tendency for head turning to the right but a deviation of the eyes to the left. He was able to reach out and touch objects presented in the left visual field better than objects presented on the right side. Spontaneous and following eye movements were normal. There was difficulty when asked to look to the right, the left, or up and down. Finally, there was definite blunting of affect with little insight into the disorder and extreme inattentiveness.

SECOND POSTOPERATIVE EVALUATION (AUGUST 5, 1971). Two weeks following surgery, little change was noted, the patient still showing marked lack of spontaneity in speech and behavior, prolonged latency for response, and frequently no response at all. On comprehension testing, he pointed to objects with greater success, repetition was still excellent, and naming was slightly improved, although he was still at times unable to identify common objects.

In summary, this 45-year-old man with some preoperative impairments showed considerable deterioration following an extensive surgical lesion in the left thalamus. The postoperative state was characterized by marked retardation in speech and behavior, inattentiveness, impaired object recognition and reaching in the visual field. Conversational speech consisted of one or two words or, less commonly, longer phrases, generally grammatically intact, the most striking feature being that of slowness and occasional perseveration. Repetition was excellent while comprehension was impaired. Most objects were named correctly, with failures suggesting an agnosic deficit. Substitutions were noted on color naming, but otherwise no phonemic or verbal paraphasias occurred. Responses were characterized by marked slowness, often without a response at all. There was also an impression of some memory loss and dementia.

Medial Geniculotomy This procedure was carried out in one patient with jargonaphasia in an attempt to mitigate the speech disorder. The case is described in full as a unique instance of a stereotaxic lesion in the medial geniculate body of the dominant hemisphere. The rationale for this operation has been previously discussed (Brown, 1975).

Case Report

A 64-year-old woman had a stable jargonaphasia for 18 months following a stroke. Neurological findings consisted of right hemiparesis with minimal right facial weakness, marked weakness in the right arm with flexion rigidity, and moderate weakness and rigidity of the right lower extremity. Response to pain was symmetrical. Deep reflexes were increased on the right side, Babinski reflexes were absent, and there was no visual field defect. Speech consisted of fluent, voluble neologistic jargon. There was active gesture and euphoria, with no evidence of speech awareness. Comprehension was nil, with no response to verbal commands, object pointing, yes/no questions, or whole-body commands. The only sign of comprehension was eye closure to command, response to her name, and puzzlement when addressed by the examiner in jargon. Repetition and naming were severely jargonized without recognizable links to test items. Reading, writing, and constructional ability were nil. Psychological testing was not possible. An EEG and previous brain scan disclosed a left posterior temporal abnormality. The patient was observed for several months prior to surgery without change in these findings.

INTRACAROTID AMYTAL TEST. Bilateral intracarotid amytal testing was carried out on separate days. Left-sided injection produced loss of speech save for a "bu, bu, bu" stereotypy. The patient remained able to close her eyes to command. On right injection, jargon persisted, with loss of eye closure. This suggested that the neologistic jargon and eye closure were left and right hemisphere dependent phenomena, respectively.

SURGERY AND POSTOPERATIVE EVALUATION. In October 1972, a cryogenic lesion was made in the left medial geniculate body, with freezing down to −90°C for 2 min at a point 1 mm below and behind the posterior commissure and 15 mm from the midline. Postoperatively, there was no attempt to speak until the sixth day, when whispered jargon similar to that on preoperative testing appeared. Speech volume gradually increased over the next 2 or 3 days up to the normal level. The patient responded to her name, and, with eyes closed, stopped talking to a whispered "shh" sound.

Neurological examination was unchanged and, although testing was difficult, there was no evidence of auditory or vestibular dysfunction. Bedside ice water calorics elicited symmetrical nystagmus on stimulation of either ear. There was no behavioral evidence of auditory hallucinations. Hearing seemed intact bilaterally, with rapid orientation to whisper or other sounds on either side and with either ear occluded. When approached from behind and her name whispered, the patient promptly turned toward the sound source. Requests for eye closure in a barely audible whisper elicited immediate correct responses. She could be aroused from sleep by noise, and there was no evidence of auditory neglect or inattention. Audiometric testing disclosed ability to turn in the direction of speech sounds in various positions of the acoustic field.

Repeat language testing over a 6-week period did not disclose a change in the fluent neologistic jargon. Other parameters of language testing remained unchanged. There was a suggestion of slightly improved speech intelligibility on conversational material.

The failure to initiate speech in the immediate postoperative period occurred with otherwise good gesture and attention. Speech returned as a whisper, with gradually increasing volume. Preoperative audiometric testing indicated that speech volume could be controlled by input volume; i.e., the patient spoke with normal volume to an input of 65 dB and whispered when the input dropped to 45 dB. This suggests that the postoperative speechlessness and whispering may have been acoustically determined.

Discussion

This review of the thalamus and disorders of language and cognition has centered chiefly on the complex of symptoms associated with different types of thalamic pathology. While it would have been preferable to consider such symptoms in relation to specific thalamic groups, this has not been possible because of the scarcity of pathological cases with restricted vascular lesions. Regarding the surgical material, only a few nuclei have been explored, and in such cases one cannot ignore the fact that the preexisting neurological deficit has an influence on the postoperative behavior.

There is some evidence to suggest that lesion of the nucleus ventralis lateralis produces mild intellectual changes similar to those following lesion of the pulvinar (Riklan & Cooper, 1975). Stereotaxic lesion of the nucleus dorsomedialis has produced memory impairment (Spiegel et al., 1955), but such cases, few in number, have not been carefully studied. Natural lesions of the anterior nucleus may also lead to memory impairment, as in the Korsakoff syndrome, although Victor et al. (1971) have attributed this to pathology in the dorsomedialis. In view of the evident difficulty in establishing correlations between lesion and symptom—no less at the thalamic than the cortical level—caution should be exercised in assigning functions to specific nuclear groups. This is even more true for stimulation studies where distant effects are always a possibility. In this regard, claims for a localization of language in anterior superior pulvinar appear to go well beyond the experimental evidence.

The effort to establish such correlations comes from the view of the thalamus as a collection of separate nuclei connected to different areas and subserving different functions. However, it can also be argued that the thalamus is a hierarchically organized structure in which levels (nuclear groups) have evolved in company with the cortical zones to which these levels project. The concept of successive levels of functional thalamic organization laid down in the course of evolution has been discussed by Riss, Pederson, Jakway, and Ware (1972). These authors have delineated six stages in the phylogenesis of the thalamus: a *spinal* or *reflex* level in relation to certain nuclei of the ventral basal complex; a *reticular* level in relation to nonspecific thalamic nuclei; a *cerebellar* level in relation to the ventral anteroventrolateral complex; a *midbrain tectal* level in relation to the primate pulvinar inferior or the lateralis posterior of other mammals; a *limbic* level in relation to the anterior nuclei and medial parts of the medial-dorsal nucleus; and a *neocortical* level in relation to the pulvinar and lateral portions of the medial dorsal nucleus.

Sanides (1970) has argued that stages in thalamic differentiation can be viewed as emergent zones which differentiate together with their cortical projection areas. Both the thalamic nucleus and its cortical projection zone can be viewed as part of the same level in brain evolution. In this way, the nuclei of the thalamus come to be understood not as control centers facilitating, inhibiting, or otherwise influencing some extrinsic area but rather as components of more widely distributed anatomical levels. The thalamic nucleus participates with its "projection" zone in the mediation of cognitive events specific to that structural level of which it is but one component.

Since thalamic differentiation follows an evolutionary course parallel to that of the neocortex, the symptomology of thalamic lesions should occur as a destructuring of this phylogenetic organization. In other words, thalamic pathology should show a level-by-level correspondence with pathology of the cortex. Symptoms of a lesion in a particular thalamic nucleus should resemble those of a lesion in the cortical zone related to that nucleus. Thus the picture of a lesion of the pulvinar should be of the same general type as that of a temporoparietal lesion, the picture of a lesion in the limbic thalamus should resemble that of the limbic cortex, and so on. With regard to language pathology, there is some preliminary evidence that this may be the case.

Thus there are two "aphasic" syndromes which have been related to thalamic lesions: one is characterized by mutism, the other by fluent jargon. Both occur with acute left thalamic lesion, but only mutism has been described in progressive bilateral cases. While it is yet unclear whether these disorders reflect the disruption of intrathalamic mechanisms, or are referred effects on overlying cortex, and if the former what mechanisms (nuclei) are involved, the approach to thalamus described above permits another interpretation of these symptoms.

Studies in primate have demonstrated prominent connections between the inferior parietal lobule and the pulvinar (Walker, 1938). Using the HRP technique, Kasdon and Jacobson (1978) have shown a more heterogeneous input to this area in monkey but have confirmed the presence of major projections to the inferior parietal lobule from the pulvinar. This arrangement is similar to that in man, where strong connections have been shown to exist between the pulvinar and the inferior parietal and posterior temporal region (Van Buren & Borke, 1969). In contrast, the anterior speech area receives the major projection from the dorsomedial nucleus. This has been demonstrated in monkey by Tobias (1975), and appears also to be the case in man. In sum, the pulvinar is in relation to the generalized neocortex of the posterior sector, and the dorsomedial nucleus is in relation to the generalized neocortex of the anterior sector.

Accordingly, the fluent-nonfluent distinction that seems to prevail in the differentiation of posterior and anterior aphasias at the "cortical" level would be expected also to prevail at the thalamic level. The aphasic jargon which is associated with a (?) pulvinar lesion, and the dysnomia which occurs on pulvinar stimulation, would correspond to the semantic jargon and verbal paraphasia, and anomia, which result from lesions of posterior (transitional and generalized) neocortex. On the other hand, the mutism that occurs with a lesion of (?) dorsomedial nucleus would correspond to the mutism that occurs as a symptom of anterior (transitional and generalized) neocortical lesion. The lack of phonological or articulatory deficit in both the fluent and nonfluent thalamic syndromes would indicate that these nuclei are in functional relationship to the generalized neocortex surrounding the Broca and Wernicke areas, *sensu stricto,* since lesions of these latter areas produce impairment at the phonological stage in language processing (Brown, 1977). Naturally, it is emphasized that this interpretation is quite speculative, and that further study is needed before it can be accepted. This is an important task for the future.

SUBCORTICAL APHASIA*

with Ellen Perecman

Subcortical Aphasia

Thalamus The possibility of cognitive changes with thalamic lesions was noted early on. Morsier (1938) reported hallucinations in thalamic cases and Grunthal (1942) described "thalamic dementia." Yet, it was not until the monograph by Penfield and Roberts (1959) that attention was focused on thalamus in relation to language function. (Figure 3-1.) Subsequently, aphasia was observed in (left) thalamic infarcts (Botez & Barbeau, 1971; Brown, 1979b; Ciemens, 1970; Elghozi, Strube, Signoret, Cambier, & Lhermitte, 1978; Fisher, 1959; Mazaux, Orgogozo, Henry, & Loiseau, 1979; Sager, Nestianu, & Florea-Ciocoiu, 1967). Series of mixed subcortical cases have been reported by Alexander and LoVerne (1980) and Lanneluc (1983). With small lesions restricted to the left thalamus, there does not appear to be a consistently enduring aphasia. Wallesch, Kornhuber, Brunner, Kunz, Hollerbach, & Suger (1983) found mainly an impairment on complex comprehension tasks. Alexander and LoVerne (1980) did not find a specific form of aphasia after thalamic lesion, though aphasic symptoms were common. Both mutism and a type of sensory transcortial aphasia have been described, the latter with jargon speech and good repetition. In transcortical sensory aphasia with thalamic lesion, the jargon appears to be of several types, either semantic (Lanneluc, 1983), neologistic (Mohr, Waters, & Duncan, 1975), or in several of our own cases, with a rhyming quality. Also, comprehension is better than in the cortical cases. With regard to mutism, this can occur at onset, or be an endstage in progressive cases. With initial mutism, it is uncertain that the recovery occurs through an aphasic phase. In cases where mutism appears in the course of deterioration, there is gradual reduction in vocalization with word search, but paraphasia has not been described. Of interest, is the occurrence of agraphia with thalamic lesions. This may appear as an isolated event or as a severe agraphia with mild oral language impairment (Grossman, Wheeler, & Brown, 1981). Lanneluc (1983) has described micrographia in thalamic cases, suggesting that the disorder may not be primarily aphasic in origin.

Thus, aphasia may occur with lesions of the left thalamus but it is usually transient. Two major forms are described, a fluent and a nonfluent type, which

*Reprinted from "Neurological Basis of Language Processing" by J. W. Brown and E. Perecman. In J. Darby (Ed.), *Speech Evaluation in Neurology*. New York: Grune & Stratton. Copyright 1985 by Grune & Stratton. Adapted by permission.

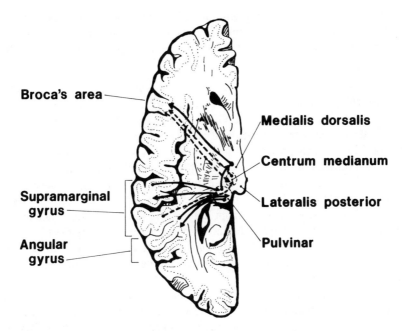

Broca's area

Medialis dorsalis

Centrum medianum

Supramarginal gyrus

Lateralis posterior

Angular gyrus

Pulvinar

FIGURE 3-1. Diagram of corticothalamic pathways after Penfield, indicating the central role given to thalamus in the mediation of anterior to posterior flow between the language zones. The arcuate fasciculus is assigned a less conspicuous role in the process.

may relate to lesions of the pulvinar and dorsomedial nucleus, though precise anatomical studies are lacking. There are several possible interpretations of thalamic aphasia:

1. The lesion may de-afferent overlying cortex so that aphasia represents cortical depression. Dysphasia on thalamic stimulation is probably a referred effect on posterior neocortex (Ojemann, 1983; Brown, 1983d). However, a recent PETT study showed normal metabolism in overlying cortex in a case of thalamic aphasia (Metter et al., 1983). Certainly, the opposite effect can occur, i.e. thalamic depression (hypometabolism) secondary to a cortical lesion (Kuhl et al., 1980).

2. The lesion disrupts linguistic mechanisms or processes mediated by (left) thalamus. This supposes a type of dominance at the thalamic level, and suggests that thalamic nuclei connected to cortical areas (e.g., pulvinar and temporoparietal cortex, dorsomedial nucleus and frontal cortex) form part of a distributed system in association with the cortical projection zones. There is also the implication that thalamic nuclei are connected to forebrain areas at the same evolutionary stage and that thalamic lesions give rise to disorders similar to those in the corresponding cortical area (e.g., limbic cortex and limbic thalamus; neocortex and neothalamus (Brown, 1979b).

3. The thalamic lesion—right or left sided—could affect nonlinguistic mechanisms which impact on language function. An effect of short-term memory, motor initiation or attention could explain language deficits with left-sided lesions.

Putamen There have been reports of aphasia due to lesions of the left putamen (Hier, Davis, Richardson, & Mohr, 1977; Naeser et al., 1982; Damasio, Damasio, Rizzo, Varney, & Gersh, 1982). Every conceivable variety of aphasia except perhaps agrammatism has been described, and there is no clear relationship between presence/absence or severity of aphasia and lesion size. Large hemorrhagic lesions may cause little or no aphasia, while small lesions may give severe impairments. Aphasia following left putamenal lesions appears to persist longer than after thalamic infarction (Wallesh et al., 1983). There is some evidence that anterior putamen lesions give motor aphasia, whereas more posterior lesions give fluent aphasia. Of parenthetic interest is the observation that patients with putamen lesions may show a loss of the blink to threat response, though visual fields are normal. Further study of this phenomenon would be of some interest.

The role of the putamen in language is unclear for several reasons. First, the proximity of the putamen and insula suggests the possibility that the aphasia is due to involvement of the latter region rather than the striatum. There is considerable evidence that the insula is important in language function. The anterior insula has been identified through CT studies as the crucial area of involvement in Broca's aphasia (Poeck, personal communication, 1982), and posterior insula plays a role in fluent aphasia (Brown, 1979a). As mentioned, PET studies suggest activation of insula in language processing. The occurrence of different types of aphasia with a putamen lesion could be explained by involvement of different parts of the insula.

Second, CT studies in the immediate post-onset period may not show atrophy of overlying cortex, but follow-up scans on such patients (Grossman et al., 1981) reveal late atrophic changes. This indicates that a direct or referred effect on cortex—though not apparent in early CT scans—should be considered. Recent PET studies of patients with lesions of putamen and hypometabolism of overlying neocortex (Mazziotta, Mettler, & Phelps, 1984) are consistent with this interpretation.

Caudate Aphasia may occur with a lesion of the left caudate (Barat et al., 1981; Cambier, Elghozi, & Strube, 1979; Lanneluc, 1983). An aphemic patient has been described (Kushner et al., 1982) with a normal CT scan and hypometabolism in left caudate on PET. Van Buren and Fedio (1976) interpret speech arrest with SMA stimulation as an inhibitory effect on the caudate. Lesions of caudate reproduce the syndrome of the dorsolateral frontal convexity in monkey. These observations indicate that close attention should be given to this structure for possible involvement in language or cognitive processing.

4
Selections on Aphasia and Lateralization

CURRENT STUDIES OF APHASIA*

Recent Studies that Support the Microgenetic Account

An important element in the microgenetic theory of language processing concerns the prediction of semantic to phonological flow. This prediction has found support in studies of deep dyslexia (Coltheart, Patterson, & Marshall, 1980), where patients with generally large left hemisphere lesions, who are unable to derive phonology from print, show semantic errors in reading, especially for concrete nouns. Such patients extract meaning from the word form even though they cannot process the word phonetically, suggesting a pre-phonological stage of lexical meaning. Similar phenomena in the auditory modality have been reported (Morton, 1980). There are reports of ability to point to semantic associates of an orally presented target on a forced-choice paradigm in patients with cortical or word deafness who are otherwise unable to point to the correct object.

Not only is word meaning extracted prior to phonology, it may be extracted prior to the conscious perception of the word. One well-known study showing semantic priming for backward-masked (and not consciously perceived) words provided important early support (Marcel, 1983a; See Holender, 1986). There are also reports of cross-field semantic priming in cases of callosal section (Gazzaniga, 1980). In our lab, we have noted that semantic priming is most pronounced in cases of severe aphasia, even when the subject has difficulty reading the target words, again suggesting that semantic processing is a preliminary stage in cognition prior to phonological analysis, prior even to conscious object or word perception.

Converging information comes from studies of pure alexia, letter-by-letter reading associated with a left occipital and, usually, splenial lesion. Recent studies suggest depressed function in the mirror right occipital area. Word-evoked potentials may be flattened over the right posterior region—in spite of normal late potentials associated with meaning—suggesting mirror diaschisis (Neville, Snyder, Knight, & Galambos, 1979). In a related study of nonalexic patients with left and right hemisphere lesions, elevated thresholds for the

---

*From *Aphasia*, F. Clifford Rose (Ed.) Whurr Publ., London, 1988.

identification of geometric shape were found in the ipsilateral field. This was present only in cases with hemianopia regardless of lesion side, and again points to mirror depression (Brown, 1980b). Patients with pure alexia have elevated tachistoscopic thresholds for object recognition. Reading errors tend to reflect the visual complexity of the stimulus. These observations, and many others, suggest that the perception of word form is impaired. In spite of this, patients with pure alexia show occasional semantic paralexias, may demonstrate semantic priming effects and show access to semantic information on words they are unable to read (Coslett & Saffran, 1983; Landis, Regard, & Serrat, 1980.) These observations provide further support for the idea that meaning can be extracted from a word (an object, etc.) prior to its conscious perception. The microgenetic model predicts that language representation unfolds from a lexical-semantic to a phonological stage. The surface of the posterior language system consists in a core zone in posterior superior temporal area for phonological processing with a lexical-semantic surround, a pattern largely confirmed by CT studies of posterior aphasia (Cappas, Cavallotti, & Vignolo, 1981) and electrocortical stimulation of the posterior language zone (Ojemann, 1983). In fact, the dissection of phonological processing into a posterior phonemic and anterior phonetic component (Messerli, Lavorel, & Nespoulos, 1983) was inherent in the earliest form of the microgenetic model. The concept that processing leads from a bilaterally represented lexical-semantic phase to a lateralized core phonological zone has developed, in part, from the interpretation of neology as a two-level (lexical, phonological) defect (Brown, 1972), an idea that is finding increasing support (Buckingham, 1981; Howard, Patterson, Franklin, Morton, & Orchard-Lisle, 1984). Studies of posterior aphasia, especially of jargon, suggest that the transition through layered semantic fields toward a target lexical item, its isolation and eventual phonemic representation, occur on a continuum which can be sliced more or less arbitrarily at innumerable points (Perecman & Brown, 1985).

With regard to some aphasic disorders:

1. The model predicts that functions do not resolve in isolation, but together with other performances as part of the same language level or processing stage. Thus, conduction aphasia was viewed as a disruption of phonological representation coextensive with a stage of cognitive analysis rather than as a deficit of repetition (see Kohn, 1984). Evidence in support of the microgenetic interpretation of conduction aphasia has been reported by Selnes, Knopman, Niccum, and Rubens (1985). These authors document that repetition is related to Wernicke's area, not to a connecting pathway, and that repetition is involved in relation to alterations in other language behaviors, especially naming and reading aloud; that is, it is not damaged with the degree of anatomical or functional specificity required by a pathway theory.

2. The description of word deafness as the disruption of an endpoint in phonological realization, a type of perceptual dysarthria, rather than an input

disorder (Brown, 1972) finds support in various recent papers, notably that of Carramazza, Berndt, and Basili (1983), demonstrating a phonological disorder in word-deaf patients. Evidence for a prephonological stage of semantic processing is also consistent with the microgenetic account.

3. The depiction of word-finding errors as moments in a process of lexical specification, and thereby the integration of anomia with other aphasic syndromes, agrees with recent interpretations of posterior aphasia—especially by the British school—that claim errors correspond to stages in lexical differentiation.

4. The concept that awareness of errors depends on error type (i.e., processing stage) and the implication that awareness develops with, or is elaborated by, language microgenesis finds some support in studies of error awareness in deep dyslexia (Newcombe & Marshall, 1980) and other conditions (Marshall, Rappaport, & Garcia-Buñuel, 1985) where awareness and self-correction accompany phonemic but not semantic errors.

5. The account of motor and conduction aphasia as disruptions of phonological processing (Brown, 1972), and the implication that the step from ape to man depended on the evolution of linked phonological (phonetic, phonemic) devices in the Broca and Wernicke area, is supported by much current work (e.g., Messerli et al., 1983).

6. The description of transcortical motor aphasia as a motoric rather than linguistic or proposition disturbance is supported by recent physiological studies in human subjects (Chauvel, Bancaud & Busen, 1985). Of interest, Jürgens (1985) reports that monkeys with bilateral supplementary motor area (SMA) lesions show a disruption of the isolation call, a self-generated vocalization, while other stimulus-dependent vocalizations are intact. This speaks for a problem in transcortical motor area in generating a vocal action (spontaneous speech) when it is independent of specific perceptual cues (repetition, reading aloud, naming) as predicted in early microgenetic accounts of this disorder.

7. A still more dramatic illustration of evolutionary levels in action comes from studies of patients with severe aphasia, unable to communicate orally or with their intact left hand, who can write (to dictation) with their hemiplegic right arm with the aid of a prosthesis (Brown, Leader, & Blum, 1983). The extent of preserved language ability in these cases has not yet been established, but we have studied one patient with severe nonfluent aphasia who produced grammatical sentences on picture description (Brown, 1985c). This phenomenon has been interpreted as the ability to access submerged or "buried" levels in language representation through the use of the older proximal motor system.

8. Studies of agrammatism have not consistently documented a disorder of grammatical knowledge in anterior aphasics differing from that in posteriors (Heeschen, 1985). Individual case studies have shown "two-way" dissociations between impairments in the comprehension of grammar and agrammatism in production (Berndt, 1985). These findings imply that an impairment in mental

grammar is not the cause of the agrammatism in production, a conclusion consistent with the microgenetic account as well as with several studies in our lab which have failed to support the usual interpretation of this disorder. Thus, motor aphasics do well on reversible sentences when the sentences are controlled for real-world plausibility, i.e., are equally implausible (Leslie, 1980), their sortings are aided by word stress (Kellar, 1978) and on a silent letter cancellation task they show sensitivity to functors (Ross, 1983).

9. The idea that error type reflects cognitive level finds support in studies by Gainotti, Carlomagno, and Craca (1986) documenting a thought disorder in posterior aphasics with semantic but not phonemic errors. Early papers on microgenetic theory (Brown, 1972, 1977) are quite explicit as to this prediction.

The Nature of the Symptom

A central hypothesis concerns the nature of pathological symptoms. Traditional neuropsychology assumes that the symptoms of brain damage result from the partial or complete destruction of an area housing certain operations, representations, processes or strategies. In this view, errors represent degraded functions, and omissions point to deficiency states. Thus, agrammatism signifies a loss or impoverishment in a mental grammar; paraphasia indicates a defective semantic or phonemic component.

However, there is reason to doubt the accuracy of this "common sense" interpretation. Errors which are typical of aphasic states are found in normal speakers, particularly in learning a second language as well as in normal sleeptalking (Brown, 1972). A study of a polyglgot aphasic (Perecman, 1985) disclosed translation errors similar to those in normal bilinguals. Studies of phonemic jargon indicate that phoneme frequencies do not differ from the normal (Perecman & Brown, 1981). Similar findings have been reported in other jargon cases (Lecours, Osborn, Travis, Rouillon, & Lavalle-Huynh, 1981). Buckingham (personal communication, 1987) consider errors in fluent aphasics to reflect normal language processing. Butterworth (1985) has interpreted errors in fluent aphasics as blends related to normal language processes. From a different perspective, Zurif, Swinney, and Garrett (1987) argue against destruction of modules as the basis for symptom formation in aphasia.

Neural Correlates

One of the earliest predictions of the microgenetic model (Brown, 1972) was that the primary cortical sensory areas were endpoints in perceptual microgenesis rather than initial stages in the building up of perceptions. This prediction, which appeared so eccentric in view of work on feature-detection theory, has been supported by studies rediscovering the so-called blindsight phenomena, the presence of residual vision in hemianopic fields, work that dates back to Bard

(1905) and Bender and Krieger (1951). The argument that these effects are artifacts of light scatter (Campion, Latto, & Smith, 1983) does not account for the occurrence of the phenomenon in cases with cortical blindness due to bilateral striate damage. Such patients can often walk confidently around obstacles without bumping into them (Brown, 1972), a behavior reminiscent of that in the destriate monkey (Humphrey, 1974). There is also the fact that comparable phenomena have been described in the auditory (Michel, Peronnet, & Schott, 1980) and tactile (Paillard, Michel, & Stelmach, 1983) modalities. Scatter does not explain denial of blindness, a phenomenon presumably reflecting a visual experience at subsurface levels, nor does it account for semantic priming in blind fields (Marcel, 1983b), a finding which indicates that more than just sensory primitives are involved.

Further support for the idea that V1 represents a late stage in object formation would be provided by PETT studies demonstrating metabolic activation of circumstriate cortex (V2) without activation of striate cortex. There are preliminary reports that this effect has been obtained. Of still greater interest is the report by Deacon (1986) on studies of the laminar distribution of corticocortical fibers in primate that the pattern of distribution from prefrontal to premotor to motor cortex parallels that from inferotemporal cortex to V3 to V2 to V1, suggesting that the direction of processing in visual perception may well be the reverse of the standard theory and instead conform to predictions of the microgenetic account.

A long-standing dogma in aphasia study concerns the idea of posterior to anterior flow mediated by intervening parietal neocortex, insula or the arcuate fasciculus. However, the microgenetic concept is that of a simultaneous unfolding over anterior and posterior systems. Although there is still little data on this question, recent work in owl monkey (Merzenich & Kaas, 1980) indicates simultaneous processing in multiple visual areas and Ojemann (personal communication, 1984) has not found posterior to anterior conduction in two craniotomy cases in which Wernicke area stimulation and Broca area recording were carried out. In fact, the study of Fried, Ojemann, and Fetz (1981) seems to suggest simultaneous processing in the two language areas.

On the microgenetic account, mesial frontal cortex (cingulate gyrus, supplementary motor area) was postulated to be entrained in the preprocessing of a vocal or limb action. Specifically, cingulate and SMA mediate preparatory stages in action generation prior to conscious awareness. This was inferred from the results of focal lesions (Brown, 1977). The argument that SMA lesion involves early stages in action generation is supported by studies of regional cerebral blood flow (Orgogozo & Larsen, 1979). Kornhuber's (1974, 1985) description of the readiness potential, a bilateral surface negative potential, the end of which begins about 90 ms before simple finger movement, and the correlation of this potential in 1980 with a paralimbic midline source, are also consistent with the microgenetic account and confirm that SMA is involved in the programming of an action at the earliest stages. The microgenetic model of action, and specifically the role of SMA, is the topic of a recent review (Goldberg, 1985).

We have studied PETT maps in subjects at rest and during language stimulation (phoneme monitoring). During the latter procedures, the resting pattern of mirror cortical and thalamic correlations tends to shift to one of correlations between cortical language areas within the left hemisphere (Bartlett, Brown, Brody, and Wolf, 1987). The strong positive correlations between left Broca and Wernicke areas (and right Wernicke but not right Broca areas) only during language activation suggests that these areas are entrained in a task-dependent manner out of a resting pattern of metabolic symmetry. The finding of coupled activity in left Broca and Wernicke areas is, of course, consistent with a number of hypotheses about how they are interrelated. The concept of simultaneous activation is in accord with the finding that the coupling is positively correlated, while the finding that asymmetric activation develops out of a symmetrical background is consistent with a microgenetic account of dominance establishment.

According to microgenetic theory, language dominance arises through a life-span growth process of regional specification (Brown & Jaffe, 1975), probably linked to changes in synaptic protein. Initial right-hemisphere growth was postulated, with left-hemisphere acceleration at the onset of language. This process was inferred from changes in aphasia type over the life span (see Brown & Grober, 1983; Joanette et al, 1983). The theory predicts greater focality of language representation in left than right hemisphere, and has implications for sex differences in degree of lateral asymmetry. Specifically, the claim is that the rate of lateralization is dependent on the sex hormones. The androgens cause an increase in (cerebral) protein synthesis and thus an accelerated rate of brain growth, with increased left hemisphere specification in males. The androgens do not have a differential effect on the hemispheres. The increase in protein synthesis accentuates the embedded trend toward left specification, which is an expression of a growth process. This theory, first proposed by Brown and Grober (1983), conflicts with that recently developed by Geschwind claiming unilateral (left) hemisphere suppression by fetal testosterone.

The microgenetic model of the maturation of language areas is in general agreement with findings that gender and IQ correlate with focality of left language representation (Mateer, 1983). Additional support comes from Buell and Coleman (1979), who document sustained dendritic growth into late life, from studies suggesting parcellation (growth through inhibition) of left hemisphere in maturation, and from studies by Scheibel et al. (1985), who report differences in dendritic structure in adult left and right Broca areas reflecting growth asymmetries. As predicted, in the Scheibel study a different pattern was found in two nondextrals, suggesting an accentuation of right-hemisphere growth early in life.

BILINGUALISM AND APHASIA*

The question of different types of aphasia in the same patient is of great theoretical interest. Albert and Obler (see footnote) describe a case of Wernicke aphasia in one secondary language and a Broca aphasia in another, with the first language sharing elements of both. Two other cases are cited, one with a fluent aphasia in the stronger language, and another with a nonfluent aphasia in the stronger language. The authors might also have mentioned Wald's case of a 63-year-old polyglot with a fluent (conduction) aphasia in Russian, the mother tongue, and a motor aphasia in her other languages. How can such dissociations be explained? It may be that site of lesion is important in determining which pattern occurs. If we consider that localization, or regional specification, is related to skill in language that develops over time, then anterior and posterior lesions might have reciprocal effects on the two languages. An anterior lesion would disrupt expression in the L1 more severely because it is more focally represented. The L2 might escape by virtue of its more diffuse representation. This might give the picture of a nonfluent aphasia in the L1 and relative preservation or fluency, though not a true "fluent" aphasia, in L2. Conversely, a posterior lesion would lead to a fluent aphasia in the strongest or earliest acquired language. Children with posterior lesions develop nonfluent aphasia. In mono-linguals, the incidence of fluent aphasia increases with age. This suggests that a more focal representation is required for a fluent aphasia, and that this takes some time to develop. The more diffusely represented (weaker) language would, as in children, show the picture of a nonfluent aphasia. Thus, in the adult bilingual a posterior lesion might cause a more fluent aphasia in L1 and a less fluent—or even nonfluent—aphasia in L2. Naturally these differences would be exaggerated according to the "distance" in age of acquisition and skill between the two languages. Whatever the interpretation, however, such cases argue against a strict localization theory and for a more dynamic process occurring over the life span.

These observations raise the question of whether the nature of a language might influence its anatomical organization and thus determine the type of aphasia that occurs after focal brain injuries. For example, it is said that agrammatism is uncommon in French speakers. This might indicate that agrammatism is related to the prominence of stressed words in the presence of disturbed intonation, since in French the stress pattern is distributed more evenly over the utterance. What then is the picture of agrammatism in an English-French bilingual? My guess is that agrammatism in English would be accompanied primarily by misarticulation errors in French. If this should be the case, it would

*Reprinted from "Review of *The Bilingual Brain*" by J. W. Brown, 1980. *Contemporary Psychology, 25,* 564–565. Copyright 1980 by name of copyright holder. Adapted by permission. (Review of Albert, M. & Obler, L. (1978). *The Bilingual Brain*. New York: Academic Press.)

help to clarify the real nature of agrammatic speech. Studies of agrammatism also suggest an interaction between the language and the lesion site. Glozman in Moscow has reported that agrammatism in Russian, which involves the system of noun declensions, can occur with posterior lesions. This is in contrast to English or German where the association is mainly with anterior pathology. In a case of aphasia in Ndebele, a Bantu language, Traill has also described agrammatism through lexical deficits. Peuser and Fittschen report a pattern of agrammatism in Turkish, an agglutinative language, comparable to that of inflected European languages; but their patient had a posterior lesion.

The comparison of two languages across aphasic patients is clearly not equivalent to the comparison of those same languages in a bilingual aphasic. In addition to the possiblity of a more bilateral representation of language in the bilingual, there is also the problem that an L1 might influence the organization of a very different type of L2. Take for example the following case: A patient of mine who had become deaf at age 8 developed a transient aphasia in sign language following a restricted left temporal (insula) stroke at age 21. While it is not known if the temporal lobe plays a role in language in the congenitally deaf, this case implies that the neural organization of L2 may be influenced by the organization of L1.

RECOVERY AND TREATMENT*

Recovery after Lesion of Broca's Area

There is no question but that documented cases exist of right-handers with focal lesion in Broca's area of the left hemisphere without, or with only transient, motor aphasia. In fact, it seems probable that about one third of a mixed group of (right- and left-handed) patients having a focal lesion in left Broca's area will show considerable functional recovery. This figure is in keeping with Luria's (1970) finding of recovery in about one third of cases with penetrating brain wounds of the primary speech zone.

The effects of age and sinistrality on recovery have long been recognized. In general, patients showing complete recovery following a later documented left Broca's area lesion are younger than those with little or no improvement. Left-handedness would also seem to favor a good recovery. Nonetheless, recovery has been described in dextrals at an advanced age while permanent aphasia may occur in left-handers or adolescents. Age and handedness are not, therefore, the sole determinants of functional restitution but rather appear to be important as rough indices of degree of left-hemispheric language specification; i.e. like

*From "Recovery and Treatment in Broca's Aphasia" by J. W. Brown, 1976. Conference report of Multinational Conference on Rehabilitation of Language Disorders, Egypt, February, 1976.

young patients, left-handers also have incomplete (immature) lateralization (Brown & Hécaen, 1976).

The fact that restitution occurs in a fair number of strong right-handers with focal lesion of left Broca's area suggests that language lateralization may be incomplete in some dextral adults. This suggests the possibility of a series of "dominance states" among adult right-handers. If this is so, then the degree of recovery after a focal lesion would tend to reflect the degree of completeness of the "lateralization" process. In this respect, other factors suggested to positively influence recovery rate, such as low educational level or illiteracy, might be considered in relation to the same mechanism.

Recovery is also linked to the nature of the pathological lesion. Patients with a congenital lesion of Broca's area may not develop aphasia following surgical excision. Presumably such a lesion acts to retard left-side specialization. This effect has been studied by Milner (1975) in patients with early unilateral lesion undergoing intracarotid amytal testing.

In several cases, excision of Broca's area has been carried out in the course of removal of an intracerebral tumor. The relative preservation of language function in some of these cases may be explained by the posterior displacement of Broca's area with only apparent surgical removal. In other cases where Broca's area is truly excised, one could assume that the slow tumor growth "prepares" the left hemisphere for subsequent surgical excision; i.e., that there is gradual adaptation prior to surgery. A similar argument would apply to the considerable degree of recovery following dominant hemispherectomy for glioma.

Theories of Recovery from Aphasia

According to Monakow (1914) there is a continuum between those patients without any aphasia, those with recovery over several days, weeks or months, and the occasional aphasic showing restitution over a period of a year or more. This continuum reflects the gradual fading away of a state of inhibition (elevated discharge threshold) induced in neighboring and distant (homologous) cortex by brain damage. This inhibitory state was termed diaschisis. The concept of diaschisis is supported by some experimental work (e.g., Kempinsky, 1958) and has been discussed in publications by Gazzaniga (1975), Smith (1972), Teuber (1974), and others. Monakow's view of transcallosal inhibition of the opposite (intact) speech area as an important factor in the symptomatology of Broca's aphasia has been developed by Kinsbourne (1974) to a theory of dominance establishment through callosal-mediated right hemispheric suppression.

In studies of posttraumatic cases, Luria (1963) proposed two categories of function loss, permanent symptoms resulting from cell destruction, and temporary symptoms due to interference with neuronal excitability and conductivity.

This latter effect was thought to result from an inactivation of a transmitter agent. Similarly, Zaimov (1965) has argued that aphasic symptoms reflect varying degress of cellular impairment in areas surrounding the lesion centre. This occurs in a manner comparable to the so-called Wedensky inhibition, an alteration in the conductivity of a peripheral nerve following acute injury. However, this concept of cellular damage in neighboring cortex does not account for negative cases without aphasia, or patients with recurrent aphasia after a second lesion in right hemisphere.

Diaschisis has often been explained on a vascular rather than neuronal basis. Meyer, Teraura, Sakamoto, and Kondo (1971) have recently confirmed findings of reduced blood flow in the hemisphere opposite an infarct. A clearing of transient ischemia in the opposite hemisphere could explain restitution in the acute stage. However, this theory does not account for similar effects occurring with trauma or intrinsic lesion, nor cases of recovery over a more prolonged period of time. Other mechanisms which have been postulated, such as neuronal regrowth or denervation hypersensitivity, are of doubtful importance in aphasia recovery (see review in Goldberger, 1974).

It is unlikely that language is actually relearned by aphasics, since many patients show rapid recovery without instruction, while others recover to a degree of fluency inconsistent with a reacquisition theory. Moreover, as Monakow (1914) pointed out, patients who have recovered from an aphasia may have a recurrence with a lesion of the previously damaged left Broca's area, in spite of the preserved right Broca's area, which should mediate the reacquisition. In this regard, theories of conceptual reorganization or "cognitive retraining" do not concern recovery *per se* but rather a type of adaptation to a deficit.

Many theories of recovery depend on the notion of an inhibitory or suppressive process involving undamaged areas of the lesioned or intact hemisphere. This inhibitory effect may occur *de novo* or may be superimposed upon (i.e., there is an accentuation of) a state of preexisting right hemisphere suppression. Theories of compensation through right hemisphere tend to favor the "unlocking" of a prior language capacity rather than the retraining of a naive hemisphere. However, such theories are basically anatomical interpretations of aphasic change and are open to all of the objections that can be raised against any anatomical account of aphasia. The alternative view would appear to be that of restitution through some sort of global reorganization.

Regression and Recovery To understand the process of restitution from the point of view of global reorganization, it is necessary to say a word about the neural organization of language prior to injury. There is some evidence to suggest that this organization is hierarchical, with evolutionary stages of brain development corresponding to levels of linguistic change (Brown, 1976). The aphasias can be viewed as manifestations of these levels when the hierarchy undergoes destructuring. According to this view, a brain area, a "centre," serves to *mediate* a transformation, i.e., tranforms a developing process to a further level, and is not bound to a specific function. If this is correct then recovery would involve a regaining of the previous performance level and not a piecemeal reacquisition of function.

Accordingly, Broca's area can be viewed not as a storehouse of speech mechanisms but as a structural level mediating a final stage in the process of speech production. In this light we may consider the four schizophrenic patients with left or bilateral removal of Broca's area without aphasia. Could one account for such cases by supposing that Broca's area mediates a level in advance of the patient's cognition? Might speech in the severely regressed schizophrenic utilize ontogenetic systems which are earlier or more preliminary, and coexistensive with the regressed cognitive level? If so, the preoperative catatonic or jargon speech of such patients would be comparable to similar productions in aphasics. One should also find less severe aphasia and/or more rapid recovery in schizophrenic than in normal patients.

Of interest in this connection is an observation on a personal case of jargonaphasia. This patient with unintelligible neologistic jargon was reported to be more coherent when sleeptalking than when awake. I have also observed aphasic speech to improve during a focal seizure arising in the damaged left hemisphere. Related to this is the common observation of improvement in aphasic speech when the utterance has a strong emotional component. All of these examples indicate that the *cognitive level* may be of importance in determining functional speech capacity. Luria has even asked if ". . . the fact that a function is preserved at a lower level (can) be used in the restoration of a deranged system?" Such considerations lead to the hypothesis that Broca's aphasia concerns not so much a destruction of the speech codes or articulatory mechanisms as a regression from, or lack of access to, an endstage in speech realization. If this should prove to be the case, one implication would be that recovery is at least a theoretical possibility in every aphasic patient with a unilateral lesion.

TREATMENT OF APHASIA*

Is there a treatment for aphasia? This is a topic which guarantees an argument at any aphasia meeting. Neurologists tend to be pessimistic, and even some speech pathologists are uncertain. We all wonder about facilitation and re-education versus spontaneous recovery, and such issues as duration, intensity and type of treatment. Studies of recovery with and without therapy seem to

---

*Reprinted from discussion by J. W. Brown, 1984. Adapted by permission. (Commentary to Peuser, G., 1984. *Language Rehabilitation after Stroke: A Linguistic Model.* New York: World Rehabilitation Fund.)

indicate that treatment has a beneficial effect, but is this a specific effect, or one that is related to a general arousal or activation of language mechanisms? Evidence for parallel change in the untreated language of bilingual aphasics suggests a nonspecific effect. So too for the apparent similarity in the recovery *pattern* of treated and untreated cases. Obviously, we need more information. We don't even know if therapy should concentrate on areas of strength or weakness. Indeed, I've often wondered whether sensory (acoustic) *deprivation* might have a salutory effect!

Data are important but it is also important to have an approach that is motivated by a theory. The approach determines the type of data that are collected. Conversely, the power of a theory can often be judged from the type of studies to which it leads. Studies of treatment and restitution in aphasia give no cause for jubilation on this point. The literature is dotted with investigations on such topics as the recovery of global aphasics to that of nonfluents, the relative improvement of comprehension in comparison to other tasks, or degree of recovery in relation to aphasia type. Perhaps these studies aid the clinician to predict which categories of aphasia or functional deficits are likely to improve, but they hardly provide the basis for a model of the recovery process. Similarly, studies on the effectiveness of treatment and the comparison of different methods, tend to show modest effects. It is time to stop asking if therapy works. First we have to define the patterns of linguistic change in recovery, and then we can develop a treatment to facilitate this change along natural lines. Only in this way can we search out the principles of a rational approach to treatment.

Concerning treatment, there are many schools of thought, but these can probably be reduced to a few major trends. By far the most prevalent, because it is also the least explicit, is the straightforward empirical management of patients, an approach with its roots in traditional concepts of aphasia classification. Performances are tested and grouped by function—impairments of naming, repetition, spontaneous speech, and so on—and therapy is given according to deficits in these functions, taking into consideration the qualitative aspects of the disorder. Within the diversity of symptom type, some workers, such as Hildred Schuell or Kurt Goldstein, have looked for common elements while others focus on the differences and take a syndrome approach. Because this approach is pragmatic and atheoretical, even opportunistic in a healthy way, it can lead to occasional innovations, such as Melodic Intonation Therapy, the use of "right hemisphere" strategies (spatial thinking, imagery), even my own studies on a writing prosthesis. These techniques are useful and provide new information on the behavior of patients. However, at the other extreme, treatment on an empirical basis can lead to a reliance on rote, automated and other mechanical aids. These are only the illusion of progress in the field.

A second approach developed through the work of Luria is based on a psychological model of language organization. This model provides the framework of a coherent—though not necessarily correct—approach to aphasia and its rehabilitation. The functional system concept (after Anokhin), and the idea of stages in psychological growth and mental structure (after Vygotsky), were responsible for a number of novel techniques in aphasia therapy. These include the use of cues and facilitators, the shifting of performance to a more automatic level, and methods which depend on links between speech and motility. One reason for the success of this approach is that for Luria, Tsvetkova and their colleagues, treatment was not just an after-thought but a form of basic research. In fact, there was no distinction between treatment and research. For example, the effect of stabilizing a semantic category on lexical search, or an attempt to aid lexical retrieval with semantic feature cues, or an examination of the hierarchy of noun declensions, might be investigated during a therapy session—the investigation was the therapy session—and the performance of patients later reported. This seems to me a perfectly acceptable strategy. Since there is no reason to consider one form of treatment superior to another, we might as well do therapy in the spirit of a research investigation.

Still another account is based on the microgenetic model of language processing, developed from a study of error types in different aphasic states and a reconstruction from these errors of the sequence of stages in the microtemporal unfolding of an utterance. The model predicts specific patterns of recovery, not across the entire heirarchy of processing levels in the anterior and posterior sectors but at particular points of transition between levels in one or another sector. The goal of therapy in this model is to facilitate the transition from one processing stage to the next.

HYPOTHESIS ON CEREBRAL DOMINANCE*

with Joseph Jaffe

Clinical Evidence

Studies of language function following acute hemiplegia of infancy (Basser, 1962) and hemispherectomy (Krynauw, 1950; McFie, 1961) indicate that damage to either hemisphere within the first year or two of life delays language development in proportion to mental retardation. However, either hemisphere can assume the language function if damage occurs sufficiently early. By the age of five, aphasia is common after left hemispheric lesion and unusual after lesion of right hemisphere (Guttman, 1942), suggesting considerable left language lateralization. When young children develop an aphasia the picture is that of

*From "Hypothesis on Cerebral Dominance" by J. W. Brown and J. Jaffe, 1975, *Neuropsychologia, 13,* 107–110. Adapted by permission.

mutism or agrammatism. This occurs with lesion in frontal, temporal or parietal lobe (Guttman, 1942; Lefévre, 1950; Alajouanine & Lhermitte, 1965). By the age of ten, left hemispheric lesions may produce mutism or agrammatism, but anomia and paraphasia also appear.

The picture of childhood aphasia, mutism or agrammatism associated with left frontal, temporal or parietal lesion is similar to that in left-handed adult aphasics (H. Hécaen, personal communication, 1973) or dextrals with crossed aphasia (Brown & Wilson, 1973; Hécaen, Mazars, Ramier, Goldblum, & Mérienne, 1971). This is consistent with incomplete language lateralization. For this reason one might suspect that the incidence of crossed aphasia in dextrals would be inversely correlated with age. In this respect it is of interest that of the eight cases of crossed aphasia in dextrals reviewed in Brown and Wilson (1978) the mean age is 41. ($SD = 13.8$) and half are under 35. In an analysis of 29 unselected cases of dextrals with crossed aphasia reported in the literature, including the eight cases found acceptable by Brown and Wilson (1978) the mean age was 44.7 ($SD = 14.0$). This is a relatively young aphasic population and further inclusion of acceptable cases of childhood aphasia might be expected to lower the mean.

With regard to adult aphasia, it has been proposed (Brown, 1972) that an inner bond exists between the expressive and receptive components of each fluent aphasic form, e.g., improvement of comprehension in neologistic jargon is accompanied by an evolution of the expressive pattern to say, the phonemic paraphasia of conduction aphasia. Thus a lesion of Wernicke's area might produce either conduction or jargonaphasia depending on the degree of comprehension preserved. Cases to this point have been described by Kleist (1962, Spratt) and Benson et al. (1973; Case 2). It is of interest that the latter patient was only 36 years old at the time of stroke, while Spratt, though 50, was ambidextrous. Jaffe (1974) has recently argued that certain patients may show left expressive dominance combined with right receptive dominance. A consequence of the present model is that such observations should be more common in younger patients.

Increasing lateralization of comprehension throughout life would led one to expect that jargonaphasia might be more common in older patients. Isserlin (1936) noted the rarity of jargon in war-wounded veterans, a youthful population. Thus, the same lesion of Wernicke's area may produce motor aphasia in a child, anomia or phonemic paraphasia (conduction aphasia) in youth and middle age, and jargonaphasia in late life.

A subsidiary hypothesis concerns a possible continuing differentiation *within* the left hemispheric speech zone, such that the anatomical correlation with a specific aphasic syndrome becomes more predictable with age. For example, a lesion in Broca's area should produce motor aphasia more predictably in an older population. In this regard it is of interest that in two cases of bilateral topectomy of Broca's area (Mettler, 1949) without subsequent aphasia, patients were aged

27 and 31. Penfield and Roberts's (1959) single case of complete surgical removal of left Broca's area of hamartoma without persistent aphasia was 18 years old at the time of operation. In his study the mean age of right-handed seizure patients undergoing surgical extirpation in and around the left hemisphere speech zone without persistent aphasia was 21. In this regard see also Hécaen and Consoli (1973).

Experimental Evidence

The hypothesis of continuous lateralization becomes even more plausible when research studies from birth to senescence are reviewed. Although the priority of the left hemisphere for articulated speech and the right hemisphere for mechanical or musical sounds has now been demonstrated in the newborn electroencephalographically, and there is related evidence of anatomical hemispheric asymmetries at birth (Wada, 1972; Tezner, Tzavaras, Gruner, & Hécaen, 1972), the "plasticity argument" still obtains (Molfese, 1973). The right hemisphere can be considered dominant in infancy, *for the type of visual and acoustic communication which is relevant to the prelinguistic child*. Evidence includes the fact that 88 per cent of unrestrained newborns spontaneously posture their heads to the right (Turkewitz, Gordon, & Birch, 1965) thus exposing their left ear and left visual field to the human environment. This would facilitate the reception of lullabyes, of other nonlinguistic environmental sounds and of visual information by the right hemisphere. Discrimination of faces is one of the earliest visual attainments and also has a special relation to the right hemisphere. Studies of infants also indicate an intimate linkage between visual and speech perception. Experimental displacement of the mother's voice from her face has been shown to be disturbing to the infant (Aronson & Rosenbloom, 1971). This is consistent with a possible reliance of decoding mechanisms on right hemispheric spatial skills. The right hemisphere has also been shown to develop sensitivity to photic driving before the left in neonates (Crowell, Jones, Kapunai, & Nakagawa, 1973), whereas driving is bilateral in the mature brain. Moreover, right-hemisphere dominance is further suggested by the report of left-hand preference in 5-month-old infants, which gives way to right-hand preference later in the first year (Seth, 1973).

The Wechsler Intelligence Test has recently been interpreted in terms of hemispheric dominance, the verbal scale for left hemisphere and performance scale for the right hermisphere (Levy, 1969). It is interesting that the WAIS norms show a decline in *performance* scores but not verbal scores with advancing age, suggestive of either continuing development or resistance to senescence of left hemispheric functions.

An additional piece of evidence derives from EEG studies of electroconvulsive therapy (ECT) in neurologically normal adults (Volavka, Feldstein, Abrams, Dornbush, & Fink, 1972). With bitemporal alternating current treatments an asymmetry develops with greater slowing of frequencies on the left side of the head. The important point is that this asymmetry increases with the age of the patient.

With regard to dichotic listening studies, there is evidence (Knox & Kimura, 1970) of a significant increase in right-earedness for verbal material between ages 5 and 8. Equivalent studies from middle to advanced age have not been performed, though from the proposed model progressive right-earedness might be predicted. Inferential evidence for progressive lateralization also derives from studies (Satz, Achenbach, & Fennell, 1967) on the relation of handedness and earedness. According to Roberts (1969) this data indicates that 10.4 per cent of test-classified dextrals are clearly left-eared. In view of the youth of this normal population, taken in conjunction with the rarity of crossed aphasia in older dextrals, one might also hypothesize a shrinkage in this percentage with age.

Discussion

The evidence cited is in support of the hypothesis that cerebral dominance is not a state but a process, and one that continues through life. In this process, expressive language *appears* to lateralize prior to language comprehension. This may reflect the fact that speech encoding is biased to the left by a left hemispheric specialization for motor sequencing, whereas speech decoding may persist longer in the right hemisphere through a relation to right-hemispheric spatial processing.

Conceivably, lateralization is the initial phase of a continuing process of specification within the dominant hemisphere. Evidence that expressive aphasia in children can be produced by widely distributed left hemispheric lesions, as well as the youth of those few patients with topectomy of left Broca's area without subsequent aphasia (Mettler, 1949; Penfield & Roberts, 1959) suggests that the eventual anterior sequestration of the expressive component follows a stage of more diffuse left hemispheric representation. The same would apply to speech comprehension though at a later age, with progressive sequestration in the left temporal region. This account bears some relation to the concept of "chronogenic localization" proposed by Monakow (1905), though the latter was chiefly an effort to explain the automatic-voluntary dissociation, viz.: through diffuse (early) as opposed to focal (late) storage.

This hypothesis has the testable consequences: (1) that there is increasing right-ear effect on dichotic listening with age, as well as more consistent conjugate deviation of the eyes to the right on verbal stimulation (Kinsbourne, 1972; Anderson & Jaffe, 1973); (2) that the clinical probability of expressive versus jargonaphasia, as well as the probability of intermediate forms, should have a strong age-correlation; (3) that the incidence of crossed aphasia in dextral patients is inversely correlated with age; and (4) that the correlation of aphasic syndrome (or degree of fluency) with anatomical region (or brain scan localization) should become more predictable with age.

Addendum

At the time of submission of this manuscript we were unaware of the articles by A. Carmon et al. (*Behavioral Biology,* 7, 1972) and by V. Fromkin et al. (*Brain and Language,* 1, 1974) which advance related hypotheses. Personal communication from J. Bogen suggests that the incidence of crossed aphasia approaches 50 per cent at the time when right-handedness is first established. E. A. Weinstein also informs us that jargonaphasics are significally older than standard aphasics.

LATERALIZATION AND LANGUAGE REPRESENTATION*

with Henry Hécaen

It is generally agreed that early in life, a state of incomplete lateralization exists. Concepts of equipotentially, plasticity, critical period, adaptation, and restitution, insofar as they concern language, have as a central feature the fact that lateralization is incomplete. The duration of the process of lateralization is not known. Anatomic findings of hemispheric asymmetry in the newborn (Wada, Clarke, & Hamm, 1975; Tezner, Tzavaras, Gruner, & Hécaen, 1972) and evidence suggesting the presence of an early physiologic bias of language to the left hemisphere (Molfese, 1973) indicate only that left hemispheric language lateralization is likely to occur, but these studies are inconclusive as to the age at which this process is completed.

Dichotic listening studies also suggest that dominance is established early, at least by the sixth year, but the technique cannot measure continuing lateralization beyond a strong right ear preference. Recent studies of childhood aphasia (Hécaen, 1976) and a case of delayed language learning (Fromkin, Krashen, Curtiss, et al., 1974) indicate that the process of lateralization may be more prolonged than previously thought, perhaps even continuing over the life span (Brown & Jaffe, 1975).

From studies of aphasia with a pathologic lesion (Zangwill, 1967; Hécaen & Ajuriaguerra, 1963), intracarotid amobarbitol injection (Milner, Branch, & Rasmussen, 1966), unilateral electroconvulsive therapy (Pratt, Warrington, & Halliday, 1971), and other parameters, it is clear that a state of incomplete lateralization may persist indefinitely. This has been referred to as cerebral ambivalence or bilateral representation. It is more common in left-handers, perhaps to a greater extent in those with familial than in those with nonfamilial sinistrality (Hécaen & Sauguet, 1971). Aphasia with a right hemispheric lesion has also been observed in strongly right-handed patients (crossed aphasia). In such patients,

---

*From "Lateralization and Language Representation" by J. W. Brown and H. Hécaen, 1976, *Neurology, 26,* 183–189. Copyright 1976 by Harcourt Brace Jovanovich Publications. Adapted by permission.

there is evidence for bilateral rather than right hemispheric language representation (Brown & Wilson, 1973). Even in standard dextral aphasics with a left hemisphere lesion, there is evidence from intracarotid amobarbitol injection (Kinsbourne, 1971) of language function in the opposite hemisphere. This may be an important factor in recovery. However, cases pertinent to the question of bilateral language representation in dextrals are lacking; thus, cases of paraphasia that both deteriorate and resolve after a second lesion of the other hemisphere have been described (Nielsen, 1946).

These findings are consistent with the possibility that cerebral dominance reflects both the degree of left lateralization in a given individual and the way language is organized in each hemisphere (Brown & Wilson, 1973; Hécaen & Piercy, 1956). This possible relationship between lateralization and intrahemispheric organization suggests that in cases of incomplete dominance, an aphasic syndrome may not so readily correspond to a lesion in a specific area as occurs in standard dextral aphasics; i.e., incomplete lateralization entails a more diffuse language representation within each hemisphere. If this is true, one should observe a close relationship between the degree of lateralization and the effect on language of a lesion in the speech zone of either hemisphere. In other words, the degree of lateralization will determine not only whether a patient will be aphasic but what type of aphasia will develop.

The concept of a relationship between the aphasic syndrome and degree of lateralization and the possibility that the process of lateralization evolves slowly over many years suggest that certain similarities should obtain with respect to aphasia type in children, in left-handers, and in those rare cases of aphasia in dextrals ("anomalous" dextrals) with a right hemispheric lesion. In all three instances, the common element is incomplete lateralization.

Aphasia in Childhood

A distinctive picture of childhood aphasia has been recognized since Guttmann's (1942) paper and subsequently verified by numerous other authors (Hécaen, 1975; Lefévre, 1950; Basser, 1962; Alajouanine & Lhermitte, 1965; Collignon, Hécaen, & Angelergues, 1968). In early childhood, aphasia is characterized by mutism or agrammatism. Word-finding difficulty and phonemic paraphasia (i.e., articulatory disorder) tend to occur in older children and adolescents. Repetition may be impaired even after resolution of the mutism.

Articulatory disorders in childhood aphasia appear in the context of a nonfluent or borderline fluent state, so that the picture of fluent phonemic paraphasia in conversation (conduction aphasia) is rarely encountered. Verbal paraphasia is distinctly less common (noted in only one of 16 patients with a left-sided lesion in Hécaen's (1976) series). Logorrhea does not occur; semantic and neologistic jargon also have not been reported. Disorders of comprehension are present in about a third of patients, perhaps more commonly in younger children, but the adult-type correspondence between comprehension loss and logorrheic jargon is not found. Recovery tends to be superior to that in adult aphasia.

At an early age (less than 2 years), there appears to be a relatively even chance that an aphasia will develop with damage to either hemisphere. However, by age 5, the incidence of aphasia with a left-sided lesion does not differ greatly from that in the adult population, although there is still a higher incidence of crossed aphasia (right-sided lesion in an aphasic dextral) than in the adult. With regard to intrahemispheric localization, mutism occurs with damage in the frontal, temporal, or parietal lobe, although more frequently with an anterior lesion. There is also a correlation between a posterior lesion and impairment of comprehension. In Hécaen's (1976) series, all three children with comprehension disorder and localized pathology had temporal lobe lesions.

Crossed Aphasia in Dextrals

Crossed aphasia refers to the combination of right hemiparesis with aphasia in a left-handed patient or left hemiparesis and aphasia in a right-handed patient. In dextrals, crossed aphasia is rare: 1.8 percent according to Zangwill (1967) 1 percent according to Gloning, Gloning, Haub, et al. (1969) and 0.38 percent according to Hécaen, Mazars, Ramier, et al. (1971). A recent review of the literature (Brown & Wilson, 1973) yielded only seven cases, in addition to that reported, in which the following criteria were satisfied: thorough language testing, a pathologic lesion limited to the right hemisphere, absence of childhood brain damage, strong right-handedness, and a negative family history of left-handedness. Recently, Wechsler (1976) has observed yet another case. Table 4-1 summarizes the clinical findings in these nine patients.

The most common feature in these patients is agrammatism, occurring in eight of nine patients. Mutism was present in six, lasting up to nine months in one patient. Phonemic paraphasia was present in four patients but marked in only one patient, with no instances of verbal paraphasia. Naming was described as good in seven patients, and as fair with rapid recovery in another patient. Repetition was either well preserved or showed defects of the same type as in spontaneous speech, i.e., agrammatism or phonemic paraphasia. Oral comprehension was described as good in four patients, moderately impaired in three, and severely impaired in two.

This picture of mutism and agrammatism with infrequent (and chiefly phonemic) paraphasia, as well as the absence of fluent jargon forms, recalls very closely the picture of aphasia in early childhood. The possibility that crossed aphasia in the dextral adult, despite strong right-handedness, represents a state of incomplete left lateralization is suggested by the finding in one patient (Angelergues, Hécaen, Djindjian, et al., 1962) of deterioration after carotid injection of amobarbitol on the left side. Evidence that language representation in

Table 4-1 Features of Crossed Aphasia in 9 Right-handed Patients

Authors	Lesion	Word finding	Phonemic paraphasia	Verbal paraphasia	Oral comprehension	Repetition	Agrammatism	Initial mutism
Marinesco et al, 1938	Anterior	-	-	-	+	+	+	-
Ettlinger et al, 1955	Posterior	-	-	-	+	+	+	+
Botez and Wertheim, et al, 1959	Anterior	-	-	-	-	+	+	+?
Angelergues et al, 1962	Central	-	-	-	-	-	+	+
Barraquer-Bordas et al, 1963	Central	+	+	-?	-	+	+?	+
Clarke and Zangwill, 1965	Central	-	-	-	-	+	+	+
Hécaen, et al, 1971	Posterior	+	+	-	+	+	-	-
Brown and Wilson, 1973	Central	+	+	-	+	-	+	+
Wechsler, 1975	Anterior	-	+	-	+	+	+	+

+ = impaired, - = intact

such patients is limited to the right hemisphere is supported only by those extremely rare cases of a left speech area lesion in a dextral without aphasia. Boller (1973) has described such a patient, a 74-year-old dextral male not observed to have been aphasic previously who was found at postmortem to have an old infarct 4 cm by 2 cm involving Wernicke's area in the left hemisphere. However, the lack of aphasia in this patient also can be explained by a more diffuse intrahemispheric language organization in the anomalous than in the standard dextral adult.

We have had the opportunity to observe a 20-year-old strongly dextral male without a family history of left-handedness who showed no signs of aphasia (preoperatively or postoperatively) following surgical removal of a left temporal lobe tumor, including Wernicke's area. However, this patient became aphasic during a postoperative intracarotid amobarbital injection on the left side. This is consistent with the idea of a more diffuse language organization within each hemisphere.

In this regard, it is of interest that of the eight dextrals with crossed aphasia previously reported, the mean age is 41 (*SD* 13.8) and half are under age 35. In an analysis of 29 unselected dextrals with crossed aphasia in the literature (Brown & Jaffee, 1975) including these eight patients, the mean age was 44.7 (*SD* 14.0). This is a relatively young aphasic population. Wechsler's (1976) 83-year-old patient might be reconciled with this finding by the fact that she was completely illiterate, since there is some evidence that literacy (Gorlitzer von Mundy, 1957; Cameron, Currier, & Haerer, 1971) and choice of writing hand (Gloning et al., 1969) may influence strength of lateralization.

Aphasia in Left-Handers

From numerous observations (Hécaen & Ajuriaguerra, 1963), we know that langauge organization in left-handed subjects is different from that in right-handed subjects. Thus, in contrast to the rarity of crossed aphasia in a dextral, the majority of left-handed aphasics have a left hemispheric lesion (Conrad, 1949; Goodglass & Quadfasel, 1954), and about 20 to 30 percent have a lesion in the right hemisphere. This tendency for bilaterality is supported by the finding that paroxysmal expressive aphasia is more frequent in left-handers than in right-handers regardless of the hemisphere damaged (Hécaen & Piercy, 1956). There is also evidence that this bilaterality is greater in familial than in nonfamilial left-handers (Hécaen & Sauguet, 1971). Conrad (1949) has suggested that in addition to bilaterality, there is a more diffuse representation of the mechanisms underlying language in each hemisphere.

There are few qualitative studies of aphasia in sinistrals. Although severe impairment of auditory comprehension has been described, even word-deafness (Goodglass & Quadfasel, 1954), aphasia of the receptive type, appears to be less common (or less intense) in left-handed patients. Paroxysmal receptive dysphasia is rare in left-handers (Hécaen & Piercy, 1956), and transient aphasia seems to be generally of the expressive type (Gloning et al., 1969). The incidence of verbal paraphasia and neologism may be lower in left-handed patients than in aphasic dextrals. This appears to be the case in several series (Conrad, 1949; Humphrey & Zangwill, 1952). According to Hécaen and Sauguet (1971), the frequency of paraphasia in aphasic dextrals with a left hemispheric lesion is similar to that in left-handers with a lesion of either hemisphere.

In order to further define the language disorder of left-handed aphasics, the charts of 39 left-handed patients with unilateral brain lesion studied on our unit were reviewed. Of these, 16 patients were selected as having some degree of impairment in oral expression or comprehension. In surgical patients only the postoperative evaluation was used. In this group of 16, there were 14 males and two females; 13 patients had a left-sided lesion, and three had a right-sided lesion. Lesions were: hematoma (4), stroke (4), tumor (5), and trauma (3). Localization was frontal (6), frontotemporal (1), frontoparietal (2), temporal (5), and temporoparietal (2). Table 4-2 shows the findings in these patients. In this table the six frontal (prerolandic) lesions are considered as anterior, the seven temporal and temporoparietal (postrolandic) lesions as posterior, and the three frontotemporal and frontoparietal lesions as central.

The findings are discussed in relation to three types of language performance: verbal fluency, comprehension, and expression. Verbal fluency refers to a test in which the patient is asked to produce words beginning with certain letters, with results expressed as the total number of words produced on three separate trials. An impairment on this test was a striking feature in these patients, with several instances of markedly reduced verbal fluency in the presence of minimal (e.g., cases 3, 4, 6) or even no (e.g., case 1) expressive aphasic impairment. There was no absolute relationship between verbal fluency and fluency in conversational speech. In 11 of the 16 patients, verbal fluency scores were 5 or less. Two of the three patients with a right hemispheric lesion had the highest scores in the series (13 and 23), while the third patient had a 0 score. A comparison of the mean score of the six patients with an anterior lesion (4.0) with that of the seven with a posterior lesion (8.7) suggests that an anterior lesion predisposes to a low score. Although the number of patients is too small to draw definite conclusions, the finding is consistent with previous observations (Milner, 1964; Benton, 1968; Ramier & Hécaen, 1970) of a relationship between reduced verbal fluency and a left frontal lesion.

Comprehension was mildly impaired in seven patients, moderately impaired in one, and unimpaired in eight. Mild impairments were revealed on the three-paper test, and moderate impairments on two-part commands using a prepositional relationship (e.g., "Place the matches *under* the pipe"). Only one patient had comprehension impairment and normal speech. Patients with good comprehension generally had articulatory disorders (i.e., phonemic paraphasia), while those with mild impairment tended to have both an articulatory disorder

Table 4-2 Clinical Features of 16 Aphasic Left-handed Patients

Case No.	Sex	Age	Lesion	Location	Index	Word finding	Phonemic paraphasia	Verbal paraphasia	Oral comprehension	Repetition	Verbal fluency
1	M	36	R	Anterior	0.82 NF	−	+	−	−	−	0
2	M	51	L	Central	0.84 NF	−	+	−	+	−	4
3	M	38	L	Posterior	0.60 F	−	+	−	−	−	4
4	M	46	L	Anterior	0.17 ?	+	−	+	++	−	5
5	M	35	L	Anterior	1.00 NF	+	+	−	−	−	3
6	M	61	L	Posterior	0.15 F	−	−	−	+	−	5
7	M	47	L	Posterior	0.44 NF	+	+	−	+	+	11
8	F	29	L	Central	0.95 F	+++	++	+	+	+++	0
9	M	40	L	Anterior	0.92 F	+	+	−	−	+	9
10	M	60	L	Anterior	0.76 NF	+	+	−	−	+	2
11	M	64	R	Posterior	0.57 F	+	+	−	+	+	13
12	M	75	R	Posterior	0.37 NF	−	+	−	+	+	23
13	M	45	L	Posterior	0.37 NF	+	+	+	+	+	0
14	F	48	L	Posterior	0.39 F	+	+	+	+	+	5
15	M	59	L	Central	0.15 F	+	++	−	−	++	9
16	M	22	L	Anterior	0.07 F	−	+	−	−	+	5

and anomia. All four patients with verbal paraphasia had mild comprehension impairment. The comprehension defect was not related to the familial : nonfamilial variable. A consideration of strength of handedness revealed a possible relationship between weak left-handedness and comprehension impairment. However, of the seven weak left-handers, four had a posterior lesion, and a relationship between posterior location and comprehension deficit was readily apparent (Table 4-3). Of all patients with comprehension impairment, the mean index (of strength of handedness) was 0.46 compared with 0.52 for the series as a whole.

Expression was not severely impaired in the majority of patients. Five patients were nonfluent in conversation, the remainder showing a borderline fluency profile. This corroborates indirectly other studies (Benson & Patten, 1967) in which left handedness was commonly found amoung aphasic patients difficult to classify as to fluency. Agrammatism was not observed, in contrast to its high frequency in dextrals with crossed aphasia and aphasic children. However, agrammatism is not common in French-speaking aphasics. Left-handers with agrammatism have been noted (Goodglass & Quadfasel, 1954; Humphrey & Zangwill, 1952; Milner, 1964; Benton, 1968; Ramier & Hécaen, 1970; Benson & Patten, 1967; Brown, personal observations, 1972).

Articulatory disorders were the most common aphasic feature, present in 14 of 16 patients. In many patients, articulatory disorders were absent or minimal in spontaneous speech and evident chiefly on repetition tests with nonsense words. Only one patient (case 8) was considered to have conduction aphasia. Similarly, 10 patients had some degree of word-finding difficulty (severe in only one patient), but of these, four patients showed verbal paraphasia. Verbal paraphasia of the type seen in Wernicke's aphasia, i.e., semantic substitutions approaching jargon, was not observed. Repetition was moderately to severely impaired in only two patients and mildly impaired in seven, with phonemic paraphasia the most common source of the impairment. Neologism was present in one patient, but no instances of logorrhea or semantic or neologistic jargon were observed.

With regard to pathologic correlation, word-finding difficulty, phonemic and verbal paraphasia, and repetition defect were distributed fairly evenly in the patients with an anterior, central, or posterior lesion. The two patients with the most severe repetition disorder each had a central lesion. Although the small number of right-sided patients does not allow a comparison with the left-sided group, phonemic paraphasia was present in all three patients, word-finding difficulty and comprehension defects each in one patient, and impaired repetition in two patients. When we consider all left-handers in the series (aphasic plus nonaphasic), there appears to be a greater relative frequency of aphasia with an anterior than with a posterior lesion (perhaps reflecting the greater likelihood of speech zone involvement in the former) and a lower frequency (three of nine patients) of aphasia with left anterior lesions (Table 4-3).

Table 4-3 Pathologic Localization and Language Distrubance in 39 Aphasic and Nonaphasic Left-handed Patients

Lesion location	Number	Word finding	Phonemic paraphasia	Verbal paraphasia	Comprehension	Repetition	Neologism	Jargon
Anterior	7	4	4	1	1	3	0	0
L Posterior	11	3	4	2	4	3	0	0
Central	9	2	3	1	2	2	1	0
Anterior	2	0	1	0	0	0	0	0
L Posterior	9	1	2	0	1	2	0	0
Central	1	0	0	0	0	0	0	0

Comment on Left-Handers

These findings tend to support previous observations on the relative mild-ness of aphasia in left-handers, regardless of the hemisphere damaged, and the similarity of aphasia type with a lesion in either hemisphere. The high incidence of crossed aphasia in this series is also consistent with previous observations. The preponderance of males (14 males, two females) appears greater than might be predicted from their higher incidence of left-handedness. In the nonaphasic group (five females, 18 males), there were four females with a left-sided lesion (two central, two posterior). The incidence of 21.7 percent females in the nonaphasic group compares with an incidence of 12.4 percent in the aphasic group.

With regard to these possible sex differences, De Agostini (1975) has reviewed the charts of 129 aphasic and nonaphasic left-handed patients with a unilateral lesion seen on our unit. In this group, there were 37 females and 92 males. Of the 61 patients with aphasia, 19 were females and 42 were males. Thus, 51 percent of the females and 45 percent of the males with a focal lesion were aphasic, while in relationship to the total aphasic group, the percentages are 32 percent and 68 percent, respectively. However, considering only patients with a left-sided lesion (23 females, 54 males), aphasia was noted in 17 females (74 percent) and 33 males (61 percent), a difference not observed in dextrals with a left-sided lesion and significant to the 0.05 level.

Aphasic features with some localizing significance include reduced verbal fluency score, associated with a (left) anterior lesion, and impaired comprehen-sion, associated with a posterior lesion. The lack of correlation for other features of the aphasic picture is consistent with the possibility of a more diffuse intrahemispheric language organization in left-handers; i.e., a lesion involving the speech zone, whether frontal, temporal, or parietal, tends to produce a similar pattern of aphasic speech. Moreover, one has the impression that left-handers may not fall into such clear diagnostic categories as dextral aphasics. Language impairments appear to be distributed more evenly over a range of performances. The high incidence of articulatory disorder and word-finding difficulty, the tendency for borderline fluency, and the absence in our material of logorrhea or jargon also should be emphasized.

The characteristics of aphasia in left-handers are similar to those in older children at an age beyond that at which mutism is the most likely symptom of a speech zone lesion. Conceivably, a relationship exists between the mutism of young children and the reduced verbal fluency scores in left-handed aphasics. It has been suggested that defective initiation may be responsible for this deficit (Ramier & Hécaen, 1970). Thus, it might be argued that reduced verbal fluency represents a kind of attenuated or mitigated mutism. This factor of reduced speech initiation might also explain the absence of logorrhea in both aphasic children and left-handers, and perhaps also the infrequency of fluent phonemic paraphasia previously noted.

Discussion

Our understanding of aphasic language derives almost completely from studies of standard right-handed patients with a left hemispheric lesion. However, there is much to be gained from considering other categories of aphasic disorders. We have studied aphasia in children, in anomalous dextrals with a right hemispheric lesion, and in left-handers with a right or left hemispheric lesion in order to determine more precisely the qualitative features of an aphasia in states of immature or anomalous lateralization. The evidence suggests that these three categories are in the nature of a continuum that relates to a gradual process of left dominance establishment.

Childhood aphasia tends to consist of mutism or agrammatism at an early age, and anomia and nonfluent phonemic paraphasia somewhat later. These two stages of childhood aphasia also represent the predominant syndromes of, respectively, crossed aphasia in dextrals and aphasia in left-handers. In early childhood, aphasia is invariably nonfluent. There is a gradual increase of fluent aphasic forms on into adolescence. Similarly, crossed aphasia in dextrals is usually nonfluent or, at the very least, fluent aphasias are extremely uncommon, while in aphasic left-handers, there is a definite bias toward nonfluency. Logorrhea and jargon do not occur in childhood aphasia or in crossed aphasia in dextrals, at least they have not been described, while in left-handed aphasics, logorrhea and jargon appear to be uncommon. This is also true of verbal paraphasia, which is rare in both young children and crossed aphasic dextrals and begins to occur only in late childhood and occasionally in aphasic left-handers (see Figure 4-1).

These considerations lead to the conclusion that aphasia type, whether in childhood, anomalous dextrals, or sinistrals, does not so much reflect the factor of handedness per se as the occurrence of brain damage in the course of a continual process of leftward lateralization that is occurring at different rates and at different levels of language learning in all three groups. From the point of view of the aphasia type, one can discern a series of dominance states leading from the anomalous dextral to the sinistral to the standard dextral. This series may correspond to an identical series of states encountered in children in the normal ontogenetic sequence. Moreover, it may prove possible to interpolate within the sinistrals two subgroups, those of familial and nonfamilial left-handedness, corresponding to increasing gradations of left hemispheric language representation. This would be consistent with the fact that nonfamilial left-handedness is more common than familial left-handedness, since the former is closer, in respect to dominance organization, to standard dextrals, while dominance in the anomalous dextral is the most "childlike" in the series and therefore the least common.

The decreasing frequency of aphasia with right-sided lesions in the course of childhood development is again recapitulated in adult groups. There is a pro-

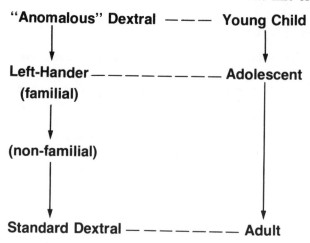

FIGURE 4-1. Degree of left-sided language representation.

gressive reduction in the incidence of aphasia with a right lesion, proceeding from familial to nonfamilial left-handers to anomalous dextrals to standard dextrals. Of course, one does not know whether an aphasia would develop in anomalous dextrals with a left-sided lesion. Some of these patients are undoubtedly included in any collection of standard aphasic adults, perhaps among those dextrals with agrammatism or mild or recovering aphasia after a left hemisphere lesion. Certainly, the similarity of crossed aphasia in dextrals to early childhood aphasia suggests that there is also a similar dominance pattern, namely, bilateral language representation, rather than a strict or truly anomalous language lateralization to the right hemisphere. If this is true, then language lateralization in the anomalous dextral represents a kind of arrest at the childhood stage. Similarly, in left-handers with right hemispheric language, as judged by aphasia with a lesion of that side, there would also be incomplete left lateralization rather than atypical lateralization to the right side. Thus, left-handers in whom an aphasia develops with a left hemispheric lesion may or may not also have right language representation, while those with an aphasia after a right hemispheric lesion would necessarily have language representation on the left side as well; i.e., aphasia would develop in the latter group with a lesion of either hemisphere.

These considerations suggest that left hemispheric language lateralization occurs to a varying degree in all individuals, but always to a greater extent than in the right hemisphere. Conceivably, handedness acts to facilitate or retard this process of dominance establishment in the left hemisphere. Since this possible influence would be accentuated in familial left-handedness but is unrelated to the actual strength of handedness, the postulated effect would be on the basis of a genetic preprogramming and not on the basis of hand use.

LATERALIZATION: A BRAIN MODEL*

In previous articles (Brown, 1975, 1976) a theory of language production has been described in which levels in normal (and pathological) language correspond (map on) to stages in the evolutionary and maturational history of the brain. The neural structure which results from this process of neocortical growth has an anterior (frontal) and posterior (temporo-parieto-occipital) component. The two main classes of aphasia, the nonfluent and the fluent aphasias, refer to these components, while the various aphasic syndromes within each class point to different levels within the anterior or posterior sector. The structure as a whole develops out of medial and paraventricular formations through several growth planes of limbic and paralimbic (transitional) cortex to a stage of generalized ("association," "integration") cortex. Within the latter, through a process of core or central differentiation, the primary motor (gigantopyramidalis) and sensory (koniocortical) zones appear (Figure 1-1).

For example, with respect to motor cortex, the evolutionary wave that had been assumed to lead from precentral to premotor strip, i.e., from primary motor cortex to "association" cortex (Campbell, 1905; Bailey & von Bonin, 1951) is actually the reverse of the true direction of neocortical growth. The premotor region, which is continous with and cytoarchitectonically indistinguishable from Broca's area, is in fact the *older* of the two areas (see Sanides, 1975). This suggests that studies of motor cortex which show a rostro-caudad topography, such as that of Woolsey et al. (1952), may be interpreted in the following way: that the proximal movements associated with more rostral stimulation represent phylo-ontogenetically (and cognitively) more ancient, i.e., earlier, phases in the elaboration of a motor act than the fine paw or digital movements elicited on precentral stimulation, which are later acquisitions. In other words, the axial and/or proximal movements of premotor stimulation point to more preliminary levels in the unfolding of a motor pattern than the highly individuated distal movements elicited on precentral stimulation. Extirpation studies in man suggest that the premotor area is part of a wider field for motor activity. In addition, the supplementary motor area, which is limbic-derived (paralimbic) cortex, has a complete representation of the body half which is less strongly contralateral in its organization than motor cortex. This suggests an evolutionary and microgenetic development of the motor act up through paralimbic, premotor, and then precentral regions.

The same interpretation applies to perceptual development, viz., object perception does not occur through a constructive phase of in-processing initiated in striate cortex (koniocortex), but rather develops in the reverse direction, over a series of levels to a koniocortical end phase. The study of disorders of perception

---

*From "Lateralization: A Brain Model" by J. W. Brown, 1978, *Brain and Language*, 5, 258–261. Copyright 1978 by Academic Press. Reprinted by permission.

supports the view that preperceptions develop through a limbic and paralimbic stage, through a parakoniocortical ("association" or generalized neocortex) phase, to a final modeling achieved through striate area (Brown, 1977).[1] Language (and cognition) also develops—is realized—over this system of structural levels. However, in man, a central point is that the transition from generalized to sensorimotor cortex occurs by way of an intermediate step, a differentiation in the course of ontogenesis within generalized neocortex of an asymmetric focal organization (Brown, 1975).

Maturation and Theory of Lateralization

The differentiation of asymmetric focal neocortex repeats the pattern established in the evolution of the sensorimotor areas, namely, a core differentiation of a specialized zone within a more generalized field. This phase is characterized by the gradual appearance, in both anterior and posterior isocortex, of an increasingly more focal and asymmetric (left lateralized) zone. The mammalian sequence from generalized → sensorimotor cortex thus becomes one from generalized → focal → sensorimotor cortex. The emergence of this interposed level out of a penultimate rather than a terminal phase is consistent with the general pattern of evolutionary branching from earlier, less individuated forms, rather than from end stages of specialization.

As inferred from pathological and other studies, the overall trend in the evolution of encephalized neocortex is from bilateral organization to unilateral hemispheric bias. This pattern is schematized in Figure 4-2. The essential feature of this model is that cerebral dominance does not come about as a (higher) stage beyond that of contralateral representation of sensory and motor cortices. Rather, *cerebral dominance—or lateral representation—occurs as an intermediate step between bilateral and contralateral representation.* The bilateral organization which is characteristic of limbic and transitional cortex develops, in man, through a stage of (left) lateral representation to one of contralateral or crossed representation. The stage of crossed representation, therefore, and not that of cerebral dominance, would be the end point of motor and perceptual (cognitive) realization.

Two further points about the model should be emphasized. First, the progression from bilateral through lateral to contralateral representation can be conceptualized, from the point of view of left hemisphere, as a successive dropping out of functional control as well as a progressive acquisition of novel organization. Second, these levels should not be understood simply in terms of

---

[1]The lesser degree of contralateral representation in auditory cortex, in comparison with somaesthetic, visual, and motor cortices, raises the possibility of selective pressures acting on the evolution of this region. The contralateral advantage, however, points in the direction of the major trend in sensorimotor cortex evolution, namely, toward contralateral representation.

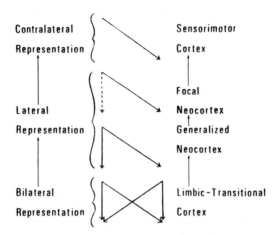

FIGURE 4-2. Although lateral representation (cerebral dominance) occurs as a final stage in neocortical evolution, it appears as a differentiation within a more preliminary level, intermediate between bilateral and contralateral representation.

connections to motor effectors or perceptual templates. Rather, they are productive levels in the representations of acts and percepts. The crossed organization of the visual half-fields, therefore, is analogous to that of motor cortex. Hemifield perception can be thought of as an end point of visual perception. It develops out of a bilaterally organized unitary field which characterizes the perception at more preliminary structural levels.

Finally, the development of lateral representation seems to have the further effect of an "asymmetrization" of earlier (bilateral) levels. In the course of maturation, these levels are gradually biased toward asymmetry, the effect being less pronounced at "deeper" than at more "superficial" stages. This process of asymmetrization may continue into late life. If so, it may account for certain psychological "deficits" of aging. These would reflect an increasing specification of the left-lateralized system rather than a process of cellular decay.

AGE, SEX, AND APHASIA TYPE*

with Ellen Grober

A major premise of most theories about the representation of language in the brain is that cerebral dominance is specified at birth (Kinsbourne & Hiscock,

*From "Age, Sex, and Aphasia Type" by J. W. Brown and E. Grober, 1983, *Journal of Nervous and Mental Disease, 170,* 431–434. Copyright 1983 by Williams & Wilkins. Adapted by permission.

1977) or is completed by age 5 (Krashen, 1972, 1973) or by puberty (Basser, 1962; Lenneberg, 1967; Zangwill, 1960). An alternative possibility is that lateralization is the expression of a growth process which continues over the life span (Brown & Hécaen, 1976; Brown & Jaffe, 1975). The latter hypothesis is consistent with age-specific trends in aphasia type that have subsequently been reported in the literature (Harasymiw & Halper, 1981; Miceli, Caltagirone, Gainotti, et al., 1981; Obler, Albert, Goodglass, & Bensen, 1978). In this paper, we present data regarding age-specific trends in aphasia type that are also gender specific. The interaction of age and sex on aphasia type seems to suggest a lateralization process that is slower in females than in males, a difference that provides a parsimonious explanation of previously reported gender related differences in lateralization (e.g., Bradshaw, Gates, & Nettleton, 1977; Lake & Bryden, 1976).

When Brown and Jaffe (1975) reviewed the clinical aphasia material, they noted an age specificity of certain aphasic disorders. For example, a lesion in Wernicke's area will produce motor aphasia in a child, conduction aphasia in middle age, and jargon aphasia in late life. This suggests a progressive differentiation or regional specification within the dominant hemisphere language zone. Language representation gradually develops from a diffuse, bilateral organization to a unilateral and focal one. In this process, expression may lateralize earlier than comprehension. The more diffuse representation of production mechanisms in younger patients accounts for the occurrence of nonfluent aphasia with more widely distributed lesions. The relative preservation of comprehension in these patients may reflect the contribution of the right hemisphere (see Searleman, 1977 for review) or intact portions of the left (Mohr & Pessin, 1978). Fluent aphasia, which is linked to comprehension deficits, rarely occurs in young patients. Rather, there is an increasing frequency of fluent aphasia into late life. Presumably this reflects the fact that comprehension is becoming more restricted to the left posterior language zone. Thus, the degree of lateralization at the time of brain damage determines not only the occurrence but type of aphasia. Nonfluent aphasia should predominate in younger patients or in subjects with relatively bilateral and diffuse language representation, whereas fluent or jargon aphasia should occur in older patients or in subjects with more lateralized and focal representation. Age is, therefore, an important predictor of aphasia type because it reflects the approximate degree of lateralization for a given individual.

Subjects

Our report is based upon the clinical records of all patients with aphasia seen at the Rheinische Landesklinik für Sprachgestörte in Bonn (Germany) between 1962 and 1975. Selection criteria included a single left-sided vascular lesion, no explicit reference to left-handedness, and a specific aphasia diagnosis. We excluded cases with questionable pathological findings, tumor and bilateral cases with traumatic or multiple lesions, and cases with progressive pathology. The majority of these patients were seen between 6 and 12 months postonset. Diagnosis was the final classification made at the Landesklinik. For example, a patient initially coded as a total aphasic, and subsequently as a mixed aphasic, was considered a mixed aphasic.

The classification is that of Leischner (1979). Total (global) aphasia refers to nonfluent speech with minimal comprehension. Mixed aphasia refers to nonfluent speech (single words or agrammatism) with moderate comprehension impairment, the so-called mixed anterior type in the American classification. Motor aphasia includes both typical Broca aphasics with good comprehension, and "motor amnestic" aphasics who also have word finding difficulty. Inasmuch as comparisons between the groups of motor and motor amnestic aphasics revealed no differences with regard to the relevant variables, they were combined into one motor aphasia group. Similarly, the categories of sensory aphasia, with severe comprehension impairment and fluent, mildly impaired speech, and "sensory amnestic" aphasia, with the addition to this picture of word finding and paraphasic errors, were combined into one sensory aphasia group. There were too few cases of phonemic (central, conduction) and amnestic aphasia for analysis. It is probable that some cases of phonemic aphasia were included in the group of sensory aphasics.

Results and Discussion

Three hundred eighty-nine patients satisfied the selection criteria. Two hundred seventy-three were male and 116 were female, a proportion reflecting the greater incidence of hypertension and stroke in the male population. Mean age for each aphasia type is given in Table 4-4. The average age for the entire population was 48.7. The average age of total and mixed aphasics was close to this average, whereas motor aphasics were younger and sensory aphasics were older than the overall group according to a median test ($\chi^2 = 33.53$, $df = 3$). The incidence of the various aphasias was compared over the life span, beginning in the second decade and ending in the seventh. The type of aphasia that occurred was dependent upon the age of onset ($\chi^2 = 52.34$, $df = 15$). Motor aphasia tended to dominate through the fourth decade of life; mixed and total aphasia, the fifth decade; and sensory aphasia, the sixth. A goodness of fit test performed on the distribution of each aphasia type by decade indicated a reasonably good fit to a normal curve: for motor aphasia ($\chi^2 = 2.92$, $df = 5$); mixed aphasia ($\chi^2 = 2.56$, $df = 5$); and total aphasia ($\chi^2 = 4.53$, $df = 5$). In contrast, the relationship between the incidence of sensory aphasia and age of onset can best be described by a linear function (correlation $= .92$, $p < .05$) beginning at about the middle of the third decade and steadily increasing through the seventh. The small number of sensory aphasics in the eighth decade might reflect the fact that elderly patients with this disorder would be less likely to be referred to a clinic that is

Table 4-4   Number and Mean Age of Patients by Sex and Aphasia Type

	Motor		Mixed		Total		Sensory		All Categories	
	N	Age	N	Age	N	Age	N	Age	N	Age
Male	106	47.2	58	50.3	76	51.2	33	55.9	273	50.0
Female	52	41.3	29	45.6	26	48.9	9	59.0	116	45.5
All subjects	158	45.3	87	48.8	102	50.6	42	56.5	389	48.7

primarily a rehabilitation service. Such cases might be considered poor candidates for speech therapy either because of advanced age or for reasons of senile changes.

Conceivably, the age specificity of aphasia type could reflect differences in lesion location between young and old subjects. We consider this unlikely for several reasons. First, the same age-specific trends for motor and sensory aphasia were present in a separate analysis of 50 trauma cases, where a random distribution of lesions might be expected. That is, motor aphasics were younger (30.7) and sensory aphasics were older (57.4) than the average age of the trauma group (34.2). The fact that this pattern has been documented for tumor cases as well (Miceli, et al., 1981) renders unlikely explanations of age specificity in aphasia type that involve differences in lesion location with age. Second, nonfluent aphasias (i.e., motor plus mixed) developed 95 per cent of the time in subjects younger than 30 and 45 per cent of the time in subjects older than 60 (Table 4-5). If this pattern were due to lesion location, and, if only anterior lesions produce nonfluent aphasias, there would have to be dramatic differences in lesion dis-

Table 4-5   Relative Incidence of Aphasic Disorders over the Life Span for Males and Females

Aphasia Type	Sex	Age				
		<30	30s	40s	50s	>60
Nonfluent aphasia	M	.95	.69	.69	.57	.44
(mixed + motor)	F	.95	.87	.72	.59	.47
Total aphasia	M	.00	.29	.22	.32	.29
	F	.05	.09	.26	.34	.13
Sensory aphasia	M	.05	.02	.09	.11	.27
	F	.00	.04	.02	.07	.40

tribution with age to account for the incidence of nonfluent aphasias among the young and old subjects in the sample. No such differences in lesion location have been described. Moreover, nonfluent aphasia occurs in children with surgically documented posterior lesions (e.g., Hécaen, 1976). In youth, posterior as well as anterior lesions produce a nonfluent aphasia. In later life, nonfluent aphasias occur primarily or exclusively with anterior lesions. Thus, nonfluent aphasias should be twice as frequent in youth as in late life, an expectation confirmed by our data.

The hypothesis of continuing lateralization over the life span provides a framework for incorporating the sex differences we found in aphasia type. Table 4-5 presents a breakdown of the relative incidence of aphasic disorders over the life span for men and women. Nonfluent aphasias are the rule in early life for both sexes. They tend to dominate the third decade as well, but more so for females than for males ($z = 1.67$, $.05 < p < .10$). During this time, total aphasia occurs more often in males than in females ($z = 1.96$, $p < .05$). During midlife (40s and 50s), males and females display the same pattern. Nonfluent aphasias are still quite common in both sexes, but total and sensory aphasias are occurring with increasing frequency. In late life, sensory aphasia occurs more often than total aphasia among women over 60 ($z = 1.66$, $.05 < p < .10$), while both occur with equal frequency in men of the same age.

We think that these patterns can be explained by different rates of regional specification for males and females. During early life, male and female brains are relatively bilateral and diffusely organized for language. Thus, nonfluent aphasias are common. The continued preponderance of nonfluent aphasias among females in the third decade suggests that lateralization proceeds more slowly than in males. The rise in total aphasia among males of the same age suggests a shift to a more lateralized and focal brain organization. In midlife, the rate of regional specification appears to decrease for males, or perhaps accelerate for females. The net effect is that the female brain becomes as lateralized and focally organized as the male brain, and both display similar patterns of aphasic disorders. The difference in regional specification rate may persist into late life, resulting in more focally organized anterior and posterior language zones in female than in male brains. This could explain why females develop sensory aphasia more often than total aphasia, whereas males display an equal incidence of both.

The hypothesis that females have a slower rate of regional specification than males, at least until midlife, is compatible with numerous experimental and clinical reports in which women are found to be less lateralized for language than men (Harris, 1978; Lake & Bryden, 1976; McGlone, 1980). Males are more likely to display hemispheric asymmetries than females in dichotic listening tasks (Harshman, Remington, & Krashen, 1974; Lake & Bryden, 1976) and in visual field studies (Bradshaw, Gates, & Nettleton, 1977; Hannay & Malone, 1976).

Left-sided lesions are less likely to produce aphasia in females than in males (McGlone, 1978). When an aphasia does develop, it tends to be less severe in females than in males (McGlone, 1978).

We suggest that the neural substrate underlying this difference is the slower rate of regional specification in females. Furthermore, lateralization considered over the life span suggests the possibility that the differential regional specification rate within the dominant hemisphere language zone may reflect differing effects of androgens and estrogens on protein synthesis. If so, lateralization—or regional specification—can be viewed as the expression of a central nervous system growth process. Specifically, age and sex interactions in aphasia type occur as the expression of cerebral growth and concomitant protein synthesis. The rate of this process would be influenced by genetic and other factors, including the effects of the sex hormones (Goy & McEwen, 1980; Hoyenga & Hoyenga, 1979). According to this interpretation, the increase in the rate of protein synthesis associated with the release of androgens in males at puberty results in a spurt in regional brain growth, whereas the outpouring of estrogens in pubescent females leads to a decrease in regional specification rate. This would explain the greater degree of lateralization that has been reported for males. The gradual decrease in androgen levels in aging males may reduce the rate of regional differentiation, whereas the precipitous decline of estrogen levels in postmenopausal females may accelerate the rate, resulting in more focally organized language zones in female brains. This would explain the higher incidence of female sensory aphasics in late life.

Finally, it should be noted that this interpretation is consistent with recent evidence of continuing dendritic growth in the human brain (Buel & Coleman, 1979), greater dendritic arborization in the left Broca area in comparison with the right (Scheibel, Fried, Paul, et al., 1982), and dendritic growth in the adult avian brain with gonadal hormones (DeVoogd & Nottebohm, 1981).

RIGHT HEMISPHERE LANGUAGE*

Lesions of the right hemisphere lead to difficulty in the comprehension of semantic material. Eisenson (1962) first noted an impairment on complex tasks, more pronounced when listening to others. Critchley (1962) mentioned cases with circumlocution and the use of odd synonyms. Language deficits in right hemisphere cases were reported by Marcie, Hécaen, Dubois, and Angelergues (1965) and Archibald and Wepman (1968). Lesser (1974) found difficulty in pointing to objects on a choice card with semantic foils, but not on comparable

*From "Hierarchy and Evolution in Neurolinguistics" by J. W. Brown, 1981. In M. Arbib, D. Caplan, and J. Marshall (Eds.), *Neural Models of Language Processes*. New York: Academic Press. Copyright 1982 by Academic Press. Adapted by permission.

tests of phonology and syntax; these findings were largely confirmed by Tägert, Chock, Niklas, Sandvoss, and Sipos (1975) and Gainotti, Caltagirone, and Miceli (1979).

The conclusion that can be drawn from these studies is that lesions of the right hemisphere, in perhaps 20–40% of cases, give rise to *semantic impairments in comprehension*. Moreover, if comprehension is sufficiently impaired, production errors may occur, with confabulation or circumlocutory speech, which is an early sign, by the way, of semantic jargon.

In contrast, motor aphasia occurs in 1–2% of dextral adults with right hemisphere lesions (Zangwill, 1967), and in about 7% of adult right-handers after right-sided amytal injection (Milner, 1974). Some years ago, I reported a case of crossed aphasia in a dextral (Brown and Wilson, 1973) and collected seven additional cases in the literature meeting certain minimal criteria: adequate description of the aphasia; right-handedness without family history of left-handedness; a unilateral lesion; and no prior history of a neurological disorder. Since then, many other cases have been described (e.g., April and Han, 1980; April and Tse, 1977; Assal, Perentes, & Diruaz, 1981; Haaland & Miranda, 1980; Trojanowski, Green, & Levine 1980; Wechsler, 1976), confirming the impression that *agrammatism* is the chief form of a right hemisphere "expressive" aphasia.

In these patients, there is evidence for *bilateral language representation*. The absence of limb apraxia and failure to observe a "hooked" writing posture in the right hand argue for a left hemisphere role in writing and skilled movement. The finding in half the cases of marked constructional impairments suggests that spatial ability is not simply shifted to the opposite side in the presence of atypical right hemisphere language. There is also a case (Angelergues, Hécaen, Djindjian and Jarrie-Hazan, 1962) with aphasic deterioration after *left* carotid amytalization. Finally, as pointed out before (Brown, 1977), the pattern of crossed aphasia in dextrals—initial mutism and agrammatism—resembles that of early childhood aphasia where bilateral language representation might be anticipated.

There is in the literature a case of crossed aphasia with agrammatism who was shown to have a left ear preference on dichotic listening (Denes & Caviezel, 1981). This result was interpreted to indicate right hemisphere language dominance in spite of the well-known problem inferring lateral asymmetries with this method. More important, perhaps, was the dramatic recovery which occurred in this case with a right Sylvian lesion, so large as to probably obviate compensation through the damaged hemisphere. This was also true in the case of Assal, Perentes, & Diruaz (1981).

More problematic are cases with fluent aphasia or jargon. Yarnell (1981) described three crossed aphasics with fluent phonemic paraphasia (phonemic or conduction aphasia). However, in two of the patients there was a history of previous neurological disease, and in none of the cases was family handedness background ascertained. This is important, as left-handedness in a parent or sib would have been grounds for exclusion of the case as a probable "crypto"-sinistral. Pillon, Desi, and Lhermitte (1979) reported two patients with crossed aphasia which resolved leaving a jargon *agraphia*. They argued that jargon writing associated with a right-sided lesion implies right language dominance. However, I doubt that Lhermitte would employ the same argument to maintain that cases of left jargonaphasia with *good* writing, such as he has previously reported, do not have language dominance in the left hemisphere! The significance of preferential involvement or sparing of writing with brain damage is not yet clear. In fact, I am aware of a case of crossed aphasia with *agrammatism* and *jargon agraphia,* certainly a peculiar combination in a typical left-damaged patient. Indeed, I have even seen a markedly nonfluent (presumably dextral) crossed aphasic with a type of neologistic jargon. Speech consisted of single-word nonsense utterances. Such cases suggest that fluency and aphasia type may dissociate.

These cases show that fluent aphasia, most often phonemic (conduction) aphasia, possibly even jargon, can occur in crossed aphasic dextrals, though it is probably infrequent. Jargonaphasia occurs in left-handers with right hemisphere lesion, but it is also infrequent (Brown and Hécaen, 1976). With regard to language laterality, there is probably a similarity between the left-hander with a right hemisphere lesion and a fluent aphasia, and the right-hander with a right hemisphere lesion and fluent aphasia. What we are probably seeing is one of a continuum of laterality states irrespective of handedness. Still, in spite of sporadic cases of fluent crossed aphasia, there does appear to be a bias toward nonfluency and, in particular, agrammatism. I do not believe this to be an accident of lesion localization in this patient group, as suggested by some writers. Indeed, the same argument has been used to explain the frequency of nonfluency in younger patients, where it has finally been laid to rest by the data from traumatic cases.

How can the pattern in right hemisphere cases of *semantic* errors in comprehension, and *agrammatism* in production, be explained? Consider first the situation with lesions of the left hemisphere. As discussed, the *left* Broca (F3) and Wernicke (T1) zones can probably be viewed as phonological processors. Damage to left F3 gives phonetic-articulatory errors in nonfluent speech; damage to left T1 gives phonemic paraphasias in fluent speech (see Figure 4-3). On the other hand, the anatomical correlation of agrammatism and semantic impairments is less precise. Agrammatism is probably associated with lesions surrounding or partly involving left F3; semantic errors in comprehension (and production) are probably associated with lesions surrounding or partly involving left T1. These are regions of "generalized" neocortex.

Now consider the situation in the right hemisphere, which to a variable extent is deprived of a Wernicke and Broca zone specified for phonological processing. These zones in right hemisphere are comparable, functionally, to the "generalized" neocortex of left hemisphere. This is the neocortical ground out of

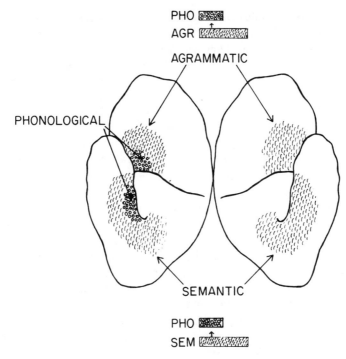

FIGURE 4-3. Regional specification of the left hemisphere leads to anterior and posterior zones mediating phonological processing. The background zone in left and right hemisphere mediates a prephonological stage. In the anterior system, this concerns a rhythmic oscillator which is linked to the intonational pattern. In the posterior system, this is a stage of lexical selection.

which the Wernicke and Broca areas differentiate. A lesion of "generalized" neocortex in right hemisphere, which therefore includes both the homologous right Wernicke and Broca zones *plus* adjacent areas, gives that form of aphasia associated with left hemisphere lesions of generalized neocortex only.

Specifically, the generalized neocortex adjacent to the Broca and Wernicke areas in the *left* hemisphere, and the "generalized" neocortex of *right* hemisphere (Broca and Wernicke zones plus adjacent neocortex) form a common level mediating a prephonological processing stage. In the anterior sector, the level mediates a rhythmic function elaborating the intonational pattern. A lesion of this level gives agrammatism. In the posterior sector, the level incorporates a multi-tiered system of word-meaning relationships. A lesion of this level gives semantic errors. The resultant form of aphasia is *level specific* regardless of hemisphere involved, though more pronounced with left-sided pathology.

Evidence that the isolated right hemisphere is deficient in syntax makes it difficult to understand on this basis the occurrence of agrammatism with right hemisphere pathology. In fact, this is more consistent with a right hemisphere bias for intonation and other rhythmic functions, and possible links to agramma-tism. On the other hand, evidence of good lexical-semantic capacity in the isolated right hemisphere explains the finding of semantic impairments in right hemisphere cases as well as clinical observations that bilateral lesions are generally required for semantically anomalous jargon (Brown, 1981b). In-cidentally, the occurrence of agrammatism and semantic impairments with right hemisphere lesions is a good illustration of the notion that pathology does not just lead to deficient performances but displays processing.

The concept of a bihemispheric semantic level, or one mediating rhythmic functions, and a left-lateralized phonological level helps to explain some observations in commissurotomy patients. Evidence for shared access to axial and/or proximal motor systems—so-called ipsilateral control—points to the unitary orgranization of primitive levels in motor behavior. It is not simply a matter of ipsilateral nerve fibers; rather, early levels in the temporal structure of a movement develop as part of a unitary bihemispheric system. There is also evidence that each hemisphere in the split has access to a unitary visual field (Holtzman, Sidtis, Volpe, & Gazzaniga, 1980; Trevarthen, 1974). Lesion stud-ies (Denny-Brown & Fischer, 1976) indicate that midbrain segmental mech-anisms construct a unified percept of the two half-fields. Even semantic content may be represented in a unitary field. There are commissurotomy cases who demonstrate semantic sharing between the "disconnected" hemispheres. Ver-balizations occur to right hemisphere stimuli, for example, the subject saying "jump" when the word *sit* is flashed in the left visual field (Nebes, 1978). Cross-field semantic priming has been demonstrated in splits (Gazzaniga, 1980).

Such observations indicate that right hemisphere contents are to some extent also in the left hemisphere but "buried" at earlier processing stages. Certainly, there is sufficient evidence from lexical decision tasks and the pathological material to identify semantic processing with preliminary cognition. The degree of semantic sharing in splits reflects the degree to which a content has "come up" in a unitary system of lexical selection. The supposed transfer of affective or experiential relations would instead represent only the most preliminary selection in this unitary system, while the achievement of an adequate conceptual field ("jump" for *sit*) reflects the capacity for a further narrowing down toward the target.

RETHINKING THE RIGHT HEMISPHERE*

Clinical and behavioral investigations of cognition have demonstrated an apparent right hemisphere bias or specialization on a variety of visuospatial or

---

*From "Rethinking the Right Hemisphere" by J. W. Brown, 1983. In E. Perecman (Ed.), *Cognitive Processing in the Right Hemisphere*. New York: Academic Press. Copyright 1983 by Academic Press. Reprinted by permission.

"holistic" tasks. Although the relationship between visuospatial capacity and the right hemisphere has been documented by numerous studies, its basis is still poorly understood. This chapter argues that the right hemisphere has neither a special role or function in cognition, nor a different style of cognition, but that the terms *holistic* and *analytic* capture differences at successive moments in a processing continuum, not parallel operations. It will be shown that symptoms of right hemisphere damage, especially to the temporoparietal region, as well as right hemisphere effects on various behavioral measures, and right-left differences in commissurotomy cases, can all be explained by a theory of perception in which the parietal lobe of the right and left hemispheres forms a *unitary* system mediating a preliminary stage in perception.

Introduction

Current accounts of visual perception assume that each visual half field is independent of the other at initial stages of perceptual processing and that the visual half fields eventually fuse into a unitary visual space. These accounts posit in-processing of stimuli over the geniculocortical system. Form perception is mediated by visual cortex, and object construction occurs as a secondary process after registration in the striate area. The object is constructed out of its sensory elements and then mapped onto spatial coordinates in relation to the position of the body. According to this view, the parietal region has a control function in the interaction between object and viewer, and provides a continual update of the perception in relation to the body surround.

Of particular interest in the context of this chapter is the position that the half fields of visual space differentiate out of a unitary preobject space. A lesion of the right hemisphere involves and so exposes the parietal segment of the object formative process. This segment, the forming left hemifield, is normally submerged within the object as a "preprocessing" stage. According to this view, the symptoms of parietal damage do not reflect disruptions of "higher order" computations subsequent to the (conscious) perception of an object but are disruptions at a point where an object is first selected out of the egocentric space of mental imagery into a three-dimensional space of objects and object relations.

The prominence of parietal mechanisms in behavior involving an interaction between viewer and object points to the transitional nature of this phase in object formation. The "interaction" reflects the incomplete separation of internal space. Both viewer and object are part of the same space field. The use of the hand on the object in reaching or constructional tasks draws upon this space in a more explicit manner. This is also true for tests of spatial relations. The space elaborated by parietal mechanisms is closer to the perceiver than the independent space of "real" objects. When the perceiver is asked to cognize spatial relations, it is this more preliminary phase that is being challenged.

It is in this sense that parietal lesions involve a preprocessing stage. They interfere with perception at the stage of interaction between the viewer and the object field, a stage in object formation prior to the complete exteriorization of perceptual space. Preprocessing is linked to object relations and conceptual mechanisms. In language perception, preprocessing is bound up with a lexical-semantic operation. End stage processing in visual perception is linked to an analysis of features defining the form of an object. The same stage in language perception involves phonological processing or the analysis of properties defining the sound form of an utterance.

The experimental procedures used to investigate object perception challenge cognition in different ways. Those which engage early stages in perception give a spurious right hemisphere effect because preliminary cognition represents a ceiling on cognitive unfolding in the right hemisphere. However, the same cognitive level which is preliminary in the right hemisphere undergoes further analysis in the left hemisphere. This is why tasks that involve late or end stage processing yield a left hemisphere effect. The right hemisphere bias for preliminary processing is an artifact due to the relative sequestration of phonological processing, and with it a feature analytic stage in perception, to the left hemisphere.

This level of perceptual processing in the left hemisphere constitutes a new stage in perception and a new level in consciousness and behavior. Specifically, the advent of phonological analysis in language perception brings with it the possibility of a finer differentiation of features in a nonverbal perceptual array. In fact, the selection of the features of a visual perception is comparable to the selection of phonemes to "fill in" the abstract frames of lexical representations. When this occurs, conceptual or object relations (semantic relations in language processing) recede into the background, and the features of the percept, whether visuospatial or linguistic, become more salient. Accordingly, the phonological level of language processing elaborates a level of cognition that is continuous with the feature analytic stage of other perceptual systems.

A by-product of this process is that the left hemisphere becomes disadvantaged in access to early cognition. Conversely, preliminary processing in right hemisphere is close to the cognitive end point of that hemisphere. A right or left hemisphere advantage arises when a task favors early or late processing. Specifically, right-left asymmetries reflect differential access to preliminary processing in a unitary cognitive system.

There is a wealth of clinical evidence for this new account of perception, coming especially from the study of hallucinatory and agnosic states (Brown, 1983b, 1983c). In the following section, the model is considered in relation to perceptual asymmetries, beginning with the problem of constructional disability in brain-damaged patients.

Constructional (Dis)ability is Equally Represented in Right and Left Hemisphere

A disorder of visuospatial cognition was first described by Kleist (1934) as a disturbance "in formative activities (arranging, building, drawing), where the

spatial part of the task is lacking although there is no apraxia of single movements." Kleist used the term *optic apraxia* since he thought that perception and
praxis were intact but that there was an interruption of an association between the
visual and the motor image. Later the term *constructional apraxia* came into use,
to indicate a relationship to other complex motor disorders with lesions of the *left*
hemisphere.

However, there was evidence of a perceptual impairment. Pick noted that
patients had difficulty understanding drawings. He claimed that there was an
impairment in the composition of the parts of the figure into a whole, that it was
a type of perceptual disturbance. Other workers proposed a regression in
the analysis of spatial relationships (see Lange, 1936), a loss in spatial structure
such that objects failed to achieve a clear perceptual organization. Disorders in localization and attention were present. Mayer-Gross (1936) found inability to analyze a real or imaginary pattern as a whole. His concept of "activity space" *(Wirkraum),* in which the disorder is bound up with the space of the
arm's reach, is relevant to modern studies of optic grasping and spatial localization.

Visuospatial impairment was first linked to the *right* hemisphere by Dide
(1938). Duensing (1953) distinguished between a perceptually based defect with
right hemisphere lesions (visuospatial *agnosia*) and a motor executive defect
with left hemisphere lesions (constructional *apraxia*). Subsequently, there were
many attempts to document right-left differences in constructional impairment.

The drawings of left-sided cases were said to show more hesitation and
greater simplification, and to be facilitated by copying from a model (Nielson,
1975) whereas those of right-damaged cases were characterized as comparable in
complexity to the model, though disorganized (Piercy, Hécaen, & Ajuriaguerra,
1960). Right-sided cases had difficulty in representing perspective, and tended to
orient the drawing on a diagonal (see Mendilaharsu, Miglionico, Mendilaharsu,
Budelli, & DeSouto, 1968). It was thought that constructional disability in
right-sided cases predicted a parietal lesion, whereas in left cases the lesion could
be frontal or parietal. These descriptive studies gradually gave way to experimental investigations, and as this occurred the right-left differences became
increasingly more difficult to substantiate.

Some hints of this were reported in the paper of Arrigoni and DeRenzi
(1964). This study confirmed the greater frequency and severity of constructional
disability with right brain damage, but attributed this to an unequal lesion size
in the two groups. When left and right cases were matched for reaction time
(i.e., presumably for lesion size), the differences were no longer significant.
Despite some methodological shortcomings, the main conclusions of this
study have been confirmed by subsequent research. The right-left difference
is due to the presence of hemispatial neglect in right-damaged cases, and to
the exclusion of severe aphasics from the left-damaged group. When allowance
is made for these factors, the difference between left and right cases is no
longer present.

Thus, *from an initial association with left, then right brain damage, the disorder is now regarded as comparable in left- and right-lesioned cases.* This conclusion is consistent with the idea that the elaboration of object space is bihemispherically mediated, and that both hemispheres participate about equally in this process. It leaves unexplained the right hemisphere bias with nonverbal measures, and the evidence in commissurotomy cases of superior right hemisphere spatial ability. The explanation of these phenomena, however, will become clearer after a consideration of the one perceptual symptom for which there is a clear right hemisphere predilection.

Left Hemispatial Neglect

The terms *hemispatial neglect, inattention,* and *agnosia* refer to an altered awareness for half of perceptual or bodily space. The disorder is chiefly associated with lesions of the parietal area of the right hemisphere. In Gloning, Gloning, and Hoff's (1968) study, a right-sided lesion was even more common among left-handers. Constructional impairment and hemispatial "agnosia" may occur independently. Patients may show marked inattention with good constructional performance and the reverse. Patients with anterior lesions may also show inattention, so-called frontal neglect, probably a mild form of the parietal disorder (Chedru, 1976). A visual field defect is common but not obligatory. The patient can "see" on the affected side but does not attend to that side. There is probably defective imagery on the impaired side (Bisiach, 1980). The deficit in right parietal cases is not material specific; both verbal and nonverbal stimuli are ignored. This may not be true in left-damaged cases.

Neglect is usually most apparent in the periphery of the field (see Zihl & von Cramon, 1979), though it often involves the entire field into the parafoveal region, and may "spill over" into the intact field. Kinsbourne and Warrington (1962) found that right hemispheric cases may neglect the left side of words presented in the "intact" right hemifield. Bisiach, Capitani, Luzzatti, and Perani (1981) have shown that the extent of neglect changes with the orientation of the body. Such cases indicate that neglect is a dynamic alteration not easily accounted for by a cortical retinal map. These observations are also consistent with the idea that the *visual half field differentiates out of a unitary space.*

Left hemispatial neglect can be interpreted in the following way. The clinicopathological data, reviewed in the preceding paragraphs, indicate bilateral processing of visuospatial information. Space perception is symmetrically organized in animals. However, in man bilateral symmetry of spatial representation is obscured by the elaboration of a phonological component. The preferential involvement of right hemisphere lesions in hemispatial neglect occurs as a result of this left hemisphere specialization. The lesion of right hemisphere involves, and so exposes, the parietal segment of the object formative process. This segment—the forming left hemifield—is normally submerged within the object as a "preprocessing" stage. The neglect occurs because the end point of cognitive processing is centered about a feature analytic level which cannot access into analytic cognition the more preliminary stage disrupted by the lesion. The neglect or inattention is the sign of the unaccessed void in the forming left hemifield (Figure 4-4); the access problem *is* the inattention.

Neglect is uncommon with left hemisphere lesions but it does occur. For either left- or right-sided neglect, a large lesion is ordinarily required. However, such a lesion in the left hemisphere will tend to involve adjacent regions in the posterior superior temporal area mediating phonological representation. The involvement of these regions obviates the access problem. This does not imply that the right half of space is not disrupted, only that the disruption is not submerged within an intact subsequent level. Nor is neglect simply obscured in left-damaged cases by a concomitant aphasia. It is not the presence of aphasia but the rarity of a lesion intersecting the parietal cortex without involving neighboring regions underlying phonological representation that accounts for the infrequency of right hemispatial neglect. Aphasia alone does not invalidate tests for spatial neglect. It is common to see global aphasics point out or hold up their hemiplegic right arm when asked about their difficulty, though this is unusual in left hemiplegics. An implicit, nonverbal, or tacit neglect of the hemiplegic right side is rare. This is because neglect points to an interlevel access limitation which is not present in patients with phonological disruption.

It should be pointed out that according to this view spatial neglect is not a disturbance of attention. The term *inattention* used for this disorder implies incorrectly that there is damage to an attentional mechanism. Some workers have looked for lateral asymmetries in such a mechanism, others an attentional "circuit" in the brain. These simplistic interpretations betray a lack of ingenuity on the part of the clinician. The first question that should be asked is, what is attention?

One can say that attention is not extrinsic to perception but is part of the perceptual process. Disorders of attention and perception do not dissociate. The state of attention reflects the state of perceptual processing at a given moment. A focused attention is the same as an articulated perception. These are different ways of describing the same state. Put differently, to cognize an object in an analytic mode requires a discrete or selective type of attention. The perception is built up around object features. Conversely, holistic or global perception accompanies a more diffuse attention which is distributed over the object field (Brown, 1983b).

The attentional state of the left hemisphere can be characterized as focused, and that of the right as diffuse; but in what sense is attention impaired in hemispatial neglect except that the right hemisphere (holistic) mode is not consistently derived to an (analytic) end stage? The situation is similar to that in the split-brain patient (discussed in what follows). However, in the split, although the limitation in access to a left hemisphere mode is more pronounced,

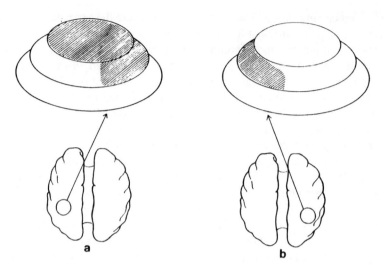

FIGURE 4-4. Hemispatial agnosia reflects a lack of access from a "surface" level to a more preliminary disruption. It is more common with right-sided lesions (b) because these do not disturb the surface level. The association is with lesions of generalized neocortex. The disorder may occur with left hemisphere lesions (a) when the pathology is interposed between levels. However, a smaller, more selective lesion is required. As illustrated here, the lesion will tend to involve adjacent structures mediating phonological realization, and thus obviate the access problem. Since the disorder requires a large lesion, it will be much less common with left hemisphere pathology.

the perception that is realized by the right hemisphere is more developed. In the case of left spatial neglect, the access limitation is incomplete but, because of the pathological lesion, there is a more preliminary object. The failure of the right hemisphere to attend to objects on the left side indicates a lack of full differentiation of its object field. The incomplete resolution of the object is accompanied by a more diffuse attention. Objects differentiate fully into the right visual field. The focal attention (perception) for the right field and the diffuse attention (perception) for the left account for much of the clinical behavior of such patients. From time to time, left field objects do complete their development, giving the mistaken impression of normal or potentially normal perceptions.

Thus, hemispatial neglect involves two symptoms: first, a disruption of contralateral space, which occurs perhaps equally with lesions of either hemisphere; second, a lack of awareness for the disrupted level, which occurs chiefly with right hemisphere lesions and reflects the inability of one cognitive mode to access another that is more preliminary. The failure to derive left visual field (right hemisphere) contents to a left hemisphere end stage is comparable to the inability in the waking state to retrieve the submerged cognition of a dream.

Behavioral Evidence for Cognitive Asymmetries

Behavioral studies of laterality in normal subjects using dichotic or hemifield presentations have consistently demonstrated a right hemisphere preference for nonverbal stimuli of various sorts (e.g., faces, dots, shapes) and a left hemisphere bias for most types of verbal and visual stimuli. Left hemisphere effects are observed for feature or component detection on various perceptual tasks, while a right hemisphere effect occurs for verbal stimuli when the task involves early processing (e.g., script, semantic priming). Changing laterality occurs for some material (faces, music, etc.) depending on the degree to which it is analyzed. The relation to skill or familiarity is also a relection of degree of analysis. Such observations indicate that it is not the material but the operation applied to this material which determines laterality. Another way of putting this is that lateral asymmetries arise according to whether the operation challenged in an experiment involves an early or late stage in cognitive processing.

Set in this light, the behavioral data can be interpreted in the same way as the lesion cases. Specifically, a right hemisphere advantage appears when the task involves initial stages of processing, a left hemisphere advantage when the task involves end stage processing. The relative proximity to end stage processing determines hemisphere bias on a particular task.

The Meaning of the Callosal Syndrome

The study of callosal patients provides what seems to be solid evidence for right-left differences in spatial capacity. However, the interpretation of these findings is not altogether clear. For one thing, the work relies chiefly on hemifield presentations and the assumption that input is restricted to a single hemisphere, an assumption which may be incorrect. Thus, Trevarthen (1970) found integration across the vertical meridian in splits, and Holtzman, Sidtis, Volpe, and Gazzaniga (1980) have demonstrated between-field spatial priming. These findings indicate that each hemisphere has access to a unitary visual field at a preliminary stage, certainly at upper brainstem, probably at even higher levels. Lesion studies in monkey have been interpreted to show that midbrain tegmental mechanisms construct a unified percept of the two half fields (Denny-Brown & Fischer, 1976). Comparable findings have been reported in humans with upper brainstem lesions (Brown, 1983b). Cases with midbrain or limbic hallucination may not show a hemianopic tendency. The visual field is replaced by a scenic, two-dimensional, at times even cycloramic hallucination. Presumably, the elaboration of a deep level, unitary space, occurs through the retinotectal system which comprises as much as 20–30% of optic tract fibers (Bernheimer, 1899).

In other studies, left field presentations in some commissurotomy cases have elicited verbal and affective responses which suggest interhemispheric transfer. Nebes (1978) has described verbalizations in splits which are semantically related to left field verbal stimuli. Interhemispheric "transfer" of affect has been reported. Gazzaniga (1980) has demonstrated cross-field semantic priming. One interpretation of these effects is that of transfer over the anterior commissure, but the phenomenon has been described in cases with section of this pathway (Zaidel, 1980). The idea that left hemisphere verbalization, semantically or affectively linked to right hemisphere stimuli, reflects cross-cueing or right hemisphere speech directly, is an ad hoc interpretation without much experimental support. It is comparable to the invocation of ipsilateral motor pathways to account for correct responses to verbal commands with the left hand, a phenomenon which might suggest that there is also a shared deep motor organization.

In my view, these findings can be explained by assuming a unified semantic representation prior to a representation of object form. Conceivably, cross-field semantic effects point to the degree to which a target can differentiate—or the degree to which it is selected—through this unified field. This is consistent with observations in aphasia which indicate that the representation of word meaning proceeds from an early stage organized about symbolic, affective, and experiential relations to a later conceptual stage (Brown, 1979a). The verbalization to the left field stimulus would reflect the degree to which the content has "come up" in this system. This interpretation of lexical-semantic phenomena in the split is identical to that for visuospatial material. Specifically, semantic or symbolic transformation, or a stage of object relations, reflects early processing; phonological or form analysis reflects end stage processing.

A second point to be emphasized is that studies of spatial capacity in splits have not consistently demonstrated right-left differences on perceptual tasks. For example, right and left field performance on block design patterns is comparable when the response involves matching to a choice card. The asymmetry appears when a manual reconstruction of the pattern is required. In fact, most studies that show lateral asymmetries for spatial ability rely on differences in copying, construction activity, or writing. Gazzaniga has stressed the role of limb behavior in this effect. It is the constructional activity of the right or left hand which introduces the asymmetry. Assuming that spatial capacity is equally represented between the hemispheres—an assumption that has not been disconfirmed by the experimental work—how does the response mode, that of vocal or limb movement, influence or determine hemispheric differences on spatial tasks?

As hand response in the split reflects the cognitive level in the contralateral hemisphere, the right hand-left hemisphere will be at a disadvantage in access to spatial cognition. This accounts for a left hand superiority on drawing tasks. Conversely, the left hand-right hemisphere will be relatively unable to analyze a lexical-semantic representation in right hemisphere into its constituent sounds or letters. This gives rise to a left-sided agraphia. In this view, writing or drawing are comparable to speech, in that they are motor performances that make underlying representations explicit, that is, they involve analysis of underlying configurations through sequential or kinetic patterns of movement.

Some recent findings in patients with right hemiplegia and severe aphasia support this conclusion (Brown, Leader, & Blum, 1983). Such patients have been found to write fairly well words to dictation using the hemiplegic right arm with the aid of a prosthesis, though they are profoundly agraphic with the intact left hand. Moreover, the ability to write words to dictation with the hemiplegic limb may be superior to the ability to produce the same words in speech. The phenomenon of hemiplegic writing is interpreted as reflecting access to preliminary lexical representations through the use of older proximal motor systems in the right arm.

Finally, the view that right and left hemisphere elaborate a unitary cognition which undergoes further processing in left hemisphere explains many other normal and pathological phenomena. For example, the underlying unity of consciousness in the split, though there is an appearance of isolated minds, cannot be explained by independent or parallel channels but can be understood through a single hierarchic system of levels. Separate consciousness does not arise from each hemisphere but reflects state-specific behavior at multiple levels in a "vertical" hierarchy. Similarly, the association between right hemisphere pathology and euphoria, or heightened affect, does not signal a difference between the hemispheres in the organization of emotion. Rather, lesions of the (posterior) left hemisphere which disrupt that level of cognition which is continuous with the cognition of the right hemisphere (i.e., a lexical semantic level in language) also give euphoria (Brown, 1982). The affect change is specific to cognitive level, not hemisphere.

II
Perception

5
Microstructure of Objects*

Jason W. Brown

INTRODUCTION

The traditional neurological approach to visual perception assumes that an object is the result of a chain of events leading over stations in a sensory pathway. This pathway leads from retina to the lateral geniculate bodies of thalamus which relay the signal to visual (striate) cortex. Cells in the visual cortex respond to various features in the stimulus array, features which are subsequently combined to a pattern perception over the circumstriate zone. From this region connections exist to convey the information to other neocortical sites for "higher" or more complex processing. For example, there are pathways to the inferotemporal region which are thought to relate percepts to meanings, or provide a constant update of the visual environment to an experiential and/or spatial map of the world.

This general model of visual perception has dominated neuropsychological thinking for a good many years, and, in fact, has served as a basis for theorizing about almost all neuropsychological functions. The centerpiece of the model is the prominence given to the geniculo-cortical pathway, and the assumption that the cortical retinal map, that this pathway elaborates, is the starting point in the brain's construction of an object. The difficulties with this account have only recently become apparent in light of anatomical and experimental studies. For one thing, we now know that the connectivity of the visual system is extremely complex with many projections not accounted for by the geniculo-cortical model; for example, extra-striate geniculo-cortical projections, extra-geniculate thalamic projections to nonstriate cortex, as well as various efferent subcortical fibers descending from visual cortex (Vastola, 1968). There are also wholly intrinsic systems which seem to have a visual function. Studies of posterior

---

*From "Microstructure of Perception: Physiology and Patterns of Breakdown" by J. W. Brown, 1983, Cognition and Brain Theory, 6, 145–184. Copyright 1983 by Lawrence Erlbaum Associates. Adapted by permission.

neocortex in primate have revealed a number of visual areas, and the connections within and between these areas are reciprocal. The actual direction of processing is unclear, with recent work suggesting simultaneous processing in widespread areas of neocortex (Merzenich & Kaas, 1980).

Another problem has to do with behavioral investigations. While initial studies of cells in the visual cortex seemed to indicate a selectivity of response, subsequent work has shown that individual cells respond to many different "features" of the stimulus, for example, shape, movement, color, even to stimulation in another modality (Pribram, 1981). This finding, together with evidence for multiple representation of the periphery, has brought about a shift from a "detector" to a "network" model, and a change from the sequential account to that of a "distributed" system underlying visual function. The concept of a distributed or functional system, in which diverse areas at different evolutionary levels interact in the elaboration of specific functions, has also been invoked to explain the finding of persistent vision after destruction of striate cortex, as well as the demonstration by Sprague (1966) and others of improvement in a cortical hemianopia with ablation of the opposite superior colliculus. These observations show the importance of brainstem and other extrastriate cortical mechanisms in visual perception, and necessitate a modification of the geniculo-cortical model to incorporate the idea of a "subcortical" visual system concerned with optic-motor responses acting together with the system of cortical pattern vision. Some theories of the function of this visual system have been summarized by Brindley, Gautier-Smith, and Lewin, (1969).

The model of visual perception outlined in this paper departs fundamentally from these prior accounts in that the perception does not begin with the detection of object features at the cortical level, nor is it the result of interaction between two or many components in a computational system. Instead, the perception develops within the phyletic core of the brain, in a direction corresponding to that of forebrain evolution. The perception is not constructed directly out of sensory material. Rather, it is proposed that a series of sensori-perceptual, or physical-mental transforms maintains an unfolding cognitive representation on a course so as to model an external object. Specifically, there is a parallel hierarchy of sensory (physical) levels and perceptual (cognitive) levels distributed over evolutionary brain structure. The sensory levels act to *constrain* the development of the perceptual levels, while the perceptual levels—wholly cognitive and representational—are the contents which undergo transformation. Levels of sensory constraint appear to be discontinuous or nodal (Brown, 1983a). One can speak of a retino-tectal or a thalamo-striate component. In contrast, the perceptual development seems to be a continuum with a gradual wave-like unfolding from one phase to the next.

According to this model, an object is an abstract multi-tiered construct unfolding over evolutionary and maturational stages in the brain. The unfolding process begins in the upper brainstem core, where it is constrained by retino-tectal input. This leads to a limbic-temporal stage, and then to a level of generalized neocortex. The final stage is that of koniocortical modeling. These neurological strata are aligned in a sequence which recapitulates the direction of forebrain evolution. At each level, visuo-sensory input acts upon an emerging cognitive form. The final object is a composite of all these representational levels.

The following sections take up each of these levels, or components, in the forming object representation. The anatomy of each component is briefly reviewed, along with the effects of pathology in man. Damage to each level in the structure gives either a perceptual *deficit,* for example, a scotoma or an agnosia, or abnormal *imagery,* such as an hallucination. This paper considers only perceptual *deficits.* A discussion of imagery and temporal aspects of this model can be found elsewhere (Brown, 1983a, 1984b).

NEURAL LEVELS IN PERCEPTION

THE SPATIAL MAP: OBJECT REPRESENTATION THROUGH MIDBRAIN MECHANISMS

The base level in the perception is presumed generated by a pon-tomesencephalic system identical to that related to dreamless sleep (Hernandez-Peon, 1966; Jouvet, 1963). The continuum between dreamless sleep and dream corresponds to a transition from upper brainstem to limbic structures. In dreamless sleep, object development is wholly endogenous. A perception occurs when this level undergoes sensory modulation by way of retinotectal input. In this way, the preliminary mental representation of dreamless sleep becomes the preliminary object of external perception. Specifically, the substrate of dreamless sleep becomes the visuospatial map out of which the object develops.

Brainstem mechanisms mediate complex behaviors (Seigel, 1979). Chronic animals with midbrain or pontine transections retain the ability to eat and drink and show defense reactions with appropriate vocalization and locomotion (Lovick, 1972). Human anencephalic infants show normal crying and sucking behavior. The various functions attributed to brainstem reticular formation (RF) includes sensorimotor function: respiration slow wave, and REM sleep. The role of RF in rhythmic swimming movements in fish (Peter, 1977), rhythmic stepping in cats (Orlovskii, 1970), as well as axial and postural movements, the involvement of RF cells in eye movements, (Baker & Berthoz, 1977), the demonstration that cells in the anterior pontine nucleus have visual receptive fields (Glickstein, Stein, & King, 1972) point to the organization in pontine and midbrain RF of an early level in behavior.

STUDIES OF THE TECTUM

A perception of some type occurs at upper midbrain. This "subcortical" or brainstem visual system involves the tectal (superior colliculi) and pretectal regions, and midbrain tegmentum. The major input to this region is by way of retino-tectal projections. In man, the retino-tectal system is quite large, and may comprise as much as 20%–30% of the fibers of the optic tract (Bernheimer, 1899).

Experimental work is consistent with the view that the tectal-midbrain system constitutes a more primitive stage in perception (see also Bishop, 1961; Diamond & Hall, 1969). Excitation of superior colliculus elicits orientation of the eyes and head towards a stimulus, or a "visual grasp" of the object (Hess, Burgi, & Bucher, 1946). Tectal stimulation produces adversive head movement and circling. Many studies confirm the importance of optic tectum in the detection of motion or rates of motion, and the saccadic displacement of the eyes to bring an object into central vision (NRP Bull. 1977). Tectal units are sensitive to movement, and may also show directional selectivity. Many units respond to a real movement of a stimulus but not a stimulus movement which is secondary to an eye movement, in contrast to cells in striate cortex which do not distinguish real from self-induced movement (Robinson & Goldberg, 1978). The tectum has also been implicated in the avoidance of large objects and possibly in simple shape and pattern recognition.

Ablation studies in monkeys have given contradictory results. In an early study, lesions of superior colliculus led to mild or transient defects (Pasik, Pasik, & Bender, 1966), perhaps because of a superficial lesion. Subsequent work has demonstrated more severe deficits (Anderson & Symmes, 1969). When the lesion penetrates into pretectal or peri-acqueductal areas, marked disturbances in visual exploration occur (Denny-Brown & Fischer, 1976). Collicular monkeys stare into space, though they can grasp large moving objects without fixation. Denny-Brown argued that midbrain-tegmental mechanisms construct a unified percept from the two half-fields.

Unilateral lesions of superior colliculus give ipsilateral ocular deviation and contralateral neglect (Trevarthen, 1968; Wurtz & Goldberg, 1972). There may also be neglect or mislocalization of tactile and acoustic stimuli on the opposite side (Sprague, 1975). Deficits for the discrimination of peripheral stimuli in collicular monkeys are abolished when the monkey is required to reach to the periphery to make the choice response (Kurtz, Leiby, & Butter, 1980) suggesting an attentional rather than a sensory impairment. The connectivity of the mammalian tectum is complex (NRP

Bull. 13:1975; Sprague, Berlucchi, & Rizzolatti, 1973). The stratified superior colliculus has been divided into superficial and deep laminae, the latter merging gradually into the midbrain tegmentum. The superficial layers receive direct fibers from the retina, in relation to the contralateral half fields, as well as from visual and other neocortical regions. The cortico-tectal projections appear to maintain a retinotopic localization. There is also an acoustic and somatic input. There is a prominent efferent connection to posterior thalamus. The deep layers receive neocortical projections and send efferents to, *inter alia,* the pontine and mesencephalic reticulum, oculomotor nuclei, and pulvinar. Wurtz and Goldberg (1972) have shown projections from superior colliculus to centers effecting the neck musculature. There is a continuous transition of tectal cytoarchitectonics into midbrain tegmentum. In lesion studies, the deeper strata appear related to the marked perceptual and behavioral deficits. The fixed staring and immobility of the acollicular monkey are also linked to the akinesia and catatonic fixity of animals with rostral tegmental lesions (Brown, 1967).

PATHOLOGY OF UPPER BRAINSTEM IN MAN

In man, damage to the tectal midbrain system results in disturbances of optic-motor, orienting and other midline responses involving the axial musculature and the space of the body surround. There is a continuum of disorders, ranging from partial disruptions of eye movements and misreaching, to more severe deteriorations of coma and akinetic mutism.

Given the behavior of acollicular and midbrain reticular animals, some predictions can be made as to the effects in man of damage to this system. Central pontine lesions below the raphe nuclei should not have pronounced cognitive effects. The damage is caudal to the postulated intrinsic system mediating sleep and early perception. This is the case in the *"locked in"* or *ventral pontine syndrome* where vascular destruction of central pons gives a subject who, though quadriplegic, is alert, conscious, and perceiving. More rostral lesions should give dreamless sleep, or *coma.* Lesions restricted to central mesencephalon give coma without eye closure, or *akinetic mutism.* With involvement of the collicular region one expects a loss of ocular saccades and eventual fixity of gaze, as well as altered motor function, especially in the axial and proximal musculature, reduced drive, vocal and affective expression, sleep disorders, and a disruption of spatial perception. These symptoms occur in *progressive supranuclear palsy (PSP).*

The Ventral Pontine Syndrome

Damage to central pons gives generalized paralysis except for eyelid and/or ocular movements through which communication may be possible, for example, blinking or shifting the gaze in response to questions requiring a yes or no answer. The disorder is termed the "locked in" syndrome, in deference to the relative sparing of mental functions in the context of severe paralysis. The term, "ventral pontine syndrome," refers to the site of pathological involvement. Such cases show that preservation of RF from the upper pontine tegmentum above the level of the fifth nerve nuclei through diencephalon is necessary to maintain consciousness. Ventral lesions (Karp & Hurtig, 1974), which spare central reticular mechanisms, may give rise to this state. The anatomy of the disorder has been studied by Nordgren, Markesbery, Fukuda, and Reeves (1971) and Hawkes (1974). It could result from partial *transection* of caudal pons or a more rostral lesion sparing the tegmentum. According to Hawkes (1974), sparing of RF in rostral pons and midbrain accounts for consciousness. The EEG may show a sleep pattern but the majority of patients have normal alpha or fast theta activity (Hawkes & Bryan-Smith, 1974).

In sum, large lesions of central pons may leave object perception intact. This is because the structural correlates of early perception are located more rostrally in brainstem.

LESIONS OF ROSTRAL BRAINSTEM

A Human Tectal Syndrome

The picture of the collicular-pretectal monkey corresponds in man to progressive supranuclear palsy (Steele, Richardson, & Olszweski, 1964). This disease involves a progressive loss of vertical and horizontal eye movements with eventual fixity of gaze, axial rigidity and dementia. The pathology affects brainstem, especially pontine tegmentum, and basal ganglia preferentially. The cerebral cortex is spared. Most importantly, the superior, but not inferior, colliculi are uniformly involved. Steele et al. (1964) found severe demyelination in all layers of the superior colliculi, especially the deeper zones. The pretectal region is also one of the most commonly and severely involved sites (Behrman, Carroll, Janota, & Matthews, 1969).

The perceptual alteration is characterized by a progressive loss or restriction of eye movements Initially, there is difficulty fixing on objects in the peripheral (vertical and horizontal) field. Vertical movements are usually first affected, especially downward gaze, and then horizontal movements. "Willed" eye movements disappear before reflex movements, and an impairment of volitional gaze precedes a gaze palsy. As the disorder continues, both volitional and following or pursuit movements will be lost, though vestibular and other ocular reflexes are retained. The fast phase of caloric and optokinetic nystagmus is lost (Dix, Harrison, & Lewis, 1971). Fixation movements are slow, hypometric and unstable (Dell-Osso & Troost, 1977). It is not clear whether the involvement of vertical before horizontal movements reflects a different substrate for these directions of gaze or if the vertical movements are more sensitive. The relationship between these deficits and pathology in the collicular and pretectal region was first suggested by Dix et al. (1971). EEG sleep patterns may be altered, and the paradoxical phase may not be obtained over several nights of observation.

There may be difficulty pointing to objects, though axial rigidity prevents thorough testing of eye-hand coordination. I have found impaired ballistic reaching in focal vascular cases. In patients who have been tested, some impairments are noted (e.g., Constantinidis, Tissot, & Ajuriaguerra, 1970). This patient also had a marked disturbance in spatial perception. Letters could be read, but there was difficulty with words and sentences. He could not see all the details of a picture. The authors concluded that there was a fragmentation of visual space, with inability to fuse multiple elements into a composite whole.

Dementia has been noted in most of the reported cases, though the first thorough study did not occur until the paper of Constantinidis et al. (1970), later by Albert, Feldman, & Willis, (1974). There is an impression that this is not a true dementia but rather a "pseudodementia" due to inertia and mumbled speech.

Focal Lesions

Large lesions of rostral pons or midbrain tegmentum give coma or coma vigil (akinetic mutism). The limbs show normal tone and reflexes but there is no spontaneous movement. The patient may stare straight ahead with weak or absent lateral eye movements, or have wandering movements through the full range of gaze. Although the patient may appear awake, even attentive, there is no objective evidence of awareness. Commonly, there is a fluctuation in and out of a more drowsy state, though the main criterion for this has been whether the eyes are open.

Segarra (1970) has linked akinetic mutism of midbrain origin to involvement in the distribution of the perforating branches of the mesencephalic artery. Smaller lesions of the midbrain tegmentum may give rise to hallucinatory states and narcolepsy. In two anatomical cases, cataplexy and narcolepsy occurred with tumors of the rostral midbrain (Anderson & Salmon, 1977; Stahl, Layzer, Aminoff, Townsend, & Feldon, 1980). Other sleep-related phenomena may occur, such as hypersomnia, twilight states, and disorders of the sleep-wake cycle. Cases with focal lesions of midbrain tegmentum or in the area of the posterior commissure have impaired object perception (Denny-Brown & Chambers, 1976).

Summary

A lesion between upper pons and midbrain tegmentum gives a state of coma in which the eyes are open (akinetic mutism) or closed (dreamless sleep), alterations of the sleep-wake cycle and hallucination. The cognition of dreamless sleep, or the "vigilance" of the akinetic mute, represents a base level in the perception which is elaborated at subsequent levels into dream and hallucinatory experience. The spatial coordinates of the tegmental map are linked with actions of the body. The map is an action schema, a program for body movement on targets which serve as triggers for actions. The tectum is an interface transforming sensory primitives into this program, which is the cognitive model at the tegmental stage. Disruptions at this point, as in progressive supranuclear palsy, lead to a disturbance in ocular saccades, loss of ballistic and axial motions of the body, and a breakdown in space perception.

These behavioral and anatomical findings converge on the view that *the wider tectal region constitutes a complex sensory processor at an early stage in percept formation which modulates an intrinsic cognitive system in the upper brainstem tegmentum.* In the tegmentum a unitary two-dimensional space may be constructed within which targets can be identified on the basis of relative motion. At this stage, these are only targets, there is no object as such and the space of the targets is part of the body space. A stimulus is fixed in a system of spatial coordinates through an orientation of the eyes, head and neck toward the target point. Space consists in a deviation or rotation within the body axis and not in a perceived space "out there." The orientation of the body towards a stimulus occurs in relation to movement about the midline of the body. The antiquity of this system is seen in its polysensory nature, the link with vestibular and labyrinthine reflexes, the close-locked character of the visual grasp; in fact the reflex-like nature of responses generally, and the relation to systems of rhythmic motility and synergic expressive movements.

EGOCENTRIC SPACE AND OBJECT MEANING: OBJECT REPRESENTATION THROUGH LIMBIC-TEMPORAL MECHANISMS

The neural substrate which elaborates midbrain perception and dreamless sleep develops through limbic mechanisms to the private viewer-centered space of dream and hallucinatory perception. The limbic object is not fully exteriorized, it is not yet positioned in the world, nor strongly biased to a visual half field. Unilateral lesions often give symptoms throughout the visual field. The bond with motility and the multimodal nature of the object are less pronounced, while object meaning, affect and symbolic changes figure more importantly.

ANATOMICAL STUDIES

The close relationship between upper brainstem and limbic regions has been demonstrated in many physiological studies (O'Keefe & Nadel, 1978). Systems underlying perceptual function involve brainstem and limbic structures identified with sleep and dream activity. An inhibitory 5-HT (serotonin) system passes from the median raphe nucleus by way of fornix and cingulum to the hippocampus, and a noradrenaline system, also inhibitory, leads from the locus coeruleus via median forebrain bundle and retrosplenial cortex. Stimulation along a path leading from the tegmental nuclei of pons and midbrain through medial hypothalamic-septal area induces hippocampal theta activity. Lesions of this pathway block theta induced by more rostral stimulation. In cats, desynchronization is produced by stimulation from the raphe nuclei through midbrain reticulum and lateral hypothalamus. Grantyn (1973) has discussed midbrain reticular inputs to hippocampus.

There is evidence for extra-striate visual input to limbic structures. MacLean and colleagues (Cuenod, Casey, & MacLean, 1965; Gergen & MacLean, 1964) have demonstrated collaterals from optic radiations to limbic structures in monkey. In microelectrode studies, visual responses are obtained from an area extending from the entorhinal region to striate cortex, perhaps identical to the "splenial visual area" identified by Kalia and Whitteridge (1973) in a photic response study. MacLean (1975) considers these responses to reflect subcortical rather than transcortical input, presumably from inferior pulvinar.

Visual evoked potentials can be obtained from hippocampus after destruction of the geniculostriate system (Sager, Nestianu, & Florea-Ciocoiu, 1967). Direct visual input to the entorhinal area may occur from optic tract by way of the anterodorsal nucleus of thalamus (Conrad & Stumpf, 1975). MacLean pointed to the antiquity of this limbic visual system, and argued that in phylogeny the temporal (Meyer's) loop of the optic radiation was connected with limbic cortex. He suggested a relation to REM activity. Evidence for direct projections from the lateral geniculate via Meyer's loop has been reviewed by Babb, Wilson, Halgren, and Crandell, (1980). These authors describe response characteristics of a posterior hippocampal unit in a human subject. Certainly, the many studies of hippocampal theta (O'Keefe & Nadel, 1978) indicate an association with learning, orientation and exploration; that is, with the isolation and/or selection of perceptual objects, as well as an association with REM activity. These findings are consistent with the view that the limbic stage is concerned with a level in object formation involved in dream cognition and object meaning.

Sanides (1975; Sanides & Vitzthum, 1965) has identified as *area prostriata* an intermediate zone between insular or limbic cortex and primary sensory cortex. This prokoniocortical visual area is located in a parasplenial position at the rostral end of the striate cortex, contiguous to inferotemporal cortex, and extends to the entorhinal region of the parahippocampal gyrus. Diamond (1979) described in the tree shrew a system from the lateral intermediate nucleus to the posterior supracallosal region. This area of posterior cingulate gyrus may be identical to Sanides' area prostriata intermediate in phylogeny between the tectal and geniculo-striate systems.

Inferotemporal Cortex

Experimental studies have demonstrated a visual perceptual organization in the limbic system and temporal lobe. A bilateral lesion of limbic and temporal cortex in monkey leads to a "visual agnosia" (Klüver & Bucy, 1937). The IT cortex includes the middle and inferior temporal gyrus back to inferior occipital sulcus (Mishkin, 1972). The region has callosal connections and receives major projections from circumstriate cortex and inferior pulvinar. IT cortex is older than koniocortex from the cytoarchitectonic standpoint (Diamond, 1979). Cells in IT cortex have large receptive fields, most are binocular and extend up to 20°–30° into both visual fields. All receptive fields include the fovea, but the stimulus response is uniform throughout the field. The more rostral extent of this zone is even more primitive and has connections through anterior commissure to the opposite hemisphere.

Recent anatomical work in pigmentarchitectonics (Braak, 1978) has defined a posterior striated region extending to the peristriate area which corresponds to primate IT cortex. The finding on behavioral studies that the IT defect is specific to visual perception is consistent with the fact that nerve cells in this region respond exclusively to visual stimuli. As noted, the majority of cells respond to stimuli in either visual field. The bilateral response is lost after commissurotomy, and the contralateral response is lost after removal of striate cortex on the same side (Rocha-Miranda, Gender, Gross, & Mishkin, 1975). This confirms that, in addition to a large projection from pulvinar, the IT cortex also receives a striate input. However, large lesions between striate and IT cortex do not lead to comparable deficits; nor for that matter do lesions of pulvinar (Mishkin, 1972).

The lesser effect of lesions between striate and IT cortex has been explained through persistence of remaining connections between these areas;

that is, incomplete interruption of the striate-IT pathway. Mishkin (1972) seems to have confirmed this with extensive bilateral lesions which reproduce the IT deficit. Although it is not known whether IT lesions depress prestriate neurons, that is, whether the effect is bi-directional, these observations, along with the lack of deficit after pulvinar lesion, have suggested to some that the IT area is a *secondary* relay zone after striatal processing. The question of whether all such unit responses might be in some sense artificial, related to the method of testing, has been at least partially answered by studies in animals with active eye movements (Wurtz & Goldberg, 1972). How then can these findings be resolved with the hypothesis that limbic-temporal processing involves a preliminary stage in the object representation?

The answer to this may be that the striate-IT pathway does not concern the *direction* of processing. The depression of activity in IT cortex after disruption of striate input may be comparable to the tectal depression following striate lesion. In the latter case, we do not suppose the direction of processing is from striate cortex to tectum; rather, the more advanced evolutionary system has reciprocal effects on more preliminary stages. Presumably, the same explanation applies to IT depression after striate lesions. It is also possible that IT depression is secondary to tectal depression.

Nakamura and Mishkin (1980) described apparent blindness in monkeys following large lesions of cortex sparing striate, prestriate, and IT regions. Unit recordings in striate cortex show poor to moderate responsiveness, but sufficient to support vision (Nakamura, DeSimone, Schein, & Mishkin, 1980). The authors concluded that the loss of visual processing responsible for the blindness must be occurring at some point beyond the striate cortex. Moreover, neurons in area 21, a visual "association area," respond to visual stimuli even if striate and pre-striate zones are destroyed. These findings are consistent with the idea that object perception develops *toward* a striate endpoint.

PATHOLOGY OF LIMBIC-TEMPORAL AREAS IN MAN

A change in object recognition, a modality-specific impairment on complex perceptual tasks, occurs in the monkey with bilateral IT lesions (Gross, 1973; Mishkin, 1972). Similar impairments may follow prestriate lesions though the latter appear related to perceptual or attentional factors, whereas those of IT lesions are related to memory and meaning in the stimulus. However, the defect is not clearly one of visual memory; there is a disturbance of visual analysis or selection (Soper, Diamond, & Wilson, 1975).

The visual "agnosia" of the Klüver-Bucy syndrome is presumably due to involvement of the same region of temporal neocortex, though it can result from bilateral limbic ablations (e.g., amygdala), especially the change in affect, passivity, and orality.

Elements of the disorder occur in man, mainly with diffuse pathology (Pilleri, 1966). However, the visual recognition defect has not been a prominent feature. Visual agnosia does occur, but it is difficult to be certain of the anatomical correlation. Pathological studies (Pilleri, 1966) suggest a relation to anterior and mediobasal temporal neocortex. Hopf (1968) correlated the visual deficits with temporal pole and its caudal architectonic continuation in fusiform gyrus. The relationship to temporal pole alone seems unlikely in view of negative results with anterior lesions in monkeys (Mishkin, 1972). However, anatomical reports of human cases of visual agnosia with focal vascular lesions confirm the importance of fusiform gyrus (see the following).

Bilateral limbic lesions in man, or bilateral anterior temporal lobectomy, give amnestic rather than agnosic disorders. Unilateral cases show perceptual impairments depending on the lesioned side; right temporal cases deficits in the estimation of numbers of dots, recognition of nonsense patterns and faces, and visual or tactile maze learning; left temporal cases, deficits on verbal tasks, word finding, and verbal recall. Impairments in visual recognition, hidden figures, and on color tasks also occur in left-damaged cases (DeRenzi, 1971). Certain of these effects may involve deeper limbic structures. Thus, maze and route learning are impaired only if the hippocampus is involved. Conversely, face recognition may be more sensitive to lesions of temporal neocortex.

The bi-temporal monkey has a defect in response selection. Teuber noted an impairment in the inhibition of irrelevant responses. This is also a disburbance in *visual selection,* in the isolation of an element from an array. The impairment is for the meaning of an object and not its visual form. This is also true in human cases. Bilateral *mesial* temporo-occipital lesions in man give rise to a visual agnosia in which errors reflect the conceptual value of the object rather than its morphological or spatial properties. Such observations indicate that *early perception involves the selection of a target through a representational network or a memory organized about relations of conceptual proximity.*

In *visual agnosia* due to bilateral lesions of the temporo-occipital area (fusiform gyrus, especially), the main symptom is impaired object recognition, not just for the name of the object but its use, its nature, in spite of a seemingly adequate perception. The patient sees the object, can describe and draw it, and may have normal ocular exploration (cf., Karpov, Meerson, & Tonkonogi, 1979).

It is important to distinguish this type of conceptual disorder (associative agnosia) from impaired *form* perception (apperceptive agnosia), with parieto-occipital lesions. In the conceptual type of agnosia, errors are semantically or conceptually related to the target object. Thus, a patient of Lhermitte, Chedru, and Chain (1973), shown a knife, said, "It's a plate." On sorting tasks, the patient could pair objects on the basis of semantic category. The case of Taylor and Warrington (1971) sorted pictures of objects into rough (superordinate) categories. The mathematics professor of Albert, Reches, and Silverberg (1975a) identified a slide rule as "something for measuring, for calculation," a Star of David as "something holy." Shown an object (tie) he could often give the correct category (clothing). Generally, there is impaired matching of objects in a category, even different instances of the same object. A disturbance in categorization has even been proposed as the basis of the disorder (Hécaen, Goldblum, Masure, & Ramier, 1974). Acuity and shape and size perception are generally normal.

The lesion in this type of agnosia involves limbic-temporal structures. The cases of Rubens and Benson (1971) and Mack and Boller (1977) had bilateral medial temporo-occipital lesions. Albert et al.'s (1975–1979) patient had bilateral lesions involving mesial posterior limbic and temporal regions. A similar localization seems probable in a case of Newcombe and Ratcliff (1974), a glioma involving deep medial structures posteriorly.

A related disorder is topographical disorientation with impaired recognition of surroundings and difficulty in retrieving prior geographical knowledge (Benton, 1969). Cases are described with preservation of well-established geographical knowledge and difficulty in new surroundings (Scotti, 1968). *Topographical disorientation and topographical amnesia* are commonly associated, though the disorientation may persist after the amnesia has cleared. The nature and style of buildings in a town, even furniture in a house, may be identified but without their familiar character. The unfamiliarity (*jamais vu*) may be linked to derealization (Zangwill, 1951). In most cases of topographical amnesia, there is also *facial agnosia* (Lhermitte & Pillon, 1975; Whiteley & Warrington, 1978). The link between these two disorders is also suggested by cases such as the lefthander of Tzavaras Merienne, and Masure (1973) with agnosia for routes and faces secondary to a left temporal lesion. Patients generally have elements of both conditions but incline toward one of the disorders. This may give the spurious impression of a lack of correlation between them.

One can say that *disorders of route finding occur on a continuum between those which are closer to a memory impairment, and those which are closer to a perceptual impairment.* The amnestic form tends to occur with bilateral posterior temporal or temporo-occipital lesions, the discrimination form with a right parieto-occipital lesion. The amnestic form (topographical amnesia) involves mental imagery. As the image is a precursor of the perception, there is also topographical disorientation, while the latter disorder may occur with preservation of route memories.

Patients with *facial agnosia* are unable to visually identify human faces, photographs of family, close friends, well-known people, or even themselves in the mirror. There may be inability to distinguish young and old faces, male and female, even human and animal faces. Recognition of facial expression may suffer; identification is accomplished by birthmarks, glasses, hair style or, more often, dress or voice. Patients may indicate errors in drawings of faces, add elements which are deleted, or embellish drawings but performance is far from normal. Visually similar items (moustache versus eyebrows) are easily confused. The difficulty is not limited to faces. There may be errors with other perceptually similar items, such as animals, flowers, fruits or automobiles. Faust's case had difficulty with furniture, DeRenzi's with wine bottles, Bornstein's ornithologist with well-known birds. A farmer could not recognize his cows and a personal case (Brown, 1972), a pilot, could not distinguish airplanes though he gave accurate descriptions by memory. In such cases impaired form perception must be present. Indeed, DeRenzi, Scotti, and Spinnler (1969) concluded that the difficulty was "not because of unfamiliarity or because of lack of verbal labels, but because they (faces) are very similar to one another and, therefore, their identification requires the ability to detect small formal differences."

This is not the whole explanation, since patients with prosopagnosia may perform well on tests of facial discrimination (Tzavaras, Hécaen, & LeBras, 1970) and patients impaired on such tests may have good facial recognition.

The central point is that *facial agnosia, like visual and topographic agnosia, comes in two varieties: one in relation to a disturbance in visual meaning or memory, and one in relation to disturbed form perception* (Benton & Van Allen, 1972; Brown, 1972; Meadows, 1974).

As to localization, Faust (1947) first emphasized the frequency of superior quadranopic defects (also Hécaen & Angelergues, 1962). Conversely, a correlation exists between left upper quadrant defects and impaired facial recognition (Newcombe & Russell, 1969). This suggests right temporal involvement. Lhermitte, Chain, Escourelle, Ducarne, and Pillon (1972) reviewed nine anatomical cases with right medial temporo-occipital lesions, especially of lingual and fusiform gyri, though there are usually bilateral lesions (e.g., Cohn, Newmann, & Wood, 1977; Gloning, Gloning, & Hoff, 1968). Thus, *in the conceptual form of topographical and facial agnosia, there is evidence for a right-sided (or bilateral) medial posterior temporal lesion. This lesion is bilateral in the conceptual form of visual object agnosia. Conversely, when visual agnosia, topographical disorientation and impaired facial recognition are based on impaired form discrimination, there is evidence for lesion of the parieto-occipital area.*

The involvement of mesial temporal cortex in the conceptual type of agnosia suggests an association with amnestic states. Could an underlying disturbance in visual memory explain the impairment for routes and faces, the link to Korsakoff states and conceptual errors in visual agnosia? Korsakoff patients are impaired in topographic orientation, and show deficits on facial recognition tasks (Butters & Cermak, 1977). Surgical and post-encephalitic amnesics have impaired facial recognition, but unlike prosopagnosics, identify faces from the pre-onset period. Prosopagnosics do not have an amnestic syndrome. Conceptual deficits in object recognition point to a disruption between amnesia proper and an alteration of form perception. In the IT monkey, an anterior lesion gives a recognition deficit and a posterior lesion a disturbance in form perception. *The central disturbance in these disorders, in my view, is a failure to fully select a visual content on the basis of its conceptual or experiential meaning.*

Summary

The two-dimensional cognitive map of ambient space represented in upper midbrain is derived through limbic-temporal mechanisms to the subjective viewer-centered space of hallucination and dream-like imagery. This is still an intrapersonal space unlike the space of objects, a fluid extension of mind into the body surround. This derivation is characterized by a selection of the object-to-be perceived through systems of symbolic and affective transformation toward increasing definition and spatial resolution. Pathology displays this segment as an hallucinatory endpoint or buried, as an agnosia, within an object which is spatially completed at subsequent levels.

The visual agnosias—object, facial and topographical agnosia—occur in two forms, each referring to a different moment in this transition. In one form, which has the appearance of a conceptual or a memory deficit, there is a disturbance in object meaning. Errors reflect symbolic or category relationships. The disorder is probably related to the Klüver-Bucy or IT syndrome of the monkey, but in man is associated with mesial temporo-occipital damage, generally bilateral but possibly with right hemisphere lesions alone. In the second form, which has the appearance of a spatial or perceptual deficit, there is a disturbance in object identification or discrimination. The abstract target is disrupted as it emerges through a system of conceptual selection toward exteriorization as a distinct spatial entity. This form tends to occur with parietal or parieto-occipital lesions, generally right-sided but with lesions of either hemisphere.

These two conditions reveal successive levels in object formation, selection for meaning and selection for form. They often occur together in the same patient, or performance fluctuates from one error type to another. In this respect, they are like the posterior aphasias, where one sees multiple levels of representation in the symptoms of a single case. Moreover, there is a deep inner relationship between semantic and phonological disorders in lexical retrieval, and conceptual and morphological disorders in object formation (Brown, 1982).

Objects are perceived as part of an object field. The object is the figural element of the field but the field is also part of the object. Presumably, object perception cannot be disturbed without a disturbance in object relations. Yet, pathology can involve these aspects separately. This is because in the development toward referential meaning an object can be disrupted prior to the space of object relations. Patients with a conceptual agnosia may not have impairments of extrapersonal space because the disruption involves a phase in the object before external space has materialized. Parietal lesions involve targets which are conceptually identified and exteriorized from the mental life of the viewer. The symptoms are no longer in a private space but in the object world. However, as we will see in the following section, the parietal object is still not fully extrinsic and independent; symptoms reflect "interaction" between object and viewer. The "interaction" shows that the object is positioned in a forming external space still influenced by a change in the action of the perceiver.

EXTERNAL SPACE AND OBJECT-RELATIONS: OBJECT REPRESENTATION THROUGH PARIETAL MECHANISMS

The object selected through limbic-temporal systems develops to an externalized three-dimensional space through parietal generalized or "integration" neocortex. Clinical demonstrations of the importance of parietal cortex in space perception have been confirmed in experiments by Mountcastle and others recording from units in the posterior parietal cortex of behaving monkeys (see Lynch, 1980). These studies have shown neurons sensitive to various aspects of space perception. Specifically, there are cells in the superior parietal lobule which are active during ballistic reaching of the arm toward an object, and cells which discharge only when the object is grasped or manipulated. These neurons do not discharge during defensive or aggressive movements, but are active when the animal is blindfolded during the behavior. Parietal lesions in monkeys lead to impairments in grasping, worse in darkness than under visual guidance. In the inferior parietal lobule, neurons have been identified that discharge during visual fixation, tracking and saccadic eye movements, as well as during peripheral light stimulation. These findings suggest that *the functional organization of this region concerns the representation of an object-centered extrapersonal space, and the behavior of the organism in that space.*

In other studies, Allman and Kaas (1974a,b) described visual areas in the temporo-parietal region of owl monkey, lesions of which give reaching impairments, even "blindness." Specifically, there is a zone in posterior middle temporal gyrus (MT) with a surrounding dorsolateral crescent (DL), which correspond in their relationship to that between areas 17 and 18. Parts of DL and MT may be included in the posterior extent of IT cortex. Just as regions in area 17 project to parts of 18 representing the same visual space, so also does MT appear to preserve topographic relations in its projections to DL. In both instances, the projections are reciprocal. Both 17 and MT have (reciprocal) subcortical inputs, the former from lateral geniculate, the latter from inferior pulvinar. Areas 17 and MT preserve topological relations to points in the visual field. Corresponding points in 17 and MT are interconnected, as may also be true for 18 and DL. Connections between DL and IT cortex have also been demonstrated (Weller & Kaas, 1980). Presumably, the system MT-DL represents the older of the two visual areas. However, the picture is extremely complex, and there is now evidence that visual association cortex—at least in owl monkey—consists of at least 10 separate visual areas (Kaas, 1978).

These studies have revealed a complex functional organization in posterior neocortex with a considerable degree of topographical specificity. Indeed, on physiological grounds, the "generalized" neocortex appears to be anything but *generalized*. The prevailing view is that of a modular organization with functional networks established through the fine connectivity of the system. The fact that lesions do not dissect functions with the specificity required by a modular theory is interpreted to indicate that networks are interlaced over widespread areas rather than regionally segregated. This concept of modular networks is not incompatible with the microgenetic theory outlined in this paper, except that the subfunctions of a network are assumed to pertain to the same microgenetic stage. Thus, the occurrence in parietal cortex of cells related to actions of the body on objects, to ocular fixation and reaching, reflect the transition of the object representation to an external but not fully exteriorized locus in object space.

PARIETAL LESIONS IN MAN

In man a lesion of the parietal neocortex results in a disruption of space perception and object relations. Other phenomena include spatial neglect, disorientation in space, disturbances of depth, location and distance judgments, and disorders of object-based ballistic movements. With a bilateral midparietal lesion, there is dissolution of object space (Balint syndrome) and inability to perceive more than one object at a time. Parietal lesions may give hallucinations, but more often illusions, distortions, and deformations of objects rather than subjective image formation. The illusion tends to mirror the perceptual deficit. Parietal disorders have a spatial quality; they are positioned in a three-dimensional exteriorizing object space, the pathology disrupting the object as it emerges from a background viewer-centered volumetric space. The interactional quality of the disorder, the impairment for activity space, the space of the arm's reach, for grasping and manipulating objects, and for drawing and constructing, point to the incomplete exteriorization of the object as an independent thing-in-the-world.

This section considers the symptoms of parietal damage, not as "higher order" deficits of computations subsequent to perceptual registration but as disruptions of an object representation as it is selected out of a conceptual organization *into* an external three-dimensional space. Damage to the parietal area alters relationships between objects, and between the viewer and objects around him. Disorders of figure-ground relations, and errors in depth and relative distance estimation are characteristic. Parietal lesions affect the interaction between object and perceiver, with impairments in ballistic reaching and grasping for objects, constructional ability, object drawing, and manipulation. The misreaching and the abnormal constructional behavior reflect a combined action-perception disturbance positioned in the object development prior to the exterioration of object space. Space has not yet detached as an independent world that can undergo change without a corresponding change in the perceiver.

In addition to these qualitative aspects, there are lateral asymmetries in the effects of a parietal lesion. Clinical and behavioral investigations have demonstrated an apparent right hemisphere bias or specialization on a variety of visuospatial or "holistic" perceptual tasks. This relationship has been documented by numerous studies and its basis is still poorly understood. In my view, the symptoms of right hemisphere damage, for example, to the parietal region, or a right hemisphere effect on behavioral measures, or right-left differences in commissurotomy cases, do not point to a special role or function of the right hemisphere, or a parallel style of cognition. Instead, the right and left hemisphere form a *unitary* system that mediates an early or preliminary stage in perception. Visuospatial or holistic cognition—perception built up around object relations—is closer to this preliminary stage than verbal (phonological) or analytic cognition, perception built up around objects and object features. This proximity to a preprocessing level gives a spurious right hemisphere bias.

How the asymmetries occur and their relation to this model of perception has been discussed elsewhere (Brown, 1983c), and will be only briefly mentioned in this paper. Instead, the unilateral and bilateral parietal syndromes of impaired spatial perception are reviewed as evidence for the thesis that parietal mechanisms mediate a stage in perception where a mental representation is transformed to an external Euclidean space (see Brown, 1977, 1983c; Critchley, 1966; DeRenzi, 1982, for clinical details).

Unilateral Lesions

Constructional disability. A disorder of visual-spatial cognition was first described by Kleist. Subsequently, Lange (1936) noted that objects failed to achieve clear perceptual organization, with impaired localization and attention. Mayer-Gross (1936) found inability to analyze and construct a pattern as a whole, and argued that the disorder occurs for the space of the arms reach ("activity space," Wirkraum).

Visuo-spatial impairment was linked to the *right* hemisphere by Dide (1938), Zangwill and Hécaen. Duensing (1953) distinguished between a perceptual defect with right (visual-spatial *agnosia*), and a motor defect with left hemisphere lesions (constructional *apraxia*).

Arrigoni and DeRenzi (1964) confirmed the greater frequency and severity with right damage, but attributed this to unequal lesion size. The conclusions of this study have been generally confirmed, that the right-left difference is due to hemi-spatial neglect in rights, and the exclusion of severe aphasics from the left-damaged group. Thus, *from an initial association with left, then right brain damage, the disorder is now regarded as probably comparable in left and right lesioned cases.* This is consistent with the view that object space is elaborated through systems in both hemispheres.

Left-spatial neglect. Hemispatial neglect refers to altered awareness for half of perceptual or body space, and is chiefly associated with right hemisphere lesions. Gloning et al. (1968) found that a right-sided lesion was more common among left-handers. Constructional impairment, neglect and visual field defects may occur independently. There is altered imagery on the impaired side (Bisiach, 1980).

Neglect is accentuated in the periphery of the field (Zihl & von Cramon, 1979), but often involves the entire field into the parafoveal region and may "spill over" to the intact field. Right hemisphere cases may neglect the left side of words presented in the right hemifield. Neglect changes with the orientation of the body; it is a dynamic alteration not accounted for by a cortical retinal map. Such observations are consistent with the idea that *the visual half-field differentiates out of a unitary space.*

Left hemispatial neglect is interpreted as follows: Space perception is symmetrically organized in animals. The predilection for right hemisphere lesion in spatial neglect reflects a left hemisphere specialization for analytic perception (through a phonological level in language). A lesion of right hemisphere exposes the parietal segment of object formation. This segment, the forming left hemifield, is normally submerged within the object as a "preprocessing" stage. The neglect occurs because the endpoint of cognitive processing is centered around a phonological level which cannot access into analytic cognition the more preliminary stage disrupted by the lesion. The neglect or inattention is the sign of the unaccessed void in the forming left hemifield. The access problem is the inattention (see Brown, 1983c). Neglect is uncommon with left hemisphere lesions, since a large lesion in the left hemisphere will involve adjacent regions mediating phonological representation, and thus obviate the access limitation.

Bilateral Lesions

The biparietal syndrome is characterized by an altered space perception, and impaired ocular and limb motility directed to objects. The case of Balint (1909) had impaired ocular fixation but normal visual fields, ocular motility, and acuity. Gaze could not be directed to peripheral objects, fixation was off target (left neglect) 30°–40° to the right, and after fixation was achieved there was inability to release the "optic grasp" and fix on other objects. There was difficulty in ballistic grasping of objects with the right hand. The patient could not seize a piece of meat with a fork, or light a cigarette, but could bring objects to the mouth. There was a tendency to perceive or report only one object at a time. For example, when the patient was asked to indicate the center of a circle, the circumference disappeared. Shortly after, Holmes (1918) reported inferior biparietal cases with defects in movement perception, relative and absolute object localization and impaired judgment of distance and position. Other biparietal cases are reported by Gloning et al. (1968).

In Balint's patients, object size was not a factor, though Pick and others have described cases in which large objects could not be recognized. This has been interpreted as a shrinkage in the field of visual attention though the "peripheral" field is intact. The cases of Luria (1959) and Hécaen and Ajuriaguerra (1954) have been explained on this basis. There is also the question of bilateral spatial neglect giving rise to apparent field constriction (Michel & Eyssette, 1972). Conceivably, a deficit in the peripheral field gives spasmodic fixation, a central deficit, labile fixation. The peripheral deficit may inhibit ocular displacement, whereas the central deficit may lead to unstable fixation. Both patterns have been described in the recovery of cortical blindness (Critchley, 1950). Conceivably, the peripheral impairment reflects a parietal lesion, the central impairment, an occipital localization.

Mountcastle (1978) found that parietal units were preferentially sensitive to peripheral targets.

Ocular saccades may be impaired to sounds as well as to objects. The impairment in ocular tracking is only for objects. Karpov et al. (1979) found normal following of a luminous dot in a dark room. There are normal slow and rapid eye movements during sleep and dream (Michel & Eyssette, 1972; though see Botez, Serbanescu, Petrovici, & Vernea, 1965).

Most studies confirm Holmes' localization of inferior biparietal lesions. The patient of Kase, Troncosco, Court, Tapia, and Mohr (1977) had bilateral superior parietal infarcts. In unilateral cases with impaired visual orientation, Ratcliff and Davies-Jones (1972) found high posterior parietal lesions.

There are three elements in the bilateral parietal syndrome: (1) simultanagnosia, which can occur with left posterior damage; (2) spatial neglect, with right posterior damage; and (3) optic ataxia (visuomotor apraxia) with unilateral lesions of either hemisphere. Spatial neglect has been discussed with constructional disability. Disturbances in simultaneous perception and optic grasping are described in the following sections.

Simultanagnosia. Difficulty perceiving multiple objects at the same time was termed simultanagnosia by Wolpert in 1924. This was described in cases where the details of a picture were enumerated though the interpretation was missed. For Wolpert this was a conceptual disorder, a failure in the comprehension of the whole together with the apprehension of its parts. The patient read letters one at a time, and had difficulty seeing words as wholes. Kinsbourne and Warrington (1962) reported an association between impaired simultaneous perception and agnosic (spelling) alexia linked to left occipito-parietal lesions.

Lange (1936) and Weigl (1964) maintained that dementia played a role, but Fogel (1966) did not find a relation between intellectual reduction and picture misinterpretation. Moreover, Lange himself cited observations in which simultanagnosia occurred with high intellectual level.

Simultanagnosia and difficulty interpreting pictures may not be manifestations of the same underlying disturbance. With bilateral lesions, it is not a question of interpreting the details of a picture but "seeing" the second of two objects held before the patient's eyes (see DeRenzi, 1982).

Impairment in visual grasping. Disordered grasping of objects in one or both visual fields may occur with unilateral parietal lesions (Ratcliff & Davies-Jones, 1972; Rondot, de Recondo, & Ribadea Dumas, 1977; Tzavaras & Masure, 1976). The principle defect is inaccurate *ballistic* movement when the patient is instructed to rapidly grasp an object at arm's length in either visual field. There may be inadequate searching for targets after the ballistic reach. These may dissociate, giving disorders of proximal or distal grasping. Tzavaras and Masure (1976) attributed these to right and left lesions respectively.

In unilateral cases, the disorder usually affects the contralateral visual field. Initially, errors may occur on grasping with either arm into the defective field, later the contralateral limb shows more accurate performance with residual deficit for grasping in the field opposite the lesion with the ipsilateral arm.

In addition to defective grasping, patients commonly show impaired optic fixation, comparable to limb movements. The patient may look to one side of an object, beyond, or in front of it. There may be difficulty maintaining fixation. Once an object is fixated, there is improved grasping. Patients can often grasp their own finger when held up for them in the defective field. Movements directed toward the subject's own body or the face are usually intact.

Haaxma and Kuypers (1975) studied grasping in monkeys with a variety of experimental lesions. Monkeys with occipital lobectomy showed deficits in grasping with the hand opposite the side of lesion. Subsequent commissurotomy increased the deficit in the contralateral hand. For example, with left occipital lobectomy the decrement in right hand grasping was increased by section of corpus callosum.

Other monkeys had a parieto-occipital leucotomy involving an extensive incision over the convexity. There was slight weakness of the arm opposite the lesion and diminished reaction to food in the opposite field, suggesting mild motor and visual deficit. Involvement of optic radiations was ruled out by anatomical study. Examination later revealed accurate reaching with either hand. After commissurotomy, monkeys showed a slight decrement in the opposite hand. The authors interpreted these findings as an interruption of occipito-frontal projections. However, the leucotomy may also entail local damage, or, as with commissurotomy, result in a suppression of target neocortex. There is a human case with bilateral interruption of the superior longitudinal fasciculus without optic ataxia (see DeRenzi, 1982). Lesions of inferior parietal cortex (MT) in monkeys produce similar deficits in grasping.

There are other problems with the disconnection account of this clinical disorder. In cases where it has been tested (Kase et al., 1977; Tzavaras, 1976, personal observations), there is defective pointing in the direction of *auditory* stimuli. Moreover, there are defects in ocular fixation; that is, in the ballistic saccade to visually "grasp" an object in the defective field. Cogan, Brooks, and Bajandas (1977) noted an associated failure of head thrusting to compensate for ocular fixation defects. Since bifrontal monkeys show normal saccadic eye movements and eye-head coordination, this would not appear to depend on a cortico-cortical pathway. This poses a problem for connectionist accounts, and suggests rather a disturbance in spatial perception on a cortical basis.

Mountcastle's (1978) findings in parietal cortex of monkeys that parietal units respond strongly to peripheral stimuli agrees with the clinical observation that the impairment is more severe for peripheral targets. As in these experiments, the behavior involves ocular fixation and pointing. The finding of ipsilateral responsiveness is consistent with the fact that spatial neglect does not always respect the Euclidian midline but may spill over into the "intact" half field, and the finding of some deficits in spatial localization in the field ipsilateral to the cerebral lesion (Ratcliff & Davies-Jones, 1972). This work provides evidence of a system in parietal lobe concerned with spatial perception, sensitive to movement and directionality, and representing to some extent the ipsilateral field.

Summary

An object resolves not through a process of construction but a suppression of alternative routes. The object-to-be first appears as an isolated content within the volumetric space of imagery. The selection of the object through fields of meaning-relationships coincides with the articulation of egocentric space to a three-dimensional moiety representing the environment within which the organism acts. This phase is mediated by mechanisms in the posterior parietal region.

Damage to these mechanisms reveals *normal* operations underlying object and space representation. For example, in simultanagnosia, the perception is contracted within a single object. The impairment of absolute distance estimation arises because space is lacking in depth when a solitary object fills the visual field. When two objects are perceived, their instability leads to impaired judgments of relative distance, because relations between objects depend on the resolution of the objects themselves. Conversely, an impairment in object relations entails a deficit in object perception. In optic ataxia, the impairment in reaching reflects a disturbance in judgments of distance and position. The very act of reaching may alter the spatial perception. This is predicted if the ballistic reach is laid down by the object perception. Generally, objects and movements on objects show a similar pattern of breakdown.

With parietal lesions, symptoms are positioned in the space of the arms reach; they are bound up with limb movement on objects in the action perimeter. Studies of eye movements show responsiveness at the neuronal level for objects which can be grasped. Parietal mechanisms elaborate an external space that lacks depth and fine articulation, perhaps like the space of an eidetic image. The further analysis and differentiation of activity space to a fully independent public space of seemingly infinite extent occurs through mechanisms in striate and circumstriate cortex.

The parietal syndrome affects a penultimate stage in the object development. The patient with a unilateral lesion has a deficit *within* the object, but the object development is completed through koniocortical mechanisms. The patient with constructional impairment does not perceive the object as it is reproduced in the drawing; the patient with optic ataxia does not perceive the object displaced in the direction of the ballistic grasp. The disruption is submerged within the object.

FEATURAL REPRESENTATION: OCCIPITAL MECHANISMS IN PERCEPTION

The object representation develops from a multi-sensory image in a unitary mental space toward modality specificity, physical reality and hemianopic exteriorization. Accordingly, the final phase of object formation occurs in a processing direction from generalized cortex *to* occipital koniocortex.

In recent years, evidence has accumulated for a revision of the traditional account of neocortical morphology, in which the "association" or "integration" cortices were viewed as the most recently evolved areas of the brain. Comparative neuroanatomical studies indicate that the direction of neocortical growth is in precisely the reverse sequence, and that the primary visual area is the more recent zone in neocortical phylogenesis (Diamond & Hall, 1969).

A similar view was expressed by Sanides (1975). "The enormous development of the supposedly secondary integration cortices was actually not understood...the most *generalized* neocortical structure is bound to become the most predominant one with the widest scope for further differentiation." The myelinogenetic studies of Flechsig (1920), that showed that the classical motor and sensory areas were among the first to begin myelination in the perinatal period, while the secondary or "association" areas showed a more drawn out pattern of myelination, were misinterpreted to indicate the evolutionary priority of the primary sensorimotor areas. In fact, these areas have the *heaviest* definitive myelin content (Vogt & Vogt, 1919) and for this reason show early myelination. The more heavily myelinated systems are more recent in phylogenesis. According to Pandya and Sanides (1973), the "development of koniocortex cores as the last wave of sensory neocortex differentiation occurred during evolution only in the *visual, auditory,* and *somatic* sensory systems mediating the sharpest objectifying and localizing representations of the periphery."

This is consistent with observations in cats of a two-stage development of visual cortex, an early primitive stage characterized by the activity of a system of fine fibers projecting to a wider extent of cortex, and a later more differentiated stage of large fibers projecting to the primary visual cortex only (Marty, 1962). In cats there is evidence for more diffuse geniculocortical projections on both anatomical (Niimi & Sprague, 1970) and electrophysiological (Bignall, Imbert, & Buser, 1966) grounds. In contrast, in monkeys, the geniculate projection is exclusively to the striate cortex. Recently, Goldman (1979) has shown, with autoradiography, that projections of the frontal association cortex in monkeys are laid down earlier in development than the thalamic projections to the primary sensory areas. These findings are in agreement with the evolutionary concept that in neocortical phylogenesis the primary "sensory" cortex differentiates out of—and develops later than—the generalized "association" cortex.

The topological mapping of the retino-geniculate system onto the visual cortex has been described in numerous publications (Reviewed in Polyak, 1957). There is a precise correspondence between points in the visual field and cortical loci in area 17, though the representation of central vision is disproportionately large. In man, the visual area has shifted medially by the enlargement of parietal cortex, whereas in monkeys the representation is distributed more extensively on the convexity. The macular zone occupies the pole of the calcarine sulcus, the periphery the rostral portion. The border of area 17 with area 18 forms the representation of the vertical meridian. There is evidence in monkeys for a "split" representation of the visual field in area 18 (Kaas, 1978), with reciprocal connections between homotopic loci in areas 17 and 18 for corresponding points in the visual field.

In monkeys, area 17 receives its major projection from dorsal lateral geniculate nucleus, but may also receive connections from pulvinar. There are reciprocal connections with area 18, "19" and area MT (superior temporal sulcus) in owl monkey and macaque (Montero, 1980). Area 17 projects to deeper layers in optic tectum as well as dorsal lateral geniculate nucleus. There are callosal fibers connecting homologous points on the vertical meridian of each hemifield, but in man the major callosal system is between homotopic points in areas 18 and 19 in each hemisphere.

Physiological studies have demonstrated cells in area 17 which respond selectively to orientation, and a separate overlapping system of ocular dominance columns. Area 18 appears concerned with more complex shape analysis, but also contains cells responsive to depth and movement (Hubel & Wiesel, 1977; Van Essen, 1979). Teuber speculated that the "simple" to more complex orientation system reflected a process of shape specification leading from orientation or edge detectors in area 17 to more complex reconstruction in area 18. In addition to orientation and binocular disparity, there are numerous cells in area 17 which respond to color, but few such cells in area 18. In man, there is evidence for color encoding in cells on the inferior bank of the calcarine fissure.

The primary visual cortex and circumstriate cortex can be viewed as a final sensory-perceptual transform in object development. This region provides the terminal modeling on the spatial image developing through posterior parietal cortex, transforming the image to a three-dimensional exteriorized object representation in an ostensibly physical space. The articulation of the object into external space coincides with the fine individuation of features in the object itself. Object and space are articulated by the same process.

The effects of lesions in area 17 and 18 are reviewed in the following pages. In brief, lesion of area 17 leads to scotoma or "blind spots" in that region of the visual field represented by the damaged area (Koerner & Teuber, 1973). Stimulation in area 17 gives phosphenes in the corresponding part of the field. Partial lesions may give selective deficits. I have seen patients with presumed ischemic damage to area 17 with difficulty perceiving *verticals*. Particular orientations may be involved in photosensitive epilepsy. Selective color vision deficits may arise from lesions of the inferior calcarine region.

Lesions of area 18 give complex impairments in form perception. Visual acuity is preserved. The patient may perceive lines, perhaps simple shapes, but there is impaired object and face perception, reading, simultaneous perception and related deficits. Stimulation in area 18 gives more complex hallucinations without the precise topographic correspondence observed in area 17.

LESIONS OF OCCIPITAL LOBE IN MAN

Cortical Blindness

Cortical blindness—or bilateral hemianopia—follows destruction of striate cortex. Sequential lesions may result in tubular (tunnel) vision with central (macular) sparing, though this can also be seen in cases with recovery first in the macular region.

Clinically, the diagnosis is not easy. A normal eye examination, retained pupillary reflexes and absent blink to threat are essential. The reflex blink to strong light may be lacking, though preserved in destriate monkeys. Alpha rhythm is usually absent acutely (Bergmann, 1957). There is usually no response to steady light or flicker on EEG and visual evoked responses tend to be abnormal. However, Bodis-Wolner, Atkin, Raab, and Wolkstein (1977) reported a case of cortical blindness with striate lesions and normal VER's. Optokinetic nystagmus (OKN) is absent in "total" blindness (cf. Ter Braak, Shenk, & Van Vliet, 1971) though present in destriate monkeys

(Pasik & Pasik, 1971; Weiskrantz, Warrington, Sanders, & Marshall, 1974).

In the initial phase, there is visual emptiness, the *vision nulle* of Dufour; Schilder described a feeling of visual expanse without form, a darkness—*vision noire*—like holding the eyes shut. The space of the altered perception ceases to exist, perhaps like the space behind the head—though probably without its inferential status. Similar observations occur in scotoma cases. The patients of Teuber described their scotoma as a blank or void. Positive scotoma were rare.

Acutely, light and dark cannot be distinguished. Yet there may be delayed glances toward a strong light, attributed to recovering areas in the periphery. Initially, there are vivid hallucinations, colored and frightening visual nightmares. Hallucinations are mainly elementary visual phenomena, photisms with sparks, flames and flickering sensations like the effects of occipital stimulation. Visual and color imagery may be involved, probably with more extensive lesions. Restricted lesions spare visual imagery (Lerebollet & Mouzon, 1917). In hallucinations, red and green are the most common colors, blue and yellow rare. Lhermitte described achromatic hallucination and achromatic imagery, Touche, a patient with achromatic dreams. After-imagery may be present though it is uncertain whether this can precede brightness perception. Bender described prolonged after-imagery in a defective quadrant but few cases have been studied in this way. The occurrence of image phenomena usually precedes the first objective visual experience. With the return of brightness perception, hallucinations disappear and nightmares may cease. In a personal case, nightmares gave way to auditory dreams impoverished in visual content and persistent REM activity.

Acutely, the patient is indifferent or denies he is blind (Anton's syndrome). This, in my view, reflects an inability to access into analytic cognition a destructured level in one perceptual modality. We do not know how soon after the onset of cortical blindness Anton's syndrome develops. The low incidence of 25%–30% for denial given by Gloning et al. (1968) probably reflects the inclusion of incomplete or recovering cases. Denial usually clears with the first return of brightness perception.

Confabulation often accompanies and disappears with denial; there is an inner relation between them. Denial is not based on hallucinatory substitution, though possibly hallucination facilitates denial (Stengel & Steele, 1946). In my view, *hallucination, denial, and confabulation reflect a common level in language and object formation.*

Residual vision. Some authors (Goldstein, Best) claimed there were completely blind scotoma, while others (Bard, Poppelreuter) demonstrated vision in blind fields. Hemianopics can see a bright light in the "blind" field when placed in a dark room. Bard (1905) noted that such cases were still hemiachromatopsic, but this could relate to inability to verbalize a preliminary cognition. Position and size were occasionally differentiated in the blind field (Bard, 1905). Klüver (1941) commented, prophetically, "it seems possible that hemianopia is not a destruction of 'recipient' cerebral areas, but a 'total blocking of attention.'" Further studies were carried out by Bender and Krieger (1951), who showed an ability to perceive luminous targets within hemianopic, quadrantic or scotomatous parts of the visual field. There was an appreciation of color when the target intensity was raised above the absolute threshold value with exposures greater than one minute. Patients could localize targets by pointing, estimate direction and distance from fixation, distinguish a steady and flickering target and had sensations of apparent movement. No form perception was demonstrated.

It has been shown that subjects can divert their gaze, fixate and point to a light source in a hemianopic field even though denying that they saw the stimulus. Poppel, Held, and Frost (1973) presented targets in the blind field at a duration (100 msec.) shorter than the latency of saccades and found the amplitude of the saccade correlated with the distance of the target to an eccentricity of about 30°. The case of Weiskrantz et al. (1974) could look at stimuli in the blind field, and guess whether a line was horizontal or vertical, though claiming not to see the stimulus. There was evidence of simple pattern discrimination. Localization of bright targets in the hemianopic field has been demonstrated in hemidecorticate subjects (Perenin & Jeannerod, 1975). Split-brain cases can compare the size, location and movement of stimuli in the peripheral fields, suggesting integration through subcortical mechanisms (Trevarthen, 1968). Trevarthen's subject noted that when he moved one hand the object on that side disappeared. A similar phenomenon can occur in the resolution of cortical blindness.

Studies in destriate monkeys confirm a moderate preservation of visual function. Initially, it was thought that the occipital monkey responded to total luminous flux, with loss of form and color discrimination. However, Klüver remarked that such monkeys did not bump into objects unless excited and, at times, changed behavior on entering an illuminated area. Subsequently, destriate monkeys were shown to reach for localized stimuli, even stimulus pairs widely separated and briefly presented. Humphrey (1974) described the behavior of a destriate monkey over 8 years. Initially, this monkey would look at and reach for objects, then it could detect a flashing light source, then a stationary light source against a dark background and, finally, a stationary black object against a white ground. There was an impression that the monkey's visual space was "a purely subjective, self-centered space in which she could place things in relation to her own body." In monkeys with documented complete removal of striate cortex, Denny-Brown and Chambers (1976) noted preserved movement perception. The animals did not collide with walls or fall over edges, and depth perception eventually returned.

The Pasiks (1971) demonstrated that destriate monkeys can learn pattern discriminations, albeit slowly, distinguish simple shapes and orientations, and reach for small objects. Most residual vision is abolished by further destruction of prestriate cortex (also Denny-Brown & Chambers, 1976).

In cats, there is persistent responsiveness of cells in area 18 following bilateral lesions of striate cortex (Donaldson & Nash, 1973; Dreher & Cottee, 1975), though the thalamocortical system in cats is not comparable to that in monkeys. Regardless of one's interpretation of residual vision, whether by way of circumstriate, temporal, or subcortical areas, these observations indicate that *perception does not begin at the level of striate cortex.*

In recovery, there is a progressive evolution toward a external object in an object-centered space. In the course of the recovery process, a variety of partial disorders occur—agnosias, alexia—that point to successive moments in the final phase of the object representation.

Recovery and Partial Deficits

Brightness perception returns first. The patient may say he can distinguish between night and day. Poppelreuter (1917) described an amorphous quantitative light sensation based on differences in illumination. Critchley (1965) described beams of bright light. However, the patient does not see a beam but a brightness diffused over the visual field. Multiple light sources give an increased illumination over the entire field without localization, space, or depth perception. Brightness gradients cannot be discriminated. Poppelreuter mentioned a twilight sensation. This was noted by Schilder, and I have observed such cases. A change in mental state accompanies perceptual recovery. With the return of sustained brightness perception, confabulation, denial, and hallucination disappear.

The next value to return is a vague sensation of movement, predominantly for large illuminated objects. There may be apparent movement of stationary objects. According to Schilder, ill-defined objects of great expanse loom up and disappear again, perhaps similar to the transient "obscurations" in brain-damaged patients on vestibular stimulation (Gloning et al., 1968) or the obscurations and extinction phenomena in "amblyopic" fields with multiple simultaneous stimuli. The world is foggy with unclear silhouettes. Positive scotoma correspond to residual field defects after recovery. Images disappear on fixation and reappear when the patient looks away.

White usually returns before the chromatic colors. Förster's (1890) patient described a dark blue as a "dark gray," a bright blue as a "bright gray." Moving objects elicit size but not form perception. While movement returns prior to form, Teuber (1960) noted that movement stimulates a wider zone with less fatigue or fading. According to Teuber, motion and contour perception are equally impaired. Gradually, small objects are perceived and movement is not necessary for size perception. About this time, there is a return of some color perception, usually red. Color seems to precede form perception. In tachistoscopic studies, Birkmayer (1951) noted that the perception of red may block the recognition of red-colored objects. Red is the last color to be lost in progressive cases. Initially, there is a monochrome vision, erythropsia (for yellow, *xanthopsia,* etc.), the "psychic Tyndall phenomenon" described by Pötzl. There seems to be no uniform order of color return, but generally the long wave length colors (red, yellow) return before the short wave lengths (blue).

As color returns, it is loose, tangible, even penetrable, diffused over the object as a type of film. When color precedes shape perception, it does not follow the object contour; there is a melting of the color beyond the object, irradiation or "illusory visual spread." Hoff described the separation of colors from objects on occipital lobe stimulation, perhaps a regression from surface to film colors. Gelb's (1920) patient distinguished differences in brightness from white to black, but colors appeared as a film above the object. When he touched a colored object, his finger seemed to sink into the color. In recovery, surface or object colors appeared in foveal vision with film colors peripherally. The distortion of color perception is termed dyschromatopsia. In addition, colors are described as grayish, dirty, lacking in intensity, that is, unsaturated, though positive after-images may be intense and vivid, and lead to illusions.

Prior to shape perception, the visual field lacks depth, though careful studies have not been carried out. Some depth impression is normally possible in a diffusely illuminated field (Katz, 1935). However, in cortical blindness there seems not to be a sensation of visual gray or depth, which returns later. Depth estimation was attributed by Pick to angular gyrus, by Poppelreuter (1917) to occipital lobe. These are not incompatible. Biparietal cases cannot estimate relative and absolute distance, whereas occipital cases have constricted subjective fields with abnormal depth appreciation. As shape perception returns, the object boundary is unstable with flickering sensations around the figure, accentuated by fixation. In recovery without scotomata, there is a transition to an (apperceptive) agnosia where the major difficulty is in form perception. At this point acuity, as measured by dot or line discrimination, is normal. Patients may detect hue differences to 7–10 mμ and differences in luminescence to 0.1 log units; tests of spatial summation and flicker fusion thresholds may show only minor deviations from normal (Efron, 1968).

The main findings are a failure to identify, describe, or copy simple objects or line-drawings, and impaired performance on matching tests. Tracing may be impaired. In contrast, objects are identified by sound though tactile identification is usually impaired (Critchley, 1965; Lange, 1936). The defect may be so severe that simple geometric figures or even straight and curved lines cannot be distinguished. Motion is ordinarily perceived and assists in recognition. Single dots cannot be counted.

As form perception recovers, the patient is left with a residual alexia, often with defects in color recognition, so-called "pure" or agnosic alexia (Alajouanine, Lhermitte, & Riboucourt-Ducarne, 1960; Brown, 1972). This disorder also occurs with occlusion of the left posterior cerebral artery. Damage to corpus callosum is common but not invariable (Hécaen & Gruner, 1974). The reading difficulty can be severe, and related to the complexity of the written material. Letters are read better than words, letters in isolation better than letter strings, and short words better than long words.

There is confusion of similar forms (R, K) hemianopic errors (I for K, N for M), occasional mirror errors (d for b) and inversions (M for W). It is important to emphasize that patients do not have intact left field perceptions. There is prolonged latency for object recognition on tachistoscopic exposures. Even Wernicke noted that patients copied or traced letters poorly, slavishly, one at a time in the same manner they read. Neville, Snyder, Knight, and Galambos (1979) described absent NI's in the visual EP to words over right occipital region in several pure alexics.

Presumably, the left occipital lesion suppresses function in the right occipital area, an effect which may be enhanced by callosal pathology. The result is a physiological lesion of right occipital lobe. When pronounced, e.g., acute hemianopia, there is cortical blindness; when moderate, impaired form perception; when mild, alexia, a residual form perception deficit (Brown, 1981).

Summary

Cortical blindness is an abolition of the final stage in object representation. With unilateral lesions, the stage of hemifield exteriorization is lost. In hemianopia and cortical blindness, visual hallucinations, changes in imagery and elementary visual phenomena occur (Brown, 1984b). These represent endogenous percepts which become the endpoint in an attenuated object development. Similarly, the preserved vision in cortically blind and hemianopic fields reflects a preliminary or preprocessing stage elaborated through midbrain, limbic-temporal or parietal mechanisms.

The patient with cortical blindness denies that he is blind. This is not surprising since there *is* a visual experience, but at a cognitive level which only anticipates that of the reporting state. In cortical blindness there is a progression from hallucination to residual "blindsight." This reflects a destructuration back through the process of object formation. Hallucination disappears with the return of brightness sensation, and a reassertion of sensory modulation at prior levels. Since an hallucination develops over the same structure as an object (Brown, 1981a), imagery is a measure of the patency of this structure prior to striate vision.

In the recovery of cortical blindness, there is a progression from a diffuse brightness sensation to a perception of brightness gradients, then a perception of movement and size. Concurrently, there is a filmy (usually red) color perception, and the visual field takes on a limited degree of depth. These changes do not occur in a piecemeal or additive manner. The expansion of the still attenuated visual field, the viscous, objectless film colors following the reacquisition of brightness differences, the vague perception and uncertainty over real and illusory movement, and the global size estimation, all reappear together in an orderly and patterned way.

These observations indicate that within the space of the external environment there is a concealed space of object-relations and limb exploration, a space generated by mechanisms in parietal cortex and transformed through striate and circumstriate mechanisms to a fine-grained analysis of object form. Damage to striate cortex deprives the developing percept of a portion of the final modeling, so that it fails to achieve a representation of the corresponding sector of external space. A scotoma is not an empty spot in the visual field. What is lost is a microgenetic endpoint and (the consciousness of) the unrealized portion. Within the scotoma, there is a persistence of subsurface content. The meaning of hallucination and residual vision is that they are truncated object developments which survive pathology *at the surface* of the perception.

The evolution of the scotoma follows a pattern corresponding to a graded reassertion of sensation at successive levels. Recovery begins with the perception of moving targets and vague size, reflecting the reestablishment of the parietal object, and the return of some shape perception. The occipital agnosias are signposts of the recovery process. The progression from cortical blindness through "apperceptive" or form agnosia to "pure" or agnosic alexia retraces the derivation of the parietal object to a stage of featural analysis through occipital mechanisms. This progression occurs in the resolution of bi-occipital lesions, or with left occipital damage. In the latter, resolution occurs through the lifting of callosal-mediated inhibition of right visual cortex.

CONCLUSIONS

This paper has surveyed the different ways that objects degrade in pathological states. Disorders that occur with focal brain damage are viewed in relation to a multi-tiered system of object formation. It is argued that these disorders are not piecemeal decompositions, but manifestations of different moments in a hierarchically organized cognitive structure. This structure is a dynamic process which unfolds in a direction from rostral brainstem toward the visual cortex. The object is represented primitively in the upper brainstem and develops to a veridical endpoint through koniocortex. The perception consists in a series of representational levels constrained at successive points by sensory input.

Disorders in somatic space perception, in space linked to the axes and orientation of the body midline, occur with upper brainstem lesions. Damage to limbic-temporal structures displays the ensuing phase of symbolic and affective transformation, and the development of the object through fields of meaning relationships to a viewer-centered mental space. From this point, the object develops to an external, object-centered space. Damage to parietal cortex involves spatial properties of the object and object relations. Yet, the object is still incompletely exteriorized. The disturbance affects not only objects but limb actions on them. Finally, through striate and circumstriate mechanisms, object space is fully articulated, exteriorized and "detached" as an independent world around the viewer.

6
Microstructure of Images*

Jason W. Brown

INTRODUCTION

Over the years from Esquirol to Henri Ey (1973) many works on hallucination have appeared. For the most part, these are accounts of hallucinations in schizophrenia or states of delirium and drug intoxication, really little more than a catalog of hallucinatory forms with no attempt to relate the hallucination to perceptual physiology or regional brain function. The result has been a complex phenomenology, a few pseudo-theories, a lack of neurological hypotheses and much scholarly disputation. The one thing that is clear from this work is that an approach to the problem of hallucination should be grounded, not in the symptom content, which is too rich for interpretation, but on **patterns** of hallucinatory experience. If such patterns can be identified, and can be shown to correspond with damage to specific brain areas, they may be comprehensible in terms of a general theory of perception (Brown 1983b).

The search for these patterns is not an easy matter, for there are many different and seemingly unique forms of imagery. Yet, all image phenomena overlap in some characteristics. A memory or a thought image and an eidetic image share the feature of an active volitional character, while the eidetic and after-image occur in relation to an external object. An hallucination, an eidetic, and a dream image may have the same content. The after-image enlarges according to the viewer's distance from the projection surface, but this also occurs in the early stages of alcoholic hallucinosis (Morsier 1938). After-images share with phosphenes or elementary visual hallucinations the characteristic of displacement with eye movements (Brindley and Lewin 1968). Objects and, in my experience, thought images may move slightly in a direction opposite a shift in gaze. Displacement does not occur for eidetic images and hallucinations. However, attempts to scan, fixate, or attend to an hallucination may result in its disappearance. This is not simply a

*From "Imagery and the Microstructure of Perception" by J. W. Brown, 1985, *Journal of Neurolinguistics*, *1*(1), 89–128. Copyright 1985 by *Journal of Neurolinguistics*. Adapted by permission.

result of eye movement. A personal case with left hemianopic hallucinations described seeing a stocking on a bed gradually drift away and disappear just as she tried to touch it. Apart from eye and limb movement, attention also plays a role. If one attends to the content of an auditory hallucination, it may diminish and fade away. A similar phenomenon occurs in hypnagogic imagery. As soon as an active relation is established, the image tends to dissipate. This change in attention or fixation is also a change in mental state, as attention shifts from a passive, or diffuse, to a more active and focal attitude.

Obviously, one cannot simply list the behavior of images and demonstrate links on this basis. Psychopathological case studies show that there is no one type of mental imagery but rather a continuum which can be understood in terms of a dynamic of image development. The image is not the result of many disparate mechanisms, nor a sort of phantom perception distinct from the world of objects. The image is a level in the realization of the object world.

This paper argues that an image is a preparatory stage in the process leading to an object representation, and that the different types of images are manifestations of different levels of object representation. The image is like an attenuated object, or an object that actualizes at an incomplete stage. Put differently, the transition from a dream to a memory or after-image occurs over the same processing stages as an object perception. Thus, in subliminal perception studies, the observation that the dream image incorporates "unseen" material from the object perception (Fisher 1954; Pötzl 1917) is explained by the fact that the dream image represents a preliminary content in the object. This is why the content is lacking (unseen) in the original perception. In dream, the image may concern the least noticed fragments of daytime perception. Freud emphasized this point. To say that a content is in the background of a perception is also to say that it is incompletely developed. The recall of an object experience in a dream involves a revival of early stages in the original perception. Like the perception, the image also unfolds over brain structural levels. Since images refer to stages on a perceptual continuum with the object the final stage, a description of the sequence of image types is a description of the process of object formation.

In the structural model proposed in this paper, the perception is assumed to develop within the phyletic core of the brain in a direction corresponding with that of forebrain evolution. The perception is not constructed out of sensory material. Rather, a series of sensori-perceptual or physical-mental transforms maintains an unfolding cognitive representation on a course so as to model an external object. Specifically, there is a parallel hierarchy of sensory (physical) levels and perceptual (cognitive) levels distributed over evolutionary brain structure. The sensory levels act to **constrain** the development of the perceptual levels, while the perceptual levels — wholly cognitive and representational — are the contents which undergo transformation. Levels of sensory constraint appear to be discontinuous or nodal. One can speak of a retino-tectal or a thalamo-striate component. In contrast, the perceptual development seems to be a continuum with a gradual wave-like unfolding from one phase to the next (Brown 1983b).

According to this model, an object is an abstract multi-tiered construct unfolding over evolutionary and maturational stages in the brain. The unfolding process begins in the upper brainstem core, where it is constrained by retino-tectal input. This leads to a limbic-temporal stage, and then to a level of generalized neocortex. The final stage is that of koniocortical modeling. These neurological strata are aligned in a sequence which recapitulates the direction of forebrain evolution. At each level, visuo-sensory input acts upon an emerging cognitive form. The final object is a composite of all these representational levels (Brown 1977, 1983b).

The following sections take up each of these levels, or components, in the forming object representation. Damage to each level in the structure gives either a perceptual **deficit**, for example, a scotoma or an agnosia, or abnormal **imagery**, such as an hallucination. This paper reviews different types of images as levels of object representation. A discussion of perceptual deficits and temporal aspects of this model is reported elsewhere (Brown 1982 and 1983b).

One must, however, concede that little is known about the brain-structural correlates of imaginal experiences. Much of our knowledge derives from the effects of electrical stimulation of the brain. The distinction of elementary (occipital) and complex (temporal) visual hallucinations owes much to this line of research. In comparison to this experimental work, clinical study offers a rich vein of phenomological description, with no attempt at a systematization of the material, much less a correlation of focal brain areas with specific hallucinatory types. There are a number of reasons for this. Many of the reported cases are tumor and epileptic foci which do not permit reliable brain localization. Pathological conditions in which hallucination is a prominent element, such as peduncular and narcoleptic hallucination, or alcoholic hallucinosis, have no firm anatomical basis, while cases with focal brain pathology usually develop hallucinations as an intermittent fluctuant symptom in the context of a more global change in conscious level. There is also the problem that hallucination occurs without a focal lesion, in normal sleep, in psychotic cases and in diffuse intoxications.

For these reasons, a model of perception based only on hallucination is not yet possible. One has also to consider the problem of the agnosias and related conditions (Brown 1983b). Hallucination and agnosia are the positive and negative side of the same disturbance, and should be captured by the same perceptual model. In the following sections, the hallucinatory states are recounted, so to say, from the "bottom up," beginning with hallucination attributable to midbrain and limbic mechanisms. Since the pathological conditions display links to normal imagery, the normal states are discussed together with their pathological fragments, with both sets of phenomena taken to refer to the same structural level.

THE SPATIAL MAP: IMAGE PHENOMENA WHICH ARE PRESUMED TO REFLECT ROSTRAL BRAINSTEM AND/OR LIMBIC MECHANISMS

Hypnagogic Hallucination

This hallucination occurs in the transitional state, most commonly the transition to sleep. The term hypnopompic is applied to the transition from sleep to wakefulness. While hallucinations of a hypnagogic character are described on awakening, these are more often like a persistent dream image or an after-image of a dream, so that it is the hallucinatory experience on **entering sleep** that has attracted the most attention.

Such hallucinations are usually colored and located about 1-2 feet before the observer. Rare cases are described (Leaning 1925) of cycloramic hallucinations located behind the viewer's head. By far the most frequent object is a human face. It usually develops as a consolidation of fragments and changes from one visage to another. The face is generally frontal and expresses some emotion. The appearance of the face and the colors in the image are often more vivid than a perception. Designs and geometrical patterns may occur, possibly similar to entoptic phenomena. Landscapes and static scenes are described, and differ from faces in that there is no movement; the scene appears complete from the beginning. Landscapes are said to be uncommon in children and may increase in frequency with age. Among other objects, animal faces or figures are most common. The hallucination may assume a circular form, has a duration of several seconds to a few minutes, and may at times be recurrent. The images may drift across the field, and approach or withdraw from the observer, but usually do not move with the eyes. The image disappears with eye opening, increasing wakefulness, attentiveness and/or fixation. It accompanies a passive, involuntary attitude and dissipates as the observer tries to exercise control. Nabokov pointed to this characteristic of hypnagogic imagery when he wrote, "They come and go, without the drowsy observer's participation, but are essentially different from dream pictures for he is still master of his senses." The observation of a vertiginous quality (Lhermitte 1922) and a possible relation to nystagmoid movements and vestibular stimulation, though an occasional occurrence during the hypnagogic state (e.g., as in the Isakower phenomenon), do not appear to be a regular part of the imagery.

Hypnagogic imagery is infrequent in other modalities. In audition, voices and sounds are more common than music. With hallucinated faces, there is often movement of the mouth as if to speak but no sound is heard. The occurrence of combined visual and auditory imagery suggests a dream rather than a hypnagogic image. Leaning (1925) wrote of "the tyranny of a rhythm or tune over the mental machinery," implying a kind of waking hypnagogic experience in the acoustic mode. Haptic, olfactory, and gustatory images have occasionally been described. On rare occasions there may be a relation to creative thinking, for example, Kekule's image of snakes and the benzene ring, or Wagner's hallucination of the Rheingold prelude. However, these are closer to the so-called autosymbolic image of Silberer where the semantic content of the image is in the foreground.

Silberer (1951) described imagery in the transitional state which combined in a symbolic manner meaning contents from the preceding day. These images, which I have personally experienced, are extremely vivid and mobile, inventive and replete with symbolic content. The image fuses together several lines of thought or experience during the daytime period. Perhaps, the autosymbolic image is intermediate between a hypnagogic image and a dream.

The frequent report of faces, not only in hypnagogic images but in a variety of other hallucinations, is a fact of considerable interest. Perhaps, this reflects the primacy of the face in early perception and/or the revival of a dominent foveal object. Our attention tends to be riveted on faces. I have experienced hypnagogic images of cards or chess pieces after several hours of play. Fluornoy described images of the chessboard, and an image of his first anatomical dissection. Gloning described a philatelist who hallucinated stamps into a left hemianopia.

There has been some thought that increased hypnagogic imagery may introduce a psychosis. Schneider thought that hypnagogic images were the initial phase in pathological hallucination, though this has not been borne out in other studies. Possibly the association may reflect the inclusion of memory images in the hypnagogic period (Vihvelin 1948). Yet, there is some connection. Patients with an hallucinatory tendency may experience an increase in hallucination during the hypnagogic state, while patients with active daytime hallucination may show a further distortion in the hallucinatory content during the transitional period.

Peduncular Hallucination

In pathological cases, hypnagogic imagery may occur in a dramatic and persistent manner. In "peduncular" hallucination, first described by Lhermitte (1922), the characteristics of the hallucination are similar if not .identical to those of hypnagogic imagery. The hallucinations occur at the close of the day or at bedtime, in the "crepuscular" period, rather than in the transition from sleep to wakefulness. They last for seconds to minutes and may recur nightly for weeks, months, or even years. Commonly, the hallucination consists of animals, faces or human figures, at times formed scenes of kaleidoscopic experiences. The images are mobile and may change in character before the subject, e.g., a young boy changing into an old woman. There is a cinematic quality. The hallucinations are primarily visual, rarely, if ever, auditory, but occasionally there is a tactile element. Lhermitte's patient saw animals walking about the room, and stated that they felt real on touching them. This patient, as in most cases, did not mistake the hallucinations for real objects. Some patients, such as the one described below, or a case of Schilders (1953), believe in the reality of the hallucination **during** the hallucinatory experience, but on later reflection will admit to its unreal character. This was described by Lafon (1951). The attitude of the patient is generally that of amusement, even wonder, though some patients do become anxious. Chronic cases may terminate in an hallucinatory psychosis. Other features which indicate a similarity with hypnagogic images include the fact that the hallucinations are ordinarily quite vivid, colored, persist and/or intensify with the eyes closed, and may disappear on opening the eyes. A relation to Emmert's law and to eye movements has not been reported.

The disorder has been described in intoxications and following vertebral angiography, but is most often associated with a vascular lesion of the upper brainstem. Lhermitte described several cases following epidemic encephalitis, presumably also with upper brainstem pathology. de Morsier (1938) reported a few cases where the lesion involved the pulvinar, suggesting to him that the hallucinations were linked to a paravisual system running from pulvinar to parieto-occipital area. This was taken to explain delirious states occurring in the thalamic syndrome. Though this pathological correlation has not been confirmed in other case studies, it is of interest that the pulvinar, which figures so importantly in current perception research, should have been emphasized in this connection. While some authors (e.g., van Bogaert 1924) have disputed the contention that these are hypnagogic phenomena, Lhermitte's interpretation has been sustained in a major review of the condition by Albessar (1934).

Hallucination in Narcolepsy

Hypnagogic hallucinations often accompany episodes of narcoleptic sleep and occur with a frequency greater than normal prior to natural sleep in narcoleptic patients.

Hypnagogic hallucinations are part of the classical tetrad of narcolepsy, the other elements being sleep attacks, sleep paralysis and cataplectic (drop) attacks with laughing or strong emotion. These four elements do not always appear together. The cataplectic and paralytic symptoms may occur in relative isolation. Some years ago, I described a family with cataplexy and sleep paralysis in which the "motor" components of the tetrad appeared to be inherited as an autosomal dominant condition (Gelardi and Brown 1967). The anatomical basis of narcolepsy is unknown. Crosby suggested a physiological disturbance in the rostral brainstem, and there are cases of narcolepsy with tumors involving this region (Anderson and Salmon 1977; Stahl *et al.* 1980).

Summary

There is evidence that hypnagogic hallucination in narcolepsy, and perhaps in normal individuals as well, occurs with sleep-onset REM periods rather than during slow wave sleep (Hishikawa *et al.* 1968; Passouant, Popoviciu, Veloki, and Baldy-Moulinier 1968). This would account for the infrequency of hypnagogic imagery in the normal population, and the greater incidence in narcolepsy. It also would suggest a link between hypnagogic and dream hallucination, though the quality of the two is very different. Possibly, hypnagogic hallucination is an incipient dream hallucination.

The characteristics of hypnagogic hallucination in narcolepsy, and in "peduncular" hallucination, are similar to those of the normal hypnagogic period. In each case, the imagery occurs in the transitional state, there is a similar form and content and in the pathological conditions there is a probable association with a lesion of upper brainstem. Of particular importance are the relatively banal nature of the hallucinations, the normal affective state, the occurrence as an isolated event in a unitary visual field, i.e., the lack of a hemifield effect, and the occasional synaesthetic (visuotactile) quality.

The transitional state may reflect the assertion of upper brainstem or limbic mechanisms, with an attenuation of neocortical function. This would account for the altered state of consciousness, the loss of objects and the onset of imagery. The relative predominance of either midbrain or limbic structures might determine the degree of organization of the image and its symbolic content. There is likely a flux between these levels throughout normal sleep. Hypnagogic images with an historical or symbolic content, images with a strong affective element in the perceiver, or images of the autosymbolic type, point to a greater participation at the limbic-temporal level.

SYMBOLIC TRANSFORMATION: IMAGE PHENOMENA WHICH ARE PRESUMED TO REFLECT TEMPORAL LOBE MECHANISMS

Hallucinations which arise with damage to limbic-temporal mechanisms are among the most interesting of all forms of pathological imagery. The usual pathology is a tumor or epileptic focus. Horrax (1923) was one of the first to establish the importance of lesions of the temporal lobe in hallucinatory states, a relationship which has been confirmed by many subsequent investigations, though the role of different subregions within the temporal lobe has not yet been explored.

In general, the auditory cortex has been related to elementary acoustic phenomena, and neighboring "association" cortex to more complex verbal and visual hallucination. Other types of temporal hallucination, olfactory, gustatory, perhaps vestibular, have been described. Hallucination also occurs from depth stimulation in limbic structures, as does, presumably, hallucination in epileptic states. These hallucinations may be more like transitional or hypnagogic experiences (Jackson's "dreamy state") than hallucinations elicited by surface stimulation.

Hallucination in schizophrenia may also reflect limbic-temporal mechanisms. There is considerable evidence for a disturbance of limbic structures in schizophrenia (see Henn and Nasrallah 1982). de Morsier (1938) claimed that organic and schizophrenic hallucinations were fundamentally identical. Chapman (1966) argued that many organic and psychotic symptoms, including hallucination, have a common basis and reflect temporal lobe dysfunction. I have discussed similar relationships between schizophrenic and organic disorders of language and action (Brown 1977). Naturally, some differences do occur, such as scotoma in organic cases, and the chronicity and the encapsulation of hallucinatory material in schizophrenics. Of interest is that the similarity between organic and schizophrenic hallucination applies regardless of the modality. Bromberg and Schilder (1934) found no difference in olfactory hallucinations for organic and schizophrenic cases.

Stimulation of the temporal lobe in schizophrenics is reported to induce hallucinatory experiences which differ from those of the schizophrenic disorder. The former are more "perceptual," the latter more "imaginary" (Ishibashi, Hori, Endo, and Sato 1964). This may reflect the greater depth of origin of schizophrenic hallucinations. The findings of Penfield and colleagues are well known. Stimulation in auditory cortex leads to elementary acoustic hallucinations (see below) whereas more lateral excitation gives rise to a range of phenomena from memory images to complex-formed visual and/or auditory hallucinations.

Horowitz and Adams (1970) carried out depth stimulation in patients with temporal lobe epilepsy, and elicited hallucinations on stimulation of posterior hippocampus and amygdala. These were in relation to the preceding mental state, and, at times, included perceptual material. The hallucinatory content was not reiterated, and frequently was forgotten by the subject after several minutes. Speech was also altered during the hallucination with bizarre utterances, slurring and neologism. Altogether, the content of the hallucinations resembled processes of dream construction, suggesting that the hallucinations occurred as part of an altered cognitive state.

The anatomical substrate of hallucinations with temporal lobe stimulation is uncertain, but limbic structures are clearly implicated. Gloor Olivier, Quesny, Andermann, and Horowitz (1982) found an association with limbic rather than temporal neocortical stimulation. This is consistent with findings in monkey by Auerbach (1978), that behavior suggestive of hallucination occurred most reliably with stimulation in posterior hippocampus. Stimulation in posterior superior temporal cortex gave responses which were less clearly interpretable. Conceivably, limbic and temporal neocortical stimulation may be associated with different types of experiential phenomena, the former being more dream-like, the latter closer to reality. Pötzl (1949) found that hallucination in organic cases was closer to reality in the daytime and underwent symbolic and affective distortion at night. Pötzl (1949) described a case with hemianopic hallucinations of letters during the day, and ghost-like faces in the evening and attributed this to a regression from a neocortical to an archicortical (limbic) level of representation. Such observations help to explain the variability of visual hallucinations with temporal lobe stimulation and pathology, some closer to memory images, others to perceptions.

Visual Hallucination

Visual hallucination occurs in association with temporal lobe lesions. Depending on the type of hallucination, a slight right-sided predilection has been noted. If the visual field is normal, the hallucination tends to occur in a unitary space regardless of the side of pathology. If there is a visual field defect, the hallucination generally appears in the defective field. Seguin (1886) first noted this association, pointing out that hallucinations were common at the onset of a hemianopia. Hallucinations in defective quadrants have been described. In rare cases, probably occipital, the hallucination itself may be hemianopic (Schröder 1925). This may occur on the side of a visual field defect or possibly with normal fields. The exceptional case of hallucination in a normal half-field probably represents an alloaesthesia (Lhermitte and de Ajuriaguerra 1942; cf. Weinberger and Grant 1940). Hallucination in the superior or the inferior meridianal field suggests an occipital lesion.

Usually, the hallucination begins in the periphery of the field or in the area of a scotoma, and progresses to the midline where it may disappear; or the hallucination may disappear when fixated. The progression is along the horizontal, less commonly the vertical meridian. Visual hallucinations may occur with the eyes open or closed, at times in only one of these conditions. The content is variable: formed scenes, animals, people, faces, some banal, others fantastic, with or without affective tonality. Changes in size (micropsia, macropsia) and shape (morphopsia), rotatory hallucinations and other distortions may occur. These may reflect a vestibular component, and may in effect be visual-vertibular synesthetic hallucinations. Generally, hallucinations of formed scenes show a correspondence between the size of the figure and its distance from the observer. Formed hallucinations are generally not three-dimensional, but objects may appear in relief. The hallucinations may be colored or achromatic. This is true for temporal as well as occipital hallucinations. If in color, the hallucination may be monochromatic or with many hues. Monochromatic hallucinations are said to be more like memory images, and can be volitionally altered. Mobile and stationary hallucinations are described. An important accompaniment of the hallucinations is the *deja vu* experience, derealization and the dreamy state.

Summary

There may be a progression from the relatively banal hypnagogic image in the transitional state to the complex hallucination in the context of dream state mentation. This progression may reflect a shift from midbrain to limbic-temporal mechanisms. The first stage is the hypnagogic image, a single or reiterated form devoid of historical context, where the affect is in the object and not in the perceiver. This image is positioned a foot or so before the viewer — the space of the visual gray or the reach of an arm — like the face of the mother to the nursing infant, and is part of a unitary space without half-field differentiation.

The hypnagogic image then gives way to the varied content of complex hallucination and dream imagery. The image undergoes condensation, symbolic and affective transformation to an hallucination with an historical character, a development over time, a link to the life of the perceiver, and a more drawn out, articulated space. Presumably, the transitional state represents the active intrusion of midbrain mechanisms into cognition, not simply a lowered level of cortical function. Dream would represent the further (limbic) development of this content, as it is derived to a network of perceptual meaning-relations.

Auditory Hallucinations

Auditory hallucinations in association with temporal lobe lesions were described in detail by Lhermitte (1951b). Unlike visual hallucinations in which animals are heavily represented, auditory hallucinations tend to consist of speech or music. Verbal hallucinations may have a rhythmic quality. They are always in the language of the subject. In polyglots, the languages are said to remain distinct. If there are different voices or different languages, they usually do not occur at the same time. However, language mixing does occur in the transitional state in polyglots (Froeschels, 1946). A voice is identified by its verbal content and not its vocal qualities. Most authors have attributed the verbal hallucination to an exteriorization of the subject's own inner speech, retaining the intonation and accent of the subject but somehow alien to him. However, the picture is more complex than this. The hallucinated voice may be that of a gender other than the subject; the subject may hear several different voices; they may be engaged in a conversation in which the perceiver does not participate, and so on.

The relation to inner speech (Brown 1982) is suggested by the so-called "echo of thought" (*echo de la pensée*) or "echo of reading" (*echo de la lecture*). In such cases, verbal hallucination precedes the actual reading by a second or less, or by 2-3 words (Morel 1936a). Increasing the rate of reading will increase the echo, while difficulty in reading will retard it. Of interest is that the echo may reproduce words missed by the reader in reading aloud. There are reports of grammatical differences between the hallucination and the thought content. Klein (1924) described a patient who **thought**, "I should go to the doctor," and **heard** "He should go to the doctor." As with visual hallucinations, verbal hallucination is often increased in the hypnagogic period, and is diminshed if the subject attends to the individual words. Seglas (1903) noted lip or oral movement during verbal hallucinations. EMG studies indicated subvocal articulatory movements during auditory hallucinations. Patients may be able to prolong or abort the hallucination through articulatory movements. There may be a suspension of hallucination during respiratory pauses (Lagache 1934). A personal case related that he could hear his own name, i.e., bring on the echo of his name, by saying it aloud.

The verbal content may vary from a syllable, or sequence of speech sounds, to isolated words, phrases, or long recitations. Commonly, the utterance is whispered, or of reduced volume. According to Kurt Goldstein, the speech sounds have a rhythmic quality which may increase or slow down in relation to normal thought. de Morsier commented that hallucinated and spoken speech do not occur at the same time. Evidently, the localization in space is variable. Pötzl described a temporal tumor case with palilalic hallucinations moving from one side of the head to the other. In schizophrenics who lateralize their auditory hallucinations, lateralization to left hemi-space is said to be more common than lateralization to right hemi-space (Steve Levick, personal communication, 1984)

Lhermitte mentioned a case with deafness and auditory hallucinations, and findings of destruction of the auditory radiations. Hoff and Silberman (1933) induced verbal hallucinations by application of ethyl chloride to the exposed auditory zone in right superior temporal convolution. Their subject also described an echo of his thought. Hécaen and de Ajuriaguerra (1956) studied a series of cases of auditory hallucination with tumor. The location of the lesions was temporal, with some cases of combined temporal-frontal and frontal lesions. However, the frontal cases had impaired mentation while the temporal patients were mentally alert. This suggests a more general alteration in the frontal cases due to increased pressure. Hallucination in frontal cases has also been attributed to involvement of fronto-temporal pathways, i.e., the uncinate fasciculus (Schneider, Crosby, Bagchi, and Calhoun, 1961) though stimulation of frontal limbic areas, such as anterior cingulate gyrus, can produce hallucination (Bancaud *et al.* 1976). Auditory or verbal hallucination in association with gustatory hallucination and swallowing movements are referred to as Bornstein's triad, and are said to indicate a lesion of the parietal operculum.

An interesting part of the verbal hallucination is the feeling of estrangement from the hallucinated voice in spite of its resemblance to the voice of the subject. Even the echo in reading which is so clearly an exteriorization of the subject's inner speech seems foreign. The case of Hoff and Silberman stated that the voices had a strange tonality. This is common in schizophrenia where the subject may believe he is receiving external messages, or is possessed by other voices, in spite of the closeness of the hallucinated voice to his own. Clerambault commented that in relation to normal speech, the content of verbal hallucination was inferior and pejorative, more concrete, affect-laden and less abstract. Verbal hallucination produced in schizophrenics by stimulation of temporal cortex does not show this affective character. As noted, the hallucinated voices on stimulation may differ from spontaneous verbal hallucinations.

Morel (1936b) studied intensity differences between hallucinated voices and real sounds. Using changing audiometric thresholds, he found that schizophrenics experienced a difference in intensity of 10-30 decibels or more. However, there was considerable variability in the results, and even some differences in threshold according to ear.

Verbal hallucination is also common in the acute stage of "word deafness," where there is generally a bilateral lesion of the auditory cortex. This condition is close to a cortical deafness, the verbal hallucination occurring as a phase on the way to auditory imperception. In this respect, it is probably analogous to visual hallucinations in the early stages of cortical blindness. Clinical studies of verbal hallucination point to •a relation to temporal lobe mechanisms. Although the association between language and the left hemisphere suggests the possibility of a predilection for left-sided lesions, studies of verbal hallucination during seizures have not demonstrated strong laterality preferences (Serafetinidis and Falconer 1963), nor has this been found in tumor cases.

Intermediate or Questionable Forms

Autoscopic Hallucination

Heautoscopic (autoscopic) hallucination is the experience of seeing one's "double" (Lhermitte 1951a). ("Negative autoscopy" is the lack of recognition of one's mirror-image, also referred to as the "mirror sign.") The double is seen as if in a mirror; it may appear thin, discolored, even transparent, though usually it is three-dimensional and realistic. The double is silent, but some tacit communication seems to take place between it and the observer. The affective tone of the experience often has a sentimental character; at times, the observer or the double is anxious. The double may be dressed and positioned like the observer; a movement of the observer's arm may be accompanied by a mirror movement in the double. It is usually located directly in front of the subject, about a yard away (Lukianowicz 1958), and ordinarily disappears after a few seconds. The similarity with hypnagogic imagery has been mentioned by several authors. Conrad (1953) pointed to the association with an altered state of consciousness, in relation to sleep or a transitional state, or an epileptic aura. This feature, along with the fact that the double usually consists of only a face or torso and its strong affective content, are consistent with this interpretation. In hypnagogic imagery, the "faces in the night" may be of familiar or more commonly unfamiliar persons; when the face is that of the observer, it is then an autoscopic hallucination.

There are few cases of this type with focal brain lesion. Conrad's (1953) case had a pituitary tumor. This was an atypical presentation, more like peduncular hallucination. Lhermitte described a case with right temporal pathology, as did van Bogaert (1934) and Lunn (1970). According to Gloning *et al.* (1968), the disorder is related to involvement of the temporal lobe, possibly the right side predominating. In cases with visual field defect, the double is seen on the hemianopic side. In addition to cases with focal pathology, the phenomenon is seen in migraine, schizophrenic and normal subjects, and may be identical to "out of the body" experiences reported at the time of imminent death.

The "Mirror Sign"

This refers to the tendency in some patients, generally those with a severe dementia, to talk with their reflection in a mirror, and fail to recognize the mirror reflection of their own face. The first description was Kahn's case of Pick's disease, then in senile dementia (Klein 1929; Sjogren, Sjogren, and Lindgren 1952; Stengel 1943). Ajuriaguerra, Strejilevitch, and Tissot (1963b) studied 30 dements and found that an inability to utilize "mirror space" was an early sign of the recognition defect. Mild dements had difficulty pointing to body parts in the mirror reflection. Some patients were unable to recognize themselves in a picture. Gaillard (1970) maintained that the lack of recognition for the mirror image of oneself and the inability to use mirror space were not clearly associated.

I have observed several cases of this type, invariably in the context of a severe dementia and associated with other visuospatial impairments. The patient's behavior is quite variable. One moment, the patient might recognize his image, the next misidentify it or carry on a conversation with the person misidentified. The image of the examiner or other individuals in the mirror is generally correctly recognized. Logorrhea and confabulation are frequent accompaniments.

Following the technique of Gallup (1970) to demonstrate self-recognition in chimpanzee, I have surreptitiously applied charcoal markings to the forehead of two such patients. Neither case recognized the marking spontaneously, though one patient did attempt to wipe off the marking when it was pointed out to her. Another patient was unable to extrapolate from the markings on the mirror reflection to himself in spite of repeated comments about this by the examiner. As noted by others, there is generally a loss of the concept of mirror space. Objects presented from behind may provoke grasping into the mirror, a behavior similar to that of young children. The disorder in mirror space probably accompanies the impairment in self-recognition, but not necessarily the reverse, and like the mis-recognition it is inconstant, present one moment and absent the next.

de Ajuriaguerra thought the mirror sign was related to an object agnosia, especially to facial agnosia (prosopagnosia). While patients with facial agnosia may fail to recognize their picture or mirror reflection, they can generally infer the identity of the mirror image from the test situation. Difficulties in mirror space have not, to my knowledge, been demonstrated in prosopagnosics. Moreover, dements with the "mirror sign" may recognize other individuals fairly well, something the prosopagnosic will fail to do. The conceptual disorder in dementia may be partly responsible, but why is the difficulty specific to the patient's own face? Francois Michel (personal communication) has shown that normal individuals have some difficulty recognizing themselves in delayed videotape recordings. This points to the fragility of self-recognition. One's own face has more of an image quality than other faces (Harding 1982). It is inferred from reflections, and not viewed directly as an object. Perhaps, it is this aspect of self-recognition that accounts for its vulnerability in cases of dementia, where the ability to construct and infer an image such as one's own face may be impaired, as a sign of impending object breakdown (agnosia).

Capgras Syndrome

Capgras and Reboul-Lachaud (1923) refer to a condition now known as the *Capgras syndrome,* in which an individual believes that a familiar person, usually a spouse or a child, has been replaced by a double or an imposter. The condition occurs in schizophrenia, but also in toxic and brain-damaged cases (Hayman and Abrams 1977; MacCallum 1973). Christodoulou (1977) reported a series of psychotic cases in which EEG abnormalities were common. Among organic patients, frontal and temporal lobe pathology, has been reported with a suggestion of a right hemisphere bias.

The Capgras syndrome seems to occur in the context of a depersonalization state with a loss of object familiarity. In some respects, it is a delusion within a "negative autoscopy," a delusion built around the failure to recognize the most familiar objects. However, it is unclear whether such patients have a disturbance of self-recognition (i.e., "mirror sign"). However, in the Capgras phenomenon the failure in recognition is associated with delusion or confabulation, and in this way differs from the mirror sign.

The Capgras phenomenon and the mirror sign illustrate the close relation between perception, hallucination, and delusion. A disturbance at an early stage in object formation affects an object in relation to its affective or experiential content. The image of the self is affected (mirror sign), or highly familiar and emotionally charged objects, because they have a strong affective and symbolic value.

The disturbance in the object is accompanied by a confabulatory element.

Confabulation may invade the mirror image and lead it to be identified as a close relative, or close relative may become imposters or doubles. In such cases, the confabulation — or the delusion — points to a prelexical conceptual phase in language production, just as an hallucination points to an image phase in object formation. One can say that an hallucination is the perceptual form taken by a delusion when it (the delusion or confabulation) was previously the cognitive element in a defective object. This is why in psychotics we say that thoughts objectify in hallucinations. The hallucination captures the delusional thought which previously involved an object which was only beginning to break down. A delusion is a transitional stage in object breakdown prior to hallucination. In senile patients, it is often difficult to distinguish between delusion and hallucination unless the subject actually reports "seeing" the described experience.

Lilliputian hallucinations

Two other types of hallucination show features of temporal lobe and/or hypnagogic imagery. These are **Lilliputian hallucinations** and the **syndrome of Charles Bonnet**. Lilliputian hallucinations were first described by Leroy in 1909, and consist of scenes of small people, objects or animals, which are seen in miniature. They are a form of microscopic hallucination, in which the hallucinatory world is miniaturized. The disorder does not seem to occur with micropsia in perception. It appears in toxic or drug states, schizophrenia, temporal lesions, and during hypnagogy. Like other forms of hypnagogic imagery, the hallucinations are commonly recognized as unreal. They may be viewed with interest or detachment, occasionally with anxiety or other affective tonality. Though generally visual, auditory and olfactory elements may be present. Hallucinated voices are said to have a Lilliputian tone, to be small and of diminished amplitude. When the content consists of animals or small creatures, the term zoopsia is applied. In the tactile sphere, this may give rise to the so-called "parasitic delirium" or "vermification" (Faure, Berchtold, and Ebtinger 1957).

The syndrome of Charles Bonnet (de Morsier 1967) is an hallucinatory disorder in the aged, similar to hypnagogic imagery and Lilliputian hallucination. The hallucinations are exclusively visual, may occur at the close of day, are recognized as hallucinatory, and have a vivid, complex, often miniature, mobile character. They may be microscopic, macroscopic or normal in size, and with illusory distortion. Of interest is that the position of the observer plays a role; the hallucination may change in size or character when the subject reaches out to touch it. The hallucinations may be lateralized, presumably to the side of a visual field defect. Some authors have claimed that the disorder is related to cataracts or other ocular pathology, though there are sufficient cases with normal vision to disconfirm this view. In many cases, there is no clear demarcation between these various hallucinatory syndromes. Elements of one disorder may blend with those of another, and features of hypnagogic imagery may alternate with those of dream-like distortion.

Summary

In all the hallucinatory forms discussed so far, which are presumed to reflect limbic-temporal mechanisms, the image comes upon the perceiver involuntarily, often beginning in the peripheral field. The hallucination occurs most often in the evening or pre-sleep period, and if present during the day undergoes symbolic transformation (distortion) in the evening. The image is vivid — at times more vivid than life; it is fluid and changing, though generally without an historical, or story-like, character. The image often has a strong affective content, or the affect may be shared between image and perceiver. There is a continuum from images that are conceptually impoverished (hypnagogic imagery) through images which fuse various lines of thought in a symbolic manner (autosymbolic images of Silberer) to images that are dynamic and conceptually rich (dream hallucination). Delusional and confabulatory elements are often prominent.

The space within which these images appear is not an empty space between hallucinatory objects but has a tangible, object-like quality. When a description can be elicited, hallucinatory space is often described as lacking in depth, rather like an extension of the perceiver, or a medium within which both image and perceiver exist. Movements of the perceiver may alter the image and its space. Touching the image, attending to it, "seizing" it visually or acoustically, may lead to changes in size and shape. The object may move nearer or farther away or disappear. This is characteristic of hallucinations referable to limbic-temporal mechanisms. They occur in an egocentric, viewer-centered space, so that actions of the viewer develop in, and so alter, the same space as that of the hallucination.

In patients with unreal or dream-like hallucination, especially when the imagery is bizarre or fantastic, and involves several modalities, there is usually poor recollection for the hallucinatory experience. The more dream-like the image, the less it is recalled. Hécaen discussed this type of hallucination and the deficient recall which accompanies it. The relation between the hallucinatory content and recall raises the question of a link between hallucination and memory imagery. One can have a memory image for an object perception and for an hallucination. We have all had the experience of uncertainty as to whether a recollection is a dream or a prior perception. In a very real sense, the memory image is what survives into waking cognition of the limbic dream image. Conversely, fantastic hallucinations emerge out of the initial stage of the memory image.

Stimulation of the temporal lobe may produce a memory image or an hallucination, depending on the clarity of the experience. In temporal lobe epilepsy, a patient may have an aura which is not recalled, but can be elicited on depth stimulation. The hallucination — or memory image — is lost when the stimulation is halted (Horowitz et al. 1970). In epileptic cases, the line between an hallucination and a memory image is not always clear; the memory image is heard or visualized like an hallucination. An epileptic aura which can be recalled tends to be closer to reality than one that is forgotten. In fact, one can say that an aura is a memory image, but one that develops involuntarily and takes on hallucinatory clarity. This type of image is sometimes called a "pseudohallucination." This is an hallucination which is not taken for a real perception. It is midway between a memory image and a true hallucination.

An hallucination is a memory image at a greater depth. Conversely, the memory image is what happens to the hallucination when it is constrained by sensory information at the parietal level in a direction toward an object perception. This transformation from a level of hallucinatory imagery to one of memory and eidetic imagery is the topic of the following section.

OBJECT RELATIONS: IMAGE PHENOMENA WHICH ARE
PRESUMED TO REFLECT PARIETAL LOBE MECHANISMS

The object representation, or the abstract image which precedes it, is selected through a limbic-temporal operation to a target object realized through perceptual mechanisms in the parietal cortex. Image phenomena at this stage are characterized by adequate representational targets, a three-dimensional spatial character, reduced affective content and the occurrence of illusions and distortions situated not in a purely subjective image but in the object itself. Memory and eidetic images, and visual illusions, fall into this category.

Memory and Thought Imagery

A memory image has a "sensory" or experiential content; it is revived after an interval from a prior object but it is weaker than an eidetic image, vague, distant and more tenuous. The memory image is seen in the "mind's eye," but it is not really seen; it is not pictured like an eidetic image or an hallucination. Individuals differ in the clarity of their memory images, from sketchy, indistinct images to vivid images of an eidetic type. The more detailed and pictural the memory image, the more it approaches an eidetic image. One difference between the two is that the structure of the scene that is recalled is preserved in the memory image, but its content is not visualized. The memory image, therefore, seems vague and indistinct in comparison to the eidetic image.

If recall for details in a memory image parallels the degree to which the image is visualized, eidetics should have better recall, a point that is still controversial. However, the superior visual recall of eidetics hardly seems in doubt after the extraordinary performance of an eidetic woman with the Julesz random dot stereogram. Her ability to fuse a real with an eidetic image to discern a geometrical pattern implies the revival of an almost limitless number of 'bits' of information in the eidetic image (see Julesz 1979; Strohmeyer and Psotka 1970). Perhaps, in eidetics the **verbalization** of detail, not the clarity of the image, is the limiting factor in visual memory.

In some respects, the indistinct content of a memory image is like the empty segment of a word one is searching for. The content of a (visual) memory image is like the content of a (verbal) memory image of a word in a "tip of the tongue" state. The indistinctness arises because the content is not fully derived into an end stage cognition. If one could withdraw into this content, that is, into a cognitive state co-extensive with the content, the vagueness would be replaced by semantic or symbolic transformation. Put differently, the selection of a verbal or visual configuration through a system of lexical or symbolic relationships is incomplete, and this incompleteness survives as the indistinct content of the memory image. I believe the continuum in visual perception corresponds in language to that from the tip-of-the-tongue state to inner speech to actual word production.

The memory image resolves out of a deeper level of symbolic transformation. It is midway between a dream and an object. As the memory image achieves a state of greater resolution, there is also a dawning sense of familiarity. The image is felt to belong to the perceiver, it is a personal object. Gradually, this, too, is lost as the image becomes an external thing belonging to a world outside the perceiver. This feeling of familiarity is related to the phenomenon of *deja vu*, where the perceiver believes he has previously had the same object experience. This feeling reappears in the first stages of object breakdown, as the object recedes back to the image which prefigured it. *Deja vu* is the feeling that an object which is positioned in the world also belongs to oneself. It is an early sign of object loss in psychotic decompensation and epileptic states.

It is said there is a difference between an image and an operation which is applied to that image. A memory image is revived and then may undergo transformation, but a genuine revival takes place first. Objects can be introduced and altered which are not a part of the original image. Novel and fantastic forms can be called up. One can imagine a three-headed elephant dancing on the head of a pin. Here, the memory image assumes the character of a productive thought or imagination image. This is really a type of complex memory image in which conventional forms are recombined in unusual ways. The degree of recombination determines whether it is a memory or thought image.

We speak of a memory image when the **reproductive** element is prominent, and of a thought image when the **productive** element is in the foreground. The memory image does not achieve the clarity of the eidetic image nor the creativity of the imagination image. Thought imagery is also volitional and can be manipulated at will, while there is a more passive attitude to the memory image. Truly creative images come unbidden. The memory image becomes a thought image when a change is induced in its content. The result is a complex image in which many memory images are blended together.

However, complexity is not the only change that occurs as the memory image undergoes transformation. The memory image may take on an autoscopic quality. The subject is included as an object in the revived scene. Attneave and Farrar (1977) suggested that the "mind's eye" has a cycloramic $360°$ field. There are even descriptions by Bleuler (1922) of "extra-campine" hallucinations where the subject sees something behind his head. Of course, there is a difference between "seeing behind the head" and "seeing" oneself in a $360°$ field. Strangely enough, the autoscopic element does not seem extrinsic to the memory image but fits quite naturally into the imaged content.

These signs of growth, lability and inventiveness in the memory image, and the link to thought or imagination images, establish a relation with limbic imagery and the level of symbolic transformation out of which the memory image developed. Conversely, the fact that the memory image is directed toward the world, toward perceptions in that world, the volitional or purposeful attitude which accompanies it, and the changed affective state, these all point to a relation with veridical objects. In these respects, the memory image is transitional between limbic temporal hallucination or dream and object perception.

There are few studies of the memory image in pathology. Some cases have been described with a loss of visualization (irreminiscence) as an isolated defect. However, the two patients described by Charcot (1883) were also seen by Freud who considered them neurotics (Schilder 1951), and the cases of Brain (1954) had a history of psychiatric disorder. There is a report of impaired mental imagery with a left mesial temporo-occipital lesion (Basso, Bisiach, and Luzzatti 1980). The case is unsatisfactory, however, because of the presence of aphasia and an incomplete evaluation. Whether a pathological loss of imagery can occur in the absence of other perceptual impairments, or more subtle verbal and cognitive deficits, is uncertain. There is some evidence for the reverse situation, disordered object perception with preserved mental imagery. This could be anticipated if the image forms the underpinnings of the perception; that is, if the perception is derived from the image and not the other way around.

Studies of visual memory have shown that defective recall for faces, geometric or nonsense patterns and routes, is associated with bilateral or right-sided pathology. For faces and routes, the mesial temporo-occipital area has been implicated. It is likely that parietal lesions, especially right-sided, also lead to impaired visual memory (Humphrey and Zangwill 1951). Certainly, the ability to image spatial relations is affected (Bisiasch 1982).

Eidetic Imagery

An eidetic image is a perception which is revived. This may occur immediately after the perception or weeks or months later. The eidetic image is seen in external space even with the eyes closed. It has a perceptual character (Gray and Gummerman 1975). Even illusions such as the Necker cube reversal may occur in the eidetic image (Leask, Haber, and Haber 1969). The phenomenon is mainly visual; auditory eideticism occurs chiefly for music. According to Jaensch (1930), the eidetic image appears on a continuum between the memory and the after-image.

In the after-image type of eidetic, the image is closely bound to the stimulus object. It is two-dimensional and can be altered by the observer only with difficulty. It is increased with fixation and may appear in complementary colors. The memory image type of eidetic is more common. It is three-dimensional, always positive to the stimulus color, not aided, at times hindered, by fixation, and accentuated by meaning in the stimulus and richness of detail. Of interest is that even within the same colored picture, detail which is meaningful or of interest to the observer will be positive, while other elements will appear in complementary colors. Moreover, like the hypnagogic image, details and colors may be brighter and more vivid than in the stimulus object.

It is especially the memory type of eidetic image that undergoes transformations and can be voluntarily altered by the observer. Klüver (1933) found that the eidetic image was often fragmentary, at times with a splitting of the stimulus into meaningless detail. These fragments could reappear minutes or hours later, and change in shape, size and color. Rotation and dislocation also occurred. In the eidetic image of printed words, letters may be omitted, scrambled or superimposed. Attention can be directed to a missing element, and the element will suddenly reappear. Certain parts of the stimulus object can be called up separately. In children, the eidetic image may disappear if it is named (Haber 1979).

Jaensch (1930) argued that the eidetic image and the perception developed out of an undifferentiated unitary ground. Klüver saw a common origin of the eidetic image and the perception. For him, these pointed to different levels of psychological reality. At one end of the scale were transient subjective phenomena; at the other, hallucinations.

It has been argued that the eidetic image is a primitive perception. In psychotic regression, the initial change in object perception is said to have eidetic characteristics. Eidetics are perhaps more inclined to develop hallucinations in toxic and other states. The predilection of eidetic imagery for children has been offered as evidence for a more preliminary position of the eidetic image on the path of object perception.

That there is a transition between an eidetic and a memory image seems indisputable. However, the transition to an after-image is less clear. Eidetics may have prolonged after-images which are said to be sustained without the usual fluctuations. However, in the original studies of Jaensch, prolonged after-imagery was used as a screening test for eidetics. Many of the resemblances between eidetic and after-images were criticized by Allport (1928) who argued that the eidetic image which behaves like an after-image is, in fact, a true after-image aroused through fixation in the process of forming an eidetic image. However, at some point, an after-image becomes an eidetic image. Quercy (1936) claimed that the after-image does not transform into an eidetic image but is "invaded" and replaced by the eidetic image. Attempts to distinguish between the two on the basis of such parameters as Emmert's law, complementary colors, or displacement with active eye movements, have not been wholly successful as these are not invariable features of after-images, and are described in some eidetics. Meenes and Morton (1936) found that the after-images of eidetic subjects did not conform to Emmert's law. Even a true hallucination may seem to move in the direction of eye movements, though a relation to the direction of the observer's "attention" is a complicating factor.

In sum, an eidetic image is a memory image which achieves the status of an almost real perception. Having the object beforehand is not the essential feature of the eidetic experience. It is the duration after exposure and the intensity of revival which distinguish the memory and the eidetic image. Both are spatial images; they behave like perceptions. The eidetic is just a later stage in the objectification of a memory image.

If the eidetic image is closer to a perception, the memory image is closer to a dream. The memory image is like a dream image which has come up to the threshold of awareness. Conversely, a dream which disappears as one awakens is like a memory image just before its content becomes known. In some ways a memory image is like an eidetic image of a dream. The line which separates the dream from the world of waking perception is no more finely drawn than that between the memory and the eidetic image. As the image unfolds through these phases, between the dream and the object, there is a loss of affective strength, of creativity and intensity in the image, and a progressive reduction in the extent to which the image brings forth new content. These are given up in the realization of a fixed and stable object world.

Illusion and Hallucination

In the parieto-occipital phase of the perception, there is a consolidation of the forming spatial, temporal, and figural elements. The object and its surround begin to conform to the spatio-temporal constraints of the external world. A disturbance at this point will appear as a change in the spatial attributes of a "real" object positioned in an extrapersonal space. Both hallucinations and illusions may occur in the same patient. In fact, the same symptom may have illusional and hallucinatory manifestations. The symptom reflects the degree to which an image objectifies. Formed hallucinations are not ordinarily associated with pathology of the occipito-parietal region, but there are cases in which this has occurred. Lance (1976) described several patients with unilateral lesions and hallucination in the defective hemifield. These were generally scenes, faces, or animals, devoid of thematic context or symbolic meaning and characteristically in color. The hallucination of verbal material, so common in auditory cases, is rare in visual hallucination. Pötzl described hallucinations of letters in a left hemianopia. A personal case with a left field defect had hallucinations of Gothic letters, especially a D, on the left side. These occurred with the eyes open, and were associated with a mild impairment in color perception and some difficulty in reading letters. This case is instructive in showing a relationship between the clinical deficit and the hallucinated material.

The more typical symptom in parieto-occipital cases is not hallucination, but illusory phenomena. These may appear at the onset of pathology, or develop in the recovery of a hemianopia or cortical blindness. A common symptom in the resolution of form perception, which also occurs as an isolated or initial change in perception, is figural distortion or metamorphopsia.

Metamorphopsia

A good example of this disorder is the case of Henschen (1927) in which people appeared bent. Lenz (1944) described a case with a right slope to horizontal surfaces. van Bogaert's patient (1934) perceived himself elongated and thinned out in a mirror. Flat objects may become convex or concave. The distortion commonly involves the human form, especially the face. The disorder is related to parieto-occipital lesions, chiefly right-sided (de Ajuriaguerra and Hécaen 1964, Mouren and Tatossian 1963). Gloning et al. (1968) found distortions of contours with lesions of either hemisphere, but predominantly right-sided cases. The effect of vestibular excitation on these symptoms is well known. Pötzl (1943) and Gloning et al. (1968) showed that caloric stimulation induced figural distortions in incomplete (partial or recovering) cases. Again, this effect was most pronounced with right posterior lesions. Their explanation was an "invasion" of the visual area by parietal vestibular impulses.

These phenomena may be related to object rotations and reversals. Oblique vision seems to be related to perception of the vertical. Deviation of the vertical was first described by Gelb. In his case, the apparent deviation was to the left while the after-image of a luminous vertical line was inclined to the right. In Hoff's case vertical stripes were inclined 30° to the right. Oblique vision is thought to be associated with occipital or occipito-parietal lesions, and is closely bound up with vestibular activity.

Klopp (1951) discussed the illusion of vision at $90°$ (Umkehrtsehen). This can involve the object of fixation or the entire visual array. Objects appear turned to a right angle. Castaigne and Graveleau (1953) described this symptom just prior to the onset of an incomplete left hemianopia. The illusion should be terminated by eye closure. There are cases in the literature (Mouren and Tatossian 1963) of $180°$ reversals. There is reversal on both the vertical and right-left axes. A case of Pötzl (1943) saw his daughter standing on her head. The patient also had vertical nystagmus. According to Mouren and Tatossian (1963) the disorder is associated with a defect in ocular motility. These object reversals can occasionally also involve the body sense. There may be a feeling of levitation or inclination of the body to one side. There is a celebrated case of Lüers and Pötzl (1941) where persistent object reversal was accompanied by the sensation that the patient was standing on her own head.

Another form of visual illusion, possibly related to the above, is alteration of stereoscopy. Objects appear flat and two-dimensional. Riddoch's (1917) case saw the contours of people but not their depth; faces seemed flattened. Scenes were like sets in the theatre. The patient of Chavany (1942) saw objects as if pictures on a wall. This occurred in the evolution of a cortical blindness. There appears to be an aspect of derealization in these phenomena. In focal cases, the anatomical correlation is chiefly right parieto-occipital. A variant of this illusion is an accentuation of the figural element; the figure may become detached from the background. This occurs in parieto-occipital and temporal cases. Perhaps, similar is the patient of Hoff who had the illusion of a recession of space though objects were unchanged.

These illusions have been attributed to a disorder of central vestibular mechanisms which becomes more prominent with damage to the parieto-occipital area. Foerster (1936) described vertigo in patients with stimulation and pathological lesions in the superior parietal lobule. de Morsier (1938) reported parietal cases with vertigo, nystagmus and other vestibular symptoms. Parietal stimulation induces visual distortion, changes in object size and apparent movement. Schilder (1933) described patients of this type. Some of the visual illusions may be related to nystagmus. Movement of the after-image can be induced by vestibular sensation. There is also a darkening of the visual field (obscurations, "foggy" vision) which has been compared to a transient cortical blindness. In toxic and psychotic states, caloric stimulation will induce an alteration and distortion in the hallucination. Hoff described a case of recovered visual agnosia where the agnosia returned during vestibular stimulation. A vestibular effect is likely in deviations of the subjective vertical. Ettlinger, Warrington, and Zangwill (1957) studied the effects of vestibular stimulation and proposed a vestibular basis for some aspects of visual disorientation and metamorphopsia.

Disorders in size and distance perception can occur with ocular and vestibular impairments, but also with lesions of the parieto-occipital region. The term

dysmegalopsia refers to changes in object size. This may occur with perimetrically normal fields, as in Bregeat, Klein and Thiebaut's (1947) case of left occipital tumor, who had the feeling that objects presented on the right side were larger. This patient also perceived objects as larger with the right eye. Generally, size alteration (micropsia, macropsia) points to a damaged field. The patient of Goldstein and Gelb (1918) had micropsia in the affected visual field though objects exposed in both fields together were seen as smaller. Usually, the illusion of an object becoming larger is associated with an illusion of it as nearer, and the reverse. In the case of Bender and Krieger (1951), micropsia increased as the object was moved peripherally. In some cases the defect may extend beyond visual perception. Pick (1904) noted that macropsia is accompanied by micrographia, and micropsia by macrographia. This occurs even with the eyes shut. Wilson (1916) had a case in whom passive movements of the right arm were imitated by the left with movements which were twice as large. Cases have been described in which movements of the hands, or manipulated objects, seemed altered in size. Such phenomena often point to a neurotic or psychotic origin. According to Lewy (1954) altered size perception is a sign of beginning ego disintegration.

In the series of Gloning *et al.* (1968) this symptom was frequently associated with dreamy states and uncinate fits, at which time it is transient and associated with an alteration of consciousness. In several cases there was a direct transition to a *deja vu* experience. Gloning *et al.* (1968) suggest that dysmegalopsia and *deja vu* are regressions in the experience of space and time perception.

Two forms can be distinguished, one closer to the perception, another more imaginal. These may relate to parieto-occipital and temporal lesions, respectively. However, the localization is not that clear. Penfield and Jasper (1954) suggested that discharges in the parainsular cortex may result in macropsia. MacLean (1975) identified some units in this area which discharged to an approaching object. There is more agreement on the interpretation of the phenomenon by Bender and Teuber (1947, 1948), as an alteration in size constancies. They noted that size constancy depends on a relative micropsia and macropsia. Constancy requires that objects enlarge to some extent as they move away, and shrink as they approach.

Alterations of motion perception can occur in parieto-occipital cases. In incomplete field defects the threshold for motion perception may be elevated, requiring that a target be moved across a wider angle or with greater acceleration (Teuber 1960). There is a change in the critical flicker frequency, and fusion may occur without an intervening phase of apparent motion. Apparent movement may also occur across a cortical scotoma. According to Teuber, these defects all occur together and have a common basis.

In rare cases, there may be a loss of the continuity of perception. The patient sees a series of more or less stationary images. More common is the illusion that events are speeded up or, less often, slowed down. There may be a slowing in central vision and acceleration in the periphery. A stimulus may seem to move excessively fast in defective areas of the visual field. According to Schilder, in vestibular cases time intervals are underrated. The time sense is also altered in depersonalization, which may be a part of this perceptual disorder. Disturbed motion perception is common in drug states and intoxications. These changes may be limited to vision or can involve other perceptual modes. A patient of Hoff and Pötzl had accelerated auditory perceptions, hallucinations of voices and music as well as a lengthening of subjective time. Wagner's (1943) cases of visual acceleration were said to have a "time agnosia." In focal cases, the lesion is parieto-occipital, possibly with a right-sided accentuation. The only explanation so far offered is that of Hoff and Pötzl who again explain it on an influx of vestibular impulses due to a breakdown in the "defenses" of the damaged occipital region.

Polyopia

Another perceptual alteration which may occur in parieto-occipital field defects or in resolving cortical blindness is **polyopia**. This condition is characterized by multiple image formation, at times monocular, and highly correlated with obscurations and elementary visual hallucinations (Gloning *et al.* 1968). Mingazzini (1908) was the first to describe it in cases of occipital trauma. Subsequently, it was found in association with peripheral visual and vestibular disorders, but it is most commonly associated with lesions of the parietal and occipital lobes. Several different forms have been described: "sun-images" which are similar to the dazzling sensation on staring at the sun; a type in which the secondary images become progressively more distant; and a "concentric" form with circular images around a central object. The secondary images tend to be less distinct than the principal image. There appears to be an illusional and hallucinatory form, the latter persisting on eye closure. According to Teuber and Bender (1949), polyopia usually requires fixation of at least five seconds or more, disappears on passive fixation of the eyes and is induced or accentuated with eye movement. The relation to disordered ocular motility seems well-established. Polyopia is associated with nystagmoid eye movements during fixation but also occurs if an object is moved and the eyes are kept stationary.

In cases of hemifield defect, polyopia occurs in the defective field and disappears as the object is moved into the intact field. Vertical polyopia may be associated with vertical nystagmus. Hoff and Pötzl (1935b) explained it as a conflict during attempts at fixation. Goldstein agreed with this and proposed an origin on the basis of a pseudofovea. These observations are incorporated in the Teuber-Bender (1949) model which postulates an imbalance during the act of fixation between intact and damaged occipital regions. The multiple images result from a conflict between the true fovea and a false (pseudo) fovea. This conflict, it is suggested, could result in either amblyopia, polyopia, or normal vision if the true macula predominates. It is probable, however, that the disorder in ocular motility is not the cause of the polyopia but a manifestation of a common underlying disturbance.

Summary

In sum, the parieto-occipital disorders reveal the spatial relationships which make up the fabric of the object world. These disorders display aspects of an object-centered Euclidean space which is derived out of the egocentric, viewer-centered space of the limbic-temporal stage. Various types of imagery which result from parietal lesions have in common the disruption of a level of object relations. This is reflected in a change in object size, distance, orientation, and position. The change can involve space perception along just one of these dimensions to give the appearance of a selective disturbance. Such isolated defects are important to the understanding of the fine organization of the level. They also allow us to infer what might be the composite function of the region; namely, that it mediates a transform in the object development which conveys the image and its subjective space to a "real" object in a space that is "external" to the viewer. The progression from the dream, to the memory image, to the eidetic image captures this transform in normal imagery.

Illusory phenomena occur with alterations of the posterior hemisphere. There may be a slight right hemisphere predilection. The parietal and parieto-occipital cortices are implicated, but temporal lobe lesions can also produce these effects. Lesion of the posterior parietal area can produce either a spatial illusion or a deficit in spatial perception. The illusion is what the viewer perceives. It is the positive aspect of the deficit. Spatial illusions have their counterparts in deficits in space perception; the spatial deficit mirrors the spatial illusion but it is the illusion that is perceived. The deficit is the illusional change when it is embedded or submerged in a completed object.

REPRESENTATION OF EXTERNAL OBJECTS: IMAGE PHENOMENA PRESUMED TO REFLECT OCCIPITAL MECHANISMS

An eidetic image is usually considered to be the trace of a perception in the immediate past. One can also say that an eidetic image is a residue of the processing of the distal segment of the object formation. The final object emerges out of the transition which leads from a memory image to an eidetic image. It is the final phase in the image development. The transformation of a spatial image to an independent "external" three-dimensional object, and the featural analysis of that object, are mediated by mechanisms at the level of striate and prestriate cortex.

Though an eidetic image is actually **seen** like an object, it is still acknowledged as a mental representation. What is the difference between a vivid eidetic image and an object? Could an eidetic image not preceded by a perception be taken for a "real" object? In my view, a three-dimensional eidetic image of comparable clarity and detail would lose its volitional, mental character and would be indistinguishable from a perception. The extent to which the image replicates the perception is the extent to which it approximates an object. The transition from an eidetic image to an object, and the relation to striate and prestriate mechanisms can be approached through a study of the after-image (AI) and related phenomena, cortical phosphenes and elementary hallucinations.

A cortical phosphene differs from an eidetic image in that it does not reveal a link to the viewer's cognition. The phosphene, or the AI, involves an object at the endpoint of its development. For this reason, the AI seems to follow a different set of rules than other mental images; it takes on certain of the inferred attributes of physical objects. For instance, the absence of size constancy in the AI is due to the fact that size and distance effects occur in the transition to the spatial image at a preceding level. This transition is lacking in the AI, which develops at the surface of the perception. Similarly, the AI is not stabilized with respect to ocular deviations, because it has not developed in relation to an action. The action, the eye movement, is correctly interpreted but the lack of a preliminary perceptual content corresponding to it obviates an adaptation (cancellation) of the apparent displacement. In other words, the displacement of the AI with eye movement is a sign that the eye movement, but not the AI, has gone through a preliminary cognitive phase. The fact that the AI does not develop into the abstract space of objects explains why it does not replace objects like other hallucinations but lies over them as a transparent two-dimensional film.

After-Images

We know a great deal more about the phenomenology of the after-image than its psychological basis. Much of the descriptive material is quite familiar. The AI is related to the intensity and duration of the original stimulus, and is of a longer duration when the stimulus is in the fovea. When seen against a light background, it is negative to the original object; that is, in the complementary color, and is positive (same color) against a dark background. The AI can be prolonged by eyeblinks or stroboscopic flashes. It undergoes a "flight of colors," though the sequence of color change may be variable. After-images of motion can be obtained with a rotating spiral. The occurrence of AI's on stimulation of an eye momentarily blinded by pressure has been taken as a sign of its retinal origin, though there are difficulties with a purely retinal interpretation (Oswald, 1957). Thus, an AI to a monocular stimulus is perceived binocularly. There is a report by Popov (1953, 1954) that after-images can be conditioned. Certain retinal phenomena, such as phosphenes, which are produced on mechanical stimulation of the eyes, are localized by the subject in the appropriate eye and are not, like the AI, projected into space. Both positive and negative after-images have been described to eidetic images. Jaensch (1930) reported an eidetic child who, on being asked to imagine a colored object, developed negative afterimages. Binet and Fere (1898) noted that subjects under hypnosis, if given a suggestion of a color, could form an AI in the complementary color. A negative AI on waking from a dream has been described. There is also the possibility of a heightened capacity for after-imagery in eidetics, and reports of alpha blocking during AI experiences.

The AI moves in the direction of active eye movements. Since the AI remains stationary relative to the retina, it can be used to measure displacement effects due to ocular movement (Yarbus 1967). In fact, Helmholtz used after-images to study his own eye movements during reading. A method has been developed to use the AI to demonstrate microsaccadic movements. Brindley, Goodwin, Kulikoski, and Leighton (1976) found that curarization of one eye eliminates the movement of the AI only in that eye. There is also a correspondence between the position of the eyes and the projected locus of the after-image (Mack and Bachant 1969).

Unlike objects, the AI is not displaced by pressure on the eyes. Karrer and Stevens (1930) found movements of the AI with passive movements of the whole body. The question of displacement of the AI with reflex movements is uncertain. The AI appears to follow the slow phase of nystagmus. This was described by Hebel and Luether (in Teuber 1960) with optokinetic and vestibular stimulation. However, Karrer and Stevens (1930) failed to observe movement during the slow phase of nystagmus induced by rotation, while the AI seemed to disappear during the fast phase. Patients with nystagmus do not ordinarily complain of movements of objects. When object movement does occur, this is usually in association with spontaneous rhythmic tremor of the eyes, or "oscillopsia." However, patients with labyrinthine disorders do show object displacement. There may be fluctuation of the horizon in vertical nystagmus. In my own experience, the AI is not displaced during eye closure in the upward rotation of the Bell's phenomenon.

When an AI is projected on an object, it appears in the plane of the object and adapts to its irregularities. The AI takes part in visual illusions. An AI of a right-angle cross which is "projected" on a perspective drawing, for example, a cube, will assume the perspective properties of the object and will appear distorted. Unlike the object, which diminishes in size with distance from the observer, the AI increases in size according to the distance of the projection surface. This is not a consistent feature, but generally the AI does retain a constant visual angle, a phenomenon referred to as "Emmert's Law." Chapanis, Uematsu, Konigsmark, and Walker (1973) have shown that this also occurs with phosphenes elicited on stimulation of the occipital lobe (see below). This would indicate that the AI does not show size constancy. However, Gregory (1968) found that Wundt's horizontal-vertical illusion (a vertical line seems longer than a horizontal of the same length) occurs in the after-image.

There are some studies of the AI in pathological states. Jung (1979) has shown that migraine phosphenes, like after-images, move with voluntary gaze and are displaced in the direction of the slow phase of nystagmus. Peatfield and Rose (1981) described a case of migrainous visual symptoms in a 38-year-old woman, enucleate since age 2 from retinoblastoma. This patient described circles, squares, triangles, oblongs and snakes of different colors, though she was unable to name the colors. Such cases provide additional support for the cortical origin of the after-image.

Morel (1933) described AI-like hallucinations in delirium tremens. These are dark with weak (unsaturated?) if any coloration, rounded or globular and occur along the horizontal axis. They are immobile but move with the eyes. They appear at the point of fixation and increase in size with increasing projection distance. As Morel put it, the patient sees "the head of a pin on his fingers, bedbugs on the bed, coins at his feet, mice at two meters and rabbits on the armoire." The hallucination is usually greeted with amusement, but anxiety may develop. There may be a progression from a positive scotoma to a zooptic illusion to an hallucination with anxiety (Bleuler 1922).

Agadjanian (1946) described changes in the AI during mescal hallucination. Monocular after-images were said to transform more easily into an hallucination, and there was an increased duration, of five-to-ten-times normal, of after-images in the mescal state. Teuber (1960) mentioned that brain-damaged subjects have increased latency and decreased duration of AI's, and an increased number and duration of dark phases. In occipital cases, the AI usually disappears on vestibular stimulation (cf. Schilder 1933). With brain damage, the AI may not follow Emmert's law. Bender and Teuber (1946) described a patient with a decrease in the apparent size of a receding object which was greater than expected by constancy effects, though AI's did not change in apparent size when projected against backgrounds of varying distances. In hemianopic or quadrantic cases, the AI may be reduced in size and extent or may be absent. There may also be a reduction in the flight of colors.

Fuchs (1921) was the first to study completion of the AI. This occurred only for patterns which were also perceptually completed. Bender (1949) noted completion of negative after-images (complementary colors) into the blind field. The AI may also be completed across a defective quadrant. Torjussen (1978), with flash-induced after-images, was unable to demonstrate completion of a half circle flashed in the intact field, nor a half circle flashed in the blind field, but did obtain facilitation of the blind field portion with whole and half-displaced circles.

Palinopsia

There are pathological states in which a type of hallucinatory persistence of an object occurs. One form which is probably a result of increased after-image activity is **palinopsia**. This is a recurrence of a perception immediately, or after a short interval. In most instances, the image recurs immediately after diverting the gaze or when the stimulus object is withdrawn. It is not affected by closing the eyes. If there is no free interval, the term visual perseveration is sometimes applied to the phenomenon. In rare cases, the image occurs hours or days later. At this point, it seems more like an eidetic image or hallucination. The content of the palinoptic image may include parts of objects, letters, faces or unnoticed details. These appear at times in relation to veridical perceptions. Pötzl (1954) described a case in which a hat seen on one person recurred in the correct position on other individuals. Bender, Feldman, and Sobin's (1968) patient had the image of his wife rubbing her face with her hands immediately after seeing an actress doing this on television. However, movement in the image is unusual, and most images do not show this contextual effect. Palinoptic images of moving objects are represented as a series of static ("stroboscopic") images over the range of movement.

The relation to after-imagery has been discussed by Bender *et al.* (1968) and Kinsbourne and Warrington (1963b). It is known that a monocular perception may be revived binocularly in the palinoptic image, that the palinoptic image is frequently achromatic and, when colored, is usually positive to the stimulus, that it may be revived by blinking and that it moves in the direction of eye movements. In Kinsbourne's cases, the image moved in a direction opposite to that of passive displacement of the eyes. Moreover, the size of the image may depend on the background. A patient of LeBeau and Wolinetz (1958) saw images as larger if they were regarded as being closer. This is reminiscent of Katz's comment (1935) that the stronger, more insistent, an AI was, the closer to the observer it appeared. However, in contrast to the AI, the palinoptic image is said to be independent of the intensity or duration of the stimulus, though this might simply reflect the heightened conditions for after-imagery in pathological cases.

Palinopsia is related to a **perceptual impairment**. In all cases with thorough perimetric testing, there has been some visual field abnormality. In patients with scotoma, the image is projected into the damaged area. Palinopsia occurs chiefly in occipital cases. This has been confirmed in cases with CT scan localization (Michel and Troost 1980).

It has been described in the recovery of cortical blindness, and in a developing or recovering visual field defect. It may disappear when a partial field defect is complete. It also occurs in visual agnosia. Pötzl (1928) described a patient who was shown a bouquet of red roses with a stalk of asparagus protruding from the center. The patient identified the roses, but, when later asked the color of the collar of an officer present in the room, he stated that he saw a green tie pin. Here, the image seems to have developed out of a subliminal perception. The association with occipital lesions was also pointed out by Critchley (1955), who described an exceptional case in association with auditory images (see below).

In palinopsia, a transposition may occur from the intact to the damaged field. The image occurs in the damaged segment, though there are rare cases where the transposition is to the intact field. This is termed (visual) **alloaesthesia**. The transposition is generally to the homologous point across fields, though alloaesthesia across quadrants in the same half field may occur. This is also associated with occipital lesions. The first such case described was a bi-occipital patient who saw on the left all objects situated on the right (Hermann and Pötzl 1928). A case of visual alloesthesia on a seizure basis was reported by Jacobs (1980). A palinoptic image was seen in the defective field, and persisted to produce "cerebral diplopia." It is likely that alloaesthesia is more common in partial than complete hemifield defects, and that this explains its infrequency in neurological patients. Moreover, the question arises of a possible relationship between the alloaesthetic content and the nature of the field impairment. Thus, a personal case with a left occipital meningioma and a partial right field deficit, with some difficulty reading, had alloaesthetic experiences of written material in the right hemifield while reading the newspaper, presumably using the intact left hemifield. There was no impairment for object recognition on the left nor was there alloaesthesia of objects. Specifically, the alloaesthesia was for material (written words) poorly processed through the left visual field.

Palinacousis

A disorder similar to palinopsia has been described by Jacobs, Feldman, Diamond, and Bender (1973) in the acoustic sphere, and is termed **palinacousis.** This condition, which appears strongly linked to temporal lobe lesions and accompanying seizure phenomena, is characterized by an hallucination of persistent or recurrent sounds. These are usually voices, single words or whole phrases. At times, noises and musical sounds may recur. Hécaen and Ropaert (1959) described a case of "palilalic" hallucination. Their patient heard spoken words repeated several times. This seems to be a type of reiterative palinacousis.

Generally, the hallucination takes place immediately after the veridical perception, but may be delayed for up to 24 hours or more. The sounds are often described as sharper and more vivid than in the original perception, and are located in the environment, usually on the side opposite the brain lesion. In this respect, they differ from peripherally induced hallucinations which are heard in the ears or in the head. The revived acoustic perceptions are at times distorted or muffled, and may contain new elements. Cases have been described in which the acoustic and visual (palinoptic) effects occurred together (Critchley 1951).

Elementary Hallucinations

Stimulation of the visual cortex may give rise to **elementary hallucinations** which share many features in common with after-images. Elementary hallucinations, or cortical phosphenes, consist of flickering lights or luminous scotoma, flames, scintillations and geometric patterns. They are usually colored, but especially with more anterior occipital stimulation may be achromatic. Similar phenomena have been described in migraine (Jung 1979), epilepsy, drug states (Kluver 1965) and with focal brain involvements. Sensory deprivation hallucinations may also begin with cortical phosphenes (Zuckerman 1969). In pathological cases the lesion tends to be occipital, though phosphenes with optic tract involvement (Pick 1904) have been reported, and the hallucination occurs in the field opposite the pathology (Gloning *et al.* 1968). Lowenstein and Borchardt (1918) first demonstrated that elementary hallucinations appeared in the appropriate sector of the visual field opposite the point of stimulation. Stimulation of the occipital pole produces an hallucination directly in front of the subject.

Foerster (1936) noted that stimulation of area 17 produced stationary phosphenes. More rostral stimulation in area 19 produced formed hallucinations which moved from the periphery to the center of the field. One doesn't need an object perception to have an elementary hallucination. It can be produced in cases of acquired blindness. The stimulation which is applied to the occipital lobe leads to an effect which is comparable to an after-image. Brindley and Lewin (1968) found that cortical phosphenes moved in the direction of voluntary eye movements, but were not displaced by passive rotation of the head. Some phosphenes persisted up to a minute or more after stimulation. In a study of three patients with implanted electrodes, Chapanis *et al.* (1973) described one patient who reported a blue rectangle against a black surround which became a faint bluish white against a white background. The electrodes were in the optic radiation. In one patient a phosphene was shown to subtend a constant visual angle. The relation to eye movements was not evaluated in this study. According to Brindley (1973), cortical phosphenes are mainly white and often flicker. Brindley obtained apparent movement when two neighboring electrodes were stimulated in succession. If the electrodes were close together and stimulated at the same time, the patient might see a line; with several points simultaneously, simple patterns or letters were seen.

Obviously, there is much in common between the AI and the elementary hallucination. It is not surprising that Krause (1924; also Brindley 1973) noted that elementary hallucinations produced by cortical stimulation do not leave after-images. This is because the AI is a type of elementary hallucination.

Comparable phenomena are described on stimulation of the auditory region. Stimulation of the "primary" auditory cortex produces elementary acoustic phenomena which are typically referred to the opposite side of space. Foerster (1936) stimulated area 22 in posterior TI and elicited sounds. Penfield and Rasmussen (1950) also obtained sounds on stimulation of auditory cortex. These consisted of tones, bells, cricket-like noises, and "rushing" sounds. The auditory perceptions of the subjects were altered during the stimulation, even to the point where some patients described a transient deafness. One patient commented that his own speech was altered during the stimulation.

With elementary auditory hallucinations, occluding the ears may alter the intensity of the sound. The hallucinations are usually rhythmic and are said to be accentuated during the hypnagogic period. The intensity is estimated at 20-40 decibels. According to Morel (1936a), they are not described by a comparison to an environmental sound, as is the case with entotic hallucination, but are directly linked to an external cause and can be localized with some precision.

The cortical phosphene which is evoked on stimulation of primary visual cortex is linked to naturally occurring elementary hallucinations, such as the fortification and other phenomena of migraine or occipital lobe lesions, as well as to normal after-images. In migraine both elementary hallucination and scotomata occur. In some ways the elementary hallucination is the active element in the scotoma.

Around the phosphene there is a normal object, except for that part of the object which the phosphene covers. This part is obscured by the phosphene which seems to adhere like a film to its surface. The impression that the phosphene is superimposed on an object is enhanced by its movement over a stationary object field. However, when an AI moves over an object, it is really the object that is changing. The AI is the filmy appearance which is taken on by an incomplete portion of the object's surface.

Summary

Lesions of striate and circumstriate cortex disrupt the object at a terminal stage of fine, featural modelling. The parietal preobject undergoes a process of form analysis, and simultaneously, is exteriorized to an independent "physical" space. The AI and related phenomena share some of the attributes of external, physical objects. The lack of constancy effects, for example, the lack of replacement by the image of that portion of object space, is different from other types of image phenomena. These effects show that the perception is disrupted at the surface of its structure, so that the resultant image displays characteristics of exteriorized (physical) objects. The lack of a pictorial quality or meaning in the image occurs because these aspects of the perception are not related to the moment in perceptual microgeny mediated by the damaged area. The effect is similar to a phonetic disturbance in motor aphasia where the endpoint of a vocal action is involved.

DISCUSSION

A Microgenetic Model of Imagery

It is natural to think that imagery and perception are different events. An object seems independent of a perceiver, real with a life of its own, a part of the public domain which will exist long after the perceiver is gone. An image, on the other hand, is insubstantial, a phantasm in the mind of the viewer, private, invented and evanescent. This is the common sense way of thinking about objects and images, and it constantly reinforces our belief that the world of mind and the world of perception are separate and irreconcilable spheres of experience.

This paper has considered the range of normal and pathological images in relation to a different concept of object perception. According to this concept, **an object is the end result of a process of image development**. This process may terminate in an object, or it may arrest prematurely in an image. Perception is a series of potential or realized mental representations leading from an image-like construction to a construction that is like an object. The final image in this series is an object representation, and this representation is the limiting point in the mind's construction of the world.

Images and objects are points on a continuum. In this continuum, imagery makes up most of the substructure of the object. Images are like ancestral objects which act as bridges to new perceptions. The various forms of imagery, dream images, memory and eidetic images, and cortical phosphenes, can be arranged in a transitional series which captures the object development. In pathological cases where a focal lesion is present, images can be shown to correspond in a general way with specific brain areas. This correspondence has a definite pattern. The pattern indicates that evolutionary stages in brain structure come into play in perception in the order of their phylogenetic appearance. In other words, the process of object development retraced in the sequence of image types maps on to successive stages in the evolutionary history of a perceptual system. A perception unfolds over antecedents in its psychological and structural past.

This progression is hypothesized to begin with a configuration elaborated in the upper brainstem at the interface of sensory and axial-motor reflex systems. This configuration represents the space of the body and the immediate body surround. It is constrained to a two-dimensional spatial map through a sensory transform at the level of the tectum. This construct develops to a subjective, viewer-centered volumetric space through limbic-temporal mechanisms. Dream-like hallucinations, hypnagogic images, hallucinations with symbolic and affective distortion, these are the objects of a perception at this level which is referentially unconstrained.

The next level in the object representation is the memory image. The memory image can also undergo a transformation to a dream hallucination. This transformation is really an uncovering of a deeper level in the memory image. The stage of the memory image is presumably realized through temporal and parietal mechanisms. Sensory input at this stage structures the representation toward a three-dimensional object-centered space. The final, detailed, featural modeling of the image, and its exteriorization as an external object, is effected through striate and circumstriate mechanisms. The after-image or cortical phosphene is a phenomenon at the surface of the object development.

This process leads from a labile mental image toward a stable "physical" object. It leads from an image which comes involuntarily, through one that is evoked in a purposeful manner, to one that is independent of the viewer. It leads from an image that is bound up with meaning and affect, to one that is independent, where affect has to be inferred. It leads from self to world, from memory to perception, from what is preconscious through consciousness, to a world "out there" in which consciousness has to be inferred.

This model of imagery has implications for many longstanding problems in the understanding of imagery and perceptual phenomena. Some of these implications are taken up in the following sections.

The Relationship between Images and Perceptions

Images replace and are replaced by perceptions but the image and the perception do not compete for the same neural space. Studies of thought imagery in normals show that the image behaves like a perception, it has a right and left side, an orientation and is scanned by an observer. On mental rotation experiments, the image has the character of a perception (Cooper and Shepard, 1983; Kosslyn, 1975). These findings in normal imagery confirm previous observations in cases of heightened or pathological images. Thus, Jaensch (1930) found altered perceptions during eidetic imagery, and Klüver (1933) noted that parts of the stimulus missing in the eidetic image retained the correct position by an "empty" space. Klüver mentioned other observations in this connection. An eidetic image of a bright object leads to contraction of the pupil, while a dark eidetic image produces dilation. One can photograph the eye movements of a subject reading an eidetic text much as in the scanning of thought images. These observations indicate that imagery and perception have a common basis. This is also the conclusion of studies of auditory and visual hallucination.

In **auditory hallucinations**, there are inadequate perceptions during the hallucinatory bouts. Morel (1936b) did audiometric testing in patients before and during auditory hallucinations. He found normal thresholds in patients when they were not hallucinating, but during auditory hallucinations marked changes in threshold occurred, even to the point of temporary deafness. This could last only a few seconds, and the next moment the patient might show a normal audiogram. Morel spoke of temporary holes, lacunae or scotoma in hearing which corresponded precisely to moments of auditory hallucination. Auditory hallucination in seizure cases may be preceded by transient deafness, or distorted perceptions. During electrical stimulation of the organ of Corti, acoustic hallucinations are accompanied by a diminution of existing auditory perceptions. There is a change in auditory perception during hallucinations resulting from stimulation of the auditory cortex. Not only organic cases, schizophrenics also have brief episodes of "word deafness" while hallucinating and are unable to recognize familiar sounds. Cases of "word deafness" usually begin with auditory hallucinations. Excision of the circum-auditory cortex leads to impaired auditory perception but reduces pre-existing auditory hallucinations (Burckhardt 1891). Stimulation of this region in schizophrenics will diminish chronic auditory hallucination (Ishibashi et al. 1964).

These and other observations already discussed indicate that **the substrate of the auditory perception and the substrate of the auditory image or hallucination are the same.**

In **visual hallucination** this is even more clear. Agadjanian (1946) found a constricted visual field during mescal hallucinations, and changes in color perception during colored hallucinations. There is a correspondence between the perceptual disorder and the hallucinatory experience. Patients with a positive central scotoma may have a central monocular hallucination (de Morsier 1938). Cases of perceptual micropsia will have micropsia in the hallucination. Hallucination involves the deficient portion of the visual field, a fact repeatedly confirmed since demonstrated by Seguin (1886) and Schröder (1925). In subjects with normal fields, hallucination commonly begins in the periphery. One can say that the hallucination has a predilection for that part of the visual field which shows the least degree of resolution. Hallucination is common at the onset of cortical blindness. Pötzl described a case of bilateral occipital lesion with hallucination where cortical blindness developed on taking mescaline. This is because the relation between visual hallucination and "cortical blindness" is one of depth. One concludes from such observations that **the hallucination and the perception develop over the same neural structures.**

The Reality of the Object

The fact that a perception has a "real" object is insufficient to distinguish it from other forms of imagery, since an object is always an inference. Hallucination may have an object that is "real" to the perceiver. The uncertainty that grips the hallucinator over the reality of his hallucinations has been experienced by the perceiver over the reality of his objects. In fact, the first stage of hallucination is often a **derealization** of perceptions prior to hallucinatory formation. The individual apprehends the fragility of his object world. We accept on faith the existence of this object world, but we cannot use its objectivity as a basis for a distinction from imagery.

And yet we do! Constantly! We say that the memory image is a revived object experience, that it points to a prior object. Conversely, hallucination is "perception without an object." But hallucination may begin as a memory image of a previous object experience. An eidetic image is close to an object, yet it is like a memory image after a brief delay. In the eidetic image, the object is revived almost immediately after it has disappeared. For this reason, the object seems **more real** than in the memory image, it is truer to the original experience. These states are all degrees of approximation to an object. They are different ways of experiencing the same object development.

The inner relation between the object and the image is seen in everyday life. We all have the experience of a "weak" perception assuming an hallucinatory character. In experimental conditions (Segal and Nathan 1964) subjects may fail to distinguish between object and image. A subjective image may be taken for a real object (Perky 1910). This has even been employed as a device in musical composition, for example, the gradually diminishing final "ewig" in Mahler's *Das Lied von der Erde* so that the listener is actually uncertain whether the song ends on an hallucination or a perception. Richardson (1969) discussed the uncertainty of the image/object boundary.

In pathological states, there is often a fluctuation between object and image. In sensory deprivation, hallucination may begin as a memory image with illusions later on. Or hallucination may begin with a change in the object. Klüver described the transformation of the negative after-image to a "pseudo-hallucination" and the latter to a true hallucination.

In sum, the fragility of the object, its basis in imagery, or its hallucinatory underpinnings, are revealed in the range of normal experience as well as in pathological states. The "reality" of the object is not a sufficient basis for a distinction of perception and imagery.

These remarks also illustrate two basic patterns of hallucinatory onset, which help to explain "real" and "unreal" images. We have seen that hallucination can develop out of a memory image, as a progression toward an object; or as a change in the object itself, a withdrawal back to the origins of the object in memory. This leads to a consideration of the apparent "reality" of the hallucination.

The "Reality" of the Hallucination

The subject's belief in the reality of an hallucination is often taken to be an essential component of the hallucinatory state and has served to distinguish true from "pseudo" hallucination. For some, the feeling of the reality of an hallucination is the basis for a distinction of image and hallucination. Yet, this aspect of hallucination is quite variable. Some patients accept the hallucination as real, others recognize it as a subjective image, and there are fluctuations from one state to another. This variability is not a fortuitous accompaniment of any type of hallucination. The awareness is **not brought to** the hallucination but is closely bound up with the disrupted level. There are two situations in which the hallucination is accepted as real.

1. In the first, an hallucination commences with an illusional experience. There is a change in a real object, as when rustling leaves seem like whispered voices, or an object undergoes a change in size or shape. The mixture of an hallucination with an object, or the instability of the object experience, begins to undermine the subject's belief in an existing world of real objects. At this stage, the hallucination may appear veridical within the relatively normal cognition of the unreplaced segment of the perception. In this situation, the "reality" of the hallucination (actually, the illusion) depends on the plausibility of its occurrence in the perceptual context. At times the image is greeted with uncertainty as to its basis in reality. In progressive cases, the attachment to a real object dissolves as the illusion takes on hallucinatory features. Eventually, the image experience converges with the second type of hallucinatory replacement.

2. In this second form, the hallucination from the beginning has the character of subjective image. The hallucination begins with an isolated memory or dream image and is recognized by the subject as a private experience. There may be an intermediate stage where the subject can no longer determine whether he is waking or dreaming, but with progression there is a gradual, eventually unshakeable, belief in the reality of the hallucination. This occurs normally in dream, and in the hallucinatory psychosis which is the endstage of both the illusional and imaginal types of hallucinatory onset. The "reality" of an hallucination of this type – that beginning with a subjective image – reflects the inability of the destructured cognitive level to assume a critical attitude towards its own hallucinatory content, not the fact that the hallucination actually takes on the characteristics of a "real" object.

An image does not exteriorize into the same space as an object. It may seem real to the perceiver but not object-like in its realness. Morgue (1932) said that a visual hallucination never exactly reproduced a perception. The feeling of the reality of an image does not depend on its object quality The hallucinatory world of the psychotic imposes its "reality" on him. The subject cannot apprehend that his images are false because he no longer has an object world for comparison. A perception which develops only to the stage of an image fails to recapture the object world. The object world, being a derivative of the image world, no longer exists. The image is real to the psychotic because it is the only object that he has.

An important part of the experience of reality seems to be the ability to verify the existence of an image through several perceptual channels. Dream hallucination is accepted as real because the visual image is supported by the other senses. We can hear and even touch the dream image, and experience it in other ways. This is also true for objects in the waking state. An hallucination which involves only one perceptual modality can be disconfirmed by the other senses. Could this be important to a judgment of the reality of images?

If the hallucination involves only one modality, the object can complete its development in other perceptual systems. Through these other systems — particularly auditory perception — the subject can maintain a relatively normal cognitive state. The object world is sustained by the other senses. On the other hand, an hallucination which shares elements of two or more modalities implies a more generalized destructuration. The object is attenuated in several perceptual modes. There is no longer an object world to inform the perceiver that his images are false. Thus, a case of Hécaen's recognized an auditory hallucination as false until the visual component of the hallucination appeared, at which point it was taken for a real perception.

There is an inner bond between these elements: one or many perceptual modes represented in the hallucination; cognitive level; and feeling of reality. At the earliest stages in perception, for example in dream, all perceptual modes co-represent an **image**. At the endstage of perception, that of our everyday waking life, all perceptual modes co-represent an **object**. The conspiracy of the senses, which is so pervasive in dream, anticipates and gives rise to the conspiracy of the senses in waking perception, by which we think to validate the reality of objects in the world.

Affect and Hallucination

Hallucinations are accompanied by differing emotional states. Some patients are amused by their hallucination, others terrified. Fear at the onset of hallucination is common in schizophrenia, whereas in organic cases anxiety may be a less frequent accompaniment. How is the affective state to be interpreted? Fear is not simply a response to the fact of an hallucination. Patients can show amusement one moment and fear another; nor is it a reaction to the hallucinatory content. A similar content may elicit quite different emotional responses. Patients can exhibit panic during the most banal hallucinatory experiences and be calm during scenic hallucinations of bizarre and unusual content. In hypnagogic states and Lilliputian or microscopic hallucinations, the image is greeted with amusement or unconcern. Patients with "peduncular" hallucinations may anticipate and even relish their hallucinatory bouts. Similarly, we have all tried to prolong an enjoyable dream. As Robert Frost said, "The finest entertainment ever known, and dirt cheap!"

A possible explanation is that the emotional state is related not to the content of the hallucination but to the structural level to which the hallucination refers. Affects or emotions undergo a microgenetic development as do objects and actions (Brown 1977). Anxiety points to an incomplete object development, it is an incompletely developed affect. Anxiety occurs in beginning states of derealization or depersonalization. If anxiety is not present, the object world is still there or it has already been lost. Anxiety is a sign that the objects of the world are in danger. In depression, a lifting of anxiety can signal a deterioration. Morbid depression recovers through a phase of agitation. The anxiety occurs as the object is about to be regained.

Anxiety points to an "in-between" stage. In hallucination as in other pathological disorders, the anxiety is as much an expression of the disturbance as is the altered perception. **Anxiety is a symptom not a reaction**. It is the form taken by the affect when an object (image) is positioned between external and mental space, that is, when the image is just exteriorizing as an object, or the object recedes to the underlying image.

Perceptuomotor Systems and Language Representation*

The anterior aphasias give evidence for a motor plan underlying the utterance, one that develops as a rhythmic series over evolutionary levels. Similarly, the posterior aphasias suggest a microgenetic development from semantic to phonological levels in retrieval. The utterance involves a simultaneous unfolding over both anterior and posterior systems. This section takes up in a more speculative vein the relationship of this model to several outstanding problems in perceptual neuropsychology.

I would like to begin with the claim that the knowledge of one's own utterance is built up on the same basis as the perception of the speech of others; that is, that an utterance is represented *as a perception*. Moreover, the perceptual development of the utterance also elaborates the awareness for that utterance. Posterior aphasia affects the speaker's representation—and thus his awareness—of his own speech. In contrast, the (anterior) motor component, the motor plan or the rhythmic structure of the utterance, does not give rise to mental content directly, but rather contributes an "intentional" quality, a "feeling of innervation" (Innervationsgefühl of Wundt) which enables us to distinguish our own speech from the speech of others. This feeling allows the speaker to determine whether the utterance has come "from within" or "from outside"; that is, whether it is an active or passive movement. The apathy and lack of spontaneity in anterior aphasia point to a disturbance in this function.

*From "Hierarchy and Evolution in Neurolinguistics" by J. W. Brown, 1981. In M. Arbib, D. Caplan, and J. Marshall (Eds.), *Neural Models of Language Processes*. New York: Academic Press. Copyright 1982 by Academic Press. Adapted by permission.

In psychotics, the distinction between speech and speech perception may break down. The subject's own voice seems foreign. The utterance takes on the quality of an alien voice, a voice speaking through the speaker. The subject may feel as if he is a vehicle for the speech of others. Speech seems like a passive movement. In such cases, and utterance has a perceptual character. The subject is repeating what another speaker has said. The utterance may also seem like exteriorized inner speech. Thoughts take on the quality of speech and speech becomes more thoughtlike. There may be a confusion of "external" or "heard" speech with inner speech. This is the basis of auditory hallucination. The subject's inner speech appears as a perception of the speech of another speaker. Inner speech seems exteriorized as a perception. Thoughts become perceptions, perceptions become thoughts.

Similar phenomena occur in normal subjects, commonly before sleep or in transitional states. A voice in a darkened room may seem like an exteriorized thought, inner speech may assume a perceptual clarity. There is a collusion of the senses which aids the speaker in making these distinctions. The confusion which may occur between inner speech and perception, or between inner speech and an utterance, points to the common basis of these seemingly disparate performances. In fact, the difficulty we experience in everyday life in trying to speak and to listen at the same time, or in listening to one's own speech while speaking, the necessity for speaker-listener conventions in conversation, the inability to comprehend a speaker when we are distracted by a private thought (inner speech), and the evidence from pathological cases, points to *the common basis of speech, speech perception, and inner speech.*

One may begin by asking, What is the relation between inner speech and auditory hallucination? How is inner speech distinguished from hallucination? One difference is the active quality of inner speech, the feeling that one is the agent or instigator of the behavior, in contrast to the more passive or receptive attitude to auditory hallucination. This difference is like that between active and passive movements. It points to the presence of a motor plan accompanying the inner speech development. This motor plan is the difference between inner speech as an active event, on the way to vocalization, and inner speech as a passive event, on the way to speech perception.

In psychosis, there is a reduced feeling of activity. The patient is no longer the agent of his own inner speech, and so inner speech takes on perceptual characteristics. This link between inner speech and hallucination is supported by numerous observations in schizophrenic patients. It is known that verbal hallucination preserves the intonation and accent of the subject, and is in the language and style of the speaker even though the "voice" seems alien. The so-called "echo of thought" points to a connection with inner speech. During reading, verbal hallucination occurs as an echo or shadow of the material which is read, *preceding* the actual reading by a second or so or a few words (Morel, 1936a). Increasing the reading rate will increase the echo. Verbal hallucination is clearly associated with temporal lobe pathology. It is common in word deafness. Hoff and

Silberman (1933) induced verbal hallucination and "echo" phenomena by application of ethyl chloride to an exposed auditory zone in the right superior temporal convolution.

Such observations suggest a continuum between inner speech and verbal hallucination. This continuum may depend on the degree to which the motor plan is activated. If a perceptual content is accompanied by a motor development, the active feeling generated by this development identifies the content as inner speech. If the content is biased toward perception, it is identified as a verbal hallucination. Thus, EMG studies during inner speech show subvocal articulatory movements. This is also true during hallucination (Lagache, 1934). Auditory hallucinations are suspended during respiratory pauses. Morsier (1938) noted that auditory hallucination and speech do not occur at the same time. Speaking also tends to interrupt ongoing verbal hallucination. This is because it biases inner speech toward a motor elaboration.

Inner speech and verbal hallucination are at a pivotal stage in thought development. Only the incipient motor development of inner speech allows the subject to separate them as distinct events. The more attenuated the motor plan, the more inner speech is like a perception. The lack of a motor development deprives the subject of an active relation to the mental content. The subject becomes a passive receiver of his own inner speech. This feeling can be recaptured in states of relaxation prior to sleep. As inner speech takes on hallucinatory features, it is not the change in vocal quality that is striking but the seeming detachment of the content, its greater liveliness, the more automatic play of ideas, and their independence from the subject. Such experiences reinforce the impression that inner speech is like a verbal hallucination oriented toward motility. Put differently, inner speech has a *perceptual* basis.

Thus, inner speech and hallucination are preliminary stages leading, respectively, to speech and to perception. Inner speech may vary from a vague, image-laden state, rich in content words or in their precursors, to a more or less well-formed mental sentence, the preverbitum or "unspoken speech." These forms of inner speech reflect a progression leading from a state that is more thoughtlike to the final articulation. Actually, these states are also successive levels of *perceptual* realization. *Inner speech develops as a perceptual series linked to levels in the motor plan.*

Now consider the relation between verbal hallucination and speech perception. There is considerable evidence from pathological studies (Brown, 1982) that hallucination is a stage leading to perception, it is a preliminary object. One can say that the cognition that fills the hallucination gives itself up in the formation of a veridical perception. The perception develops out of the same ground—or over the same substrate—as the hallucination. This is why hallucination and perception do not occupy the same space. *Hallucination is a phase in a perceptual series which terminates in a veridical object.* Accordingly, verbal hallucination is a stage on the way to speech perception.

Thus, the deep level in perception that gives rise either to inner speech or verbal hallucination can develop in two directions. One direction, accompanied by an unfolding motor plan, leads through the series of inner speech forms and is the microgenetic path of speech production. Here the perceptual content is represented—perceptually—as an utterance in the mind of the speaker. That is, an utterance consists of a perceptual development, which elaborates the mental representation of the utterance, and a parallel or complementary motor development, which elaborates a feeling of "intentionality." Each level in the perceptual representation corresponds with a level of rhythmic organization in motility. An attenuated development of the parallel motor and perceptual hierarchies gives rise to inner speech. This development is completed in the spoken utterance.

The other direction is to speech perception, and this is also a complex story (Brown, 1982). Briefly, I would suggest that the autonomous content which in the absence of acoustic stimuli gives rise to hallucination is constrained at successive levels by sensory input. The product of the development would then be an object representation oriented to perception and the external world rather than a subjective image formation. That is, the perception is not built up from sensory material, which rather acts to constrain an endogenous system so as to model the external world. In object perception the accompanying motor development would be attenuated. The result would be that the passive or receptive attitude which was so prominent in hallucination, and which reflected the lack of "intentionality" which the motor development provided, is now even more pronounced as the image (object) exteriorizes and seems to detach as an independent thing in the world. The central point is that, from the point of view of mental content, *both speech and speech perception develop over the same set of perceptual levels.*

The view of inner speech as a perceptual content linked to verbal hallucination has implications for aphasia study. Goldstein (1948) thought that inner speech developed in relation to perceptual mechanisms, and maintained that phonemic (conduction, central) aphasia involved a disruption at the stage of inner speech. In contrast, Luria assigned inner speech to the anterior region and the motor component of language. This was based on the failure of the motor aphasic to regulate other nonverbal motor activities and the presumed role of inner speech in such regulative functions. However, one might as well argue that nonverbal motor functions are disturbed because motor aphasia represents a disturbance in a motor system rather than a distrubance of language apart from motility. Of course, Luria was also thinking of Vygotsky's characterization of inner speech as predicative and the disruption of predication in agrammatism. Actually, both Goldstein and Luria may be correct. Inner speech should be disrupted by both posterior and anterior lesions but in a different way. Because inner speech is a perceptual content linked to a motor develop-ment, anterior lesions should disrupt the motor development and alter the active quality of inner speech. Inner speech might be passive, imaginal, even hallucinatory (see Critchley, 1955). In contrast, a posterior lesion would disrupt the representational content of inner speech, while its intentional quality should be preserved. Certainly, the posterior aphasic gives the impression of a retained active, if not fully critical, attitude to his defective language and toward the world.

Image and Object*

For Hilgard there are links between different types of images, and between images and perceptions. Neuropsychological study supports this contention, and also provides evidence for the stronger claim that imagery unfolds over the same neural substrate as perception, and that images represent stages in object formation.

Studies of thought imagery show that the image has a perceptionlike character, it has a right and left side, an orientation and is scanned by an observer. Eidetic phenomena also show this relationship. Jaensch (1925) found altered perceptions during the eidetic phase. Klüver (1965) noted that parts of the stimulus missing in the eidetic image retained the correct position by an "empty" space; that is, the perception "exists" as a void in the eidetic image. An eidetic image of a bright object is said to lead to pupillary constriction, the reverse for a dark eidetic image. There are many other observations in normals that one could cite.

The link between perception and imagery is even more evident in pathological case study. Subjects with *auditory* hallucination have inadequate perceptions during hallucinatory bouts. Morel (1936b) found normal audiometric thresholds in patients when they were not hallucinating, but marked changes during hallucinatory periods, even to the point of temporary deafness. He spoke of holes, lacunae or scotoma in hearing which corresponded precisely to moments of auditory hallucination. In seizure cases, auditory hallucination may be preceded by transient deafness or distorted perceptions. During electrical stimulation of the organ of Corti, acoustic hallucinations are accompanied by a diminution of existing auditory perceptions. There is a change in auditory perception during hallucinations resulting from stimulation of the auditory cortex. Brain-damaged and schizophrenic cases have transient "word-deafness" while hallucinating, and are unable to recognize familiar sounds. Cases of "word-deafness" with lesions of auditory cortex begin with auditory hallucination. Excision of the auditory cortex leads to impaired auditory perception and at the same time reduces preexisting auditory hallucination.

Similarly in *visual* hallucination, there is a correspondence between the perceptual disorder and the hallucinatory experience. Agadjanian (1946) found constriction of the visual field during mescal hallucinations, and changes in color perception during chromatic hallucination. Patients with a positive central scotoma may have central monocular hallucination. Visual micropsia appears also in hallucination. Since the work of Seguin (1886), Henschen and Schröder, we know that hallucination involves the defective portion of the visual field. In subjects with normal fields, hallucination commonly begins in the periphery, that is, that part of the field with the least degree of

---

*From "Image and Object" by J. W. Brown, 1981, *Journal of Mental Imagery*, 5, 26–27. Copyright 1981 by Brandon House, Inc. Adapted by permission. (Commentary upon issues relating to the work of E. R. Hilgard.)

resolution. Hallucination may coexist with perception but not in the same locus of space. Unlike after-images, hallucinations do not occur as a film over an object but replace the pathological segment. Hallucination is common at the onset of cortical blindness. Pötzl (1928) described a case of bilateral occipital lesion with hallucination where cortical blindness developed on taking mescaline. Morel (1936) claimed that hallucination involved the functions lost in agnosia. Obviously, these phenomena can be interpreted in a variety of ways, but they all have in common the fact that changes in perception involve changes in imagery, and imply that *the substrate of the perception and the substrate of the image are the same*.

Hilgard also discusses the "reality" of the hallucination. In pathological cases, hallucination does not exteriorize into the same space as objects. The space of hallucination is lacking in depth; it is more viscous and tangible. The hallucination may seem real to the perceiver but not objectlike in its realness. A visual hallucination never exactly reproduces a perception. The feeling of the reality of an image, therefore, does not depend on its object quality, but on a change in the cognition which the hallucination generates. Hallucination accompanies a more preliminary cognition, which may be specific to the modality of the hallucination. The hallucination is like a submerged part of the object formation. The subject cannot apprehend that his images are false because he no longer has an object world for comparison. A perception which develops only to the stage of an image fails to fully recapture the object world which, being a derivative of the image, no longer exists. The image is real to the psychotic, or the dreamer, or subjects in hypnotic or trance state cognition, because it is the only object that they have.

The multisensory nature of some hallucinations may be important to the veridicality of the image experience. Dream hallucination is accepted as real because the visual image is supported by the other senses. We hear and touch the dream image, and experience it in other ways. This is true for objects in the waking state. An hallucination which involves only one perceptual modality can be disconfirmed by the other senses.

If an hallucination involves only one modality, the object can complete its development through other perceptual channels. Cognition is sustained by the other senses. An hallucination which shares elements of two or more modalities implies a generalized destructuration. There is no longer an object world to inform the viewer that his images are false. Thus, a case of Hécaen and Ropaert (1959) recognized an auditory hallucination as false until the visual component of the hallucination appeared, at which point it was taken for a real perception.

According to this view, images are like ancestral objects which act as bridges to new perceptions. The forms of imagery Hilgard reviews—dream images, memory and eidetic images, and cortical phosphenes—comprise a transitional series developing just beneath the surface of the object. This series leads from a deep, viewer-centered space of dream and hallucinatory distortion, through intermediate stages, to a three-dimensional object-centered space of exteriorized and independent forms. The object which is the end result of this process is only an image of a different type than those which are part of its preparatory stages. Pathological study indicates that images correspond in a general way with certain brain areas. These areas refer to levels in the evolutionary history of perceptual systems. An analysis of the clinical material indicates that the sequence of image types maps on to levels in the microstructure of the perception. More study of these problems, expecially the relations between images and perceptions, and their neural substrates, as Hilgard points out, are important goals for future research.

7
Essay on Perception*

What is the world? How are we to conceive it? The problem is posed in our everyday experience. Presently, there is before me a wide river, trees and a great bridge that tapers into the distance. The scene has depth, movement, light and color. The clean smell of the water, the warmth of the sun, are part of my perception; there are sounds and voices around me. I am aware of a multitude of other things in the background, my discomfort on the bench where I am sitting, the pen in my hand, the image I am calling up. I am aware also that the perception is given to me all at once in its entirety. I have no sense that it is constructed out of elements. I seems whole and invulnerable. I shift my attention and the world remains fixed. It will be there again when I look away. It presents itself before me and I ingest it with my organs of sense. My body is an object that exists for the perception of others. And on the rim of this perception is an awareness of self. This self-awareness is bound up with an inner commentary. My concept of self as experienced is replete with this commentary, which seems to be the equivalent of mind in the context of this perception. But unlike mind, the perception is not experienced as in the mind or even through the mind but as something outside mind in a space which could be vacant if deprived of the objects with which it is so abundantly filled.

This seems a fair account of an everyday experience of such force and immediacy as to encumber any theory of mind that runs counter to its appeal. Yet every day we are reminded of the fragility of the world. We are dizzy and the world spins around us. We struggle to maintain our balance even as the world disintegrates. Object constancies and perceptual illusions remind us that we are *thinking* objects, not just seeing them. In the evening the object gives way to a dream imagery that may be more vivid than waking perception. We question the reality of dream only on waking as we regain the world of objects. Now the perception is stable and outside us. But how fixed and stable is this object? Even as we gaze at it we are aware that it is never perceived in the same way. It is noticed differently, it changes with our feelings and interest; the object itself changes in our perception. We ignore this instability to the degree to which the reconstruction is successful. Yet the fragility of the object helps us to recognize its basis in the mind, it helps us to recognize the continuum which exists from the image of the dream to the object in perception in the enlarging representation of a cognized world.

*From *Neuropsychology of Visual Perception,* by J. Brown (Ed.). Copyright 1988 by Lawrence Erlbaum, Associates.

I Preliminaries to a Theory of Object Formation

Let us begin by asking, in what way is perception built up? Is it constructed like a building out of the units of experience? Are the edges, colors, and contours of objects the formative material of which objects are composed?

The conventional approach to perception assumes that an object is the result of a chain of events leading over stations in a sensory pathway. Features of the object are extracted by cells in the visual cortex and reconstructed to patterns that are then relayed to other cortical zones for spatial mapping, recognition and association to prior experience. On this basis, we patch together an object representation. This theory of perception is grounded on parameters of an object itself, its shape, movement, brightness, depth or color, and correlations with cell discharge at various points in the visual pathway. On this account, attributes or isolates of an object are elements in its mental reconstruction, while other aspects of an object experience—affect, imagery, awareness, recognition—are added on as secondary effects after registration.

Pathological Objects The symptoms of pathology are the data for a different theory of perception. The symptoms of a perceptual disorder are not piecemeal dissolutions of normal objects but a shift to objects of another type. Objects do not degrade into constituents but to more preliminary objects; or the symptoms of a disrupted perception intrude into a completed object as earlier phases in its formation. The pathological fragment is the nucleus of a preobject— a formative stage in the object representation. At times this change is brief and restricted to a small part of the visual field, for example, a migrainous blindspot or scotoma, a distortion or an hallucination that appears as part of an otherwise normal object. However, the pathological segment can persist and replace the perception entirely. Here the preobject character of the symptom is apparent; it more clearly constitutes an incompletely developed object embedded in the object field.

Perceptual deficits and hallucinations may occur together in the same modality. Morel (1936a, 1936b) thought that hallucination involved the functions which were lost in a perceptual disorder and that hallucination and perceptual disorders were different ways of looking at the same perception. Following Morel, one might say that a deficit points to a disrupted stage in percept formation which is embedded in a fully developed object, while an hallucination is the representation deposited at that stage when it becomes a (truncated) endpoint in percept formation.

The inner bond between hallucination and perceptual deficit is illustrated by cases of agnosia. In such cases, an individual may misidentify objects on the basis of their conceptual relationships. Thus, a *fork* might be called a "plate." This is not a language or naming disorder but a disturbance in perception, a disruption of *object meaning*. In dream, the substitution of an object is also determined by its meaning, though affective and symbolic elements predominate. Unlike deficient perceptions, an object substitution in dream is really *seen*. Of course, the target of a dream perception is an inference from the dynamics of the dreamwork. Were a waking patient to see the objects of his misidentification (seeing a plate instead of a fork)—and there is no evidence that he does—he would be hallucinating like a dreamer. It seems that what is characteristic of the dream perception is the very thing that is lacking in agnosia. However, the form of agnosia that involves object meaning is related to neural substrates—limbic and temporal lobe mechanisms—which are probably also implicated in dream hallucination. Specifically, conceptual errors in agnosia and substitutions in dream hallucination are both linked to similar (identical?) brain areas.

The mechanisms of the dreamwork, substitution, condensation, and fusion reflect an *incomplete selection* of the object representation out of its background field. An hallucination is an alternative (pre)object conceptually related to the target. The relationship between the target and the hallucination is determined by the degree to which the hallucinatory preobject develops. In sleep, the lack of external stimulation facilitates autonomous image formation and cognitive withdrawal and leaves an incomplete object—an hallucination—as an endpoint in percept formation.

Disorders of object meaning constitute only one type of visual agnosia. Impaired discrimination of object form is another type. Errors of object form and meaning may occur in the same patient. The change in performance moment-to-moment reflects the depth of processing for each object formation. When morphological or form-based errors occur we are more likely to think the patient *sees* the misnamed object. For example, when a *button* is called a "coin" we have no difficulty supposing that the perception is rather more "coinlike" and we explain this deviation on a visuosensory basis. This is not so clearly the case for conceptual errors when object meaning is involved. The symptom is different because it involves a different level in the object. Disorders of object meaning and disorders of object form correspond to the difference between hallucination and illusion which also differ as to momentary depth.

Moreover, as hallucination and disturbed object meaning are related to similar brain areas, disorders in the analysis or specification of object form and distortions or illusional phenomena in imagery are also linked to similar or identical brain areas. However, object meaning and hallucination are linked to *older* brain areas, object form and illusional phenomena are linked to areas of evolutionary *recency*.

Object Formation and Evolutionary Growth The relation to evolutionary structure is important because it corresponds with direction of processing. That is, given that disorders of object meaning are related to brain structures more archaic than those mediating processing stages underlying form analysis, the implication is that meaning is encoded prior to form in object perception. Specifically, areas supporting analytic perception are entrained subsequent to the activation of semantic or conceptual stages. However, the patient with a disruption of object meaning still appears to see the target object, not the one resulting from the conceptual derailment. In other words, the disruption of early stages in percept formation may not impact on the completion of subsequent stages. How can this be explained?

On the microgenetic theory, sensory information arriving distal to the disrupted segment constrains the process of object formation to model the external object. What survives in an adequate object is the trace of an incompletely traversed conceptual phase. This trace, the incomplete selection of the object, is the symptom of the disorder.

Put differently, errors in object recognition are the substitutive element of an hallucinatory image displayed in a veridical perception. In other words, misrecognition in agnosia is the price the object must pay in order to avoid the fate of an hallucination. Implicit is the idea that object formation proceeds unidirectionally *from* a stage of conceptual analysis *toward* a stage of form analysis and not, as commonly supposed, in the reverse direction.

These remarks establish a core and highly controversial feature of the microgenetic theory of perception, that a conceptual or symbolic stage in the processing of an object representation *precedes* a stage of form analysis. The implications of this theory are profound, for they entail that the meaning of an object is extracted prior to its form, that we understand and recognize objects before they are perceived consciously and that, in a very real sense, an object is remembered into perception, recollected like a dream into the world of external objects.

The Meaning of Associated Symptoms The symptoms of a perceptual disorder are usually accompanied by other manifestations of preliminary cognition. There may be changes in behavior, affect, language, emotion and awareness. These changes are inferred to be intrinsic to the perceptual disorder because they fluctuate moment-to-moment according to the symptom type. In other words, the affective content or error awareness associated with a perceptual disorder does not depend on the disorder itself but on the particular symptom at a given moment. On these grounds, many nonperceptual symptoms can be construed to be level-specific alterations that reflect stages in the elaboration of a behavior coextensive with that of the disrupted object.

To take an example, objects have an affective content. We may adore an object or the object can be terrifying. We can be amused by hallucinations or frightened by them. The affect may be located in the viewer or in the object representation. An individual may be frightened by a banal hallucination, or the hallucination itself may be frightening. Intense affect is a feature of early cognition. In contrast, partial, derived, or exteriorized affects characterize fully unfolded objects. Strong affective content in a behavior is a sign that the object is incompletely exteriorized. Unlike the final object, which seems to exist for its own sake as an object in the world, the preobject is fixed in the mind of the perceiver as a content that has not yet attained the status of an independent object. For this reason the object experience is imbued with subjective content from the perceiver. Emotion is a bridge to external objects; it is a sign that the object is not as independent as it seems but that it flows out from the perceiver as an extension of his affective life.

Summary From such observations we can recover the hidden infrastructure of the perception as it is displayed in pathology, an infrastructure not simply bypassed on the way to the final object but one that accounts for the greater though unexpressed part of its content. Stages given up in the process of object formation persist in the final object as manifestations of early cognition. The feeling of familiarity with the object, the memory or recognition of that or similar objects, its location in a system of concepts and affective tonality, are residues of preliminary phases in object formation. The space of the object and its relation to other objects, depth, distance and constancies, are also achieved in the course of a development in which one level is derived into the next, building a context around that object—in other words, building up mind within the object—in sum, elaborating the perceiver for whose pleasure the object seems to exist.

Imagery The nature of mental imagery is a critical problem in perception, for it addresses the interface between private and public experience. Apart from feelings, events experienced as mental can be interpreted as images of one type or another, so that a theory of perception that incorporates a theory of images is also a theory on the boundaries of mind in the world.

In the microgeny of perception, images and objects are points on a continuum. An image unfolds over the same neural substrate as a perception. An image is an object that is attentuated, while an object is an image that has undergone a further development. One can say that an image is an object in the mind, whereas an object is built up on a phase of image development. Conversely, an object is a late stage in the microgeny of images. The progression from image to object enlarges mind to embrace the world of perception. This means that a memory or thought image is not simply a revived and transformed perception, but a stage on the way to an external object. When we remember an experience we do not uncover a secondary association but recapture an earlier phase in the original object.

Similarly, dream and hallucination are not fictitious reveries constructed on the remnants of an object experience, but signposts on the way to an object that actualize prematurely. The often bizarre content of these images does not indicate a reworking of the perception along independent lines, but the application of subsurface rules that differ from those at a subsequent stage. A dream of events from the preceding day does not entail the transmission of a perception to an image or memory store for later retrieval; in dream, an object recedes into the formative cognition out of which it first emerged.

In psychosis the memory image can be the start of an hallucination and result in an almost real perception, or a fully intrapersonal hallucination can result from an object that begins to degrade. Hallucination can proceed outward to the world, or inward to the mind. We all know the frightening reality of many dreams just as the psychotic knows the frightening unreality of many object experiences. Such observations confirm that objects are retrieved out of long-term memory into short-term memory and perceptual awareness, that the recognition and identification of the object occur early on in perceptual processing so that objects are known before they are consciously seen, and that, far from objects existing for mind to scrutinize, mind and mental imagery are elaborated in the course of perceptual growth.

II Microgeny of Objects

On the microgenetic theory of perception, a representation unfolds from image to object within the phyletic core of the brain, not pieced together from peripheral input. The object begins in upper brainstem as a unified act/percept in a two-dimensional map of the body surface. There is a parallel hierarchy of sensory (physical) and perceptual (mental) levels at successive points corresponding to growth planes in the evolution of the forebrain. The sensory levels act to *constrain* the perceptual development, but do not enter directly into the object construction, while the perceptual levels—wholly cognitive and representational—are the contents that undergo transformation. There is no constructive process in which perceptions are build up on the raw material of sensation; rather, objects are "sculpted" in the mind as sensation restricts the degrees of freedom in cognitive processing. An object representation emerges through the inhibition of alternative pathways.

The application of sensory constraint at successive levels to an emerging mental representation leads to a model of an external object that captures successive levels in the representation of physical space. The withdrawal or interruption of sensation (levels of constraint) at one or more levels in percept formation results in a suspension of this modeling effect on the unfolding perceptual configuration. This leads to an attentuated object formation and an object representation that develops along autonomous lines to mental imagery or hallucination. The different types of hallucination and imagery can be viewed as incompletely developed objects that model the world up to a certain point.

The outcome of the microgenetic sequence is an abstract multitiered construct unfolding in the brain over evolutionary and maturational stages. Within this construct are successive planes in space formation, in memory and in personality organization. These planes provide a perceptual and cognitive foundation for the development of every object representation. The object grows out of this infrastructure. It does not come to the organism but is a product, an output, very much like an action or a behavior. Moreover, the position in the world to which the object unfolds is like a point on an extended body surface, a point that is not sensed by the body or brought into relation with it but one that extends mind's reach as it expands the body into a world without limits.

Sensation and Perception On this account, sensation is part of the physical world around the viewer, extrinsic to mind and something to be inferred from the perceptions it generates. Sensations do not become perceptions through an increase in their complexity, nor is the perception a distal phase in a chain of sensory processes. Perceptions are not elaborated or built up from sensations but are distinct from sensations from their inception.

Perceptions develop through intrinsic mechanisms, that is, mechanisms through which mind also develops. In fact, mind and perception are almost synonymous. The configurational series that constitutes the perception elaborates a representation that is mental and autonomous in that it does not utilize external sensory material. Sensation is applied at each level or processing stage in the perceptual series. There is a hierarchy of sensory input that corresponds with the structure of the perceptual representation. Specifically, sensation shapes the developing object representation but does not enter directly into its construction. The representation is modulated at successive points (moments in the object microgeny), the final object being determined by input that is not part of the developing representation.

Presumably, the perception lays down a track—a configurational series—that is the trace of its development. This track has an influence on subsequent experiences in which a similar configuration is encountered. The original track is activated to the degree to which a novel configuration approaches the (latent) configuration of the preceding experience. Since a perception involves the selection of an object, not its piecemeal construction, and since every object has to be selected from a great many other potential object representations, the recognition, feeling of familiarity, experiential and affective content of the final perception are activated early in the forming object to the extent to which similar prior configurations are approximated. In this way sensory experience enters perception as learning.

A corollary to this theory is that there are no *raw feels* or primitive sensations. The perception of pain does not involve a sensory prime but a percept that is archaic or rudimentary in comparison with other objects. The quality of pain may differ from other perceptual experiences—the pain may not be located in a well-defined body part; it is not objectlike, it is subjective and in-trapersonal—but the processing underlying the pain is experienced, or elaborates a representation, that is basically like any other perceptual object. As long as an object experience (pain, touch) is in awareness, it is by definition a perception, embedded in mind with other cognitive contents.

III Stages in Perceptual Microgenesis

Roots of Perception The perception begins in the upper brainstem reticular core, or tegmentum, as a two-dimensional map of ambient space in which targets are identified on the basis of relative motion, size, and perhaps simple shape and pattern detection. The spatial coordinates of the map are linked to actions of the body. The map is an action schema, a program for body movement on targets which serve as triggers for action. This core is modulated or constrained by sensory input through the wider tectal region, an interface for the transformation of sensory primitives into the spatial map and its action program. Although tectal cells appear to show hemifield organization, the tegmental map is presumed to represent a unitary space.

At this stage, however, space has not exteriorized and there is no external object. The space of the target is part of a private space organized about the body midline. A stimulus is fixed through an orientation of eyes, head, and neck, toward the locus of the target and seized through a movement of the eyes, or another body part such as the tongue or a limb. There is a tight bond between perception and action. The perception of a stimulus is linked to, one could even say manifested by, an orientation toward the stimulus, and this orientation is implemented through older axial and proximal motor systems.

Cases with injury or disease of the brainstem confirm the role of this system in early perception. There may be impaired ballistic (rapid, proximal) reaching of an arm, and neglect or inattention (failure to orient) to one side of space. With bilateral damage, there is complete failure of orientation to stimuli, giving rise to a state of "akinetic mutism," a type of catatonia. This condition is similar to a coma with the eyes open. With large lesions of upper brainstem an individual is comatose, or in a state of persistent sleep.

In normal perception, this level appears as, or represents, a state of dreamless sleep. That is, dreamless sleep reflects the autonomous (sensory-free) operation of this system as a ceiling on cognitive unfolding. The coma that results from extensive damage to upper brainstem displays the contribution of this system to normal perception. Specifically, the cognition of dreamless sleep, coma, and the "eyes-open" coma of the akinetic mute, represent a base level in the microgeny of percepts, a level that elaborates a state of perceptual vigilence preparatory to a ballistic movement or an optic grasp, organized about axial and proximal motility in an archaic, unextended, two-dimensional, intrapersonal preobject space.

The World of Dream The two-dimensional cognitive map represented at the level of upper brainstem is derived through mechanisms in the limbic and temporal lobe to a viewer-centered, volumetric space of dream and hallucination. A spatial map of targets for action develops to a preliminary object representation. At the same time, the object representation—at this stage an image or hallucination—enlarges and fills mental space with content, creating an intrapersonal object in opposition to a viewer that is equally intrapersonal, an observer as much a part of the image development as the image itself.

The limbic preobject is an image in a transitional space that is not wholly intrapersonal but rather a fluid extension of mind into the body surround. The opposition that is set up between image and viewer—which are contents in the same mental surface—is part of the feeling that the image is not wholly intrapersonal. The image is separate from the self though it has not yet achieved the space of an independent object. The space of dream and hallucination has an object quality; an hallucination may be accepted as real but it is not objectlike in its realness. The fact that dreamers and psychotics believe in the reality of their hallucinations should make one pause over the reality of waking percepts, but it is not a sign that hallucinatory objects mimic "real" ones. Hallucination is labile and changing and confluent with a space that has a tangible, viscous quality, not yet the empty medium in which independent objects, fixed and solid, are so reliably situated.

The distortions of dream imagery reveal aspects of the process of object selection. The object-to-be-perceived is derived through systems of symbolic, experiential and affective transformation toward increasing definition and spatial resolution. The emerging perceptual configuration differs from that of the preceding stage in that the bond with motility is less pronounced, responses are less automatic, the target is unreal and its meaning, its affective and conceptual relationships more important in determining the nature of the content that is represented. There is some direct sensory input to this stage by way of collaterals from the optic radiations, but relative freedom from sensory modeling may be necessary for the object to develop autonomously through a stage of personal experience and conceptual knowledge. Specifically, the relaxation of sensory constraints at this transition permits the tectal-derived spatial image to traverse— to be selected through—a stage of symbolic relations and dreamwork mechanisms preliminary to the resolution of the image as a fixed object in the world (Figure 7-1; Figure I-1).

Pathology in this region disrupts the image as it traverses a memory organized about experiential and conceptual relations. Damage to lateral and inferior temporal cortex in monkey gives an impairment in the selection of a visual target from an array of objects. The condition has been interpreted as midway between a memory and a perceptual disorder; retrieval and discrimination are intact. On the microgenetic account, one could say that the lesion disrupts (displays) a stage where the target configuration is emerging within a system of meaning-relations with other potential object representations. In humans with comparable injuries

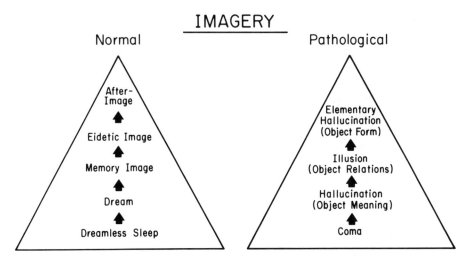

FIGURE 7-1. Microgenetic levels in object formation with reduction of sensory constraint: normal and pathological imagery.

involving the mesial temporo-occipital area, there may be difficulty recognizing common objects, faces or familiar routes. These are forms of visual agnosia (see above) where the problem concerns a conceptual derailment in object selection. Object form and detail are perceived adequately—the object can be described and drawn—but there is a change in the meaning of the object or its relation to prior experience so that the individual can no longer name or categorize the object or describe its function.

Pathology of limbic and temporal lobe regions can produce hallucination. Stimulation of limbic regions produces an hallucination that is more like a dream, while stimulation of temporal neocortex appears to produce an hallucination that is more like a perception. The greater the microgenetic depth of stimulation or evocation of the image, the greater the symbolic and/or conceptual distortion, the more subjective and storylike the experience, and the stronger its affective content. There may be a similarity between normal hypnagogic and "autosymbolic" images (introductory dream images) on falling asleep at night and some cases of hallucination due to temporal lobe damage. The derailment, fusion and condensation that characterize dreamwork mechanisms capture changes in the object representation as it traverses this level.

However, hallucinations are often isolated events without the historical character of dream. In this sense, they are like dream fragments. As with dream, hallucination can range from fantastic images to almost veridical objects. The quality of the hallucination reflects its momentary depth. Thus, cases with temporal lobe lesion may show banal hallucination during the day and bizarre distortion toward evening. Or, the hallucination may first appear at the close of day. These observations suggest that with sleep approaching, imagery recedes to a form characteristic of early cognition, or conversely, that a twilight cognitive regression recaptures an hallucinatory phase in object formation.

According to this account, the spatial map and action program, and the stage of dreamless sleep laid down in upper brainstem as the beginnings of the object representation, are derived through limbic-temporal systems to a stage of affective, experiential and conceptual relations. Aided by a lessening of sensory constraints on object microgeny, an image is transformed along more autonomous paths toward a veridical object. Pathology displays this segment as an hallucinatory endpoint, or the conceptual derailment is buried as an agnosia within an object that is spatially completed at subsequent levels. In deficiency states such as agnosia, object meaning is incomplete, or derailed, though the correct object is achieved, while dream hallucination and dreamlike hallucinations in waking mentation reflect the persistent or brief actualization of this level as an endpoint in percept formation.

Object Relations and Mental States The hallucination and its volumetric space are selected through the preceding stage and develop to a "real" external (veridical) object in a three-dimensional Euclidean space. This transition is accomplished through mechanisms in parietal cortex. The object exteriorization occurs from a fluid, subjective space to a space of limb exploration. This is a "manipulation" or grasping space that is not fully independent but that is centered on the action perimeter, the space of the arm's reach. Through this stage there is a consolidation of the forming spatial, temporal and figural qualities of the object as object and surround conform to the constraints of the external world.

Damage to the parietal cortex reveals normal operations underlying object and space representation. In imagery, the change is centered in a perception that is more like an object than a private image. One can say that the image achieves the status of an object so that alterations in real objects (illusions) predominate. Hallucinations may occur, but more commonly there are distortions and deformations of object size, shape, distance or motion (metamorphopsia). The shift from the hallucination of the preceding stage to illusional change in real objects reflects the microgenetic progression toward the final object representation.

Deficiency states tend to mirror changes in pathological imagery. Deficits occur in an external space with impairments of object relations and an alteration in the relation between a viewer and the objects around him. There are disorders of figure-ground perception, depth and relative distance estimation, impaired reaching and grasping of objects, drawing and manipulation. There are a number of disorders related to unilateral and bilateral parietal lobe damage, including such conditions as constructional disability, impaired simultaneous judgments (simultanagnosia), the Balint syndrome, impaired visumotor reaching (optic apraxia), spatial inattention, inability to dress oneself (dressing apraxia), and related conditions. These disorders have in common the fact that they are centered in an interactive space between object and viewer, bound up with limb movement on objects in the action perimeter. This occurs because the preobject has exteriorized to an object-centered space that is extrapersonal but not yet fully independent of the viewer.

Many of the spatial impairments associated with parietal lesion are referred to as part of the "right hemisphere syndrome," indicating a preferential link to right-sided damage. The right hemisphere bias appears to be restricted to deficiency states, for hallucination and other forms of abnormal imagery do not show strong laterality effects. The problem of the asymmetric effect of lesions on spatial and other performances, the assimilation of this phenomenon to the microgenetic model and its implication of "parallel" rather than "vertical" processing, are discussed in Brown (1983c).

Normal image phenomena referable to this stage are characterized by adequate representational targets, similarity to real percepts and a reduced affective content. Memory and eidetic images fall into this category. The memory image is like a dream image that has "come up" to the threshold of awareness, midway between private experience and its perceptual target. If a memory image of a recent event becomes so clear and picturable that it is actually "seen" as if it were still present, it is referred to as an eidetic image. Eidetic images usually follow rapidly on object perceptions, but the eidetic image can also occur after a delay. There is a gradual change from eidetic to memory imagery (and to dream) in the forgetting of a perception. This is because hallucination, memory, and eidetic imagery lie on a continuum leading to the object perception. Dream hallucination may surface to a memory image. Amnestics describe their memory disorder as like the fading of a dream on awakening. In the same way, one can say that an eidetic image is a memory image that has surfaced to an almost real perception.

As the image unfolds through these phases, from dream to memory image to eidetic image and "real" object, there is a loss of affective strength, of creativity and inventiveness in the image and a progressive reduction in the extent to which the image brings forth new content. These are markers of the subjective origins of the object that are given up in the realization of a fixed and stable world. There is also a change from an image that comes spontaneously and unbidden (dream) to one that occurs to some extent volitionally (memory image), to one that is entrained by an external object (eidetic image), to one that is a fully independent ("real") object. The feelings of spontaneity, purposefulness, or independence that are attached to different types of images are generated as manifestations of a single process of object representation at various moments in its completion. These feelings complement those of automaticity, purposefulness and volition that accompany the action microgeny. Both actions and objects lead out into and elaborate the external world. The active nature of action (the feeling that one is an agent that acts) develops within the action itself, just as the feeling of passivity to images and the feeling of the independence of objects develop within the process of object formation.

A World of Real Objects In the final segment of the microgenetic process, sensory modeling of the emerging object representation results in the individuation of featural detail and the full exteriorization and "detachment" of an ostensibly real object in an independent, extrapersonal space. This transition is accomplished through mechanisms in primary visual cortex and the circumstriate zone. Specifically, on the microgenetic account, this region is not the initial point of registration for a perception, but a sensory-perceptual transform that provides the final modeling to a mental image that has all but completed its perceptual development. The spatial image, which has exteriorized into a space of limb activity, is analysed to an independent object in a space that seems public and physical. The articulation of the object into external space coincides with the individuation of features in the object. Relations between objects, between object and space, and between object and perceiver recede into the background of a fully unfolded perception in which object, viewer and space are independent elements.

Thus, within the space of the external environment, submerged in the final percept, there is a concealed space of object relations and limb exploration generated by mechanisms in parietal cortex, a space in which a change in object or perceiver, or the actions of the perceiver on an object, visibly alters the entire perception. This level of space relations, like the preceding stage of recognition and conceptual meaning, persists in the background of the completed percept and provides a context and an underpinning out of which the analysis of object features is derived.

Damage to circumstriate cortex gives disorders of form perception affecting objects, faces and letters. A disturbance of reading (alexia) and object identification (form agnosia) occurs with involvement at this point. The various forms of this disturbance, whether the impairment affects colors, written material, or objects, depends on the particular point in the process where the pathology has its maximum impact, and/or the stage of restitution or decay. These disorders are not the result of a piecemeal disarray of independent mechanisms; they are not deletions or fragments but successive moments in a single unfolding process.

Damage to the primary visual cortex results in scotoma or blind spots in the visual field; in severe cases with bilateral damage, cortical blindness. Such patients are not really blind since it is possible to demonstrate perceptions at a more preliminary level. Vision in hemianopic fields ("blindsight") was first demonstrated by Bard in 1905, and confirmed by Bender and Krieger in 1951. There is perception of movement, shape, size, some form, and perhaps color. The degree of perception in patients without a striate cortex may be considerable. Semantic priming has even been reported in blind fields (Marcel, 1983b; see also Holender, 1986).

Hallucinations are common at the onset of a scotoma or in cortical blindness. These hallucinations represent endogenous percepts that become the endpoint in an attenuated object development. Patients are often unaware of cortical scotomata or blindness. This indicates that the scotoma is not an empty spot in the object field, but a failure to realize a microgenetic endpoint—and thus to elaborate a consciousness of the unrealized portion. The significance of hallucination and residual vision is that they are truncated object developments that survive destruction of the surface of the perception.

Patients with scotoma may show completion of patterns across gaps in the visual field. There is a celebrated story about the neuropsychologist Hans-Lukas Teuber, who used to recall how Karl Lashley one day "beheaded" him in a migraine scotoma, leaving unaffected the geometric pattern on the wall. Such observations along with the experimental studies support the idea of subsurface perceptual gestalts. Parenthetically, the fact that there is completion *in the mind* across "holes" in the brain, though explicable in terms of microgenetic or gestalt theory, could provide an argument for dualism.

Pathological images include elementary hallucinations—lights, flames, geometric patterns—and illusory persistence or multiplication of objects. These phenomena are related to after-images (the residues of a bright object when one looks away) and represent equivalents in imagery of pathological deficiency states. One could say that the image is the mental content within the scotoma, a content oridinarily not accessed into the consciousness of a fully completed object. The after-image and related phenomena differ from eidetic images and hallucinations in that they do not replace but are *superimposed* on object perceptions. They also undergo a change in size in relation to projection distance; that is, the after-image does not show constancy effects. In other words, the after-image takes on certain of the attributes of *physical* objects. This is because the after-image arises through primary visual cortex and is extrinsic to—one could say, at the surface of—the developing object perception.

Summary of Perceptual Microgenesis To sum up, object and space are formed more or less instantaneously over a series of microstructural transitions. This multitiered process proceeds over a set of autonomous cognitive transformations constrained at successive levels by sensory input to model an external object. There is a transition from an archaic two-dimensional map of somatic space elaborating dreamless sleep and the spatial underpinnings of the object, to the egocentric or volumetric space of dream and hallucination. The object is selected through fields of meaning relations to a three-dimensional Euclidean space. The preobject, or image, has a holistic or relational quality in the interactive space of limb exploration. From this stage the perception is transformed to an articulated object in a fully independent and extrapersonal "physical" space. At the same time the self "detaches" from the forming object so that self and object, which are both laid down by the same process, become distinct and separate representations.

Early stages in this process lay down relations between object and body movement, the link to experience and memory, affective content, relations with self and other objects and the situational context within which the object appears. These stages persist abstractly in the final object as a background of knowledge and feeling. At the same time, the object proceeds from a representation bound up with action about the body axis to one that is linked to the proximal and distal musculature. In other words, the articulation of an object into external space is accompanied by a parallel microgenesis of action as the act unfolds into discrete and asymmetric digital movements on external objects.

This process is retraced in normal imagery, in the transition from dreamless sleep to dream hallucination, through memory imagery to eidetic images, and finally to the after-image. This sequence leads:

1. From an image that comes involuntarily (dream); through one that is purposeful or volitional (memory images); to an independent object that seems to interact with the perceiver.

2. From a dream image that is filled—or the perceiver who is filled—with intense affect; to a memory image that is accompanied by a mild or subtle affective tonality; to an eidetic image devoid of affective content; to an external object where feelings in the object have to be inferred.

3. From perceptual or symbolic distortion linked to past experience and distant memory; through a stage of spatial and conceptual resolution; toward increasing referential stability as a memory and then eidetic image; and finally to an independent object.

4. From the unconsciousness of deep sleep; through the archaic consciousness of dream; to the introspective consciousness of the memory image; to an awareness distributed over a world of objects that mind itself has created.

In the course of this process, affect and meaning are drawn out from their positions in mind to infiltrate surrounding objects. To imbue an object with meaning and emotion is to recede for a moment to a preobject phase. When we do this, we withdraw from externality to a stage of imagery that prefigures the object, and we recapture the affect and meaning that were part of the preliminary object development. From a microgenetic point of view, this state is midway between dream and object perception, beyond the vagueness of a memory image that is struggling to the surface and prior to the clear perusal of an object field. Introspection is not a higher state but a regression from the world of objects to an antecedent phase of mental imagery.

IV Self-Knowledge and Object Awareness

Objects and Mental Representations The view that the worlds of inner and outer perception lie on a continuum within the same mental state entails that the knowledge of external objects and self-knowledge are the same kind of knowledge and share common underlying properties. An object is represented as an image in private space or as a "real" object in public space; it develops with, and is qualitatively changed into different mental spaces, but the same process of object and space representation is involved.

A mental representation—a *conscious* content of the mind, such as an idea or an image—is an object that is truncated in its development. Conversely, an external object—an utterance, an action or a "real" perception—is a mental representation that undergoes further processing. A mental representation, a thought, is a phase in percept formation. Put differently, thoughts make up the infrastructure of objects. The series of states from dream to introspection to percepts retraces the microgeny of objects. From this it follows that observations on inner states, and verbal reports of those observations, are subject to the same limitations as observations directed to external objects. Specifically, both introspection and exteroception (perception) suffer from the same deficiency: namely, an inability to access the physical object within the representation and an uncertainty as to the accuracy with which this physical object is represented.

In this view, a representation is the content of a mental state, the nature of which is determined by the surface to which the processing sequence develops. In theory, the process that elaborates a mental state can terminate—or with pathology be attentuated or "sliced"—at any of a possibly infinite number of points on a continuum. The spatiotemporal configuration collapsed over the duration required to generate a representation comprises the content of the mental state.

A representation requires time to develop, and the duration of that development has to be incorporated in a definition of a mental state. The state has a temporal context. The content of that state, the representation, is the sum of the potential configurations traversed in the processing, while the degree or extent of processing—the endpoint of the processing sequence—determines the level to which the representational content is realized.

Dream and Waking Reality In this view, there is no clear boundary between inner and outer events, but rather a succession of spatial planes leading outward from an intrapsychic core. Of course, in everyday life the distinction of inner and outer is sharply drawn. We peer out of our mental cells and ruminate on a world around us. Objects and ideas could not be more different. Yet in pathological cases, perceptions can actualize at the transition between image and object and the individual dose not know whether he is dreaming or awake. This can persist as a more or less permanent condition. Images can appear to invade and replace perceptions or objects can withdraw to imagelike states. What is actually happening is that the object, or a part of the object field, has receded to the image that anticipates it, resulting in illusion, hallucination or, more specifically, some level in a preperception.

Surely, many of us at one time or another have had a momentary glimpse of this feeling: a perception that is like a remembered dream or an uncertainty as to whether an experience is a dream or a recollection. For many, the whole of life is a dream that is experienced. The record of one's life *(Lebensfilm)* unfolds at the moment of death as a dream that has been lived. Shakespeare's remark that life is a dream surrounded by a sleep captures this feeling. What is the difference between a vague memory image of a real experience that is incompletely revived and the memory image of a dream? The microgenetic position is that there is no difference. We are usually able to distinguish the two because objects developing through sensory constraints can be revived with greater resolution into waking consciousness. Except for dreams that are like vivid hallucinations and break through into conscious awareness, most dreams are submerged and "trapped" in subsurface cognition. A dim memory image that recedes to deeper levels in mentation is like a dream that has come up to the threshold of awareness.

The apprehension of this similarity—one could say continuity—between dream and memory images helps us to understand the anguish of the brain-injured patient, for example the patient of Luria (1972) unable to distinguish dream from wakefulness, fixed at a point in object representation that for others is but a feeling insight. In such a state, objects are invested by thoughts, and feel as if they are still part of the perceiver's mind.

Dreams appear distinct from conscious mental states, which form a separate domain of knowledge. Conscious mentation is more real to us than dream even though it may be less vivid. There are different modes of thought during dream and introspection. In spite of these differences, conscious mentation is built on a foundation of dream cognition. Unlike objects, dreams and ideas are positioned in the mind. We find plausible a transition from dream image to idea or mental representation, but not a transition from mental representation to object. The world is more real to us than thought, which seems to be a secondary acquisition. Dreams and ideas seem to be deposited by sensory experience, not there before experience and giving rise to it. After all, how can the world we apprehend in perception be an extension of mind if the world was there before mind developed?

Of course, the transformation of ideas to objects has to be quantal or molar—there has to be an emergent step underlying the transition from inner to outer space—or there would be no world at all. The deception of a mind that interacts with real objects is total and unshakable. But the exteriorization of acts and objects is a graded process that can be followed along in its course. An idea is not projected or thrust into the world, but develops with the world in stages, only gradually becoming independent of the mind, where it originated. We have to understand that the deception of a real world has to be a strong one—there is survival value in the strength of this deception—for otherwise we could not manage in the world—there would be no world to manage in—nor could we consciously interact with minds and objects other than our own.

The implication is that awareness of, or consciousness of other objects, is part of the consciousness of our own mental states; one cannot exist without the other. The question of the evolutionary selection value of consciousness is, then, bound up with the selection value of an awareness of other objects—not just a state of attentiveness to objects and actions, but an awareness that entails an independent self that is extrinsic to and looking on those external objects. In this view, introspection is another form of object awareness, the objects being the inner objects (images) or ideas that anticipate external objects, rather than the objects themselves.

Other Objects and Other Minds There are other similarities between introspection and the awareness of external objects. Introspection has for its object the content of a mental state, not the physical (brain) state for which that content is a type of correlate. This is also true for exteroception, or the perception of objects. We see an object as a whole, we hear its sound and see its color, not the physical processes responsible for these phenomena. These have to be inferred through analysis or experimentation. The physical process(es) underlying mental representations can be investigated in the same manner if appropriate methods are employed. This follows because the physical correlate of an object perception is of the same kind as the neural correlate of a mental representation. There is continuous flow from the physical world to the neurophysiological underpinnings of mind. A theory of the nature of external objects and the brain states that correspond to object perceptions is also a theory of brain states underlying ideas and of the sensory elaboration of ideas to model external objects. In fact, one can go even further and say that there is a still deeper theory of the common basis of mind and world.

The basis in mind for the objects of perception and the ideas of introspection, and the argument that ideas and objects lie on a continuum, entails the solipsistic conclusion that one knows only one's own mental content. If the world embracing a mind is continuous with, and another manifestation of, the representational content of that mind, then the incapacity to break through a world of mental representation is matched by the incapacity to perceive a world beyond that of our object representations. Introspection has for its data only mental content, whether internal or external.

But even one's mental content is largely inaccessible to introspection; there is no way to be sure that we are not deluded by the content of our mental states. We may perceive dream images or waking hallucinations as real. The dream or hallucination obtains across different modalities—it is seen, touched, heard—and its apparent reality is confirmed by the collusion of the various perceptual channels. In pathological cases, there are many instances of dissociation (or, rather, incongruity) between awareness and behavior. For example, there may be lack of awareness for a defective utterance, for a paralysis of a limb or even for blindness! An individual may insist his aphasic speech is accurate, that he can move his paralysed arm or that, in spite of failed performances, he can see objects clearly. The implication of these observations is that deviant mental representations entail or generate deviant states of the self and alterations in awareness of mental content, and that what is true in pathology is also true in normal individuals.

Apart from the unreliability of (normal or pathological) introspection, and the fact that the momentary content determines what the self of that moment is, there is the added problem that we enjoy but limited knowledge of our own mental states. We are aware, and incompletely at that, of only the surface of a mental or object representation, of only that fraction of the mental representation that entails awareness. We know only what we are aware that we know, only that part of the representation presented in awareness. What doesn't enter into awareness—and that is the major part of the representational content, including all of that potential content given up in the realization of the final representation—is excluded from the scrutiny of the introspecting state.

But this is only the beginning! There are still greater problems for introspection to resolve. Among these is the fact that the self of the introspective state (the self that is supposedly doing the introspecting) is regenerated each moment by the representational content. The self is a product, not an agent. This means that the content that is surveyed in introspection is not there waiting to be reviewed by an onlooking self, but is thrust into and generates the awareness by which it is accompanied. In other words, mental states introspect themselves and elaborate a self as a part of the available content. Introspection applies to a representation that includes a self-concept.

On these grounds, solipsism, though a logical outcome of microgenetic theory, is disingenuous, for we know as little of our mental states as of the world beyond observation. What proof that mental representations are accurate or complete or correspond to experience and memories of lived events? What proof that objects are real or hallucinatory or correspond to objects in the physical world? The corollary to solipsism, that one cannot access any event beyond one's mental representation of it, appears the more primary datum.

Introspection As mentioned, pathological studies indicate that the awareness of a mental representation is bound up with the representation itself, as a part of that representation, and not the expression of a mind's eye gazing on mental content. There is a change in the awareness for a given content—a perception, an utterance—when there is damage to the content in question or to the cognitive domain of that content. The change in awareness or introspection is specific to error type and perceptual modality.

For example, an aphasic patient who makes both phonological and semantic errors will tend to be aware of the phonological ones but not the semantic ones. Similarly, a patient with "blindness" due to damage to the visual cortex may be unaware that he is blind, but very much aware of a limb paralysis. The lack of awareness or denial of blindness occurs because the patient is no longer able to generate a memory of (i.e., reperceive) the (attentuated) world of visual object representations. Awareness is structured, it is elaborated in relation to domain-specific mental representations and is not a general or unitary faculty that floats above or surveys any mental content that surfaces.

Another way of saying this is that a representation incorporates its own awareness; the awareness is *in* the representation. Contents are not derived or accessed into consciousness, but elaborate conscious states consistent with their level of derivation. This means that there is no self that introspects mental content; rather, the representational content (usually, a language representation) displays itself in the nature of the introspection that it elaborates. Introspection is not a state or component in addition to the state or component that is the object of the introspection. Introspection is a particular state that arises as a coincidence of linguistic and perceptual representations at a given moment. Actually, in the microgenetic view introspection is a kind of withdrawal from the perception of objects to the mental images that anticipate them. The self and other mental contents are deposited by the object development before the object exteriorizes.

Specifically, there are two oppositions set up in the course of object development: (1) an opposition between viewer and external objects; (2) an opposition between viewer and internal representations. In the microgenetic view, these are comparable states, the latter anticipating the former. Both phenomena are a result of the outward development of objects. In the course of this development, a sphere of inner mental (verbal, perceptual) imagery precedes the derivation of the external object. As the object draws outward and becomes independent of mind, mind—that is, the internal or subjective phase of the object development—persists as a type of subjective object in opposition to the objects of the external world. This is the basis for exteroception, the belief in independent objects that impinge on a mind distinct from those objects. Introspection is simply attenuated exteroception, mind gazing on preliminary object representations.

This leads to the apparently paradoxical conclusion that the introspective state is a precursor to a state of object awareness, even though object awareness would appear to be the more primitive function. There is a difference, however, between an awareness or attentiveness to objects and an awareness in which a self surveys an object field that is external and independent of the viewer. Thus, Piaget's description of an awareness of objects and an awareness of activity as early stages in the ontogeny of self-awareness does not obtain when a conscious self scrutinizes objects. An awareness of objects in which the observer is not yet an agent distinct from the objects being viewed is prior to the emergence of a self that is independent of mental contents and external objects.

In this view, introspection is an expression of a perceptual or language behavior, a state of an organism that needs to be explained, not a method of psychological investigation. There are problems in the characterization of the self or self-concept that is supposedly doing the introspection; there are problems with the observer's access to his own mental content; and there are problems with the reliability of verbal report. These problems do not arise through the inability of others to verify mental states and their verbal description, or through the potential for bias, deception or dissimulation on the part of the subject. There is a

deeper problem inherent in the nature of introspection that defines the limits of
self-knowledge and the knowledge of other objects that has to do with the way in
which representations emerge and the nature of intrapsychic content. A fuller
understanding of the process through which representations develop is likely to
erode the comon-sense belief in the existence of a self that scans mental content
and vitiate theories of mind built up on metalinguistic data.

The Self as Mental Representation The feeling of apartness and interaction
of a self with objects and other mental contents is a central feature of our
conscious life and cannot be simply disregarded. A theory of mind has to account
for these phenomena. It also has to account for the structure of mind and how that
structure develops. But it need not attribute causal efficacy to contents generated
into the introspective state. These contents, like leaves on a tree, are outgrowths
of the effective (agentive) or formative structure of mind, part of the crust of new
form pouring out from below and not components in mind's creative engine. In
this view, introspection is not a shaping activity, but rather is a shadow of mental
content as it rapidly decays to the past, always a step behind the dynamic of mind
and, ultimately, less informative, less genuine, than intuitions developing naturally as the direct manifestations of subsurface processes.

The central point is that the self is also a representation, a self-representation, that is part of the representational content. The self-representation is not
confined to one perceptual mode but spans the modalities at a given moment in
perception. Contents elaborated in each of the modalities contribute to part of the
self-representation. In pathological cases, damage to the perceptual modalities
chips away at the self concept. The self is derived from multiple perceptual
contents.

How are the various elements of the self-concept integrated across the
different modalities? Given that mental contents are like objects in subjective
space, the opposition or contrast between self and mental representation is not
found across contents in different perceptual modalities. The content of a tactile,
an auditory or visual representation seems part of the same object, unlike the
self, which seems to observe its own representations. In other words, the
opposition is between a self and other mental objects, not among those other
mental objects. Moreover, how does a construct such as the self-concept stand in
opposition to other mental representations if the self-concept is composed of
elements that develop within those representations? The self is generated by, and
decomposes in relation to, the representational content of the perceptual modalities—but the self has to be more than a composite representation.

One way out of this bind is to think of the self as a type of background
configuration that embraces contents in each modality. The process that generates the self-concept, along with other representational content, traverses and
revives formative levels in the personality that are not part of the surface content
of the separate modalities. That is, the self-concept is laid down in early,

formative stages in perceptual microgenesis as a unitary preobject, and it is out of this unitary representation that the contents of the separate modalities differentiate. To return to the metaphor of a tree, one can think of the self as deposited early in the upward growth of structure as it articulates into ever finer arborizations. The fact that the modalities show surface differentiation but are unitary at their base accounts for the unity of a self-representation in which all the modalities have a share. The unity of the self, therefore, is not accomplished secondarily through an interaction or integration across the modalities, but is a unity that underlies the modalities and distributes itself into them.

III
ACTION

8
Frontal Lobes and the Organization of Action*

GENERAL REMARKS

The frontal lobes, it is often said, are the regions of the brain which have undergone the greatest expansion in evolution, represent the highest centers of human intelligence, and are the sites of the most complex and highly evolved mental functions. In human and animal studies, the frontal lobes have been associated with self-consciousness, moral behavior and foresight, the awareness of social norms, habituation, drive, abstract thinking and judgment. Frontal lobe mechanisms which have been proposed to underlie these capacities include synthetic or integrative functions, motivation, recent memory, selective attention, and planning.

In view of these claims, therefore, it is surprising that experimental and clinical studies have not yet succeeded in defining a set of symptoms or deficits clearly associated with damage to the frontal lobes, nor in isolating those aspects of behavior, apart from movement and speech, which depend on frontal lobe mechanisms. There are several reasons why this is so. Symptoms of frontal lobe damage are often subtle and appear only on careful testing. Neuropsychological studies tend to compare performance on a few tests in disparate populations, while case reports with anatomical correlation are often incomplete from the linguistic and psychological standpoint. The literature on prefrontal lobotomy has led to more confusion than insight, while problems in left frontal cases are often confounded by the presence of aphasia.

In spite of these difficulties, there is still much to be said regarding the functions of the frontal lobes. This article will review behavioral effects of frontal lobe damage in several different populations: cases of frontal lobotomy or lobectomy; mixed pathological groups; and single case studies. The frontal syndrome in monkey will also be discussed. The article will not deal with motor, oculomotor or autonomic

---

*From "Frontal Lobes and the Microgenesis of Action" by J. W. Brown, 1985, *Journal of Neurolinguistics, 1,* 31–63. Copyright 1985 by *Journal of Neurolinguistics.* Adapted by permission.

deficits associated with frontal lesions. It is argued that an interpretation of the nature of frontal lobe function can be aided by a careful analysis of the disorders of speech and motility which occur with focal lesions. As in other areas of neuropsychological study, evidence from the aphasias and apraxias can provide a framework for a general theory of behavior.

ANATOMY

In the human brain, the frontal lobes are usually divided into three major sections moving rostrally from the rolandic fissure: (1) The **precentral cortex** consists of the motor strip, Brodmann area 4; (2) anterior to this zone is the **premotor cortex,** consisting of areas 6, 8, and 44, (3) excluding the opercular zone, the remainder is **prefrontal cortex.** This includes Brodmann areas 9-12, also referred to as non-motor or granular frontal cortex. In the monkey, the caudal border of the prefrontal cortex is defined by the arcuate sulcus. While it is true that a major increase in the volume and fissuration of the prefrontal cortex has occurred over the mammalian series leading to man, this increase may not be disproportionate to the overall increase in brain size (Passingham, 1979). However, the extent of integration cortex in man is certainly larger than in lower primates.

All areas of granular prefrontal cortex in the monkey (Kievit and Kuypers 1977) and human brain (van Buren and Borke 1972) have reciprocal connections with mediodorsal (MD) nucleus of thalamus. According to Tanaka (1976), the older magnocellular portion of MD projects mainly to the orbital surface, whereas the more recent parvocellular portion projects to the convexity. The relationship between MD and the prefrontal cortex is so striking that it is often used as a means of following the evolution of the latter region over the phyletic scale, and for comparisons across widely different evolutionary forms (Nauta 1972). Prefrontal cortex has even been defined as that region of the frontal lobe connected to MD nucleus (Fuster, 1980). However, lesions of MD in monkey do not reproduce the behavioral deficits that occur with dorsolateral lesions (Rosvold, 1972). Of interest is that regions of prefrontal cortex receiving projections from MD also receive dopaminergic projections from midbrain (Divac, Bjorklund, Lindvall, and Passingham 1978).

The prefrontal cortex also projects to caudate nucleus and other basal ganglia structures. Autoradiographic studies have shown efferents to the entire length of the caudate nucleus (Goldman and Nauta 1977). In contrast to MD lesions, caudate lesions in monkey reproduce all of the behavioral deficits of prefrontal lesions (Rosvold 1972). In addition to these projections, there are diffuse thalamic projections (Kievit and Kuypers 1977), and afferents from brainstem tegmentum, amygdala (Llamas, Avendano, and Reinoso-Suarez 1976) and hypothalamus (Jacobsen, Butters, and Tovsky 1978).

The major cortico-cortical connections have been reviewed by Nauta (1972), Pandya and Vignolo (1971), Jones and Powell (1970), and Jacobsen and Tro-janowski (1977). There are reciprocal connections with the secondary visual, auditory and somatosensory "belt" areas, and prominent limbic efferents, including projections to hippocampus and cingulate cortex (Rosene and van Hoesen 1977). The ventral and orbital regions are connected through uncinate fasciculus to the rostral temporal neocortex.

FRONTAL SYNDROME IN MONKEY

Early observations on the effects of frontal lesions carried out in monkey and subprimate did not show clear evidence of impaired learning or perception. Ferrier (1875) noted a lack of curiosity, difficulty in carrying out planned or purposive activity and aimless behavior. Bianchi (1895) gave the first thorough description of the frontal syndrome in monkey, noting impaired recognition of the significance of, or relationships between, objects. Memory loss, lack of initiative, and changes in the emotional aspects of behavior were described. An important advance was the development of conditioned reflex techniques (Pavlov 1902) and the invention of the problem box (Franz, 1902; Thorndike, 1911) which led to the demonstration in animals of deficits on delayed response and alternation tasks. Since these early studies, a great deal has been learned about the "frontal monkey," though it is not clear that we are much closer to an understanding of the lesion effects.

The monkey with bilateral frontal lesions does about as well as animals lesioned in other areas on many simple discrimination and learning tasks (Brutkoski 1965) but has particular difficulty when stimuli are presented in succession or when a delay is introduced. This is especially marked on "go – no go" paradigms, where the animal is required to respond to one stimulus and withold a response to another stimulus. In such instances, the monkey makes many errors of commission. Similar deficits occur in human cases, especially with mesial frontal lesions (Drewe 1975). There is also great difficulty in reversing discrimination habits for stimuli and their location (place reversal) once these habits are established. The animal persists in responding to the previously rewarded stimulus or location.

The most widely studied task is the delayed response paradigm, developed by Jacobsen (1936). In a typical task, food is placed under one of two covers and then screened from view before the monkey makes a choice. The normal animal can respond correctly after delays of 1-2 minutes, but the frontal monkey may fail after delays of only a few seconds. In contrast, patients with frontal trauma do well on this task (Ghent, Mishkin, and Teuber 1962) and chimpanzees show mild or transient impairments.

Variations of this task have been intensively studied over the years (Fuster

1980), with no consensus as to the basic deficit. It is known that the most critical area is the sulcus principalis, especially the middle third though lesions of adjacent areas also give impairments. The initial interpretation was that the deficit occurred because of an impairment in short-term memory, but there are reasons for thinking this is not the whole explanation. For example, animals kept in the dark during the delay perform well on the task (Malmo 1942). This and other findings (Grueninger and Pribram 1969) suggest a susceptibility to interference from extraneous stimuli during the delay interval. This formulation is similar to Luria's interpretation of frontal deficits in human cases. The distractibility of the frontal monkey has been attributed to a preference for novel objects (Pribram 1961), increased alerting responses and decreased habituation.

In addition to distraction, the frontal monkey also shows perseverative errors of various types. Harlow (1950) maintained that frontal lesions lead to perseveration of stimuli (i.e., sensory perseveration), but perseveration of responses and persistence of preferences and orientation biases have all been noted. Mishkin (1964) argued that the perseveration is not a peripheral phenomenon but involved the central set or attitude established by the task. This is certainly consistent with the experience in human cases. In general, lesions of orbital cortex and the inferior convexity affect reversal tasks where perseveration of behavioral sets is an important factor. Orbital lesions are also related to changes in autonomic function, emotional reactivity and social behavior.

There is also an age effect in the behavioral consequences of frontal lesions. *In utero* resections of dorsolateral cortex in infant monkeys (Harlow, Akert, and Schiltz 1964) do not give impairments later in life, nor is there degeneration of dorsomedial nucleus (Goldman and Gelkin 1978). However, there is a well-known human case of severe perinatal frontal lobe damage with defective personality development (Ackerly and Benton, 1948).

In addition to the cognitive changes, the frontal monkey is more fearful and withdrawn, though inappropriate aggressive behavior may occur (Deets, Harlow, Singh, and Bloomquist 1970). There is mutism or decreased vocalization, reduced facial mimicry, decreased grooming and other social behaviors. The alteration in social interaction (Warren, 1972) recalls changes in human lobotomy cases. Hypoactivity has been described, especially with orbital lesions. This may be present initially or follow a hyperactive phase. The hyperactivity which is so characteristic of the frontal monkey may not reflect a primary disorder of motility but an increased responsiveness to stimuli. Aimless pacing has been described with posterior orbital lesions, along with stereotyped rhythmic or perseverative movements.

Although it is difficult to relate the various behaviors of the frontal monkey to distinct subdivisions of prefrontal cortex, some general patterns have emerged (see Rosenkilde 1979). Sulcus principalis lesions or stimulations give deficits on spatial delayed response and alternation tasks, and there have been suggestions that this region is involved in spatial memory, or in spatiotemporal processing (Rosvold 1972). Superior convexity lesions may disrupt movement-produced kinaesthetic cues. Inferior convexity lesions tend to give perseverative errors, especially on reversal tasks, while orbital lesions lead to changes in emotional and social behavior.

In view of the complexity of the data, and the difficulty interpreting the significance of defective performance in lesioned animals, it is not surprising that there are few general formulations of the role of frontal cortex based on the animal studies. Such theories as do exist tend to emphasize anatomical factors. Nauta (1964; 1972) argues that frontal cortex is the major neocortical representative of limbic system and functions to modulate limbic activity. In this role the frontal cortex, through its close relation to posterior exteroceptive cortex, integrates information about the environment.

Pribram (1975) distinguishes three sectors of prefrontal cortex: medial transitional cortex in relation to anterior thalamic nuclei; dorsolateral homotypical cortex in relation to medial thalamus; and posterior orbital cortex in relation to medial thalamus, anterior insula, temporal pole and periamygdaloid cortex. Both dorsolateral and limbic sectors are involved in the inhibition of interference among brain events. According to Pribram, the function of frontal cortex is to organize goal directed behavior in context-sensitive or environmentally cued conditions.

Fuster (1980) emphasizes the importance of evolutionary aspects of frontal lobe organization, and the idea that the frontal lobe is involved in the temporal structuring of behavior. A behavior is an action which is directed toward a goal, and its structure and temporal unfolding are mediated by frontal mechanisms. Perhaps, because it is so general, this approach seems most consistent with the interpretation to be developed from a consideration of the human material.

CLINICAL STUDIES OF THE "FRONTAL SYNDROME"

The study of frontal deficits in man is usually taken to begin with the celebrated crowbar case of Harlow (1848; 1868) in which an injury to the left frontotemporal region with bilateral damage led to intellectual change, impulsiveness, profanity and inability to plan and direct behavior toward future goals. Oppenheim (1890) was the first to describe Witzelsucht or moria, the tendency for manic and/or facetious behavior.

The first major study of the "frontal syndrome" was by Feuchtwanger (1923), who examined 200 cases of frontal lobe injury and compared the psychological effects to those of lesions elsewhere in the brain. He found changes in mood and initiative, with euphoria and disorders of attention in the majority of cases.

Witzelsucht, sexual erethism with childish and at times tasteless wisecracks, mood swings, hypomanic behavior and schizoid states were noted. The majority of patients showed no intellectual or memory deficits, though impaired concentration, difficulty initiating a task and following through on it, and lack of full awareness of the problem, were present in many cases.

Under the term alogia, Kleist (1934b) described impairments of abstraction in frontal patients, using tests of definitions, analogies, proverbs, similarities and differences, and emphasized a change in drive *(Mangel an Antrieb)* as a fundamental impairment. Kleist's contribution, however, was marred by his overly zealous attempt to localize different faculties in cytoarchitectonic regions of the frontal lobes, as well as other areas of the brain, though he did anticipate studies of the frontal monkey in assigning the emotional changes in human cases to orbital lesions and the intellectual changes to lesions of the convexity.

Schilder (1934) thought that the intellectual and the emotional changes after frontal lesion were not independent but stemmed from an underlying restructuration of the personality. This was also the view of Goldstein (1936) who considered the change in affect a part of an altered ability to abstract. Whether a patient was apathetic or euphoric was determined by the degree of his understanding of a situation. In addition to the changes in mood and initiative, apathy or euphoria, impulsiveness and inappropriate behavior, frontal patients had impairments in thinking and planning, and in the awareness of their own disability. Excellent reviews of this early work can be found in Brickner (1936) and Denny-Brown (1951).

Prefrontal leucotomy

The relatively independent lines of research in primate and human brain-damage came together in 1936 when Moniz and Lima (Moniz 1936) described the results of leucotomy in a series of agitated mental patients. This operation developed on observations by Jacobsen and Fulton (Fulton 1953) that chimpanzees with prefrontal lesions did not show normal anger and frustration when deprived of a reward. The procedure used by Moniz involved the insertion of a leucotome, a hollow needle with a stylet and a flexible wire loop at the top, at different angles through the skull with 4-6 1 cm cores of white matter cut out *in situ* in the frontal lobe on each side. This approach was subsequently replaced by the Freeman-Watts (1950) procedure in which the leucotome severed frontal connections on each side through a lateral burr hole. Other procedures include transorbital lobotomy, topectomy and serial coagulations (Valenstein, 1973). According to Meyer and

McLardy (1948) and Denny-Brown (1951), section of the mesial frontal white matter, involving the connections of the orbital surface, was the most effective method.

The more posterior lesions generally gave better results, though such lesions were associated with greater side-effects. Pathologically, there is cystic degeneration in the orbito-frontal area (Denny-Brown 1951). CT studies confirm the presence of sizable cystic lesions in post-leucotomy patients (Banna, Admas, Tunks, and Finlayson 1978). However, there is evidence that schizophrenics who do well after leucotomy have *larger* orbital lesions than schizophrenics with modest or poor recovery (Naeser, Levine, Benson, Stuss, and Weir 1981). We have had the opportunity to study a single case many years post-lobotomy, where there was a considerable cognitive and psychiatric impairment.

The initial description by Moniz on the effects of leucotomy has been repeatedly confirmed in subsequent studies. At first, there is apathy or somnolence, transient incontinence, masked facies or grimacing, at times mutism and catatonic attitudes or akinesia. This gradually resolves over several days to a state of decreased initiative and variable changes in behavior. These include tactlessness, lability, a change in social habits, distractibility, disturbances in judgment and emotional shallowness. There may also be changes in IQ testing, especially during the immediate postoperative period. This has been clearly demonstrated in nonpsychotic cases (neurotics, chronic pain) where thorough pre- and postoperative testing can be carried out (Rylander, 1943; Koskoff, Dennis, Lazobik, and Wheeler, 1948). Over time, there is usually some recovery toward the preoperative level, and psychotic patients are described where the IQ has shown a subsequent rise over previous testing. Decrements may occur on a variety of psychological tests but it has not been possible to extract a central or core deficit which is consistently present in these cases. Of interest is that recent studies of post-leucotomy patients demonstrate fairly good performance on IQ and memory testing, as well as on a variety of attentional tasks, finger tapping, hand sequencing and go/no-go tests (Stuss *et al.* 1981). Moreover, since patients with good recovery have both higher test scores and larger frontal lesions, the mild decrements that occur in some patients may reflect an incomplete lesion, or a combination of the latter and the persistent psychiatric impairment, rather than a pure consequence of the surgery. A similar interpretation has been proposed for discrepancies in the lobectomy data (see below). Generally, the various interpretations of the change in personality after lobotomy are similar to those which have been proposed for patients with frontal damage, viz an impairment in abstract or categorical behavior; a deficit in planning, synthesizing and/or in the temporal organization of experience; a loss of anticipation or the ability to predict future events and their consequences; and an alteration in affect and initiative.

In addition to neurotic obsessional and psychotic states, lobotomy has been carried out for morbid anxiety (Meyer and McLardy 1949) and for the relief of intractable chronic pain (Freeman and Watts 1950). Benefit has been reported in cases with neuralgic pain, pain in association with carcinoma, even to some extent phantom pain (Horrax 1946). Denny-Brown (1951) noted that unilateral lobectomy could relieve the anxiety attached to the pain though pain reactions were preserved. Various studies demonstrated that the relief of pain did not depend on a change in the pain threshold but an alteration of the emotional reaction to pain. Similar findings have been demonstrated in animals with frontal lesions, where an altered response latency to painful shock is reported without a change in the pain threshold (Zielinski 1972). Of parenthetic interest is the observation by Mettler (1972) that no cases of aphasia were reported as a complication of lobotomy, in spite of the common insertion of the leucotome through the pars opercularis (Broca's area) bilaterally.

In sum, there is general agreement that the patient with a prefrontal leucotomy (lobotomy) may be less motivated than prior to surgery, less concerned with past events and future goals, and more affected by immediate experience, that he may be tactless, euphoric and subject to emotional outbursts, and may have mild deficits on some psychological tests. There is also evidence, though controversial, that certain patients are helped by the procedure and that improvement is related to lesion size and localization.

Lobectomy

Unilateral frontal lobectomy ordinarily does not give rise to severe cognitive disturbances, though some changes do occur (Jefferson 1937). Penfield and Evans (1932) described several cases of lobectomy, including Penfield's own sister who had a right frontal lobectomy for a glioma. In some patients there were subtle changes, mainly reduced initiative and impaired planning. Rylander (1939) found alterations of mood, initiative, social behavior, and abstraction, without a difference between right and left lobectomy cases. Stooky, Scarff, and Teitelbaum (1941) suggested that personality changes occurred only in patients with incomplete removal of the frontal lesion, usually a tumor.

Bilateral frontal lobectomy, in contrast to one's expectations, does not lead to a greater deficit than unilateral cases. Hebb and Penfield (1940) reviewed the material and presented an important negative case. Their patient underwent a removal of the anterior third of both frontal lobes without demonstrable psychological deficit. However, this was a post-traumatic seizure patient where some degree of re-organization may have occurred prior to surgery.

There are difficulties with the lobectomy data. In tumor cases, normal prefrontal tissue is compressed and displaced and may not be removed at operation. There may also be an adaptation effect during the period of tumor growth, so that the lobectomy occurs as a relatively late event in a multistage destruction. One has to agree with the conclusion of Freeman and Watts (1950) that "a great deal more has been learned about the function of the brain without the frontal lobes than has been learned about the function of the frontal lobes themselves."

Psychological Studies of Patients with Frontal Lesions

There have been many attempts to demonstrate objective deficits on psychological testing in patients with frontal pathology. However, while such patients commonly have disturbances in behavior, these are subjective impressions which do not readily correspond to impairments on assessment batteries. One of the most extensive programs of research on frontal lobe function in man was carried out by Teuber and his colleagues (1972) on cases with unilateral and bilateral frontal damage. Overall, the frontal cases performed as well as other patient groups on a variety of cognitive, intelligence, and problem-solving tasks, including the Army General Classification Test. Though changes in social behavior are reported in frontal patients, this was infrequent in their population. The frontal patients also did as well as other brain-damaged cases on digit-span (Ghent et al. 1962) and nonverbal short-term memory tests such as memory for line tilt, and the position of visual or tactile points (Teuber 1972).

The poverty of findings in frontal patients has been confirmed in other patient groups. Delany, Rosen, Mattson, and Novelly (1980) found that epileptic patients with unilateral frontal foci performed well on a battery of memory tests, in contrast to cases with temporal foci who did poorly. Stuss et al. (1981) studied postleucotomy schizophrenic patients with large bilateral orbitofrontal lesions and found good memory function on an assessment battery, though sensitivity to distractors was noted. Of interest was the lack of a deficit on Stroop testing, where interference effects should be maximal.

Frontal patients do, however, show impairments on certain tasks. Teuber (1972) found deficits on perceptual tests such as visual search, judgments of the vertical with body tilt, and reversible figures. Impairments in visual search were also noted by Luria et al. (1966), though this can also occur in patients with posterior lesions. The basis of these deficits is unclear. They do not appear to represent a primary perceptual disturbance, but the frontal lobes do play a role in visual perception. Denny-Brown (1951) thought the frontal lobes were "the chief executive organ of visual directed behavior," with damage giving rise to an inability to project events visually in time, that is, a disturbance in the visualization of the consequences of a situation. Teuber (1972) thought that the perceptual deficits were due to a disturbance in the corollary discharge from motor structures, such that there was an altered tuning or expectancy in sensory systems. The role of perseveration, distractibility and inability to shift set, however, should not be discounted in the interpretation of these findings.

In other studies, patients were found to have difficulty with the Porteus maze (Porteus, Demonbrun, and Kepner 1944), especially cases with right frontal lesion, and the stylus maze (Milner, 1964). Left, and to some extent right, frontal cases have difficulty on tests of verbal fluency, where items have to be generated according to a certain rule or category (e.g., words beginning with a certain letter; animals, etc.). This is not related to the presence of aphasia (Milner, 1964; Ramier and Hécaen 1970) or to the specific lesion site within the frontal lobe (Hécaen and Ruel, 1981).

In early studies, Teuber reported that frontal patients did fairly well on the Wisconsin Card Sorting Test, but Milner (1964; 1982) later found impairments, and Teuber (1972) reinterpreted his data in agreement with Milner's findings. The impairment seems to be greatest in patients with left dorso-lateral lesions. More recent studies have confirmed the usefulness of the WCST in frontal cases (Nelson, 1976; Robinson, Heaton, Lehrman, and Stilson 1980). Of interest is that patients are often able to recognize and comment on their errors on this test, though they are unable to use this information to correct their performance (Teuber 1972; Konow and Pribram, 1970). This suggests that the problem is not in "categorical behavior" but reflects "stimulus bound-ness," or perseveration, and that errors largely reflect an inability to shift set from one category (performance) to another.

In other studies, Milner (1982) has demonstrated that frontal patients are impaired on same-different comparisons using clicks, flashes or colors over a 60 second interval with distraction. Milner asked patients to indicate the recency of an item in a series of either abstract visual designs or compound words. Frontal cases recognized items but not positions. Right-damaged patients had difficulty with the visual material, while left-damaged patients had difficulty with the verbal material. With a similar paradigm, Doreen Kimura found impaired recognition of recurring nonsense figures, though this may reflect perseveration or response bias rather than a recognition defect. Frontal patients are also impaired on sequential memory tasks, for example, when required to identify a stimulus two items prior to another stimulus in a series of presentations (Collier and Levy 1982). Petrides and Milner (1982) found deficits, especially in left frontal cases, for a self-ordered task of pointing responses to visual and verbal material, suggesting an impairment in active, working memory. On these tasks, the difficulty is described as an inability to "initiate a sequence of responses in a given situation and to carry them out with constant monitoring of their execution."

This is similar to Luria's (1969) description of the incapacity of frontal patients to carry out a sequential pattern of action. He noted a lack of inhibition of impulsive or extraneous movements, and an inability to restrain a tendency towards fixed reiteration, leading to repetition and perseveration. Luria thought this was due to a failure in the verbal control or regulation of behavior, but it may represent a general disturbance in complex action development of which verbal behavior is one manifestation.

Symptoms of Frontal Lesion

1. Memory impairments

There is some evidence that extensive damage to the frontal lobes bilaterally can give rise to memory impairments. Of course, such cases are confounded by uncertainty as to the extent of the lesion, particularly involvement of subcortical structures, possible hydrocephalus in tumor and trauma cases, the role of associated language deficits and increased intracranial pressure. Nonetheless, Hécaen (1964) argued that memory impairments, which occurred in about 20 percent of frontal tumor cases, were independent of elevations in intracranial pressure. When this is not taken into account the incidence of memory loss is much higher, for example, 70 percent in Messimy's (1939) study. Luria (1976) studied patients with large bilateral lesions and found memory deficits which were modality-nonspecific (see Lewinsohn, Zieler, Libet, Eyeberg, and Nielson 1972). These were interpreted as secondary to inhibition of traces rather than impaired storage, and retrieval disorders occurred through a confabulatory trend brought on by impulsiveness and random associations.

There are scattered reports of patients with bifrontal infarcts and memory impairments, for example, the case of Mabille and Pitres (1913) with bilateral softenings adjacent to the caudate, but there is little evidence for major impairments of memory in patients with focal pathology.

However, there is evidence for an unusual type of Korsakoff syndrome in some frontal cases. Whitty and Lewin (1961) described a case following bilateral cingulectomy. There are cases with confabulation and relative preservation of memory on the usual tests. Stuss, Alexander, Lieberman, and Levine (1978) and Kapour and Coughlin (1980) have described cases of this type. The disturbance is generally interpreted as an expression of impulsivity but a retrieval deficit seems likely. One more complex material, such as stories, or on the retrieval of lengthy episodes from long term memory, there is a tendency for derailment and elaboration, perhaps due to distractibility and the inability of such patients to selectively attend to a task. The meaning of the memorial content is usually preserved in spite of the elaborated recall. The anatomical substrate of this phenomenon is not certain, but presumably it reflects either direct involvement of frontal limbic structures, e.g., orbital or mesial frontal cortex, or is a referred effect on temporal lobe through uncinate fasciculus. Apart from frank confabulation, frontal patients do tend to give bizarre, perhaps inpulsive or confabulatory answers on tests of cognitive estimation (Shallice and Evans 1978).

2. Personality Changes

A change in personality or behavior is a central aspect of the "frontal syndrome." Patients are described as lacking in initiative or motivation, as apathetic or indifferent to their affairs. Euphoria occurs in frontal cases, but may not be as specific a frontal sign, since euphoric states are common in temporal lobe disorders as well, for example, in fluent aphasics and confabulating Korsakoff patients. There is often disinterest in work, and involvement only with events in the immediate environment.

The "stimulus boundness" of frontal patients was described by Kurt Goldstein as an inability to detach oneself from momentary objects. The other side of this impairment is the lack of concern with events in the past or future, in other words, for events outside the immediate experience of the subject. Patients are commonly said to be impulsive, with poor judgment, impaired concentration and a tendency toward inappropriate or irresponsible behavior.

Some striking changes in personality have been described in patients with slow growing tumors of the frontal lobes, especially meningiomas involving the poles or mesial and subfrontal surfaces. A variety of psychiatric disorders have been described, including typical schizophrenia (Davison and Bagley 1969; Carlson 1977). Personality changes, depressive illness, and antisocial behavior have been described following frontal head injuries. Conversely, studies of various psychiatric populations with so-called "frontal lobe tests" have revealed deficits (Gorenstein 1982). Regional cerebral blood flow studies (Franzen and Ingvar 1975) and positron emission tomography (Farkas et al. 1980; Buchsbaum et al. 1982) have demonstrated frontal hypometabolism in schizophrenic patients, though at this stage it is uncertain whether this represents a state-dependent phenomenon (e.g., increased visual imagery, dream-like states, relation to anxiety) or is specific to the psychiatric disorder. Nonetheless, the changes in behavior that can occur after frontal lesions, evidence for "frontal" signs in psychiatric populations, and hypo-frontality on metabolic studies in schizophrenic patients, do support the idea of an important role of frontal lobe mechanisms in personality organization.

Luria (1969) carried out extensive studies of patients with frontal lesions. He pointed out the disinterest and inactivity of such patients, the inability to selectively attend to a task, along with the increased orientation ("orienting reflex") to novel or irrelevant stimuli. This gives the picture of inattention with distractibility. Perseveration arises as a "pathological persistence of action," reflecting a disturbance in successive movements. Perceptual disorders arise out of defective scanning and impaired analysis of complex objects. While Luria denied a primary disorder of memory in frontal patients, retrieval errors occurred (see above) in the recall of complex story material through the same impairment as in the motor sphere, a difficulty in selective retrieval and a tendency toward irrelevant associations.

One difficulty with the clinical studies is the lack of comparison with other patient groups. For example, many of Luria's tests of sequential action, or "motor Stroop" tests involving conflicting actions or commands, are troublesome for patients with posterior lesions as well, though perhaps for a different reason. A major problem is the disambiguation of the effects of subtle motility disorders, perseverative trends and impulsivity, on the memory and cognitive tests. These factors have also confounded the psychological test data.

3. Frontal dementia

Although many neurologists consider dementias to be so similar that a specific diagnosis is not possible on purely clinical grounds, there is some evidence for a different presentation of dementia according to whether the pathology involves the frontal or posterior regions preferentially.

Dementias which tend to have a frontal onset, as in some cases of Pick's disease, differ from Alzheimer cases in the greater lack of spontaneity, reduced speech leading to mutism, and relative preservation of memory and constructional ability in the early stages (Goldstein and Katz 1937). Frontal dements also tend to show inappropriate behavior, loss of social constraints and poor hygiene. Incontinence is also more common. Ferraro and Jervis (1936) described a fluctuation in attention, lack of initiative, affective changes and jocularity. However, confabulation is unusual, and Witzelsucht does not occur as often as might be expected. About 25 percent show aphasic symptoms, largely word-finding difficulty progressing to diminished speech production, though true Broca's aphasia is rare (Ley, Titeca, Divry, and Moreau 1934). Echo phenomena in speech, movement and writing are described, and some authors have noted, as occurs in the frontal monkey, an early stage of hyperactivity followed by a stage of hypoactivity.

This picture differs from that of Alzheimer's disease where there is early memory loss, fluent aphasia with paraphasic errors, relatively well-preserved social behavior and impaired visuo-spatial ability. However, there are variants of Pick's disease which can be present with a fluent aphasia. Adam Wechsler has described a case with involvement of the left temporal lobe.

An example of a frontal dementia is described in Figures 6 and 7. This patient had progressive mutism leading to a state of passivity, disinterest, almost an ambulatory catatonia. Some repetition was elicited on language testing, and writing showed logoclonic (perseverative) jargonagraphia. The enlarged frontal horns and fronto-temporal atrophy are consistent with Pick's disease (McGeachie et al. 1979).

4. Spatial neglect and attention

Monkeys with frontal lesions show reduced orienting reactions to novel stimuli suggesting an impairment of attentional processes. The relation between frontal cortex and the contingent negative variation (Walter, 1973) is consistent with this association. Frontal patients show alteration in event-related potentials during tasks of selective auditory attention (Knight, Hillyard, Woods, and Neville 1981).

Spatial neglect occurs with frontal lesions in monkey (Welch and Stuteville 1958) and in man (Heilman and Watson 1977); Damasio, Damasio, and Chui, 1980). The impairment is not directly related to involvement of the frontal eye fields, nor to gaze shifts, but is similar to neglect with parietal lesions (Chedru, personal communication) except that it is usually milder and less persistent. Patients in whom bifrontal lesions are superimposed on a state of bilateral posterior lesions may go from a state of labile fixation with a Balint syndrome, to one of spastic fixation where the eyes are centrally fixed without deviation (Hécaen and de Ajuriaguerra, 1954).

5.   Miscellaneous Disorders

Damage to the frontal lobes may give rise to impairments of various aspects of musical ability, affect and motility, apart from apraxia. These will be briefly mentioned.

Musical Functions: While there are many studies of lateral asymmetries on tasks which involve musical capacity (Gates and Bradshaw 1977), and some work on the differential effects of right and left hemisphere lesions (Milner 1962), there is little evidence to suggest a specific role of the frontal lobes in musical ability, much less a difference between right and left frontal lobe mechanisms. Henschen (1926) thought the right hemisphere, especially the right Broca area, played a subsidiary role in musical expression, with compensation through the right Broca area after left frontal damage. There is a case of expressive amusia with aphasia and dysprosody due to a right frontal lesion (Botez and Wertheim 1959). Cases of expressive amusia with right frontal involvement without aphasia have been described (Jossman 1927; Benton 1977), though such cases are usually dysprosodic.

Patients with left frontal lesions and aphasia may show dysprosodic speech, with a loss of the normal intonation contour. This also occurs in the rare dextral with a right lesion and aphasia, but it is unusual in right frontal cases without aphasia. After prefrontal lobotomy, speech becomes monotonous and lacks normal inflection. This is more pronounced with posterior section but is not associated with abnormalities of articulation, language or singing (Freeman and Watts 1950). There is no evidence as yet for a different role of right and left frontal lobe in prosody though as noted, clinical impairments appear more often after left frontal involvement in association with aphasia.

Affect: While there have been speculations concerning a different function of the right and left hemisphere in emotional tone and expression, there are few studies which look specifically at changes in affect in patients with left and right frontal lesions in comparison with other brain-damaged groups. This is essential, since posterior cases can show affective disorders similar to those of frontal cases, for example, the euphoria of patients with temporal lobe lesion, or the depression of posterior anomics which can mimic the apathy and/or depression of motor aphasics. Moreover, frontal lesions can produce a variety of changes in affect and emotional expression, from labile or hypomanic states to a lack of sponteneity, inertia and catatonic behavior.

The clinical impression that left frontal cases with motor aphasia tend to be apathetic or depressed has not been confirmed in psychological studies. Buck and Duffy (1980) found diminished facial expression in right more than left brain damaged patients, though they did not determine lesion site within the hemisphere. Borod, Koff, Perlman, and Nicholas (1983) compared right and left frontal patients with posterior cases and found that left frontals had the best preserved facial expression while right frontal cases were the least expressive. This is consistent with reduced emotionality with right frontal damage, though spontaneous facial expression, not emotional state, was evaluated. In my view, evidence that right hemisphere, or right frontal lobe, plays a dominant role in processing intonation contours, melodies or emotional behavior can be interpreted, not as an asymmetric organization of these performances, but as a reflection of a spurious right hemisphere effect on cognitive tasks which involve early processing stages (Brown 1983b).

Hallucination: There are reports of hallucination in patients with frontal lesions. Hallucinations may occur in Pick's disease, though it is probably explained by involvement of temporal lobe. Similarly, hallucination occurs in some patients with frontal lobe tumor (Hécaen and de Ajuriaguerra 1956), but this may be a referred effect through the uncinate fasciculus (Schneider, Crosby, Bagchi, and Calhoun 1961). Cases of frontal tumor with hallucination tend to be less alert than temporal lobe patients, suggesting that increased intracranial pressure may play a role. There are also reports of hallucination as an infrequent result of leucotomy, and on stimulation of anterior cingulate gyrus.

Alien Hand and Motor Initiation: This disorder was first described by Goldstein (1908) in a patient with a resolving left hemiparesis, who stated that she could no longer control her left limb. There was diminished sensation on the left, poor object recognition and difficulty releasing the grasp with the left hand, though objects were manipulated correctly. Transient difficulty relaxing the grip has been described in some callosal patients. Brion and Jednyak (1972) noted a feeling of estrangement for the left hand referring to the condition as *la main etrangere*. Other features include a tendency for the arm to drift off and assume odd postures, especially when the eyes are closed or attention is diverted, inter-manual conflict or competition, and the patient's own report that he cannot will or command the limb to act.

The conclusion of Brion and Jednyak that the disturbance represents a callosal syndrome is disputed by Goldberg, Mayer, and Toglia (1981) who reported two patients with lesions of left supplementary motor area involving the **right** hand. In a personal case with a left mesial frontoparietal infarction, the right hand assumed unusual flexor postures when the eyes were closed or the patient was distracted. With the eyes closed and arms extended, the right hand began to clench and drift posteriorly and superiorly. When the patient was instructed to open his eyes, he reached out with the left hand to grasp the right limb and draw it down. The left hand, then, forcibly released the right hand grasp. Once relaxed, the right hand remained in a normal posture, so long as the eyes were open and attention was not diverted to a specific task. In this case there were mild sensory deficits in the right hand. I have observed other similar cases where the sensory deficits were more severe, and thought, perhaps incorrectly, to be the basis of the disorder.

In sum, the alien hand is an unusual disorder which appears to follow a lesion of the mesial frontal or fronto-parietal cortex of either hemisphere, possibly involving SMA. There is a disturbance of motor initiation which may, with frontal involvement, be especially marked for extensor movements resulting in a persistent grasp or flexion posturing of the hand, and at times wandering movements of the limb. The disorder is determined by tactual stimulation, is greater in the arm than leg, and is mitigated by visual attention to the affected limb. It differs from a grasp reflex in the relation to attention, and the awareness of difficulty initiating the action. Moreover, in forced grasping the problem is not a failure of "willed relaxation" but a persistence of stimulation (Denny-Brown, 1951).

Lesions of the frontal lobe may also give rise to "motor neglect," with difficulty initiating actions with the affected limbs (Laplane and Degos 1983). The disorder is usually greater in the arm than leg and there is a predilection for right hemisphere lesions. This condition is probably related to motor initiation disorders with SMA lesions and elements of the alien hand syndrome.

Perhaps, related in the phenomenon of levitation described by Denny-Brown, Meyer, and Horenstein (1952) in association with parietal lesions. Their patient assumed *extensor* postures of the left fingers and wrist. When attention was directed to her hand, she could relax it and assume a normal posture. Schilder described a case of this type, and Hécaen and de Ajuriaguerra (1954) also reported patients with peculiar hand postures.

DISORDERS OF SPEECH AND ACTION WITH FOCAL LESIONS

Population studies of psychological test performance, and case reports of the frontal syndrome, usually consist of patients with massive, often bilateral, lesions. Such cases are useful in displaying aspects of the frontal syndrome but have limited value in the understanding of the contributions to neurolinguistic and neuropsychological functions of different regions within the frontal lobe, or defining the way these regions, and the subfunctions they presumably mediate, are integrated into a particular behavior. In other words, they do not help us greatly to understand the infrastructure of pathological change and the nature of the cognitive disturbance.

Cases with focal lesions within the frontal lobe provide an opportunity to study the contributions of specific regions. These cases usually present with partial disorders of speech and/or motility. The regions that are most commonly implicated in such disorders are the anterior cingulate gyrus, the supplementary motor area (SMA) and the inferior premotor region. A consideration of the disorders which result from damage to these areas can provide a framework for a concept of frontal lobe organization. This material can serve as a basis for a general interpretation of the frontal syndrome, and the role of frontal mechanisms in the construction of the mental life.

Anterior Cingulate Gyrus

A bilateral lesion of anterior cingulate gyrus (Brodmann area 24) leads to akinetic mutism. Nielsen and Jacobs (1951) described the first such case but other reports have followed (e.g., Buge, Escourolle, Rancurel, and Poisson 1975; Jurgens and von Cramon 1982). The clinical picture differs from akinetic mutism with periacqueductal lesions in that the akinesia is punctuated with bouts of excitement, rather like the excited phases in the course of a catatonic stupor. Mutism with excitation after bicingulate lesions has also been observed in monkey.

The patient with anterior cingulate lesions is not only speechless but aphonic with no attempt at vocalization, nor is there evidence for preserved language comprehension. With recovery, speech returns through whispering and hoarseness rather than dysarthria or aphasia. Mutism has been reported following callosal section in man (Bogen 1976) where damage to cingulate gyrus or cingulum is likely. These patients also recover through a phase of hoarseness. Akinetic mutism has been described as an end stage in Marchiafava-Bignami disease, presumably through damage to cingulum rather than mid-callosum. Small bilateral stereotactic lesions of anterior cingulate gyrus (cingulotomy) give placidity with little in the way of language, motor or cognitive deficit (Corkin, Twitchell, and Sullivan 1979). Placidity has been reported in animals with destruction of anterior cingulum (Ward 1948) and in humans with naturally occurring lesions (Poeck 1975). These effects may be partial expressions of the more pronounced akinetic disorder with extensive destructions.

In monkey, there is evidence from ablation, stimulation and recording studies that the anterior cingulate gyrus plays a role in vocalization. Destruction of anterior cingulate cortex impairs trained vocalization in monkey, and recordings from units in anterior cingulate gyrus indicate that activity associated with vocalization occurs early in the phonation process (Sutton, Samson, and Larson 1978). Stimulation studies have demonstrated that anterior cingulate gyrus is part of a limbic and brainstem system mediating vocalization (Jurgens and Pratt 1979). In man, stimulation of anterior cingulate gyrus produces integrated motor behavior and affective change. Movements induced by stimulation of cingulate cortex are largely contralateral, though bilateral and ipsilateral movements occur. Integrated oral movements, postural distortions, reactions of fear and hallucinations have also been described. From these effects, Bancaud et al. (1976) concluded that the region mediates a primitive or archaic level in behavior.

Morphological studies of the anterior cingulate gyrus are consistent with the view that it is part of an older evolutionary system. Braak (1980) considers the anterogenual region to be a limbic-derived or proisocortical ganglionic core zone in contact with retrosplenial cortex posteriorly, as well as amygdala and hippocampal formation. The relationship between anterior cingulate and retrosplenial cortex is consistent with clinical evidence that these regions mediate primitive stages in motility and perception.

Supplementary Motor Area (SMA)

Interest in SMA has been sparked by recent findings of bilateral increase in cerebral blood flow during language tasks (Larsen, Skinhoj, and Lassen 1978) though it has been known for some time (Penfield and Welch 1949; Penfield and Roberts 1959) that the area is involved in speech production.

Stimulation of either SMA gives (motor) speech arrest or vocalization, hesitation, distortion and palilalic reiterations. The vocalizations are often rhythmic or "quasi-sinusoidal," and accompanied by limb movements, facial contractions and awareness for the speech alteration (Chauvel 1976). The limb movements are chiefly proximal, tonic and contralateral, mainly involve the arm with abduction and elevation. Bilateral movements may occur, but ipsilateral movements are uncommon. Adversive movements of the head and eyes to the opposite side occur, usually as part of a postural "seizure" (Laplane, Talairach, Meininger, Bancaud, and Bouchareine 1977). With irritative lesions of either side, palilalic iterations, cries and vocalizations have also been reported, though clinical deficits seem to occur only with left hemisphere lesions (Jonas 1981).

With damage to left SMA, there is usually mutism at onset resolving to transcortical motor aphasia (Brown 1977; Rubens 1975). The patient evolves to a state of little or no spontaneous speech with some repetition and naming. Repetition may be agrammatic, or if normal, agrammatism may appear in spontaneous speech and/or writing as these performances return. Repetition is usually deliberate, not echolalic. Speech may have few aphasic errors, with difficulty largely for initiation, such that repetition and naming survive as simpler performances. The patient with a left SMA lesion has a type of partial mutism, i.e., impaired initiation of spontaneous speech, but also a partial akinesia affecting primarily the upper limbs. Ambulation is usually good, though inertia or slowness resembling Parkinsonism may occur.

There is often marked difficulty initiating upper limb action, especially for the contralateral arm. When asked to lift or lower the arm, the patient may require initiation of the movement by the examiner. A touch of the patient's finger in the direction of the movement often suffices for it to be completed. There may be an impression that the patient is uncooperative, for strength and tone are normal, and he may stare at the examiner without attempting to carry out the command. Motor neglect (Waltregny 1972) may occur after surgical lesions, but appears related to large ablations, probably involving cingulate gyrus (Chauvel 1976). Contralateral grasping has also been described (Penfield & Jasper 1954). Unusual movements of the arm are uncharacteristic, but perhaps there is a relation to the alien hand syndrome with mesial frontal and parietal lesions.

Cases of limb apraxia which occur with mesial frontal lesion, particularly with anterior cerebral artery occlusion, interpreted on a callosal basis, may also reflect SMA involvement. Of interest is that stimulation in SMA gives contralateral or bilateral movements involving the proximal (e.g., shoulder) musculature (van Buren and Fedio 1976), while hypertonia at the shoulders is reported as a consequence of ipsilateral ablations in monkey (Travis 1955).

The effects of bilateral SMA lesions are unknown. Presumably, a persistent deficit occurs since unilateral cases tend to show recovery. In monkey, unilateral lesions lead to changes in posture and tonus (Travis 1955). The SMA has been surgically extirpated in epileptic cases (Penfield and Welch 1949; Laplane et al. 1977) with few residual motor or speech impairments. There is a report of increased regional blood flow in SMA with movements of the lower limbs (Orgogozo et al. 1979).

The connections of the SMA have been reviewed by Chauvel (1976) and Goldberg (1985). There are projections from Somatosensory areas I and II and area 5, reciprocal connections with ipsilateral and contralateral motor cortex (area 4), cingulate gyrus, thalamus and callosal projections. There are efferent connections with caudate and putamen, and ipsilateral projections to midbrain tegmentum and red nucleus (see Kuypers and Lawrence 1967; Kievit and Kuypers 1977; Pandya and Kuypers 1969). This system of connections is consistent with the idea that SMA is part of an older evolutionary network, and agrees with the results of cytoarchitectonic studies (Sanides 1969), indicating that SMA is an archaic level in sensorimotor control.

Left Premotor Area

The limits of Broca's area are imprecisely known, since the area is defined by its association with Broca's aphasia, and there is little agreement on what constitutes this disorder. Two major components of Broca's aphasia are a phonetic-articulatory defect — with sequencing errors, "verbal apraxia," perseverations and "cortical anarthria" — and agrammatism. These components may refer to different anatomical substrates: for example, agrammatism to the premotor cortex around posterior inferior F3, and misarticulation to focal lesions of posterior inferior F3 (Broca area proper).

1. Agrammatism

Agrammatism (telegrammatism) describes utterances in nonfluent aphasics consisting of strings of content words (e.g., nouns and uninflected verbs in English) with a relative lack of small grammatical or function words (e.g., prepositions and articles). Articulation may be good without dysarthria or phonemic paraphasia. There is difficulty with inflections and auxilliaries and a dropping out of unstressed syllables—especially initial unstressed ones—and simplification of syntax. The normal intonation contour is lost. There is a monotony of speech and a reliance on lexical stress in production. Some studies of syntactic of deficits in anterior aphasics are reviewed in Caramazza and Zurif (1978).

There are two major interpretations of this disorder: that it represents a loss of grammatical knowledge due to a damaged syntactic device in the inferior premotor region; or that it reflects a disruption of a cognitive rhythm underlying the speech melody so that only the stressed words survive (see Brown 1979). In recent years, evidence has accrued to challenge the syntax model. Motor aphasics have been shown to understand actor-object relations (Heeschen 1980) and reversible sentences (Leslie 1980); they can interpret the structural as well as lexical meaning of prepositions, and can sort function words reasonably well, if they are stress bearing (Kellar 1978). Moreover, agrammatic errors on tests of syntactic knowledge occur in fluent aphasics who are not agrammatic in production.

Alternatively, agrammatism can be approached as a disturbance of the speech rhythm, the functors dropping out because, unlike the stressed content words, they lie in the troughs of the intonation pattern. Stress aids motor aphasics in production (Goodglass 1968). There is evidence for a disturbance in the physiological aspects of intonation (Ryalls, personal communication). The attempt to interpret agrammatism as an alteration of the rhythmic structure of the utterance is consistent with a motor account of other frontal speech disorders, as well as with linguistic interpretations of the putative grammatical defect on a phonological basis (Kean 1980).

There are few studies of the anatomical pathology of agrammatism, but the impression from a few case studies is that the responsible lesion is usually in the premotor area anterior or superior to pars opercularis of F3 (Goldstein 1948; Luria 1970). A case of agrammatism with lesion of Broca's area proper has been reported by Miceli, Mazzucchi, Menn, and Goodglass (1983). Of interest is that agrammatism occurs with anterior lesions of the right hemisphere in crossed aphasic dextrals with a frequency surprising in view of its rarity in left frontal cases. Agrammatism is a major form of aphasia in young children with a left hemisphere lesion involving frontal or temporal regions (Brown and Hécaen 1976).

Clinically, there are links between agrammatism and transcortical motor aphasia. Agrammatics show better (less agrammatic) repetition, an observation responsible for the earlier interpretation of agrammatism as a type of speech economy. There is the appearance of agrammatism in children and crossed dextrals out of an initial stage of mutism. The difficulty initiating actions with the upper limbs typical of transcortical motor aphasias with SMA lesions now appears as a limb apraxia, where the movement is initiated properly but is derailed as it unfolds toward the target. Similarly, instead of inability to initiate vocalization, there is now oral apraxia with substitutions, omissions and poorly executed orofacial movements.

2.   Broca's Area and Broca's Aphasia

Lesions restricted to the foot of F3 (area 44) give phonetic-articulatory defects in utterances which may be syntactically normal. The misarticulation does not show a clear word class effect, and the intonation pattern is closer to normal. A phonetic disturbance in motor aphasics has been documented in studies by Blumstein (1981). Luria (1970) described impairments in initiation and sequencing of speech sounds in motor aphasia. Speech production errors in patients with Broca area lesions have been best described in surgical and traumatic cases (Hécaen and Consoli 1973; Luria 1970). In these populations, a phonetic-articulatory defect has been demonstrated with various sub-classifications (kinetic, kinaesthetic aphasia, verbal apraxia, phonetic disintegration, etc.) depending on the dominant error type. Though vascular cases have been described with involvement of Broca's area, selective defects are usually not observed. There are cases with inferior pre-central and/or premotor lesions where mis-articulation has been the major residual (Hécaen & Consoli 1973; Mohr, Pessin, and Finkelstein 1978; Masdeu and O'Hara 1983. Tonkonogy & Goodglass 1981).

There has always been a lively discussion on the limits of Broca's area (see Brown 1979). Broca (1863) maintained that the frontal speech zone included the posterior portion of the inferior or third frontal convolution (F3), that is, the pars opercularis and possibly, the pars triangularis, and perhaps also part of the middle frontal gyrus (F2). Various authors have included the inferior precentral convolution (i.e., the "face area"), although this zone is generally distinguished from Broca's area proper. Some writers (e.g., Goldstein 1948; Mills and Spiller 1907) included the anterior insula in an extended frontal speech zone. Niessl von Meyendorff (1911) maintained that the frontal operculum was the motor speech center.

For Monakow (1914), Broca's area included F3, anterior insula, the connecting gyrus between F3 and the precentral convolution, and the Rolandic operculum. This is similar to the description given by Dejerine (1914): the posterior part of left F3, frontal operculum, and neighboring cortex ("cap" of F3 and "foot" of F2), extending to the anterior insula but excluding Rolandic operculum. Henschen (1920) argued that the cap of F3 (pars triangularis) was not a part of the motor speech zone on the basis òf a negative case with bilateral lesion reported by Bonvicini (1926).

More recent discussions of the evidence concerning the limits of Broca's area can be found in Whitaker and Selnes (1975), Brown (1979) and Levine and Sweet (1982). There is agreement on the importance of posterior F3 (area 44) or pars opercularis and the inferior precentral region. There is strong evidence that anterior insula is involved in speech production, while the role of pars triangularis and posterior F2 remains controversial. In my view, the inferior premotor region including anterior insula should be viewed as a type of field, with a qualitative gradient from the periphery of the field to area 44 and inferior precentral gyrus mediating successive moments in motor speech production.

Broca's aphasias also have oral and limb apraxia (DeRenzi, Pieczuro, and Vignolo 1966; Poeck and Kerschensteiner 1975) though perhaps not the same type as in patients with agrammatism. In misarticulation cases, one has the impression of a dyspraxic impairment, with clumsiness in the distribution of the distal (oral and limb) innervation rather than para-praxic substitutions, though there are no studies which look at these differences within motor aphasics.

Interpretation of Frontal Aphasias

Impairments of speech and action with frontal lesions have traditionally been viewed as disruptions of, or disconnections between, components in a complex functional system. On this view, each deficit reflects a normal mechanism situated in the damaged area, or an interruption of information flow between these areas. More recently, the different clinical syndromes have been proposed to reflect processing stages in the unfolding of the utterance or the action (Brown 1977).

According to this view, a base level (motor envelope) elaborates an archaic stage in speech and motility, combining the incipient vocal and somatic movement in a space centered on the body axis. The action is organized about the axial and proximal musculature, linked to respiratory and other rhythmic automatisms, and close to motivational and drive-like states. Disruptions of this stage give rise to akinetic mutism. As it develops, the action undergoes specification of its motor components, with an isolation of limb, body and vocal motility. Pathology can give rise to selective impairments of vocalization (TMA) and initiation of limb action. This phase in the action is mediated by frontal paralimbic formations, (bilateral) anterior cingulate gyrus and (mainly left) SMA. This deep rhythmic structure is derived through left generalized (premotor) cortex to an oscillator elaborating the speech melody. Disruption at this point leads to a prominence of stress-bearing content words (agrammatism). The speech melody is, then, derived to the fine temporal program of sound sequences, through left inferior premotor cortex. Disruption exposes a stage of phonological (phonetic) encoding (Broca's aphasia) and its articulatory realization through inferior precentral cortex (phonetic disintegration). As the utterance undergoes progressive specification, limb action develops from a global, axial movement to independent upper limb motility (impaired initiation), through a stage of the sequential laying down of the movement (apraxia) to the fine distal innervation (dyspraxia).

CONCLUSIONS

Since the studies of Bianchi in 1895 and the crowbar case of Harlow, research on the frontal lobes has been a faithful mirror of progress in neurolinguistics, behavioral neurology, and neuropsychology. As in other fields of psychological research, the early fascination with unitary concepts gave way to more a pragmatic approach, as researchers discovered that these concepts were too general in scope to address the diversity of symptoms and deficits which make up the "frontal syndrome." For example, speculations as to a loss of a synthetic or integrative capacity could apply to the effects of lesions of many parts of the brain, while theories of a central predictive or anticipatory function, a sequential ordering or an abstraction ability, are not really explanatory constructs but re-statements of the very deficits that need to be explained.

Gradually, the symptoms of frontal damage were fractionated into partial disorders and new conditions were described. These advances made it increasingly difficult to attribute the variety of frontal deficits to a single underlying disturbance or mechanism, and the unitary concepts of the early workers were replaced by present day componential and modular theories. The frontal lobes were now viewed as a mosaic of inter-connected functional units, each subserving a different aspect of behavior. The role of each area was inferred *ad hoc* from the effects of stimulation or ablation. Such components might share a role in phenomena of expectancy or temporal ordering, or in mediating between inner states and external experience, but these formulations, as helpful as they are, serve mainly to highlight a particular feature of behavior among operations that on the surface appear to have little else in common. We still do not have an explicit model of the functional organization of the frontal lobes.

Observations of focal cases with disorders of speech and skilled movement provide clues to the building of a model of this type. These observations are consistent with the idea that an action is comprised of a series of oscillatory systems or temporal programs (Bernstein 1967; Turvey 1977; Brown 1982). The clinical material suggests that these programs are distributed over stages in the evolution of the forebrain, and that the action develops or unfolds over these stages in a microtemporal framework.

On this view, each response of an organism represents a more or less complete action structure, the structure being the stages through which the movement sequence develops. Pathology disrupts the action at different moments in this process. The site of the lesion determines the moment in the action sequence which is disturbed, and this moment, or processing stage, is the symptom of the lesion. The different symptoms which occur with frontal damage can be assigned to three major groups, which correspond with successive evolutionary systems. Damage to frontal limbic formations leads to impaired activation (response bias or perseveration, motor neglect, and lack of initiation); damage to "integration" cortex on the convexity leads to derailment of the action after adequate initiation (distractibility, confabulation); and damage to pre-motor and pre-central cortices leads to a defect of the final implementation (misarticulation, dyspraxia).

Impaired initiation with lesions of mesial or orbito-frontal cortex may involve the action as a whole, or partially. The patient may be unable to initiate any action (akinetic mutism) or show hypoactivity, inertia and lack of spontaneity. These latter symptoms may represent attenuated forms of akinetic mutism. Perhaps, the degree of encroachment on, or distance from, core regions of frontal limbic cortex (e.g., anterior cingulate gyrus) determines the extent of hypoactivity.

In the partial disorders there is difficulty initiating a vocal act (mutism, trans-cortical motor aphasia) or limb action (alien hand, SMA syndrome and related disorders). Perseveration also occurs with damage to frontal limbic areas and is related to disturbed initiation. The persistence of a performance is the other side of an inability to go on to the next. Impaired initiation may occur without perseveration, but it is questionable whether the reverse is true. In fact, in persevera-tion, the initiation deficit often seems primary, for perseveration is greater for tasks which are more difficult, and it tends to involve previously successful performances.

With convexity lesions the action is disrupted at a stage subsequent to its activation. Derailments occur at serial points in the unfolding of the action toward a goal. Apraxia, a substitution or defective selection of partial movements with lesions of left premotor cortex, is due to an alteration of motor timing, or a change in the kinetic pattern for a particular motor sequence. Other frontal disorders may have a similar basis. Agrammatism, dysprosody and expressive amusia probably represent the disruption of an oscillator which elaborates the rhythmic or prosodic contour of an utterance or vocal action.

Lesions of adjacent areas, especially bilateral lesions, lead to distractibility and inattention. There is a derailment within a specific task, midway between the activation of a behavior, i.e., a response, an action structure, and its final imple-mentation.

Pre-motor and pre-central cortex mediate final processing stages in the action sequence. Involvement of these areas leads to a change in the motor realization of preliminary phases which may have undergone a normal development. In speech there are phonetic and articulatory substitutions leading to "cortical anarthria"; in limb action, substitution of partial movements (parapraxia) gives way to dyspraxia or clumsiness of the distal innervation.

In sum, the evolutionary progression from limbic to convexity ("integration") to pre-motor and pre-central cortex retraces the sequence of processing stages in the microtemporal elaboration of an action. Disruption at successive points gives a change in initiation, derailments in the flow of an action once initiated, or defects of the final implementation or articulation of the target movement. Motor symptoms occur when focal areas in each evolutionary system are involved, whereas cognitive symptoms occur with (bilateral) damage to neighboring regions. Specifical-ly, bilateral lesions of areas adjacent to specialized limbic and convexity zones give general cognitive changes (e.g., orientation biases, impulsiveness, lack of motivation) which have their motor correlates in, for example, the perseveration, apraxia and akinesia with focal lesions. This is true for each phyletic division: limbic, convexity ("integration"), pre-motor and pre-central cortex.

The presumed role of frontal cortex in the elaboration of action structures, that is, the rhythmic or oscillatory components of an action, can explain other seemingly non-motor phenomena which occur with frontal lobe damage. For example, perceptual disorders may arise, not from a primary deficit of perception, but from impairments in the visual exploration of space, including changes in visual search, orientation, and ocular displacement (see Konorski 1972).

The lack of drive or motivation in frontal patients can also be approached from a motor standpoint. I have suggested that base levels in the action elaborate the experience, or feeling, of drive (Brown 1977) and that this experience, like the *Innervationsgefühl* of Wundt, arises as an accompaniment of the action development rather than as an energy or a force which is only an underpinning. In other words, drive undergoes a development together with action. Some actions appear to be motivated by drives or instincts, others are purposeful or goal-oriented, and still others are volitional, in the sense that decisions are made, actions can be delayed and even witheld in pursuit of a goal. My guess is that these feeling states — drive, purposefulness, volition — correspond with evolutionary levels in the action development, and that this is why damage to the action structure impacts on the feeling state specified by the damaged processing stage.

Finally, actions also elaborate intentions, the feeling that one is an agent who acts on an environment. This is part of the temporal unfolding of the action and its continual surge toward a future state. It is the basis for our distinction of passive and active movements. This feeling, and the other affects which the action generates, are bound up with the sense of anticipation and forward growth. The loss of, or a change in, this direction toward the future has the consequence of a greater responsiveness to ongoing stimuli and an apparent tendency to live for the immediate present. The loss of this active or volitional relation to the world is, ultimately, the most profound effect of damage to the frontal lobes.

9
The Microstructure of Action*

INTRODUCTION

This chapter describes a model of frontal lobe organization based on the idea that the symptoms of a frontal lobe lesion can be understood as disruptions in the microgenetic unfolding of an action. According to the microgenetic account, every behavior or mental state has a submerged infrastructure distributed over evolutionary planes in the forebrain. Cognitive processing retraces the direction of phyletic growth, so that evolutionary levels, and correlated processing stages, are entrained in behavior in the order of their evolutionary appearance. In a very real sense, microgeny recapitulates phylogeny as cognition rapidly unfolds over evolutionary structure.

We can begin by defining an action as a cognitive structure consisting of multiple representational planes, each of which is reconstituted moment to moment in the flow of behavior. In the course of the unfolding of an action, movements are deposited at successive points. However, there is a difference between an action and a movement. Movements are what actually happen in the behavior; they are physical events or chains of events that are extrinsic to cognition (mind). In contrast, an action is a mental event that participates in private experience. Actions are representations that are read off into movements. An action is a cognitive precursor that lays down or instantiates a movement in physical space, in the same way that a perception is a mental event that is configured by, or modeled through, external (physical) sensory experience.

MICROGENESIS OF ACTION

An action unfolds over a stratified system of levels that retraces the pattern of evolutionary growth. These levels instantiate the action through discharge into

---

*From "The Microstructure of Action" by J. W. Brown, 1987. In E. Perecman (Ed.), *The Frontal Lobes Revisted*. Copyright 1987 by IRBN Press. Adapted by permission.

keyboards at successive moments in the microgenetic sequence. The progression is from an archaic motility centered in the axial and proximal musculature and a body-centered space (Yakovlev, 1948), a stage in the action that is sensitive to or dependent on "internal context," toward discrete, asymmetric movements with the distal musculature that are "goal oriented," context-free, and directed to external objects. Early phases distribute into postural systems within body space, then into a space of body-on-body movement to a manipulation space of the arm's reach, and finally to action on outer objects.

In the course of this unfolding, the action proceeds "bottom up" as a type of propagated wave from a core system in upper brainstem and basal ganglia through structures on the mesial aspect of the frontal lobe, to systems on the frontal convexity, and finally to the contralateral motor cortex. Early stages constitute an "envelope" of the action, in a bodily space incorporating all of the to-be-realized constituents of the action. The forming postural, limb, respiratory, and vocal movements are prefigured in this preparatory phase. Early stages in the action structure have a unitary or global character with all of the incipient elements of the final act embedded in the same matrix of primitive motility and discharging at the same time. At these early stages, the act is bilaterally represented in the brain. Later stages are asymmetric in relation to neural structure. The action undergoes a progressive articulation into discrete motor elements that eventually appear to gain some independence. Yet speech, digital movement, and locomotion, which on the surface have little in common, are linked as the twigs of a tree to a single root.

In the microgenetic view there is no action plan that has been worked out or script guiding the movement sequence in the sense of a conscious representation of what the action is going to be. We plan actions for the future, but the plan is not the framework on the basis of which the action develops. Rather, the action unfolds according to intrinsic constraints—one could say microgenetic imperatives—in the action structure. The conscious awareness of the plan of an action does not generate the action that it appears to forecast but is secondarily elaborated by actions that are automatically laid down.

Neural processes underlying the action microgeny have the nature of rhythmic or oscillatory programs that may be derived as a series of harmonics from fundamental rhythms at the core of the action structure, possibly linked to other patterns of rhythmic motility such as respiration, and even circadian rhythms (Bernstein, 1967; Brown, 1982; Schepelmanns, 1979; Turvey, 1977). For example, a deep nodal rhythm might support a system for postural tone, while successive derivations of this rhythm might transform postural tone into actions such as rocking or walking and ultimately to selective limb action and digital movements, and the individuated vocal movements of speech. Speech, of course, can also be viewed as a type of rhythmic activity (Lashley, 1951; Martin, 1972). Rhythmic factors, tonality, and the engagement of respiratory mechanisms are important at the earliest stages of speech production.

The fundamental unit of an action, therefore, is a rhythmic, hierarchic module distributed over evolutionary stages in forebrain development, unfolding in a direction that retraces the pattern of evolutionary growth "bottom up" from archaic to recent motor systems. Successive moments or processing stages in the module discharge into keyboards at each evolutionary stage, and in this way sequentially lay down the movement, in milliseconds, as the structure of the action is serially traversed. Complex behaviors are bundles of individual action structures; they are reiterated packets of unfolding representations and the secondary perceptual representations that they leave behind.

THE ACTION PROGRAM

An action begins in a two-dimensional spatial map elaborated through mechanisms in the upper brainstem. Postural, vestibular, orienting, and locomotor mechanisms establish the core of the action structure. Ballistic movements emerge out of this core as the orientation precipitates into global action patterns. A target—for example, a prey—is seized by a sudden shift of the eyes or a rapid thrust of the body or jaw. The perception of a stimulus coincides with an action pattern targeted to that stimulus. The action discharges into symmetrical, axial, or midline motor systems. Some motor patterns that might result from the discharge of a configuration at this level (i.e., when it is not transformed to the next stage) are crying and sucking movements in the newborn, swimming, crawling, or other locomotor synergies.

This stage in the action development is as close as any to an action plan. Vestibular orienting and tonic postural and locomotor mechanisms are activated preparatory to a shift in orientation, that is, a commitment to a direction, signaling the ensuing motor sequence. This phase constitutes an embryonic core, a framework or "envelope" of the action embracing *in status nascendi* all of the elements of the action-to-be, none of which as yet have differentiated. The isolation of segmental movements and the increasing resolution and exteriorization of action and space are accomplished at later stages. Subsequently, the action will unfold through limbic mechanisms to a configuration representing segmental movement patterns. As this occurs, the object accompanying that action development also unfolds from a two-dimensional map at a tectal phase of object formation to an egocentric, volumetric space of limbic cognition.

We can examine this stage in the action development when it is displayed as a symptom in pathological cases. Damage to rostral brainstem gives rise to coma or akinetic mutism, a type of coma but with eyes open. This disorder has been interpreted as a loss of will or a loss of the impulse to act, without true paralysis. In fact, disruption of the core of the action exposes the action program at its inception, with inability to initiate any body movement (akinetic mutism) at an instinctual or motivational level in drive organization (the loss of drive or impulse to act) and a regression to an archaic pre-object level in perceptual space (coma). Unilateral lesions of rostral midbrain may lead to impaired ballistic movements in hemispace. We learn from this that the action program anticipates a stage of labile and precipitate motility discharging through the proximal muscles into a space beyond the body confines.

ACTION ON THE BODY

The action unfolds into the volumetric space of limbic cognition, a space of dream and hallucination (Brown, 1985f). The action moves outward beyond the body itself to an extrapersonal field of body movement that is still part of and continuous with subjective mental space. This is not a grasping or manipulation space, for objects have not yet exteriorized. The emerging action is read off into keyboards innervating the proximal musculature. Actions leave the body axis and are distributed through the proximal muscles into the space around the body or onto the body itslef. At this stage, the first separation appears between perceiver and object, actor and object acted upon, agent and action. The motor envelope differentiates into partial actions, objects begin to clarify, and space begins to expand, fractionate, and draw away from the perceiver.

This phase of action development is mediated by extrapyramidal or basal ganglia mechanisms in relation to other limbic components. Disorders of these structures in man (e.g., Parkinson's disease) are characterized by difficulty in body and limb motility not directed outward to objects (Yakovlev, 1948). Changes in mood, hallucination, and impaired spatial perception in these disorders are predictable consequences of the disruption. Pathological objects and affects accompany action disorders in a level-specific manner. Lesions of basal ganglia have their maximal impact on the action microgeny, but other behaviors are affected in a manner referable to the same cognitive level.

The role of limbic mechanisms in action is brought home even more clearly by conditions in which there is damage to limbic-derived neocortex on the mesial aspect of the frontal lobe. Bilateral damage to the anterior cingulate gyrus gives rise to a state of akinetic mutism resembling that which can occur with damage to the upper brainstem. The patient appears to be in a catatonic stupor and, as in catatonia, there are periodic bouts of excitement that give way to a persistent vegetative state (Buge, Escourolle, Rancurel, & Poisson, 1975; Nielsen & Jacobs, 1951). Stimulation of this region in man produces motor and affective responses suggestive of "a primitive or archaic level in behavior" (Bancaud et al., 1976).

Stimulation adjacent to the anterior cingulate gyrus in the supplementary motor area (SMA) causes iteration or arrest of vocalization and proximal movement, especially of the upper limbs. With damage there may be a "release" of automatisms and primitive synergies of the arm and hand (alien hand) or difficulty initiating action with the arm though strength and coordination are intact (Brown, 1977, 1985a; Goldberg, 1985). There may also be difficulty initiating speech. This can lead to selective mutism or selective akinesia, that is, ambulatory mutism or good speech with imparied initiation of limb movement. Selective difficulty initiating movements with the lower extremities occurs in the so-called gait apraxia, or magnetic gait, often associated with hydrocephalus. Gerstmann and Schilder (1926) related this disorder to lesions of the medial and basal parts of the frontal lobe, and this was also found by Denny-Brown (1958; see Knutsson & Lying-Tunnell, 1985).

In the microgenetic theory set out in Brown (1977), the SMA mediates preparatory stages in action generation prior to conscious awareness. Lesions of this area disrupt speech, limb, and body action in a common manner early in the processing of the action, prior to the specification of constituent movement patterns. The disturbance of speech was viewed as motoric, not linguistic or propositional.

This account was based on an interpretation of clinical disorders with mesial and lateral frontal lesions. Subsequent physiological research has confirmed these speculations. Kornhuber's (1974, 1985) description of the readiness potential led to its correlation in 1980 with a paralimbic midline source. These findings have been confirmed and extended by Goldberg (1985). P. Chauvel and J. Bancaud (personal commmunication, 1984) have reported slow wave activity from the SMA preceding limb movement and motor cortex discharge in human subjects. Recent studies (Chauvel, Bancaud, & Buser, 1985) confirm the view that SMA speech disorders are motoric. Indeed, Jürgens (1985) notes that SMA lesions in the monkey decrease only spontaneous (isolation call) vocalizations, and not those elicited by perceptual stimuli.

Arguing from the neurophysiological literature primarily, Eccles (1982) claimed that the SMA was a locus for the initiation of voluntary movement. This idea recalls the old concept of *Willenlosigkeit,* a loss of the volitional impulse, described in early neuropsychology. In the microgenetic view, however, the sense of volition is a product of action development; it is realized with the action and is not something that gives rise to it. Volition is not a faculty that can be independently impaired. Disturbance of volitional or skilled action as in apraxia (see below) is associated with damage to subsequent levels of the action microgeny.

In sum, the motor envelope, a base level or early processing stage, elaborates an archaic stage in speech and motility, combining the incipient vocal and somatic elements of the action in a space centered on the body axis. The action is organized about the axial and proximal musculature, linked to respiratory, locomotor, and other rhythmic automatisms, and close to motivational and drivelike states. As it develops, the action undergoes specification of its motor components with an isolation of limb, body, and vocal motility. Pathology can give rise to selective impairments of vocalization (mutism) and of initiation of action involving both the upper limbs (inertia, alien hand) and lower limbs (gait apraxia). This phase is mediated by frontal paralimbic formations, including the anterior cingulate gyrus and the supplementary motor area. The action system is bilaterally represented at early stages with a gradual bias to a left-hemisphere representation, first apparent at the level of the supplementary motor cortex.

ACTION IN THE WORLD

The emerging representation is transformed to a phase of real actions on real objects in a space apprehended as real and independent of the action. This transition carries the representation from a rhythmic configuration that is bilaterally organized and centered in the proximal musculature to one that is asymmetrically organized—reflecting the degree of hemispheric dominance[1]— and distributed into the distal musculature. The generalized background configuration arising through paralimbic regions undergoes a progressive specification into its constituent elements, a transition mediated by left premotor and motor cortices.

The premotor phase in action development is characterized by a transition through a space of object manipulation, the perimeter of the arm's reach. The action proceeds from an incomplete exteriorization where the object is still part of an extended action space toward an eventual exteriorization of discrete, partial actions on fully independent external objects. Lesions of the convexity of the dominant hemisphere give rise to limb apraxia, with substitution and derailment of partial acts, chiefly on tasks in which object use is pantomimed. The disruption displays a stage in the unfolding of the act linked to the manipulation space of proximate objects. From this point the action configuration develops into the precentral motor keyboard as the distal structure of the act instantiates. Disruptions at the end point of the action development give rise to impairments of the highly individuated speech and limb musculature. In speech, there are phonetic, articulatory deficits leading to the so-called syndrome of phonetic disintegration (Alajouanine, Ombredane, & Durand, 1939; Lecours & Lher-

---

[1]The transition from *bilateral* representation in paralimbic cortex to crossed or *contralateral* representation in motor cortex may occur by way of an intermediate stage of unilateral *asymmetric* representation in the dominant hemisphere (Brown, 1978). That is, the action pattern develops first in both hemispheres, then through the left hemisphere, and finally through the contralateral hemisphere. Put differently, early stages in action development are bilaterally represented in both hemispheres, late stages are unilaterally represented in the opposite or contralateral hemisphere, with a stage of (dominant) left hemisphere representation of bilateral action interposed in the microgenetic sequence. This interpretation entails that evolutionary advances in brain organization, such as dominance, do not spring from highly adapted systems of evolutionary recency but from earlier, more plastic stages.

mitte, 1976), with "peripheral" disorders of the vocal apparatus, including paresis and hypotonicity. In limb movement, there is the so-called limb kinetic apraxia, with disruption of separate distal movement patterns, leading to paresis and altered motor tone. The transition from a central to a more peripheral manifestation of an action disorder captures stages in the "physicalization" of the act as it passes from an origin in mind to an effectuation in external space.

The more intense affective content of early stages, which is expressed in the form of instinctual drive or motivational state, for example, will or the impulse to act, undergoes a simultaneous analysis into partial affects. These partial affects—depression, apathy, euphoria—are revealed by frontal lobe lesions (Borod, Koff, Perlman, & Nicholas, 1983) and reflect a transitional stage in affect development, a stage that is midway between deeper instinctual drive and subsequent affect-free behaviors. One can say that the affective tonality of the act discharges into a world of independent acts and objects. In other words, affect and action distribute together into extrapersonal space, the affective content discharging along with the action as it exteriorizes. The discrepancy between the intense affect at the depths of the action development and the affect-free nature of surface motility contributes to the sense of an active movement going out toward the world and the experience of agency and volition.

The analysis of an action into constituent elements or features is accompanied by an elaboration of its underlying rhythmic structure into oscillators that mediate the rapid and discrete digital and articulatory sequences. For example, an oscillator(s) linked to respiratory and other rhythms that elaborates the speech melody or the prosodic contour of an utterance would be derived to one that mediates the programming of phonetic units in speech. An oscillator that organizes axial and proximal motility would be derived to one that mediates the serial unfolding of separate motor units in limb, orofacial, and other finely individuated movements. One can envision a stratified system of oscillators, each discharge or peeling off into motor templates at successive evolutionary planes, creating an action structure that is a dynamic pyramid of rhythmic or vibratory levels.

THE FRONTAL SYNDROME

There are many other symptoms of action disorder in animals and man that can be related to this structural model. For example, damage—usually bilateral—to the orbital and mesial area and the convexity of the frontal lobes gives rise to a number of changes—the "frontal syndrome"—that can be interpreted on a motoric basis. These changes include an increase or decrease in activity level (hyper- or hypoactivity), apathy and impaired initiation of movement, impulsiveness and distractibility, persistence or recurrence of limb or vocal actions (perseveration), difficulty in shifting set or changing response patterns from one task to another (response bias), and substitutions in speech and recall (paraphasia and confabulation) as well as in limb movement (apraxia).

These disorders appear to be quite distinct from each other and this fact alone has made attempts at a unitary explanation somewhat unconvincing. The elements of the frontal syndrome are not easily reduced to a single underlying deficit, particularly a deficit that is so general as to account for almost any pathological change. Interpretations of the syndrome as a disturbance of a synthetic, regulatory, or integrative function, as a disorder of abstraction, prediction, anticipation, or temporal processing, as an uncoupling between inner states and outer experience, or as a loss of will or self-consciousness achieve a unitary character by extracting one variable from the richness of (abnormal) behavior and then resolving all of this richness in terms of this variable. The element that is *ad hoced* from the diversity of symptoms becomes an explanatory principle under which all of the symptoms are grouped. This problem is avoided in the microgenetic approach by positing a single process in continuous transformation, where symptoms are deposited as signposts of pathology at successive points. Here, symptoms are processing stages that differ with respect to their positions in the transformational sequence. The unity in this account is thematic in that different symptoms reflect a single coherent process unfolding from one state to another. In the microgenetic view, each response represents a bundle of action structures, consisting of the series of stages through which the action develops. Pathology disrupts the action at different points in this process. The site of the lesion determines the point in the sequence that is disrupted, and this point or processing stage constitutes the symptom or abnormal behavior.

Microgeny maps onto patterns of phyletic growth. The structure of an action and the symptoms that correspond to levels in this structure are distributed over stages in forebrain evolution. Damage to older orbital and mesial frontal limbic formations leads to impaired activation (response bias or perseveration and lack of initiation), damage along the convexity leads to derailment of the action after adequate initiation (distractibility, apraxia, and confabulation), and damage to premotor and motor cortices leads to a defect in implementation of distal targets (misarticulation, clumsiness, and weakness).

Specifically, the evolutionary progression from limbic to motor cortices retraces the sequence of processing stages in the microtemporal elaboration of an action. Disruption at successive points—at deep bilateral levels, at unilateral surface levels—gives rise to symptoms that reflect this progression:

1. Damage at the base of the system produces an impairment in the initiation of an action (inertia, apathy, hypomotility, or mutism). This difficulty can appear as a failure to begin an act (impaired initiation) or an inability to switch from one action to the next (perseveration, response bias). There can also be a heightened transition to successive behaviors, a lability of initiation, with distractibility and impulsiveness or "dyscontrol." The activation of an action module, the switching from one module to the next, persistence or lability of the

transition across modules, and the maintenance or interruption of set are all phenomena of the early stages of action microgeny.

2. Damage at intermediate stages derails the flow of an action after it has been initiated. This can appear in a more general way (impulsiveness and distractibility) or it can affect specific performances, for example, substitution in limb action (apraxia) or in retrieval (confabulation). In limb action the disruption will involve the more distal musculature according to that point in the sequence that is interrupted. In confabulation, the general meaning of the utterance is preserved in the presence of an extravagance of detail. For example, on story recall the subject may free-associate but eventually retrieves all of the salient elements. Such performances show that the base organization is preserved but that there is a disturbance in the serial elaboration of the action out of this base level.

3. Damage at the surface or end point of the action development produces a defect at the final implementation. The disturbance involves the digital and/or articulatory musculature with misarticulation (Broca's aphasia) and clumsiness (dyspraxia) proceeding to slurring of speech (dysarthria) and limb weakness (paresis).

The elements of the frontal syndrome reflect subtle disorders of action, not complex or high-level cognitive impairments. The action disorder is subtle in that it is a step removed from pure motility and simulates an impairment in planning or self-monitoring. In part, the impression of a cognitive deficit arises from the dissociation between action and awareness. The subject seems unable to inhibit or regulate his own actions. This occurs because the action disorder is a manifestation of a subsurface content to which the surface perceptual representation lacks access. That is, the fully unfolded perceptual development, which maintains awareness, is unable to penetrate submerged processing stages in the action, and these early encapsulated stages represent the nucleus of the action disorder. There is also the more general problem of awareness of an action—how this awareness arises and what action contributes to cognition. Before taking up these questions, however, it is useful to consider the problem of subsurface action in greater detail, in relation to a recently described motor analogue of "blindsight" (see below).

SUBSURFACE ACTION AND MENTAL REPRESENTATIONS

A dramatic illustration of the role of evolutionary levels in action comes from studies of patients with damage to the left hemisphere, paralysis of the right side, and severe aphasia. Such patients may be unable to communicate in speech or in writing with the left hand, and they cannot type or use block letters to construct words. The right arm is paralyzed, though usually some shoulder movement is possible.

A prosthesis has been designed that enables the paralyzed right arm to write by means of steering movements from the residual shoulder musculature (Brown, Leader, & Blum, 1983). With this device, patients with total aphasia are able to produce words to dictation and even write complete and fully grammatical sentences when asked to describe a picture. This is all the more astonishing in view of the loss of articulate speech and the complete inability to write with the normal left hand. Moreover, the performance of global aphasics with the prosthesis is often superior to that of milder aphasics without hemiparesis, suggesting that severe aphasia and hemiplegia are required to "release" or access preliminary language levels. It is also our observation that patients do not appear to have full awareness of their correct performances, which often come as something of a surprise to them.

Although the basis for this phenomenon is not clear, one interpretation might be that the destruction of the distal phase of the action development permits the more archaic proximal motor system to tap into coordinate levels in language representation. Specifically, the older proximal motor system actualizes as an end point in the action microgeny when the distal limb is centrally paralyzed. This system is instantiated through the residual shoulder movement, which is able to penetrate (i.e., is coextensive with) submerged or "buried" levels of language processing. In other words, deep levels in the representation of an action express deep levels in the representation of language. The phenomenon is akin to preserved vision ("blindsight"), audition, and tactile perception with destruction of the primary perceptual zones in the cortex. Hemiplegic writing, like blinksight and related conditions, provides strong evidence that action as well as perception are ordered from bottom to top in the brain, and that actions, like perceptions, do not begin with arousal in the primary cortical areas but are emergent phenomena issuing out of deeper evlutionary strata.

ACTION AND PERCEPTION

In the microgenesis of a perception a neural configuration unfolds so as to represent an object in a progressively more articulated and externalized form (Brown, 1983). Perception is an active process that builds up, partitions, and arborizes external space. Objects in the world are like tributaries that draw out and at the same time punctuate an external space that is like a body for the perceptual process. This is also the case for action.

The microgenesis of action proceeds in a parallel manner and fractionates movement into discrete elements. Unlike perception, where early processing stages are bypassed on the way to the final object, early stages in action appear as postural, orienting, or locomotor (axial and proximal) components of the action structure, discharging early in the movement sequence. This is one way that acts and objects differ. We are aware of an object and not the object development, the object being realized at the expense of its formative structure. In action the development is displayed in the unfolding of the movement.

According to the microgenetic concept, objects are not "out there" in the world waiting for acts to engage them but have to be constructed in parallel with developing actions. Although there are differences between action and perception, there are deep inner similarities. Early stages in object formation provide the contextual background from which objects develop and persist abstractly as levels of conceptual or symbolic content within the object itself. Similarly, early stages in action elaborate the instinctual and affective bases that drive the action forward to its goal. Act and object also undergo a similar development. The "zeroing in" on target movements in the specification of an action has its correlate in the featural modeling of object form. Both act and object are analyzed into finer units. The exteriorization of a target movement and its effectuation on extrapersonal objects correspond with the realization of an external object field. Act and object exteriorize together. A world of real objects and the effects of actions in that world are part of the same microgenetic end point. The deception that a movement is voluntary or willed by the self as an agent corresponds to the deception that we are independent of our own objects. The increasing passivity and then final detachment of an object representation mirror the activity of an action and the realization of an intentional attitude to movements directed toward those object representations.

The tightly locked character of act and object is more prominent at early stages. As action and object undergo increasing differentiation they diverge into widely distributed neural systems. Movements can be interrupted with minimal impact on perceptions, and the reverse, giving the mistaken impression that act and object are independent constructions. But every action has a perceptual residue and every object has an action to which it corresponds. This is true for the most highly differentiated functions. Damage to a phonetic device mediating articulation can lead to an equivalent disturbance of speech perception, and disturbed speech production can occur when there is impaired "phonemic hearing." Acts and percepts both lead outward to the world, they carve up and elaborate space, and, though implemented by different neural mechanisms, they entail a fundamentally unitary psychological process.

Action is required for the development of spatial perception. Animals that are passively moved through environments do not acquire normal depth judgments and other spatial cues. Infants show a preference for objects that can be manipulated. Infants who wear a cast or brace show altered acquisition of spatial perception. Similarly, the space of action is disturbed when perception does not develop normally. The congenitally blind have a distortion of space built up on the action perimeter.

Damage to areas in the temporal and parietal lobes produces a perceptual deficit that is displayed in the context of an action disorder. Parietal lesions give rise to impairments in drawing and other constructional tasks. Posterior aphasic and apraxic errors reflect an underlying perceptual disruption. The idea of a disturbance in speech and limb action secondary to a sensory impairment has a lengthy history. Bastian (1898/1984; Brown, 1984b) and Luria (1962/1966) have both interpreted motor aphasias on a kinaesthetic basis. The work of Mountcastle (1976; Lynch, 1980), demonstrating responsiveness of parietal cells to reaching in relation to an object, provides experimental support for the concept that action and perception share a common perceptuomotor space.

This common space of act and object provides a basis for the tacit knowledge of which movements to make in relation to an object, that is, the more or less automatic sequence of movements that corresponds to levels in object formation. These levels represent different perceptual spaces with a different movement sequence linked to each level in the object representation. In other words, the hierarchy of motor responses is built up in relation to the layered space of perception. One could perhaps go even further and say that the movements in a movement sequence are an expression of successive levels in the transition leading to the final object; they are the residues of an object construction. In a very real sense an action pursues an object, for phases laid down in the action appear before the final object individuates.

AWARENESS OF AN ACTION

These observations demonstrate an inner bond between act and object that is fundamental to the problem of volition and awareness for action. The phenomenon of hemiplegic writing and the occurrence of impaired regulation of behavior in frontal cases are relevant to this problem and to our understanding of the way in which the action development builds up or enters mental representation.

A consideration of the problem of awareness for an action begins with the recognition that the action microgeny does not contribute a content directly to awareness. The awareness of an act and the act itself are contents *in perception* that the action lays down. There is no act that is experienced. The experience of an action is a feeling of its forward development, not an awareness of a particular content. The action generates a feeling of effort or tension, an awareness that an action has or has not taken place, in other words, a self-initiated or "intentional" quality. This is the only *direct* contribution to mind of the dynamic of the action structure.

This is an old problem in neuropsychology. William James (1890) argued that "in perfectly simple voluntary acts there is nothing else in the mind but the kinaesthetic idea . . . of what the act is to be." On the other hand, Wundt believed there was only a feelng of the current of outgoing energy, the *Innervatsionsgefuhl*. Experimental studies of this problem (see Roland, 1978) tend to emphasize techniques of peripheral paralysis or anesthesia rather than the nature of central processes. Thus, passive and active motions have a different effect on perception. Since passive motion can stimulate the peripheral receptors, the perception of this difference (the distinction between passive and active motion) indicates a contribution from the central structure of the action. This contribution could be a motor effect, or it could arise through recurrent collaterals activated in the motor discharge.

For example, object stability depends on whether an action is volitional or passive. Objects are displaced when the eyes are passively moved. If an eye movement is weak or prevented an effort to divert the gaze in the direction of the deficit may result in object displacement. With total paralysis the illusion of movement disappears (Brindley, Goodwin, Kulikoski, & Leighton, 1976; Siebeck & Frey, 1953). During total paralysis from curare an attempt to move the eyes is accompanied by a feeling of spatial displacement even though the object does not move. An effort to move a paralyzed limb may result in illusory displacement, or the action may occur several moments after the attempt with uncertainty as to whether it occurred or to what point the limb has been displaced (Stevens, 1978). Myasthenics have been described who continue to have the feeling they are speaking even after the articulators are paralyzed. These observations indicate that the central action structure deposits a perceptual representation of the act and that the effects of this representation are not erased by an abolition of peripheral motility.

Conversely, a change in perception can give a change in action. In a sense, a perception is a movement, a disposition to act (Bergson, 1896/1959). Patients may have a limb paralysis secondary to a sensory, not a motor deficit. Sensory impairments of the hand lead to pseudo-athetoid or writhing movements of the fingers of which the subject is often unaware. Phantom limb phenomena in amputees offer a rich source of material relevant to this question. There can be an experience of willed or passive action without movement, with a different feeling for volitional as opposed to spontaneous displacement. An effort to move the absent limb gives rise to stronger impressions. In such cases, imagined movements of the phantom may be accompanied by movements of the stump. These are not the cause of the phantom. Such movements are comparable to subvocal articulatory movements during inner speech. The image calls up the movement. There is a similarity between the imagined movements of the phantom and the feeling of motility in a dream. These observations demonstrate the close bond, indeed the common basis, of action, space, and perception. They also show that awareness for an act is built up on perception.

In sum, the action contributes to awareness a feeling of activity, an intuition that the subject is the agent of his or her actions, while the content or description of the act, the awareness that a particular act has taken place, is built up on perceptual residues laid down by the action as it unfolds. Patients with frontal lesions have an alteration in the feeling of agency, which appears in various forms of inertia and dyscontrol. It is not clear whether there is also a deficit in the perception of the act generated by collaterals of the action discharge.

VOLUNTARY ACTION

Volition is the feeling that one is an agent who reflects upon, chooses, and implements an action. It implies more than a direction toward a goal. Action of that type we call purposeful, and purposeful action is not necessarily volitional. An individual can be in a trance or hypnotic state and engage in purposeful action, but we would not say that the act is voluntary. There is a decisional element in volition and a sense in which an action can be withheld. One can choose not to act, and that would also qualify as volitional behavior. A central part of the feeling of volition seems to be the idea of choice, and the implication of an opposition between the self and its actions. The self initiates and guides actions *at will*.

The term *will* is often used interchangeably with volition, but it seems to presume or take on the status of a separate faculty or agency in the mind. Will applies to the engagement of self in a volitional act. Will and volition imply essentially the same mode of action, though will is more thing-like and volition more like a process. Free will entails a belief in the autonomy of the self in the initiation and propagation of acts. The free will problem can be linked to the issue of social and biological constraints on action; the fewer there are, the more the freedom (Dennett, 1985).

The concept of control over action and degrees of constraint, however, shifts the problem outside the intrapsychic context, where it belongs, and in so doing sidesteps many fundamental issues, for example, the nature of the self that is deciding which actions to take, the question of what is involved in the neuropsychology of choice, and the nature of the interaction, if any, between the self (construed as a mental or biological entity) and a motor apparatus. These are the more crucial issues, for which it matters little to what extent an act is obligated by environmental conditions. The first question that needs to be asked is: What is an action?

THE PHYSIOLOGY OF WILL

The old idea that voluntary movement begins with discharge in motor cortex is inconsistent with the clinical material. A consideration of the variety of motor and speech disorders occurring with frontal lesions obligates an interpretation of volitional action as a series of states unfolding in a direction *toward* motor cortex, not away from it. Each state is accompanied by a different awareness experience, so that one can reconstruct from this material the emergence not only of action but of consciousness of action and the volitional attitude. The conclusion of a microgenetic analysis of this material is that consciousness, volition, and action all develop together as a reiterated series of hierarchic modules, and that this development unfolds over evolutionary brain structure (Brown, 1977).

Physiological research has demonstrated that the initiation of an act begins well before cell discharge in motor cortex. There is a bilateral surface negative potential (*Bereitschaftspotential;* Kornhuber, 1974), the end of which begins about 90 msec before simple finger movement. Mesial frontal slow activity has been described .2–.3 sec (P. Chauvel & J. Bancaud, personal communication, 1984; Goldberg, 1985) prior to motor cortex activation, prior even to the conscious decision to act. Libet, Gleason, Wright, and Pearl (1983) found that neural activity associated with voluntary action occurs prior to the conscious decision to act. Discharge in basal ganglia prior to motor cortex during "purposeful" limb movement in the monkey (Evarts, 1979) and the work at Haskins Laboratories demonstrating that purposeful movements arise at the peaks of physiological tremor are also consistent with early programming of the action at subsurface levels.

One interpretation of these observations is that areas associated with activation preceding an action are the same areas that mediate volition. It is claimed that brain correlates of early slow wave activity constitute the substrate of volition, and that these areas are also responsible for the motor plan and the initiation of movement. Some have found in this work physiological evidence for a mind–brain interaction, that is, the effects of mental states on physical brain states (Eccles, 1982). Alternatively, these findings show that an action commences prior to awareness, that it is a result or outcome of early preparatory stages whether or not the action is volitional, and that the decision to act occurs prior to introspective access to decisional content. In other words, the decision to act rises into consciousness on the heels of the action development. Put differently, the consciousness of an act, or the choice involved in the decision to act, appears in awareness subsequent to the onset of the act that is being decided upon. The will, it seems, rises to the occasion a split second too late.

THE PATHOLOGY OF VOLITION

An action is not a concatenation of movements but has a momentary prehistory of some complexity. Weakness and paralysis are only a fraction of the ways in which actions can degrade. Some action disorders are characterized by automatic behaviors, others are purposeful, and still others involve volitional behaviors. The degree to which the action is willed is related to the type of action that appears and the brain region that is involved. Pathological actions expose part of the structure of volition.

A disruption at the core of the action produces inertia and an inability to initiate any action at all. This is not due to a loss of the will because there is no evidence of a self that is deciding, or even trying, to act. One cannot infer a loss of volition from the simple absence of movement. Moreover, preservation of this system associated with initiation disorder with destruction of the distal segment of the action hierarchy may "release" automatic behaviors—brief latency laughing or crying, even rage attacks that are explosive and not directed at objects. The individual has little control over these behaviors and is unable to acknowledge their conceptual or affective content. The appearance of automatic behaviors and "sham" displays reflects discharge of submerged levels in action structure for which subsequent levels associated with content awareness lack access.

From such cases one can surmise that there is an inner relationship between a stage of onset of an action and the features of lability and automatism. The action discharges early in its development prior to the full microgenetic derivation of its content. The action is not truly released or disinhibited from higher control, but expresses directly the characteristics of early cognition. The strong affective tonality of the behavior, its brief latency, and its lack of object orientation point to archaic cognition. The fact that lesions of deep action systems give rise to either automatisms or impaired initiation indicates that actions are not instigated by the will or the self but rather the initiation process is automatic because it is subsurface, and automaticity is the expression of early or subsurface cognition. Moreover, it confirms that the initiation of an action is prior to consciousness of the action and that, by inference, the feeling of willed or voluntary action is elaborated by the action development, not the other way around.

Subsequent to the initiation of the envelope of the action, damage can produce selective impairments of initiation—the initiation of partial (limb, vocal) actions—while stimulation of the pertinent brain areas (the SMA) leads to automatisms that are quasi-purposeful, such as grasping, lip smacking, or similar behaviors. Seizures involving mesial frontal limbic cortex can lead to stereotypical actions of a purposeful type, such as scratching one's head, manipulating imaginary objects, or pacing. The alien hand syndrome also represents a type of released automatism (see Goldberg, 1987). Here a more complex integrated behavior of a purposeful but not volitional type is associated with damage or stimulation to zones intermediate in the action microgeny. The inner relationship between (impaired) initiation and ("released") automatism recurs but now in the context of a more differentiated action pattern, involving segmental or vocal movements. The more intense affective, instinctual, or motivational states associated with the preceding stage fractionate to partial affects that still have a heightened intensity. The developing action is accompanied by a developing object, and the greater degree of object resolution draws the action outward to a space of object manipulation. This gives direction and goal orientation to the emerging action, and elaborates a feeling of purposefulness. The developing action hones in on a developing object.

With dominant convexity lesions there is apraxia, a condition affecting skilled movements requested in pantomime, such as hammering a nail or snapping one's fingers. These actions are disturbed instead of actions done spontaneously or with objects. The disruption involves an action in its most volitional context, when the subject deliberately performs a given behavior. Pantomime lacks the context of an object development to constrain and facilitate its development. In limb apraxia, the action is initiated properly and is usually correctly targeted to a goal, but there is a disturbance in the seriation of partial movements. Apraxia is the primary disorder of voluntary action. The affective state of a patient with apraxia approaches the norm because the affect development has largely completed its course. The volitional character of the disorder reflects involvement of late processing stages in action microgeny. The disorder is for an action in response to verbal request; a conscious decision and a representation— in propositional form—of the action are required. Apraxia satisfies the description of a disorder of voluntary action but it is elaborated late in the action development near the surface of the action structure. One can say that the action penetrates a level in mind coextensive with introspection and awareness of perceptual content.

The erroneous idea that impaired initiation reflects a disturbance of volition derives from the concept of volition as a faculty that initiates action, whereas the phase of initiation actually precedes that of awareness and the feeling of agency. Disorders of this stage do not involve volition in the sense of a separate faculty but rather action in a volitional framework, again demonstrating that volition is an effect or an accompaniment of the action development, not something that instigates the action from the beginning.

There are many other observations that provide insight into the relationship between action and volition. Stimulation of motor cortex, for example, gives rise to limb movements, but the individual may be uncertain as to whether the movement was deliberate. Many of us experience a similar feeling with jerks of the legs just before falling asleep. Patients with choreic movements may round out the choreic twitch to a completed action sequence, such as transforming a sudden jerk of the arm to rubbing the chin, not to mask the movement disorder but because they are unsure whether or not they have activated the behavior.

Such observations show that the automatic nature of an action, its purposefulness, and its volitional quality are not descriptions of a relation between a self and its behavior, but are features of the action generated by the action development and determined by the degree to which the action is completed. Similarly, we learn that the feeling that an action is willed and the distinction of active and passive movement are fragile sensitivities that can be challenged by a variety of pathological disturbances. The individual may (falsely) believe that a spontaneous and fragmentary twitch is willed and so complete it (i.e., the action completes itself) to produce a meaningful sequence, or there may be uncertainty as to whether it is automatic, passive, or active and self-generated.

The pathological material is instructive in showing that automaticity, purposefulness, and volition characterize actions at successive points in their development. A corollary to this is that an action that is automatic is not identical to one that is volitional. One can walk automatically or in a deliberate manner, but these two types of walking are not quite the same. Of course automaticity is to be desired in the acquisition of skills where deliberation can be disadvantageous (Brown, 1984d).

THE MEANING OF VOLUNTARY ACTION

The implication of these observations is that the volitional feeling that accompanies an action has to be achieved along with and as part of the action itself. It is not the specific action that establishes the volitional attitude but the microgenetic stage that is realized in the action development. Volition is not applied to an action from outside but is intrinsic to the unfolding sequence, and in pathological conditions follows the same fate as the action development. The persistence of a prior act, the maintenance of a present state or a resistance to change, and further action are all nonetheless actions. It is the developmental level, not the specific behavior, that determines its volitional quality.

Volition inheres in an action but what, more precisely, is the volitional state? Clearly more than the action is required—a self has to be constructed and there have to be objects for actions to impinge upon. The action contributes an active attitude to behavior, a sense of agency, a feeling that the act is self-generated. This feeling follows the formative direction of the action. The surge and flow of the action outward—its forward growth in this one direction—are part of the feeling of (inter)action with external objects and events. Actions carve out the space of perception; they help to define objects. They flow into a space they have helped to articulate. This too is part of volition, the deception that an action that begins in the mind ends in the world when, after all, the action is only distributed into the mind's extrapersonal component.

The feeling that actions externalize and are active events that influence real objects parallels the passive or receptive quality that we experience in relation to our own objects. Both acts and objects are products of an emergent cognition, but objects "detach" and become independent. In contrast, the self exteriorizes in acton, that is, actiuon carries the self outward into the world. We are convinced that objects act on us and that we act on objects, when in truth the object development is laying down the action while the action deposits in advance of the object and sees always in pursuit.

ACTION AND CAUSATION

If cognitions and actions emerge from below and the programming of the action is preset before reaching awareness, then conscious deliberations—which are in any event also products of subsurface mentation—do not propel behavior but inform us of actions that have already been initiated. A decision state preceding an action is itself an action (an inaction or a covert action) and is not a preparation for an ensuing behavior. There is simply a train of actions of different types, some leading to decision states and others to overt behaviors. The precedence of one state over another is not a sign of causality. The configuration that gives rise to a conscious state provides the context that configures an ensuing state, but the causation is across subsurface configurations, not contents in awareness. In other words, causation, if it applies at all in an emergent system, pertains to the sequence from depth to surface, not from one surface phenomenon to another.

This does not mean that we are propelled by hidden forces and secret motives. Nor does it mean that we have no control or responsibility for our own actions. Indeed, precisely the opposite conclusion can be drawn. Since in its development an action traverses, and in a sense lays down, levels in affect and experience (levels that are part of the concept of a personality), the action can be said to develop out of the very core of one's being. The action is driven by the self—not the self that is exposed in awareness, but a subsurface phase in the development of the self out of which awareness also develops.

ACTION AND PERSONALITY

The observation that damage to the frontal lobes seems to alter complex aspects of behavior and the interpretation of the frontal syndrome as a disturbance in the microgeny of action imply that action plays a critical role in elaborating and maintaining the personality. Certainly, there is some evidence that personality development reflects early patterns of motor activity. The direction of postural preferences in infancy may predict subsequent handedness (Coryell & Michel, 1978), suggesting that manual dominance may derive out of a primitive vestibular or orientation bias. Infants with forceful grasping and active Moro reflexes (sudden tensing and opening of the arms with startle) may show greater assertiveness and a more forceful personality as they grow older. Conversely, children with cerebellar disease or Down's syndrome with hypotonicity tend to be more passive and docile (Goldstein, 1938; Schilder, 1964). There is a well-known case of early frontal damage with abnormal personality development (Ackerly & Benton, 1948).

Such observations show that a personality is not just a set of traits for which an action is a means of expression; instead, the process that lays down the action flows through and elaborates aspects of the personality. We say, "You know a man by his deeds, not his words." Action is less prone to dissimulation than speech. Gestures, facial expressions, and body language are markers of the authenticity of statements. These movements are deposited on the path to conscious ideas and serve as guides to underlying motives. Actions emerge out of memory and layers in the infrastructure of the self. Actions express these early layers in cognition but do not themselves generate mental contents; rather, actions generate an attitude, an orientation or approach to the environment, confidence, participation and withdrawal, going out into the world, and a sense of control over objects. Stages in the exteriorization of an action are also stages in the realization of other mental contents. The self and its actions are reconstituted each moment to the degree to which the action unfolds.

10
The Problem of Perseveration*

with Karen Chobor

Summary of Previous Work

The literature on both diffuse and focal deficits involving frontal lobe in man characteristically describes perseveration in terms of impaired: (1) initiation; (2) modulation; or (3) termination of the executive control of action, with a neurophysiological basis in either a pathological form of facilitation or inhibition.

Much of our thinking on perservation dates back to Hughlings Jackson (1894) who ascribed perseveration to a "release" from cortical inhibition. The concept of inhibition and disinhibition of function has strongly influenced subsequent writings. Thus, Cameron (1933) noted a similarity between perseveration and the conditioned inhibition of brain function described by Pavlov. Jaspers (1913) and Hudson (1969) suggested that perseveration in language reflected an impaired inhibitory system that leads to increased facilitatory activity and the involuntary recall of recently established memory. Kinsbourne and Warrington (1963b) proposed that visual perseveration represented a pathological overactivity of brain systems underlying visual perception through release from inhibitory control.

Subsequent to Jackson, Liepmann (1905) described three types of perseveration. This classification has become quite influential, and consists of three major forms:

1. *Intentional* perseveration, involving the repetition of a performance when a new performance is intended, is regarded as an ideational disorder with an impasse in the sensory preparation of movement. The result is that new stimuli excite a previous idea and the associated movements. Wilson (1908) interpreted this type as a passive preponderance of the perseverating idea as a consequence of diminished activation of others. In contrast, Von Solder (1899) argued for an active preponderance of the perseverating idea.

2. In *clonic* perseveration, once a performance is initiated it is repeated

---

*From "Frontal Lobes and the Problem of Perseveration" by J. W. Brown and K. L. Chobor. In Pena-Casanova, J. (Ed.). (1988). *Memorial Volume for A. R. Luria*. Copyright 1988 by *Journal of Neurolinguistics*. Adapted by permission.

indefinitely without interruption. This, too, is considered ideational (see also Wilson & Walshe, 1914).

3. *Tonic* perseveration is a passive motor disturbance (e.g., a patient is unable to let go of an object in his grasp). Pick (1905) described cases where the patient, at the end of a given act, came to a standstill in a fixed attitude that was maintained indefinitely.

Freeman and Gathercole's (1966) cases of "impaired switching," described by Goldstein (1943) as secondary rigidity, suggest the "intentional" perseveration of Liepmann, while his "compulsive" type, the primary rigidity of Goldstein (1943a), is reminiscent of Liepmann's "clonic type." The intentional and clonic types of aphasic perseveration described by Yamadori (1981) are similar to those of Liepmann.

There have been other functional approaches to perseveration. Perseveration may be most pronounced when the patient is at capacity level or with difficult tasks (Jaspers, 1913, Goldstein, 1943; cf., Werner, 1946). There may be a relation to anxiety (Allison, 1966), amount of effort (Eisenson, 1954), attention (Wepman, 1972), and reaction time (Cameron, 1933). Hebb (1949) compared perseveration to the initial learning stage of an organism where repetition of behavior leads to cortical adaptation, which is lost with brain damage, resulting in a reversion to repetitive behavior. In diffuse pathology, perseveration is said to be the most persistent part of a complex of symptoms involving memory, learning, and orientation. With focal lesions, perseveration is more pronounced in the acute stages and occurs primarily at the beginning of testing sessions (Allison, 1966).

Luria's Concept of Perseveration

Luria distinguished two kinds of motor perseveration. The "efferent" type—which occurs with deep posterior frontal and basal ganglia lesions—is due to a "pathological inertia" of a response that has already been initiated. The intention to act, the action program and the ability to switch from one action to another are unimpaired. This appears to be a type of blocking or compulsive persistence of movement that sets in within a particular task or response mode after the onset of that task or with several repetitions of the same response. The perseveration is mitigated by a change in set, or switching to a different task.

The second form—occurring with massive prefrontal lesions—involves the action program. Once initiated, the program becomes inert and there is inability to switch to the next action, with the result that fragments of several performances may be combined in a single behavior. There is particular difficulty carrying out movements to visual models or verbal commands, an impairment in the monitoring of ongoing activities.

These two forms differ in that the first involves a persistence within an action unit, sparing the ability to switch to, or the activation of, the ensuing unit, whereas in the second type there is defective initiation of serial movements but preservation of a given unit once it is correctly activated. In other words, the disturbance is either within an action structure or across separate action structures. In the first type, the inability to suppress a persistent innervation within the same unit is not clearly linked to an inability to go on to the next unit in the sequence, and the reverse seems to be the case in the second type; specifically, the difficulty in switching is not part of a general impairment in the activation of individual action units or bundles of complex movements.

Perhaps independent of type of perseveration, deep lesions were thought to produce perseveration across different behaviors (language, drawing, limb movement), while superficial lesions give rise to perseveration within performance categories.

Goldberg and Tucker (1979) have extended this work and documented the complexity of perseverative responses. They described persistence not only of motoric elements but of conceptual features such as closedness versus openness, concavity versus convexity, and symmetry. Their work demonstrates that perseveration involves the persistence of complex action structures that are hierarchically organized and bound up with cognitive processing.

More recently, Sandson and Albert (1984) described some cases of perseveration and proposed a new classification. In *continuous perseveration,* the repetition is for simple movements, probably corresponding with Luria's efferent form. "*Stuck-in-set*" perseveration is compared with Luria's switching disorder, though the impairment seems to be rather a persistence of the set or framework of ongoing actions. A third form, *recurrent perseveration,* is a type of contamination or intrusion error.

Case Report: MD is a 76-year-old, right-handed woman, who had a CVA in 1984, resulting in decreased spontaneity, reduced initiative, and paucity of speech and other motor responses; perseveration in speech and writing; and word-finding difficulty. CT was reported to demonstrate an infarct in the left basal ganglia region, with dilatation of the left lateral ventricle and widening of the Sylvian fissure. MRI scan in June, 1986, revealed focal atrophy in the left hemisphere consistent with prior infarction, T2 prolongation in the left temporoparietal region, diffuse periventricular T2 prolongation with several foci in the right frontal white matter. A single focus of T2 prolongation in left mesencephalon was also noted.

Neurological examination disclosed some general slowness of movement and speech, and decreased facial expression, with mild plastic rigidity of the upper extremities, vaguely suggestive of a Parkinsonian state. Slowness of rapid and fine movement was noted, without tremor, cogwheeling or ataxia. Cranial nerve examination, sensory and reflex testing were normal. Babinski reflexes were absent. There was no grasp reflex, echo phenomena or perseveration of motor behavior.

Description of Perseverative Behavior

Perseveration was present mainly on writing and drawing tasks—only rarely in speech. In speech, errors consisted of occasional lexical perseverations on naming and, rarely, reiteration of the initial sound of a word on naming or repetition tasks. Occasionally, behavior was observed that suggested perseveration in everyday activities, for example, ringing the doorbell three or four times. The perseveration did not increase with fatigue over a 2-hour session, although MD tended to assume a rigid and reticent set when tired. Frequency of perseverative errors did not change in relation to the position of letters within words or words within sentences, nor in relation to the style of drawing (e.g., closedness or openness). The perseveration did not increase with persistence in a given task. In fact, maintaining the patient in a task over time appeared to mitigate the perseveration, which was most pronounced on switching within and across behaviors (see below).

Awareness of Perseveration

MD was incompletely aware of perseverative errors in writing and in drawing. She showed little or no frustration over drawings that might be quite deviant, there was infrequent self-correction and she could not improve a drawing when errors were pointed out to her. For example, in one series the self-correction of "hat" showed a lack of separation of the preceding drawing, and possibly a revival of elements from the second and third in the series. The initial item "house" was drawn as *chair*, a contamination from a previous exercise. She recognized this error but was unable to correct it. This behavior is well described in frontal patients, and is further discussed below.

In contrast, MD was often able to correct perseverative errors in productions of the examiner. Thus, she could cancel extraneous letters in a sentence such as in *Bringg the cat insside* or *The ssunn is shinhing*. In this respect, MD resembles the majority of aphasic and brain-damaged patients (and, for that matter, normal subjects as well) in that errors she produces are less well recognized than those occurring in test material provided to her.

Characteristics of Perseveration

MD demonstrated most of the conceptual features of perseveration described by Goldberg and Tucker (1979). For example, the enclosedness of a preceding circle contaminated the second attempt at drawing a table. In another drawing, a man had a cat tail, while the second drawing of a cat was upright and human in appearance, in contrast to the initial attempt.

The majority of perseverative errors consisted of incorporating form elements from preceding items and, less commonly, semantic errors. Contaminations were generally proximate or adjacent to the contaminating figure, but occasionally the perseveration did skip over correct intervening items. There was a suggestion that the perseveration tended to involve certain categories preferentially. For example, perseveration across animate objects (cat, man) seemed more likely than from a physical object (house, chair) to an animate one. The closeness of animate objects may be a factor. In one instance, the feature of closedness was carried over from an apple to a table, so perseveration does occur across organic and physical objects.

Perseveration was not present when MD was asked to copy a series of drawings. In contrast, when asked to produce a set of three different pictures, she produced, for example, an apple and two catlike animals. This performance is comparable with that on verbal fluency tasks. MD produced 4 instances of animals with one repetition in 60 seconds.

Interactions between Speech and Drawing

Perseveration was markedly reduced when MD was asked to name or describe an object before going on to the next item in the series. This effect was present regardless of whether the naming or description occurred before drawing the item or after drawing it. It appeared that perseveration was mitigated by initial or subsequent verbal participation in the drawing process (e.g., when the object concept was explored verbally in labeling or when she was asked to provide descriptive features).

The patient was given a series of 10 different categories (e.g., fruit, clothing) and asked to draw an item within that category. This was done without perseveration, and suggests that if the examiner facilitates the activation of the semantic category of the next item in a series this aids the subject to gain a degree of freedom from the preceding item. Similarly, the patient had no difficulty giving an exempler from the category and then drawing another item in the same category. Her success on this task indicates an absence of contamination of pictorial by lexical representations once access to a specific category has been achieved.

Interactions between Writing and Drawing

MD was asked to draw an item in a series of different objects (e.g., chair) and then write the name of the item beneath the object before going on to the next item. This maneuver resulted in some perseveration across written object names as well as across object drawings. This is of interest in that perseveration did not occur or, alternatively, correct performance was facilitated, when the object name was spoken (see above), suggesting an effect of the motoric system (limb gesture) linked to the object category, rather than an effect related to the category alone.

If the facilitation is largely related to verbal processes and the perseveration is linked to right arm gestural systems, analogous effects might appear if gestures were employed rather than written or spoken namings. This is described in the next section.

Interactions between Gesture and Drawing

As with language facilitation, perseveration was also decreased by certain gestures. MD performed well when asked to gesture the use of an item before drawing it, or if she was asked to gesture the use of an item (e.g., put on your hat) and draw another (given) item in the same category (tie). Although occasionally present, this effect was not as pronounced if irrelevant gestures were used. For example, when she was asked to gesture the use of a needle and thread, and then to draw a toothbrush, contaminations were noted from the preceding drawing (mop), not the preceding gesture.

Distraction

Perseveration was absent when the patient was distracted by 3 minutes of irrelevant conversation between drawings in a series. With on-line distraction such as diversion by radio noise or blinking lights during rote number writing, there was no effect. Conversely, over a long testing session there was no increase in perseveration with fatigue.

Discussion

Discordance between knowledge and behavior In frontal cases, there is a relatively intact verbal description of a failed or inadequate behavior. The patient is aware of and can describe inappropriate performances but cannot correct them. A classic example is the ability of frontal patients to describe the strategies that are required on a test such as the Wisconsin Card Sorting Test (WCST), but in spite of the correct description they continue to perform in a deficient manner. Another example would be the awareness that frontal patients have of confabulatory responses even while they are engaging in confabulation. The presence of error awareness and an ability to describe the correct activity without being able to alter it has been observed by many authors.

In MD's case, there was incomplete awareness of perseveration and a limited ability to correct errors that were pointed out. Generally, frontal cases are reported to have relatively intact awareness of disability, so that the incomplete awareness present in this patient was unusual, perhaps representing the effect of nonfrontal (left temporoparietal) lesions. The difficulty in correcting errors once she was made aware of them, however, is consistent with the behavior of other frontal patients, though it is unclear whether this is an intrinsic part of the perseveration symptom.

The dissociation between intact knowledge or verbal report and impaired behavior that occurs in frontal patients is quite different from the dissociation common to patients with posterior or callosal lesions. Such patients may have little insight into their paraphasic errors. In callosal cases without aphasia, there may be visual or tactile misnamings (left field, hand) without self-correction and confabulation when the patient is confronted with his errors. Conversely, there are also patients who are unaware of—or unable to report—behaviors that may be performed well: for example, the deficient verbal access to "right hemisphere" content in split-brain cases; "blindsight" phenomena; and hemiplegic writing (Brown, 1986). In the latter case, a more or less correct behavior is accompanied by a lack of awareness for the behavior or an inability to access it into language and verbal report. These dissociations can, perhaps, be explained as the discharge or completion of a performance at early processing stages prior to the derivation of that performance to a later stage of verbal or perceptual awareness (Brown, 1983c; Brown, 1986). How can we account for the reverse dissociation in frontal patients?

The Problem of Verbal Regulation One possibility is simply that of disturbed monitoring, an impairment in verbal regulation as postulated by Luria. The patient understands the task and can describe what is required, but is unable to use this linguistic or conceptual knowledge to direct the target action. This, of course, seems intuitively to be the case in such patients. However, there are problems with this interpretation.

First, the inability to carry out a behavior to a verbal request though the patient is able to verbally describe the requested activity may have to do with increased complexity. Certainly, this is the case with many of the Stroop tasks designed to demonstrate this deficit. The fact that verbal cueing does not aid a performance does not implicate (failure in) a system mediating the cue. We do not postulate a regulatory system for cued response or cross-modal effects in other channels.

Alternatively, the test conditions might involve a dual-task effect. Two tasks are set before the patient instead of one—a motor task and its linguistic equivalent—and the patient is required to resolve the two in the performance. In some ways this is a production analogue of perceptual sorting tasks where patients have difficulty resolving two or more object attributes (e.g., color and form). This is certainly the case in the description of motor decrements in aphasics when the mouth is held open or a bite block is employed. Rather than an interruption of inner speech and a lack of verbal regulation, the patient now must focus on two tasks, the required motor activity and the verbal deprivation procedure.

Moreover, severe aphasics with an impairment or "loss" of language, and presumably a loss of verbal regulation, may not show the same deficits as frontal cases where language function is relatively intact. Why should there be disconnection effects that are not reproduced by a loss of one (the driving or regulating) component? In addition, it is not always clear to what extent perseveration and distractibility, as the cause (result?) of a disturbance in action, can be distinguished from failed regulation. Is the regulation of action impaired or do these factors overwhelm an intact regulatory system? Can one infer a system underlying regulation from proactive verbal interference or from a disruption in action control?

However, there is a more serious objection to the idea of failed verbal regulation, and that is that it restates as an explanation the very phenomenon in question without probing more deeply into the basis for the presumed monitoring or regulating activity.

The Conceptual Base of Actions In Luria's account, it is not altogether clear whether control of action is a conscious or unconscious effect. On the one hand, there is the directive function of language and the presumed role of inner speech. This entails conscious mediation. On the other hand, there is an early decisional element that seems to require a conceptual or linguistic organization appearing in the preliminary action plan. There are studies to indicate that actions are programmed prior to an awareness of the decision to act (Brown, 1977; Libet, 1985). How does this fit in with conscious verbal regulation? More specifically, one might ask how regulation would occur in real time as actions unfold? Does an action ensue from a conceptual base that is intrinsic to the action or do extrinsic conceptual systems feed into a set of motor keyboards? Is there, as Luria supposed, an action plan or hypothesis that serves as conceptual anchor and guide to the action sequence?

It seems to us that the central question in perseverative behavior of the type we have described is how language and concepts are brought to bear on action (or perception, memory, etc.). In spite of the common-sense view, this is not a simple implementational or directive process. Thoughts and language representations are not read off into a series of movements. This is not the way actions develop. Neuropsychological study has shown that actions have a dynamic stratification distributed over phyletic stages in forebrain growth. Actions develop in archaic brain systems bound up with early stages in cognitive processing and lead with increasing specification to neocortical formations of evolutionary recency. The action unfolds in concert with levels in language and perception. Actions are subjective, cognitive events, movements the physical output of keyboards at successive points in the action structure.

Dual Task Effects From this perspective, consider studies of dual-task interaction deriving from the observation that dowel balancing is impeded in the right but not left hand by concurrent verbalization (Kinsbourne & Cook, 1971). These studies were interpreted to show interference effects between a verbal processor in left hemisphere and the proximate control system for right hand movement. However, it is reasonable to assume—but to our knowledge the study has not been done—that if the verbalization was directed toward the right hand activity and not to another topic, the right hand decrement would disappear. The prediction is that right hand performance would improve if the subject could freely verbalize on the activity of dowel balancing. This would indicate that it is not the verbal task that interferes with the motor one, nor a result of limited "functional space," but a condition of divided attention. More specifically, the crucial element is the requirement that two separate conceptual systems or two concurrent states of focussed attention are active in the same hemisphere.

Verbalization can facilitate many different behaviors. Reading aloud is an aid in the understanding of difficult texts. Active repetition of word lists gives enhanced recall over passive listening. Are reading and memory "regulated" by verbalization? Or does the facilitation occur through the incorporation of the behavior into a wider system of lexical concepts?

Speech or inner speech is a form of action. Areas of the brain concerned with speech production are derived from motor systems. Speech develops in relation to action. The facilitation or regulation of action by language may reflect the incorporation of the forming action into, or its conceptual expansion by, the preliminary conceptual determinants of the language behavior. This would not be a verbal or linguistic effect, but a nonspecific facilitation by dual tasks that arise out of the same conceptual base.

This assumes that actions are facilitated (regulated) by nonverbal as well as verbal processes, and it also assumes the reverse effect, that language production can be facilitated by actions. There appears to be evidence that this is the case. Thus, an action can be facilitated by another action that provides a context for the target act; i.e., partial actions are facilitated by more generalized ones. Finger tapping is aided by bilateral synchrony. There are patients with brain damage who are unable to carry out partial actions without first assuming the appropriate posture, for example, a patient unable to throw a punch "like a prizefighter" unless he assumes a fighting stance. In some individuals, gesture or pacing may facilitate speech production. Signing may facilitate speech in language-delayed children, and gesture is employed as a cue in aphasia retraining. Exaggerated oral postures in some patients precede and may facilitate speech production.

One can say that a partial action may be aided by the assimilation of its base structure to a broader system involving deep, preconscious levels in language or conceptual organization, even early stages in the formation of another action. This assimilation provides a contextual background within which the act can differentiate. A common element may be the enlargement of the conceptual underpinnings of the act to be performed. Moreover, the same explanation accounts for facilitation in the reverse direction; the initiation or activation phase of a speech act may be aided by combining it with gestural or other motor activity.

Applications to Clinical Observations: In the case presently discussed, the perseveration largely involved limb motility on drawing and writing tasks. As in other cases in the literature, there was contamination of a conceptual nature from earlier items, often across adjacent performances. Rather than demonstrating the failure of verbal regulation, these observations confirm that conceptual elements mesh or are intertwined with the action and persist, or are unusually prolonged, into succeeding activities. This prolongation points to an exaggerated overlap across successive deep levels in action generation. Conversely, one could say there is incomplete specification of the action out of a base organization coextensive with nonmotor conceptual systems. That is, the conceptual core out of which the action unfolds reappears when the action is incompletely specified.

That verbal "regulation" was present in our patient is indicated by the mitigation of perseverative behavior when the patient was required to name items prior to drawing them. The selection of the verbal label facilitates access to the target category underlying the derivation of the action sequence. The fact that writing the name does not have a facilitatory effect comparable to oral naming argues against facilitation as an effect of inner speech. The specific channel into which the action develops plays a central role. Moreover, the facilitation was not specific to verbalization as demonstrated by the marked reduction in perseveration when the patient was required to gesture the use of an object prior to drawing it. This facilitatory effect—comparable to that of oral naming—did not occur for irrelevant gestures, indicating that the facilitation is not due to distraction or "release" from a persistent motor innervation by switching to another task.

In our view, the enhanced retrieval (selection, specification) of the action and the consequent decrease in perseveration are accomplished through an augmentation of the base conceptual structure of the forming action-to-be. This augmentation is achieved through gesture, or naming or describing the object, but only when these are conceptually related to the target action. Writing does not have the same effect as limb gesture, for it involves the specification of a lexical concept into the same target keyboard (the digital musculature) as is entrained on drawing tasks. In this case, the base structure of the action—the concept—has to be reactivated. In oral naming, the distal specification is into a different target organ, and the activated concept can undergo completion into an "uncluttered" production device.

In sum, the common element in these performances is that they develop out of a shared system of concepts. Gesture and naming facilitate action through an activation of the base concept through which the action develops. These observations point to the existence of a deep level of conceptual structure in which spoken and gestural semantic content, together with perceptual information, co-occur with early stages in the generation of action. This level of shared conceptual structure underlies and gives rise to these components. The limbic and mesolimbic ring may provide an anatomic substrate for a system of this type. Presumably, the pathologic lesion displays (through a processing delay?) this level in relation to the action component.

IV
MEMORY AND TIME

11
Toward a Microgenetic Theory of Memory

Usually we think of memory as an image of a past event surveyed at leisure in the "mind's eye," or as the fragments of the preceding day that are reworked in dream hallucination; but memory is also active when we recognize objects and retrieve the words to describe them, in the bonds and habits that pattern our everyday experience, the unconscious processes that structure behavior, and in movements like dancing or typing, even walking—indeed, in all actions and automatic mechanisms. Memory is idea or representation, but it is also the process of remembering and the way this process shapes actions, percepts, feelings and thoughts.

With such diversity it is not surprising that the goal of many studies of memory and its disorders has been mainly that of classification and analysis. As a result, memory has been fractionated into separate forms, each localized to a store in which information about preceding events is deposited. The various types of memory assume a location within the network of the store(s) in relation to anatomical region or stage in information processing. Of course, the idea that a memory function is localized to a store does not imply that the store itself is localized. A store could be woven into other components, but the idea does entail some degree of functional encapsulation or the store would be indistinct from the components it innervates.

There are consequences of this point of view for a theory of mind, apart from the problem of memory. For example, a store that updates or matches information received from sites of registration implies that recognition is nonperceptual, or a function that is secondarily recruited to perception, and obligates a theory of perception that is little more than an account of sensory primitives. A similar explanation of the selection and insertion of words into slots in a sentence frame supposes word-equivalent configurations (labels) in a lexical store. Attaching a mental lexicon to a language device, however, obscures the fact that word finding is a constructive process intrinsic to language no less than are the semantic and syntactic "rules" that guide word finding along.

Perhaps because of difficulties with a faculty account of memory, another version has appeared, duplicating the structure of memory for each mental component, a component consisting of a sensorimotor system or some knowledge base. For example, there might be a separate motor memory, a memory for tactile or visual perception, or for a system underlying mathematical ability, language function or musical skills. In the first theory memory processes impinge on other functions from outside, whereas in the second theory they are organized within the function itself. For example, a single long-term memory store could be shared or accessed by multiple components, or there could be long-term memory processes specific to each component.

One memory system or many, however, the essential question is whether memory within or across components—regardless of what the components are— is an independent faculty or a way of looking at those components in operation. Is there a system of memory capable of being described independently of the cognitions and the modalities through which it is expressed, or is memory a description of states of those cognitions and modalities without a structure independent of this description?

Recognition and Retrieval

Consider these two extremes of memory: recalling the face of a friend from the past, and recognizing the friend on a subsequent encounter. The first one involves the suspension of activity during a more or less vivid, purposeful mental image in a state of introspection; the other is an experience that is immediate, external, involuntary and seemingly part of the activity in which it occurs. In the first, the feeling of familiarity develops out of a context leading to the image. The context guides the search for the image but there is no experience of recognition. We do not recognize our own images. We may be aware of the degree to which the image recaptures an object experience—there is, it seems, a standard against which the accuracy of the image is gauged—but we do not say of a mental image, "That's him, I recognize that face!" In the the second case, the feeling of familiarity is in the object, not the viewer. The object itself seems to drive or trigger the recognition process. Now we say, "That's a familiar face", and begin to search for the contextual background within which the act of recognition develops. In the first instance, a mental representation emerges spontaneously out of some context; in the second instance, the mental representation is replaced by an object and the context is revived secondarily.

Conventional theories of memory explain differences between recognition and recall by assuming a match of a perception to a memory trace for recognition and the spontaneous activation of the (same?) trace in the retrieval process. The trace that corresponds to the face of my friend is activated as a memory image in a state of reminiscence or matched to a sensory configuration when the face is actually seen. Following on this assumption a good deal of work has been done on the effects of stimulus type and context, duration and capacity, all of which serve largely to obscure problems in the underlying assumption. It is not that the theory is wrong; rather it is too narrow to account for what is important in memory study. The situation, in fact, is a reminder that the parsimony required by a theory is a parsimony to be exacted in the decision between competing accounts, not in the phenomena the theory seeks to explain.

Thus, one might ask whether the idea of a match between a percept and a memory image or trace explains intermediate phenomena, (such as an hallucination or eidetic image of a face), experiential effects on perception, or growth and change in memory (for example, a change in the appearance of a face and one's memory of it over time), all pointing to constructive aspects of perception and recall. One should ask also whether the theory explains transitional states between the mental image and the object perception or similarities between the two, which point to problems in the distinction of intra- and extrapersonal space. Thus, the familiarity that permeates the memory image replaces the tacit recognition of the object experience during such phenomena as *deja vu*, a state in which the feeling of familiarity surfaces in an object perception. Transitional states such as *deja vu* point to the commonality of objects and images and the continuum from mental space to externality.

If we reflect on these and similar problems we realize that a theory of memory is closely bound up with a theory of perception. In fact, one determines the other to such an extent that a new approach to memory organization obligates an overhaul of perceptual theory. The central question is how objects are formed. The microgenetic theory of perception leads to a very different concept of memory than that to which we are accustomed from traditional accounts. The theory entails, for example, that images and objects are mental constructs in a layered hierarchy of space representation and that differences between stages in mental representation, not memory operations, underly the problem of retrieval and recognition. In short, the claim is that what seem like memory components are actually manifestations of processing stages in object formation.

There is, after all, a good deal of work on the common basis of image and object; there are transitions between memory images, imagination and eidetic images and "real" perceptions, and there is a way of thinking about perception as a process leading from mental imagery to external objects. These and similar observations converge on the idea that image and object represent stages on a processing continuum. Further, in this continuum the image anticipates and unfolds over the same structures as the object. Specifically, an image is an object that is incomplete in its development, while an object is an image that has undergone further processing.

If one accepts this point of view, and there is much evidence in its favor, differences in stage rather than component would account for the mnestic or perceptual characteristics of a given phenomenon. In other words, whether an event is experienced as an occurrence in memory or perception depends on the extent of processing of a given object representation. A representation that unfolds to a position in external space is perceived as an object, while a representation that has an attenuated development is apprehended as a mental image. The nature of the memory operation depends on how far the object develops. Thus, on this theory, the implicit recognition of a familiar face involves the same cognitive processes as the feeling of familiarity accompanying a revived image of the face. In the case of a memory image, the feeling actualizes with the image, while in the case of a perception it comprises a preliminary phase and is traversed, buried or submerged on the way to the external object.

Memory in Act and Object Formation

If a mental image is a precursor of an external object and if the retrieval of mental content occurs through some form of mental imagery—that is, if recall involves an incomplete percept—there is no need for a function of retrieval in addition to that of perception. Retrieval is not an operation applied to a trace in a memory store. Contents are not accessed, a representation is not searched for. The search is the struggle of the representation to realize its own content. Retrieval, therefore, is just a term for the process of act and image production. A memory image that is retrieved into awareness, movements that are revived and laid down automatically, or words that mesh into utterances, are not static contents looked up and printed into performances arising through activities in other domains, but are the end stage of a dynamic process that proceeds along the same path as action and perception.

There are many consequences of this approach that impact on memory theory. One consequence mentioned above is that the retrieval of a perceptual experience, even from the distant past, involves the same mechanisms as the original percept. Retrieval is re-perception, unfolding over the same cognitive structure as the original object. In this structure, mechanisms identified with long-term memory (object meaning, recognition) refer to early or deep levels in percept formation, whereas mechanisms identified with short-term or iconic memory refer to surface levels associated with registration. Specifically, long- and short-term memory—and related forms such as intermediate, working, semantic, etc.—refer to stages or segments in object formation, not independent procedures or stores. Object formation is a continuous process that can be "sliced" at successive points. The segment that is sliced determines the nature of the object representation and the particular form of memory appropriate to that representation. But the form of memory is a characteristic of the representation, not an extrinsic component.

A core element of this approach is the idea that object perception involves the derivation of a target through a type of sensory modeling, not a piecemeal construction from featural elements. An object is selected—isolated—through fields of meaning and form specification. Recognition—the attribution to an object of experiential and conceptual meaning—is elaborated early in the selection phase, and mechanisms underlying recognition are the same as those mediating the selection of a mental representation in imagery or an object representation in perception. Recognition, like retrieval, therefore, is not a part of the memory problem, since the microstructure of these operations is identical to that of the system or modality through which the operations are realized.

From this it follows—or the theory obligates—that long-term memory processes are entrained *prior* to those mediating short-term memory. This is true for both perception and mental imagery. Since imagery constitutes an intrapsychic phase in object formation, the retrieval of an image and, therefore, the recognition of the object toward which the image leads would be accomplished before the representation of the image as an external perception.

Another implication concerns the problem of capacity. The capacity of a memory state now has to be conceived in relation to the capacity of the representation elaborating that state and/or the number of reiterated sequences— the number of representations—that can be generated for the duration of the memory component. Put differently, capacity reflects the content of a number of related or unrelated object representations that are elaborated over the time frame of the type of memory under investigation. There is an appearance of decreasing capacity as one proceeds from long- to short-term to immediate and iconic memory—in other words, as percept formation approaches an external object. There is also a decrease in the duration of the memory state and there is an assumed change in the material on which the memory operates. Since the object is specified over levels from depth to surface, the surface content is more restricted than the base level out of which that content is selected. Deep levels appear to have a greater capacity than surface levels. However, since base and surface levels constitute the extremes of a single object formation there is a sense in which all memory forms or levels should have the same capacity.

In sum, retrieval is perception, the reiterated unfolding of mental representations into images or external objects. Depending on whether this process terminates in an image or an object, the experience is that of a memory image in the mind or a perception in the world. Long-term memory applies to preliminary phases in this process, the feeling of familiarity attached to the revival of remote percepts or the feeling of recognition (or novelty) that inheres in independent objects. Short-term memory applies to the distal phase of the process, the realization of an external object or a mental image that is objectlike in clarity. This sequence is reiterated for every percept. Even unfamiliar or impossible objects (or neologisms) transit a stage of object meaning (through which they are recognized as being unfamiliar or "meaningless").

The Trace and the Store

What is a memory trace and how is it activated in recall? In one sense, a trace is a persistent neural change associated with learning, presumably related to cellular and/or synaptic events. Conceivably, a compounding of changes at the neuronal level underlies learning in complex systems. In such systems, however, the trace would have to be more than a collection of synapses strengthened by repeated traversals. The problem is that it is unclear how synaptic change achieves sensitivity to stimulus configurations unless this change translates to a network or population dynamic. That is, to encode the many features in an object, the trace would have to include many (and probably widely distributed) cell populations, so that the pattern (code, etc.) of change over many cells rather than the change in a particular cell would be the important factor. In this sense, the trace is not just an effect of learning but encodes a stimulus pattern. On a mechanism of this type, a given cell population could engage in innumerable configurations through the differing strengths of synaptic connectivity among the cells. The trace, the neural change linked to the specific memory or experience, would apply to the configurational properties of the network and not the connectivity.

If this is accurate, it implies that the trace has neither anatomical nor psychological localization but consists in a network of potential synaptic relations. The trace would depend on the relative strengths of a myriad of synapses and would include similar complex networks at all levels through which retrieval occurs. Since the representation unfolds over a series of hierarchic levels, the trace would embrace a wave of configurational change passing over all of the levels through which the representation develops. Since the final representation is not retrieved *in statu quo* from a store but differentiates through a sequence of transitions there is no physical trace that corresponds to a mental or perceptual representation.

Most models of memory assume that a trace is analogous to or isomorphic with an experienced event and that change in the trace occurs through interference or decay or is an effect of other operations applied to the trace. We are also lead by common sense to think that the nature of the trace must capture in some sense the nature of the experience that is stored. Otherwise, why does the world appear as it does? If traces consist of codes, procedures or mathematical transforms, why do we see and recall objects and events? However, something is deeply wrong with trace theory. We recognize that there are cognitive elements in a perception or a memory image that are not in the physical object— constancies or affect, for example—so that the trace must at least include additional content; and the effect of experience on perception and recall indicates the presence of dynamic factors not accounted for in trace models.

The concept of microgeny provides another difficulty for the idea of a memory trace, in that objects and images *develop* over stages, so that the trace either does not exist—at least in the sense in which it is usually employed—or it includes an entire microgenetic series. Specifically, the content of a representation in awareness—an object, an image, a lexical item—is the endpoint of a transitional series so that the trace corresponding with this content has to include segments of the transition that anticipate or prefigure the final content. In other words, the content of a representation consists also of preliminary stages leading to that content. Since the final representation is not a "bit" but an outcome, preparatory phases in the representation have to be included as an obligatory part of the representational content. It is futile, therefore, to search for the memory trace of an object, say a trace for the word "chair," since the word chair is not isomorphic to a given configuration, but rather the realization of a series of formative stages.

According to this view, a trace is not an entity that can be searched for and localized, but the probability of the recurrence of a given configuration at a particular stage in the retrieval (perceptual) process. The memory store is the sum of traces so defined or, put differently, the resting state of all realizable sets (i.e., all potential configurations). This concept of the memory trace is related to the idea of competence. In the sense of a knowledge of or capacity to perform a given behavior, competence refers to the range of configurations activated or brought to bear on the emergence of a given configuration. It refers to the contextual background out of which performances are selected; that is, to relations between incipient configurations activated spontaneously in recall or by a stimulus in perception.

On the other hand, competence in relation to production or performance strategies has to do with factors influencing the selection of a given configuration—that is, why one performance and not another occurs. The capacity to generate a specific performance depends on processes at multiple stages, so that it is impossible to pinpoint one level of organization where the competence resides. In the psychological sense, competence resembles less, say, the program of a computer than the potential of an embryo to develop to a specific phenotype.

Microstructure of Retrieval

Retrieval mirrors percept and action formation. The succession of configurations called up in the original formation of an act or an object constitutes the trace of the resultant behavior or representation. This series of configurations is hypothesized to arise in upper brainstem and/or limbic structures and to unfold over evolutionary stages in the growth of the forebrain. The configurational series passing over this structure is common to perception and to spontaneous recall. That is, both objects and images unfold over the same system. In perception the series underlying spontaneous recall (imagery) is constrained or modulated by sensory input to model an external object. Sensation is a physical event outside of cognition and enters hierarchically at successive stages in the derivation or selection of a mental representation. The representation is a purely cognitive or mental phenomenon that is constrained by sensory input to model an external object. In other words, sensation constrains image production so that the image it produces is an object; but sensations do not enter directly into the object construction. The different forms of normal and pathological imagery—hallucination and illusion, memory, eidetic, and imagination or thought images—reflect specific levels in this unfolding sequence.

At the earliest stages in percept formation, a construct develops from sensory modulation of autonomous brainstem and tectal systems to a viewer-centered, volumetric space through mechanisms in limbic and temporal lobe. The primitive schema is transformed—or the object is selected—through a network of symbolic and experiential relations. There is direct sensory input to limbic-temporal lobe, but the poverty of constraints on the developing representation at this level obligates selection through a system of personal memory. Image phenomena occur in the absence of sensation at more distal microgenetic stages. Such phenomena have an hallucinatory quality. There are features of dreamwork mentation and the object is bound up with instinctual drive and a strong affective tonality. This level in the object representation appears normally in dream hallucination. The shift between dream and dreamless sleep reflects the momentary dominance in the perception of limbic-temporal or upper brainstem mechanisms.

As the percept develops, a limbic image and its egocentric, volumetric space are transformed (selected) through fields of conceptual relationships to a three-dimensional Euclidean or object-centered space. This occurs by way of mechanisms in the parietal lobe. In this transition, the representation achieves a kind of referential adequacy. There is an object in an external space, but object and space are not fully independent of the viewer. This is a space of the arm's reach, a space bounded by the perimeter of limb action. Damage to parietal lobe mechanisms leads to deficits in the perception of object relations, particularly when limb action or object manipulation are involved. Illusions occur, reflecting distortions of object relations. With reduced sensory input, there is mental imagery rather than object perception. The hallucinatory stage of the preceding level is transformed to a memory image. The memory image is at the threshold of awareness. The link between hallucination and memory imagery is experienced normally when a memory image survives a dream that is fading as one is awakened. A memory image can also be confused with a dream recollection when the context around the event is forgotten. An effort to reconstruct the prior and/or subsequent history of the event may provide the continuity that is characteristic of living memory and help to disambiguate the experience.

The representation derived through parietal lobe mechanisms is then submitted for featural modelling and exteriorization through mechanisms in striate and circumstriate cortex. Sensory input at this stage analyzes the gestalt to its featural elements and at the same time establishes the object as an independent thing in the world. This is the surface of everyday perception. When the level discharges spontaneously or is deprived or sensory input, there are elementary hallucinations (for example, in migraine and afterimages). Damage to this stage impairs identification of object features—reading, perceiving form and colors—and may induce scotoma. In the case of scotoma, the finding of residual vision points to levels in the object completed prior to the surface disruption.

Thus, a configuration arises through constraints imposed on a resting state by sensory primitives. The configurational pattern is shaped by the input to model certain aspects of the physical object. In imagery, there is a suspension of external stimulation. The pattern is now constrained by inner relations and develops along autonomous lines. In either case, however, in imagery or perception the initial configuration incorporates diverse potential objects evoked to the extent their patterns share in the configuration that is first activated. In other words, sensation acts on the resting pattern to delimit the range of configurations that might develop. One can say that objects develop—or are, in a sense, sculpted—through inhibitory effects at successive stages in image formation.

As the configuration unfolds over these stages, many patterns or potential objects subsumed in the initial set become untenable given the sequence that is being laid down. These incipient but unselected objects evoked at each processing stage persist in the final object as a contextual background out of which the object develops, and they provide for much of the affective and semantic richness of the object experience. That is, the conceptual background of the object is not a store of knowledge to which the object must appeal but a phase in the microstructure of the object prior to conscious perception. To reflect on an object is to draw on preliminary phases in the object itself. It is to revive as incomplete objects (thoughts, images) those unselected representations bypassed on the way to the original object.

In this view, an object develops out of a history of prior encounters through a network of conceptual relations to a stage of perceptual awareness. An attenuation of this process results in a mental image rather than an external object. If the attenuation is early, involving experiential and affective relations, there is a dream or hallucination. If the attenuation is at a later stage of conceptual or lexical-semantic relations, the content is that of inner speech or other forms of mental imagery. Memory obtains at each of these stages but differently at each stage. Initially, memory appears as an activation, scanning or search procedure, then as a semantic or conceptual operation, finally as the segmentation or analysis of an object into its component features. In sum, the appearance of different types of memory operations—activation, long- and short-term memory—results from the reiteration of the same process at multiple stages in a continuum, with the type of memory at a given moment determined by the content that emerges at that moment rather than by an operation applied to that content.

Forgetting

In forgetting, the path of the perception is unpeeled in a direction from surface to depth. Forgetting is the degree to which retrieval is attenuated. Events recede like the falling spray of a fountain, with each moment in object formation recaptured in the course of the decay. First, the analysis of object form gives way to a stage of object gestalts and object relations. This stage in turn gives way to one of object concepts, a stage where the object-to-be is co-represented with other possible objects. Underlying this stage is a level of experiential and affective relations. The retreat of the object back through these stages elaborates forgetting. Specifically, forgetting is not a loss of elements or a failure of traces to consolidate but an *uncovering* of bypassed stages in the unfolding of an object representation. This occurs because the changed sensory conditions no longer favor the individuation of objects out of early, multivalent and more generalized configurations. The degree of resolution and specificity is insufficient to derive once more the same object. The perception must be revived spontaneously over the same series of levels, unaided by sensory information. The nature and extent to which short- or long-term recall deviates from the target object reflects characteristics of a stage in the object deprived of sensory modeling. That is, deficiencies or errors in recall are not aberrations of targets but descriptions of the content of levels within the object when the level is not modulated by sensation to derive a specific item.

Iconic Recall

Within the first second or so after an object is perceived, the object can be revived almost completely and most of its content recaptured. We can appreciate this stage of memory by viewing a scene, then closing our eyes and, for a brief moment, "seeing" the scene in our mind's eye. In some eidetic individuals this ability may be extremely well developed. This "iconic" stage of memory is usually attributed to an input buffer, or to a low-level sensory phenomenon, or a type of afterimage or persistent excitation. In fact, it can be explained as the reiterated unfolding of the object representation over almost the entire infrastructure through which it was generated. A preobject achieves an almost objectlike clarity. Perhaps in eidetics there is an unusual persistence of the effects of sensory modulation, especially at surface levels in the object representation.

Short-term Recall

An object that is revived—re-perceived—during the next 15–30 seconds shows a loss of information and "chunking" of the available content. Similarity of sound and form or, to a lesser extent, of meaning, may influence recall. In contrast to the physical character or iconic memory, short-term memory displays features of a cognitive or reconstructive nature. This is explained by the fact that the representation corresponding to the short-term content is positioned earlier in the continuum leading to an external "physical" object.

Characteristic of short-term memory is that its content can be analyzed into segments or features. The serial or spatial array of the original percept is available but elements are lacking. A string of words or sounds, the location of a set of objects, can be revived but there are limits on capacity. Language is retrieved better than other perceptual material. Rehearsing a string of digits (for example, repeating a telephone number) aids in recall. The evocation of the content in inner speech reiterates the percept and prolongs the retrieval period. The spatial frame of the sequence—the number of slots in the span—can be imaged though specific items are lost, and items can be imaged though the order is incorrect. This is easily demonstrated at the span limits in normal or pathological cases. These observations confirm that a spatial gestalt emerges in imagery (and is maintained in perception) before it is analyzed into segments that mirror the physical features (e.g., spatial and temporal order) of the external object.

If the distal segment of the perception becomes refractory at a too rapid rate there will be an accelerated attenuation of retrieval and "deficits" in short-term memory. This will impact on the capacity to revive a perception quickly without necessarily affecting long-term memory. Rapid fading at the perceptual surface should be accompanied by heightened sensitivity to new percepts. Interference effects should be prominent and arise spontaneously from competing stimulation, as occurs in confusional states. The observation that phonetic material is more susceptible to interference than is semantic material and that interference effects are most pronounced within the same modality suggests a sort of "perceptual erasure."

Long-term Memory

Over time, the perception retreats to a stage of an unanalyzed gestalt in long-term, semantic or conceptual memory. Retrieval is sketchy, contextualized and integrated with other experience. As in short-term memory, temporal order (episodic memory) is more vulnerable than item recall. However, order is reconstructed in relation to other events, not to other items within the retrieved content. The episodic or temporal seriation of an event, its time tagging, refers to the position of the event in the flow of experience and its role in building up the life of the individual, as well as its position in the original percept.

Long-term verbal memory is conceptual and influenced by the semantic category of the item to be recalled. Some theorists distinguish between semantic knowledge that is unrelated to temporal order (for example, word or object memory) and the recall of episodes. Yet all experience is initially episodic, so that we need to ask why some memories remain episodic and others become part of conceptual knowledge. One interpretation might be that the structure of a semantic category, the concept of a word or an object, is extracted or averaged from repeated exposures to instances of that word or object, with each instance or episode fading in relation to further encounters with instances of the same type. If one takes a train to work every day as I do, each trip is an event in episodic memory, but one that is lost in the succession of daily commutations. These episodes go into the topographical knowledge of routes rather than persisting as unique instances of one's experience with them. The same thing happens when we are repeatedly exposed to instances of the object *chair* or its verbal label. The averaging of like encounters builds up our knowlege of the world and the conceptual store. Accordingly, it is a matter of degree whether a representation is episodic or conceptual, since retrieval never exactly reproduces the original perception. The conceptual element is active to the extent to which the representation deviates from the to-be-remembered event.

The gradient in forgetting from episodic to conceptual is to be expected, given the greater difficulty retrieving a specific event as opposed to retrieving the knowledge derived from many such events. However, conceptual knowledge may not be retrieved in the same way as episodic knowledge. Conceptual memory is implicit in retrieval; it has an effect on the way in which any content is retrieved. Conceptual knowledge is applied at successive points in the recall of episodes. The real issue, therefore, in the question of the permanence of memory is the possibility of a loss of conceptual memory, not episodes, because episodes naturally disappear in the constant building up of categories. The enrichment of these categories is the other side of normal forgetting.

Along these lines, it may be that the episodic-semantic distinction applies also to short-term memory, for example, to the difference between a phonological sequence and an abstract phonological code. In short-term memory the sequence of sounds that represent an utterance or the flow of objects before the viewer comprise an episodic component linked to spatiotemporal events in the world. From the chunks that constitute the short-term span, common properties may be extracted that concern phonological rather than semantic categories, or the spatial attributes of objects rather than their meanings. In both long- and short-term memory, episodic memory would refer to the retrieval of a unique event, and conceptual memory to the retrieval of an average or ideal of many related events.

Learning

Surface levels show a "magic writing pad" effect; events fade rapidly to make way for new impressions. The opposite seems true of deep levels. There is a long-term persistence of traces, consolidation and growth. However, this difference, which appears so fundamental, may be exaggerated. Learning inheres at every stage in perceiving. The more we study an object the more we perceive its detail. When a piece of music is fully learned the notes are heard selectively. The fine tuning of attention to the features of a familiar object is an instance of learning at the perceptual surface. What is lacking, perhaps, are the contextual effects and averaging of like configurations prominent at early stages. Of course, there are other differences. Surface objects are facts in the world, not in the mind. Learning "at the surface" is a phenomenon outside the self. The stability of the world depends on such learning. One can say that learning at deep levels in perception establishes the growth and continuity of the personality, while learning at surface levels in perception establishes the endurance and continuity of the external world.

Microgenetic theory predicts that cognitive processing is allied to organic growth trends. Cognition repeats the pattern of evolutionary and, to a lesser extent, ontogenetic growth. There is a profound relation between process and growth. Growth is process etched in over time, while process is like instantaneous growth. Process seems impersistent compared to growth, but the element of growth in process is learning.

After all, the brain itself is an ancestral memory. Patterns of cell growth and connectivity established during learning are the same as those laid down in fetal life and early development. Thus, line detection in visual cortex of newborn kitten, its loss with visual deprivation and enhancement with stimulation, constitute a model of genotypic memory, trace decay or forgetting, and learning as a continuation of organic growth trends. Similarly, left-right asymmetries in dendritic arborization have been described in Broca's area, indicating that the neural change accompanying the learning of vocalization may an expression of a normal growth trend.

Skill

Skill is retrieval (action or perception) in the absence of representation, when a performance is overlearned and the representation is rapidly traversed, or when a representation is not involved from the beginning. In learning a task a representation is prominent. If the task is well learned and proceeds rapidly, the representation is lost. This is the meaning of the automatization of a skill. The accelerated processing traverses the stage of the representation. This interpretation depends upon the view that the representation is a preliminary stage in the unfolding of a behavior and not a plan that precedes it. This is why, when a learned task is obstructed, the representation reappears.

Early learned tasks are said to be "wired in" to the brain. Skills learned early in life or highly overlearned may be more "tightly wired" and less accessible to consciousness. The amnesia for childhood is a sacrifice of representation for skill. The forgotten memories of childhood are the ground out of which other representations arise. One can say that cognition is built up from these early memories, which have become unconscious skills.

The tendency for certain behaviors to become automatized leads to a consideration of the nature of a "rule," because the more skillful or automatized a performance, the more rule governed it seems. Performances like speaking or walking or perceiving are more or less automatic. They are regular and lawful, and give the impression of rules applied to subsurface elements. Rules are principles that interpret the predictability of a behavior. They are descriptions of relations between representations and not determinants that act upon them. In perception or in language, in constancy effects or in the rules of syntax and phonology, the rule is a description of the recurrence of an event in a certain context. The event is the representation, the context is the set of relations configuring the event. Rules are inferences about relationships between object representations that guide the processing along.

As a performance becomes a skill, we lose those representations that appeared as signposts of incompleteness in the performance. The representations become actualized in the behavior and are lost as mental events. A skill is like a well-traveled path in action or in object formation. The landmarks along the path can be described, the shrubs, the rocks, and the valleys; these are events in perception, but where is the path? It exists in the relations between these events. The choice of a path over other paths, the logic of the path, these are the rule, while the facility that comes of repeated encounters is the skill. Put differently, skill is an account of cognitive processing highly constrained in relation to a specific performance. Rules are attempts to capture the relations that govern this process, and representations are the actual configurations that undergo transformation.

Amnestics can learn skills that are not composed of representations. These are activities in which the behavior does not lead to a representation if it is terminated prematurely. These "procedures" are like the interstices of representations, involving relational values that are not pegged on static events. In this respect, the procedure is like a rule, a relational feature unaccompanied by conscious representation. A relational feature can serve as a basis for introspection; one can represent—talk or think about—a procedure or a rule. But one can also think about unicorns and three-headed fairies. The ability to conceptualize something does not imply that the thing conceptualized is real. In the case of procedural memory, an amnestic subject may retrieve skills that are rule governed, though event memory is lost. This entails the effectuation of perceptual or action patterns guided by relations laid down between the patterns in the absence of a mental representation. The observation that procedural memory may survive a loss of event memory—but apparently not the other way around—tells us that representation is more vulnerable to pathology than skill. The one-way dissociation is interpretable in terms of level of disruption and/or differences in perceptual and action learning, not in terms of separate systems underlying these activities (see below).

Action Memory

We do not have mental representations of actions, only their perceptual correlates. Actions do not participate directly in conscious experience—an action is not a conscious representation. This means that the conscious recall of an action is not a true action memory but a perceptual image derived from motor elements in the behavior. Put differently, motor skill is an example of retrieval in the absence of representation; there is nothing to be retrieved in the elaboration of an action but the action itself. There are, of course, representations that accompany the learning of a skill, but these are laid down as perceptual correlates that do not mediate the skill—once it is learned or even at the beginning.

Motor learning, therefore, is learning pure and simple, the facilitation of a series of transformations through repetition. Motor learning is expressed directly, in the degree to which an act is automatized, or indirectly, in the mastery of procedures that are extracted—averaged—from recurrent behaviors. Conceivably, a regularity in the transformational sequence through which the action configuration develops establishes a pattern, not for the sequence but for the elicitation of that sequence in a given context.

Motor learning is closely linked to learning in perceptual systems. Action involves configurations that are like perceptual representations; in both there is a reiterated process in which partial components are selected out of background formations with an appearance of rules—relations between representations—guiding the process along. These rules constitute a type of "grammar" for action and perception, as in language. The analogy to a grammar is demonstrated in the retention of performances in amnestics (for example, the Tower of Hanoi puzzle) that involve a strategy of recursive embedding. Such rules or processing interactions appearing in the absence of (conscious) representations account for the learning of procedures as opposed to the learning of motor routines.

The sparing of *procedural* memory in some amnestics is perhaps based on common perceptual and motor mechanisms. The profoundly amnestic patient HM has procedural memory along with the ability to learn certain motor and perceptual tasks. Skills acquired through "rule" learning in procedural memory do not flow from a separate memory, but are linked to processing constraints in the realization of act and object representations.

Acts develop outward from the body axis to the distal extremities and individuate like objects into featural elements positioned in an external world. The progression of an action from an archaic motility about the midline of the body to the fine digital movements parallels the course of object development from deep contextual layers to an analysis of features at the surface of the representation. Actions, like objects, proceed through a series of context to item transformations.

The similarity between act and object implies that motor learning is more complex than a strengthening of the concatenations between motor elements. For one thing, there are state changes at successive points in the transitional series. Archaic motility is characterized by intense affectivity or drivelike states and the discharge or "release" of well-organized instinctual behaviors—for example, sexual or other displays. These behaviors are encapsulated "action memories" and point to early stages in the action program. This behavior is comparable to dream hallucination in the perceptual series. In both, an archaic level—normally intermediate—constitutes a cognitive endpoint. Moreover, just as in waking perception an incomplete series may result in memory images and ideas, so there is the possibility that attentuated actions have residual cognitive effects though it is unclear what form these effects would take. Does an incompletely retrieved action generate "unconscious" representations equivalent to those at the same stage in the perceptual series? Are action configurations "read off" through recurrent collaterals as incomplete percepts and secondarily represented in mental imagery (inner speech, kinaesthetic imagery, etc.)?

Habit

Habits are complex actions that have become stereotyped or ritualized. According to Bergson, habit memory is habit illuminated by memory rather than memory itself. I would interpret this to mean that the condition of habit can be represented as an idea but it is the representation, not the thing represented, that illustrates the process of memory. Habit unfolds like a procedure and does not have the character of a representation. Moreover, the problem of habit as memory is a reminder that the memory image is the crucial instance of remembering, or there is a danger of being overtaken by the immensity of the memory problem. In a sense, all behavior and all of one's mental life is an expression of memory. Is a motor tic distinguishable from more complex daily habits or these from the overall pattern of behavior? Where is the line between habit and routine, or between a routine and a life-style? Each day, after all, is built on the experience of the past, and both the past and its experience have to be continuously renewed. In perception, the image is given to us; it is a construction of a personality even though there is a feeling that a person reaches into a memory to retrieve it. The memory image is an artifact of the way in which objects develop. Actions undergo a development in which conscious representation does not play a part. In action, memory is realized directly in spite of an impression that the act is hunted up and consciously motivated. Memories of actions are images in perception, not action memories. The action memory is the action itself.

Habit reveals to us in recurrent or compulsive activity the reiterative quality of everyday behavior. Habit is the intuition of a deeper reality, that actions, both simple and complex, are not invented but retrieved. The action calls itself up and elaborates the feeling of agency and volition. In other words, actions are not willed, but are recalled into behavior. However, since actions, like perceptions, are not looked up but derived, and since the process of derivation involves a transition through a multitude of competing configurations, including those laid down by the immediately preceding behavior, the same action cannot be selected more than once. The probability of growth at deep levels in action organization, and the fact that actions emerge through a transitional series, provide a basis for novelty in behavior. Novelty, which reflects a deviation at some point in the context-to-item sequence, is part of the problem of memory, for the element of imprecision in habit is the key to an understanding that habit and originality are variants of the same operation.

However, it is not habit that claims our attention, but patterns in the life history of the individual of which habits are only one manifestation. If habit is construed as an action memory, and if a continuum is accepted between creativity and automatism—one that reflects the degree of deviation in the course of object formation—and if a state of decision making (the awareness of action and the decision to act) is something that is deposited by the action, not something propelling it, at what point does action as memory become action as spontaneous behavior? We come at last to see that actions are not instigated but revealed, and that in a very real sense, a personality—habits and all—unfolds as a sort of living memory, reconstructed each moment as a mental representation—a memory image—of oneself.

Pathology of Memory

In amnestic disorders there is a failure in the spontaneous evocation of a mental image, though other aspects of thinking, perception and language appear to be relatively normal. The gradient in severity from an impairment in recognition to a more severe impairment in retrieval is characteristic of most amnestic states and reflects the fact that, in retrieval, spontaneous evocation is required. Recognition is the simpler performance because sensory information aids in the elicitation of the target configuration. Put differently, the more the performance depends on spontaneous image formation the greater the disruption of recall. In some cases the disparity is enough to suggest a problem limited to retrieval. The central defect, however, is an inability to select a configuration through stages in long-term memory to the point of a conscious mental representation. The content remains unevoked or insufficiently evoked, submerged in preliminary cognition unavailable to ongoing perceptual awareness.

Amnesia

In amnesia, the disruption seems to be at the point where a configuration is first activated out of the resting state through brainstem or limbic mechanisms. Lesions of basal forebrain, medial thalamus, limbic system and upper brainstem give the picture of impaired evocation. The symptom is the mirror of the normal processing at the point of disruption. Depending on the degree of selection of the object, something of the configuration may survive, though generally with some alteration in awareness of content. It is not that something is lacking in the recollection; the unretrieved content has features of preliminary cognition.

This may explain evidence of memory without awareness, and cases where material that is incorrectly retrieved has a conceptual link to the target content. For example, severe amnestics may show dream recall for unrecollected fragments of the preceding day. This is an exaggeration of a normal phenomenon that was first described by Freud. There is also the preservation of affect memory described by Korsakoff in alcoholics with neuropathy undergoing painful nerve stimulation as a form of therapy. The patients did not recall the sessions but refused to return for further treatment. In a celebrated observation, Claparede concealed a pin in his palm while shaking hands with amnestics. On a subsequent encounter, the patients did not recall meeting him before but refused to shake his hand again. The amnestic HM could not recall his father's death but became sad when his father was mentioned in a conversation. These and similar observations indicate that contents that are missing in recall persist as symbolic or affective precursors or formative stages in the to-be-remembered event.

The idea that amnesia is not the failure to retrieve items but an incomplete object formation helps to explain the findings of Betlheim and Hartmann (1951), who described Korsakoff patients with dreamlike transformations on story recall. For example, patients might recall the story of a violent rape as a woman burned to death in a fire. Such phenomena reflect the arousal of prefigurative content in the memory image to a stage of affective, symbolic and experiential relations prior to the conceptual and spatial resolution of the image and its final conscious representation.

Context and Item

One source of amnesia might be a disruption in the contextual assimilation of novel events with past experience. The process of assimilation occurs in the consolidation phase of learning, that phase during which an electrophysiological state is thought to be transformed to a durable trace. But consolidation is more than the laying down of new memories. Recent events have to be woven into the life history of the individual. We know that retrieval from long-term memory is context-sensitive; the context around an event is essential for the activation of patterns leading to the selection of that event, so that the establishment of context for an item, the integration of the item within the network of past experience, is part of what consolidation involves.

Contextual effects, moreover, occur at each stage in retrieval, and at each stage it is necessary to arouse the context around a configuration in order for that configuration to be accessed. The event is isolated from the context and then serves as context for the next derivation. Since the context really consists of all of the other potential events that are part of the same concept or category, the transition from context to event is very much like the transition from one processing stage to the next. For this reason it is doubtful that an event can be stored independent of the context required to elicit it. The event is a phase in a continuum; one moment it is event, the next moment it is context for another event. There is a reiterated ground-to-figure, surround-to-center, or context-to-item process, always in the same direction and so evanescent that the distinction of context and item is fundamentally a theoretical, not a practical issue.

Dream and Confabulation

Dream aids or is an expression of this integration process. Events that are incompletely revived reappear in dream but with distortion. Head-injured cases with retrograde amnesia often forecast in dream their eventual recall of amnestic experiences. There is a common basis of dream, confabulation (fabrication) and intrusion (reiterative or substitutive) errors. In confabulation, a subject is said to "fill in a gap" in memory with false recollection. But the patient may confabulate on future events, and confabulation may occur with little in the way of memory disorder. This is because confabulation represents a deviation in the path of recall, a displacement at a conceptual, a phrasal or intersentential stage in language formulation.

There is, in fact, a continuum from the conceptual derailment of confabulation (where ideas or whole concepts are substituted) to the lexical derailment of aphasia (where words are substituted), and cases occur with fluctuation from one symptom to another. Like the symbolic distortions of dream, which point to an early stage in object development, confabulation is a sign of incomplete verbal recall. Dream and confabulation are parallel phenomena in the microgenesis of percepts and utterances. The intrusion phenomena that occur spontaneously and on learning experiments are like confabulations at the word level. In each of these cases, dream, confabulation, intrusion errors, the nature of the content that is retrieved characterizes a particular stage in the perceptual or verbal specification of the event out of long-term memory or, put differently, out of preliminary stages in the original percept.

Retrograde Amnesia

In retrograde amnesia, the contextual arousal of contents in long-term memory pertaining to a certain period of time is impaired. In cases of head injury there is often an initial amnesia covering a duration of several weeks or months, which may then shrink down to include only those few moments before impact. After recovery, there is a persistent gap, though memory is otherwise normal. One way of thinking about an island of amnesia is to compare it to the *normal* amnesia for sleep and the immediate presleep period. In some respects, retrograde amnesia is like a capsule of the amnesia problem. In fact, HM compared his amnesia to the forgetting of a dream on awakening.

The amnestic syndrome is like a permanent retrograde amnesia, or one that is continuously reinstated. When one considers what is involved, it is no wonder that injury to temporal lobe and limbic structures disrupts recall. The arousal of a pattern of activity associated with an event must entrain millions of neurons. Pathology disengages these patterns, however subtly, altering the complex series of context-to-item transforms in recognition and retrieval through which events develop. The more severe the disruption the more it erodes into the ongoing contextualization of prior events. This in turn impacts on the duration of retrograde amnesia and the impairment of new learning. Object perception is preserved, less so in some categories of amnesia, through constraints provided by the object stimulus. The knowledge of familiar objects and their function is relatively normal, but recognition of recent objects (events) is impaired. The intensity of the disorder across these various performances reflects the interaction of recency (contextualization) and constraints on context-to-item processing afforded by the presence of an object and the object situation.

In addition, there is in retrograde amnesia the factor of conscious state, or state-specificity. It seems likely that contents can be retrieved no further than—if as far as—the level to which they were originally processed. An event experienced in a dream or trance state, a state of preliminary cognition, cannot be derived to normal wakefulness. The shift in conscious state on falling asleep, like that in concussion, explains part of the period of retrograde amnesia. Of course, in sleep, contextualization of recent material up to the brief presleep amnesia continues in a normal manner, in fact through the very limbic and temporal lobe systems that are active in dream cognition, whereas in concussion it is precisely these systems that are damaged.

Contextualization and the Function of Dream

The world of independent objects develops in the private space of long-term memory, with context appearing at the beginning of the object experience, not added to the object at a later stage. Though objects develop out of memory, they do seem to undergo subsequent growth and change. However, it is unclear whether changes in memory over time reflect a reworking of the item or an uncovering of formative stages as the object undergoes regression.

The growth of an object in long-term memory parallels the withdrawal of the object to an early phase in object formation. The reappearance of the object in preliminary cognition—for example, dreaming about an object experience—is linked to the time course of decay in normal forgetting. Preliminary stages in the original object, recaptured in the course of forgetting, are liberated from the constraints of daytime perception to participate with other prefigurative contents. In other words, objects from the preceding day(s) withdraw as forgetting proceeds, a withdrawal that continues to a level coinciding with that of dream cognition. Since in dream these preliminary stages are not constrained to conscious images or objects but actualize as endpoints, the regression of the object releases a dynamic there in the background, and this regression allows formative elements in the object to be incorporated by or assimilated to other dream contents.

According to this interpretation, normally submerged dream contents surface as an endpoint in object formation when sensory information is insufficient to constrain processing to an external object. The lack of external stimulation leads to a disinhibition of the dream content and an active play of imagery. The failure to derive preliminary cognition to the mental representations of waking life permits a free and unconstrained flow of unconscious material and, as a result, a reconfiguration of existing content. The destructuration of an object as it decays brings the context underlying that object into relation with that of dream and promotes the assimilation of the new with the old and novel recombinations of both. This process is bound up with and dependent on the rate of memory decay so that forgetting—the retreat of an object and its return to buried or traversed processing stages—is an essential part of the growth of new form.

Dream rises to meet receding memory patterns and envelops the content in an archaic mode of thinking centered in affective tonality and symbolic transformation. In this way, early stages in the microtemporal history of the object are assimilated with early stages in the life history of the organism. The function of dream, therefore, is a commingling of the antecedents of object representations, and the enrichment of deeper form-building contextual layers giving rise to the objects of the ensuing day.

In cases of dream deprivation or pathological imagery these early stages reappear as hallucinations or intrusive memory images. The deprivation studies indicate that the reworking of perceptual material in dream is essential to the maintenance of normal object perceptions. Perhaps an interruption of the dream-work results in a discontinuity of perceptual objects and a dissociation of these objects from the inner life of the perceiver. There is a failure to weave new objects into the life story, a rupture of links between past and present, and a breakdown of the perceptual world. The disintegration of objects in people who are deprived of dream accompanies an emergence of subsurface content: imagery, hallucination and associated changes in affect and behavior. Such cases demonstrate that objects are not neutral entities in a disinterested outer space, but mental products flowing from the life experience of the observor.

In perceiving, categories are combed for instances with a progression from the general to the specific. Recognition involves relations of similarity and the averaging of like configurations. In dream, other mechanisms come into play, or operations that are in the object but are inobtrusive come to the fore. Condensation, fusion and displacement are correlates of underlying physiologic events. Configurations are evoked that reflect thematic, experiential relations of the object or object class and serve as bridges to new categories. Properties of objects aroused as anticipatory contents call up like attributes of unrelated objects. This gives rise to fusions across objects that are otherwise disparate (e.g., the fusion of blood and fire-engine, mediated by the shared color red). Perceptual attributes bind objects (e.g., knife = penis) along a psychoanalytic dimension. Fragments of these transformations in language and perception are also seen in pathological cases.

Accuracy in Recall

An old problem in memory study concerns the basis for the assessment of accuracy in recall. How is recollection judged as inaccurate or incomplete unless there is a template of the memory, a standard of comparison, against which the recollected event is gauged. Donald Norman (in Malcolm, 1977) put the issue directly: "If you know the answer for which you are looking, then you wouldn't need to look. But if you don't know the answer, then how can you recognize it when you find it?" This implies a sort of match between bits and memoranda or items in a store and items in recall. Conversely, the appeal to unretrieved traces in judgments of accuracy exposes the partial or reconstituted character of contents that are retrieved, underscoring the idea of a base level out of which surface representations differentiate.

In pathological cases with simple amnesia, there is awareness of the memory deficit, but this awareness is usually lost in patients with fabricated or deviant recollection, especially in cases with florid symptoms. This implies an awareness that is intrinsic to the representational content. That is, configurations laid down in the course of retrieval elaborate the awareness state within which the judgment of accuracy will be made. Put differently, the judgment is part of the representation, not a critique elaborated through independent processes.

Incomplete recall is judged inaccurate by virtue of a surface representation that insufficiently realizes the underlying content. The feeling of inaccuracy in the representation is a feeling of incompleteness; like a word that is searched for, it is a sign that anticipatory stages in that representation are undepleted and that the object that is selected, if any, is inadequate to actualize content latent in its own preparatory phases.

The feeling of reality of a representation is linked to the judgment of accuracy. A memory image that achieves a perceptual quality, as in hallucination, may be taken for an object, not a recollection. The mental image loses its mnemonic character, its subjectivity and relation to the life of the perceiver, when it attains an objectlike status. There is a transition from a memory image that is recognized as corresponding with a prior (subsurface) event to an object representation that is apprehended as external and independent. When a memory image develops to this point—or, more commonly, when an object undergoes a momentary attenuation—there is a *deja vu* experience, the evanescent feeling, actually the intuition, that objects, even novel ones, have a basis in personal memory.

12
Emergence and Time

Emergence

Emergence is the idea that qualitative changes in a system may occur which have characteristics not anticipated by preceding states. Bunge (1977) has argued that emergence is a characteristic of the aggregate of a system; otherwise, each component would be required to have the properties of the whole. In principle, emergence could be accounted for by interaction among the components of a system. The question, then, is what is the emergent property that is explained in this way?

In evolution, the idea of emergence has been resisted by those who consider it a metaphor for entelechy or *élan vital*. The problem is that the emergent step does not lend itself to analysis. Can an emergent system have causal properties? Presumably, if we knew all there was to know of a particular state, what appears as an emergent from this state could be explained or predicted on a quantitative basis. For example, when ice melts to water and then vaporizes to steam, each appears as a different *qualia* but occurs on a continuum of physical change. Are emergents really "resultants" awaiting physical explication? In evolutionary theory the question of emergence is difficult to assess. It is not even clear what would be required to confirm or disconfirm the idea.

In some instances, emergence refers to the appearance of a behavioral (mind) state out of a physiological (brain) state—that is, to the mind-body problem. Or, emergence is used to describe successive levels in a systems organization, e.g., molecular → biological → mental → social. In neuropsychology, emergence can be applied to the problem of part:whole relationships. Partial functions may coalesce in a manner to suggest emergent phenomena. This was the view of the Gestalt theorists, and it has recently been advocated by Sperry (1976). Of course, it is not clear how the effect occurs. One interpretation is that the frequencies of different oscillators (cells, machines) are mutually entrained, or synchronized, by virtue of their belonging to a single interconnected group. There is certainly good reason to believe that oscillatory systems play an important role in speech and motor function (Brown, 1982).

*From "Emergence and Time in Microgenetic Theory" by J. W. Brown, 1983, *Journal of the American Academy of Psychoanalysis, 11,* 35–54. Copyright © 1983 by John Wiley & Sons, Inc. Adapted by permission.

Dewan (1976) has indicated various ways in which the coupling of oscillators might lead to a superordinate regulator, and has drawn an analogy between the emergence of such a regulator and the idea that mind emerges out of a distributed neural system. The problem with this analogy is that new levels in a physical or neural series are still neural and not mental levels.

Still, cell columns and modules do enter into circuits which elaborate new levels of organization. Individual cells probably participate in many different behaviors, making it impossible to specify the function of a particular neuron. The "function" of a brain area is not a composite of the functions of cells in that area but emerges out of the constituent routines of networks of cells. This has been shown for brainstem neurons (Seigel, 1979) and can also be argued for neocortical systems (Butter, 1980). These considerations suggest that emergence applies within, but, perhaps not across, a mental or a physiological series. Emergence characterizes the progression over levels in behavior, or transitions over physiological states, but not the elaboration of a behavioral state or a series of states by a physiological one. This is a more focused use of the term for transformations within a series of the same generic type.

The few experimental studies that investigate this issue generally have not addressed this interpretation but rather the possibility of an emergent passage from the physical to the mental—for example, categorical perception studies which show that discrete intervals in a physical (acoustic) series of synthetic speech sounds do not regularly conform to differences in perception: perception imposes categories upon these stimuli. The *physical* continuum between two sounds within the same phonetic category is continuous with sounds in a neighboring phonetic category. However, a subject will discriminate two sounds adjacent on the physical continuum best at the category boundary. This shows that physical or acoustic differences between the sounds are less salient than the abstract category to which the sounds belong. These findings are of a piece with data on perceptual illusions and constancies, which also indicate that contents in the mind do not run parallel to external stimuli. But the question that should be asked is, does emergence occur across levels in cognition? Is there a gap which qualifies as an emergent step?

In an emergent system, the relationship between levels in behavior is not that of domination of the lower by the higher but rather, as Bunge (1977) states, one of precedence. This is in contrast with the Jacksonian concept that "higher" levels hold in check the "lower" ones. In neurology, it is common thinking that lower centers are "released" when inhibition from above is interrupted. But one can also say that a disruption of "higher" levels results in a prominence of more preliminary states, not because they are disinhibited but because they are not derived to the "higher" level. The labile and precipitate quality of "released lower levels" is the natural expression of preliminary cognition when it actualizes prematurely.

In microgenetic theory there is a fixed and reiterated sequence of levels underlying every act of cognition. Although successive levels reciprocally modulate preceding ones, a behavior does not result from the interaction between two or more levels but is a manifestation of the unfolding sequence. That is, the unfolding lays down the behavior which is itself hierarchically structured. The question of emergence in a system such as this, whether it occurs over the series of physiological or cognitive levels, depends on our concept of the nature of a level and the transition from one level to another.

What is a Level?

In a microgenetic system, as in evolution or development, the unfolding of events occurs in one direction only. Microgenesis involves a forward transition from one cognitive level to another. It is this unfolding from one level to the next which may have emergent properties. But what is a level and what is a transition? How does something which is one moment transitional become the next moment a level?

The problem has to do with the stability of psychological levels, whether they are fixed components in mental structure or determined by whatever psychological events happen to crystallize at a given moment. If they are fixed components, one might ask whether cognitive change occurs in the transition from one level to another. That is, is a transition a bridge between components or an active transformation? If the latter, this would mean that the transitional segment is also a kind of level. Alternatively, cognition may unfold as a continuum, like waves piling upon the shore. In this case, levels would be arbitrary demarcations without significance other than as conceptual anchors.

In principle, a continuum could terminate at any point, and the point of termination would constitute a level. The "level" would be the end stage of a processing sequence. But what happens to stages which are traversed on the way to this end stage? Are they given up in the formation of the next segment in the sequence, or do they persist in some manner in the final state?

One way of thinking about levels concerns their relationship to memory. The retrieval of an experience in memory involves a calling up of past—or subsurface—content which is still in some sense available to the subject in the present. When we retrieve a memory in the past we access a content that is buried within the present at a deeper level of processing. It may well be that retrieval and microgenesis involve the same set of operations. This means that the mental state of an ongoing perception develops *out of* memory components, and that these memory components are active in the formation of the state, not deposited after the state has occurred. Later on in this paper it is proposed that the ability to access a memory might be a function of the distance—or depth—of the memory from the end-stage cognition. For example, when we speak of a "subconscious idea" we are referring to content in long-term memory which has, because of the depth of its representation, limited access to the present state.

This implies that in some ways a level is a hypothesis about the structure of memory. The idea of discrete mental levels is probably untenable if there is a graduated access to preliminary contents, or if the series leading to the end stage decays in a constant manner, that is, if each stage in the processing sequence decays according to its position in the temporal series. A system of stratified levels would seem to require a discontinuity in the decay of preliminary points, i.e., both access and decay would be determined by the level within which the event falls, not by its relative position in the processing sequence, and thus there would be a kind of "all or none" phenomenon in retrieval (see below).

In addition to the "vertical" extent of a level there is also the question of its "horizontal" distribution. Does a level incorporate all neural components at the same phyletic stage? Is a level specific to one perceptual system or does it consist of all perceptual channels which achieve a comparable stage of processing? Presumably, the level established in each perceptual modality has access to concurrent depositions in other modalities at or about the same end point. On this the pathological material is helpful, indication that under certain conditions an end-stage level may lack access to preliminary contents in another destructured modality (Brown, 1983b). Thus, in cortical blindness the phenomena of "blind-sight," in which subjects are unaware of their rudimentary perceptions, or "Anton's syndrome," in which they deny their blindness, occur because there is incomplete access of the waking cognitive level to the level of the destructured perception.

Saltatory or Continuous?

In part, certain of the problems which arise on attempting to define a level occur because it is unclear whether processing is nodal or continuous. If it is nodal, then a level would correspond to a node, and a transition would correspond to a conduction system between nodes. The situation is more complex in a continuous system. One could still have a level, but the level would have emergent properties.

To make this clearer, consider a series of transitional states. One can speak of the *distance* of the transition from the starting point of the series to the end point. Along this transition, there may be a maximal distance or interval over which one state can access another prior state. In order to be accessed by— incorporated in—a subsequent state of greater total distance, i.e., a more fully unfolded cognition, the interval between two states ought not to exceed a certain critical distance. Perhaps a term such as *segment* could be applied to the maximum length of access over a continuous series of states. A segment would then be an average critical distance.

In this transitional sequence, there may be a finite number of segments within which a set of end points is clustered (saltatory) or the segment may be an arbitrary construct. In other words, the continuum may be segmented so that the end points fall into one segment or another, or the segments may be determined by the end points. In the first case, a cluster of states within a segment would be isolated from a cluster just outside of that segment. In the second case, clusters would overlap so that access would depend on the relative psychological distance between discharge points, i.e., on the critical distance of a segment (Figure 12-1).

If the segmentation is nonarbitrary, there would be a kind of emergence across transitions between each segment (level). In the case of an arbitrary segmentation, the reinstantiation of a segment would require a match of one end point to another. An emergence would not occur across points in the continuum. Rather, the constant flux of differing though overlapping segments would somehow coalesce to form an average segment which would give the appearance of one or more stable levels in the mind. Stated differently, in the case of a fixed (saltatory) segmentation (Figure 12-1A), there would be an emergence from one mind state to another across the segment boundaries. The stability of a mind state would be guaranteed by the reproducibility of the segmentation. In the case of an arbitrary segmentation (continuum), a mind state would emerge from a succession of everchanging segments (Figure 12-1B). This would appear to have the consequence of an infinite number of mind states, given that a level is determined by an arbitrary end point. The process would be that of a continuous forward surge with a rapid and incessant turnover of innumerable end states. The distillation of these segments into a unitary self which is stable over time, and the continuity of the self developing out of repeated approximations to the same discharge point would constitute an emergence of a different type than that occurring in a system of fixed segmentation.

These two ways of viewing the microgenetic process recall the debate among evolutionary theorists over sudden quantum advance as opposed to gradual incremental change. How could one decide which of these two organizations prevails? In the first system, that of fixed levels, one might assume an equal access to all states falling anywhere within a segment. In the latter, access within

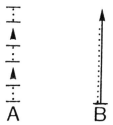

FIGURE 12-1. In a system of fixed segmentation (A), discharge points (dots) fall within a level. The transitions between levels may have an emergent character. In a continuum (B), there is a perhaps infinite number of discharge points. Levels would arise as emergents from the repeated approximations of successive discharge points to the same locus.

a segment depends on the distance between states. Perhaps this could be assessed in maturation, where successive states are spread out over development. One example is amnesia involving early childhood, a type of forgetting on a state-dependent basis. It would be of interest to know whether the ability to access the first few years of life declines gradually into adolescence, or whether it shows a sudden drop at some point in childhood, say at or about the latency period.

These reflections on the nature of levels in a microgenetic system, and the possibly emergent character of transitions between them, the forward direction of these transitions, and the idea that levels in memory are recaptured in the microgenetic sequence, lead to a consideration of the *structure* of a microgenetic traversal, the time course of this traversal, and how a succession of individual brain states builds up and sustains the cognitive flow.

Brain State and Minimal Perceptual Duration

In the foregoing account, psychological events are assumed to occur as reiterated unfoldings over brain structural levels. Each unfolding retraces the same path as the preceding one. The reiteration of the same structural level in every performance establishes a continuity in the mental life which the system generates, while the dynamic nature of the configurations which unfold allow for the possibility of change, creativity and mental growth. In other words, a single microgenetic traversal constitutes a kind of minimal or irreducible unit of cognition. According to this view, a *brain state* refers not only to the end point of a microgenetic series but to the immediate temporal program through which the end point is laid down. This is because the meaningful unit of cognition is the complete series, and not an individual level. In this way a state and a level differ. The level is an inference about the stages through which a state has developed. The state incorporates all such "levels" traversed in the development. A state does not provide a starting point from which another series ensues, but gives way to a new development rising from below.

A *brain state,* therefore, is not a momentary activity pattern but one that arises in a certain spatiotemporal context. The temporal context is analogous to the minimal perceptual duration (see below), and represents the transition time of a single microgenetic series. The brain state is the activity pattern at the beginning of this series up to and including the end stage. The spatial context refers to the distribution of components within each microgenetic level. The brain state is distributed *spatially* over evolutionary structure, and *temporally* over the microgenctic transition time.

The Now

The immediate present, the Now, corresponds to a brain state as defined above. The "perceptual moment hypothesis," in which the immediate present is conceived as a series of about 0.1-sec perceptual frames (Stroud, 1956;

Blumenthal, 1977), provides the basis for a concept of the duration of the Now. This duration comes from numerous psychophysical studies, particularly simultaneity judgments, and is variable depending on modality and task (Efron, 1967; Thatcher & John, 1977). The microgenetic approach takes the perceptual moment hypothesis one step further, in proposing a substrate for the phenomenon, and an account of what transpires during the interval, namely a single unidirectional traversal, from the bottom up, over the infrastructure of cognition (perception).

The immediate present is the experience *within* a perception, the perception experiencing itself. In the succession of microgenetic states, each new state replaces the preceding one as it trails off in the decay of short-term memory (STM). The present decomposes and is renewed as a new present emerges over the replenished surface of the past. The Now is maintained through a continuous outpouring from STM and LTM (Figure 12-2).

This is not a movement into the future; the direction of the process is from depth to surface, not from past to future. Moreover, the succession is not clearly linked to an extrinsic physical series, but is a *replacement of one state by another*. States develop and subside like reverberating chords that grow ever dimmer. The Now of one moment recedes as the Now of the next is developing. In this way, the succession of microgenetic states maintains the continuity of the mental life. The "stream of consciousness" is not a flow from one operation to the next but a tidal surge of innumerable microgenetic traversals repeatedly unfolding to a common end point.

Short-Term Memory and the Immediate Past

While the Now persists for only a fraction of a second, its *apparent psychological* duration is somewhat longer, depending on the duration of STM included as part of the immediate present. Lashley (1951) pointed to this problem in his celebrated example, "Rapid righting with his uninjured hand saved from loss the contents of the capsized canoe." Is "rapid righting" part of the immediate

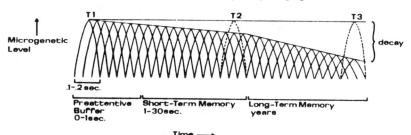

FIGURE 12-2. Each new state (T) develops over previous states which are attenuated. The degree of attenuation, or decay, of a past state within a present state determines the "component" in memory which is retrieved in the present state. The Now of brain state T_1 decays to STM within the Now at T_2, and to LTM within the Now at T_3.

present when the Now is filled by the word "canoe?" This is just a more convincing example of the everyday experience, that one retains over fairly long intervals the thread of a conversation, the development of a visual scene, the progression or inconsistency of an idea or story, the referential content of pronouns, or the sequence of changes in the position of an object. The fact that these contents are available to the Now for about 10–30 seconds has suggested that the duration of the present, the "specious present" of William James, extends over a longer period than the minimal perceptual duration. Lashley's idea of a mechanism which scans memories in the space-coordinate system does not account for the phenomenon, but only adds another mechanism to be explained. The problem is that there is no clear limit as to the duration of memory included in the immediate present. If contents in STM are part of the Now, why not still earlier contents in "working memory?"

How can we understand the role of STM in the consciousness of the immediate present? Viewed as a flow of events from one moment to the next, the Now seems like the cutting edge of STM. Similarly, the Now of a moment ago seems part of an immediate past which is held onto. But as a flow from moment to moment, what knowledge could the Now have of a past already in decay? How does the Now lay claim to something that lies behind it? The answer to this is that STM is not really in the past of the present Now; it is not something that the Now has to search out as a secondary process. The Now unfolds over the residue of the past, a past which is active and alive in the substructure of the Now. Events decaying in STM, working memory, or LTM continue to influence events in the Now because these components are levels through which the Now is derived. The perception, the Now, incorporates these levels as part of its preliminary development. It is structured out of LTM and STM. This is why a perception is never entirely free of influences from preceding perceptions.

Neural structures active in the elaboration of the Now comprise a series of distributed systems—actually evolutionary growth planes—leading from archaic limbic formations to more recent primary sensory (konio)cortex (see Brown, 1983b). These systems can be thought of as levels in the perception which mediate successive moments in its unfolding. The developing percept sweeps over these levels and so activates LTM and STM contents as the percept is generated. In this view, the infrastructure of the object is multitiered and stratified, with earlier levels persisting abstractly even as the final stage of processing is realized (Figure 12-3).

Attention and Temporal Disorientation

The state of attention is the behavioral signal for whatever cognitive level predominates at a given Now. Attention is the behavioral manifestation of a perception. Focal attention is perception at the surface, a perception individuated about features in an object-centered space. Diffuse attention is an attenuated perception organized about subsurface components.

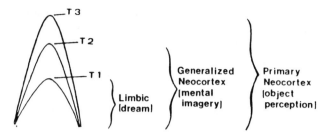

FIGURE 12-3. Attenuated percepts from earlier Nows at T_1 and T_2 form processing stages in the elaboration of the Now at T_3. These earlier stages correspond to neural systems over which the percept unfolds. T_1 corresponds to limbic processing and LTM; the more recent Now of T_2 corresponds to processing at generalized neocortex and STM. T_3 represents the derivation of T_1 and T_2 to a stage of primary cortex and object perception.

The perception of time cannot be dissociated from the state of attention. Patients with attention disorders are disoriented in time, not just clock time, the date or hour of the day, but in the apparent temporal succession of mental events. There is an inability to cognize instances in an object array. Perception is less differentiated and attention is dispersed over the object field.

Attentional disorder is part of a confusional state; it is what confusion is. A disturbance of focal attention gives rise to a state of diffuse attention. Diffuse and focal attention refer to preliminary and end-stage perceptions. With preliminary objects, attention is equally distributed over the object field. With focal attention, there is the ability to attend to specific objects and their features. Focal attention characterizes a completed object development. In states of diffuse attention, in confusional states, the Now coincides with preliminary cognition. Other signs of this are prominent imagery and hallucinations, pronounced affective tonality, and aphasic symptoms. There is an inability to maintain the thread of a conversation, with derailment or confabulation in discourse; the speaker becomes incoherent. Presumably the speech of others seems incoherent as well.

These symptoms occur with an attentuation of the Now. One could say that STM becomes the surface of preception. The result should be a more rapid transition time, though not necessarily a change in the rate of replacement of one state by another, and thus a decrease in the minimal perceptual duration. This change would have the effect of abolishing the fine incrementation of the immediate past, which depends on the normal decay of the Now to STM. Incoherence in speech and perception would result from a disturbance in the implicit effects of STM on the Now, the lack of structuring of the Now within the context of the immediate past, and a loss of the continuity of mental life.

Ordinarily, we attribute the confusion to bilateral or diffuse brain involvement. It can also occur with bilateral thalamic lesions (Brown, 1974). Efron thought the left temporal lobe was responsible for time judgments. If this were true, temporal disorientation should occur in posterior aphasia. So far, the results are not encouraging (Kreindler & Fradis, 1968). Even global aphasics show up "on time" for therapy visits. Still, there are cases of temporal lobe pathology where time seems to accelerate or stand still. This also occurs in schizophrenics (Schilder, 1936; Arieti, 1974). Thus, psychotics with a loss or emptiness of the time experience were described by Fischer (1929). Lewis (1932) found cases with an inability to evoke the past, or a difficulty in distinguishing between past and future. This seemed to occur in patients with depersonalization, regardless of the etiology. Arieti also noted a tendency in schizophrenics for a progressive restriction to the present. There are, in fact, experimental studies which indicate that schizophrenics have impairments in anticipating short intervals (King, 1962), in estimations of duration (Hamon & Goldston, 1956) and sequence (Jenkins & Winkelman, 1966). The possibility of temporal lobe dysfunction in schizophrenics might help to explain these alterations of the time sense.

Patients with bilateral temporal lesions are often confused during the acute period. This is characteristic of "cortical" and "word" deafness. Generally, the confusion abates in the post-onset period and is not present in chronic cases. Indeed, I have studied a case of bilateral temporal lobe pathology with incomprehensible jargon, where there was no obvious confusion (Perecman and Brown, 1981). The phonological deficit in this patient should have precluded a Now organized solely about auditory language perception. Similarly, patients with acute cortical blindness are usually confused and may have a Korsakoff syndrome. This too may gradually disappear and is not necessarily related to a change in vision. Such cases indicate that the Now is constructed about visual *and* auditory perceptions and that it can be disturbed transiently when one modality is disrupted bilaterally.

The confusional state is a disturbance of incremental time, an inability to estimate and feel brief durations. Whether the feeling for the distant past is affected is not known, though most likely there is a comparable change. In my view, it is a microgenetic imperative that processes underlying judgments of duration for STM in the "specious present" are identical to those for LTM in the distant past. This is because duration is computed from decay, and STM and LTM are markers of the decay process. What, then, is the "feeling for duration" and how does it arise in relation to levels in memory?

The Feeling of Duration

In general, the concept that evolutionary and maturational time are collapsed within the cognitive dynamic applies equally to the problem of temporal integration in perception. The idea that the history of a perception is not really in the past of that perception but is submerged within its structure raises the possibility that the depth of the past within the Now is the source of the feeling of duration. In other words, the feeling for duration is linked to the progressive attenuation of STM and LTM within the microgenetic structure of the immediate present

(Figure 12-2). Specifically, the "vertical separation," or interlevel distance between levels in STM and LTM is interpreted as a longitudinal axis extending back into an illusory past.

Knowledge and Memory

The duration of the past can be *known* and can be *felt*. These two ways of experiencing the past are ordinarily bound up together, but they may dissociate in pathological states. The ability to date a remote event and the relatedness of the event to others about the same time build up a framework of knowledge that masquerades as a sense of duration for time past, and a feeling for the precedence of past events. However, to place an event 10 years in the past is not the same as to have a feeling for a 10-year interval. Does anyone truly *feel* the passing of an hour or a day? Do we not exclaim how hard it is to believe (feel) that 10 years have gone by? We say that an experience 10 years ago or even the past weekend *feels* like only yesterday. Yet the past can be reconstructed. To a limited extent, we can also say that an event of one year preceded or followed an event of another, though probably there is inaccurate assignment of precedence for remote events within a particular year. This kind of reconstruction is like the recounting of a story about oneself and is not really a part of the time problem. The reconstruction extends the feeling for duration secondarily. It is not a true duration judgment. Without such reconstruction, there would be a dramatic contraction in the genuine feeling for the past. This is because perceptions in LTM are compressed, with a kind of foreshortening effect of depth on duration judgment. Studies of amnestic patients, where there may be a diminished reconstructive effect, could provide some support for this hypothesis.

We know that the sense of duration persists through sleep, anesthesia, perhaps even through periods of coma. Subjects required to awake after a number of hours commonly awake at the determined time (Zung & Wilson, 1971). If they are awakened during the night, they can often give a reasonable estimate of the correct time. I have confirmed this in my own spontaneous awakenings. It seems not to be the correct time that is apprehended but the time inferred from sleep duration. Ehrenwald showed that hypnotized subjects estimated time intervals during sleep even more accurately than normals.

Korsakoff cases, known since Korsakoff's own observations to have difficulties in the temporal ordering of events, are said to show good time appreciation under hypnosis. I have seen postencephalitics who reported some feeling of time passing in spite of a total lack of recall for the amnestic period. Richards (1973) reached a different conclusion in a study of time reproduction in H.M., a patient with a bilateral surgical lesion of the temporal lobes and a profound learning deficit following the procedure. This patient had minimal recall for new material over many years following the operation, and a retrograde deficit extending back one or two years. Such cases raise the question of time perception for an extended interval for which there is little if any recall. In this patient, normal reproductions were found for the STM span, but there was a systematic contraction for longer intervals. Richards speculated that several years would seem to H.M. like several hours. If so, this would represent the true *feeling* for duration deprived of its autobiographical reconstruction.

On the other hand, the pathological may only be an exaggeration of the normal tendency in this direction. In psychophysical studies, intervals beyond the STM span are normally underestimated. In my experience, if one simply asks Korsakoff patients for estimates of the duration of an interview, or the duration of their hospital stay, they are usually fairly accurate. I am less certain of their accuracy for longer periods—for example, the duration of their amnesia. Schilder mentioned a patient with a memory loss of one month who felt that about a month had passed since his last recollection. There is an amnestic like H.M. studied by Squires and his colleagues, who has shown normal personality development over the amnestic gap.

The Nature of Duration Judgments

These signs of a feeling for time passing and personality growth point to a preliminary cognition which underlies the present moment. This preliminary cognition is still active in sleep, presumably during anesthesia and over an amnestic gap. This indicates that the inability to retrieve content in LTM during an interval does not directly affect the estimation of the duration of that interval, and that the feeling of duration does not require that the events which fill an interval be recalled. This is because the duration estimate is not computed from storage during the interval but in relation to the decay of the onset point.

However, events during an interval may extend its apparent duration in two ways. First, the lack of interference might slow the rate of normal forgetting and lead to a contraction of duration judgments. Second, the lack of recall would prevent secondary reconstruction, and this would have essentially the same effect. In other words, excessive contraction or underestimation of duration in amnestics compared to normals could reflect either a lack of interference or an absence of reconstruction or both, since these would lengthen the feeling for duration. In the one case, this would occur through increased attenuation of the onset point; in the second, through the interplay of knowledge structures. Still, the feeling for an "unfilled" duration should be present. In fact, this model predicts that in a hypothetical case where cognition is suspended for an interval but normal forgetting for the last recalled event is allowed to occur—perhaps as in coma—the vacant interval could be computed when the Now is reestablished.

In sum, duration judgments are inferences derived from the depth of events in STM or LTM in relation to the end point of the Now. The extent of retrieval influences the feeling for interval length. For events in the distant past there is a contraction of the interval such that durations of 5, 10, or 20 years can be distinguished *(felt)* only indirectly through an autobiographical reconstruction. What is recalled is the saga of one's life, not the temporal encoding of the events which have transpired. New events are simply added on to an existing story. This gives rise to an idea about the duration of time past but not a true feeling for interval length. The outcome is that the *feeling* of duration does not truly extend beyond a matter of days, weeks, perhaps months, except as it is reconstructed from the life story. Events are not encoded in terms of time, they are not lined up in a sequence which recaptures their order of occurrence. Rather, time is encoded in terms of the depth of events in relation to the unfolded level of the Now.

The Content of the Interval

The importance of amount or complexity of information processed during an interval on judgments for the duration of that interval has been stressed in psychophysical theories of temporal distrimination (Allen & Kristofferson, 1974). Most studies show that, at least for brief durations, "filled" intervals are judged longer than "unfilled" ones. The idea is that an increased amount or complexity of information requires more "storage space" and that this is reflected in longer durations. But what is the meaning of "storage space," or complexity, or amount of processing? What is more complex, watching a display of lights in a laboratory chamber, or gazing out of a crowded room at a panoramic view of east side Manhattan? Does the latter require more storage space, more processing time? Does it seem to last longer?

While filled intervals are judged longer, "empty" time seems to pass slowly. Hartocollis (1975) has explained this through a focusing of attention on time or events. This suggests that the degree to which events are actively cognized plays a role in duration judgments. One prediction of the microgenetic account is that the extent to which an event is retrieved should influence the feeling of its recency. Specifically, the interval following a past event should shrink as the event approximates the original perception. If a past event is retrieved to the point where it is actually perceived, for example, an hallucination, it is felt as an experience in the present. Conversely, intervals expand in relation to forgetting. "Empty" time seems longer because there is nothing to remember. This enhances interlevel distance and exaggerates the feeling of duration. Time filled with exciting events passes quickly because the events are vivid and their imprint mitigates somewhat the degree to which retrieval is attenuated. Now the interlevel distance is narrowed and the duration seems shorter.

However, there is a limit to the influence of affect, interest and event complexity on time perception. Interlevel transitions, memory decay and retrieval, and the relationships between levels should be relatively independent of the information which is fed into them. The information determines the processing level, which determines the nature of the information stored; but fundamentally, it is the rhythmic replacement of microgenetic states and the orderly decay of each state within the next that underlies the time sense. In other words, the overall framework of time perception is derived from the intrinsic properties of the system and not from the input.

The "Clock" of Subjective Time

The iteration of perceptual moments at a frequency on the order of 10 per second suggests the possibility of a "biological clock," not one that simply ticks off moments in psychological time but a rhythmic generator underlying the minimal perceptual duration. The frequency of the clock would not be interpreted as a natural increment of subjective duration. It is not even clear that subjective time is incremented in this way. The "clock" would be a biological rhythm initiating the microgenetic series at its base and determining the tempo of replacement of one state by another.

There are two basic intervals to be considered, the duration within and between states. First there is the *Microgenetic transition time,* the minimal perceptual duration, the time required for a single state to unfold depending on the degree of completion. Second, there is the *replacement time,* the "pulse rate" for the succession of microgenetic states. This is probably quite regular, though possibly it is altered in fever or hypothermia, mania, depression, perhaps in other conditions. The replacement time is the basis for duration judgments since it determines the interval between successive Nows, and thus the decay period for each Now in relation to the next. Conceivably, there is a correspondence between the replacement frequency and refractory period of the base level. Perhaps there is also a correspondence between the microgenetic transition time and the replacement frequency.

With regard to mechanism, there is considerable evidence for intrinsic rhythms in different brain structures. In particular, oscillators have been demonstrated in the upper brainstem, organized about the sleep/wake cycle (Buser, Bouyer, & Buser, 1978) and in locomotor and respiratory synergies (Schepelmann, 1979). Conceivably, the fundamental frequency of the base rhythm elaborates a series of (harmonic?) derivations through oscillators at successive microgenetic levels. If so, this would mean that the base or nodal frequency is considerably slower than its subsequent derivations. The resultant rhythmic structure would be the physiological carrier of the cognitive process (Brown, 1982).

A biological rhythm of this type may underlie temporal discrimination, but does not explain the continuity of the self over time. As long as there is a Now there can be no discontinuity in mental life. It is not the continuity from Now to Now that is crucial—not the linkage of successive Nows—but the continuity from depth to surface in the unfolding of each Now. The Now does not have a critical frequency for "psychological fusion"; it is not like a frame in a movie reel. The continuity of the self is guaranteed by the fact that the Now is generated over levels confluent with LTM and STM. Each Now is a microcosm of the personality. The distant past and the immediate present, one's history and thus one's self, are revived in every perception.

References

Ackerly, S. & Benton, A. (1948). Report of a case of bilateral frontal lobe defect. *Association for Research in Nervous and Mental Disease, 27,* 479–504.

Adams, J., & Malamud, N. (1981). Severe chorea with degeneration of the nucleus centrum medianum. *Archives of Neurology (Chicago) 24,* 101–105.

Agadjanian, K. (1946). *Le mécanisme des troubles perceptives-associatifs en rapport avec l'origine de l'hallucination et du delire.* Paris: Peyronnet.

Ajuriaguerra J. de, & Hecaen, H. (1956). *Revue Neurologique, 94,* 434–435.

Ajuriaguerra, J. de (1957). Considération sur les troubles de la conscience à partir de faits anatomo-cliniques, In *Les états de conscience en neurologie.* Proceedings, Premier Congress International des Sciences Neurologiques, Brussels.

Ajuriaguerra, J. de, & Hécaen, H. (1964). *Le cortex cerebrale,* Paris: Masson.

Ajuriaguerra, J., de, Strejilevitch, M., & Tissot, R. (1963b). A propos de quelques, conduites devant le miroir de sujets atteints de syndromes dementiels du grand age. *Neuropsychologia, 1,* 59–73.

Alajouanine, T. (1956). Verbal realization in aphasia. *Brain, 79,* 1–28.

Alajouanine, T., Lhermitte, F., & Riboucourt-Ducarne, B. (1960). Les alexies agnosiques et aphasiques. In *Les Grandes Activites du Lobe Occipital.* Paris: Masson.

Alajouanine, T., & Lhermitte, F. (1963). In L. Halpern, (Ed.), *Problems in dynamic neurology Jerusalem.* p. 201–216.

Alajouanine, T. & Lhermitte, F. (1964). Aphasia and physiology of speech. In D. Rioch & E. Weinstein (Eds.), *Disorders of communication.* Baltimore: Williams & Wilkins.

Alajouanine, T. & Lhermitte F. (1965). Acquired aphasia in children. *Brain, 88,* 653–661.

Alajouanine, T., Lhermitte, F., Ledoux, M., Renaud, D., & Vignolo, L. (1964). Les composantes phonémiques et sémantiques de la jargonaphasie. *Revue Neurologique, 110,* 5–20.

Alajouanine, T., Ombredane, A., & Durand, M. (1939). *Le syndrome de desintegration phonetique dans l'aphasie.* Paris: Masson.

Alajouanine, T., Sabouraud, P., & Ribaucort, B. de (1952). Le jargon des aphasiques: désintégration anosognosique des valeurs sémantiques du language. *Journal de Psychologie Normale et Patkologique, 45,* 158–80; 293–329.

Albert, M., Feldman, R., & Willis, A. (1974). The subcortical dementia of progressive supranuclear palsy. *Journal of Neurology, Neurosurgery and Psychiatry, 37,* 121–130.

Albert, M., & Obler, L. (1978). *The bilingual brain.* New York: Academic Press.

Albert, M., Reches, A., & Silverberg, R. (1975–1979). Associative visual agnosia without alexia. *Neurology, 25,* 322–326; *29,* 876–879.

Albert, M., Reches, A., & Silverberg, R. (1975). Hemianopic colour blindness. *Journal of Neurology, Neurosurgery and Psychiatry, 38,* 346–349.

Albessar, R. (1934). *L'hallucinose pédonculaire.* Paris: Doin.

Alexander, M. P., & LoVerne, S. R. (1980). Aphasia after left hemisphere intracerebral hemorrhage. *Neurology, 30,* 1193–1202.

Allen, L. & Kristofferson, A. (1974). Psychophysical theories of duration discrimination. *Percept. Psychophys., 16,* 26–34.

Allen, C., Turner, J., & Gadea-Ciria, M. (1966). Investigations into speech disturbances following stereotactic surgery for Parkinsonism. *British Journal of Disorders of Communication, 1,* 55–59.

Allison, R. (1966). Perseveration as a sign of diffuse and focal brain damage. *British Medical Journal* 1095–1101.

Allman, J., & Kaas, J. (1974a). A crescent-shaped cortical visual area surrounding the middle temporal area (MT) in the owl monkey (Aotus trivirgatus). *Brain Research,* 1974, *81,* 199–213.

Allman, J., & Kaas, J. (1974b). The organization of the second visual area (V II) in the owl monkey: A second order transformation of the visual hemifield. *Brain Research, 76,* 247–265.

Allport, G. (1928). The eidetic image and the after-image. *American Journal of Psychology, 40,* 418–25.

Anderson, J. (1978). Arguments concerning representations for mental imagery. *Psychological Review, 85,* 249–77.

Anderson, K., & Symmes, D. (1969). The superior colliculus and higher visual functions in the monkey. *Brain Research, 13,* 37–52.

Anderson, M., & Salmon, M. (1977). Symptomatic cataplexy. *Journal of Neurology, Neurosurgery and Psychiatry, 40,* 186–191.

Anderson, S. & Jaffe, J. (1973). Eye movement bias and ear preference as indices of speech lateralization in brain. (*Scientific Report* No. 15). *Department of Communication Sciences,* New York State Psychiatric Institute.

Angelergues, R., Hécaen, H., Djindjian, R., & Jarrie-Hazan, N. (1962). Un cas d'aphasie croisée. *Revue neurologique, 107,* 543–545.

April, R., & Han, M. (1980). Crossed aphasia in a right-handed bilingual Chinese man. *Archives of Neurology, 30,* 342–346.

April, R., & Tse, P. (1977). Crossed aphasia in a Chinese bilingual dextral. *Archives of Neurology, 34,* 766–770.

Archibald, Y., & Wepman, I. (1968). Language disturbance and non-verbal cognitive performance in eight patients following injury to the right hemisphere. *Brain, 91,* 117–130.

Arieti, S. (1974). *Interpretation of schizophrenia*. New York: Basic Books.

Arkin, A. & Brown, J. W. (1971). Resemblances between NREM associated sleep speech, drowsy speech, and aphasic and schizophrenic Speech. In *Association for the Psychophysiological Study of Sleep, 253*, First International Congress, Bruges, Belgium, June 19–23.

Aronson, E. & Rosenbloom, S. (1971). Space perception in early infancy: perception within a common auditory-visual space. *Science, 172,* 1161–1163.

Arrigoni, G., & DeRenzi, E. (1964). Constructional apraxia and hemispheric locus of lesion. *Cortex, 1,* 170–197.

Assal, G., Perentes, E., & Deruaz, J. P. (1981). Crossed aphasia in a right-handed patient. *Archives of Neurology 38,* 455–458.

Attneave, F., & Farrar, P. (1977). The visual world behind the head, *American Journal of Psychology, 90,* 549–68.

Auerbach, A. (1978). Experimentally induced visual hallucinations in the rhesus monkey. In D. Chivers and J. Herbert (Eds.), *Recent advances in primatology* (Vol. 1). New York: Academic Press.

Babb, T., Wilson, C., Halgren, E., & Crandell, P. (1980). Evidence for direct lateral geniculate projections to hippocampal formation in man. *Neuroscience Abstracts, 6.*

Bailey, P., & von Bonin, G. (1951). *The isocortex of man.* Urbana, IL: University of Illinois Press.

Baker, R., & Berthoz, A. (Eds.). *Control of gaze by brain stem neurons. Developments in neuroscience* (Vol. I). Amsterdam, Elsevier.

Balint, R. (1909). Seelenlahmung des "Schauens," optische Ataxie, raumliche Störung der Aufmerksamkeit. *Monatschrift fur Psychiatrie und Neurologie, 25,* 51–81.

Bancaud, J., Talairach, J., Geier, S., Bonis, A., Trottier, S., & Manrique, M. (1976). Manifestations comportementales induites par la stimulation electrique du gyrus cingulaire antérieur chez l'homme, *Revue Neurologique, 132,* 705–724.

Bancroft, J., & Barron, D. (1937). The genesis of respiratory movements in the foetus of the sheep. *Journal of Physiology, 88,* 56–61; *91,* 329–361.

Banna, M., K. Adams, E. Tunks, and M. Finlayson (1978). Computed tomography after psychosurgery. *Journal of Computer Assisted Tomography 2,* 98–99.

Barat, M., Mazauz, J., Bioulac, B., Giroire, J., Vital, C., & Arne, L. (1981). Troubles du langage de type aphasique et lesions putamino-caudees. *Rev. Neurol., 137,* 343–356.

Bard, L. (1905). De la persistance des sensations lumineuses dans le champ aveugle des hemianopsiques. *Semaine Medicale, 25,* 253–255.

Barlow, T. (1877). *British Medical Journal, 2,* 103.

Barraquer-Bordas, L., Mendilaharsu, C., Peres-Serra, J., et al. (1963). Estudio de dos casos de afasia cruzada en pacientes manidextros *Acta Neurologica Latino America, 9,* 140–148.

Bartlett, E., Brown, J. W., Wolf, A., & Brody, J. (1987). Correlations between glucose metabolic rates in brain regions of healthy male adults at rest and during language stimulation. *Brain and Language, 32,* 1–18.

Basser, L. (1962). Hemiplegia of early onset and the faculty of speech with special reference to the effects of hemispherectomy. *Brain 85*, 427–447.

Basso, A., Bisiach E., & Luzzatti, C. (1980). Loss of mental imagery: a case study. *Neuropsychologia, 18*, 435–441.

Bastian, H. C. (1869). On the various forms of loss of speech in cerebral disease. *The British and Foreign Medico-Chirurgical Review 43*, 209–236, 470–492.

Bastian, H. C. (1898). *Aphasia and other speech defects*. London: (Reprint, AMS Press, New York, 1984)

Bateman, F. (1980). *On aphasia and localization of the faculty of speech* (2nd Edition). London: Churchill.

Behrman, S., Carroll, J., Janota, I., & Matthews, W. (1969). Progressive supranuclear palsy: Clinicopathological study of four cases. *Brain, 92*, 663–678.

Bell, D. (1968). Speech functions of the thalamus inferred from the effects of thalamotomy. *Brain, 91*, 619–638.

Bender, M., Feldman, M., & Sobin, A. (1968) Palinopsia, *Brain 91*, 321–338.

Bender, M. & Krieger, H. (1951). Visual function in perimetrically blind fields. *Archives of Neurology and Psychiatry, 65*, 72–99.

Bender, M., & Teuber, H.-L. (1946). Nystagmoid movements and visual perception. *Archives of Neurology and Psychiatry, 55*, 511–29.

Bender, M., & Teuber, H.-L. (1947/1948). Spatial organization of visual perception following injury to the brain. *Archives of Neurology and Psychiatry 58*, 721–739; *59*, 39–62.

Bender, M., & Teuber, H.-L. (1949). *Psychopathology of vision*. In E. Spiegel (Ed.), *Progress in Neurology and Psychiatry*, New York: Grune & Stratton.

Benson D. & Patten D. (1967). The use of radioactive isotopes in the localization of aphasia-producing lesions. *Cortex 3*, 258–271.

Benson, D., Sheremata, W., Bouchard, R., Segarra, J., Price, D., & Geschwind, N. (1973). Conduction aphasia. *Arch. Neurol. 28*, 339–346.

Benton, A. (1968). Differential behavioral effects in frontal lobe disease. *Neuropsychologia 6*, 53–60.

Benton, A. (1969). Disorders of spatial orientation. In P. Vinken, & G. Bruyn (Eds.), *Handbook of clinical neurology*. Amsterdam: North-Holland.

Benton, A., & Van Allen, M. (1972). Prosopagnosia and facial discrimination. *Journal of the Neurological Sciences, 15*, 167–172.

Benton, A. (1977). The amusias. In M. Critchley & R. Henson (Eds.), *Music and the brain*. Springfield, MA: Charles C. Thomas.

Bergmann, P. (1957). Cerebral blindness. *Archives of Neurology and Psychiatry, 78*, 563–584.

Bergson, H. (1896). *Matter and memory*. (Engl. Trans., Doubleday, New York, 1959)

Berndt, R. (1985). A multicomponent deficit view of agrammatic Broca's aphasia. In: M-L Kean (Ed) *Agrammatism*. New York: Academic Press.

Bernheimer, S. (1899). Die Wurzelgebiete der Augennerven. *Handbuch der gesamte Augenheilkunde*, (Vol. VI, Part 2). Berlin: Springer.

Bernstein, N. (1967). *The coordination and regulation of movements*. London: Pergamon.

Bettelheim, S, & Hartman, H. (1951). On parapraxes in the Korsakow psychosis. In D. Rapaport (Ed.), *Organization and pathology of thought*. New York: Columbia University Press.

Bianchi, L. (1895). The functions of the frontal lobes, *Brain 18*, 497–530.

Bignall, K., Imbert, M., & Buser, P. (1966). Optic projections to nonvisual cortex of the cat. *Journal of Neurophysiology, 138*, 396–409.

Binet, A. & Fere, C. (1898). *Le magnétisme animal*. Paris: Alcan.

Birkmayer, W. (1951). *Hirnverletztungen*. Vienna: Springer-Verlag.

Bishop, G. (1959). *Journal of Nervous and Mental Disease, 128*, 89.

Bishop, G. (1961). The cortex as a sensory analyzer. In R. Jung, & H. Kornhuber (Eds.), *The visual system: Neurophysiology and psychophysics*. Berlin: Springer.

Bisiach, E. (1966). Perceptual factors in the pathogenesis of anomia. *Cortex, 2*, 92–95.

Bisiach, E. (1980). Commentary. *Behavioral and Brain Sciences, 3*, 499–500.

Bisiach, E., Capitani, E., Luzzatti, C., & Petani, D. (1981). Brain and conscious representation of outside reality. *Neuropsychologia, 1981, 19*, 543–551.

Bleuler, F. (1922). L'origine et la nature des hallucinations, *Encéphale 17*, 537–553.

Blumenthal, A. (1977). *The process of cognition*. Englewood Cliffs, NJ: Prentice-Hall.

Blumstein, S. (1970). In C. Gribble (Ed.), *Studies presented to Professor R. Jakobson by his students* (pp. 39–43). Cambridge: Slavica.

Blumstein, S. (1973). *A phonological investigation of aphasic speech*. The Hague: Mouton.

Blumstein, S. (1981). Phonological aspects of aphasia. In M. Sarno (Ed.), *Acquired Aphasia*. New York: Academic Press.

Bodis-Wolner, I., Atkin, A., Raab, E., & Wolkstein, M. (1977). Visual association cortex and vison in man. *Science, 198*, 629–631.

Bogen, J. (1976). Linguistic performance in the short-term following cerebral commissurotomy, In H. Whitaker & M. Whitaker (Eds.), *Studies in neurolinguistics* (Vol. 2, pp. 193–224). New York: Academic Press.

Boller, F. (1973). Destruction of Wernicke's area without language disturbance. *Neuropsychologia, 11*, 243–246.

Boller, F., & Green E., (1972). Comprehension in severe aphasics, *Cortex 8*, 382–394.

Bonvicini, G. (1926). *Wiener klinische Wochenschrifft 44*, 47.

Borod, J., Koff, E., Perlman, M., & Nicholas, M. (1983). *The expression and perception of facial emotion in patients with focal brain damage*. Presentation at the International Neuropsychology Society, Mexico City.

Botez, M., and Barbeau, A. (1971). Role of subcortical structures, and particularly of the thalamus in the mechanism of speech and language. *International Journal of Neurology, 8*, 300–320.

Botez, M., & Wertheim, N. (1959). Expressive aphasia and amusia following right frontal lesions in a right-handed man. *Brain, 82*, 186–203.

Botez, M., Serbanescu, T., Petrovici, I., & Vernea, I. (1965). Clinical and electrooculographic findings in Balint's syndrome and its minor forms. *Rapports du 8th Congress International de Neurologique, 3*, 183–187.

Braak, H. (1978). The pigment architecture of the human temporal lobe. *Anatomy and Embryology, 154*, 213–240.

Braak, H. (1980). *Architectonics of the human telencephalic cortex*. Berlin: Springer.

Brain, R (1954). Loss of visualization. *Proceedings of the Royal Society of Medicine, 47*, 288–290.

Brain, R. (1961). *Speech disorders: Aphasia, apraxia and agnosia*. Washington, DC: Butterworth.

Bramwell, B. (1898). *Brain, 21*, 343–373.

Bregeat, P., Klein, M., & Thiebaut, F. (1947). Hémianopsie homonyme droite et tumeur occipitale gauche, Revue d'Oto-Neuro-Ophtalmologie, *19*.

Brickner, R. (1936). *The intellectual functions of the frontal lobes*. New York: Macmillan.

Brindley, G. (1973). Sensory effects of electrical stimulation of the visual and paravisual cortex. In Richard Jung (Ed.), *Handbook of Sensory Physiology (Vol. 7/3B)*. Berlin: Springer.

Brindley, G., Gautier-Smith, P., & Lewin, W. (1969). Cortical blindness and the functions of the nongeniculate fibers of the optic tract. *Journal of Neurology, Neurosurgery and Psychiatry, 32*, 259–264.

Brindley, G., Goodwin, G., Kulikoski, J. & Leighton, D. (1976). Stability of vision with a paralyzed eye. *Journal of Physiology, 258* 65–66.

Brindley, G. & Lewin, W. (1968). The sensations produced by electric stimulation of the visual cortex. *Journal of Physiology, 258*, 479–493.

Brion, S. & Jednyak, C. (1972). Troubles du transfert interhémisphérique: A propos de trois observations de tumeurs du corps calleux. Le signe de la main etrangère. *Revue Neurologique, 126*, 257–266.

Broca, P. (1863). Localisation des fonctions cérébrales. Siege du language articulé. *Bull. Soc. Anthrop., 4*, 200–202, 208.

Broca, P. (1865). Du siege de la faculté du langage articulé. *Bull. Soc. Anthrop., 6*, 377–393; Discussion, 412–414, 417.

Bromberg, W. & Schilder, P. (1934). Olfactory imagination and olfactory hallucinations. *Archives of Neurology and Psychiatry, 32*, 467.

Browman, C. (1978, August) (1978). Tip of the tongue and slip of the ear: implications for language processing. *UCLA Working Papers, 42*.

Brown, J. W. (1967). Physiology and phylogenesis of emotional expression. *Brain Research, 5*, 1–14.

Brown, J. W. (1972). *Aphasia, apraxia, and agnosia: Clinical and theoretical aspects*. Springfield, IL: Charles C. Thomas.

Brown, J. W. (1973). Observations on cryopulvinectomy. In Cooper, I., Riklan, M., & Rakic, P. (Eds.), *The Pulvinar-LP Complex*. Springfield, IL: Charles C. Thomas.

Brown, J. W. (1974). Language, cognition and the thalamus. *Confinia Neurologica, 36*, 33–60.

Brown, J. W. (1975). On the neural organization of language: Thalamic and cortical relationships. *Brain and Language, 2,* 18–30.

Brown, J. W. (1976). The neural organization of language: Aphasia and lateralization. *Brain and Language, 3,* 482–494.

Brown, J. W. (1977). *Mind, brain and consciousness: The neuropsychology of cognition.* New York: Academic Press.

Brown, J. W. (1978). Lateralization: a brain model. *Brain and Language, 5,* 258–261.

Brown, J. W. (1979a). Language representation in the brain. In H. Steklis & M. Raleigh (Eds.), *Neurobiology of social communication in primates.* New York: Academic Press.

Brown, J. W. (1979b). Thalamic mechanisms in language. In M. Gazzaniga (Ed.), *Handbook of Neuropsychology* (pp. 215–236). New York: Plenum.

Brown, J. W. (1980a). Brain structure and language production: a dynamic view. In D. Caplan (Ed.), *Biological studies of mental processes.* Cambridge, MA: MIT Press.

Brown, J. W. (1980b). Visual discrimination after lesion of the posterior corpus callosum [Letter]. *Neurology, 30,* 1251.

Brown, J. W. (1981a). Image and object. *Journal of Mental Imagery, 5,* pp. 26–28.

Brown, J. W. (1982). Hierarchy and evolution in neurolinguistics. In M. Arbib, D. Caplan, & J. Marshall (Eds.), *Neural models of language processes.* New York: Academic Press.

Brown, J. W. (1983a). Emergence and time in microgenetic theory. *Journal of the American Academy of Psychoanalysis, 11,* 35–54.

Brown, J. W. (1983b). Microstructure of perception: Physiology and patterns of break-down. *Cognition and Brain Theory, 6,* 145–184.

Brown, J. W. (1983c). Rethinking the right hemisphere. In E. Perecman (Ed.). *Cognitive processing in the right hemisphere* (pp. 41–52). New York: Academic Press.

Brown, J. W. (1984a). Frontal lobe syndromes. In P. Vinken, G. Bruyn & H. Klawans (Eds.), (2nd ed.). Amsterdam: Elsevier. (Reprinted with additions in *Journal of Neurolinguistics, 1,* 31–77, 1985)

Brown, J. W. (1984b). Hallucination, imagery and the microstructure of perception. In P. Vinken, G. Bruyn & H. Klawans (Eds.), *Handbook of clinical neurology* (2nd ed.). Amsterdam: Elsevier. (Reprinted with additions in *Journal of Neurolinguistics, 1,* 89–141, 1985)

Brown, J. W. (1984c). Introduction to Bastian (1898).

Brown, J. W. (1984d). Review of *The expression of knowledge,* R. Isaacson and N. Spear (Eds.). *Journal of Nervous and Mental Disease, 172,* 232–234.

Brown, J. W. (1984e). Review of *Neuropsychology of human emotion,* K. Heilman and P. Satz (Eds.). *Journal of Nervous and Mental Disease, 172,* 628–629.

Brown, J. W. (1985a). Cognitive microgenesis: review and current status. *Progress in Clinical Neurosciences* (Vol. 2). Proceedings of the 35th Annual Conference of the Neurological Society of India, December, 1985.

Brown, J. W. (1985b). Commentary. In *The Behavioral and Brain Sciences, 8,* 588–589.

Brown, J. W. (1985c). Electrophysiological studies of aphasia: review and prospects. *Language Sciences 7*, 131–142.

Brown, J. W. (1987). The microstructure of action. In E. Perecman (Ed.), *The frontal lobes revisited*. New York: IRBN: Press.

Brown, J. W. & Grober, E. (1983). Age, sex and aphasia type. *Journal of Nervous and Mental Disease, 170*, 431–434.

Brown, J. W. & Hécaen, H. (1976). Lateralization and language representation. *Neurology, 26*, 183–189.

Brown, J. W. & Jaffe, J. (1975). Hypothesis on cerebral dominance. *Neuropsychologia, 13*, 107–110.

Brown, J. W., Leader, B., & Blum, C. (1983). Hemiplegic writing in severe aphasia. *Brain and Language 19*, 204–215.

Brown, J. W. & Perecman, E. (1985). Neurological basis of language processing. In J. Darby (Ed.), *Speech evaluation in Neurology*. New York: Grune Stratton.

Brown, J., Riklan, M., Waltz, J., Jackson, S., & Cooper, I. (1971). Preliminary studies of language and cognition following surgical lesions of the pulvinar in man (cryopulvinectomy). *Int. J. Neurol. 8*, 276–299.

Brown, J. & Wilson, F. (1973). Crossed aphasia in a dextral. *Neurology, 23*, 907–911.

Browne, W.A.F. (1890). Impairment of language, the result of cerebral disease. *West Riding Lunatic Asylum Medical Reports, London* (1872). Cited in *On aphasia and the localization of the faculty of speech* F. Bateman (Ed.), (2nd Edition). London: Churchill.

Brutkowski, S. (1965). Functions of prefrontal cortex in animals. *Physiological Review 45*, 721–746.

Bruyn, G. & Gauthier, J. (1969). The operculum syndrome. In P. Vinken and G. Bruyn (Eds.), *Handbook of clinical neurology* (Vol. 2). Amsterdam: North-Holland.

Buchsbaum, M., Ingvar, D., Kessler, R., Waters, R., et al. (1982). Cerebral glucography with positron tomography. *Archives of General Psychiatry, 39*, 251–259.

Buck, R. & Duffy, R. (1980). Nonverbal communication of affect in brain-damaged patients, *Cortex, 14*, 351–362.

Buckingham, H. W. & Kertesz, A. (1976). *Neologistic jargon aphasia*, Amsterdam: Swets & Zeitlinger.

Buckingham, H. W. (1981). Where do neologisms come from? In J. W. Brown (Ed.), *Jargonaphasia*. New York: Academic press.

Buell, S. & Coleman, P. (1979). Dendritic growth in the aged brain and failure of growth in senile dementia. *Science, 206*, 854–856.

Buge, A., Escourolle, R. Rancurel, G., & Poisson, M. (1975). Mutisme akinétique et ramollissement bi-cingulaire. *Revue Neurologique 131*, 121–137.

Bunge, M. (1977). Emergence of the mind. *Neuroscience, 2*, 501–509.

Burckhardt, G. (1891). Uber Rindenexcisionen als Beitrag zur operativen Therapie der Psychosen. *Allgemeine Psychiatrie, 57*, 463–548.

Buser, A., Bouyer J., & Buser, P. (1978). Transitional states of awareness and short term fluctuations of selective attention. In A. Buser & P. Buser (Eds.), *Cerebral correlates of conscious experience*. Amsterdam: North-Holland.

Butter, C. (1980). Commentary. *Behavioral and Brain Sciences, 3,* 500.

Butters, N., & Cermak, L. (1977). *How do amnesic patients encode faces?* International Neuropsychology Society Meeting, Oxford.

Butterworth, B. (1979). Hesitation and the production of paraphasias and neologisms in jargonaphasia. *Brain and Language 8,* 133–61.

Butterworth, B. (1985). Jargonaphasia: Processes and strategies. In S. Newman & R. Epstein (Eds.), *Current perspectives in dysphasia* (pp. 61–96). Edinburgh: Churchill Livingstone.

Cambier, J., Elghozi, D., & Strube, E. (1979). Hemorragie de la tete du noyau caude gauche. *Revue Neurologique, 135,* 763–774

Cameron, D. (1933). Mensuration in the psychoses. *American Journal of Psychiatry, 90,* 153.

Cameron, R., Currier, R., & Haerer, A., (1971). Aphasia and literacy. *British Journal of Disorders of Communication, 6,* 161–163.

Campbell, A. (1905). *Histological studies on the localization of cerebral function.* Cambridge.

Campion, J., Latto, R., & Smith, Y. (1983). Is blindsight an effect of scattered light, spared cortex and near-threshold vision? *Behavioral and Brain Sciences, 6,* 423–486.

Capgras, J. & Reboul-Lachaud, J. (1923) Illusion des sosies dans un delire systematise chronique. *Bulletin de la société clinique de médecine mentale, 2,* 6–16.

Caplan, D., Kellar, L., & Locke, S. (1972). Inflections of neologisms in aphasia. *Brain 95,* 169–172.

Cappas, S., Cavallotti, G., & Vignolo, L. (1981). Phonemic and lexical errors in fluent aphasia: correlation with lesion site. *Neuropsychologia, 19,* 171–177.

Caramazza, A., & Zurif, E. (1978). *Language acquisition and language breakdown.* Baltimore: Johns Hopkins.

Caramazza, A., Berndt, R., & Basili, A. (1983). The selective impairment of phonological processing: A case study. *Brain and Language 18,* 128–174.

Carlson, R. (1977). Frontal lobe lesions masquerading as psychiatric disturbances. *Canadian Psychiatric Association Journal, 22,* 315–318.

Castaigne, P., Buge, A., Cambier, J., Escourolle, R., Brunet, P., & Degos, J. (1966). Démence thalamique d'origine vasculaire par ramollissement bilatéral. *Revue Neurologique, 114,* 89–107.

Castaigne, P. and Graveleau, D. (1953). Aspects particuliers de certaines crises occipitales. *Revue Neurologigue, 88,* 286–287.

Cénac, M. (1925). 1976 *Les glossolalies.* Thèse, Faculté de Medecine, Université de Paris, Cited in A. R. Lecours, and M. Vanier-Clément.

Cermak, L and Butters, N. (1973). "Information processing deficits of alcoholic Korsakoff patients. *Quarterly Journal of Studies on Alcoholism, 34,* 1110–1132.

Chapanis, N., Uematsu, S., Konigsmark, B., & Walker, A. (1973). Central phosphenes in man: A report of three cases. *Neuropsychologia 11,* 1–19.

Chapman, J. (1966). The early symptoms of schizophrenia. *British Journal of Psychiatry 112,* 225–251.

Charcot, J. (1883). Un cas de suppression brusque et isolée de la vision mentale des signes et des objects, formes, et couleurs. *Progrès Médical*, 568–571.

Chauvel, P. (1976). *Les stimulations de l'aire motrice supplementaire chez l'homme.* Paris: These.

Chauvel, P., Bancaud, J. & Buser, P. (1985). Participation of the supplementary motor area in speech. *Experimental Brain Research, 58,* A14.

Chavany, J. (1942). Contribution à l'étude des localisations cérébrales. *Gazettes des Hôpitaux, 25,* 281–285

Chavany, J. & Rougerie, J. (1978). *Presse Médicale, 66,* 1191–1192.

Chedru, F. (1976). Space representation in unilateral spatial neglect. *Journal of Neurology, Neurosurgery and Psychiatry, 39,* 1057–1061.

Cheek, W., & Taveras, J. (1966). Thalamic tumors. *Journal of Neurosurgery, 24,* 505–513.

Christodoulou, G. (1977). The syndrome of Capgras. *British Journal of Psychiatry, 130,* 556–64.

Ciemins, V. (1970). Localized thalamic hemorrhage. *Neurology, 20,* 776–782.

Clarke, P., Wyke, M., & Zangwill, O. (1958). Language disorder in a case of Korsakoff's syndrome. *Journal of Neurology, Neurosurgery and Psychiatry, 21,* 190–194.

Clarke, P., & Zangwill, O. (1965). A case of "crossed aphasia" in a dextral. *Neuropsychologia, 3,* 81–86.

Cogan, D., Brooks, B., & Bajandas, F. (Eds.). (1977). *Eye movements.* New York: Plenum.

Cohn, R., & Neumann, M. (1958). Jargon aphasia. *Journal of Nervous Mental Disorders, 127,* 381–99.

Cohn, R., Neumann, M., & Wood, D. (1977). Prosopagnosia: A clinicopathological study. *Annals of Neurology, 1,* 177–182.

Collier, H., & Levy, N. (1982). Presentation, cited in Gorenstein (1982).

Collignon, R., Hécaen, H., & Angelergues, R. (1968). A propos de 12 cas d'aphasie acquise de l'enfant. *Acta Neurol Belg. 68,* 245–277.

Coltheart, M., Patterson, K. and Marshall, J. (Eds.). (1980). *Deep dyslexia.* London: Routledge & Kegan Paul.

Conrad, C., & Stumpf, W. (1975). Direct visual input to the limbic system. *Experimental Brain Research, 23,* 141–149.

Conrad, K. (1949). Über aphasische Sprachstörungen bei hirnverlezten Linkshänder. *Nervenarzt, 20,* 148–154.

Conrad, K. (1953). Un cas singulier de 'fantôme spéculaire.' *Encéphale 42,* 338–352.

Constantinidis, J., Tissot, R., & Ajuriaguerra, J. (1970). Dystonie oculo-facio-cervicale ou paralysie progressive supranucleaire de Steele-Richardson-Olszweski. *Revue Neurologique, 122,* 249–262.

Cooper, L. & Shepard, R. (1983). Chronometric studies of the rotation of mental images. In W. Chase (Ed.), *Visual information processing* New York: Academic Press.

Corkin, S., Twitchell, T., & Sullivan, E. (1979). Safety and efficacy of cingulotomy for pain and psychiatric disorder. In E. Hitchcock et al. (Eds.), *Modern concepts in psychiatric surgery.* Amsterdam: Elsevier.

Coryell, J. & Michel, G. (1978). How supine postural preferences of infants can contribute toward the development of handedness. *Infant behavior and development, 1,* 245–257.

Coslett, H. & Saffran, E. (1983). Preservation of lexical access in a patient with alexia without agraphia. Presentation, INS.

Cotman, C., Matthews, D., Taylor, D., & Lynch, G. (1973). *Proceedings of the National Academy of Sciences. 70,* 3473–3477.

Cremieux, A., Alliez, J., Toga, M., & Bruno, M. (1959). Tumeur thalamique à évolution démentielle rapide. *Annales Medico-Psychologiques, 117,* 508–517.

Creutzfeldt, O. (1977) Generality of the functional structure of the neocortex. *Naturwissenschaften, 64,* 507–517.

Critchley, M. (1950) Metamorphopsia of central origin. *Transactions of the Ophthalmological Society* (1949–1950), *69,* 111–121.

Critchley, M. (1951). Types of visual perseveration: "Paliopsia" and "illusory visual spread." *Brain, 74,* 267–99.

Critchley, M. (1955). Further remarks upon the phenomenon of visual perseveration. *Geseusch zu Würzburg, 67,* 26–37.

Critchley, M. (1955). Verbal symbols in thought. *Transactions of the Royal Medical Society, 71,* 179–194.

Critchley, M. (1962). Speech and speech-loss in relation to the duality of the brain. In V. Mountcastle (Ed.), *Interhemispheric relations and cerebral dominance.* Baltimore: Johns Hopkins Press.

Critchley, M. (1965) Acquired abnormalities of colour perception of central origin. *Brain, 88,* 711–724.

Critchley, M. (1966) *The parietal lobe.* New York: Hafner. (Reprint of 1953 edition).

Crosby, E., Humphrey, T., & Laner, P. (1962). *Correlative anatomy of the nervous system.* New York: Macmillan.

Crowell, D., Jones, R., Kapunai, L., & Nakagawa, J. (1973) Unilateral cortical activity in newborn humans, *Science. (New York), 180,* 205–208.

Cuenod, M., Casey, K., & MacLean, P. (1965) Unit analysis of visual input to posterior cortex. I. Photic stimulation. *Journal of Neurophysiology, 28,* 1101–1117.

Curtiss, S. (1977). *Genie: A psycholinguistic study of a modern-day "wild child."* New York: Academic Press.

Damasio, A., Damasio, H., & Chui, H. (1980). Neglect following damage to frontal lobe or basal ganglia. *Neuropsychologia, 18,* 123–32.

Damasio, A., Damasio, H., Rizzo, M., Varney, M., & Gersh, F. (1982). Aphasia with nonhemorrhagic lesions in the basal ganglia and internal capsules. *Arch. Neurol., 39,* 15–20.

Daniels, A. (1969). Thalamic degeneration, dementia and seizures. *Archives of Neurology (Chicago), 21,* 15–24.

Davison, K. & Bagley, C. (1969) Schizophrenia-like psychoses associated with organic disorders of the central nervous system. In R. Herrington (Ed.), *Current problems in neuropsychiatry.* Kent: Headley.

Deacon, T. (1988). Neuroanatomy applied to neuropsychology. In E. Perecman (Ed.). Integrating theory and practice in clinical neuropsychology. Hillsdale, N.J.: Lawrence Erlbaum Associates.

Deets, A., Harlow, H., Singh, S., & Bloomquist (1970). Effects of bilateral lesions of the frontal granular cortex on the social behavior of rhesus monkeys. *Journal of Comparative Physiology and Psychology, 72,* 452–461.

Dejerine, J. (1885). Étude sur l'aphasie. *Revue de Médecine, 5,* 174–191.

Déjerine, J. (1914). *Semiologie des affections du système nerveux.* Paris: Masson.

Dejerine, J., and Roussy, G. (1906) Le syndrome thalamique. *Revue Neurologique, 12,* 521–532.

Delaney, R., Rosen, A., Mattson, R. & Novelly, R. (1980). Memory function in focal epilepsy. *Cortex, 16.* 103–17.

Delay, J., & Brion, S. (1962). *Les Démences Tardives* Paris: Masson.

Dell-Osso, L., & Troost, B. (1977). The ocular motor system: Normal and clinical studies. In B. Brooks & F. Bajandas (Eds.), *Eye movement.* ARVO Symposium, 1976; New York: Plenum.

Denes, G., & Caviezel, F. (1981). Dichotic listening in crossed aphasia. *Archives of Neurology, 38,* 182–185.

Dennett, D. (1985). *Elbow room.* Cambridge, MA: MIT Press.

Dennis, M., & Whitaker, H. (1976). *Brain and language, 3,* 404–433.

Denny-Brown, D. (1951). The frontal lobes and their functions. In A. Feiling (Ed.), *Modern trends in neurology.* London: Butterworth.

Denny-Brown D., Meyer, J., & Horenstein, S. (1952). The significance of perceptual rivalry resulting from parietal lesion. *Brain, 75,* 433–471.

Denny-Brown, D. (1958). The nature of apraxia. *Journal of Nervous and Mental Disease. 216,* 9–32.

Denny-Brown, D., & Chambers, R. (1976). Physiological aspects of visual perception. *Archives of Neurology, 33,* 219–227.

Denny-Brown, D., & Fischer, E. (1976). Physiological aspects of visual perception. *Archives of Neurology, 33,* 228–242.

DeRenzi, E. (1971). Visual agnosia and hemispheric locus of lesion. *Fortbildungskurse schweize. gesamte Psych., 4,* 57–65.

DeRenzi, E. (1982). *Disorders of space exploration and cognition.* New York: Wiley.

DeRenzi, E., Scotti, G., & Spinnler, H. (1969). Perceptual and associative disorders of visual recognition. *Neurology, 19,* 634–642.

DeRenzi, E., Pieczuro, A., & Vignolo, L. (1966). Oral apraxia and aphasia. *Cortex, 2,* 50–73.

De Voogd, T., & Nottebohm, F (1981). Gonadal hormones induce dendrite growth in the adult avian brain. *Science, 214,* 202–204.

Dewan, E. (1976). Consciousness as an emergent casual agent in the context of control systems theory. In G. Globus, G. Maxwell, and I. V. Savodnik (Eds.), *Consciousness and the brain.* New York: Plenum.

Diamond, I. (1979). The subdivisions of neocortex: A proposal to revise the traditional view of sensory, motor and association areas. *Progress in Psychobiology and Physiological Psychology, 8,* 1–43.

Diamond, I., & Hall, W. (1969). Evolution of neocortex. *Science, 164,* 251–262.

Dide, M. (1938). Les desorientations temporo-spatiales et la preponderance de l'hemisphere droit dans les agnoso-akinesies proprioceptives. *Encephale, 33,* 277–294.

Divac, I., Bjorklund, H., Lindvall, O., & Passingham, R. (1978). Converging projections from the mediodorsal thalamic nucleus and mesencephalic dopaminergic neurons to the neocortex in three species. *Journal of Comparative Neurology, 180,* 59–72.

Dix, M., Harrison, M., & Lewis, P. (1971). Progressive supranuclear palsy. *Journal of the Neurological Sciences, 13,* 237–256.

Donaldson, I., & Nash, J. (1973) Interaction between visual cortical areas. *Journal of Physiology, 234,* 77–78.

Dreher, B., & Cottee, L. (1975). Visual receptive field properties of cells in area 18. *Journal of Neurophysiology, 38,* 735–750.

Drewe, E. (1975). "Go—no go" learning after frontal lobe lesions in humans. *Cortex, 11,* 17–21.

Duensing, F. (1953). Raumagnostische und ideatorisch-apraktische Störung des gestaltenden Handelns. *Deutsch Zeitschrift Nervenheilkunde, 170,* 72–94.

Dufour, L. (1881). *De l'aphasie liée a la lésion du lobule de l'insula de Reil.* These, Nancy.

Eccles, J. (1982). The initiation of voluntary movements by supplementary motor area. *Archiv für Psychiatrie und Nervenkrankheiten, 231,* 423–441.

Efron, R. (1968). What is perception? In *Boston Studies in the Philosophy of Science* (Vol. IV). Holland: Reidel.

Efron, R. (1967). Time and psychopathology. *Annals of the New York Academy of Science 138,* 798–821.

Eisenson, J. (1954). *Examining for aphasia.* New York: Psychological Publishing Corporation.

Eisenson, J. (1962). Language and intellectual modifications associated with right cerebral damage. *Language and Speech, 5,* 49–53.

Elghozi, D., Strube, E., Signoret, J. L., Cambier, J., & Lhermitte, F. (1978). Quasiaphasie lors de lesions du thalamus. *Rev. Neurol., 134,* 557–573.

Ettlinger, G., Jackson, C., Zangwill, O. (1955). Dysphasia following right temporal lobectomy in right-handed man. *Journal of Neurology, Neurosurgery and Psychiatry, 18,* 214–217.

Ettlinger, G., Warrington, E., & Zangwill, O. (1957). A further study of visual-spatial agnosia. *Brain, 80,* 335–361.

Evarts, E. (1979). Brain mechanisms of movement. *Scientific American,* September.

Ey, H. (1950–1954). *Etudes psychiatriques* (Vols. 1–3). Paris: Desclée de Brower.

Ey, H. (1973). *Traite des hallucinations* (2 Vols.). Paris: Masson.

Eyzaguirre, C., and Fidone, S. (1975). *Physiology of the nervous system.* Chicago: Year Book Medical Publishers.

Farkas, T., Wolf, A., Cancro, R., Friedhoff, A., Christman, D., Fowler, J., van Gelder, P., Brown, J. W., & Brill, A. (1980). The application of 18 F-2 deoxy-2 fluoro-D-glucose and positron emission tomography in the study of psychiatric conditions (Abstract). *12th CINP Congress,* Goteborg.

Farris, A. (1969). *Neurology, 19,* 91–96.

Faure, H., Berchtold, R., & Ebtinger, R. (1957). Sur les parasitoses délirantes. *Evolution Psychiatrique, 2,* 357–75.

Faust, C. (1947). Partielle Seelenblindheit nach occipital Hirnverletzung. *Nervenartz, 18,* 294–297.

Ferraro, A. & Jervis, G. (1936). Pick's disease. *Archives of Neurology and Psychiatry, 36,* 739–67.

Ferrier, D. (1875). Experiments on the brain of monkey. *Philosophical Transactions of the Royal Society of London, 165,* 433–88.

Feuchtwanger, E. (1923). Die Funktionen des Stirnhirns. *Monographs of Neurological Psychiatry, 38,* 194.

Fischer, F. (1929). Zeitstruktur und Schizophrenie, *Zeitschrift der gesamte Neurologie und Psychiatrie, 121,* 544.

Fisher, C. (1954). Dreams and perception, *Journal of the American Psychoanalytic Association, 3,* 380–445.

Fisher, C. (1959). The pathologic and clinical aspects of thalamic hemorrhage. *Transactions of the American Neurological Association, 84,* 56.

Flechsig, P. (1920). *Anatomies des menschlichen Gehirns und Ruckenmarks.* Leipzig: Thieme.

Fogel, M. (1966). Picture description and interpretation in brain-damaged patients. *Cortex,* 433–448.

Förster, O. (1890). Uber Rindenblindheit. *Graefes Archives Ophthalmologie, 36,* 94–108.

Förster, O. (1936). Sensible corticale felder. In *Handbuch der Neurologie,* Bumke & Förster, O. (Eds.), *6,* 358–448. Berlin: Springer.

Franz, S. (1902). On the function of the cerebrum. *American Journal of Physiology, 8,* 1–22.

Franzen, G., & Ingvar, D. (1975). Abnormal distribution of cerebral activity in chronic schizophrenia. *Journal of Psychiatric Research, 12,* 199–214.

Freedman-Stern, R., Ulatowska, H., Baker, T., & Delacoste, C. (1984). Disruption of written language in aphasia: A case study. *Brain and Language, 28,* 181–205.

Freeman, T., Gathercole, C. (1966). Perseveration—the clinical symptoms—in chronic schizophrenia and organic dementia. *British Journal of Psychiatry, 112,* 27–32.

Freeman, W., & Watts, J. (1950). *Psychosurgery,* Springfield, IL: Charles C. Thomas.

Freud, S. (1891). *On aphasia.* New York: International Universities Press. (Reprinted in 1953)

Freud, S. (1900). *The interpretation of dreams* (Standard Edition). London: Hogarth Press.

Fried, I., Ojemann, G., & Fetz, E. (1981). Language related potentials specific to human language cortex. *Science, 212,* 353–356.

Froeschels, E. (1946). A peculiar intermediary state between waking and sleep. *Journal of Clinical Psychopathology, 7*, 825–833.

Fromkin, V., Krashen, S., Curtiss, S., et al. (1974). The development of language in Genie: A case of language acquisition beyond the "critical period." *Brain and Language, 1*, 81–107

Fuchs. W. (1921). Untersuchung über das Sehen der Hemianopiker und Hemiamblyopiker. *Zeitschrifft für Psychologie, 86*, 1–43.

Fulton, J. (1953). *Physiologie des lobes frontaux et du cervelet*. Paris: Masson.

Fuster, J. (1980). *The prefrontal cortex*. New York: Raven Press.

Fuster, J. (1987). Single-unit studies of the prefrontal cortex. In E. Perecman (Ed.), *The frontal lobes revisited*, New York: IRBN Press.

Gaillard, J. (1970). *Journal of Psychol. Norm. et Pathol., 67*, 443–472.

Gainotti, G., Caltagirone, C., & Miceli, G. (1979). Semantic disorders of auditory language comprehension in right brain-damaged patients. *Journal of Psycholinguistic Research, 8*, 13–20.

Gainotti, G., Carlomagno, S., Craca, A., & Silveri, M. (1986). Disorders of classificatory activity in aphasia. *Brain and Language, 28*, 181–195.

Gallup, G., (1970). Chimpanzees: self-recognition, *Science, 167*, 86–87.

Garcin, R., Brion, S., and Khochneviss, A. (1963). Le syndrome de Creutzfeldt-Jakob et les syndromes corticostriés du presenium. *Revue Neurologique, 109*, 419–441.

Gates, A., & Bradshaw, J. (1977). The role of the cerebral hemispheres in music. *Brain and Language, 4*, 403–431.

Gazzaniga, M. (1975). The concept of diaschisis. In: K. Zulch, O. Creutzfeldt, & G. Galbraith (Eds.), *Cerebral localization*. New York: Springer.

Gazzaniga, M. (1980). *Right hemisphere language: A 20 year perspective*. Paper presented at the Conference on Cognitive Processing in the Right Hemisphere, Institute for Research in Behavioral Neuroscience, New York.

Gelardi, J., & Brown, J. W. (1967) Hereditary cataplexy. *Journal of Neurology, Neurosurgery and Psychiatry, 30*, 455–456.

Gelb, A. (1920). Uber den Wegfall der Wahrnehmung von "Oberflachenfarben." *Zeitschrift für Psychologie, 84*, 193–257.

Gergen, J., & MacLean, P. The limbic system. Photic activation of limbic cortical areas in the squirrel monkey. *Annals of the New York Academy of Sciences, 117*, 69–87.

Gerstmann, J. and Schilder, P. (1926). Uber eine besondere Gangstörung bei stirnhirnerkrankung. *Wiener Medizinische Wochenschrift, 3*, 97–102.

Ghent, L., Mishkin, M., & Teuber, H. L. (1962) Short-term memory after frontal lobe injury in man. *Journal of Comparative Physiology and Psychology, 55*, 705–9.

Glick, S. & Greenstein, S. (1973). *British Journal of Pharmacology, 49*, 316–321.

Glickstein, M., Stein, J., & King, R. (1972). Visual input to the pontine nuclei. *Science, 178*, 1110–1111.

Gloning, I., Gloning, K., & Hoff, H. (1968) *Neuropsychological symptoms and syndromes in lesions of the occipital lobe and the adjacent areas*. Paris: Gauthier-Villars.

Gloning, I., Gloning, K., Haub, G., et al. (1969). Comparison of verbal behavior in right-handed and non right-handed patients with anatomically verified lesion of one hemisphere. *Cortex, 5,* 43–52.

Gloor, F., Olivier, A., Quesny, L., Andermann, F., & Horowitz, S. (1982). The role of the limbic system in experiential phenomena of temporal lobe epilepsy. *Annals of Neurology, 12,* 129–44.

Goldberg, E., & Tucker, D. (1979). Motor perseveration and long-term memory for visual forms. *Journal of Clinical Neuropsychology, 1,* 273–288.

Goldberg, G., Mayer, N., & Toglia J. (1981). Medial frontal cortex infarction and the alien hand sign. *Archives of Neurology, 38,* 683–686.

Goldberg, G. (1985). Supplementary motor area structure and function: review and hypotheses. *Behavioral and Brain Sciences, 8,* 567–616.

Goldberg, G. (1987). From intent to action: Evolution and function of the premotor systems of the frontal lobe. In E. Perecman (Ed.), *The frontal lobes revisited.* New York: IRBN Press.

Goldberger, M., Recovery of movement after CNS lesions in monkeys. In J. Rosen & N. Butters, (Eds.), *Plasticity and recovery of function in the central nervous system.* New York: Academic Press.

Goldberger, M., & Murray, M. (1972). *Recovery of function after partial denervation of the spinal cord: A behavioral and anatomical study.* Meeting of the Program and Abstracts Society for Neuroscience, Houston, Texas.

Goldman, P. (1976). *Advances in the study of behavior, 7,* 1–90. New York: Academic Press.

Goldman, P., & Nauta, W. (1977). An intricately patterned prefronto-caudate projection in the rhesus monkey. *Journal of Comparative Neurology, 171,* 369–84.

Goldman, P., & Gelkin, T. (1978). Prenatal removal of frontal association cortex in the fetal rhesus monkey. *Brain Research, 152,* 451–85.

Goldman, P. (1979). Presentation, Cornell Medical Center.

Goldstein, K. (1908). Zur Lehre von der motorischen Apraxie. *Zeitschrift Physiologische Neurologie,* Bd XI, *4/5,* 169–187.

Goldstein, K. (1912). *Die Halluzination,* Wiesbaden: Bergmann.

Goldstein, K. (1915). *Die transkortikalen Aphasien.* Jena: Fischer.

Goldstein, K. (1927). Die Lokalisation in der Grosshirnrinde, *Handbuch der Normalen und Pathologischen Physiologie.* Berlin: Springer.

Goldstein, K. (1936). "The significance of the frontal lobes for mental performances," *Journal of Neurology and Psychopathology, 17,* 27–40.

Goldstein, K. (1938). Moro reflex and startle pattern. *Archives of Neurology and Psychiatry, 40,* 322–327.

Goldstein, K. (1939). Clinical and theoretic aspects of lesions of the frontal lobe. *Archives of Neurology and Psychiatry, 41,* 856–867.

Goldstein, K. (1943a). Concerning rigidity. *Character and Personality, 11,* 209–226.

Goldstein, K. (1943b). The significance of psychological research in schizophrenia. *Journal of Nervous and Mental Disease, 97,* 261–279.

Goldstein, K. (1948). *Language and language disturbances*. New York: Grune & Stratton.

Goldstein, K., & Gelb, A. (1918). Psychologische Analysen hirnpathologischer Fälle auf Grund von Untersuchungen Hirnverletzter. *Zeitschrifft gesamte Neurologie und Psychiatrie, 41*, 1–142.

Goldstein, K., & Katz, S. (1937). The psychopathology of Pick's disease, *Archives of Neurology and Psychiatry, 38*, 473–490.

Goltz, F. (1881). *Uber die Verrichtungen des Grosshirns*. Bonn: Strauss.

Goodglass, H., & Quadfasel, F., (1954). Language laterality in left-handed aphasics. *Brain, 77*, 521–548.

Goodglass, H. (1968). Studies on the grammar of aphasics. In S. Rosenberg & J. Kaplan (Eds.), *Developments in applied psycholinguistic research*. New York: Macmillan.

Goodglass, H. (1971). *Transactions of the American Neurological Association, 96*, 144–145.

Goodglass, H., & Kaplan, E. (1972). *Assessment of aphasia and related disorders*. Philadelphia: Davis, 1972.

Gorenstein, E. (1982). Frontal lobe functions in psychopaths. *Journal of Abnormal Psychology 91*, 368–79.

Gorlitzer von Mundy V. (1957). Zur Frage der paarig veranlagten Sprachzentren. *Nervenarzt, 28*, 212–216.

Gould, S. (1977). *Ontogeny and phylogeny*. Cambridge, MA: Harvard University Press.

Goy, R. W., & McEwen, B. S. (1980). *Sexual differentiation of the brain*. Cambridge, MA: MIT Press.

Grantyn, A. (1973). Postsynaptic responses of hippocampal neurons to subcortical stimulation. *Acta Physiologica Hungarica, 43*, 329–345.

Gray, C., & Gummerman, K. (1975) The enigmatic eidetic image. *Psychological Bulletin, 82*, 383–407.

Gregory, R. (1968). Perceptual illusions and brain models. *Proceedings of the Royal Society of Medicine, 171*, 279–96.

Green, E. (1969). Phonological and grammatical aspects of jargon in an aphasic patient: A case study. *Language and Speech, 12*, 103–18.

Green, E., & Howes, D. (1977). The nature of conduction aphasia. In H. Whitaker & H. Whitaker (Eds.), *Studies in neurolinguistics* (Vol. 3). New York: Academic Press.

Gross, C. (1973). Visual functions of infero-temporal cortex. In R. Jung (Ed.), *Handbook of sensory physiology, Vol. VII/3*. New York: Springer.

Grossman, M., Wheeler, D., & Brown, J. W. (1981). Paper presented at the Annual Convention of the Academy of Aphasia.

Grueninger, W., & Pribram, K. (1969). Effects of spatial and nonspatial distractors on performance latency of monkeys with frontal lesions. *Journal of Comparative Physiology and Psychology, 68* 203–09.

Grunthal, E. (1942). Ueber thalamische Demenz. *Monatsschrift für Psychiatrie und Neurologie, 106*, 114–128.

Guttman, E. (1942). Aphasia in children. *Brain, 65*, 205–219.

Haaland, K., & Miranda, F. (1980). *Case of crossed aphasia in a dextral*. Paper presented at the meeting of the Academy of Aphasia, Cape Cod.

Haaxma, R., & Kuypers, H. (1975). Intrahemispheric cortical connexions and visual guidance of hand and finger movements in the Rhesus monkey. *Brain, 98,* 239–260.

Haber, R. (1979). Twenty years of haunting eidetic imagery. *Behavioral and Brain Sciences, 2,* 583–629.

Hamanaka, T., Kato, N., Ohashi, H., Ohigashi, Y., & Hadano, K. (1976). *Studia Phonologica, 10,* 28–45.

Hamon, W., & Goldston, S. (1956). The time sense: Estimation of one second durations by schizophrenic patients. *Archives of Neurology & Psychiatry, 76,* 625.

Hannay, H., & Malone, D. (1976). Visual field effects and short-term memory for verbal material. *Neuropsychologia, 14,* 203.

Harasymu, S. J., & Halper, A. (1981). Sex, age and aphasia type. *Brain and Language, 12,* 190–198.

Harding, D. (1982). On having no head. In D. Hofstader & D. Dennett (Eds.), *The mind's I*. New York: Bantam.

Harlow, H. (1950). Analysis of discrimination learning by monkeys. *Journal of Experimental Psychology, 40,* 26–39.

Harlow, H., Akert, K., & Schiltz, K. (1964). The effects of bilateral prefrontal lesions on learned behavior of neonatal infant and preadolescent monkeys. In J. Warren & K. Akert (Eds.), *The frontal granular cortex and behavior*. New York: McGraw-Hill.

Harlow, H., & Settlage, P. (1947). Effect of extirpation of frontal areas upon learning performance of monkeys. *Research Publications Association in Nervous and Mental Disease, 27,* 446–459.

Harlow, J. (1848). Passage of an iron rod through the head. *Boston Medical Surgery Journal, 39,* 389–393.

Harlow, J. (1868). Recovery from the passage of an iron bar through the head. *Massachusetts Medical Society Publication, 2,* 329–347.

Harris, L. (1978). Sex differences and spatial ability. In Kinsbourne, M. (Ed.), *Asymmetrical functions of the brain*. London: Cambridge University Press.

Harshman, R., Remington, R., & Krashen, D. (1974). *Sex, language and the brain, Part II: Evidence from dichotic listening for adult sex differences in verbal lateralization.* Paper presented at the UCLA Conference on Human Brain Function, Los Angeles.

Hartocollis, P. (1975). Time and affect in psychopathology, *Journal of the American Psychoanalytic Association, 23,* 383–395.

Hawkes, C., & Bryan-Smith, L. (1974). The electroencephalogram in the "locked-in" syndrome. *Neurology, 24,* 1015–1018.

Hawkes, H. (1974). The "locked-in" syndrome: Report of seven cases. *British Medical Journal, 4,* 379–382.

Hayman, M., & Abrams, R. (1977). Capgras syndrome and cerebral dysfunction. *British Journal of Psychiatry, 130,* 556–64.

Head, H. (1926). *Aphasia and kindred disorders of speech*. New York: The Macmillan Co.

Hebb, D. (1949). *The organization of behavior*. New York: Wiley.

Hebb, D., & Penfield, W. (1940). Human behavior after extensive bilateral removal from the frontal lobes. *Archives of Neurology and Psychiatry, 44*, 421–438.

Hécaen, H. (1964). Mental symptoms with tumors of the frontal lobe. In J. Warren and K. Akert (Eds.), *The frontal granular cortex and behavior*. New York: McGraw-Hill.

Hécaen, H. (1976). Acquired aphasia in children and the ontogenesis of hemispheric functional specialization. *Brain and Language, 3*, 114–134.

Hécaen, H., & Ajuriaguerra, J. de (1954). Balint's syndrome (psychic paralysis of visual fixation) and its minor forms. *Brain, 77*, 373–400.

Hécaen, H., & Ajuriaguerra, J. de (1956). *Troubles mentaux an cours des tumeurs intracraniennes*. Paris: Masson.

Hécaen H., Ajuriaguerra, J. de (1963). *Les gauchers: prévalence manuelle et dominance cérébrale*. Paris: Presses Universitaires de France.

Hécaen, H., & Angelergues, R. (1962). Agnosia for faces. *Archives of Neurology, 1962, 7*, 92–100.

Hécaen, H., & Consoli, S. (1973). Analyse des troubles du langage au cours des lesions de l'aire de Broca. *Neuropsychologia, 11*, 377–388.

Hécaen, H., Goldblum, M., Masure, M., & Ramier, A. Ramier, A. (1974). Une nouvelle observation d'agnosie d'object. *Neuropsychologia, 12*, 447–464.

Hécaen, H., & Gruner, J. (1974). Alexie "pure" avec integrite du corps calleux. In F. Michel & B. Schott (Eds.), *Les syndromes de disconnexion calleuse chez l'homme*. Lyon.

Hécaen, H., Mazars, G., Ramier, A., Goldblum, M. & Mérienne, L. (1971). Aphasie croisee chez un sujet droitier bilingue. *Revué Neurologique, 124*, 319–323.

Hécaen, H., Penfield, W., Bertrand, C., & Malmo, R. (1956). The syndrome of apractognosia due to lesions of the minor cerebral hemisphere. *Archives of Neurology and Psychiatry, 75*, 400–434.

Hécaen, H., & Piercy, M. (1956). Paroxysmal dysphasia and the problem of cerebral dominance. *Journal of Neurological and Neurosurgical Psychiatry, 19*, 194–201.

Hécaen, H., & Ropaert, R. (1959). Hallucinations auditives au cours de syndromes neurologiques. *Annales Médico-Psychologiques, 117*, 257–306.

Hécaen, H. and Ruel J. (1981) "Sieges lesionnels intrafrontaux et deficit au test de 'fluence verbale'," *Revue Neurologique* 137:277–284.

Hécaen, H., & Sauguet, J. (1971). Cerebral dominance in left-handed subjects. *Cortex, 7*, 19–48.

Heeschen, C. (1980). Strategics of decoding actor-object relations by aphasic patients. *Cortex, 16*, 5–19

Heeschen, C. (1985). Agrammatism versus paragrammatism: A fictitious opposition. In M. L. Kean (Ed.), *Agrammatism*. New York: Academic Press.

Heilman, K., & Watson, R. (1977) The neglect syndrome. In S. Harnad et al. (Eds.), *Lateralization in the Nervous System*. New York: Academic Press.

Henn, F., & Nasrallah, H. (1982) *Schizophrenia as a brain disease*. New York: Oxford.

Henschen, S. (1920). *Klinische und anatomische Beiträge zur Pathologie des Gehirns*. Stockholm: Nordiska.

Henschen, S. (1926). On the function of the right hemisphere of the brain in relation to the left in speech, music and calculation. *Brain, 49*, 110–23.

Henschen, S. (1927). Über die Lokalisation einiger psychischer Prozesse. *Zentralblat für Neurologie, 45*, 65.

Herrmann, G., & Pötzl, O. (1928). *Die optische Alaesthesie*, Berlin: Karger

Hermann, K., Turner, J., Gillingham, F., & Gaze, R. (1966). The effects of destructive lesions and stimulation of the basal ganglia on speech mechanisms. *Confinia Neurologia, 28*, 197–207.

Hess, W., Burgi, S., & Bucher, V. (1946). Motorische Funktion des Tektal-und Tegmentalgebietes. *Monatsschrift Psychiatrie and Neurologie, 112*, 1–52.

Hier, D., Davis, K., Richardson, E., & Mohr, J. (1977). Hypertensive putaminal hemorrhage. *Ann. Neurol. 1*, 152–159.

Hillier, W. (1954). *Neurology, 4*, 718–721.

Hernandez-Peon, R. (1966). A neurophysiological model of dreams and hallucinations. *Journal of Nervous and Mental Disease, 141*, 623–650.

Hishikawa, Y., Man'no, H., Tachibana, M., Furuya, E., Koida, H., & Kaneko, Z. (1968). The nature of sleep attack and other symptoms of narcolepsy. *EEG and Clinical Neurophysiology, 24*, 1–10.

Hoff, H. and Silberman, M. (1933). Änderungen der akustischen Wahrnehmingswelt bei Temporallappenläsionen. *Zeitschrifft gesamte Neurologie und Psychiatrie, 144*, 657–664.

Hoff, H., & Pötzl, O. (1935a). Über Störungen des Tiefensehens bei zerebraler Metamorphopsie. *Monatschrifft für Psychiatrie, 90*, 305.

Hoff, H., & Pötzl, O. (1935b). Zur diagnostischen Bedeutung der polyopie bei Tumoren des Okzipithalhirns. *Zeitschrifft gesamte Neurologie und Psychiatrie, 152*, 433.

Holender, D. (1986). Semantic activation without conscious identification. *Behavioral and Brain Sciences, 9*, 1–66.

Holmes, G. (1918). Disturbances of visual orientation. *British Journal of Ophthalmology, 2*, 449–468.

Holtzman, J., Sidtis, J., Volpe, B., & Gazzaniga, M. (1980). Attentional unity following brain bisection in man. *Neurscience Abstracts, 6*, 195.

Hopf, A. (1968). Photometric studies on the myeloarchitecture of the human temporal lobe. *Journal für Hirnforschung, 10*, 275–297.

Horowitz, M., & Adams, J. (1970) Hallucinations on brain stimulation. In W. Kemp (Ed.), *Origin and mechanism of hallucination*. New York: Plenum.

Horrax, G. (1923). Visual hallucinations as a cerebral localizing phenomenon. *Archives of Neurology and Psychiatry, 10*, 532–547.

Horrax, G. (1946). Experiences with cortical incisions for the relief of intractable pain in the extremities. *Surgery, 20*, 593–602.

Howard, D., Patterson, K., Franklin, S., Morton, J., & Orchard-Lisle, V. (1984). Variability and consistency in picture naming by aphasic patients. In F. Rose (Ed.), *Progress in aphasiology*, Raven Press, New York.

Hoyenga, K. B., & Hoyenga, *The question of sex differences*. Boston: Little, Brown.

Hubel, D., & Wiesel, T. (1977). Functional architecture of macaque monkey visual cortex. *Proceedings of the Royal Society of London, 198*, 1–59.

Hudson, A. (1969). Perseveration. *Brain, 91*, 571–582.

Humphrey, G. (1963). *Thinking*. New York: Wiley.

Humphrey, M., & Zangwill, O. (1951). Cessation of dreaming after brain injury. *Journal of Neurology, Neurosurgery and Psychiatry, 14*, 322–326.

Humphrey, M., & Zangwill, O. (1952). Dysphasia in left-handed patients with unilateral brain lesions. *Journal of Neurology, Neurosurgery and Psychiatry, 15*, 184–193.

Humphrey, N. (1974). Vision in monkey without striate cortex: A case study. *Perception, 3*, 241–255.

Isakower, O. (1938). A contribution to the pathopsychology of phenomena associated with falling asleep. *International Journal of Psychoanalysis, 19*, 331–345.

Ishibashi, T., Hori, H., Endo, K. & Sato, T. (1964) Hallucinations produced by electrical stimulation of the temporal lobes in schizophrenic patients. *Tohoku Journal of Experimental Medicine, 82*, 124–139.

Isserlin, M. (1936). Aphasie. In O. Bumke & O. Förster (Eds.), *Handuch der Neurlogie* Berlin: Springer.

Jackson, J. H. (1894). The factors of insanities. Medical Press and Circ. (Reprinted in J. Taylor (Ed.), *Selected writings of John Hughlings Jackson*. London: Staples Press, 1931)

Jackson, J. H. (1931). J. Taylor (Ed.), *Selected writings of John Hughlings Jackson*. London: Staples Press.

Jacobs, L. (1980). Visual alloaesthesia. *Neurology, 30*, 1059–1063.

Jacobs, L., Feldman, M., Diamond, S., & Bender, M. (1973) Palinacousis. *Cortex, 9*, 275–287.

Jacobsen, C. (1936). Studies of cerebral function on primates. *Comparative Psychology Monograph, 13*, 3–60.

Jacobsen, S., Butters, N., & Tovsky, J. (1978). Afferent and efferent subcortical projections of behaviorally defined sectors of prefrontal granular cortex. *Brain Research, 159*, 279–291.

Jacobsen, S., & Trojanowski, J. (1977). Prefrontal granular cortex of the rhesus monkey. *Brain Research 132*, 209–233.

Jaensch, E. (1930). *Eidetic imagery*. London: Kegan Paul.

Jaffe, J. (1974). Coupling between a symmetric and an asymmetric neural system. *Mount Sinai Journal of Medicine, 41*, 153–155,

Jakobson, R. (1964). Discussion. In A.V.S. deReuck & M. O'Connor (Eds.), *Disorders of language*. London: Churchill.

James, W. (1890). *The principles of psychology*. New York: Holt.

Jaspers, H. J. (1913). Is perseveration a functional unit particular in all behavioral processes? *Journal of Social Psychology, 2*, 28–51.

Jefferson, G. (1937). Removal of right or left frontal lobes in man. *British Medical Journal, 2*, 199.

Jefferson, G. (1949). *British Medical Bulletin, 6,* 333–340.

Jenkins, S., & Winkelman, A. (1966). Inverted perception of time sequence in mental disorders. *International Journal of Neuropsychiatry, 2,* 122–128.

Joanette, Y., Ali-Cherif, A., Delpuech, F., Habib, M., Pellissier, J., & Poncet, M. (1983). Evolution de la semiologie aphasique avec l'age. *Revue neurologique 139,* 657–664.

Johnson, J., Sommers, R., & Weidner, W. (1977). *Journal of Speech & Hearing Research, 20,* 116–129.

Jonas, S. (1981). The supplementary motor region and speech emission. *Journal of Communication Disorders, 14,* 349–379.

Jones, E., & Powell, J. (1970). *Brain, 93,* 795–820.

Jossman, P. (1927). Die Beziehungen der motorischen Amusie zu den apraktischen Störungen. *Monatschrifft Psychiatrie und Neurologie, 63,* 239.

Jouvet, M. (1963). A study of neurophysiological mechanisms of dreaming. The *physiological basis of mental activity: EEG Clinical Neurophysiology Supplement, 24,* 133–156.

Julesz, B. (1979). Discussion. In R. Haber (1979).

Jung, R. (1941). Physiologische Untersuchungen uber den Parkinsontremor und andere Zitterformen beim Menschen. *Zeitschrifft Neurologie, 173,* 263–332.

Jung, R. (1979). Translokation corticaler Migrainephosphene. *Neuropsychologia, 17.* 173–185.

Jürgens, U. (1985). Implications of the SMA in phonation. *Experimental Brain Research, 58,* A12–A14.

Jürgens, U., & Pratt, R. (1979). The cingular vocalization pathway in the squirrel monkey. *Experimental Brain Research, 34,* 499–510.

Jürgens, U., & von Cramon, D. (1982). On the role of the anterior cingulate cortex in phonation: A case report. *Brain and Language, 15,* 234–248.

Jurko, M., & Andy, O. (1973). Psychological changes correlated with thalamotomy site. *Journal of Neurology Neurosurgery and Psychiatry, 36,* 846–852.

Kaas, J. (1978). The organization of visual cortex in primates. In C. Noback (Ed.), *Sensory systems of primates.* New York: Plenum.

Kähler, O., & Pick, A. (1879). *Vierteljahresschrift für praktische Heilkunde,* 1:6.

Kalia, M., & Whitteridge, D. (1973). The visual areas in the splenial sulcus of the cat. *Journal of Physiology, 232,* 275–283.

Kapour, N., & Coughlin, A. (1980). Confabulation and frontal lobe dysfunction. *Journal of Neurology, Neurosurgery and Psychiatry, 43,* 461–463.

Karis, R., & Horenstein, S. (1976). *Neurology, 26,* 226–230.

Karp, J., & Hurtig, H. (1974). "Locked-in" state with bilateral midbrain infarcts. *Archives of Neurology, 30,* 176–178.

Karpov, B., Meerson, Y., & Tonkonogi, J. (1975). Eye movement in visual agnosics. *Zh. Neuropat. i. Psik., 75,* 1806–1814.

Karpov, B., Meerson, Y., & Tonkonogi, J. (1979). On some perculiarities of the visuomotor system in visual agnosia. *Neuropsychologia, 17,* 281–294.

Karrer, E. and Stevens, H. (1930). The response of negative after-images to passive motion of the eyeball and the bearing of these observations on the visual perception of motion. *American Journal of Physiology, 94,* 611–614.

Kasdon, D., & Jacobson, S. (1978). The thalamic afferents to the inferior parietal lobule of the rhesus monkey. *Journal of Comparative Neurology, 177,* 685–705.

Kase, C., Troncosco, J., Court, J., Tapia, J., & Mohr, J. (1977). Global spatial disorientation. *Journal of the Neurological Sciences, 34,* 267–278.

Katz, D. (1935). *The world of color.* London: Kegan Paul

Kean, M. (1980). Grammatical representations and the description of language processing. In D. Caplan (Ed.), *Biological studies of mental processes.* Cambridge, MA: MIT Press.

Kellar, L. (1978). *Stress and syntax in aphasia.* Paper presented at the meeting of the Academy of Aphasia, Chicago.

Kelso, J., Holt, K., Kugler, P., & Turvey, M. (1980). On the concept of coordinative structures. In G. Stelmach and J. Requen (Eds.), *Tutorials in motor behavior.* Amsterdam: North-Holland.

Keminsky, W. (1958). Experimental study of distant effects of acute focal brain injury. *Archives of Neurology and Psychiatry, 79,* 376–389.

Kennard, M. (1936). *American Journal of Physiology, 115,* 138–146.

Kertesz, A. (1981). The anatomy of jargon. In J. W. Brown (Ed.), *Jargonaphasia* (pp. 63–112). New York: Academic Press.

Kertesz, A., & Benson, D. F. (1970). Neologistic jargon: A clinicopathological study. *Cortex, 6,* 362–386.

Kievit, J. & Kuypers, H. (1977). Organization of the thalamo-cortical connections to the frontal lobe in the rhesus monkey. *Experimental Brain Research, 29,* 299–322.

King, H. (1962). Anticipatory behavior: Temporal matching by normal and psychotic subjects. *Journal of Psychology, 53,* 425–440.

Kinsbourne, M. (1971). The minor cerebral hemisphere as a source of aphasic speech. *Archives of Neurology, 25,* 302–306.

Kinsbourne, M. (1972). Eye and head turning indicates cerebral lateralization. *Science, 176,* 539.

Kinsbourne. M. (1974). Lateral interactions in the brain. In M. Kinsbourne & L. Smith (Eds.), *The disconnected cerebral hemisphere.* Springfield, MA: Charles C. Thomas.

Kinsbourne, M., & Cook, J. (1971). Generalized and lateralized effect of concurrent verbalization on a unimanual skill. *Quarterly Journal of Experimental Psychology, 23,* 341–345.

Kinsbourne, M., & Hiscock, M. (1977). Does cerebral dominance develop? In S. Segalowitz & F. Gruber (Eds.), *Language development and neurological theory.* New York: Academic Press.

Kinsbourne, M., & Warrington, E. (1962). A disorder of simultaneous form perception. *Brain, 85,* 461–486.

Kinsbourne, M. and Warrington, E. (1963a). Jargonaphasia. *Neuropsychologia 1,* 27–37.

Kinsbourne, M., & Warrington, E. (1963b). A study of visual perseveration. *Journal of Neurology, Neurosurgery, and Psychiatry, 26,* 468–475.

Klein, H. (1924). Gedankenhören bei Affektion im linken Schlafenlappen. *Zeitschrift die gesamte Neurologie und Psychiatrie, 84.*

Klein, H . (1929). *Zeitschrift für die gesamte Neurologie und Psychiatrie, 118.*

Kleist, K. (1934a). *Gehirnpathologie.* Leipzig: Barth.

Kleist, K. (1934b). Kriegsverletzungen des Gehirns in ihrer Bedeutung fur die Hirnlokalisation und Hirnpathologie. In O. von Schjerning (Ed.), *Handbuch der ärztlichen Erfahrungen im Weltkriege* (Vol. 4) (pp. 343–393). Leipzig: Barth.

Kleist, K. (1962). *Sensory aphasia and amusia: The myeloarchitectonic basis.* New York: Pergamon.

Klopp, H. (1951). Über Umgekehrt und Verkehrtsehen. *Deutsche Zeitschrift Nervenheilkunde, 165,* 23.

Klüver, H. (1933). The eidetic type. *Association for Research in Nervous and Mental Disease, 14,* 150–68.

Klüver, H. (1965). Neurobiology of normal and abnormal perception. In P. Hoch & J. Zubin (Eds.), *Psychopathology of perception.* New York: Grune & Stratton.

Klüver, H., & Bucy, P. (1937). "Psychic blindness" and other symptoms following bilateral temporal lobectomy in rhesus monkeys. *American Journal of Physiology, 119,* 352–353.

Knight, R., Hillyard, S., Woods, and Neville, H. (1981). The effects of frontal cortex lesions on event-related potentials during auditory selective attention. *EEG Clinical Neurophysiology 52,* 571–582.

Knox, C., & Kimura, D. (1970). Cerebral processing of nonverbal sounds in boys and girls. *Neuropsychologia 8,* 227–237.

Knutsson, E., & Lying-Tunnell, U. (1985). Gait apraxia in normal-pressure hydrocephalus. *Neurology, 35,* 155–160.

Koerner, F., & Teuber, H. (1973). Visual field defects after missile injuries to the geniculo-striate pathway in man. *Experimental Brain Research, 18,* 88–113.

Kohn, S. (1984). The nature of the phonological disorder in conduction aphasia. *Brain and Language, 23,* 97–115.

Konorski, J. (1972). Discussion. *Acta Neurobiologica Exp., 32.*

Konow, A., & Pribram, K. (1970). Error recognition and utilization produced by injury to the frontal cortex in man. *Neuropsychologia, 8,* 489–491.

Kornhuber, H. (1974). Cerebral cortex, cerebellum and basal ganglia. In F. Schmitt & F. Worden (Eds.), *The neurosciences: Third study program.* Cambridge, MA: MIT Press.

Kornhuber, H. (1985). Bereitschaftspotential and the activity of the supplementary motor area preceding voluntary movement. *Experimental Brain Research, 58,* A10–A11.

Kosslyn, S. (1975). Information Representation in Visual Images. *Cognitive Psychology, 7,* 341–370.

Koskoff, Y., Dennis, W., Lazovik, D., & Wheeler, E. (1948). The psychological effects of frontal lobotomy performed for the alleviation of pain. *Association for Research in Nervous and Mental Disease, 27,* 723–753.

Krashen, S. D. (1972). Language and the left hemisphere. *UCLA Papers on Phonetics, 24,* 1–72.

Krashen, S. D. (1973). Lateralization, language learning, and the critical period: Some new evidence. *Language and Learning, 23,* 63–74.

Krause, F. (1924). Die Sehbahn im chirurgischen Beziehung und die faradischen Reizung der Sehzentrums. *Klinische Wochenschrifft, 3,* 15–24.

Kreindler, A., Calavrezo C., & Mihailescu, L. (1971) Linguistic analysis of one case of jargonaphasia. *Revue roumaine de neurologie, 8,* 209–228.

Kriendler, A., & Fradis, A. (1968). *Performances in aphasia,* Paris: Gauthier-Villars.

Kreindler, A., Nereantiu, F., & Botez, M. (1962). Tulburari de constiinta intr-un caz de ramolisment thalamic bilateral. *Neurologia (Bucuresti), 7,* 121–129.

Krynauw, R. (1950). Infantile hemiplegia treated by removing one cerebral hemisphere. *Journal of Neurology, Neurosurgery and Psychiatry, 13,* 243–267.

Kuhl, D., Phelps, A., Kowell, A., Metter, E., Selin, C., & Winter, J. (1980). Effects of stroke on local cerebral metabolism and perfusion. *Ann. Neurol. 8,* 47–60.

Kuhlenbeck, H. (1957). *Brain and consciousness.* Basel: Karger.

Kurtz, D., Leiby, C., & Butter, C. (1980). Reaching to the periphery abolishes deficits in peripheral vision of monkeys with superior colliculus lesions. *Neuroscience Abstracts, 6,* 481.

Kushner, M., Reivitch, M., Alavi, A., Greenberg, J., Stern, M., Dann, R. (1982).. A PET study of the physiopathology of pure word mutism. *Neurology, 32* (abstract).

Kussmaul, A. (1877). Disturbances in Speech. In H. von Ziemssen (Ed.), E. Buchanan Baxter, G. Shattuck, & J. A. McCreery, (Trans.), *Encyclopaedia of the Practice of Medicine, Vol. XIV: Disease of the Nervous System and Disturbances of Speech.* New York: William Wood & Co.

Kuttner, H. (1930). *Archiv. f. Psychiat. m. Nervenkr 91,* 691–693.

Kuypers, H., & Lawrence, D. (1967). Cortical projections to the red nucleus and the brain stem in the rhesus monkey. *Brain Research, 4,* 151–188.

Ladame, P., & Monakow C. von. (1908). *Encephale, 3,* 193–228.

Lafon, M. (1951). Le problème de l'hallucinose pédonculaire. *Paris Medicale, 141,* 181–187.

Lagache, D. (1934). *Les hallucinations verbales et la parole.* Paris: Felix Alcan.

Lake, D. O., & Bryden, M. P. (1976). Handedness and sex differences in hemisphere asymmetry. *Brain and Language, 8,* 266–282.

Lance, J. (1976). Simple formed hallucinations confined to the area of a specific visual field defect. *Brain, 99,* 719–734.

Landis, T., Regard, M., & Serrat, A. (1980). Iconic reading in a case of alexia without agraphia caused by a brain tumor: A tachistoscopic study. *Brain and Language, 11,* 45–53.

Lange, J. (1936). Agnosien und Apraxien. In O. Bumke, & Förster, O. (Eds.), *Handbuch der Neurologie. 6,* 807–960.

Lanneluc, B. (1983). *Troubles due comportement linguistic et lesions sous corticales.* These, Bordeaux.

Laplane, D., & Degos, J. (1983). Motor neglect. *Journal of Neurology, Neurosurgery and Psychiatry 46,* 152–158.

Laplane, D., J. Talairach, V. Meininger, J. Bancaud, & A. Bouchareine (1977). Motor consequences of motor area ablations in man. *Journal of the Neurological Sciences, 31,* 29–49.

Larsen, B., Skinhoj, E., & Lassen, N. (1978). Variations in regional cortical blood flow in the right and left hemispheres during automatic speech. *Brain, 101,* 193–209.

Lashley, K. (1951). The problem of serial order in behavior. In L. Jeffress (Ed.); *Cerebral mechanisms in behavior.* New York: Wiley.

Lassen, N., Larsen, B., & Orgogozo, J. (1978). *Encephale 4,* 233–249.

Leaning, F. (1925). An introductory study of hypnagogic phenomena. *Proceedings of the Society for Psychological Research, 10,* 287–409.

Leask, J., Haber, R., & Haber, R. (1969). Eidetic imagery in children. *Psychonomic Monographs, 3,* Supplement, 25–48.

LeBeau, J., & Wolinetz, E. (1958). Le phénomène de persevération visuelle. *Revue Neurologique 99,* 524–534.

Lecours, A. R., & Lhermitte, F. (1972). Recherches sur le langage des aphasiques: Analyse d'un corpus de néologismes; notion de paraphasie monetique. *Encéphale, 61,* 295–315.

Lecours, A. R., & Lhermitte, F. (1976). The "pure form" of the phonetic disintegration syndrome (pure anarthria): Anatomo-clinical report of a historical case. *Brain and Language, 3,* 88.

Lecours, A., Osborn, E., Travis, L., Rouillon, F., & Lavallee-Huynh, G. (1981). Jargons. In J. Brown (Ed.), *Jargonaphasia.* New York: Academic Press.

Lecours, A. R., & Rouillon, F. (1976) Neurolinguistic analysis of jargonaphasia and jargonagraphia. In H. Whitaker & H. Whitaker (Eds.), *Studies in Neurolinguistics* (Vol. 2), pp. 95–144. New York: Academic Press.

Lecours, A. R., & Vanier-Clément, M. (1976) Schizophasia and jargonaphasia: A comparative description with comments on Chaika's and Fromkin's respective looks as "schizophrenic" language. *Brain, 3,* 516–565.

Lefévre, A. (1950). Contribuicao para estudo da psicopatologia da afasia em criancas. Arq Neuropsiquiatr *8,* 345–393.

Leischher, A. (1979). *Storungen der Sprache: Aphasien und Sprachentwicklungs-Störungen.* Stuttgart: Thieme

Leischner, A., & Peuser, G. (1975). Presentation, Aachen, November.

Lenneberg, E. (1967). Biological foundations of language. New York: Wiley.

Lenz, H. (1944). Raumsinnstörungen bei Hirnverletzungen. *Deutsche Zeitschrift für Nervenheilkunde 157,* 27–64.

Lereboullet, F., & Mouzon, J. (1917, July 7). Hallucination de la vue et crises jacksoniennes dans un cas de lesion du cortex visuel. *Paris Med.*

Leroy, E. (1926) *Les visions du demi sommeil.* Paris: Alcan.

Leslie, C. (1980). *The interactive effects of syntax, pragmatics, and task difficulty in aphasic language.* Unpublished doctoral dissertation, Columbia University.

Lesser, R. (1974). Verbal comprehension in aphasia. *Cortex, 10,* 247–263.

Lesser, R. (1976). Presentation at European Brain-Behavior Conference, Oxford.

Levine, D., & Sweet, E. (1982). The neuropathological basis of Broca's aphasia and its implications for the cerebral control of speech. In M. Arbib et al. (Eds.), *Neural Models of Language Processes.* New York: Academic Press.

Levy, J. (1969). Possible basis for the evolution of lateral specialization of the human brain. *Nature, 224,* 614–615.

Lewis, A. (1932). The experience of time in mental disorder, *Proceedings of the Royal Society of Medicine, 25,* 611–620.

Lewinsohn, P., Zieler, R., Libet, J., Eyeberg, S., & Nielson, G. (1972). Short-term memory. *Journal of Comparative Physiology and Psychology, 81,* 248–255.

Lewy, E. (1954). On micropsia. *International Journal of Psychoanalysis, 35,* 13–19.

Ley, J., Titeca, J., Divry, P., & Moreau, M. (1934). Atrophie de Pick: Étude anatomoclinique. *Journal Belgique de Neurologie, 34,* 285–314.

Lhermitte, J. (1922 November 9) Syndrome de la calotte du pédoncule cérébral. *Société de Neurologie.*

Lhermitte, J. (1951a). Visual hallucinations of the self. *British Medical Journal 1,* 431–434.

Lhermitte, J. (1951b). *Les hallucinations.* Paris: Doin.

Lhermitte, J. & Ajuriaguerra, J. de (1942). *Psychopathologie de la vision.* Paris: Masson.

Lhermitte, F., Chain, F., Escourelle, R., Ducarne, B., & Pillon, B. (1972). Etude anatomo-clinique d'un cas de prosopagnosie. *Revue Neurologique, 126,* 329–346.

Lhermitte, F., Chedru, F., & Chain, F. (1973). A propos d'un cas d'agnosie visuelle. *Revue Neurologique, 128,* 301–322.

Lhermitte, F., Derouesné, J., & Lecours, A. (1971). *Revue Neurologique 125,* 81–101.

Lhermitte, F., & Derousine, J. (1974). Paraphasie et jargonaphasíe dans le langage oral, *Revue Neurologique, 130,* 21–38.

Lhermitte, F., & Pillon, B. (1975). La prosopagnosie. *Revue Neurologique, 131,* 791–812.

Libet, B., Gleason, C., Wright, E., & Pearl, D. (1983). Time of conscious intention to act in relation to onset of cerebral activity (readiness-potential). *Brain, 106,* 623–642.

Libet, B. (1985). Unconscious cerebral initiative and the role of conscious will in voluntary action. *Behavioral and Brain Sciences, 8,* 529–566.

Lieberman, P. (1967). *Intonation, perception and language.* Cambridge, MA: MIT Press.

Liepmann, H. (1905). *Ueber Störungen des Handelns bei Gehirnkranken.* Berlin: Karger.

Liepmann, H. (1920). Apraxie. *Ergebnisse der gesamte Medizin, 1,* 516–543.

Liepmann, H. (1926). Das Krankheitsbild der Apraxie ("Motorischen Asymbolie"). *Monatsschrift fur Psychiatrie und Neurologie, 8* (1900), 15–44, 102–132, 181–197.

Llamas, A., Avendano, E., & Reinoso-Suarez, E. (1977). Amygdaloid projections to prefrontal and motor cortex. *Science, 195,* 794–796.

Lovick, T. (1922). The behavioral repertoire of precollicular decerebrate rats. *Proceedings of the Physiology Society, 226,* 4–6.

Lowenstein, K., & Borchardt, M. (1918). Symptomatologie und elektrische Reizung bei einer Schussverletzung des Hinterhauptlappens. *Deutsche Zeitschrifft Nervenheilkunde 58,* 264–294.

Lüers, T., & Pötzl, O. (1941). Über "Verkehrtsehen" nach Insult. *Wiener Wochenschrift, 53,* 625.

Lukianowicz, M. (1958). Autoscopic phenomena, *Archives of Neurology and Neurosurgery 80,* 199–220.

Lunn, V. (1970). Autoscopic phenomena. *Acta Psychiatria Scandinavia, 219* (Supplement) 118–125.

Luria, A. R. (1959). Disorders of "simultaneous perception" in a case of bilateral occipito-parietal brain injury. *Brain, 82,* 437–449.

Luria, A. R. (1961). *The role of speech in the regulation of normal and abnormal behavior.* New York: Liveright.

Luria, A. R. (1962). *Higher cortical functions.* (English translation, Basic Books, New York, 1966)

Luria, A. R. (1963). *Restoration of function after brain injury.* Oxford: Pergamon.

Luria, A. R. (1964). Factors and forms of aphasia. In A.V.A. DeReuck & M. O'Connor (Eds.), *Disorders of Language.* Boston: Little, Brown.

Luria, A. R. (1965). Two kinds of motor perseveration in massive injury of the frontal lobe. *Brain, 88,* 1–10.

Luria, A. R. (1969). Frontal lobe syndromes. In P. Vinken and G. Bruyn *Handbook of clinical neurology* (Vol. 2, pp. 725–757). Amsterdam: North-Holland.

Luria, A. R. (1970). *Traumatic aphasia,* The Hague: Mouton.

Luria. A. R. (1972). *The man with a shattered world.* New York: Basic Books.

Luria, A. R. (1973). The frontal lobes and the regulation of behavior. In Pribram, K. & Luria, A. R. *The psychophysiology of the frontal lobes.* New York: Academic Press.

Luria, A. R. (1976). *The neuropsychology of memory.* Washington, DC: Winston.

Luria, A. R. (1977). The theory of aphasia. In D. Armstrong & C. H. Van Schooneveld (Eds.), *Roman Jakobson: Echoes of his scholarship.* Lisse: The Peter de Ridder Press.

Luria, A. R. (1977). On quasi-aphasic speech disturbances in lesions of the deep structures of the brain. *Brain and Language, 4,* 432–459.

Luria, A. R., Karpov, B., & Yarbuss, A. (1966), Disturbance of active visual perception and lesions of the frontal lobes. *Cortex, 2* 202–212.

Luria, A. R., Pribram, K., & Homskaya, E. (1964). An experimental analysis of the behavioral disturbance produced by a left frontal arachnoid endothelioma (meningioma). *Neuropsychologia, 2,* 257–280.

Lynch, G. (1974). *Functional recovery after lesions of the nervous system.* In E. Eidelberg & D. Stein (Eds.), Bulletin 12, No. 2.

Lynch, J. (1980). The functional organization of posterior parietal association cortex. *Behavioral and Brain Sciences, 3,* 485–534.

Mabille, H., & Pitres, A. (1913). Sur un cas d'amnesie de fixation postapoplectique ayant persiste pendant 23 ans. *Revue de Medecine, 33,* 257.

MacCallum, W. (1973). Capgras syndrome with an organic basis, *British Journal of Psychiatry, 123,* 639–642.

Mack, A., & Bachant, J. (1969). Perceived movement of the after-image during eye movements. *Perception and Psychophysics, 6,* 379–384.

Mack, J., & Boller, F. (1977). Associative visual agnosia and its related deficits. *Neuropsychologia, 15,* 345–351.

MacLean, P. (1975). An ongoing analysis of hippocampal inputs and outputs. In R. Isaacson and K. Pribram (Eds.), *The hippocampus* (Vol. 1). New York: Plenum.

Malcom, N. (1977). *Memory and mind.* Ithaca, NY: Cornell University Press.

Malmo, R. (1942). Interference factors in delayed response in monkeys after removal of frontal lobes. *Journal of Neurophysiology, 5,* 295–308.

Mandler, G. (1985). *Cognitive psychology.* Summit, NJ: Erlbaum.

Marcel, T. (1983a). Conscious and unconscious perception. *Cognitive Psychology. 15,* 197–237.

Marcel, T. (1983b). Presentation. INS, Deuville, France.

Marcie, P., Hécaen, H., Dubois, J., & Angelergues, R. (1965). Les réalisations du langage chez les malades atteints de lésions de l'hemisphere droit. *Neuropsychologia, 3,* 217–245.

Marinesco, G., Nicolesco, J., and Nicolesco, M. (1935) Lésions bilatérales du thalamus. *Encéphale, 30,* 153–170.

Marinesco, G., Grigoresco, D., Axente, S. (1938). Considérations sur l'aphasie croisée. *Encephale, 33,* 27–46.

Mark, V, Ervin, E., & Yakovlev, P. (1963). Stereotactic thalamotomy. *Archives of Neurology (Chicago), 8,* 528–538.

Marshall, R., Rappaport, B., & Garcia-Bunuel, L. (1985). Self-monitoring behavior in a case of severe auditory agnosia with aphasia. *Brain and Language, 24,* 297–313.

Martin, J. (1966). Troubles psychiques dans une atrophie primitive des noyaux thalamiques dorso-medians. *Revue Neurologique, 114,* 215–219.

Martin, J. (1972). Rhythmic (hierarchical) versus serial structure in speech and other behaviors. *Psychological Review, 79,* 487–509.

Marty, R. (1962). Development post-natal des responses sensorielles du cortex cerebral chez chat et le lapin. *Arch. Anat. Micr., 51,* 129–264.

Masdeu, J., & O'Hara, R. (1983). Motor aphasia unaccompanied by facialbrachial weakness. *Neurology, 33,* 519–521.

Mateer, C. (1983). Localization of language and visuospatial functions by electrical stimulation mapping. In A. Kertesz, (Ed.), *Localization in neuropsychology.* New York: Academic Press.

Mayer-Gross, W. (1936). The question of visual impairment in constructional apraxia. *Proceedings of the Royal Society of Medicine, 29,* 1396–1400.

Mazaux, J. M., Orgogozo, J. M., Henry, P., & Loiseau, P. (1979). Troubles du langage au cours des lesions thalamiques. *Rev. Neurol. 135,* 59–64.

Mazziotta, J., Metler, E. J., & Phelps, M. (1984). *Strategies for the use of positron emission tomography (PET) in the study of normal and abnormal language function.* Paper presented at the Annual Meeting of the Academy of Aphasia. Los Angeles.

McEntee, W., Biber, M., Perl, D., & Benson, F. (1976) Diencephalic amnesia: A reappraisal. *Journal of Neurology, Neurosurgery and Psychiatry, 39,* 436–441.

McFie, J. (1961). The effects of hemispherectomy on intellectual functioning in cases of infantile hemiplegia. *Journal of Neurology, Neurosurgery and Psychiatry 24*, 240–259.

McGeachie, R., Fleming, J., Sharer, L., & Hyman, R. (1979). Diagnosis of Pick's disease by computed tomography. *Journal of Computer Assisted Tomography, 3*, 113–115.

McGlone, J. (1978). Sex differences in functional brain asymmetry. *Cortex, 14*, 122.

McGlone, J. (1980). Sex differences in human brain asymmetry: A critical survey. *Behavioral and Brain Sciences, 3*, 215–263.

Meadows, J. (1974). The anatomical basis of prosopagnosia. *Journal of Neurology, Neurosurgery and Psychiatry, 37*, 489–501.

Meenes, M., & Morton, M. (1936). Characteristics of the eidetic phenomenon. *Journal of General Psychology, 14*, 370–391.

Mendilaharsu, C., Miglionico, A., Mendilaharsu, S., Budelli, R., & DeSouto, H. (1968). A propos d'une epreuve d'etude de l'apraxie constructive pour differentier les lesions de l'hemisphere droit et du gauche. *Acta Neurologica Latinoamericana, 14*, 138–154.

Merzenich, M., & Kaas, J. (1980). Principles of organization of sensory-perceptual systems in mammals. *Progress of Psychobiology and Physiological Psychology, 9*, 1–42.

Messerli, P., Lavorel, P., & Nespoulos, J. L. (1983). *Neuropsychologie de l'expression orale*. Paris: Ed. CNRS.

Messimy, R. (1939). Les effets chez l'homme des lesions prefrontales. *Annals of Medicine 45*, 321–360.

Metter, E., Riege, W., Hanson, W., Kuhl, D., Phelps, D., Squire, L., Wasterlain, C., & Benson, D. (1983). Comparison of metabolic rates, language, and memory in subcortical aphasias. *Brain and Language 19*, 33–47.

Mettler, F. (Ed.). (1949). *Selective partial ablation of the frontal cortex*. New York: Hoeber.

Mettler, F. (1972). Discussion. *Journal of Speech and Hearing Disorders, 37*, 278–279.

Meyer, A., & McLardy, T. (1948). Posterior cuts in prefrontal leucotomy. *Journal of Mental Science 94*, 555–564.

Meyer, A., & McLardy, T. (1949). Clinico-anatomical studies of frontal lobe function based on leucotomy material. *Journal of Mental Science, 95*, 403–417.

Meyer, J., Teraura, T., Sakamoto, K., & Kondo, A. (1971). Central neurogenic control of cerebral blood flow. *Neurology, 21*, 247–262,

Miceli, G., Caltagirone, C., Gainotti, G. et al. (1981). Influence of age, sex, literacy, and pathologic lesion on incidence, severity and type of aphasia. *Acta Neurologica Scandinavia, 64*, 370–382.

Miceli, G., Mazzucchi, A., Menn, L., & Goodglass, H. (1983). Contrasting cases of Italian agrammatic aphasia without comprehension disorder. *Brain and Language, 19*, 65–97.

Michel, E., & Troost, B. (1980). Palinopsia. *Neurology, 30*, 887–889.

Michel, F., & Eyssette, M. (1972). L'Ataxie optique et l'ataxie du regard dans les lesions bilaterales de la jonction parieto-occipitale. *Revue d'Oto-Neuro-Ophtalmologie, 2,* 177–186.

Michel, F., Peronnet, F., & Schott, B. (1980). A case of cortical deafness. *Brain and Language, 10,* 367–377.

Mihailescu, L., Voinescu, I., & Fradis, A. (1967) Relative phoneme-frequency in aphasics. *Revue Roumaine de Neurologie, 4,* 181–189.

Mills, C., & Spiller, W. (1907). *Journal of Nervous and Mental Disease, 34,* 624–650.

Milner, B. (1962). Laterality effects in audition. In V. Mountcastle (Ed.), *Interhemispheric relations and cerebral dominance.* Baltimore: Johns Hopkins Press.

Milner, B. (1964). Some effects of frontal lobectomy in man. In J. Warren & K. Akert (Eds.), *The frontal granular cortex and behavior* (pp. 313–334). New York: McGraw-Hill.

Milner, B. (1974). Hemispheric specialization. In F. Schmitt and F. Worden (Eds.), *The neurosciences.* Cambridge, MA: MIT Press.

Milner, B., (1975). *Hemispheric specialization and interaction.* Cambridge, MA: MIT Press.

Milner, B. (1982). Some cognitive effects of frontal lobe lesions in man. *Philosophical Transactions of the Royal Society of London, 298,* 211–236.

Mingazzini, G. (1908). Über Symptome infolge von Verletzungen des Occipitallappens durch Geschosse. *Neurologische Zentralblatt, 27,* 1112.

Miraillie, C. (1896). *L'Aphasie sensorielle,* Paris: Steinheil.

Mishkin, M. (1964). Perseveration of central sets after frontal lesions in monkeys. In J. Warren & K. Akert (Eds.), *The frontal granular cortex and behavior.* New York: McGraw-Hill.

Mishkin, M. (1972). Cortical visual areas and their interactions. In A. Karczmar, & J. Eccles (Eds.), *The brain and human behavior.* Berlin: Springer.

Mohr, J. (1973). *Archives of Neurology 28,* 77–82.

Mohr, J., Watters, W., & Duncan, G. (1975). Thalamic hemorrhage and aphasia. *Brain and Language, 2,* 3–17.

Mohr, J., Pessin, M., Finkelstein, S., et al. (1978). Broca's aphasia: Pathological and clinical. *Neurology, 28,* 311–324.

Molfese, D., Freeman, R., & Palermo, D. (1975). *Brain and Language, 2,* 356–368.

Molfese, D. (1973). Cerebral asymmetry: the development of speech perception in the human brain. Paper presented at the Midwest Psychological Association, Chicago.

Monakow, C. von (1905). *Gehirnpathologie.* Vienna: Halder.

Monakow, C. von (1914). *Die Lokalisation im Grosshirn.* Wiesbaden.

Moniz, E. (1936). *Tentatives operatoires dans le traitement de certaines psychoses.* Paris: Masson.

Montero, V. (1980). Patterns of connections from the striate cortex to cortical visual areas. *Journal of Comparative Neurology, 1980, 180,* 45–59.

Moreau, (1864). *Gazette des Hopitaux, 70,* 70–71.

Morel, F. (1933). Les scotomes positifs et les hallucinations visuelles du delirium tremens. *Revue de Oto-Neuro-Ophtalmologie, 11,* 81–88.

Morel, F. (1936a). Des bruits d'oreille, des bourdonnements, des hallucinations auditives élémentaires, communes et verbales. *Encéphale, 31,* 81–95.

Morel, F. (1936b). "De l'application de l'audiométrie en neuropsychiatrie," *Revue de Oto-Neuro-Ophtalmologie, 14,* 161,

Morgue, R. (1932). *Neurobiologie de l'hallucination.* Bruxelles: Lamertin.

Morsier, G. de (1938). Les hallucinations. *Revue Oto-Neuro-Ophtalmologie, 16,* 244–352.

Morsier, G. de (1967). Le syndrome de Charles Bonnet. *Annales Médico-Psychologues, 125,* 677–702.

Morsier, G. de (1969). Etudes sur les hallucinations. *Journale de Psychologie Normale et Pathologique 3,.* 281–318; *4,* 421–432.

Morton, J. (1980). Two auditory parallels to deep dyslexia. In: M. Coltheart, K. Patterson, & J. Marshall (Eds.), *Deep dyslexia.* London: Routledge & Kegan Paul.

Mountcastle, V. (1976). The world around us: Neural command functions for selective attention (The F. O. Schmitt Lecture in Neuroscience, 1975). *Neurosciences Research Program Bulletin, 14* (Supplement), 1–47.

Mountcastle, V. (1978). An organizing principle for cerebral function. In E. Edelman, & V. Mountcastle, *The mindful brain.* Cambridge, MA: MIT Press.

Mouren, P. & Tatossian, A. (1963) Les illusions visuospatiales: étude clinique. *Encéphale, 5,* 380–438; *6,* 517–573.

Moutier, F. (1908). *L'Aphasie de Broca.* Paris: Steinheil.

Myers, R. (1976). In S. Harnad et al. (Eds.), Origin and evolution of language and speech. *Annals of the New York Academy of Science, 280,* 745–747.

Naeser, M. A., Alexander, M. P., Helm-Estabrooks, N., Levine, H. L., Laughlin, S. A., Geschwind, N. (1982). Aphasia with predominantly subcortical lesion sites: description of three capsular/putaminal aphasia syndromes. *Arch. Neurol. 39,* 2–14.

Naeser, M., & Hayward, R. (1978). Lesion localization in aphasia with cranial computed tomography and the Boston diagnostic aphasia exam. *Neurology, 28.* 545–551.

Naeser, M., Levine, H., Benson, F. Stuss, D., & Weir, W. (1981). Frontal leukotomy size and hemispheric asymmetries on computerized tomographic scans of schizophrenics with variable recovery. *Archives of Neurology, 38,* 30–37.

Nakamura, R., Desimone, R., Schein, S., & Mishkin, M. (1980). Visually responsive units in striate cortex of blind monkeys. *Neuroscience Abstracts, 6,* 578.

Nakamura, R., & Mishkin, M. (1980). Blindness in monkeys following non-visual cortical lesions. *Brain Research, 188,* 572–577.

Nauta, W. (1964). Some efferent connections of the prefrontal cortex in the monkey. In J. Warren and K. Akert (Eds.), *The frontal granular cortex and behavior.* New York: McGraw-Hill.

Nauta, W. (1972). Neural associations of the frontal cortex. *Acta Neurobiologica Experimentalis, 32,* 125–140.

Nayrac, P., Arnott, G., and Warot, P. (1965). Lesions thalamiques et troubles mentaux. *Lille Médical, 10,* 692–698.

Nebes, R. (1978). Direct examination of cognitive function in the right and left hemispheres. In M. Kinsbourne (Ed.), *Asymmetrical function of the brain*. Cambridge: Cambridge University Press.

Nelson, H. (1976). A modified card-sorting test sensitive to frontal lobe defects. *Cortex, 13*, 313.

Neville, H., Snyder, E., Knight, R., & Galambos, R. (1979). Event related potentials in language and nonlanguage tasks in patients with alexia without aphasia. In D. Lehmann & Callaway (Eds.), *Human evoked potentials*. New York: Plenum.

Newcombe, F., & Marshall, J. (1980). Response monitoring and response blocking in deep dyslexia. In Coltheart, M., Patterson, K., & Marshall, J (Eds.), *Deep dyslexia*. London: Routledge & Kegan Paul.

Newcombe, F., & Ratcliff, G. (1974). Agnosia: A disorder of object recognition. In F. Michel (Ed.), *Les syndromes de disconnexion calleuse chez l'homme*. Colloque Internat'l de Lyon.

Newcombe, F., & Russell, W. (1969). Dissociated visual perceptual and spatial deficits in focal lesions of the right hemisphere. *Journal of Neurology, Neurosurgery and Psychiatry, 32*, 73–81.

Nielsen, H. (1975). Is constructional apraxia primarily an interhemispheric disconnection syndrome? *Scandinavian Journal of Psychology, 16*, 113–124.

Nielsen, J. (1944). *Bulletin of the Los Angeles Neurological Society, 3*, 67–75.

Nielsen, J. (1946). *Agnosia, apraxia, aphasia*. New York: Harper & Row.

Nielsen, J., & Jacobs, L. (1951). Bilateral lesions of the anterior cingulate gyri. *Bulletin of the Los Angeles Neurological Society 16*, 231–234.

Niessl von Mayendorff, E. (1911). *Die aphasischen Symptome und ihre kortikale Lokalisation*. Leipzig: Barth.

Niimi, K., & Sprague, J. (1970). Thalamo-cortical organization of the visual system in the cat. *Journal of Comparative Neurology, 138*, 219–250.

Nordgren, R., Markesbery, W., Fukuda, K., & Reeves, X. (1971). Seven cases of cerebromedullospinal disconnection: The "locked-in" syndrome. *Neurology, 21*, 1140–1148.

Obler, L., Albert, M., Goodglass, H., & Bensen, D. (1978). Aphasia type and aging. *Brain and Language, 6*, 318–322.

Ojemann, G. (1976). Subcortical language mechanisms. In H. Whitaker (Ed.), *Neurolinguistics* (Vol. 1 pp. 103–138). New York: Academic Press.

Ojemann, G. (1983). Brain organization for language from the perspective of electrical stimulation mapping. *Behavioral Brain Sciences* 6:189–230.

Ojemann, G., Fedio, P., & Van Buren, J. (1968). Anomia from pulvinar and subcortical parietal stimulation. *Brain, 91*, 99–116.

Ojemann, G. & Ward, A. (1971). Speech representation in ventrolateral thalamus. *Brain, 94*, 669–680.

Ojemann, G. & Whitaker, H. (1977). Presentation: Academy of Aphasia, Montreal.

O'Keefe, J., & Nadel, L. (1978). *The hippocampus as a cognitive map*. Oxford: Clarenden Press,

Oppenheim, H. (1890). *Arch Psychiatrie und Nervenkrankheiten, 21*, 22–27.

Orgogozo, J., Larsen, B., Roland, P., Melamed, E., & Lassen, N. (1979). Further studies on the supplementary motor area in man with the CBF method. *Acta Neurological Scandinavia, 72*(Supplement), 8–9.

Orgogozo, J., & Larsen, B. (1979). Activation of the supplementary motor area during voluntary movement suggests it works as a supramotor area. *Science, 206,* 847–850.

Orlovskii, G. (1970). Work of the reticulo-spinal neurones during locomotion. *Biophysics, 15,* 761–771.

Osborne, J. (1833). On the loss of faculty of speech depending on forgetfulness of the art of using the vocal organs. *Dublin Journal of Medical and Chemical Science 4,* 157–171.

Oswald, I. (1957). After-Images from retina and brain. *Quarterly Journal of Experimental Psychology, 10,* 88–100.

Paillard, J., Michel, F., & Stelmach, G. (1983). Localization without content: A tactile analogue of "blind sight." *Archives of Neurology, 40,* 548–557.

Pandya, D. and Kuypers, H. (1969). Cortico-cortical connections in the rhesus monkey. *Brain Research, 13,* 13–36.

Pandya, D., & Vignolo, L. (1971). Intra- and interhemispheric projections of the precentral, premotor and arcuate areas in the rhesus monkey. *Brain Research, 26,* 217–233

Pandya, D., & Sanides, F. (1973). Architectonic parcellation of the temporal operculum in rhesus monkey and its projection pattern. *A. Anat. Entwicklgesch, 139,* 127–161.

Pandya, D. (1987). In E. Perecman (Ed.), *The frontal lobes revisited.* New York: IRBN Press.

Paradis, M. (1977). Bilingualism and aphasia. In *Studies in Neurolinguistics* (Vol. 3, pp. 65–121). H. Whitaker & H. A. Whitaker (Ed.), New York: Academic Press.

Paradis, M. Goldblum, M., & Abidi, R. (1982). Alternate antagonism with paradoxical translation behavior in two bilingual aphasic patients. *Brain and Language, 15,* 1.

Pasik, T., Pasik, P., & Bender, M. (1966). The superior colliculus and eye movements. *Archives of Neurology, 15,* 420–436.

Pasik, T., & Pasik, P. (1971). The visual world of monkeys deprived of striate cortex: Effective stimulus parameters and the importance of the accessory optic system. *Vision Research Supplement, 3,* 419–435.

Passingham, R. (1979). Specialization and the language areas. In H. Steklis & M. Raleigh (Eds.), *Neurobiology of social communication in primates.* New York: Academic Press.

Passouant, P., Popoviciu, L., Velok, G., & Baldy-Moulinier, M. (1968). Étude polygraphique des narcolepsies au cours du nycthémère, *Revue Neurologique, 118,* 431–441.

Pavlov, I. (1902). *The work of the digestive glands.* (W. Thompson, Trans.) Philadelphia: Lippincott.

Peatfield, R., & Rose, C. (1981). Migrainous visual symptoms in a woman without eyes. *Archives of Neurology, 38,* 466.

Penfield, W., & Evans, J. (1932). Functional defects produced by cerebral lobectomies. *Association for Research in Nervous and Mental Disorders, 13,* 352.

Penfield, W., & Faulk, M. (1955). *Brain, 78,* 445–470.

Penfield, W., & Jasper, H. (1954). *Epilepsy and the functional anatomy of the human brain.* Boston: Little, Brown.

Penfield, W., & Rasmussen, T. (1950). *The cerebral cortex of man.* New York: Macmillan.

Penfield, W., & Roberts, L. (1959). *Speech and brain mechanisms.* Princeton: Princeton University Press.

Penfield, W., & Welch, K. (1949). The supplementary motor area of the cerebral cortex of man. *Transactions of the American Neurological Association, 74,* 179–184.

Perecman, E. (1980). *Semantic jargon over time.* Paper presented at Meeting of International Neuropsychological Society, San Francisco, February.

Perecman, E. (Ed.) (1983). *Cognitive processing in the right hemisphere.* New York: Academic Press.

Perecman, E. (1984). Spontaneous translation and language mixing in a polyglot aphasic. *Brain and Language, 23,* 43–63.

Perecman, E. (1985). Language mixing in polyglot aphasia: conscious strategy or preconscious necessity? A reply to Grosjean. *Brain and Language, 26,* 356–359.

Perecman, E., & Brown, J. W. (1981). Phonemic jargon: A case report. In J. W. Brown (Ed.), *Jargonaphasia.* New York: Academic Press.

Perecman, E. & Brown, J. W. (1985). Ukeleles, condessors and fosetch: Varieties of aphasic jargon. *Language Sciences, 7,* 177–214.

Perenin, M., & Jeannerod, M. (1975). Residual vision in cortically blind hemifields. *Neuropsychologia, 13,* 1–7.

Perky, C. (1910). An experimental study of imagination. *American Journal of Psychology, 21,* 422–452.

Peter, R. (1977). Effects of midbrain tegmentum and diencephalic lesions on swimming and body orientation in goldfish. *Experimental Neurology, 57,* 922–927.

Petras, J. (1971). *Journal Psychiatric Research, 8,* 189–201.

Petrides, M., & Milner, B. (1982) Deficits on subject-ordered tasks after frontal and temporal-lobe lesions in man. *Neuropsychologia, 20,* 249–262.

Peuser, G., & Temp, K. (1981). The evolution of jargonaphasia. In J. W. Brown (Ed.), *Jargonaphasia* (pp. 259–294). New York: Academic Press.

Pick, A. (1904). The localizing diagnostic significance of so-called hemianopic hallucinations, with remarks on bitemporal scintillating scotomata. *American Journal of Medical Science, 127,* 82–92.

Pick, A. (1905). *Studen über motorische Apraxie* Deuticke. Leipzig.

Pick, A. (1913). *Die agrammatischen Sprachstörungen* Berlin: Springer.

Pick, A. (1973). Aphasia. In *Handbuch der normaler und pathologische Physiologie 15*(2), 1416–1524. J. W. Brown (Trans.). Springfield, IL: Charles C. Thomas. (Originally published 1931. Berlin: Springer)

Piercy, M., Hécaen, H., & Ajuriaguerra, J. de (1960). Constructional apraxia associated with unilateral cerebral lesions—left and right sided cases compared. *Brain, 83,* 225–242.

Pilleri, G. (1966). The Klüver-Bucy syndrome in man. *Psychiatria et Neurologia, 152,* 65–103.

Pillon, B., Desi, M., & Lhermitte, F. (1979). Deux cas d'aphasie croisée avec jargonagraphie chez des droitièrs. *Revue Neurologique 1,* 15–30.

Poeck, K & Kerschensteiner, M. (1975). Analysis of sequential motor events in oral apraxia. K. Zulch (Ed.), In *Cerebral localization.* Heidelberg: Springer.

Polyak, S. (1957). *The vertebrate visual system.* Chicago: University of Chicago Press.

Poppel, E., Held, R., & Frost, D. (1973). Residual vision function after brain wounds involving the central visual pathways in man. *Nature, 243,* 295–296.

Poppelreuter, W. (1917). *Die psychischen Schädigungen durch Kopfschuss im Krieg.* (1914–1916).

Popov, N. (1953–1954). Le conditionnement dans l'écorce cérébrale chez l'homme. *Comptes Rendus Hebdomadaires de Seancs de l'Academic des Sciences, 236,* 744–746; *238,* 2026–2028.

Pötzl, O. (1917). The relationship between experimentally induced dream images and indirect vision. *Psychological Issues, 2,* 41–120, 1960, Monograph 7. (Originally Published: *Zeitschrift die gesamte Neurologie und Psychiatrie 37,* 278–349)

Pötzl, O. (1928). *Die optisch-agnostischen Störungen.* Leipzig: Deuticke.

Pötzl, O. (1943). Über verkehrtsehen. *Zeitschrifft gesamte Neurologie und Psychiatrie, 176,* 780.

Pötzl, O. (1949). Zur Pathophysiologie des Uncus-Syndroms. *Archive der Psychiatrie und Neurologie, 117,* 153–170.

Pötzl, O. (1954). Über Palinopsie. *Wiener Zeitschrift für Nervenheilkunde 8,* 161–186.

Porteus, S., Demonbrun, E., & Kepner, M. (1944). *Genetic Psychology Monographs, 29,* 3–115.

Pratt, R., Warrington, E., & Halliday, A. (1971). Unilateral ECT as a test for cerebral dominance. *British Journal of Psychiatry, 119,* 79–83.

Pribram, K. (1961). A further experimental analysis of the behavioral deficit that follows injury to the primate frontal cortex. *Experimental Neurology, 3,* 432–466.

Pribram, K. (1975). The primate frontal cortex: Progress report 1975. *Acta Neurobiologica Experimentalis, 35,* 609–625.

Pribram, K. (1981). The brain, the telephone, the thermostat, the computer, and the hologram. *Cognition and Brain Theory, 4,* 195–122.

Pribram, K. (1982). Localization and distribution of function in the brain. In J. Orbach (Ed.), *Neuropsychology after Lashley,* Hillsdale, NJ: Erlbaum.

Quercy, P. (1936). *Les hallucinations* (2 Vols.). Paris: Alcan.

Raisman, G. (1969). *Brain Research, 14,* 25–48.

Ramier, A., & Hécaen, H. (1970). Role respectif des atteintes frontales et de la latéralisation lésionelle dans les déficits de la "fluence verbale." *Revue Neurologique, 23,* 17–22.

Ratcliff, G., & Davies-Jones, G. (1972). Defective visual localization in focal brain wounds. *Brain, 95,* 49–60.

Reyes, M., Chokroverty, S., & Masdeu, J. (1976). Thalamic neuroaxonal dystrophy and dementia in Hodgkin's disease. *Neurology, 26,* 251–253.

Richards, W. (1973). Time reproductions by H. M., *Acta Psychologica, 37,* 279–282.

Richardson, A. (1969). *Mental imagery.* New York: Springer.

Riddoch, G. (1917). Dissociation of visual perception due to occipital injuries, with special reference to appreciation of movement. *Brain, 40,* 15–47.

Riese, W., & Goldstein, K. (1950). *Journal of Comparative Neurology, 92,* 133–168.

Riklan, M., & Cooper, I. (1975). Psychometric studies of verbal functions following thalamic lesions in humans. *Brain and Language, 2,* 45–64.

Riklan, M., & Levita, E. (1969). *Subcortical correlates of human behavior.* Baltimore: Williams & Wilkins.

Riss, W., Pederson, R., Jakway, J., & Ware, C. (1972). Levels of function and their representation in the vertebrate thalamus. *Brain Behavior and Evolution, 6,* 26–41.

Robb, J. (1948). *Assoc. Res. Nerv. Ment. Dis. 27,* 587–609.

Roberts, L. (1969). In P. Vinken and G. M. Bruyn (Eds.), *Handbook of clinical neurology, 4.*

Robinson, D., & Goldberg, M. (1978). The visual substrate of eye movements. In J. W. Senders, D. F. Fisher, & R. A. Monty (Eds.), *Eye movements and the higher psychological functions.* Hillsdale, NJ: Erlbaum.

Robinson, A. Heaton, R., Lehman, B. & Stilson, D. (1980) The utility of the Wisconsin Card Sorting Test in detecting and localizing frontal lobe lesions. *Journal of Consulting Clinical Psychology, 48,* 605–614.

Robinson, B. (1977). In *Annals of the New York Academy of Science.*

Rocha-Miranda, C., Gender, C., Gross, C., & Mishkin, M. (1975). Visual activation of neurons. *Journal of Neurophysiology, 38,* 475–491.

Rochford, G. (1974). *British Journal of Disorders of Communication, 9,* 35–44.

Roland, P. (1978). *The Behavioral Brain Sciences, 1,* 129–171.

Rondot, P., Recondo, J. de, & Ribadea Dumas, J. Visuomotor ataxia. *Brain,* 1977, *100,* 355–376.

Rosene, D., & van Hoesen, G. (1977). Hippocampal efferents reach widespread areas of cerebral cortex and amygdala in the rhesus monkey. *Science, 198,* 315–317.

Rosenkilde, C. (1979). Functional heterogeneity of the prefrontal cortex in the monkey: A review. *Behavioral Neural Biology, 25,* 301–345.

Ross, P. (1983). Phonological processing during silent reading in aphasic patients. *Brain and Language, 19,* 191–203.

Rosvold, H (1972). The frontal lobe system. *Acta Neurobiologica Experimentalis 32,* 439–460.

Rubens, A. (1975). Aphasia with infarction in the territory of the anterior cerebral artery. *Cortex, 11,* 239–250.

Rubens, A., & Johnson, M. (1976) *Aphasia with thalamic hemorrhage.* Presentation at Academy of Aphasia, Miami.

Rubens, A. (1977). In Harnad et al (Eds.), *Lateralization in the nervous system*. New York: Academic Press.

Rubens, A., & Benson, D. (1971). Associative visual agnosia. *Archives of Neurology, 24*, 305–316.

Rylander, G. (1939). *Personality changes after operations on the frontal lobes*. London: Oxford University Press.

Rylander, G. (1943). *Mental changes after excision of cerebral tissue*, Copenhagen: Munksgaard.

Sager, O., Mares, A., & Nestianu, V. (1965). *Formatia Reticulata*. Bucharest: Ed. Acad. RSR.

Sager, O., Nestianu, V., & Florea-Ciocoiu, V. (1967). EEG studies on the transmission of visual stimuli to the hippocampus. *EEG Clinical Neurophysiology, 22*, 576.

Sandson, J., & Albert, M. (1984). Varieties of perseveration. *Neuropsychologia, 22*, 715–732.

Sanides, F., & Vitzthum, H. (1965) Zur Architektonik der menschlichen Sehrinde und den Prinzipien ihrer Entwicklung. *Deutsche Zeitschrift für Nervenheilkunde, 187*, 680–707.

Sanides, F. (1969) Comparative architectonics of the neocortex of mammals and their evolutionary interpretation. *Annals of New York Academy of Science, 167*, 404–423.

Sanides, F. (1970). Functional architecture of motor and sensory cortices in primates in light of a new concept of neocortex evolution. In C. Noback & W. Montagna (Eds.), *Advances in primatology*. New York: Appleton-Century-Crofts.

Sanides, F. (1975). Comparative neurology of the temporal lobe in primates including man with reference to speech. *Brain Language, 2*, 396–419.

Sargent, W., & Slater, E. (1954). *An introduction to physical methods of treatment in psychiatry* (3rd Edition). Edinburgh: Livingstone.

Satz, P., Achenbach, K., & Fennell, E. (1967). Correlations between assessed manual laterality and predicted speech laterality in a normal population. *Neuropsychologia, 5*, 295–310.

Saundby, R. (1911). *British Medical Bulletin*, 605–608.

Scheibel, A., Fried, I., Paul, L., et al. (1982). *Annals of Neurology, 12*, 76.

Scheibel, A., Paul, L., Fried, I., Forsythe, A., Tomiyasu, U., Wechsler, A., Kao, A., & Slotnick, J (1985). Dendritic organization of the anterior speech area. *Experimental Neurology, 87*, 109–117.

Schepelmann, F. (1979). Rhythmic patterns of motor activity after lesions of the central nervous system in man. *Acta Neurochirurica, 49*, 153–189.

Schilder, P. (1933). The vestibular apparatus in neurosis and psychosis. *Journal of Nervous and Mental Disease, 78*, 1–23.

Schilder, P. (1934). Discussion. *Archives of Neurology and Psychiatry, 31*, 1121.

Schilder, P. (1936). Psychopathology of time, *Journal of Nervous and Mental Disease, 83*, 530–546.

Schilder, P. (1951). *Brain and personality*. New York: International Universities Press.

Schilder, P. (1953). *Medical psychology*. New York: International Universities Press.

Schilder, P. (1964). *Contributions to developmental neuropsychiatry*. L. Bender (Ed.). New York: International Universities Press.

Schilder, P., Pasik, P., & Pasik, T. (1972). Extrageniculostriate vision in the monkey. *Experimental Brain Research, 14*, 436–448.

Schneider, G. (1974). In (E. Eidelberg and D. Stein, Eds.), *Functional recovery after lesions of the nervous system*. *NRP Bulletin, 12*, No. 2.

Schneider, R., Crosby, E., Bagchi, B., & Calhoun, H. (1961). Temporal or occipital lobe hallucinations triggered from frontal lobe lesions. *Neurology, 11*, 172–179.

Schoenle, P. (1979). *Speech and respiration in normals and aphasic patients*. Paper presented at the meeting of the Academy of Aphasia, San Diego, 1979.

Schröder, P. (1925). Über Gesichtshalluzination bei organischen Hirnleiden. *Archives für Psychiatrie und Nervenkrankheiten, 73*, 308–777.

Schulman, S. (1957). Bilateral symmetrical degeneration of the thalamus. *Journal of Neuropathology and Experimental Neurology, 16*, 446–470.

Schuster, P. (1936–1937). Beitrage zur Pathologie des Thalamus opticus. *Archiv für Psychiatrie und Nervenkrankheiten, 105*, 358–432, 550–622, *106*, 13–53, 201–233.

Scoville, W. and Milner, B. (1957). *Journal of Neurology, Neurosurgery and Psychiatry, 20*, 11–21.

Scotti, G. La perdita della memoria topografica: Descrizione di un caso. *Sistema Nervoso, 20*, 352–361.

Searleman, A. (1977). A review of right hemisphere linguistic capabilities. *Psychological Bulletin, 84*, 503–528.

Segal, S., & Nathan, S. (1964). The Perky effect. *Perception Motor Skills 18*, 385–395.

Segarra, J. (1970). Cerebral vascular disease and behavior. *Archives of Neurology, 22*, 408–418.

Seglas, J. (1903). *Sémiologie des affections mentales. Traite de pathologie mentale*. Boin: Ballet.

Seguin, E. (1886). A clinical study of lateral hemianopsia. *Journal of Nervous and Mental Disease, 13*, 445–454.

Seigel, J. (1979). Behavioral functions of the reticular formation. *Brain Research Rev., 1*, 69–105.

Selnes, O., Knopman, D., Niccum, N., & Rubens, A. (1985). The critical role of Wernicke's area in sentence repetition. *Annals of Neurology, 17*, 549–557.

Semmes, J. (1968). *Neuropsychologia, 6*, 11–26.

Serafetinidis, E., & M. Falconer (1963). Speech disturbances in temporal lobe seizures. *Brain, 86*, 333–346.

Serres, E. (1860). Cited in Gould (1977).

Seth, G. (1973). Eye-hand coordination and handedness: A developmental study of visuo-motor behaviour in infancy. *Brit. J. educ. Psychol., 43*, 35–49.

Shallice, T., & Evans, M. (1978). The involvement of the frontal lobes in cognitive estimation. *Cortex, 14*, 294–303.

Siebeck, R., & Frey, R. (1953). Die Wirkungen muskelerschlaffender Mittel auf die Augenmuskeln. *Anaesthesist, 2,* 138–141.

Siegel, J. (1979). Behavioral functions of the reticular formation. *Brain Research Review, 1,* 69–105.

Silberer, H. (1951). Report on a method of eliciting and observing certain symbolic hallucination phenomena." In D. Rapaport (Ed.), *Organization and pathology of thought,* New York, Columbia University Press.

Sjogren, T., H. Sjogren, & Lindgren, A. (1952). *Acta psychiatrica et neurologica scandinavia supplementum, 82,* 1–152.

Smith, A. (1972). Dominant and nondominant hemispherectomy. In W. Smith (Ed.), *Drugs, development and cerebral function.* Springfield, IL: Charles C. Thomas.

Smith, A., & Burklund, C. (1966). *Science, 153,* 1280–1282.

Smyth, G., & Stern, K. (1938). Tumours of the thalamus—a clinico-pathological study. *Brain, 61,* 339–374.

Soper, H., Diamond, I., & Wilson, M. (1975). Visual attention and inferotemporal cortex in rhesus monkey. *Neuropsychologia, 33,* 409–420.

Spear, P. (1979). Behavioral and neurophysiological consequences of visual cortex damage: Mechanisms of recovery. *Progress in Psychobiology and Physiological Psychology, 8,* 45–90.

Sperry, R. (1976). Mental phenomena as causal determinants in brain function, In G. Globus, G. Maxwell, & I. V. Savodnik (Eds.), *Consciousness and the brain.* New York: Plenum.

Spiegel, R., Wycis, H., Orchinik, C., & Freed, H. (1955). Thalamic chronotaraxis. *Archives of Neurology and Psychiatry, 73,* 469–471.

Sprague, J. (1966). Interaction of cortex and superior colliculus in mediation of visually guided behavior in the cat. *Science, 153,* 1544–1547.

Sprague, J. (1975). Sensorimotor function of the midbrain tectum. *NRP Bulletin, 13,* 204–213.

Sprague, J., Berlucchi, G., & Rizzolatti, G. (1973). The role of the superior colliculus, etc. In R. Jung (Ed.), *Handbook of sensory physiology, Vol. 7/3. Central processing of visual information. Part B. Visual centers in the brain.* New York: Springer-Verlag.

Sprague, J., Levy, J., DiBernardino, A., & Berlucchi, G. (1977). Visual cortical areas mediating form discrimination in the cat. *Journal of Comparative Neurology, 172,* 441–488.

Stahl, S., Layzer, R., Aminoff, M., Townsend, J., & Feldon, S. (1980). Continuous cataplexy in a patient with a midbrain tumor. *Neurology, 30,* 1115–1118.

Starr, M. A. (1889). The pathology of sensory aphasia, with an analysis of five cases in which Broca's centre was not diseased, *Brain, 12,* 82–101.

Steele, J., Richardson, J., & Olszweski, J. (1964). Progressive supranuclear palsy. *Archives of Neurology, 10,* 333–359.

Stein, D. (1974). In (D. Stein, J. Rosen, & N. Butters (Eds.), *Plasticity and recovery of function in the central nervous system.* New York: Academic Press.

Stengel, E. (1943). *Journal of Mental Science, 89.*

Stengel, E., & Steele, G. (1946). Unawareness of physical disability. *Journal of Mental Science, 92,* 379–388.

Stern, K. (1939). Severe dementia associated with bilateral symmetrical degeneration of the thalamus. *Brain,* 1939, *62,* 157–171.

Stevens, J. (1978), Commentary. *Behavioral and Brain Sciences, 1,* 163–165.

Stookey, B., Scarff, J., Teitelbaum, M. (1941). Frontal lobectomy in treatment of brain tumors. *Archives of Surgery, 113,* 161.

Strohmeyer, C. & Psotka, J. (1970). The detailed texture of eidetic images, *Nature, 225,* 346–349.

Stroud, J. (1956). The fine structure of psychological time. In H. Quastler (Ed.), *Information Theory in Psychology.* IL: Free Press.

Stuss, D., Alexander, M., Lieberman, A. & Levine, H. (1978). An extraordinary form of confabulation. *Neurology, 28,* 1166–1172.

Stuss, D., Kaplan, E., Benson, D. F., Weir, W., Naeser, M., & Levine, H. (1981) Long-term effects of prefrontal leucotomy. *Journal of Clinical Neuropsychology, 3,* 13–32.

Sugishita, M., Ishijima, B., Hori, T., Fukushima, T., & Iwata, M. (1973). "Pure" agraphia after left CM-thalamotomy (Japanese). *Clinical Neurology, 13,* 568–574.

Sutton, D., Samson, H., & Larson, C. (1978). Brain mechanisms in learned phonation of Macaca mulatta. In D. Chivers and J. Herbert (Eds.), *Recent advances in primatology* (Vol. 1). New York: Academic Press.

Sweet, R., McDowell, F., Feigenson, J., Loranger, and Goodell, H. (1976). Mental symptoms in Parkinson's disease during chronic treatment with levodopa. *Neurology, 26,* 305–310.

Tägert, J., Chock, D., Niklas, J., Sandvoss, G., & Sipos, J. (1975). Linguistische Funktionsstörungen bei Patienten mit rechtshirnigen Läsionen. *Nervenarzt, 46,* 249–255.

Tanaka, D. (1976). Thalamic projections of the dorsomedial prefrontal cortex in the rhesus monkey *(Macaca mulatta). Brain Research, 110,* 21–38.

Taylor, A., & Warrington, E. (1971). Visual agnosia: A single case report. *Cortex, 7,* 152–161.

Ter Braak, J., Schenk, V., & Van Vliet, A. (1971). Visual reactions in a case of long-lasting cortical blindness. *Journal of Neurology, Neurosurgery and Psychiatry, 34,* 140–147.

Teszner, D., Tzavaras, A., Gruner, J., & Hécaen, H. (1972). L'asymmétrie droite-gauche du *planum temporale, Revue Neurologique 126,* 444–449, 1972.

Teuber, H.-L., & Bender, M. (1949). Alterations in pattern vision following trauma of occipital lobes in man. *Journal General Psychology, 40,* 37–57.

Teuber, H.-L. (1960), Perception. In J. Field (Eds.), *Handbook of physiology,* Section I. Neurophysiology (Vol. III). Washington, DC: American Physiological Society.

Teuber, H.-L., Battersby, W., & Bender, M. (1960). *Visual field defects after penetrating missile wounds of the brain.* Cambridge, MA: Harvard University Press.

Teuber, H.-L. (1972) Unity and diversity of frontal lobe functions. *Acta Neurobiologia Experimentalis, 32,* 615–656.

Teuber, H.-L. (1974). In E. Eidelberg & D. Stein (Eds.), *Functional recovery after lesions of the nervous system. NRP Bulletin, 12,* No. 2.

Thatcher, R., & John, E. (1977). *Functional neuroscience,* (Vol. I). Hillside, NJ: Erlbaum.

Thorndike, E. (1911). *Animal intelligence.* New York: Macmillan.

Tobias, T. (1975). Afferents to prefrontal cortex from the thalamus mediodorsalis nucleus in the rhesus monkey. *Brain Research, 83,* 191–212.

Tonkonogy, J. (1968). Insult and aphasia (Russian). Leningrad: Meditsina.

Tonkonogy, J., & Goodglass, H. (1981). Language function, foot of the third frontal gyrus, and Rolandic operculum. *Archives of Neurology, 38,* 486–496.

Torjussen, T. (1978). Visual processing in cortically blind hemifields. *Neuropsychologia, 16,* 15–21.

Torrey, & E. Peterson, M. (1974). *Lancet,* 942–946.

Travis, A. (1955). Neurological deficiencies following supplementary motor area lesions in Macaca mulatta. *Brain, 78,* 174–198.

Trelles, J., & Lagache, D. (1932). Intoxication barbiturique récidivante s'accompagnant d'hallucinose pédonclulaire. *Annales de Médico-Psychologie, 90,* 565–572.

Trevarthen, C. (1968). Two mechanisms of vision in primates. *Psychologische Forschung, 31,* 299–337.

Trevarthen, C. (1970). Experimental evidence for a brain stem contribution to visual perception in man. *Brain, Behavior and Evolution, 3,* 338–352.

Trevarthen, C. (1974). Functional relations of disconnected hemispheres with the brain stem and with each other. In M. Kinsbourne & W. Smith (Eds.), *Hemispheric disconnection and cerebral function.* Springfield, IL: Charles C. Thomas.

Trojanowski, J., Green, R., & Levine, D. (1980). Crossed aphasia in a dextral: A clinicopathological study. *Neurology, 30,* 709–713.

Turkewitz, G., Gordon, E., & Birch, H. (1965). Head turning in the human neonate: spontaneous patterns. *Journal of Genetic Psychology, 107,* 143–158.

Turvey, M. (1977). Preliminaries to a theory of action with reference to vision. In R. Shaw & J. Bransford (Eds.). *Perceiving, acting and knowing.* Englewood Cliffs, NJ: Erlbaum.

Tzavaras, A., Hécaen, H., & LeBras, H. (1970). Le probleme de la specificite du deficit de la reconnaissance du visage humain lors lesions hemispherique unilaterales. *Neuropsychologia, 8,* 403–417.

Tzavaras, A., Merienne, L., & Masure, M. C. (1973). Prosopagnosie, amnesie et troubles du langage par lesion temporale gauche chez un sujet gaucher. *Encephale, 4,* 1–13.

Tzavaras, A., & Masure, M. (1976). Aspects differents de l'ataxie optique selon la lateralization hemispherique de la lesion. *Lyon Medicale, 1976, 236,* 673–683.

Ungerstedt, U., & Arbuthnott, G. (1970). *Brain Research 24,* 485–493.

Valenstein, E. (1973). *Brain control.* New York: Wiley.

Van Bogaert, L. (1924). Syndrome inferiour du noyau rouge," *Revue Neurologique, 1,* 417.

Van Bogaert, L. (1934). "Sur la pathologie de l'image de soi," *Annales de Médico-Psychologie, 92,* 519–555, 744–759.

Van Buren, J., & Borke, R. (1969). Alterations in speech and the pulvinar. *Brain, 92,* 255.

Van Buren, J. M., & Borke, R. C. (1972). *Variation and connections of the human thalamus.* Berlin: Springer.

Van Buren, J. & Fedio, P. (1976) Functional representation on the medial aspect of the frontal lobes in man. *Journal of Neurosurgery, 44,* 275–289.

Van Essen, D. (1979). Visual areas of the mammalian cerebral cortex. *Annual Review of Neuroscience, 3,* 227–263.

Veyrac, G. J. (1931). *Etude de l'aphasie chez les sujets polyglottes.* These pour le doctorat en médecine. Paris.

Von Monakow, C. (1914). *Die Lokalisation im Grosshirn.* Wiesbaden: Bergmann.

Von Solder, F. (1899). Perseveration. *Journal of Psychiatry and Neurology, 18,* 479.

Von Weizsaecker, V. (1958). *Le cycle de la structure.* Bruges: Desclee de Brouwer. (Translation of *Der Gestaltkreis,* Thieme, Stuttgart, 1939)

Vastola, E. (1968). Localization of visual functions in the mammalian brain: A review. *Brain, Behavior and Evolution, 1,* 420–471.

Victor, M., Adams, R., & Collins, G. *The Wernicke-Korsakoff syndrome.* Philadelphia: Davis.

Vihvelin, H. (1948). On the differentiation of some typical forms of hypnagogic hallucinations. *Acta Psychiatria Neurologica, 23,* 359–389.

Vilkki, J., & Laitinen, L. (1976). Effects of pulvinotomy and ventrolateral thalamotomy on some cognitive functions. *Neuropsychologia, 14,* 67–78.

Vogt, C., & Vogt, O. (1919). Allgemeinere Ergebnisse unserer Hirnforschung. *Journal für Psychologie and Neurologie, 25,* 279–462.

Volavka, J., Feldstein, S., Abrams, R., Dornbush, R. & Fink, M. (1972). EEG and clinical change after bilateral and unilateral electroconvulsive therapy. *EEG Clinical Neurophysiology, 32,* 631–639, 1972.

Wada, J. (1972). Morphological hemispheric asymmetry and cerebral speech lateralization. Cited in Teszner et al. (1972).

Wada, J., Clarke, R., Hamm, A. (1975). Cerebral hemispheric asymmetry in humans. *Archives of Neurology 32,* 239–246.

Wadham, W. (1869). *St. George's Hospital Reports, 4,* 245–250.

Wagner, W. (1943). Anosognosie, Zeitrafferphanomen und Uhrzeitagnosie als Symptome der Störungen in rechten Parieto-Occipitallappen. *Nervenarzt, 16,* 49.

Walker, A. (1938). *The primate thalamus.* Chicago: University of Chicago Press.

Wallesch, G., Kornhuber, H., Brunner, R., Kunz, T., Hollerbach, H., & Suger, G. (1983). Lesions of the basal ganglia, thalamus and deep white matter: differential effects on language functions. *Brain and Language, 20,* 286–304.

Walter, W. (1959). Intrinsic rhythms of the brain. In H. Magoun (Ed.), *Handbook of Physiology Section 1: Neurophysiology, 1,* 279–298.

Walter, W. (1973). Human frontal lobe function in sensory-motor association. In K. Pribram & A. R. Luria (Eds.), *Psychophysiology of the frontal lobes*. New York: Academic Press.

Walther, H. (1945). Uber einen Dammerzustand mit triebhafter Erregung nach Thalamusschädigung. *Monatsschrift für Psychiatrie und Neurologie, 3,* 1–16.

Waltregny, A. (1972). L'epilepsie de l'aire motrice supplementaire. *Médicine de Hygiéne,* 815–816.

Waltz, J., Riklan, M., Stellar, S., & Cooper, I. (1966). Cryothalamotomy for Parkinson's disease. *Neurology, 16,* 994.

Ward, A. (1948). The anterior cingular gyrus and personality. *Research Publications of the Association for Nervous and Mental Disorders, 27,* 438–445.

Warren, J. (1972). Evolution, behavior, and the prefrontal cortex. *Acta Neurobiologica Experimentalis, 32,* 581–593.

Wechsler, A. (1976). Crossed aphasia in an illiterate dextral. *Brain and Language, 3,* 164–172.

Weigl, E. (1964). Some critical remarks concerning the problem of so-called simultanagnosia. *Neuropsychologia, 2,* 189–207.

Weiler, R., & Kass, J. (1980). Connections of the dorsolateral visual area (DL) of extrastriate visual cortex of the owl monkey. *Neuroscience Abstracts, 6,* 579.

Weinberger, L., & Grant, F. (1940) Visual hallucinations and their neuro-optical correlates. *Archives of Ophthalmology, 23,* 166–199.

Weinstein, E Lyerly, O, Cole, M. and Ozer, M. (1966). Meaning in jargonaphasia. *Cortex* 2.165–88.

Weinstein, E., & Kahn, R. (1952). Nonaphasic misnaming (paraphasia) in organic brain disease. *Archives of Neurology and Psychiatry, 67,* 72–80.

Weiskrantz, L., Warrington, E., Sanders, M., & Marshall, J. (1974). Visual capacity in the hemianopic field following a restricted occipital ablation. *Brain, 97,* 709–728.

Welch, K. and Stuteville, P. (1958). Experimental production of neglect in monkeys. *Brain, 81,* 341–347.

Wepman, J., & Jones, L. (1964). Five aphasias: A commentary on aphasia as a regressive linguistic phenomenon. In D. Rioch & E. Weinstein (Eds.), *Disorders of communication*. Baltimore: Williams & Wilkins.

Wepman, J. (1972). Aphasia therapy: a new look. *Journal of Speech and Hearing Disorders, 37,* 203–214.

Werner, H. (1946). The concept of rigidity: a critical evaluation. *Psychological Review, 53,* 43–54.

Wernicke, C. (1874). *Der aphasische Symptomenkomplex*. Breslau: Cohn, and Weigart.

Whitaker, H., & Ojemann, G. (1977). *Stimulation in human speech area*. Presentation at Academy of Aphasia, Montreal.

Whitaker, H., & Selnes, O. (1975). Broca's area. *Linguistics, 154/155,* 91–103.

Whiteley, A., & Warrington, E. (1978). Selective impairment of topographical memory. *Journal of Neurology, Neurosurgery and Psychiatry, 41,* 575–578.

Whitty, C., & Lewin, C. (1961). A Korsakoff syndrome in the post-cingulectomy confusional state. *Brain, 83,* 648–663.

Wieser, H. (1983). Depth recorded limbic seizures and psychopathology. *Neuroscience Biobehavioral Reviews, 7,* 427–440.

Wilson, S. (1908). Perseveration. *Brain, 31,* 164.

Wilson, S., & Walshe, F. (1914). Perseveration. *Brain, 37,* 199.

Wilson, S. (1916) Dysmetropsia and its pathogenesis. *Transactions of the Ophthalmological Society, U.K., 36,* 412–444.

Witelson, S., & Pallie, W. (1973). *Brain, 96,* 641–647.

Wolpert, I. (1924). Die Simultanagnosie. Störung der Gesamtauffassung, *Ztschr. ges. Neurol. Psychiatr., 93,* 397–415.

Woolsey, C., Settlage, P., Meyer, D., Sencer, W., Pinto-Hamuy, T., & Travis, A. (1952). Patterns of localization in precentral and "supplementary" motor areas and their relation to the concept of a premotor area. *Research Publication of the Association for Nervous and Mental Disease, 30,* 238–264.

Wurtz, R., Goldberg, M., & Robinson, D. (1980). Behavioral modulation of visual responses in the monkey: Stimulus selection for attention and movement. *Progress in Psychobiology and Physiological Psychology, 9,* 43–83.

Wurtz, R., & Goldberg, M. (1972). Activity of superior colliculus in behaving monkey. *Journal of Neurophysiology, 35,* 575–596.

Yakovlev, P. (1948). Motility, behavior and the brain. *Journal of Nervous and Mental Diseases, 107,* 313–335.

Yakovlev, P. (1972). In C. Hockman (Ed.), *Limbic system mechanisms and autonomic function.* Springfield, IL: Charles C. Thomas.

Yamadori, A. (1981). Verbal perseveration in aphasia. N*europsychologia, 19,* 591–594.

Yarbus, A. (1967). *Eye movements and vision.* New York: Plenum.

Yarnell, P. (1981). Crossed dextral aphasia: A clinical radiological correlation. *Brain and Language, 12,* 128–139.

Yeni-Komshian, G. (1977). Presentation. Conference on Aphasia, CUNY, NY.

Zaidel, E. (1976). *Cortex, 12,* 191–211.

Zaidel, E. (1977). *Neuropsychologia, 15,* 1–18.

Zaimov, K. (1965). *Uber die Pathophysiologie der Agnosien Aphasien, Apraxien.* Jena: Gustav, Fischer.

Zangwill, O. (1951). Discussion of parietal lobe syndromes. *Proceedings of the Royal Society of Medicine, 44,* 343–346.

Zangwill, O. (1960). *Cerebral dominance and its relation to psychological functions.* Edinburgh: Oliver & Boyd.

Zangwill, O. (1967). Speech and the minor hemisphere. *Acta neurologica et psychiatrica, 67,* 1013–1020.

Zangwill, O. (1975). In K. Zulch et al. (Eds.), *Cerebral localization.* Berlin: Springer.

Zielinski, K. (1972). Effects of prefrontal lesions on avoidance and escape reflexes. *Acta Neurobiologia Experimentalis, 32,* 393–415.

Zihl, J., & von Cramon, D. (1979). The contribution of the 'second' visual system to directed visual attention in man. *Brain, 102,* 835–856.

Zuckerman, M. (1969). Hallucinations, reported sensations and images, In J. Zubek (Ed.), *Sensory deprivation.* New York: Appleton-Century-Crofts.

Zung, W., & Wilson, (1971). Time estimation during sleep, *Biological Psychiatry, 3,* 159–164.

Zurif, E., & Caramazza, A. (1976). Psycholinguistic structures in aphasia. In H. Whitaker & H. A. Whitaker (Eds.), *Studies in neurolinguistics* (Vol. 1). New York: Academic Press.

Zurif, E., Swinney, D., & Garrett, M. (1988). Lexical processing and sentence comprehension in aphasia. In A. Caramazza (Ed.), *Advances in cognitive neuropsychology and neurolinguistics*. Hillsdale, N.J.: Lawrence Erlbaum Associates.

Author Index

Subject Index